Environmental Jurisdiction in the Law of the Sea

Victor Alencar Mayer Feitosa Ventura

Environmental Jurisdiction in the Law of the Sea

The Brazilian Blue Amazon

Springer

Victor Alencar Mayer Feitosa Ventura
João Pessoa, Brazil

Dissertation zur Erlangung des Doktorgrades der Rechtswissenschaft an der Fakultät für Rechtswissenschaft der Universität Hamburg, Albrecht Mendelssohn Bartholdy Graduate School of Law
vorgelegt von Victor Alencar Mayer Feitosa Ventura
Erstgutachter: Prof. Dr. iur. Stefan Oeter
Zweitgutachter: Prof. Dr. iur. Henning Jessen
Tag der mündlichen Prüfung: 29.05.2019

ISBN 978-3-030-50542-4 ISBN 978-3-030-50543-1 (eBook)
https://doi.org/10.1007/978-3-030-50543-1

This Springer imprint is published by the registered company Springer Nature Switzerland AG.
The registered company address is: Gewerbestrasse 11, 6330 Cham, Switzerland

Acknowledgements

A book is never an individual's work. I have to thank my family, Marco and Maria Luiza, fantastic parents, and my brothers, Danilo and Felipe, who encouraged me to embark on the adventure of a PhD abroad and stood by that idea at all times.

My deepest gratefulness to Valeria, a companion who offered much-needed backing, especially in the darkest hours. This work, if anything, is the direct result of our love, mutual support, and delightful cultural escapades in Hamburg and Elmshorn.

A special thank you to both my supervisors, Prof. Dr. Stefan Oeter and Prof. Dr. Henning Jessen, for the patience to dialogue with my ideas and for offering valuable insights for this work. Also, my appreciation for the constant helpfulness and efficiency of the staff of the Faculty of Law of the University of Hamburg, in particular Ms Claudia Zavala and Ms Dinah Cassebaum.

This work would not have been made possible without the support of several scholars and institutions, where I had the treasured opportunity to conduct research and collect feedback. Those scholars are Prof. Dr. Anne Peters and the Max Planck Institute of Comparative Public Law and International Law, for the opportunity to attend the Institute's Masterclasses; Prof. Dr. Bjorn Kunoy, the University of the Faroe Islands, where I concluded the Summer Academy on the Continental Shelf; Prof. Dr. Erik Molenaar, the Netherlands Institute for the Law of the Sea (NILOS), University of Utrecht, under whose supervision I carried out a two-month long research stay; Dr. Jo König and Prof. Dr. Doris König, for setting up the best summer academy on ocean governance of the world, in Hamburg; and, finally, Prof. Dr. Clive Schofield, of the Global Ocean Institute, of the World Maritime University, for welcoming me into the premises of the Institute for a short research stay.

I am equally indebted to the International Tribunal for the Law of the Sea (ITLOS), for having me assist the Registry during the 46th Session of the Tribunal, and to the wonderful multinational colleagues I met there, with special remark to Sebastian Gomez, Brigitte Rakatomalala, Julia Ritter, Antje Vorbeck, and Anke Egert.

In Hamburg, this work would not have been possible without the monthly debates in my beloved Portuguese language at the Brazilian Debate Group (GDTB, *Grupo de Discussão de Temas Brasileiros*), especially with Emília Castro, Ana Quintão, Cristina Francisco, and Renata do Val. My particular thanks to the "Brazilian Directorate," Fernando Magrão Preusser de Mattos, Rômulo Lima, Eduardo Gresse, and Júlio de Rizzo. Likewise, my deepest gratitude to Júlia Mandil and Bettina Zbinden. To my colleagues and friends of the Albrecht Mendelssohn Bartholdy Graduate School of Law, of the University of Hamburg, namely Rustam Atadjanov, Gregor Lamersdorf, Matthias Packeiser, Annalisa Morticelli, Pipitsa Kousoula, Tomas Restrepo, Giuseppe Bitti, Raoul Veit, Barbara Germann, Reem Harok, Lucas Bento, and many more. You all made the PhD mission one worth enjoying.

Finally, I am appreciative of the Albrecht Mendelssohn Bartholdy Graduate School of Law and the PIASTA Program, both of the University of Hamburg, as well as the Brazilian Foundation for the Development of Higher Education Personnel (CAPES), for having funded different stages of the research that gave life to this book.

Contents

Abbreviations

ABNJ	Areas beyond national jurisdiction
AMAZUL S/A	Blue Amazon Defense Technologies Corporation
CBD	Convention on Biological Diversity
CCAMLR	Convention on the Conservation of Antarctic Marine Living Resources
CIRM	Brazilian Interministerial Commission for Marine Resources
CITES	Convention on International Trade in Endangered Species of Wild Fauna and Flora
CLCS	Commission on the Limits of the Continental Shelf
CONAMA	Brazilian National Council for the Environment
CPLP	Community of Portuguese-Speaking Countries
CSC	Continental Shelf Convention
EEZ	Exclusive economic zone
FAO	United Nations Food and Agriculture Organization
GOOS	Global Ocean Observing System
IBAMA	Brazilian Institute of the Environment and Renewable Natural Resources
IBAS	India, Brazil, and South Africa Dialogue Forum
ICCAT	International Commission for the Conservation of Atlantic Tunas
ICJ	International Court of Justice
ILA	International Law Commission
IMO	International Maritime Organization
IOC	International Oceanographic Commission
ISA	International Seabed Authority
ITLOS	International Tribunal for the Law of the Sea
LEPLAC	Brazilian Continental Shelf Survey Plan
MARPOL	Convention for the Prevention of Pollution Caused by Ships
MEA	Multilateral environmental agreement
MGR	Marine genetic resources
MMA	Ministry for the Environment

MPA	Marine protected area
MSR	Marine Scientific Research
MSRA	Brazilian Marine Scientific Research Act
NAFO	Northwest Atlantic Fisheries Organization
NEAFC	North East Atlantic Fisheries Commission
OILPOL	Convention on Civil Liability for Damage Caused by Oil Pollution
OPRC	International Convention on Oil Pollution Preparedness, Response and Co-operation
PMN	Brazilian National Maritime Policy
PNM	Brazilian Marine Nuclear Program
PNCMar	Brazilian National Policy for the Conservation of the Marine Biome
PNMA	Brazilian National Policy for the Environment
PNRM	Brazilian National Policy for Marine Resources
PSRM	Brazilian Sectorial Plans for Marine Resources
PROAREA	Brazilian Program for the Prospection and Exploration of Mineral Resources of the International South Atlantic and Equatorial Area
PROSUB	Brazilian Submarine Development Program
REMPLAC	Brazilian Program for the Assessment of the Mineral Potential of the Brazilian Legal Continental Shelf
REVIMAR	Brazilian Action for the Assessment, Monitoring and Conservation of Marine Biodiversity
REVIZEE	Brazilian Program for the Assessment of the Sustainable Potential of EEZ Living Resources
RFMO	Regional Fisheries Management Organization
SISGAAZ	Management System of the Blue Amazon
SISNAMA	National Environmental System
SPLOS	Meeting of the State Parties to UNCLOS
UNCLOS	United Nations Convention on the Law of the Sea
UNEP	United Nations Environment Programme
UNFSA	United Nations Fish Stocks Agreement
WWF	World Wide Fund for Nature
ZOPACAS	South Atlantic Zone of Peace and Cooperation

Chapter 1
Introduction: Setting the Stage

1.1 Factual Background and Theoretical Framework

The world ocean is a giant of nature, occupying more than 70% of the Earth, adored and feared by countless civilizations. It is home to a multitude of marine ecosystems, each responsible for performing different *ecosystem services*, such as those of provisioning protein-rich food and valuable sea-lanes; supporting the production of biomass from plankton, indispensable for balancing the marine food cycle; and regulating the planet's temperature, the absorption of carbon dioxide, as well as regulating other biological, chemical, and physical processes which take place in the oceans and benefit human well-being. It also offers cultural services which benefit all peoples, such as tourism and the locus for ancestral traditions and rituals associated with the oceans.

Yet, humankind has increasingly looked at the oceans as an apparently inexhaustible source of marine goods indispensable to today's capitalistic world-system. Decades of aggressive anthropogenic interference, motivated by the hunt for food, energy, and swift navigational operations have set the world ocean under a multitude of stresses and risks. Nobody can deny the fact that a changing climate and the sea-level rise have been leading to drastic changes in the world's coasts, where approximately 2.8 billion people currently live.[1] Ocean acidification, a phenomenon still under-investigated and under-regulated, but known to exist, has caused devastating impacts on marine habitats such as coral reefs worldwide. Intense urban occupation of coastal areas has resulted in a high level of use and severe pollution of coastal waters, as 13 of the world's 20 megacities with a population above 10 million are located at the shoreside.

Given that those problems are by no means fresh, and in order not to fall into repetition, it suffices to refer *à vol d'oiseau* to other environmental strains the ocean

[1]World Ocean Report (2017).

V. Alencar Mayer Feitosa Ventura, *Environmental Jurisdiction in the Law of the Sea*,
https://doi.org/10.1007/978-3-030-50543-1_1

currently undergo, such as eutrophication of coastal waters, marine pollution by micro-plastic, oil spills and the degradation of coastal habitats, land-based pollution, over-fishing, among others.[2] On top of those stresses, data of the United States National Oceanic and Atmospheric Administration (NOAA) evidence how little is known about the oceans, as scientists stipulate that less than 20% of the world ocean has been mapped, observed and explored.[3]

In light of the prevailing economic and geopolitical interests in the oceans, it would not be too radical to see them as a battlefield of multiple (and sometimes opposing) interests from distinct actors. On the one hand, different ocean uses include leisure, tourism, commerce, fishing ground, hydrocarbons exploration and exploitation, mining, scientific research, preservation, communication, among others. On the other hand, different actors include flag, researching, coastal, port states, among others, which on occasion may have conflicting interests in the oceans. Opposition stems from the fact that oceans are both an important economic and geopolitical variable in every nation's socioeconomic and security calculations, respectively. From a realist perspective, those considerations comprise the so-called core of "high politics" surrounding the ocean uses, while "low politics" issues can be framed as the scientific and environmental variables—matters that are not perceived as absolutely vital to the existence of the state.[4] In other words, in the battlefield of the ocean, states look primarily forward to asserting geopolitical influence and economic exclusivity rather than advancing pure scientific knowledge on the oceans or conserving habitats and ecosystems.

Since medieval times, the oceans have lain amidst disputes between sovereign states, largely due to the conflicting interests and unilateral jurisdictional assertions seawards. Issues of *jurisdiction*, i.e. of *rights* and *duties* over specific physical media,[5] have since long occupied a central role in the traditional law of the sea. Those disputes were focused on navigation and communication, because of the fact that the oceans were predominantly seen as unidimensional. That scenario changed after World War II, when the law of the sea incorporated new features: pluri-dimensionality, situational nature, focus on the coastal states and the evolution from a law of communication to a law of resources, among others.[6] In fact, since

---

[2]More on each of these environmental challenges in WWF (2016), pp. 6, 39.

[3]National Oceanic and Atmospheric Administration of the United Sates (NOAA), Ocean Facts, *How much of the ocean have we explored?* Available online at: https://oceanservice.noaa.gov/facts/exploration.html Accessed 30 March 2020.

[4]For more on the distinction between "low" and "high" politics, based on the concept of "complex interdependence" in international relations, *see* generally Keohane and Nye (1977).

[5]The generic reference to jurisdiction in the law of the sea as the ensemble of rights and duties over particular maritime spaces or activities is backed by the formulation of the concept sketched in the work of Alex Mills. Thus, jurisdiction is to be conceived not only as a "ceiling" (limit) to state powers, but also as a "floor", containing the minimum requirements for the exercise of regulatory powers. Such approach is embraced in this work and further detailed in Chap. 4. *See* Mills (2014), p. 210.

[6]*See* Marotta Rangel (1985), p. 388.

1945 it has become pluri-dimensional, encompassing the dimensions of surface, atmosphere and the seabed and subsoil underwater. Upon the discovery of riches of the seabed and subsoil, the law of the sea was no longer a mere communicational law, but rather a law of resources, aimed at regulating more than just the water surface.

Increased economic interests in the various dimensions of the oceans reinforced developing states' disagreement with the short length of the territorial sea, traditionally fixed at 3 nm. Moreover, the unequal access to the oceans and its resources by states with larger capabilities and greater technical knowledge prompted developing countries to seek for exclusive access to a share of marine resources adjacent to the shore. Prior to the signature of the 1982 Convention on the Law of the Sea (UNCLOS),[7] and within the highly politicized and ideological context of the Cold War, the oceans served as a thermometer to estimate the political and economic tension between the maritime powers (a category usually equivalent to the "industrialized North") and developing coastal states (a category usually associated with the "global South"). In this sense, the decades preceding UNCLOS were marked by bolder jurisdictional assertions of coastal states who dismissed the traditional dual division of the seas and the prevalence of the Grotian freedom of the seas as unfair towards developing states and, therefore, conflict-prone.

Upon the adoption of UNCLOS, the international community migrated from a dual- to a multiple division of the oceans, in which several newly codified maritime zones reflected political and not ecological boundaries.[8] The freshly conceived partition encompassed the contiguous zone (CZ), the exclusive economic zone (EEZ), the continental shelf (CS), the high seas (HS) and the Area, among others, each endowed with a particular legal regime. To make it even more complicated, the maritime zones often overlap, and so do their legal regimes.[9]

In order to enable the functioning of such a complex system, UNCLOS grounded the new division on a few basic premises. Firstly, the distinction between marine sovereignty and jurisdiction, according to which coastal states were accorded sovereignty, or very extensive rights, over the territorial sea, but *functional jurisdiction* over other adjacent zones. The concept of functional jurisdiction is much more restrictive than that of sovereignty, and thus limited *ratione materiae* and *ratione loci*, depending on the maritime space in question. Materially, jurisdiction in the newly created zones relates to specific functions or activities of coastal states. *Ratione loci*, the competences of coastal states were limited to the boundaries of the maritime space at stake. Another key premise which inspired the new division of the oceans was the principle of *regression*, in line with which coastal states' powers

---

[7]UN Convention on the Law of the Sea, UNTS vol. 1833, 10 December 1982.

[8]Klemm (1999), p. 431.

[9]The author of this book has published a paper in the Brazilian Journal of International Law, on the clash between the principles of freedom of the seas and that of territorial sovereignty, and how it has been shaping the law of the sea since the birth of the discipline. *See* Ventura (2015), p. 52.

gradually weakened the farther away from the shore one is.[10] In this sense, coastal states were to exercise fewer substantial rights (and were less strictly obliged) on the EEZ or the continental shelf than in the internal waters, territorial sea, and contiguous zone.

Among the series of compromises that enabled the crafting of such new and complex division[11] was the possibility of lawfully delineating a continental shelf that extends beyond the default 200 nautical miles (nm) applicable to the EEZ by virtue of Art. 57 UNCLOS.[12] In other words, coastal states were to be acknowledged functional jurisdiction over the natural prolongation of their land mass beyond 200 nm, provided they comply with the scientific and technical formulae contained in Art. 76 (4) to (6) UNCLOS, and perform the complete delineation procedure before the UN Commission for the Limits of the Continental Shelf (CLCS).[13] The Commission, one of the three treaty-based bodies devised by UNCLOS, is charged with entertaining the geographic, geodesic and oceanographic data submitted by coastal states, and making recommendations on the outer limits of the continental shelf claimed in these submissions.[14] The continental shelf laying beyond 200 nm has been commonly referred to by the literature as "outer", "extended" or "legal" continental shelf, expressions which will be used as synonyms throughout this work.[15]

Thus far, 77 states have lodged submissions for outer continental shelves, among which Australia, France, UK, Canada and *Brazil*. This last country, which is at the core of the present work, was the second state to forward to the CLCS a submission for the delineation of the outer limits of its continental shelf, as early as 2004. Altogether, it claimed outer limits that should have approximately 911.000 km^2 of seabed and subsoil fall under some degree of Brazilian jurisdiction. Yet, only approximately 80% of the claimed area has been accepted. The initial submission was followed by revised partial submissions in 2015 and 2017.[16] National ambitions towards exclusive rights over an amplified Brazilian continental shelf is a significant part of the "Brazilian Blue Amazon", concept coined in 2004 by the Brazilian Navy to raise public awareness to the economic, geopolitical, scientific and environmental

[10]Gavouneli (2014), p. 15.

[11]UNCLOS' negotiators opted for the "package deal" methodology, according to which all key (and polemic) topics were negotiated in packages (or groups), and to be approved in its entirety by consensus, so that no particular self-interests could prevail in the process. *See* Tanaka (2012), p. 28.

[12]The continental shelf of broad-margin states may extend up to 350 nm from the baselines or to a distance not exceeding 100 miles from the 2500-meter depth isobath. The most beneficial variable shall apply for coastal states, in line with Art. 76 (4) to (6) UNCLOS.

[13]Art. 76, paragraph 8, UNCLOS.

[14]Art. 76, paragraph 9, UNCLOS.

[15]In French, the expression "plateau continental étendu" shows preference for the term "extended". *See* generally Tassin (2013).

[16]*See* Brazilian Executive Summary, "*Continental Shelf and UNCLOS*", presented to the CLCS, 8 September 2017, available at: https://www.un.org/Depts/los/clcs_new/submissions_files/submis sion_bra.htm. Accessed 30 March 2020.

relevance of the ocean adjacent to the country's paradisiac shore.[17] Let us keep that in mind, as the Brazilian policy and legal marine environmental framework stand on the spotlight of this book's last chapters.

The very possibility of coastal states having extended jurisdiction seawards, even if limited, results from the traditional clash between freedom of the seas (*mare liberum*) and territorial sovereignty (*mare clausum*) in the law of the sea. Yet, more importantly, it seems that such dichotomy has been lately coexisting with another rather recent one: the trichotomy between those principles and principles of marine environmental protection, thus rendering it a de facto trichotomy. By the time UNCLOS was signed, the wave of *prise de conscience environmentale* had marine environmental concerns inchoately permeate the international agenda, and Parts V and XII of the Convention, alongside its Preamble, undeniably reflect those concerns. In line with this new "conscience", oceans are a common good that must be cared for by governments, having such task been entrusted to governments by the public.[18] Two chief ecological concerns of the time made their way into the wording of the Treaty, namely over-fishing and marine pollution (from land, seabed, and shipping activities).

Agreeing upon an internationally binding instrument punctuated with audacious, environment-oriented norms was certainly a much important step to enhance the overall ocean health. Drafters of the Convention believed that decisive action by national states constituted a key part of the solution to environmental issues. Yet, for environmental norms to be effectively implemented, two further steps ought to supplement the entry into force of international rules, and those steps take place in the national sphere: the exercise of *prescriptive* and, subsequently, *enforcement* jurisdiction by states parties to the treaty.[19] In other words, the implementation of environmental norms heavily depends on the states' domestic action. That ascertainment implied a shift in the perception that the international community had on coastal states: from enemies of the marine environment, to guardians of the common goods; from part of the problem, to part of the solution, to put in a simplistic manner.[20] Hence, alongside the "nationalization" of marine natural resources adjacent to the shore, coastal states were awarded a key role in advancing the environmental conservation of the world ocean.[21]

Such jurisdictional expansion did not (and does not) go unquestioned. As early as 1956, Josef Kunz criticized the "doctrine and practice of the continental shelf",

---

[17]Carvalho (2005).

[18]That theory is referred to as the "public stewardship of the oceans" and it claims that "the government should exercise environmental and economic control over these with a broad sense of responsibility toward all citizens and their long-term interests". *See* Sand (2007), p. 521.

[19]For more on the "three step approach" to environmental law implementation, *see* Hafner (2006), p. 347.

[20]Tassin (2013), p. 31.

[21]As Garrett Hardin's theory on the "tragedy of the commons" suggests, natural resources considered as global commons would not escape soon depletion, given the clear incentives to exploit without caution. *See* Hardin (1968), p. 1243.

abhorring the "triumphant upsurge of national sovereignty" against the long-established customary principle of freedom of the seas.[22] Similarly, Richard Bilder claimed that "any coastal state extension of jurisdiction into the contiguous high seas, even if functionally limited, tends over time to expand to include more claims, until it becomes the functional equivalent of a territorial sea, in substance if not in name".[23] More recently, and in the very same line, Bernard Oxman has famously sounded the sirens on the "territorial temptation" of states,[24] in order to raise the international community's awareness to an alleged insatiable hunger of coastal states for increased jurisdiction seaward. That extended jurisdiction, so James Kraska, can be cloaked as environment-based measures, which admittedly enjoy more persuasive justification power in the eyes of the international community.[25]

In an age when environmental concerns occupy a more relevant place than ever in international rule- and decision-making, it is important to permanently reshape the balance between freedom of the seas, coastal state jurisdiction over the seabed, and those principles of environmental protection of marine areas. In light of the expansion of coastal states' sovereign rights to explore and exploit, it is relevant to assess whether that expansion was accompanied by greater powers to legislate and enforce locally designed environmental regulations on one specific part of the ocean: the outer continental shelf. In an area that embodies the jurisdictional ambitions of coastal states, such as the outer continental shelf, it is pressing to define the precise environmental regime applicable therein.

1.2 Subject Matter

In light of the factual background introduced above, it should rest clear that this work focuses on the environmental jurisdiction of coastal states on the continental shelf. As such, it is narrowed down to the study of the relationship between the *sovereign rights* to explore and exploit the resources of the continental shelf within and beyond 200 nm, and the *obligations* to protect and preserve the marine environment of the seabed under national jurisdiction.[26] Those rights are confronted with environmental considerations and obligations that fall upon coastal states when conducting activities in the depths.

Together with the Preamble, UNCLOS' Parts V (on the EEZ), VI (on the continental shelf) and XII (on the marine environment) provide a general

[22]Kunz (1958), p. 828.

[23]Bilder (1973), p. 104.

[24]In his critique, Oxman labels territorial temptation as "a unilateralist impulse often born of narrow agendas, impatience, frustration or politic and bureaucratic ambitions". This concept was inspired on Jean-François Revel's expression "totalitarian temptation" (1978). *See* Oxman (2006), p. 24.

[25]Kraska (2011), pp. 1–9.

[26]Arts. 76, 77 and 78 of Part VI, UNCLOS.

intra-conventional framework applicable to the marine environment. In the Preamble, whose normativity has been repeatedly reaffirmed by the international legal literature, the signatories recognize the "desirability of establishing a legal order for the seas and oceans which will [...] promote the conservation of their living resources, and the study, protection and preservation of the marine environment". In addition to that, Art. 56 (1) (a) and (b) grant coastal states not just sovereign rights to manage and conserve the marine environment of the EEZ, but jurisdiction with regard to the "protection and preservation of the marine environment". When it comes to Part XII, Arts. 192 to 194 codify states' general obligation to protect the marine environment, alongside the duty to exploit natural resources taking into account their duty to protect and preserve the marine environment. Furthermore, the Convention has several provisions on special duties to prevent, reduce and control marine pollution, including from seabed activities.[27]

In addition to that, the legal environmental regime applicable to the continental shelf is also to be found in other international environmental agreements, such as the 1992 Convention on Biological Diversity (CBD),[28] which states in Art. 3 the general principle according to which states have "the sovereign right to exploit their own resources pursuant to their own environmental policies, and the responsibility to ensure that activities within their jurisdiction or control do not cause damage to the environment of other States or of areas beyond the limits of national jurisdiction". Complementing such general principle, states parties are equally obliged to, as far as possible and as appropriate, identify and monitor components of biological diversity, as well as to take measures to promote the *in-situ* and *ex-situ* conservation of that biological diversity.[29]

With that in mind, this work has attempted at all costs to avoid a solipsistic view of the international law of the sea, thus fostering a porous relationship between the international law of the sea and international environmental law. It was at no time intended to stimulate the bracing of an excluding view, one that praises the "epistemic domination" of one special legal regime by another, as it is also not about asserting the superior epistemic validity of the continental shelf regime over the regimes applicable to other maritime zones; nor the superiority of the law of the sea rules against environmental rules.[30] It is rather an exercise of mapping out and asserting the valid rules for continental shelf activities, be them in law of the sea instruments or environmental ones.

Results obtained in the initial phase of the investigation are, then, complemented by a case study research on the state practice of a particular state: Brazil. Why Brazil and its Blue Amazon? For one, because the country has undoubtedly been a major

[27] Arts. 192, 193, 194, as well as Arts. 208 to 222, UNCLOS, on the international rules and national legislation to prevent, reduce and control pollution of the marine environment.

[28] Convention on Biological Diversity, 1760 UNTS 69, 5 June 1992.

[29] Arts. 8 and 9, CBD.

[30] A critique to the so-called "superior epistemic validity" of certain subsystems of international law can be found generally in Crawford and Koskenniemi (2012) Introduction.

player in international ocean negotiations and law-making. To start with, reference ought to be done to the country's participation in international negotiations for current binding and non-binding oceanic instruments. Here, Brazil has played a proactive role in shaping the contemporary law of the sea, with emphasis on its participation in international negotiations and promulgation of international binding and non-binding instruments during the second half of the twentieth century. The great number of international instruments regarding maritime activities signed and ratified by the Brazilian state suggests the country's dedication to the international rule of law applied to oceans.

Another reason for selecting Brazil as the target of a case study stems from the fact that the environmental governance of the Brazilian continental shelf has earned the spotlight in the wake of the 2009 CLCS recommendation acknowledging Brazilian sovereign rights over a large portion of the seabed of the South Atlantic Ocean beyond 200 nm. Such recognition has raised questions, *inter alia*, as to the adequateness of existing domestic rules and regulations to manage—in the sense of protecting and exploiting—such submarine universe. Studies within the country have revealed the abundance of marine life abounds in several parts of the Brazilian continental shelf, within and beyond the claimed 200 nm.[31] The conservation of fragile ecosystems, as the seamounts neighboring the Atlantic islands of Trindade and Martim Vaz, or the coral reefs off the Amazon river delta, in the Northern cone of Brazil, have inspired this research and the need for regulating the management and uses of the continental shelf, so that the national ecological patrimony does not vanish by virtue of inadequate domestic laws and policies, nor deficient enforcement.

1.3 Problemfelder

Despite the apparent "glut" on legal continental shelf-related investigations, suggested by the reduced number of recent publications on that topic in comparison with the early 2000s, the legal regime of the continental shelf has still not been entirely understood, in particular the environmental jurisdiction of coastal states in the portion of the seabed beyond 200 nm. This work assumes, thus, an original and necessary character for several reasons. For one, it is never too late to discuss the complex interaction between law of the sea and environmental law in the overlapping zones of the continental shelf, the high seas and the Area. Secondly, the likelihood of exploitation activities on the outer continental shelf has never been

[31]The project *Atlas Mar*, of the Brazilian Institute for Geography and Statistics (IBGE) has pinned several entries of marine life around the seamounts of Martim Vaz e Trindade, as well as in the Vitoria-Trindade Chain and the Northern Amazonas Cone, portions of the seafloor that Brazil claims to pertain to the country's continental shelf, but which have been rejected by the CLCS following the first Brazilian submission. *See* IBGE, *Atlas geográfico das zonas costeiras e oceânicas do Brasil*. Available at: http://www.atlasmar.ibge.gov.br/ Accessed 30 March 2020.

as concrete as it is now, a situation which has awaken the interest of practically every broad-margin state worldwide to delineate its outer limits. The extension of the continental shelf does not come without responsibilities for coastal states, especially in light of the overall precarious condition of the marine environment worldwide. So, this work also highlights the need to assess the precise implications of the extension of the continental shelf in terms of environmental duties and obligations for the coastal states, so as to, subsequently, map out the environmental jurisdiction of coastal states on that zone. Finally, this work offers a detailed insight into the domestic legal and policy framework of a particular state with respect to the management of the continental shelf, namely Brazil.

The continental shelf, especially beyond 200 nm, is one of the maritime zones where major challenges to the sustainable governance of the oceans are expected to occur, namely the need to accommodate economic activities therein with the protection of the marine environment and the conservation of its biodiversity. Practical examples include illegal fishing for crustaceans and sedentary species; illegal marine scientific research on the continental shelf; illegal sampling of marine genetic resources; marine pollution from oil and gas exploitation activities and deep-se mining, among others. Scientific reports have recently concluded that "the marine environment is not improving",[32] and the United Nations Environmental Programme (UNEP) has warned that "the outlook is poor and alarming for the continuing wellbeing of marine biodiversity".[33] Those concerns are not purely hypothetical or academic, as exploration activities are already taking place in continental shelves beyond 200 nm around the world, the two most prominent examples in this regard being Canada and Norway.[34] In short, exploitation of the ocean seabed seems inevitable.[35]

In this context, it is undeniable that UNCLOS has permanently influenced the behavior of states and shaped the landscape of international relations regarding the oceans for better. The Convention's significance in regulating oceanic uses lies, among others, on the fact that "it provides a comprehensive regulatory regime for all maritime matters, without being the typical framework convention so frequently encountered in other branches of international law."[36] In fact, the much-praised

---

[32]Dimento and Hickman (2012), p. 80.

[33]UNEP (2010), p. 5.

[34]Canada is expected to bid areas for exploitation as late as early 2019, while Norway has stepped domestic debate on how to best implement the country's obligation to make financial contributions to the International Seabed Authority (ISA), in line with Art. 82 UNCLOS. Information on this regard has been obtained with Wylie Spicer and Rodrigo More, lawyers that have been engaging for a long time in continental shelf matters.

[35]On a rather sensational and tabloid tone, yet informative, *see* Klare (2012), pp. 20–22. According to the magazine "Maritime Executive", there is a growing demand for the exploitation of nonliving resources in the continental shelf. *See* "Global deepwater expenditure expected to increase by 69 percent between until 2019, to reach a total of US$ 210 billion", Maritime Executive, April, 2015.

[36]Gavouneli (2006), p. 205.

"constitution of the oceans"[37] remains, in the view of some commentators, "the one example of a successful integral document, which has come to prevail over any other expression of State power by the sheer force of its existence".[38]

UNCLOS, however, does not offer enough clarity on the *activities* that may be regulated by the coastal state, nor the *material extent* of the jurisdiction to regulate seabed activities under national jurisdiction. When disciplining the environmental jurisdiction of states—flag, coastal and port states alike—on the outer continental shelf, the Convention has embraced ambiguous terms and relied on generalized formulations.[39] For instance, it does not specifically address some environment-related questions, such as the regulation of the establishment of marine protected areas by coastal states on the outer continental shelf; nor has it clearly regulated the practice of bioprospection or the sampling of genetic resources in areas within national jurisdiction. The very definition of bioprospection is not consensual in the law of the sea, as views differ: to industrialized states, bioprospecting ought to be considered as marine scientific research, whereas to coastal developing states it clearly is a commercial activity that ultimately profits from resources inhabiting the seabed.

In addition to that, confusion still exists as to the precise rights and powers of coastal states on the continental shelf's entirety. As rightfully pointed by Joanna Mossop, one regime of the continental shelf does not fit all, as certain rules vary between the shelf within and beyond 200 nm.[40] Take, for instance, the case of the right to regulate and authorize marine scientific research on the continental shelf, regulated by Art. 246 UNCLOS. According to that provision, marine scientific research shall be conducted with the *consent* of the coastal state, which may not withhold consent in specific situations—paragraph 5. The situations which restrict the right of coastal states to withhold consent to research projects on their maritime spaces vary between the continental shelf within and beyond 200 nm, what suggests the existence of a dual legal treatment for the issue. On the continental shelf within 200 nm, coastal states shall grant consent under normal circumstances, whereas beyond 200 nm, those states may not withhold consent, except for specific situations. In light of that, some coastal states' interpretations of the right to regulate marine scientific research vary so much that certain states, such as Brazil, claim the right to regulate all kinds of research both on the inner continental shelf and on the area claimed outer limits.[41]

This work aims to map out and understand coastal states' competencies to regulate activities which may impact the marine environment of that specific maritime space—particularly in light of the normative overlaps between the continental shelf, the EEZ, the high seas and the Area. The exercise of environmental powers in

---

[37]Koh (1982) Speech.

[38]Boyle (2005), pp. 563–567.

[39]*See* generally Ong (2010).

[40]Mossop (2016), p. 193.

[41]Resolution no. 003/2010, Interministerial Commission for Marine Resources (CIRM).

areas farther and farther away offshore is not usually well-seen by maritime powers, as coastal states have, on occasions, allegedly cloaked territorialist intents under the premise of advancing regulatory mechanisms for marine ecological conservation.[42] The augment of domestic jurisdiction seawards is, thus, often regarded as coastal states' sheer "territorial temptation".

Another critique to the very concept of an outer continental shelf has been formulated on the theoretical level, based on the perception that the symbolism of coastal states' increasing powers seaward reinforces a traditional logic of appropriation or enclosure of common goods, such as the high seas.[43] The present work entertains that argument and also discusses whether a renewed balance between the principles of environmental protection and sovereign rights over marine natural resources is possible, or whether the extension of continental shelves necessarily represents a detrimental move to marine environmental protection efforts around the globe.

The problems referred to above affect several coastal states worldwide. Yet, one particular country holds great ambitions towards the oceans, seeks regional *oceanopolitical* influence in the South Atlantic Ocean and holds a contested record of territorialist stances when interpreting the law of the sea. That country is Brazil, whose aims to exploit mineral resources farther away offshore, technologically backed by the worldwide renowned expertise of its state-owned oil company, Petrobras, raises questions as to the adequacy of the country's domestic legal framework to sustainably manage the entirety of the "Brazilian Blue Amazon", in particular the continental shelf. Thus, this work departed from the need to assess the consistency of Brazil's national policies and legislation with UNCLOS relevant provisions, to evaluate the country's legal and policy adequacy to face the challenges of managing approximately 4.5 million km^2 of jurisdictional maritime zones. Such a study has not been thoroughly conducted yet, neither in Brazil, nor abroad, and not only serves as legal guidelines to Brazilian future regulations in the field, by highlighting the corresponding international duties, but also identifies domestic lacunae in terms of marine environmental legislation and policies.

1.4 Research Questions

This contribution is part of a larger scholarly effort to tackle traditional and isolated approaches within the law of the sea. It joins such efforts and offers no finished solutions, but reflections and insights into two main questions: firstly, what is the material extent of coastal states' environmental jurisdiction—to legislate and to enforce—on the continental shelf within and beyond 200 nm?

---

[42]It is the case of Kraska's critique (2011), p. 9.

[43]This view can be found in the work of Pahuja (2012), pp. 398–401.

The marine environment is complex, and its regulation should adopt a holistic and integrated perspective. Precisely this vastness and complexity calls for the specification of the object under scrutiny, if the research is to succeed in conducting analyses and reaching credible conclusions. In fact, every scientific study is narrowed down to the analysis of a particular aspect of a broader whole, which does not mean it denies the need for integrated solutions to problems affecting that particular universe. Hence, this work does not aim at exhausting the comprehension of possible conflicts and lacunae concerning the whole of the marine environment. To the contrary, it aims at offering a detailed examination of the legal environmental treatment given to one maritime zone within Brazil: the continental shelf.

Secondly, and on an empirical basis, are the Brazilian marine environmental policies and legislation consistent with general international law and the law of the sea, namely UNCLOS? The national statutes analyzed within the efforts to answer that second question include the Federal Constitution, the Ocean Act (Act n° 8.716 of 1993) and a plethora of sparse legislation aimed at regulating specific marine activities which take place on or may affect the quality of the marine environment of the continental shelf.[44] Incidentally, this work entertained the question whether the procedure of delineating outer continental shelf limits has triggered specific legal-environmental obligations for the Brazilian state, in particular the adaptation of domestic rules to UNCLOS and general international law provisions.

Basically, the arguments embraced in this work are the following. Firstly, that because of a long-established narrative contrary to coastal states' jurisdictional expansion seawards, coastal states' environmental jurisdiction on the continental shelf has been said to be significantly more limited than it actually is. This work maps coastal states' rights and duties, prescriptive and preventive jurisdiction over activities which may affect the seabed marine environment to confirm that argument. To that task, it is paramount to refer to UNCLOS and to international environmental instruments, so that identified coastal states' environmental powers do not reinforce skepticism among the international community concerning the rights of other states in maritime zones intersecting with the continental shelf.

Brazil has partially implemented its environmental jurisdiction over the continental shelf. Yet, national policies comprise a complex and confusing web of provisions, which not always leads to a good grasp of the country's powers and obligations over the Blue Amazon. Besides, some pieces of legislation are either inconsistent with UNCLOS, or do not incorporate UNCLOS key provisions, such as those on the revenue-sharing mechanism of Art. 82, into the domestic legal framework.

[44] Some of the domestic statutes examined in this work include the Decree no. 96.000/1988 (Marine Research Decree); Act no. 9.985/2000, which regulates the designation of environmental protected areas, including in the ocean; Act no. 9.605/1998 (Environmental Crimes Act); Decree-Law no. 227/1967 (Mining Code), among others.

1.5 Structure

From the outset, this investigation was meant to combine a research on (i) environmental law and the law of the sea; (ii) on the outer continental shelf; and (iii) the Brazilian marine environmental framework in the context of the "Brazilian Blue Amazon". That is how the investigation was split in two main titles: 1. The environmental jurisdiction of coastal states over the continental shelf; and 2. The consistency of the Brazilian marine environmental policies and legislation with international law, in particular UNCLOS. Chapters were organized in a logical manner, so as to facilitate the formulation of the book's main arguments.

Hence, Chaps. 2 and 3 start the discussion by defining the object under investigation, namely the continental shelf within and beyond 200 nm. Several key concepts to the international legal regime of the continental shelf are presented and debated in those early pages. Subsequently, Chaps. 4, 5 and 6 dwell into the equally core concepts of sovereignty and jurisdiction in the international law of the sea. Those pages shed light on the complex intersections between the different regimes of the continental shelf, high seas, EEZ and the Area, in order to justify the need for clearer rules on coastal states' powers on the specific zone of the continental shelf. Furthermore, a critique against the widespread use of the phrase "creeping jurisdiction" is formulated, as a means to pave that the way for the following chapters.

Chapters 7 and 8 consist of one of the work's two cores and scrutinize the material extent of coastal states' environmental jurisdiction on the continental shelf, in an assessment which categorized environmental rights and duties in three main axes: conservation of living resources; prevention, reduction and control of pollution arising from the commercial development of non-living resources, and the regulation of marine scientific research. Finally, and based on the findings reached until then, Chaps. 9 and 10 complete the second *nucleum* of this work, and contain the detailed case study of the Brazilian domestic policy and legal framework applicable to the marine environment, as part of a broader effort to assess the country's adequateness to pursue the sustainable management of the "Brazilian Blue Amazon", especially with respect to its continental shelf.

1.6 Methodology

To answer the questions detailed above, this work has adopted the methodological techniques of a typical interdisciplinary research in public international law. The research techniques employed in both parts of this work include *bibliographic and documental revision*. Vast literature was consulted and summarized on sustainable development, the principle of governance of the oceans, marine environmental jurisdiction, rights and duties of coastal states on the continental shelf, the intricacies of the procedure to delineate the outer continental shelf, among others. Several theories and theses have been examined, ranging from the theory of "*mare nostrum*", by Phillip Allot,[45] to the one which sees UNCLOS as a "living treaty", by Jill Barret and Richard Barnes,[46] and many more.

The investigation was also grounded on the analysis of *primary sources*, mainly UNCLOS and the CBD, their respective drafting histories, and doctrinal commentaries to them. For that, intense use of purpose-oriented hermeneutics of law of the sea provisions and environmental principles is to be expected in the coming pages, in line with the famous Art. 31 of the Vienna Convention on the Law of Treaties. Besides, abundant resort was also made to case law from international and national tribunals.

Another research technique actively employed was the investigation of *state practice*, in particular the Brazilian one, via resort to history books and documents which maintain a track of the Brazilian stances in law of the sea negotiations throughout the last decades. Regarding the study of state practice, this work had due regard to the method of "ideational positivism", advanced by Anne Peters, consisting in the search for a "via media" between infertile alienation from and fetishism with international legal practice.[47] In this sense, attention will be paid to the legal practice of states, but not exclusively, as theoretical considerations shall also permeate the arguments put forward throughout this work. Other relevant methodological works are the ones by Olivier Corten[48] and Phillip Allott,[49] both profound analysts of language and method in Public International Law.

This research has also relied on valuable information provided in personal, unrecorded *interviews* with diplomats of the Brazilian foreign service, Navy officials, legal consultants to the Navy and the Brazilian Ministry for Foreign Affairs, maritime lawyers and professors of law. The interviews were collected between November 8 and December 27, 2016, in the federal capital, Brasília, as well as in the city of Fortaleza. The following authorities were interviewed: Lieutenant Kenia Piccoli, Blue Amazon Division of the Interministerial Commission for Marine Resources (CIRM), linked to the Brazilian Navy—November 17, 2016; Prof. Dr. iur. Marcelo Dias Varella, Legal Advisor and Legislative Advisor to the Ministry of Justice—November 18, 2016; Prof. Dr. iur. George Rodrigo Bandeira Galindo, Legal Advisor to the Ministry of Foreign Affairs—November 22, 2016; Prof. Dr. iur. Carina Costa Oliveira, Professor of Environmental Law and International Law of the Sea at the University of Brasília—November 25, 2016; and Prof. Dr. Rodrigo Fernandes More, Lawyer and Legal Advisor to the Brazilian delegation responsible for drafting the revised proposal for outer continental shelf limits before the CLPC—November 28, 2016.

The criteria used to select the interviewees were: (i) their direct or indirect participation in the elaboration of the Brazilian request for extension of the

---

[45] Allott (1992), p. 764.

[46] Barrett and Barnes (2016), p. 3.

[47] Peters (2016), p. 2.

[48] *See* generally Corten (2009).

[49] Allott (1971), p. 81.

continental shelf to the CLCS; (ii) acting as active formulator of public policies in the Ministries, Commission or Groups mentioned above; (iii) their consolidated knowledge of the doctrine of international environmental law and law of the sea. All interviews lasted approximately 50 min. The questionnaire initially envisaged was adapted to the authorities' time availability, in order to extract more quality inputs for the research. Direct contact with the interviewed authorities enabled access to official documents of different shades, which were of crucial relevance to this work.

Due to confidentiality clauses, the precise content of the interviews is not present in this book. Yet, the possibility of enquiring high-ranking public authorities of the Brazilian state that are directly engaged with the management of the country's Blue Amazon has granted this study valuable insights and contributed with first-hand information on that issue in Brazil. The last part of this work relies on the triangulation of the content obtained in those interviews, with the findings reached through bibliographic revision and the consultation of primary sources.[50] Such triangulation made it possible for this study to assess the conformity of the official discourse in Brazil, regarding the country's jurisdiction over the continental shelf, with current laws and the actual practice of the state in that regard.

Finally, the investigation counted on an *empirical axis* as well, namely on the method of case study. Understood as the "intensive study of a single case which draws on observational data and promises to shed light on a larger population of cases".[51] The case of the Brazilian Blue Amazon offers the possibility to explore the argument according to which, without a domestic legal and institutional framework consistent with international law, namely UNCLOS and CBD, the expansion of the continental shelf may reinforce suspicions against the detrimental effects of an enhanced territorial temptation of coastal broad-margin states. In short, this part of the research has chosen depth over breadth by sticking to the study of one country's legal marine environmental framework.

1.7 Terminological Notes

Prior to entering into the merits of any discussion, a few terminological notes are due, so that author and reader share the same meaning of key concepts and possibly controversial expressions used throughout the work. Firstly, this book mostly refers to the plural form "coastal state*s*", while most of the works in the field adopt the singular version. That should be interpreted as a deliberate, political statement in favor of treating coastal states as a group, not a singularity, particularly so in light of the historical strategy of coastal (developing) states to coalize in larger groups, such

[50] For more on the methodological technique of triangulating information obtained through field research, see Flick (2004), p. 178.

[51] John Gerring calls this sort of highly specialized study a "small-C study", as it deals with either one or very few cases. *See* Gerring (2017), p. 28.

as the Group of the 77. In any case, the reference to states in plural does not affect the meaning of the expression nor the clarity of the argument.

Still on the employment of the word "state", this study adopted the lowercase form, another political statement. This time, it relates to the struggle against hierarchy between the subjects of international law: as long as persons are referred to in lowercase, so should be international organizations and states. In addition to the political motivation, that also reflects an option of style. Whenever the study quotes the writings of other scholars, though, capital letter is preserved.

The words "oceans" and "seas" *in abstracto* are used interchangeably, in order to refer to massive bodies of water separating land that possess their own chemical dynamics and functioning.[52] Respect will be paid, nonetheless, to the kind of fixed expressions referred to supra, such as "territorial sea" or "regional seas programme".

With respect to the expression "continental shelf beyond 200 nautical miles", the literature has more often than not chosen to use of a shorter version for it, as "outer" or "extended" continental shelf. Whereas UNCLOS Art. 76 (5) to (9) refers to the "outer limits of the continental shelf", nowhere in the Convention are the phrases "outer" or "extended" continental shelf to be read. Within international courts and tribunals, the full expression is favorited: "continental shelf beyond 200 nm". The Arbitral Tribunal in the *Barbados v. Trinidad and Tobago case* refused to use the term "extended" continental shelf, for it could lead to the false impression that the shelf was being factually extended,[53] when, as a matter of fact, it was not; it has been there *ab initio*. Just the outer limits over which the coastal state exercises sovereign rights on the continental shelf are increased, in a purely legal move that prompts scholars to indicate a "legal continental shelf".[54] That same Arbitral Tribunal opted to use the expression "outer continental shelf".

Yet, it is tempting to use the shorter description for reasons of practicability, so as to enable the text a better flow, particularly in light of the need to constantly refer to that maritime area. Besides, the context of the work suffices to clear confusions regarding to meaning of the shorter expressions. Hence, this work will rely on previously used forms "outer" and "extended" continental shelf interchangeably. Eventually, the expression "shelf" may come unaccompanied of the additional "continental", as the meaning of the concept is understandable from the context of the discussion. As a standard for this kind of work, it should also be noted that the meaning of "outer continental shelf" adopted here differs from that of American

[52]This work is aware of the distinction adopted by NOAA, according to which "seas are smaller than oceans and are usually located where the land and ocean meet. Typically, seas are partially enclosed by land". See NOAA, *What's the difference between an ocean and a sea?*, available online at: https://oceanservice.noaa.gov/facts/oceanorsea.html. Accessed 30 March 2020.

[53]PCA *Arbitration between Barbados and the Republic of Trinidad and Tobago, relating to the delimitation of the exclusive economic zone and the continental shelf between them*, vol XXVII, 11 April 2006, 165.

[54]Suarez (2008), p. 13.

legislation which considers "outer" to comprise the submerged land beyond 3 geographical miles of the baselines, which fall under jurisdiction of the United States.[55]

Apart from that, the use of "nm" to refer to nautical miles may also be scientifically inaccurate,[56] but it is widespread in the international legal literature. So, will this work refer to nautical miles as "nm". Other key concepts to this work will be defined in the beginning of their respective chapters, for stylistic reasons. As such, the definitions of "sovereignty", "sovereign rights", "functional jurisdiction", "marine environment" and "environmental jurisdiction", among others, are found throughout this work. Now, to the beginning of the story.

References

Allott P (1971) Language, method and nature of international law. Br Yearb Int Law 45:79–135

Allott P (1992) Mare nostrum: a new international law of the sea. Am J Int Law 86(4):764–787

Barrett J, Barnes R (eds) (2016) Law of the sea: UNCLOS as a living treaty. BIICL, London

Bilder R (1973) The Anglo-Icelandic fisheries dispute. Wisconsin Law Rev 37(1):37–132

Boyle A (2005) Further development of the law of the Sea Convention: mechanisms for change. Int Comp Law Q 54:563–584

Carvalho RG (2005) A Amazônia azul. Folha de São Paulo, 11 May, 2005

Corten O (2009) Méthodologie du Droit Internationale Public. Editions de l'Université de Bruxelles, Bruxelles

Crawford J, Koskenniemi M (eds) (2012) The Cambridge companion to international law. Cambridge University Press, Cambridge

Dimento J, Hickman A (2012) Environmental governance of the great seas: law and effect. Edward Elgar, Cheltenham

Flick U (2004) Triangulation in qualitative research. In: A companion to qualitative research. SAGE Publications, London, pp 178–183

Gavouneli M (2006) From uniformity to fragmentation: the ability of the UN Convention on the law of the sea to accommodate new uses and challenges. In: Unresolved issues and new challenges to the law of the sea: time before and time after. Nijhoff, Leiden

Gavouneli M (2014) State jurisdiction in relation to the protection and preservation of the marine environment. In: The IMLI manual on international maritime law. Oxford University Press

Gerring G (2017) Case study research: principles and practices. In: Strategies for social inquiry, 2nd edn. Cambridge University Press, Cambridge

Hafner G (2006) Meeresumwelt, Meeresforschung und Technologietransfer. In: Handbuch des Seerechts. Beck, Munich, pp 355–462

Hardin G (1968) Tragedy of the commons. Science 162(3859):1243–1248

IBGE (2019) Atlas geográfico das zonas costeiras e oceânicas do Brasil. http://www.atlasmar.ibge.gov.br. Accessed 30 Mar 2020

Keohane RO, Nye JS (1977) Power and interdependence: world politics in transition. Little Brown & Co, Boston

Klare MT (2012) The race for what's left: the global scramble for the world's last resources. Metropolitan, New York

[55]Outer Continental Shelf Lands Act, 7 August 1953, United States of America.

[56]In hard sciences, the abbreviation for nautical miles is "N", whereas "nm" stands for nanometers.

Klemm C (1999) Fisheries conservation and management and the conservation of marine biological diversity. In: Developments in international fisheries law. Brill, Leiden, pp 431–455
Koh TB (1982) A constitution for the oceans. Third United Nations Conference on the Law of the Sea
Kraska J (2011) Maritime power and the law of the sea: expeditionary operations in world politics. Oxford University Press, New York
Kunz LJ (1958) Continental shelf and international law: confusion and abuse. Am J Int Law 50 (4):828–853
Mills A (2014) Rethinking jurisdiction in international law. Br Yearb Int Law 84(1):187–239
Mossop J (2016) The continental shelf beyond 200 nautical miles: rights and responsibilities. Oxford University Press, Oxford
NOAA (2018) Ocean facts. How much of the ocean have we explored? https://oceanservice.noaa.gov/facts/exploration.html. Accessed 30 Mar 2020
Ong D (2010) The 1982 UN Convention on the law of the sea and marine environmental protection. In: Research handbook on international environmental law. Edward Elgar, Cheltenham
Oxman BH (2006) The territorial temptation: a siren song at sea. Am J Int Law 100(4):830–851
Pahuja S (2012) Conserving the world's resources? In: The Cambridge companion to international law. Cambridge University Press, Cambridge, pp 398–414
Peters A (2016) The refinement of international law: from fragmentation to regime interaction and politicization. MPIL Research Paper Series 2016–2019: 1–29
Rangel VM (1985) Le plateau continental dans la Convention de 1982 sur le Droit de La Mer. Collect Courses Hague Acad Int Law 194:269–428
Sand PH (2007) Public trusteeship for the oceans. In: Liber Amicorum Judge Thomas A. Mensah. Brill, Leiden, pp 521–544
Suarez SV (2008) The outer limits of the continental shelf. Beiträge Zum Ausländischen Öffentlichen Recht Und Völkerrecht 199. Springer, Heidelberg
Tanaka Y (2012) The international law of the sea. Cambridge University Press, Cambridge
Tassin VJM (2013) Les défis de l'extension du plateau continental: la consécration d'un nouveau rapport de l'État à son territoire. Pedone, Paris
UNEP (2010) Global synthesis: a report from the regional seas conventions and action plans for the marine biodiversity assessment and outlook series. Nairobi, Kenya
Ventura VAMF (2015) Tackling illegal, unregulated and unreported fishing: the ITLOS advisory opinion on flag state responsibility for IUU fishing and the principle of due diligence. Br J Int Law 12(1):50–67
WOR (2017) Coasts – a vital habitat under pressure. World Ocean Review. Maribus, Hamburg
WWF (2016) Living planet report 2016: risk and resilience in a new era. WWF International, Geneva

Jurisprudence

PCA (2006) Arbitration between Barbados and the Republic of Trinidad and Tobago, relating to the delimitation of the exclusive economic zone and the continental shelf between them. Decision of 11 April 2006. In: Reports of International Arbitral Awards, Vol. XXVII, UN, New York

Chapter 2
The General International Legal Regime of the Continental Shelf

The new law of the sea received this qualifier in the years following the adoption of UNCLOS to mark the paradigmatic shift between maritime provisions that had existed before it and those which were born after it. The negotiation of the Convention, a herculean task which aimed at regulating all known uses of the oceans and redefining powers and obligations over newly crafted zones, is still praised as a landmark in international law. In fact, for some authors, it marked the beginning of a new era for the law of the sea, one that features a more balanced distribution of rights and duties over the seas, in accordance with the emergence both of independent states following the decolonization wave of the 1960s and modern technologies enabling intense commercial uses of the oceans.

A renewed regime that was forged on systematic opposition to the traditional order of the oceans, and on the practice of territorialization and disorder in the pre-UNCLOS ocean system. Such subversive behavior by several states was important, as it defied the model of colonial spoliation which inspired the traditional international law of the sea (customary and convention) until that time. The "new" law of the sea, as opposed to the old one, was thus sensitive to social, economic and human needs, which sees in maritime spaces not just the ideal landscape for navigation, but also the treasures capable of satisfying various needs of peoples. In short, a law of the sea focused on enhancing life conditions of each people and of humanity as a whole.[1] It is juridically accurate, thus, to refer to special regimes in international law, the new law of the sea being case in point.

In order to make that clear, this chapter undertakes a brief incursion into issues dear to the theory of international law, namely the emergence of special regimes and the mutual relationship between them, so as to pave the way for material discussions on the legal regime applicable to the continental shelf.

---

[1] *See* generally Rangel (1966).

V. Alencar Mayer Feitosa Ventura, *Environmental Jurisdiction in the Law of the Sea*,
https://doi.org/10.1007/978-3-030-50543-1_2

2.1 The Law of the Sea as a Special Legal Regime of Public International Law

The definition of regime will change accordingly if one navigates from law into international relations and political theory. For a legal audience, regimes are a set of codified legal norms (which excludes implicit rules) shaping individuals and state behavior, backed by a particular institutional and organizational edifice. In line with the international relations' theory, regimes are "sets of implicit or explicit principles, norms, rules and decision-making procedures around which actor's expectations converge in a given area of international relations".[2] Whereas from a political theory standpoint, regimes would be rather be described broadly as "governing arrangements constructed by states to coordinate their expectations and organize aspects of international behavior in various issue areas. They thus comprise a normative element, state practice, and organizational roles."[3] Note the emphasis on "arrangements", instead of rules, which are set in motion to "coordinate expectations", and not to shape behavior.

In international law, regimes may be qualified as "self-contained", "special", among others. In a 2006 Report on the fragmentation of international law, the International Law Commission (ILC) spoke against the misleading use of the term "self-contained regime", which could imply a hermetically closed set of primary and secondary rules, non-existent in international law. Not even the law of diplomatic relations is that closed.[4] Although no regime should ever be described as entirely self-contained, it is correct to speak of "special" regimes, understood as a set of rules and principles concerned with a particular subject-matter.

For the purposes of this work, here are key assumptions concerning the idea of law of the sea as a special regime of international law. Firstly, regimes are "sets of norms, decision-making procedures and organizations coalescing around functional issue-areas", which deal deals with specific areas of international life, such as human rights law, humanitarian law, environmental law, refugee law, among others.[5] In addition to that, it ought to be clear that regimes are sets of rules "dominated by particular modes of behavior, assumptions and biases" of those making, implementing and enforcing international law.[6] In short, they are part of the social construction of law, and of law as a cultural product.

The specialty of some regimes was at the root of much concern during the 2000s, when international lawyers voiced fears that international law could be losing its unity and becoming helplessly fragmented. As newer regimes emerged and consolidated, such as international environmental, trade and climate change law, new treaty

[2]Krasner (1982), p. 2.

[3]Kratochwil and Ruggie (1986), p. 759.

[4]Koskenniemi (2006), p. 11.

[5]Young (2012), p. 9.

[6]*Id.* 11.

clauses and rules followed suit, which sometimes were not entirely compatible with traditional general law or previous specialized law.[7] The debate went on for some years, with fragmentation at the center of the debate, embraced as inevitable (though not necessarily good) by some, demonized by others,[8] until a conciliatory position gained momentum. As it seemed, fragmentation was (and remains) rather "natural" to international law, as it is constantly being shaped by the emergence of new values and by the specific demands of subjects in a pluralistic global society.[9]

In that sense, the "functional specialization" of international law partially helps explain the emergence of special legal regimes, based on the Weberian idea of formal rationality and functional specialization in modern bureaucracies[10] to understand the *emergence* of special international rules. Partially, because that theory does not apply in its entirety to the law of the sea, which is not the result of a perceived need for rules to regulate the ocean, but the consequence of a long-standing clash of interests that had been dragging on for the past four centuries. First, in the form of custom, then as treaties.

That said, it does make sense to refer to a certain degree of "functional specialization" in the law of the sea since the end of World War II, when a new set of qualities were attributed to oceans which entirely changed the significance of those large bodies of water in the eyes of states. Until the end of that conflict, the traditional dual division took only two dimensions of the seas into account: water surface and water column. Oceans were essentially vectors for the carriage of goods and transport of persons (surface), as well as sources of food and vectors of communication, via submarine cables (water column).

After 1945, technological breakthroughs added other dimensions to the equation, i.e. subsoil and airspace. At stake were not only living resources (fisheries), but especially non-living resources, such as hydrocarbons and minerals on and underneath the seafloor. Humankind was finally able to explore and exploit natural resources, namely hydrocarbons, in depths unknown to men before. In addition to that, technologically advanced states were able to capitalize on energy resources from the airspace above water, such as wind and solar energy. In a nutshell, perception of the economic and strategic meaning of this pluri-dimensionality of the seas played a most relevant role in precipitating objection not only to the traditional dual division, but also to the preponderance of untouchable freedoms. It became clear to international lawyers that the law of the sea was undergoing profound changes, to such an extent that even during negotiation on a binding treaty

---

[7]Koskenniemi (2006), p. 14.

[8]Prominent scholars such as Teubner and Fischer-Lescano embraced the rhetoric of fragmentation. *See* Fischer-Lescano and Teubner (2004), p. 999. On the other side, dismissing fragmentation and calling for unity was Cançado Trindade (2010), p. 37.

[9]The discussion has cooled off recently, with the overriding conclusion that the unity of international law was never at stake, but was just forced to coexist with newer types of rules and newer demands. It is the case of Anne Peters, to whom international law has entered a benevolent phase of "regime interaction" and politicization. *See* Peters (2016), p. 1.

[10]Weber (1978), p. 85.

for the oceans, statements of a "new international law of the sea" were common in literature.[11] Such pluridimensionality may be looked at from the perspective of a "functional specialization", which prompted the need for renegotiations on the fundamental rules and principles grounding the law of the sea.

Thus, the law of the sea is a special regime of international law, one of the oldest ones. As such, it is also susceptible to suffering from some of the threats that affect special regimes as a whole in international law. One of them is the *essentialization* or *reification* of certain *lex specialis*, in which the notion itself of regimes blurs the generality of international law and jeopardizes a correct understanding of the international legal system. The use of metaphors and allegories in referring to legal regimes, such as "islands", "ships", "platforms" etc., as if to show that they stand alone, mirrors that essentialization and results in an imprudent and counter-productive effort of describing how international law functions. As rightfully pointed out by Koskenniemi, an extreme functional differentiation between special regimes may even lead to path dependency, higher transaction costs, "tunnel vision", and "solipsistic and imperial tendencies" from stronger and more consolidated sets of rules.[12]

In this context, the conduct expected from international lawyers is to perceive international law as a general system of rules and principles, without limiting one's understanding to a specific set of functional rules. On a broader picture, the only way international law can reflect the interests and needs of the international society is through the regime interaction, which may lead to a more responsive and effective international legal system than merely the sum of individual regimes. Such a mindset is extremely valid for the law of the sea, a regime that heavily relies on interdependence with other regimes, in a complex relation dictated by the multifaceted nature of oceans.

On that regime interaction, especially law of the sea and environmental law, lies one of the main pillars of this work: the analysis of the environmental jurisdiction of coastal states over the continental shelf before and after the delineation of the outer limits of that shelf. To this quest, it is not sufficient to restrict the research to legal provisions pertaining to the law of the sea. One must read beyond UNCLOS—the "bible", and employ provisions, principles and rules of international environmental law instruments. In light of the evolution of environmental values and standards worldwide, it would be unwise to envisage the law of the sea as a static and self-contained system. To the contrary, the law of the sea, as a special regime, cannot be

[11]The theory of pluridimentionality (or multidimentionality) of the oceans was originally formulated by Marotta Rangel, with the difference he labeled the newer dimension as "depth", whereas to our understanding the dimension of depth had already been exploited via the setting of submarine cables since mid-nineteenth century. The appended dimensions were the subsoil of submarine areas and the air column above the sea. *See* Rangel (1981), p. 41.

[12]Koskenniemi (2012), p. 305.

understood without reference to later developments in the realm of international environmental law.[13]

2.2 UN Convention on the Law of the Sea: Cornerstone of the New Law of the Sea

The new law of the sea emerged, at least formally, upon the adoption of the 1982 UNCLOS and its Annexes I to IX, followed by other international binding and non-binding instruments which unified previous regulations and created a true legal order for the oceans. The main purpose of such order is to facilitate international communications, promote the peaceful use of the seas, and the equitable and efficient use of its resources.[14] For that reason, UNCLOS is commonly described as "a comprehensive constitution for the oceans",[15] perhaps "the most significant international agreement since the Charter of the United Nations". It is the most iconic document for the law of the sea, finishing-line of almost 10 years of hard-fought negotiations between different formal and informal groups of states, each one upholding specific interests while shaping the new *ordre publique* for the oceans.[16]

The entry into force of UNCLOS can be portrayed as an earthquake in the traditional international ocean law landscape. The negotiation efforts praised many times in academic publications, and the comprehensiveness of that treaty increase its relevance for the regulation of ocean matters. UNCLOS was, indeed, the first document to codify a comprehensive legal framework for the rational and

[13]It was the case of the 1992 Rio Declaration and the Convention on Biological Diversity, among several others. For more on such necessary inter-relation between those regimes, *see* Birnie et al. (2009), p. 384.

[14]Other instruments include the Implementation Agreement of Part XI of UNCLOS (1994), and the UN Agreement on Straddling and Highly Migratory Stocks, A/CONF.164/37, 8 September 1995.

[15]Koh (1982).

[16]UNCLOS' negotiations were particularly tough, in light of the chosen "package deal approach", i.e. the Convention's provisions as constituting a coherent whole. *See* Harrison (2011), pp. 44–45. A direct consequence of such drafting methodology is that states may not make reservations or exceptions to the Convention, as posited in Art. 309 UNCLOS. In addition to that, Art. 310 allows signatory states to make declarations, provided they do not "purport to exclude or to modify the legal effect of the provisions of this Convention in their application to that State". An example is the case of Brazil, which has expressed concern over the possibility of foreign military vessels conducting military exercises in water off the Brazilian coast. The Brazilian Declaration reads: "The Brazilian Government understands that the provisions of the Convention do not authorize other States to carry out military exercises or maneuvers, in particular those involving the use of weapons or explosives, in the exclusive economic zone without the consent of the coastal State". Brazil (1988) UNCLOS Declarations and Statements (n. 52). Such refrain might be connected to the country's history of foreign interventions since colonial times and, in recent history, due to US Navy presence, in the case of the Operation *Brother Sam*, a movement by the United States Navy to support the military coup d'état in 1964. *See* Cavalcanti (2015) chap. 3.

sustainable exploitation of marine natural resources, while continuously recognizing the relevance of navigational freedoms.[17]

The main modifications (or advancements, if one may) operated by the adoption of UNCLOS are the following. Firstly, it shifted the balance of powers between flag states, more interested in maintaining freedom of navigation, and coastal states, dedicated to regulating and controlling activities off their coast. Traditionally, the conflicting nature of the law of the sea could be summed up to the ancient and opposing doctrines of "open seas" (*mare liberum*) and "closed seas" (*mare clausum*). Based on such fundamental opposition, the law of the sea has always been "made, changed, challenged and remade."[18] Each doctrine gives birth to different principles of the law of the sea. On the one hand, the *mare liberum* thesis is supported by the freedom of the seas' principle, which had in Hugo Grotius its main defender.[19] On the other, the *mare clausum*, defended by authors such as William Welwood.

Nowadays, prevalence of the principle of freedom of the seas was called in question and the balance leaned towards the principle of sovereignty, as the Convention codified additional powers to coastal states. A most relevant factor during negotiations was the participation of newly independent African and Asian states, which embraced positions significantly different from those of their colonial predecessors. Conjointly with other third world countries, sympathetic to the political orientation of the Group of 77,[20] they played an important role during the III UN Conference on the Law of the Sea. Against this backdrop, the Conference may be associated to the phenomenon of the "rise of coastal states", one that fulfilled old demands of exclusive jurisdiction over marine resources. The solution found by the international community to balance such antagonistic views was to crystalize in UNCLOS a primordial logic for the law of the sea: "as the maritime zones become more distant from the coast, coastal State jurisdiction reduces and the strength of high seas freedoms increases".[21]

Secondly, that power shift has also been potentialized by the emergence of a key principle for the management of the oceans, namely their seabed. In fact, the common heritage of mankind (CHM) principle altered dramatically the previous balance between the ancient principles of *mare liberum* and territorial sovereignty. The common heritage principle will trigger profound changes on the continental shelf regime, in special given the limitation of national continental shelves and the establishing of a hybrid treatment for activities on the continental shelf beyond

[17]Birnie et al. (2009), p. 383.

[18]Pirtle (2000), p. 7.

[19]*See* Grotius (2004), p. 95.

[20]The Group of 77 advocated a more radical form of "common heritage of mankind" principle, based on the ideology underpinning the so-called New International Economic Order (NIEO), designed to rebalance economic relations between industrialized countries of the North and poorly developed states of the South, as discussed in Chap. 5.

[21]Mossop (2016), p. 8.

200 nm. However, the principle, its origin, definition and relationship with the continental shelf regime will be analyzed in detail in Chap. 3. For now, it suffices to mention its codification as one of the greatest developments in international law (not just of the sea), a development that approves the innovative and ground-breaking character of UNCLOS.

From an environmental perspective, UNCLOS has moved from an initial focus on responsibility and liability for environmental damage to one on international regulation and cooperation, without ignoring the relevance of attributing liability and the respective compensation.[22] In fact, the Convention incorporated some of the inchoate environmental discussions held at Stockholm in 1972, during the Conference on the Human Environment, and developed stronger environmental standards on a reactive basis, following oil tanker disasters, namely the Torrey Canyon in 1967 and the Amoco Cadiz in 1978.[23] While the Torrey Canyon oil spill triggered the adoption of the OILPOL Convention in 1969, focuses primarily on liability and compensation schemes, UNCLOS laid emphasis on the preventive role of international law, through the codification of a duty to cooperate, as well as to enact measures to prevent, reduce and control pollution of the marine environment.[24]

The 45 articles comprising UNCLOS Part XII on the protection and preservation of the marine environment represented a revolutionary step taken by the international community towards an increased *prise de conscience environmentale*,[25] placing the Convention amongst the first binding documents (perhaps the first on a global scale) to regulate environmental uses of the ocean and set protection and conservation principles and standards. The innovative character of UNCLOS was such that Wolfrum and Matz-Lück enquired whether the Convention could even be considered an environmental treaty, having righteously concluded for the negative.[26] In short, the Convention was born ahead of its time. Remained, however, a product of its time, i.e. facing increased limitations in light renewed challenges posed by rapidly advancing technologies. It is not to be hailed as the beginning and end of the law of the sea, the answer to current questions may lie in the interface between UNCLOS and instruments of other special regimes.[27]

---

[22] Art. 195 ff. UNCLOS. Liability is dealt particularly with regard to pollution from oil. On the other hand, provisions on international cooperation include Art. 283 and others.

[23] *See* 1972 Stockholm Declaration, UN Conference on the Human Environment, A/RES/2994, 15 December 1972.

[24] Arts. 194 UNCLOS, on the duty to adopt measures to reduce, prevent and control pollution of the marine environment, and 197, on the duty to cooperate on a global or regional basis.

[25] Kiss (2005), p. 115.

[26] For Wolfrum and Matz-Lück (2000), p. 42, despite the plurality of environmental provisions punctuating UNCLOS, it must not be forgotten that the treaty is rather of a liberal nature, much more trade and communication-oriented.

[27] In this regard, there have been plenty of works examining the relationship between UNCLOS and other treaties, in particular the "major" environmental law treaty, the 1992 Convention on Biological Diversity. For further detail, *Id.* 445–480.

In light of such limitations, posed by unforeseen challenges such criminal jurisdiction on the EEZ (as faced by the International Tribunal for the Law of the Sea in the *Enrica Lexie* case),[28] climate change, ocean acidification *et al.*, a possible approach is to envisage the Convention as a "living instrument". In other words, a treaty that enjoys continuous vitality and evolves over time as a result of reiterated interpretation of its provisions, thereby growing and evolving, just like a living organism. For Barrett and Barnes, for instance, UNCLOS can adapt to changing circumstances and to address major challenges not foreseen at the time of negotiations.[29] Such growth is made possible by heteronomous inputs, which use the text of the Convention itself. In other words, it does not take an amendment to change UNCLOS, but interpretations by treaty-based institutions and informal processes of change.

If seen as a constitution (which establishes a system of institutions, and organizes the governance of the oceans alongside other legal regimes), UNCLOS should not be read in isolation. "Lives beyond the terms of any individual text".[30] There is an intrinsic relevance of further interaction between formal and informal processes of change, and the role of actors interested in the implementation of UNCLOS's provisions. Concerning internal mechanisms of change, one could mention the amendment conference; and a simplified procedure or procedure for amendments to Part XI.

In the process of evolving, there is an undeniable role to be played by UNCLOS's institutions: the International Tribunal for the Law of the Sea, ITLOS; the International Seabed Authority, ISA; and the Commission for the Limits of the Continental Shelf, CLCS. Take, for instance, ITLOS' decision to recognize advisory jurisdiction to the full court in the 2015 Advisory Opinion on Flag State Responsibility for Illegal, Unregulated and Unreported Fishing, which, due to the ground-breaking interpretation of the Convention, was faced with resistance by members of the international community. The United Kingdom, for example, rejected the possibility of reading UNCLOS as "living instrument" with powers of its own, particularly so in matters of assessing jurisdiction.

Another important actor in advancing homeopathic changes in the Convention is the Meeting of the State Parties (SPLOS), an organ that has the competence to pass non-binding resolutions, which are nonetheless meaningful for the purpose of "breathing life" into UNCLOS. They are not supposed to interpret UNCLOS, but do it anyway. In addition to the SPLOS, one could not obliviate the GAIRS, or Generally Accepted International Rules and Standards—reference to external rules that are essential to the implementation of UNCLOS.[31]

---

[28]ITLOS *"Enrica Lexie" Incident (Italy v. India), Provisional Measures*. Order of 24 August 2015, ITLOS Reports 2015.

[29]Barrett and Barnes (2016), p. 14.

[30]*Id.* 14.

[31]*Id.* 21.

Finally, state practice and the production of soft law do play a role in equipping UNCLOS for contemporary challenges. On the side of state practice, evolution occurs via "subsequent agreements" (two of which adopted during the 1990s), or reiterated action, which may contribute to a "subsequent practice", pursuant to Art. 31 of the Vienna Convention on the Law of Treaties.[32] General rule to interpret in good faith, respecting the meaning of the terms used, but also in the light of the object and *purpose* of the treaty. On the soft law level, the Agenda 21 and the adoption of a clear sustainable development goal, via the adoption of the precautionary principle for instance, has heavily influenced UNCLOS' interpretations regarding marine environmental affairs.[33]

Regardless of the standpoint adopted by the legal operator (whether optimistically facing UNCLOS as a living instrument, or rather pessimistically seeing the Convention as flawed body of provisions on several fields), one cannot deny the profound change it effected on the continental shelf regime. Prior to the examination of those changes, in particular relating to the possibility of a legal outer continental shelf that may extend beyond the traditional 200 nm, this work ought to present the state-of-the-art regarding principles and rules for the continental shelf as codified in the Convention. Chapter 3 will then closely dissect the implications inherent to the delineation of outer continental shelf limits.

The most relevant Part of UNCLOS for the purpose of this work is the Part VI, which sets out the rules and principles applicable to the continental shelf and concerns exclusively the *natural resources* present therein. In general, Part VI provides a definition of continental shelf, features the formulae and methods for delimiting its outer limits, creates the CLCS, displays the rights of coastal states over that maritime space and specifies the legal status of the superjacent waters to the continental shelf. It also provides rules for the laying of submarine cables and pipelines on the shelf, as well as rules on contributions and payments demanded from coastal states exploiting continental shelf resources beyond the 200-nm limit—the so-called "revenue-sharing mechanism" of Art. 82. Finally, it contains commands regarding the delimitation of continental shelves between states with opposite or adjacent coasts.

---

[32]Vienna Convention on the Law of Treaties, 23 May 1969, United Nations, Treaty Series, vol. 1155, at 331.

[33]The much spoken-about precautionary principle consists of a legal norm, gradually developed in the past 40 years, that essentially imposes an obligation to take preventative measures in case of risk to the environment and human health. In the realm of the law of the sea, namely in the case of deep seabed mining, an activity inherently dangerous the precautionary principle remains as one of the most relevant legal tools to be implemented by ocean-related organizations, such as the International Seabed Authority (ISA). A discreet element of precaution can be found in Art. 3(1), Annex III, UNCLOS, on exploration and exploitation of the seabed.

2.3 Definition of Continental Shelf Within and Beyond 200 nm

UNCLOS Part VI positivizes rules and principles applicable to the continental shelf, a juridical definition of which is provided straightforwardly by Art. 76 (1):

> The continental shelf of a coastal State comprises the seabed and subsoil of the submarine areas that extend beyond its territorial sea throughout the *natural prolongation* of its land territory to the outer edge of the *continental margin*, *or* to a distance of 200 nautical miles from the baselines from which the breadth of the territorial sea is measured where the outer edge of the continental margin does not extend up to that distance (emphasis added).[34]

It is juridical, for it does not coincide with the strictly geologic or geomorphological characteristics of the shelf.[35] From this definition, some expressions stand out, namely "natural prolongation", "continental margin" and "or" (used in order to mark an alternative to the first, essentially geological, concept of continental shelf), which mark the complex interdisciplinarity of the continental shelf regime, and the entangled relationship between law and science in this particular regard. In order to understand the legal concept of continental shelf, one must be familiar with the geographical notion of "continental margin". As such, the margin consists of "the seabed and subsoil of the shelf, the slope and the rise", excluded the deep ocean floor and its oceanic ridges or subsoil.[36]

An authoritative definition was provided by the International Court of Justice (ICJ) in the North Sea Continental Shelf cases, in which the continental shelf was described as

> the natural prolongation of its land territory under the sea exist ipso facto and ab initio by virtue of the State's sovereignty over the land and by extension of that sovereignty in the form of the exercise of sovereign rights for the purposes of the exploration of the seabed and the exploitation of its natural resources.[37]

A key development in the continental shelf regime established by UNCLOS is the possibility given to broad-margin coastal states to exercise rights over a submerged area stretching out beyond 200 nm from the baselines. Such area is still labelled as "continental shelf", but due to some particularities, it has also been tagged *outer continental shelf* by academic works in the field. A definition for that "extra" seafloor describes the outer continental shelf as "the area of sea-bed and subsoil ranging from the 200-nm EEZ limit to the seaward limit of the legal continental shelf, incorporating the geological continental shelf, rise, slope and margin but not including the

---

[34] UNCLOS Art. 76, paragraph 1, on the definition of the continental shelf.

[35] A geological definition of the continental shelf describes it as a strip of submerged land existing on the entire coast of every continent, which, on a gradual inclination, stretches seaward until the continental slope.

[36] UNCLOS Art. 76, paragraph 3, still on the definition of the continental shelf.

[37] ICJ *North Sea Continental Shelf Cases*, judgment of 20 February 1969, Reports, 1969, 3, para 19.

superjacent water column above it."[38] There occurs, thus, a separation between law and science. The concept of continental shelf adopted in UNCLOS Art. 76 (4) is different from the scientific one. In fact, the continental shelf as regulated by UNCLOS is a legal fiction, which justifies its popular nomenclature as "juridical" or "legal continental shelf".[39] In UNCLOS definition, the seabed itself has a limited role; only distance is preferred.[40]

Historically, the continental shelf can be portrayed as an infant concept within the law of the sea, the birth of which dates back to the well-known Truman Proclamation in 1945. At the outset, however, it should be noted that an in-depth discussion of the history of continental shelf provisions in the law of the sea escapes the purpose of this work. For now, some brief commentaries on the most paradigmatic events leading up to the current continental shelf regime can be of aid in understanding the main rules, functioning and, eventually, weaknesses and deficiencies of that regime.

On a brief, panoramic overview on the evolution of the law governing the seabed, it is no novelty that ground zero was that policy document by the US Presidency. However, a cardinal precursor of such document was the 1942 Treaty Between the United Kingdom and Venezuela on the submarine areas of the Gulf of Paria,[41] which sought to extend coastal rights beyond the traditional 3 nm territorial sea. That agreement was followed by a UK Council Order stipulating the annexation of the British part of the Gulf, using a language that strongly indicates British belief of being entitled to exercise territorial sovereignty over the "submarine areas" of the Gulf, in the first modern reference to "submarine areas".[42] As such, the treaty amounted to the first exercise of sovereignty over the seabed beyond the traditional length of the territorial sea.

In this context, the 1945 Truman Proclamation, popular term for the "Presidential Policy of the United States with Respect to Natural Resources of the Subsoil and Sea Bed of the Continental Shelf",[43] unilaterally declared the natural resources of the subsoil and the seabed of the continental shelf to be under the jurisdiction and control

[38] *See* ILA (2002), p. 11. Also, a definition for the phrase "superjacent waters" may be found in a report by the UN Office for Ocean Affairs and the Law of the Sea (DOALOS) as "the waters lying immediately above the seabed or deep ocean floor up to the surface".

[39] In this sense, Suarez considers that the "legal continental shelf" was the result of a battle between the objective and the subjective. During UNCLOS III negotiations, two proposals on the definition of continental shelf were at the table: the distant-based model and the one based on geology and geomorphology. A compromise was struck by adopting both models. *See* Suarez (2008), p. 13. *See* also Magnússon (2017), p. 8.

[40] Due to the continental shelf's legal character, in particular the space beyond 200 nm, the Brazilian Navy refers to it as "juridical continental shelf", or *plataforma continental jurídica*, in Portuguese. *See* LEPLAC—Plan for the Assessment of the Brazilian Continental Shelf. Available at: https://www.marinha.mil.br/secirm/leplac. Accessed 30 March 2020.

[41] Treaty Between the United Kingdom of Great Britain and Northern Ireland and the Republic of Venezuela Relating to the Submarine Areas of the Gulf of Paria, 1942, LNTS 205, 201.

[42] For more, *see* Proelss (2017a) commentaries to Art. 77, para. 5.

[43] US Presidential Proclamation 1667, 28 September 1945.

of the US. From the document one can extract premises, which inspire the policy being adopted by the American at the time, and the legal content of provisions. Such premises range from a variety of economic, geographical, geopolitical and conservational motives. Firstly, the document was inspirited by clear economic motivations. 1945 marked the end of World War II, a historic event out of which the United States emerged as the world's uncontended industrial power, with insatiable energy needs—in particular, petroleum and gas.

However, technological developments enabled companies to pump oil out of not-so-shallow waters but were confronted with legal insecurity of not being able to exploit a specific oil field with exclusivity, in case it would be located beyond the 3 nm jurisdictional scope of the coastal state. Invariably, that "inability to obtain secure legal title – exclusive rights – was very frustrating to an industry aware of the production potential beyond the three-nautical mile limit".[44] This was the turning point towards a "jurisdictional shift" in the law of the sea, so as to grant companies secure grounds to invest, a reasonable justification for the "jurisdictional preemptive strike" by the federal government of the United States. Hence, the express clause of the Proclamation aiming at encouraging "efforts to discover and make available new supplies of these resources".

Secondly, there was a *geographical motivation*, in line with which "the continental shelf may be regarded as an extension of the land-mass of the coastal nation and thus naturally appurtenant to it". Indeed, the main argument used to back the American claim for extended jurisdiction over the continental shelf was the *natural prolongation of the landmass*, or "land that simply happens to be covered by ocean".[45]

Thirdly, there was a latent security reason, inserted on broader geopolitical (or *oceanopolitical*) concerns, according to which "self-protection compels the coastal nation to keep close watch over activities off its shores which are of the nature necessary for utilization of these resources". Last, but not least, the US also identified the conservation and rational use of marine resources, as early as 1945, as an important premise for the extension of coastal states jurisdiction seaward. In fact, they saw the coastal state as a key player in promoting the rational use of finite marine resources, or as the Proclamation puts it, "jurisdiction over these resources is required in the interest of their conservation and prudent utilization when and as development is undertaken".

Politically, the Truman Proclamation is a master-piece of realism in international politics. In a concise instrument, the US condensed all the necessary dimensions of statehood, supporting the extension of jurisdiction over the submarine shelf seaward. From a legal standpoint, the Proclamation embraced a resource-oriented jurisdiction, in which natural resources of the seabed and subsoil of the continental shelf shall appertain to the US and be subject to their jurisdiction and control. Exercise of such jurisdiction was based on the ideas of *reasonableness and fairness of the claim*, to be

[44]Townsend-Gault (2014), p. 77.

[45]*Id.* 78.

reached via preservation of the "character as high seas of the waters above the continental shelf and the right to their free and unimpeded navigation are in no way thus affected". Hence, the Proclamation did not alter the limits of the territorial waters of the US, making it clear that the expansion of jurisdiction obeyed a functional-economic purpose: the conservation and prudent utilization of natural resources of the continental shelf.

Noticeable in that document was the clear-cut distinction between seabed and superjacent waters, as the Proclamation does not extend coastal state powers to the water column above the shelf, so as not to threaten freedoms of navigation. To make this distinction even clearer, President Truman published another proclamation on fisheries, instead of treating it within the instrument on the continental shelf, in other to pinpoint the difference between seabed and water column. Interestingly, the Proclamation established exclusive resource jurisdiction to the US, but does *not* determine the breadth of the continental shelf under national jurisdiction. The Press Release of the Proclamation suggests the adoption of a depth criterion to assess the continental shelf under US jurisdiction, in line with which "submerged land which is contiguous to the continent and which is covered by no more than 100 fathoms (600 feet) of water is considered as the continental shelf". That would imply, roughly, 182 meters deep.

Following the 1945 Proclamation, several developing states in Central and South America welcomed wholeheartedly the measure and, in their turn, made own unilateral declarations based on the US documents. A detailed list of countries forwarding such claims is provided in Chap. 4, in the scope of the analysis of the "rise of coastal states" and the practice of creeping jurisdiction both before and after the adoption of UNCLOS. For now, it suffices to highlight that a plethora of unilateral jurisdictional claims succeeded, varying in nature, some of them without a single reference to the expression "continental shelf",[46] a phenomenon that led to the need to clarify the limits of coastal State's jurisdiction over maritime zones off their shores.

Thus, after the move by the US President, there was considerable inconsistency on the extent and nature of continental shelf claims by coastal states—some claimed jurisdiction, some claimed sovereignty. The need to place limits on clearly extensive continental shelf claims has triggered the work of the International Law Commission (ILC), which adopted the first draft articles on the continental shelf by 1951.[47] A final version of those draft articles was adopted in 1956, one that combined two criteria for limiting the continental shelf: water depth and exploitability.[48] The draft articles served as the basis for the 1958 Geneva Convention on the Continental Shelf (CSC), which defined continental shelf as the submarine areas adjacent to the coast (but outside the territorial sea) up to a depth of 200 meters *or* to a depth where

---

[46]For an early critique on the phenomenon of jurisdictional claims, *see* Lauterpacht (1950), p. 376.

[47]International Law Commission, *Memorandum on the Regime of the High Seas*, A/CN.4/32, 1950.

[48]Report of the International Law Commission, 8th Session, A/CN.4/102/Add.1, II YB ILC, 1956, at 251.

exploitation of natural resources is possible.[49] Hence, the main feature of the 1958 CSC was the dual criteria for the delimitation of the shelf, i.e. depth and exploitability, following the ILC approach.

Moreover, the CSC already contained the embryo of the "sovereign rights" concept in Art. 2, by indicating the creation of maritime zones with *functional jurisdictions*. There, sovereign rights over natural resources were exclusive, meaning that no other state could, without consent from the coastal State, explore or exploit resources therein. The wording of Art. 2 was copied *ipsis litteris* into Art. 77 UNCLOS. Coastal states are also acknowledged the right to "take reasonable measures for the exploration of the continental shelf and the exploitation of its natural resources".

As clear as in the Truman Proclamation, the rights of coastal States over the continental shelf shall not affect the legal status of the superjacent waters as high seas.[50] Coastal States, when exercising their sovereign rights, are bound by a duty of reasonableness, and may not interfere with high seas freedoms. In fact, coastal States have the right to "take reasonable measures" over the continental shelf, but shall not exercise jurisdiction on the water column beyond 12 nm.[51] The CSC prohibited any unjustifiable interference with: laying of cables and pipelines; navigation; fishing; conservation of the living resources of the sea; and fundamental oceanographic or other scientific research with *intention of open publication* (not applied commercial research).[52] The legislators went as far as possible in the preservation of freedom of navigation above the continental shelf, establishing the illegality of interferences with activities that have an *indirect impact* on the shelf resources, anticipating debates on coastal state measures to limit fishing in the superjacent waters, with an aim at protecting sedentary species of the continental shelf.

An innovation of the CSC lied on the fact that it consistently positivized the obligation to take "all appropriate measures for the protection of the living resources" from harmful agents around the installations.[53] To our understating, this represented a first timid attempt to impose an environmental due diligence obligation to States, but restricted to the 500 meters safety zones. Apart from that, the CSC offered inspiration for several provisions of UNCLOS Part VI, with the exception of Arts. 76 and 82, which relate to the outer continental shelf, a concept not yet in discussion during the 1950s.

---

[49] Art. 1 CSC, on the definition of the continental shelf.

[50] Art. 3 CSC, on the legal status of superjacent waters of the continental shelf.

[51] Art. 4 CSC, on the rights of coastal states to explore the continental shelf and exploit its natural resources.

[52] In the case of "purely scientific research", States shall not withhold consent, but have the right to participate or to be represented in the research, according to Art. 5, paragraph 8, CSC.

[53] Art. 5 CSC, paragraph 7, on the right of coastal states to protect living resources of the continental shelf.

For some authors, particularly in Latin America, the "exploitation criterion" of the CSC benefited exclusively advanced countries, and not just that.[54] In an era of rapidly evolving exploitation techniques as applicable to the oceans, that definition was already outdated upon its entry into force in 1964, due to intense technological progress in the post-war years.[55] Indeed, the length of the continental shelf was obscure and juridically uncertain, while depth and exploitability criteria cared for dissatisfaction over the undefined limits of the continental shelf, which would be subject to forceful adaptation every time new technological advancements allowed for resource extraction in deeper waters, further and further offshore.

Moreover, despite some advantages brought by the 1958 CSC, there was still plenty of uncertainty regarding the limits of maritime claims, such as the territorial sea, or the waters under coastal sates exclusive economic jurisdiction. The increasing amount of States unilaterally extending their territorial seas and maritime spaces under some sort of functional jurisdiction led to the need for a compromise, which ultimately materialized around UNCLOS Art. 76 and the rules on the delimitation of the continental shelf. From 1946 to 1958 alone, fifteen Latin American states changed their maritime borders, whereas in the 1960s some forty states expanded their territorial sea. Such trend could prove deleterious to the principle of freedom of navigation, dear to the United States and to other maritime powers. In fact, there was no consensus on relevant issue, such as the breadth of the territorial sea, or "marginal sea", as phrased by Fraser.[56]

Thus, the birth and development of the continental shelf regime may be compared, for didactic reasons, to that of a strong plant.[57] After the sowing of the seed of extended maritime jurisdiction, the international community witnessed the germination of coastal State authority over living and non-living resources of both the seafloor and the water column in an area much larger than the 3-nm territorial sea. The evolution of the doctrine of the continental shelf, as observed with the regime of territorial waters, revealed a tendency towards the expansion coastal states jurisdiction.

2.4 Core Principles of the Continental Shelf Regime

In international law, legal principles have strong value connotation, as axioms, and are therefore subject to being influenced by different elements, such as historical, cultural, psychologic, political and legal factors. Such a volatile nature may lead to a different approaches and interpretations, depending on the operator actively interpreting a given principle. Menezes believes that the specialization of certain

---

[54]Opinion espoused by Cançado Trindade (2014), p. 209.

[55]On the limitations of the criteria adopted by the 1958 Convention, *see* Poyoyo (1997), p. 247.

[56]Fraser (1925), p. 456.

[57]*See* Schofield (2012), p. 43.

fields of law has contributed to the establishment of a coordinated chain of principles, which work in a systemic and coordinated way.[58] According to Menezes, "the law of the sea is the result of an international normative dialectic, it is an autonomous field, but linked and coordinated axiologically by general international law". Such "dialectics" consists of the dual sources of principles informing the law of the sea, offering guidance and "steering" interpretation and application: general international legal principles,[59] and specific ones, as devised in UNCLOS.

Take, for instance, some of the main principles inspiring the law of the sea system, as the principle of the "common heritage of mankind", an elaboration of the "common concern of mankind", as read in the 1959 Antarctic Treaty;[60] the principle of equality, which involves the equally shared obligation to protect and preserve the marine environment; or the principle of the promotion of "social and economic progress", a norm that can be rather linked to a goal, an aspiration present already in the Preamble of UNCLOS,[61] but still filled with normative content, to the extent of informing other norms of the law of the sea, such as the rule of technology transfer, pursuant to Art. 62 (4) (j), on the transfer of fisheries technology, and Art. 144 of the Convention, on the transfer of deep-sea mining technology between developed and developing states. Those are but a few examples of how much entrenched legal principles are to the law of the sea.[62]

Concerning the relatively short continental shelf regime (in comparison with the set of rules comprising other parts of UNCLOS), the key principles for this study are the natural prolongation, the principle of inherent entitlement of the coastal state to the continental shelf, and the sovereign and exclusive rights of the coastal state over the continental shelf for the purpose of its exploration and exploitation of its resources.

---

[58]Menezes (2015), p. 50.

[59]Examples of the so-called general principles of international law include the principle of consent, reciprocity, equality of states, good faith, finality of awards and settlements, among others. Those are "primarily abstractions and have been accepted for so long and so generally as no longer to be directly connected to state practice". *See* Crawford (2012), p. 37.

[60]The 1959 Antarctic Treaty, 12 UST 794; 402 UNTS 71; 19 ILM 860 (1980).

[61]"*Believing* that the codification and progressive development of the law of the sea achieved in this Convention will contribute to the strengthening of peace, security, cooperation and friendly relations among all nations in conformity with the *principles of justice and equal rights* and will promote the *economic and social advancement* of all peoples of the world, in accordance with the Purposes and Principles of the United Nations as set forth in the Charter". UNCLOS, Preamble, emphasis added.

[62]Take, as a few examples more, the principles of peaceful settlement of dispute, freedom of the seas, territorial sovereignty, pollution prevention, amongst many others within the Convention for the Law of the Sea.

2.4.1 *Natural Prolongation* vs *Distance*

The definition of continental shelf employed in Art. 76 (1) UNCLOS gave a new meaning to the principle of natural prolongation, one radically different from the one adopted in the 1958 CSC,[63] which defined the continental shelf in terms of depth and ability of the coastal state to exploit natural resources of the seabed. In other words, the CSC did not expressly require the need for physical continuity between seafloor and landmass, although such requirement be implicit in the depth criterion and the need for the shelf to be not too distant from the surface. That criterion was different from UNCLOS' physical identity (or natural prolongation) and distance.

The element of physical identity of the submerged land could be seen already in the 1945 Truman Proclamation, where the continental shelf was construed as "the extension of the landmass of the coastal nation and thus *naturally appurtenant* to it" (emphasis added). In fact, if the geological connection of the continental shelf with the landmass was the chief argument espoused by the Proclamation, it followed logically that the contiguous nations may exercise exclusive jurisdiction over continental shelf resources. That was the birth of the principle of natural prolongation of the territory of the coastal state that happens to be covered by ocean.[64] Despite the principle's slight neglection in the 1958 CSC, it was later absorbed and complemented at UNCLOS, which additionally bonded natural prolongation with the geomorphological notion of continental margin, so as to reinforce the physical relationship between them. According to newer provisions, the continental margin equals the continuous and uninterrupted natural prolongation of the landmass seawards, pursuant to UNCLOS Art. 76 (4) (a) (i).

The other criterion, of *distance*, attributed to coastal states a continental shelf of up to 200 nm, "where the outer edge of the continental margin does not extend up to that distance".[65] Practically, to say that coastal states have a continental shelf of 200 nm even where the continental margin does not "naturally prolong" until that breadth, is to say that states will exercise functional jurisdiction over natural resources of the seafloor up to that limit, whatever those resources may be. It does not mean that the Convention sees a geological continental shelf where none exists, but simply that it awards coastal states exclusive and sovereign rights over natural resources of the seafloor until 200 nm, even if that seafloor is the oceanic crust.

As noticeable from the above, the notions of natural prolongation and continental margin are closely interrelated.[66] However, natural prolongation is not the same as continental margin, nor outer continental shelf. Those are similar, but separate concepts. Whereas the continental margin is the geomorphological notion of the

---

[63]Kwiatkowska (1991), p. 157.

[64]Townsend-Gault (2014), p. 78.

[65]UNCLOS, Art. 76, paragraph 1, on the definition of continental shelf.

[66]That finding was confirmed by ITLOS. See *Dispute concerning delimitation of the maritime boundary between Bangladesh and Myanmar in the Bay of Bengal (Bangladesh/Myanmar)*, Order of 14 March 2012, ITLOS Reports 2011, 4, para 437.

seafloor sharing sediment affinity with the mainland, i.e. natural prolongation is a feature, a condition for that affinity. In other words, the continental margin is made possible by the natural prolongation of the terrestrial territory. In addition to that, natural prolongation is the most relevant feature of the outer continental shelf, one that demands the shelf, rise and slope to be part of the natural prolongation of land territory, allowing for the set-in motion of the formulae of Art. 76 (5) UNCLOS.

The practical consequences of the concept of natural prolongation are twofold. Firstly, because of that concept, rights over the continental shelf do not depend on occupation or on any express proclamation, in consonance with Art. 77 (3) UNCLOS. In other words, the right to a continental shelf is an *inherent* right. Besides, natural prolongation constitutes the legal basis of title to an outer continental shelf, to be delineated in line with Art. 76 UNCLOS.[67] As noted by Judge Oda "the concept of natural prolongation for the continental shelf was suggested with a view to defining the international sea-bed area".[68] In fact, evidence of natural prolongation is a condition for the entitlement to a continental shelf beyond 200 nm.[69]

Politically, the concept has shown considerable relevance. For instance, during the Third Conference, Nicaragua reaffirmed that the continental shelf is the natural prolongation of a state's territory.[70] Such a principle was equally reinforced by Uruguay in the country's declarations upon signature and ratification of UNCLOS, according to which "the continental shelf is the natural prolongation of the territory of the coastal State to the outer edge of the continental margin".[71] Those are but a few states which have taken a similar path.

In jurisprudence, there was a period of substantial confusion and controversy surrounding the principle of natural prolongation, in special with regard to maritime

[67]For a contrary view, *see* Hyun Jung Kim (2014), p. 383, for whom the principle of natural prolongation has been eroded to the point of having little legal effect, particularly in maritime boundary delimitation disputes. In fact, the natural prolongation had been weakened due to the artificial emergence of the EEZ and to the need to establish more objective criteria for the determination of the outer limits of the continental shelf. Such changes would have turned the natural prolongation into an irrelevant circumstance in delimitation, "whether the continental shelf extends beyond 200 nm or not". With due respect to that scholar, it seems that the principle of natural prolongation was preserved in UNCLOS, still playing a significant role in determining the outer edge of the continental margin, a pre-requisite for the delineation of the outer limits of the continental shelf. In fact, one of the criteria for determining the outer edge is the *sedimentary affinity* between the seafloor and mainland, pursuant to Art. 76, paragraph 4 (a) (i) UNCLOS. What is sedimentary affinity if not an evidence of the natural prolongation of the land mass seawards? It is, thus, premature to dismiss the principle of natural prolongation as a myth for the continental shelf regime, in particular regarding the shelf beyond 200 nm. That provision will be examined in further detail in the next chapter.

[68]McWhinney (1993), p. 424.

[69]In Jia's opinion, "the notion of natural prolongation still has currency in today's legal regime of the continental shelf". *See* Jia (2013), p. 102.

[70]A/CONF.62/SR.104 104th Plenary meeting Extract from the Official Records of the Third United Nations Conference on the Law of the Sea, Volume IX.

[71]Republic of Uruguay. Declarations made upon signature (10 December 1982) and confirmed upon ratification (10 December 1982).

delimitation disputes. The ICJ was provoked in different occasions to settle boundary disputes involving the continental shelf of coastal states. In the Anglo-Norwegian fisheries case,[72] for instance, the Court professed the famously known dictum of land dominating over the sea, or "it is the land which confers upon the coastal State a right to the waters". A few years later, the same Court attested the connection between the principle of natural prolongation and the determination of continental shelves, in the North Sea Continental Shelf cases.[73] In with the Court's decision,

> a natural prolongation of its land territory into and under the sea exist ipso facto and ab initio, by virtue of its *sovereignty over the land*, and as an extension of it in an exercise of sovereign rights for the purpose of exploring the seabed and exploiting its natural resources. *In short, there is here an inherent right*. In order to exercise it, no special legal process has to be gone through, nor have any special legal acts to be performed. Its existence can be declared (and many States have done this) but does not need to be constituted (emphasis added).[74]

Then, UNCLOS and the idea of a continental shelf beyond 200 nm followed suit, and with them, the need to emphasize the existence of a single continental shelf governed by slightly different rules, instead of two different maritime spaces.[75] Here as well, states had entitlement to the maximum potential geographical extent of jurisdiction over the continental shelf. Maritime delimitation cases involving continental shelves beyond 200 nm demanded courts and tribunals to determine the title, i.e. the area of the shelf itself, to which coastal states were entitled. However, the notion of a single continental shelf is of little help in cases of maritime delimitation beyond 200 nm, where the delimitation methodology will necessarily be different from that of the continental shelf within 200 nm. It was the case of the findings of the ITLOS in the *Bay of Bengal* case, opposing Myanmar and Bangladesh, which will be examined in Chap. 3.

2.4.2 Inherent Entitlement

The principle of inherent entitlement to the continental shelf (within and beyond 200 nm) is intimately connected to that of natural prolongation of the landmass. In

[72]ICJ *Fisheries (United Kingdom v. Norway)*, judgement of 18 December 1951, ICJ Reports, para. 133.

[73]ICJ *North Sea Continental Shelf (Federal Republic of Germany/Netherlands)*, judgment of 20 February 1969, ICJ Reports 1969, at 3.

[74]ICJ *North Sea Continental Shelf Cases (Federal Republic of Germany v. Netherlands/Denmark)*, Judgment of 20 February 1969, ICJ Reports (1969) para 19.

[75]As reinforced by Kunoy (2013), p. 1, "in international law there is only a single continental shelf regardless of whether the zone is beyond or within 200 nautical miles". International jurisprudence also attests the existence of a single continental shelf. See *Dispute concerning delimitation of the maritime boundary between Bangladesh and Myanmar in the Bay of Bengal (Bangladesh/Myanmar)*, Judgement of 14 March 2012, para 361.

fact, entitlement of the coastal state to the continental shelf stems from its sovereignty over the land territory. In other words, "*entitlement* to the continental shelf, as to any other coastal State maritime zone, is based on the *title* of the coastal State over the land".[76] That has been an undisputed assumption in the law of the sea since at least the 1969 North Sea Continental Shelves cases,[77] which has acquired the status of customary international law.[78]

Coastal states' entitlement to the continental shelf is inherent, *ipso facto* and *ab initio*, implying that the shelf does not need to be proclaimed. For the sake of comparison with other maritime zones under national jurisdiction, the right to a continental shelf is always there, due to the coastal state's sovereignty over the land territory from which the continental shelf originates. The contiguous zone and the EEZ, on the other side, need express proclamation by coastal states. Those three zones have a "*sui generis* character"[79] and relate to specific functions, giving birth what is called in the law of the sea as "functional jurisdiction".

The implications of inherent entitlement play out especially regarding the outer continental shelf, where broad-margin states are entitled to a continental shelf beyond 200 nm even if they have not yet established the outer limits, nor forwarded a submission to the CLCS. That is to say, the absence of outer limits established in consistency with Art. 76 does not threaten the entitlement of coastal states to an outer continental shelf, pursuant to Art. 76 (4) to (7) UNCLOS.[80] However, a state's inherent right to an outer continental shelf does not eliminate the burden of demonstrating its entitlement to that area,[81] a topic lying at the core of Chap. 3.

---

[76] *See* ILA (2004), p. 2. It should be noted that there is a subtle distinction between entitlement and title. According to Kunoy (2013), p. 6, "entitlement to the continental shelf corresponds to coastal States' maximum potential geographical extent of jurisdiction, while title corresponds to the area landward the boundaries which the relevant judicial or arbitral forum declares". Hence, in delimitation procedures before international tribunals, courts determine title, and not entitlement, to the area under dispute.

[77] However, it has not been always so, and this discussion is detailed in Chap. 4, on jurisdiction in the law of the sea.

[78] Wolfrum (2008), p. 5.

[79] Molenaar (2015), p. 297.

[80] Detailed discussions on the implication of the inherent entitlement to an outer continental shelf will be further explored in Chap. 3. For instance, whether having entitlement mean that states may exercise sovereign rights over that area before the clear establishment of the outer limits or not.

[81] McDorman (2010), p. 520.

2.4.3 Sovereign and Exclusive Rights

In line with Art. 77 (1) UNCLOS, coastal states exercise *sovereign rights* for the purposes of exploring the continental shelf and exploiting its natural resources.[82] This provision mirrors Art. 2 (2) CSC. By natural resources, UNCLOS means mineral non-living resources (particularly hydrocarbons and minerals of the seabed and subsoil) and living organisms known as sedentary species, i.e. "organisms which, at the harvestable stage, either are immobile on or under the seabed or are unable to move except in constant physical contact with the seabed or the subsoil".[83] Besides, sovereign rights over the continental shelf resources are *exclusive*, in the sense that "if the coastal State does not explore the continental shelf or exploit its natural resources, no one may undertake these activities without the express consent of the coastal State".[84]

States are, thus, recognized a functional jurisdiction, enjoying rights to explore the *territory* (physical medium) of the continental shelf, as well as rights to exploit the resources thereon. References have been made in literature to a "resource jurisdiction" or "economic jurisdiction" of coastal states over the shelf, phrases that, although not wrong, only incompletely depict the rights and duties of coastal states in that zone.[85] In this regard, there seems to be considerable confusion between the notions of continental shelf, sovereign rights and territory, as some authors have described the continental shelf as the "terrestrial territory" of the coastal state, in contrast with the EEZ, which would amount to the "maritime territory" of that state.[86] That is a rather loosen way to refer to a key element of statehood, that of

[82]There is also a debate on the range of the notion of "natural resources", as some domestic legislations seem to adopt an expansive interpretation of this phrase to include "other resources", such as archeological as well as other submerged objects into the hall of resources under its jurisdiction. It must be clear, however, that UNCLOS does not allow for such a broad interpretation. Natural resources are defined in Art. 77, paragraph 4, and contain solely "mineral and other non-living resources of the seabed and subsoil together with living organisms belonging to sedentary species". Such sedentary species are generally accepted as including "clanks, clams, oysters, mussels, scallops, sponges, corals, and crustaceans such as shrimps, prawns, lobsters, and crabs". *See* generally Kojima (2008). According to the ILC Commentaries to the law of the sea, paragraph 3, "the rights in question do not cover so-called bottom-fish and other fish which, although living in the sea, occasionally have their habitat at the bottom of the sea or are bred there". Finally, it should be noted that coastal States have also rights over the *genetic resources* abounding on their continental shelves.

[83]Art. 77, paragraph 4, UNCLOS.

[84]Art. 77, paragraph 2, UNCLOS, which coincides with the ILC Commentaries to the Law of the Sea, of 1956, paragraph 2, 297.

[85]More on the insufficiencies of the phrase "resource jurisdiction" applied to the continental shelf in Chap. 7.

[86]It is the case of Rangel (1995), p. 484, to whom the continental shelf beyond 200 nm meant, imprecisely, that the terrestrial territory of the coastal state could extend beyond the "maritime territory" of that same state.

territoriality. It is often the case with the "political" use of the continental shelf concept, especially beyond 200 nm.

While lawyers usually look at that maritime space in term of rights and obligations, military analysists and domestic policy-makers envisage the continental shelf in terms of "territory" of the coastal state. In fact, the "last boundary" of the Brazilian state, according the Brazilian Navy, is the outer continental shelf.[87] Even though coastal states mostly exercise sovereign rights over the natural resources of the continental shelf (but not just that), geopolitical strategists think in terms of establishing "spheres of influence" seawards. There, an undeniable potential for conflicts emerge, which is a variable of international relations theory that must be taken seriously by international lawyers as well.[88]

Such befuddlement has been addressed by the International Law Association (ILA), upon the assessment that sovereign rights have been commonly "misconstrued as conveying territorial sovereignty and jurisdictional powers available only on land. Thus, sovereign rights are treated as conferring full title and ownership over the continental shelf's natural resources".[89] To be clear, an running the risk of diverging form the ILA findings, having sovereign rights over the natural resources of the continental shelf equates, for the purposes of this work, to having *ownership* over those resources, but not ownership of the entire area. In other words, the natural resources of the continental shelf are *property* of the coastal state. It is following this rationale that the Brazilian Constitution, to quote but one example, considers the natural resources of the exclusive economic zone and the continental shelf as *property* of the Union, and rightfully so.[90] As such, the seafloor itself is not taken as an asset of the state, nor is it territory of the state, but the state has ownership over the natural resources.

It seems logical that coastal states exercise jurisdiction over seabed *activities*, as a consequence of the sovereign rights exercised over the natural resources thereof.[91] For a concise definition of offshore activities, over which the coastal state exercises some degree of jurisdiction, reference can be made to the OSPAR Convention, Art. 1, according to which "offshore activities" mean activities carried out in the maritime area for the purposes of the exploration, appraisal or exploitation of liquid and gaseous hydrocarbons.[92]

---

[87] *See* Marinha do Brasil (2013), p. 1.

[88] Discussions on jurisdictional claims over the continental shelf are the core of Chap. 5.

[89] *See* ILA (2002), p. 14.

[90] Art. 20, paragraph 5, Brazilian Federal Constitution, on the properties of the Union. It should be borne in mind that Brazil is a Federal State divided into three federative entities: Union, States and Municipalities, each with a certain degree of autonomy. In this political scheme, the assets pertaining to the Union are those essential to the preservation of the country's sovereignty and independence.

[91] For instance, UNCLOS grants coastal states the exclusive right to regulate and authorize any drilling of the continental shelf for all purposes, pursuant to Art. 81.

[92] Convention for the Protection of the Marine Environment of the North-East Atlantic, concluded on 22 September 1992, 2354 UNTS 67; 32 ILM 1069 (1993).

Interestingly, the original phrase of "sovereign rights" was crafted during the 1950s by the ILC upon assessing the potential threat to freedoms of the high seas posed by claims of extended jurisdiction beyond the territorial sea—in particular, the continental shelf. Such examination resulted not only in draft articles for the first United Nations Conference on the Law of the Sea (UNCLOS I), but in a series of detailed commentaries to those articles. Hence, in the commentaries to draft article 68 of the law of the sea, which inspired both Art. 2 of the 1958 CSC and Art. 77 (1) UNCLOS, the Commission justifies the chosen wording with the need to prevent interpretations prone to infringing a decisive element of the continental shelf regime, i.e. the "full freedom of the superjacent waters and the airspace above it".[93]

The legal construct of "sovereign rights" emerged from the need to regulate the uses of recently created maritime spaces, the EEZ and the continental shelf, with one ambitious mission: to conciliate respect for the principle of *permanent sovereignty over natural resources* and the restriction of coastal state powers, in order to prevent undue interferences with freedom of navigation.[94] The Commission was reluctant to endorse full sovereignty of coastal states over the seabed and subsoil, out of fear that such sovereignty might ground excessive sovereignty claims to superjacent waters. Hence, the Commission decided to employ a softer expression and to devise a new category of rights, one deriving from state sovereignty but signifying less than full sovereignty. A right addressing specifically one legal good: natural resources.

Hence, the concept of sovereign rights does not mingle with that of sovereignty, it is but "an extract of the broader concept of sovereignty".[95] Firstly, because it relates uniquely to coastal state's rights over natural resources of the continental shelf, not the water column above. As such, the coastal state may not exercise powers that the idea of sovereignty carries along, such as the unrestricted application of national laws to that area. Secondly, because the coastal state exercises only a limited jurisdiction over the continental shelf, its resources and activities thereon.[96] Such state had, thus, a functional/resource jurisdiction, as well as the jurisdiction to prevent and punish violations to the law. With the principle of sovereign rights of coastal states, the ILC believed to achieve a formulation simultaneously compatible with the principle of freedom of the seas and with the needs of the international community as a whole.[97]

Concerns of the ILC as to the menace of coastal state expansion to freedoms of the seas were mirrored in negotiations throughout the second half of the twentieth century. The legal solution was to grant sovereign rights over natural resources, without curtailing traditional high seas freedoms to navigate, to lay submarine cables and pipelines and to fly over the zone. The 1958 CSC codified that particular status

---

[93]*See* generally UN (1956), p. 297.

[94]*See* Ventura (2017), p. 615.

[95]Proelss (2017b), p. 424, mn 9.

[96]The distinction between sovereignty and jurisdiction in international law and in the law of the sea is analyzed in further detail in Chap. 4.

[97]UN (1956), p. 298.

of the water column above the continental shelf, providing that "the rights of the coastal state over the continental shelf do not affect the legal status of the superjacent waters as *high seas*, or that of the air space above those waters".[98] The equivalence of the superjacent waters with the high seas was later dropped, following the appearance of the EEZ, a *sui generis* zone which is neither territorial sea nor high seas. Thus, UNCLOS adopted in its Art. 78 (1), almost the same wording as the CSC, except of the high seas part.[99] Under UNCLOS, superjacent waters to the continental shelf either come under the regime of the EEZ (for the portion up to 200 nm) or the high seas (for the waters beyond that).

That the status of superjacent waters not be confused with sovereign rights over the continental shelf was a guarantee not only for maritime powers, but also landlocked and geographically disadvantaged states, as to their freedom to navigate the oceans.[100] Such freedom was, furthermore, secured by the provision contained in Art. 78 (2) UNCLOS, on the rights of other states in the waters above the shelf, according to which coastal states "*must not* infringe or cause any unjustifiable interference with navigation and other rights and freedoms of other States as provided for in this Convention" (emphasis added). The choice for the expression "must not" was no coincidence, as it accentuates the unambiguous character of the obligation, as wished by the ILC. When commenting upon the relationship between the continental shelf regime and the principle of freedom of the seas, the ILC was of

[98]1958 CSC, Art. 3, paragraph 1. Since the waters above the seafloor within national jurisdiction were, back then, considered as high seas, other freedoms did also apply, namely to navigate, to fish, to conserve living resources and to conduct "fundamental oceanographic or other scientific research". Coastal states were to respect those activities and not to unjustifiably interfere with them, in consistency with Art. 5, paragraph 1, CSC.

[99]UNCLOS Art. 78, paragraph 1, on the legal status of the superjacent waters and air space and the rights and freedoms of other States: "The rights of the coastal State over the continental shelf do not affect the legal status of the superjacent waters or of the air space above those waters".

[100]UNCLOS does not make any prejudice among coastal and land-locked states, having made the high seas open to both categories and awarded freedoms therein for both (Art. 87, paragraph 1). Besides, every state, whether coastal or land-locked, has the right to sail ships flying its flags, in line with Art. 90 UNCLOS, on the right to navigation. According to the Virginia Commentaries, the inclusion of paragraph 2 to Art. 78 "addressed the concerns of states – in particular landlocked states and geographically disadvantaged states – that the extension of coastal state jurisdiction over the continental shelf would infringe on the rights and freedoms granted to those states under other provisions of the Convention". Virginia Commentaries, at 907. It is perhaps exaggerated to credit pressure towards the preservation of the high seas freedoms *particularly* to land-locked states, as maritime powers (which are coastal states) have also displayed much concern as to the possibility of having a limited set of freedoms in the high seas. For that reason, the United States Proclamation expressly preserved the legal status of the superjacent waters to the continental shelf. Later on, during the 1960s, the United States Navy created the Freedom of Navigation Program (FON), in order precisely to counter bold jurisdictional assertions, mostly by developing coastal states, in the years preceding UNCLOS III negotiations. Chapter 4 of this work addresses the expansion of coastal state jurisdiction in further depth.

the view that the former had to be taken as "subject to and within the orbit of the paramount principle of the freedom of the seas".[101]

Amongst the rights of other states sustained by the continental shelf regime was the right to lay submarine cables and pipelines on that maritime space.[102] Such freedom is tempered by several rights attributed to coastal states, namely the right to explore and exploit its natural resources; the right to prevent, reduce and control pollution from pipelines, in accordance with UNCLOS Art. 79 (2); the right to be consulted and to grant consent to the delineation of the trajectory of cables and pipelines; the right over cables and pipelines penetrating its territorial sea; the right to exercise jurisdiction over submarine cables and pipelines on its continental shelf, which is not be understood as a right to without consent for the laying of those objects, pursuant to paragraph 5 of that same provision.

At the end of the day, the insertion of the phrase "sovereign rights" into UNCLOS, so as to govern the regime of the continental shelf, represented a critical compromise in the negotiations for the Convention, continuing a work which date back to 1958, with the CSC. In short, the phrase is a legal construct, developed and adopted to "make it clear that the coastal State did not own the seabed, as advocated by some states",[103] but had the exclusive right to explore and exploit natural resources therein. Freedoms exercised over the water column were duly kept, in order to satisfy the interests of maritime powers, while giving to the interests of coastal states in natural resources offshore. The emergence of the continental shelf regime represents, thus, a vigorous yet not the last step towards the "enormous extension of coastal State rights offshore".[104] In fact, the outer limits of the continental shelf stretching further out beyond the 200 nm are still to be defined.

2.5 Partial Conclusions

Whenever the expression "legal regime" is used, it refers to a body of rules and principles applicable to a particular branch of international law. A central regime to this work is that of the continental shelf, or in other words, "the law of the continental shelf". To approach a fragment of the content of the law of the sea is deemed

[101] UN (1956), p. 298, commentary to Art. 69: "The articles on the continental shelf are intended as laying down the regime of the continental shelf, only as subject to and within the orbit or the paramount principle of freedom of the seas and of the airspace above them. No modification of or exceptions to that principle are admissible unless expressly provided for in the various articles."

[102] Such right to lay cables and pipelines is also preserved in the EEZ regime, according to Art. 58, which incorporates high seas provisions as long as they are not incompatible with Part V, on the EEZ. Here, there is a clear overlap between regimes, which, if nothing, strengthens that specific right of other states in the maritime spaces beyond 12 nm under national jurisdiction.

[103] Jayakumar (2013), p. 6.

[104] Schofield (2012), p. 46.

pedagogical and systematic, allowing an enhanced academic analysis and understanding of the topic.

On the regime of the continental shelf, it has been there for approximately 60 years, since a legal theory on the continental shelf began. Prior to the 1958 CSC, there was only international practice. Since then, expected wealth has been the main motor behind the rush for the ocean floor and for enlarged jurisdiction over natural resources thereof. The continental shelf regime has experimented a monumental development and evolution, with few areas of the law of the sea having developed or evolved as much as part VI UNCLOS. Other fields that have greatly developed are the Area (Part XI) and Protection and Preservation of the Marine Environment (Part XII). It is in the interaction between the continental shelf regime and the regime for marine environmental protection that lies the core of this work: the assessment of the coastal state's environmental jurisdiction over the continental shelf within and beyond 200 nm.

Within the very definition of continental shelf embraced at the Convention, it is possible to observe some of the legal principles governing that maritime space. "Sovereign rights" impersonated a tempered form of jurisdiction over the EEZ and continental shelf, where the coastal state exercised a set of limited powers, not to compare with the powers comprised by the attribute of sovereignty. The aim was, thus, to uphold the overriding principle of freedom of the seas in the water column above the continental shelf.

References

Barrett J, Barnes R (eds) (2016) Law of the sea: UNCLOS as a living treaty. British Institute of International and Comparative Law, London

Birnie P, Boyle A, Redgwell C (2009) International law and the environment. Oxford University Press, Oxford

Cavalcanti P (2015) Fatos do meu tempo: memórias políticas. CEPE, Recife

Crawford J (2012) Brownlie's principles of Public International Law. Oxford University Press, Oxford

Fischer-Lescano A, Teubner G (2004) Regime-collisions: the vain search for legal unity in the fragmentation of global law. Mich J Int Law 25(4):999

Fraser HS (1925) Extent and delimitation of territorial waters. Cornell Law Q 11:455–480

Grotius H (2004) The free sea. Liberty Fund, Indianapolis

Harrison J (2011) Making the law of the sea: a study on the development of international law. Cambridge University Press, Cambridge

Jayakumar S (2013) The continental shelf regime under UNCLOS. In: The regulation of continental shelf development: rethinking international standards. Nijhoff, Leiden, pp 1–12

Jia BB (2013) The notion of natural prolongation in the current regime of the continental shelf: an afterlife? Chin J Int Law 12(1):79–103

Kim HJ (2014) Natural prolongation: a living myth in the regime of the continental shelf? Ocean Dev Int Law 45(4):374–388

Kiss A (2005) Réflexions sur l'interêt general de l'humanité. In: Liber Amicorum Judge Cançado Trindade. Sérgio Antônio Fabris Editor, Porto Alegre

Koh TB (1982) A constitution for the oceans. Statement at the Final Session of the Third United Nations Conference on the Law of the Sea, 11 December 1982, New York

Kojima C (2008) Fisheries, sedentary. In: Max Planck Encyclopedia of Public International Law [MPEPIL], Oxford

Koskenniemi M (2006) Fragmentation of international law: difficulties arising from the diversification and expansion of international law. International Law Commission, New York

Koskenniemi M (2012) Hegemonic regimes. In: Regime interaction in international law. Cambridge University Press, Cambridge, pp 305–324

Krasner S (1982) Structural causes and regime consequences: regimes as intervening variables. Int Organ 36(2):185–205

Kratochwil F, Ruggie JG (1986) International organization: a state of the art or an art of the state. Int Organ 40(4):753–775

Kunoy B (2013) The delimitation of an indicative area of overlapping entitlement to the outer continental shelf. Br Yearb Int Law, pp 1–21

Kwiatkowska B (1991) Creeping jurisdiction beyond 200 miles in the light of the 1982 Law of the Sea Convention and state practice. Ocean Dev Int Law 22(2):153–187

Lauterpacht H (1950) Sovereignty over submarine areas. Br Yearb Int Law 27:376–433

Magnússon BM (2017) The continental shelf beyond 200 nautical miles: delineation, delimitation and dispute settlement. Int J Mar Coast Law 32: 603

Marinha do Brasil (2013) Amazônia azul: a última fronteira. Centro de Comunicação Social da Marinha, Brasília

McDorman TL (2010) The outer continental shelf in the arctic ocean: legal framework and recent developments. In: Law, technology and science for oceans in globalisation. Brill, Nijhoff, Leiden, pp 499–520

McWhinney E (1993) Judge Shigeru Oda and the progressive development of international law: opinions (declarations, separate opinions, dissents) on the International Court of Justice, 1976–1992. Nijhoff, Leiden

Menezes W (2015) O Direito do Mar. FUNAG, Brasilia

Molenaar EJ (2015) Port and coastal states. In: The Oxford handbook of the law of the sea. Oxford University Press, Oxford, pp 280–303

Mossop J (2016) The continental shelf beyond 200 nautical miles: rights and responsibilities. Oxford University Press, Oxford

Peters A (2016) The refinement of international law: from fragmentation to regime interaction and politicization. MPIL Research Paper Series 2016–2019:1–29

Pirtle CE (2000) Military uses of ocean space and the law of the sea in the new millennium. Ocean Dev Int Law 31(1–2):7–45

Poyoyo PB (1997) Cries of the sea: world inequality, sustainable development and the common heritage of humanity. Nijhoff, The Hague

Proelss A (ed) (2017a) United Nations Convention on the law of the sea: a commentary. C.H.Beck/Hart/Nomos, Munich/Oxford/Baden-Baden

Proelss A (2017b) Article 56: rights, jurisdiction and duties of the coastal state in the exclusive economic zone. In: United Nations Convention on the law of the sea: a commentary. C.H.Beck/Hart/Nomos, Munich/Oxford/Baden-Baden, pp 419–438

Rangel VM (1966) O conflito entre o direito interno e os tratados internacionais. Revista da Faculdade de Direito, Universidade de São Paulo 62(2):81–134

Rangel VM (1981) O novo Direito do Mar e a América Latina. Revista Da Faculdade de Direito Da Universidade de São Paulo 76:75–85

Rangel VM (1995) A problemática da zona econômica exclusiva: vamos perder as 200 milhas? Revista da Faculdade de Direito, Universidade de São Paulo 90:483–492

Schofield C (2012) Parting the waves: claims to maritime jurisdiction and the division of ocean space. Penn State J Law Int Aff:40–58

Suarez SV (2008) The outer limits of the continental shelf. Beiträge Zum Ausländischen Öffentlichen Recht Und Völkerrecht, 199. Springer, Berlin

Townsend-Gault I (2014) The 'territorialisation' of the exclusive economic zone: a requiem for the remnant of the freedom of the seas? In: The limits of Maritime Jurisdiction. Nijhoff, Leiden, pp 65–78
Trindade AAC (2010) Os tribunais internacionais contemporâneos e a busca da realização do ideal da justiça internacional. Revista da Faculdade de Direito da UFMG 57:37–68
Trindade ACC (2014) Direito do Mar: indicações para a fxação dos limites laterais marítimos. In: Reflexões Sobre a Convenção de Direito do Mar. FUNAG, Brasilia, pp 167–222
Ventura VAMF (2017) A força normativa do princípio do uso racional e sustentável dos recursos naturais marinhos no Direito Internacional Ambiental e do Mar: soft norm ou regra cogente? análise da jurisprudência do Tribunal Internacional de Direito do Mar. In: Direito do Mar: reflexões, tendências e perspectivas. D'Plácido, Salvador, pp 615–652
Weber M (1978) Economy and society. University of California Press, Los Angeles
Wolfrum R (2008) The outer continental shelf: some considerations concerning applications and the potential role of the International Tribunal for the Law of the Sea. Statement presented at the 73rd ILA Conference, Rio de Janeiro, August 21, 2008
Wolfrum R, Matz-Lück N (2000) The interplay of the United Nations Convention on the law of the sea and the United Nations Convention on biological diversity. Max Planck Yearb U N Law 4:445–480
Young MA (ed) (2012) Regime interaction in international law: facing fragmentation. Cambridge University Press, Cambridge

Reports

ILA (2002) Preliminary report of the Committee on the Legal Issues of the Outer Continental Shelf. International Law Association, New Delhi
ILA (2004) Legal issues of the outer continental shelf. International Law Association, Berlin
LEPLAC (2020) Plan for the assessment of the Brazilian continental shelf. https://www.marinha.mil.br/secirm/leplac. Accessed 30 Mar 2020
UN (1950) Memorandum on the regime of the high seas, prepared by the Secretariat, Doc. A/CN.4/32, 14 July 1950. Yearbook of the International Law Commission II (69). United Nations, New York
UN (1956) Yearbook of the International Law Commission, 8th Session, Doc. A/CN.4/102/Add.1, II. United Nations, New York
UN (1989) The Law of the Sea. Baselines: an examination of the relevant provisions of the United Nations Convention on the Law of the Sea. Appendix I. Glossary of Technical Terms. United Nations, New York

Jurisprudence

ICJ (1951) Fisheries (United Kingdom v. Norway). Judgement of 18 December 1951. International Court of Justice Reports
ICJ (1969) North Sea Continental Shelf Cases (Federative Republic of Germany v. Denmark). Judgment of 20 February 1969. International Court of Justice Reports
ITLOS (2012) Dispute Concerning Delimitation of the Maritime Boundary Between Bangladesh and Myanmar in the Bay of Bengal (Bangladesh v. Myanmar). Judgement of 14 March 2012, ITLOS Reports
ITLOS (2015) 'Enrica Lexie' Incident (Italy v. India), Provisional Measures. Order of 24 August 2015. ITLOS Reports

Chapter 3
The Continental Shelf Beyond 200 nm: Innovations in Art. 76 UNCLOS

Prior to the adoption of UNCLOS, several circumstances leveled the ground for the emergence of the continental shelf beyond 200 nm and the adoption of scientific formulae disciplining the exact extension of the outer continental shelf. The goal formally announced by the international community was to *limit the expansion of coastal state jurisdiction seawards.*

3.1 Enlarged Coastal State Jurisdiction Over the Continental Margin

To begin with, there was widespread dissatisfaction with the 1958 dual criteria of water depth and exploitability to determine the limits of the continental shelf. Both criteria were imprecise and inadequate in many cases,[1] namely because technical innovation allowed exploitation in increasing depths, continuously widening the regions that were considered exploitable. It is the case with the petroleum and gas offshore industry, which swiftly developed techniques to extract oil from increasing depths, such as the semi-submersible oil rigs.[2]

---

[1] A review of the criticisms to the exploitability and water depth criteria adopted in the 1958 CSC is made later in this chapter.

[2] The "Ocean Driller", built in 1963, designed and owned by ODECO, but operated by Texaco. The history of impressive advancement goes all the way to the current days. In October 2014, Petrobras began exploring a well (Iracema Sul) 2300 m below the surface. Available at: https://www.offshore-technology.com/projects/iracema-sul-field-santos-basin/. Accessed 06 April 2020.

V. Alencar Mayer Feitosa Ventura, *Environmental Jurisdiction in the Law of the Sea*,
https://doi.org/10.1007/978-3-030-50543-1_3

Secondly, agreement had been reached on the principle of common heritage of mankind, following the proposal by Arvid Pardo in 1967,[3] which would render the ocean floor and subsoil beyond national jurisdiction unfit for appropriation by any particular state. For that principle to produce legal effects, it was paramount to define the precise limits of national jurisdiction over the continental shelf.

Thirdly, the straw that broke the camel's back was the adoption of the UN General Assembly Resolution 2574 A of 15 December 1969, upon considering that the 1958 CSC did not "define with sufficient precision the limits of the area over which a coastal state exercises sovereign rights". In addition to that, delegates took customary international law on the matter for "inconclusive".[4] These circumstances can be said to have led to the "protracted, difficult and at times highly technical negotiations on the limits of the continental shelf which followed, first in the Seabed Committee and later at UNCLOS III".[5]

The dawn of the outer continental shelf was, thus, the result of a *critical compromise* between broad- and narrow-margined states. Together with the creation of the category of sovereign rights,[6] the adoption of formulae determining the geographical extension of the continental shelf beyond 200 nm was, beyond doubt, the second chief accord between states with opposing interests.[7] The rules for delineating the outer continental shelf, as well as the rights and duties exercisable thereon stood out as two of the most contentious topics of the III Conference.

Hence, debates and compromises preceded the international agreeance on the possibility of a coastal state's continental shelf extending beyond 200 nm.[8] The bulk of pressure pro-extension stemmed from broad-margin states, which nurtured interests in the potential resources offshore. As such, the crafting of the outer continental shelf, has been described as a "profound reallocation of resource rights from international to national jurisdiction".[9] Currently, more than 30 million km^2 of potential extended continental shelf areas are subject to submissions to the CLCS.

---

[3]*Note verbale* of the Permanent Mission of Malta to the United Nations addressed to the Secretary-General to the United Nations, A/6695, 18 August 1967. In the note, Malta requested the inclusion of a supplementary item in the agenda of the 22nd session of the UNGA.

[4]United Nations General Assembly, Resolution 2574 A, "Question of the reservation for exclusively peaceful purposes of the sea-bed and the ocean floor, and the sub-soil thereof, underlying the high seas beyond the limits of present national jurisdiction and the use of their resources in the use of mankind" of 15 December 1969, Vol. I, 169.

[5]Nordquist et al. (2002), p. 829.

[6]According to Jayakumar, those compromises regarding the continental shelf are but an example of the "carefully constructed compromises characteristic of the provisions in UNCLOS". Jayakumar (2013), p. 5.

[7]Art. 76, paragraphs 4 to 6, UNCLOS, on the scientific formulae that determine the size of the continental margin, as well as the outer limits of the continental shelf beyond 200 nm.

[8]The political struggles that preceded the phenomenon known as the "rise of coastal states" and the expansion of coastal state jurisdiction seawards in the second half of the twentieth century are further analyzed in Chap. 4.

[9]Schofield (2012), p. 46.

Of those, over 2.7 million km^2 of continental shelf areas beyond 200 nm from the coast are subject to overlapping submissions.[10]

One of the reasons for the overlapping claims is the existence of living and non-living resources on the seafloor in the disputed area. Although estimates have suggested that 87% of the world's known submarine oil deposits would fall within 200 nm from the baselines,[11] researchers and scientists have been working with the possibility of a rush to the deep seas.[12] Firstly, because of the stark decline in the availability of land-based resources worldwide, in particular the much-demanded conventional hydrocarbon reserves. Secondly, due to the estimated vastness of natural resources occurring on the deep seabed, both within and beyond national jurisdiction.

On the first causation for the expected increase in deep-sea exploitation of natural resources, specialists point to the inevitable depletion of land-based resources and minerals, thus grounding the argument that seabed exploitation at greater depths is inescapable, if mankind wishes to sustain ongoing life standards and economic growth.[13] Such premise has not been without criticism. Several environmental initiatives, such as the Deep Sea Conservation Coalition,[14] have questioned the true need for new minerals and advocated the search not only for an alternative and more efficient recycling schemes, but also an overall minerals reduction worldwide. For the purposes of this work, it is realistic to estimate that humankind, immersed as we are in a capitalistic socioeconomic system, will continuously and increasingly demand rare minerals, as well as hydrocarbons (oil and gas), until alternate production techniques and an unlikely revolution in consumption patterns has been achieved. Soaring need for minerals, combined with the foreseeable depletion of land mining sites and rapid technological progress, are expected to pose great strain on the deep ocean floor. In such a scenario, it matters most for lawyers to understand reality and discuss legal constructs in order to anticipate and hopefully solve societal conflicts.

A second cause for the probable near- to mid-term surge in deep-sea exploitation relates to the speculated vastness of resource reserves of the ocean floor within national jurisdiction. A report by the ISA has sketched a comprehensive picture of non-living resources potential of outer continental shelves worldwide, despite the

[10]*See* generally Van de Poll and Schofield (2010).

[11]Churchill and Lowe (1999), p. 162.

[12]A possible definition of "deep sea" follows the depth criterion and equals it to the seafloor deeper than 500 m. See *Study to investigate the state of knowledge of deep-sea mining*, Final Report under FWC MARE/2012/06 - SC E1/2013/04, drafted by ECORYS for the European Commission, 28 August 2014, 21–22.

[13]Klare (2012), pp. 1–5.

[14]According to information extracted from the organization's website, the Deep Sea Conservation Coalition was founded in 2004 to address the issue of bottom trawling in the high seas, in the absence of an effective regime for the management of deep-sea fisheries in the high seas and in response to international concerns over the harmful impacts of deep-sea bottom trawling.

Available at: http://www.savethehighseas.org/about-us/.

intrinsic limitations of collecting data in a venture of that magnitude. The study found that "the major resource potential within the ELCS [extended legal continental shelf] regions is held in iron-manganese nodules and crusts, conventional oil and gas, and gas hydrates",[15] scientists arriving at the estimated sum of approximately US$ 10 trillion in commercial value.[16] Even if some of those resources remain uncompetitive in relation to land-based ones in the mid-term, except for hydrocarbons, their commercial value is not expected to reduce (again, provided there will not be a technological revolution which dismisses the precious minerals currently employed in all kinds of industries worldwide).

Abundance of mineral riches on the ocean floor beyond 200 nm has been a stark argument pro-ratification of UNCLOS within the United States. Then and again, the American government has been blamed for neglecting the "immense value" of marine resources occurring beyond the country's EEZ by not ratifying the Convention. According to some, the United States would be voluntarily and irrationally embracing blurred jurisdiction and legal uncertainty, both disincentives for economic investments in exploitation that far offshore.[17] Moreover, "in many coastal nations, the development of outer continental shelf oil and gas resources is a part of government's commitment to encourage the economically and environmentally sound expansion of diverse energy resources".[18] That has been the case in countries such as the United States, Norway, Canada, Brazil, among others, albeit in a still inchoate stage.

Apart from oil and gas, there are also non-hydrocarbon resources, such as seafloor massive sulfide deposits and hydrothermal systems, which may offer viable commercial exploitation in the coming decades. Deep-sea hydrothermal vents have attracted significant market interest in recent years due to their tendency to host rich deposits of valuable metals. However, vent sites also concentrate endemic and fragile biota that might be damaged, if not eliminated, by mining operations in or around them. Exploitation of exploitation of sulfide deposits is underway in the Southern Pacific Ocean, where Pacific Island States, such as Papua New Guinea, have agreed with mining companies, such as Nautilus Minerals Inc., of Canada, on

[15]Murton et al. (2001), p. 7.

[16]The precise commercial value of deep-sea resources is quite hard to grasp, as the ISA Study itself works with contradicting numbers. First, in the introduction, it highlights the sum of US$ 10,328 trillion, p. 7. However, the concluding remarks close with the estimated amount of US$ 11,934 trillion. The Report collected data from the London Metal Exchange (LME), the United Stated Geological Survey (USGS) and the Oil and Gas Journal (OGJ), from the turn of the millennium. See *Id.* (2001), p. 53.

[17]Thomas Donoghue on the resource potentiality of the outer continental shelf and the benefits for the United Stated in ratifying UNCLOS: "immense value of the resources that would be made subject to the United States' exclusive sovereign jurisdiction". Donoghue (2012), US Senate, 5.

[18]Kelly (2004), p. 413.

the commercial development of those resources in areas under national jurisdiction.[19]

From the perspective of *biodiversity*, the continental shelf is known to host diverse marine life. There are, for instance, rhodolith beds consisting of a diversity of living organisms and spatially dynamic ecosystems. In a study published in 2016, on the structure of Brazilian rhodolith beds, Paulo Horta describes those ecosystems as "colorful, unattached, branching, crustose benthic marine red algae", which increased in size and decrease in abundance in areas with a gentle slope.[20] In contrast, rhodoliths from narrow shelves and steep slopes decreased in size but increased in abundance. Such rhodolith beds provide habitat for a plethora of benthic living organisms, a function which has rendered them the fame of ecosystem engineers.

In short, expectancy of abundant resources on the continental shelf beyond 200 nm is commonly embraced by scientists, industry consultants, decision-makers and, consequently, international lawyers. In regard of the appropriation and extraction of those marine resources in those areas, this work has identified two different narratives among environmental advocates and international lawyers for what is happening: claims of an on-going "wild-west race to resources", opposed to the narrative of an "orderly development of marine resources".

The first narrative has been fueled by the perception of disorder in "hot" areas, where adjacent and opposing coasts interact with each other—a disarray which could stem political and diplomatic tensions. A case in point is the Arctic region, where Russian claims to secure access to natural resources of the continental shelf have attracted the world's attention and sounded an alarm as to the increasing use of *Machtpolitik* in the region.[21] There, worries of a "race to continental shelf resources", as Timo Koivurova has put it,[22] or a "race for what's left",[23] to Michael Klare, have taken the spotlight. Some have also mentioned, in a quite sensationalistic manner, a "scramble for the Arctic", a process allegedly corresponding to the world's last colonial scramble.[24]

[19]Nautilus Minerals Inc. has launched an exploration programme for the exploration of massive sulfides in 2007. At the time of publishing, Nautilus has obtained the first mining exploitation lease for deposits within its Solwara 1 and 2 Projects, offshore of Papua New Guinea, and has research permits for other regions including Tonga, the Solomon Islands, and other sites in the South West Pacific. *See* Gena (2013), p. 227. *See* also Nautilus Minerals Inc. (2016), *Annual Report*, Toronto, 5.

[20]Horta et al. (2016), p. 121.

[21]The concept of "power politics" stems from the realist school of International Relations theory, which depicts international relations as the constant competition for absolute power capacities and access to natural resources. One of the school's most representative intellectuals was Hans Morgenthau. *See* generally Morgenthau (1948).

[22]According to Koivurova, "it is important to take the 'race to the resources' description seriously because it is not only the media that perceive such a development in the Arctic, many researchers do as well". Koivurova (2011), p. 212.

[23]Klare (2012), p. 237.

[24]*See* generally Sale and Potapov (2009).

Such narrative, despite some level of hyperbolism, may offer useful insights to the analysis of resource development in areas where maritime borders are relatively well-defined. In other words, it does not take a region such as the Arctic, with the aggravating factor of climate change melting ice-covered areas that will allow for unseen exploitation of the Arctic seabed, to identify a "race to resources" of the continental shelf. Within national jurisdiction, coastal states are enticed not only by the riches, but also by interests of enhanced *oceanopolitical influence* offshore.[25] That is the case, *inter alia*, of Brazil, as Chaps. 9 and 10 show.

An alternative discourse is that coastal states do nothing less than what is expected from rational agents: to claim jurisdiction over a maritime space that was attributed to them by an international legal treaty, so as to exercise their rights and obligations in line with international law. That is the core of the narrative that detects in the law of the sea, namely UNCLOS, the elements for an "orderly development" of marine natural resources.[26] For sympathizers of this discourse, UNCLOS has effectively supported the interests of broad-margin states with an array of rules for the delineation of outer limits of the continental shelf. Hence, it would be outright irrational not to make use of such rules and exercise jurisdiction in the terms of the Convention.[27] Applied to the Arctic, such a discourse emphasizes the role of international cooperation in the orderly exploitation of marine resources, proof of which is the Ilulissat Declaration,[28] in which the five Arctic states have agreed to pursue continental shelf entitlements in an orderly fashion.

However rational and desirable that "orderly development" may be, one must not forget the enormous enforcement challenge placed upon international law. It should not be forgotten that international law consists, in essence, of a malleable set of rules and principles, some of which deliberately vague and self-contradicting, which can serve multiple constituencies and interests.[29] One ought, thus, to approach the "orderly development" narrative with caution, not taking international law as a belief, but as an earthly tool for shaping behavior and influencing policy in a highly decentralized international system. All the more so in light of the potential for conflict regarding the outer continental shelf, where the opposition between UNCLOS' provisions, CLCS recommendations, and coastal states' own political strategies form an explosive mix of variables with capacity to undermine any wishful orderly development of continental shelf resources.

In short, the estimated value of those resources, added to the fact that more than 30 million km^2 of ocean floor is currently under some sort of jurisdictional claim by coastal states, make it urgent to understand the exact legal regime applicable to the

[25]The concept of "oceanopolítica", from the Spanish, has been broadly used by Chilean scholars and military strategists, so as to emphasize the need for a national policy aimed at ensuring Chilean interests over its "oceanic territory". Busch (1993), pp. 203–207.

[26]Koivurova (2011), p. 216.

[27]*Id.* 221.

[28]Ilulissat Declaration, Arctic Ocean Conference, Ilulissat, Greenland, 27–29 May 2008.

[29]Criticisms of this kind to international law are to be found in Koskenniemi (2012), p. 306.

outer continental shelf. That is the reigning perception amid petroleum, gas, and mining industry representatives that more clarity and legal certainty must be reached before private and state-owned petroleum companies inject massive investments into projects in lease sites beyond 200 nm. In a speech before the United States Senate, Thomas Donoghue quoted a note by ExxonMobil, which states that "legal certainty in the property rights being explored and developed" precedes investments.[30] Sure, a good deal of certainty with regard to the continental shelf beyond 200 nm is to be found in UNCLOS', particularly the legal procedures established for the delineation and delimitation of outer continental shelves around the world. However, it is the case to assess with precision which are the implications of such outer continental shelf delineation both for the coastal state and for the international community. This chapter aims at shedding initial light on that issue.

3.2 *Formulae* to Precise the Outer Edge of the Continental Margin and the Outer Limits of the Continental Shelf

The adoption of UNCLOS meant the creation of a maritime space with a variable geographic formation, the continental shelf. In fact, following pressures from broad-margin states, the Convention stipulates that the continental shelf may extend beyond the default 200 nm, provided the extension respects a set of complex scientific formulae, aimed at assessing the geological affinity of the continental shelf between seabed and landmass, as well as at limiting the outer continental shelf limits of extreme-margin states, such as Canada, Australia and New Zealand. For that, it was necessary to elaborate a juridical definition which, in order to be accepted, had to be based on technical-scientific criteria, which culminated in Art. 76 UNCLOS, a piece of exceptional law-making virtuosity.[31] To monitor the implementation of the established criteria, the CLCS was created.[32]

Upfront, it is worth noting that the *basic principles* governing the continental shelf within 200 nm are valid for the portion of the seabed extending beyond 200 nm, pursuant to the theory of the "single shelf".[33] However, the set of rules applicable to the outer continental shelf, hereinafter named the "outer continental shelf regime", rests on specific legal backbones, which vary significantly from those basic principles. Firstly, the outer continental shelf depends on the declaration of the respective

[30]Donoghue (2012).

[31]That is the opinion of Luis Soares, shared by this author. *See* Soares (2014), p. 301.

[32]Art. 76, paragraph 8; and Annex II, UNCLOS, on the Commission on the Limits of the Continental Shelf.

[33]The theory of the single continental shelf was discussed during the negotiations of the Convention and has recently been affirmed by international jurisprudence. See *Dispute concerning delimitation of the maritime boundary between Bangladesh and Myanmar in the Bay of Bengal (Bangladesh/Myanmar)*, Order of 14 March 2012, ITLOS Reports 2011, 4.

coastal states, whereas the continental shelf does not.[34] Secondly, an internationally cogent delineation of outer limits is subject to a complex technical procedure, which is overseen by the CLCS, an eminently technical body. Thirdly, it is the coastal state, not the Commission, that sets the outer limits. The trick is that the chosen limits will only be final and binding if identical to the CLCS recommendations.[35]

Even though the *delineation* of the outer limits of the continental shelf is a *unilateral* act (for states are inherently entitled to the natural prolongation of the land mass seaward), its validity before the international community depends on international law. Note, thus, that the action required by Art. 76 (7) UNCLOS is one of delineating, not delimiting. To delineate is a unilateral act done in absence of a conflict or dispute, whereas to delimit is an act following a dispute as to the trajectory of a certain line.[36] To delimit is to mark or fix the limits of a borderline, while to delineate equals the sketching out or tracing a line. In practical terms, a delimitation presupposes a dispute, an area of "overlapping entitlements",[37] and shall be governed by Art. 83 UNCLOS, whereas none is needed in the process of delineating the outer lines of the continental shelf.

Regarding delineation, Art. 76 UNCLOS sets out a complex methodology, based on geological and geomorphological criteria, which are very briefly examined in this item. First, the Convention compels the coastal state to identify the *outer edge* of their *continental margin*, in order to assess the exact length of that geological feature,[38] "wherever the margin extends beyond 200 nautical miles from the baselines from which the breadth of the territorial sea is measured".[39] In so doing, coastal states must follow one of the two formulae at hand in the Convention. Firstly, the "Irish formula", based on a line delineated with reference to the outermost fixed points, each point with a thickness of sedimentary rocks of at least 1% of the shortest distance from such point to the foot of the continental slope (item "i")—the so-called

[34]Art. 76, paragraph 7, UNCLOS, requires the coastal state to "delineate the outer limits of its continental shelf", differently from Art. 77, paragraph 3, which states that the rights over the continental shelf do not depend on any proclamation.

[35]A similar classification is to be found in Armas-Pfirter (2010), p. 477.

[36]For more on the distinction between delineation and delimitation, see Oystein (2013), pp. 278–279.

[37]*Dispute concerning delimitation of the maritime boundary between Bangladesh and Myanmar in the Bay of Bengal (Bangladesh/Myanmar)* para. 397.

[38]The notion of "continental margin", as in Art. 76, paragraph 3 UNCLOS, was approached in the previous chapter. It consists of the "submerged prolongation of the landmass of the coastal state".

[39]The intricacy of the issue increases if one takes into account the Statement of Understanding concerning a Specific Method to be Used in Establishing the Outer Edge of the Continental Margin, approved upon the closing of the III UN Conference on the Law of the Sea by states sharing the Bay of Bengal. In particular, the SoU was meant to govern the geographical conditions off the Southeastern coast of India and the coast of Sri Lanka, due to specific sedimentary circumstances of the Bay of Bengal. The technicalities of the debate on the determination of the continental in that particular portion of the ocean floor, albeit elucidating, escapes the main purpose of this chapter. See *Final Act of the United Nations Conference on the Law of the Sea*, A/CONF.62/121, 27 October 1982, Annex II, Official Records XVII, 138.

sediment thickness criterion; or the "Hedberg formula", consisting of a line delineated by reference to fixed points not more than 60 nautical miles from the foot of the continental slope (item "ii").

The "Irish formula" is essentially based on the thickness of sedimentary rocks and aims at measuring the *sedimentary affinity* between mainland and seabed.[40] The "Hedberg formula", on the other hand, focuses on the determination of the *foot of continental slope*. Intrinsic difficulties in finding the precise base (or foot) of the continental slope led to the establishment of a "boundary zone", which was set in 60 nm as the "minimum technically practical width of the boundary zone".[41]

Once the outer edge of the continental margin has been determined, coastal states rely on Art. 76 (5) UNCLOS to ascertain the fixed points comprising the outer limits of the continental shelf, where the state will exercise sovereign rights. Here, two other criteria are available for states, to be used alternatively. The first criterion is grounded exclusively on distance: the outer limits shall not exceed 350 nm from the baselines from which the territorial sea is measured. The second criterion is slightly more complicated, resulting from the combination of distance and depth criteria: the outer limits shall not exceed 100 nm from the 2500-meter isobath.[42] The resulting outer limits may extend beyond 350 nm, in case the water depth be relatively shallow.[43]

When demonstrating the sedimentary affinity between landmass and continental margin, coastal states must take into account rather complex geological and geomorphological features, such as "submarine ridges", "submarine elevations" and "oceanic ridges", "caps", "banks", "spurs" etc.[44] The thorny process of defining and understanding those features has been a learn-by-doing experience, in which coastal states and the CLCS interact in fixing the feature's meanings. Submarine elevations are considered "natural components of the continental margin, such as its plateaus, rises, caps, banks and spurs".[45] The full content of paragraph 5 applies to submarine elevations, i.e. the two criteria: depth [350 nm], and depth *plus* distance [2500-meter isobath + 100 nm]. Submarine ridges are not natural components of the continental margin, but are taken as "natural prolongation" of the land mass. As such, once that feature is found on the seabed, the outer limit of the continental shelf shall not exceed 350 nm. Oceanic ridges, in line with paragraph 3, are neither a feature of the continental margin nor the "natural prolongation" of the mainland. Thus, they are not to be taken into account in the extension of the continental shelf beyond 200 nm.

---

[40] The "Irish formula" was proposed in the 75th Informal Meeting of the Second Committee of UNCLOS III, in 15 April 1976.

[41] See Hedberg (1972).

[42] The 2500-meter isobath is a line connecting the depth of 2500 m, as stated in Art. 76, paragraph 5, UNCLOS.

[43] When applying the depth criterion, the identification of the relevant coasts becomes "redundant", so Kunoy (2013), p. 2.

[44] The definition of caps, banks and spurs can be found in the online glossary of the International Hydrographic Organization (IHO).

[45] Art. 76, paragraph 6 UNCLOS.

For the rest, it escapes the purpose of this work to examine in detail the technicalities and intricacies of Art. 76, such as the definition of "foot of slope", "fixed points", the selection of the 2500-meter isobath, amongst others.[46]

3.3 Delineating: The Commission on the Limits of the Continental Shelf

One of the institutions brought to life by UNCLOS, the CLCS was given the legal mandate to entertain requests for extended continental shelves worldwide and to make recommendations to coastal states on matters related to the establishment of those limits.[47] The CLCS is, thus, tasked with confronting submissions by national governments with the formulae and criteria laid down in Art. 76, and issuing recommendations accepting (partially or entirely), or denying the outer limits claimed.[48] The institution is a sort of "referee" of Art. 76 application, a role imbued with an "important stimulus for the peaceful settlement of disputes related to law of the sea is also provided by the CLCS".[49] Yet, that role has not always been easy to fulfill, as the Commission faces large challenges concerning, *inter alia*, funding, workload, criticisms on its abidance to the law, lack of transparency, among others which are inspected below.

---

[46]Several legal and technical publications have addressed those technical provisions, such as Magnússon (2017), Suarez (2008) and ILA (2002).

[47]During the Third Conference, early proposals for a body on the limits of the continental shelf called for a *Continental Shelf Boundary Commission*, as in the Canadian Proposal during the 4th Session of the Conference, in 1976. In line with the position adopted by Canadian negotiators, the establishment of such a body, to be bound by special procedures, could prove very useful. In fact, it would be a necessary first step, so as to prevent a multitude of conflicts that could (and did in fact) emerge from the application of the complex and intricated formulae of Art. 76. In short, because, "it was difficult to envisage dispute settlement with respect to the exploration and exploitation of the resources of the sea-bed and subsoil of the continental shelf. The same was true for fisheries management, except in the case of a coastal State failing to meet its obligations in respect of conservation or the full utilization of resources". See A/CONF.62/SR.65 65th Plenary meeting Extract from the Official Records of the Third United Nations Conference on the Law of the Sea, Volume V, para. 10. The first references to a "Commission on the Limits of the Continental Shelf" were made by Ireland and the Soviet Union, members of the Negotiating Group 6 (NG6), at the seventh session of the Conference, in 1978. See A/CONF.62/WP.10/Rev.1, 1979. More information on the historical negotiations preceding the establishment of the Commission can be found in Nordquist et al. (2002), pp. 1003–1014.

[48]Note that the CLCS is *not* an international organization, but rather a treaty-based body created by UNCLOS, albeit with secretarial aide of the UN. As such, it is not an independent organization and does not possess legal personality. That the CLCS is not an international organization was also a conclusion reached by the International Law Association (ILA) in its 2002 Report on the Outer Continental Shelf, 5.

[49]Kwiatkowska (2013), p. 221.

The *functions* of the Commission are basically twofold: to scrutinize data submitted by coastal states concerning the outer limits of the continental shelf beyond 200 nm; and to provide scientific and technical advice, if requested by the coastal state, during the drafting of the submission.[50] In order to accomplish those functions, the CLCS is presumed to have the necessary competences, albeit limited materially to the application of Art. 76.

Ted McDorman accurately considers the Commission to have three main *roles*, although it may other roles may be recognized. For that author, the Commission is a legitimator of the delineation process comprised in Art. 76 UNCLOS, a role slightly different from the granting of legal or political approval. Secondly, the Commission has a procedural role, in that its actions are inspired by provisions of the Convention and by its own Scientific and Technical Guidelines (STGs) concerning the delineation process. Finally, it is informed by an informational role, once the procedural phase is overcome, consisting of publishing charts and information relating to outer limits of outer continental shelves for access by the international community.[51]

To those, two more roles may be added. An *advisory* role, which allows the Commission to offer scientific and technical advice to states drawing up their submissions;[52] and a considerably neglected role, one of massive scale and complexity, of reducing (and eventually zeroing) undefined maritime boundaries between continental shelves and the Area—the role of *pacifier*. Thereby, the Commission is expected to tackle a major uncertainty in the law of the sea provisions concerning exploitation of the seafloor.

Only the outer limits which are established "on the basis of" the Commission's recommendations are "final and binding", so Art. 76 (8) UNCLOS. This provision is particularly relevant, because even though "the establishment of the outer limits is an act within the sole discretion of a state", those very limits will only be vested with finality and bindingness if pursuant to the recommendations issued by the Commission.[53] The phrase "on the basis of" implies limited maneuver room for coastal states when determining the outer limits of their continental shelf, without being contrary to the recommendations of the Commission. States may even define the outer limits of their continental shelf in disagreement with the Commission, for this is their prerogative, based on the inherent nature of the right to a continental shelf and based on the fact the CLCS does not emit decisions nor orders.[54] However, such limits would not be final and binding, for the purpose of evidence in a dispute before an international tribunal, and would not "easily attract international recognition".[55] In

[50]Art. 3, paragraph 1, Annex II, UNCLOS.

[51]McDorman (2002), p. 301.

[52]Art. 3, paragraph 1 (ii), Annex II, UNCLOS.

[53]Kunoy (2012), p. 109.

[54]The phrase "final and binding" refers to the outer limits of the continental shelf adopted in accordance with the Commission's recommendations; not to the recommendation *per se*, which could not, by its very essence, be binding.

[55]ILA (2004), p. 22.

short, that prerogative does not obliterate coastal state's *obligation* to establish the outer limits in accordance with Art. 76 (4) to (6) UNCLOS.[56]

The Commission does not have the mandate to inspect whether a state's outer limits were established "on the basis of" its recommendations.[57] The command given to the CLCS by the Convention is not as broad as to encompass such a function. In this sense, analogies suggesting a link between the Commission and police tasks regarding the issue of the continental shelf would be inappropriate. Only states have the power to challenge outer limits that they suspect were not established "on the basis of" the Commission's recommendations, triggering UNCLOS Part XV and the compulsory settlement system.

As to the "final and binding" character of outer limits established in consistency with the Commission's recommendations, it should be noted that the phrase may be divided in two, for the sake of examination. Firstly, those limits will be final, meaning that they become permanently fixed and not amenable to later change, "even if the parameters on which it is based, such as the baseline, change".[58] Secondly, they are binding for other states, including to non-parties to the Convention, given the customary nature of the Art. 76 delineation procedure, in a sense that those states have the obligation to accept the outer limits fixed by the coastal state.

Once the CLCS has issued its recommendations and the coastal state has delineated the outer limits its continental shelf on the basis of those recommendations, the next step is for the state to give *publicity* to the limits before the international community. Hence, it is expected from states to deposit with the UN Secretary-General the charts "permanently describing the outer limits of the continental shelf".[59] The Secretary-General shall then give publicity to those charts, as means to inform the other states of the space beyond national jurisdiction, where the international seabed starts and the common heritage principle applies. Noteworthy is the character of *permanency* of those charts, which confirm the final nature of the outer limits established on the basis of the Commission's recommendations. That act of depositing the charts certifies the closure of the delineation procedure, in consonance with Art. 76 UNCLOS, and marks the moment when the outer limits line becomes binding both on the coastal state and on other state parties to the Convention, unless the line is subjected to a judicial dispute.

For the rest, Annex II of the Convention specifies the composition and functions of the Commission, the obligations of coastal states towards the Commission, the procedure within the Commission in the delineation of outer limits of the continental shelf beyond 200 nm, amongst others. Thus, the Commission is composed by

---

[56]That obligation is inscribed in Art. 76, paragraph 2, UNCLOS, according to which "the continental shelf *shall* not extend beyond the limits provided for in paragraphs 4 to 6" of Art. 76 (emphasis added).

[57]McDorman (2002), p. 315.

[58]ILA (2004), p. 23.

[59]Art. 76, paragraph 9, UNCLOS. Such requirement is complemented by Art. 84, paragraph 2, UNCLOS, which compels the coastal state to "give due publicity" to charts and geographical coordinates of the outer limits of the continental shelf.

21 members, experts in geology, geophysics and hydrography, nominated and elected by states parties to UNCLOS on the basis of "equitable geographic representation", conforming to Annex's Art. 2.[60]

Regarding the Commission's legal and technical framework, it is basically restricted to UNCLOS Art. 76 and Annex II, alongside other rules of international law directly pertinent to the delineation process. In addition to those provisions, the CLCS has made use of the *Kompetenz-Kompetenz* principle in order to design its own rules of procedure. In other words, the Commission has invoked a power common to international organization and bodies to approve its own statute and working guidelines, a fundamental step to the performance of the Commission's duties. This understanding is compatible with the 1949 Advisory Opinion by the ICJ on the compensation for damage occurred while serving the UN. Hence, the Commission has adopted its Rules of Procedure[61] and the Scientific and Technical Guidelines,[62] an attempt to unify procedures before the CLCS and to uniformize recommendations.[63]

3.3.1 Challenges to the Work of the Commission

During UNCLOS' negotiations, states expected no more than 35 submissions for outer continental shelves.[64] Nowadays, there are 78 submissions and 4 revised submissions under analysis,[65] i.e. more than the double of what was expected. If, on the one hand, that shows an almost universal use of Art. 76 and its procedures, it also implies a gigantic amount of work for a body comprised of only 21 members, who meet for no longer than 20 weeks each year on a *pro bono* basis, without any

[60]The Commission is allowed to work in cooperation with the International Oceanographic Commission (IOC) of UNESCO and the International Hydrographic Organization (IHO), when necessary and useful, through the exchange of scientific and technical information. It is not just a permission for the Commission, but in fact, it could be seen as a recommendation.

[61]Rules of Procedure of the Commission on the Limits of the Continental Shelf. CLCS/40/Rev.1, adopted on 17 April 2008. Available at: http://www.un.org/depts/los/clcs_new/commission_rules.htm. Accessed 06 April 2020.

[62]Scientific and Technical Guidelines of the Commission on the Limits of the Continental Shelf. CLCS/11, adopted on 13 May 1999. Available at: http://www.un.org/depts/los/clcs_new/commission_guidelines.htm. Accessed 06 April 2020.

[63]Besides, the CLCS developed methodologies for states to present submissions: joint submissions and partial submissions—such terms and methods are not in UNCLOS. However, Annex I provides the needed avenues for interstate cooperation.

[64]*See* generally Carrera (2017).

[65]The complete list of submissions is to be found at the website of the Commission: http://www.un.org/depts/los/clcs_new/commission_submissions.htm. Accessed 06 April 2020.

sort of subsidy or salary. Despite those limitations, the Commission has issued 26 recommendations thus far.[66]

In entertaining a submission, the CLCS may invoke powers that are not restricted to technical prerogatives *strictu sensu*¸ but assume a legal nature.[67] In fact, the Convention must make recommendations in accordance with rules inherent to UNCLOS Art. 76, and this task unavoidably implies some form of treaty interpretation. In that process, the Commission has found itself in the position of having to precise, from a scientific perspective, some concepts mentioned in the Convention, such as "seafloor highs", "submarine elevations", "submarine ridges" and "oceanic ridges". To interpret the Convention is, therefore, not an excessive and illegal action by the CLCS. However, every act of interpretation ought to be examined on an ad-hoc basis, in order to prevent abuses, such as excessive hermeneutics of the meaning of Art. 76 provisions or even the creation of new law.[68] That delicate task has rendered heated debates within the Commission itself and has put its Commissioners in the spotlight, with several publications discussing the extent of the Commission's mandate to interpret the Convention.

In the delineation procedure, solely two parties are active: the submitting coastal states and the CLCS. Basically, the work of the Commission is called for when a coastal state triggers the procedure present in Art. 76 (4) to (10) UNCLOS.[69] Questions have arisen as to the *participation of third states* in the analysis of a submission. Despite the current architecture lacking a legal tool allowing for protests and interventions within the CLCS, third states may not be deprived of the right to voice out concerns, provided that direct interests of theirs be at stake. As the ILA rightly observed, states should not in principle object to each other's submissions because Art. 76 (10) UNCLOS is sufficient to protect their interests.[70] However, third states' views on the matter ought to be taken into account. In line with the ILA,

> a third State may hold that the consideration by the CLCS of a submission made by a State party to the Convention may impair its rights existing outside the Convention. In such a case, a third State can lodge a diplomatic protest with the State concerned or take any other steps at its disposal to address the issue"[71]

[66]States must deposit charts "permanently describing the outer limits" of their continental shelf in accordance with the recommendations before the UN Secretary-General and the Secretariat of ISA, in order to fulfill the duty enshrined in Art. 76, paragraph 9, UNCLOS. As of the time of writing, only seven states have deposited those charts.

[67]Kunoy (2012), p. 109. In fact, for some authors, the Commission seems a key, but fragilized institution in the delineation procedure, due to its limited mandate, as in Tassin (2013), p. 419.

[68]In order for the Commission to avoid unwanted violations of its legal mandate, important parcel of the law of the sea literature is of the view that the Commission should seek, when needed, "some form of legal guidance, one of which could be the application of the legal services offered by the Legal Counsel of the United Nations". It is the case of Kunoy (2011), p. 334.

[69]*Scientific and Technical Guidelines of the Commission on the Limits off the Continental Shelf*, Doc. CLCS/11 of 13 May 1999, p. 12, para. 2.2.3.

[70]See Serdy (2011), p. 379.

[71]ILA (2004), p. 27.

A case in point was the Russian submission, which raised three notes from states, one of which non-party to the Convention: Canada and Denmark and the United States. For the ILA, "there was no objection to the fact that third States indicated their views on the submission".[72] Whether their views will be heard and shape the work of the CLCS is another question. Another practical case concerned the Brazilian submission, parts of which were objected by the United States in a *note verbale* to the Commission. Nonetheless, the CLCS still analyzed the claim, instructing the sub-commission charged with the analyzing the Brazilian submission to disregard the objection, since it was not a dispute between countries with adjacent or opposite coasts, nor one of unresolved land or maritime dispute.

Finally, the CLCS is not allowed to act upon submissions involving *delimitation* matters (or disputes) of the continental shelf between states with adjacent or opposite coasts.[73] That limitation is reinforced by Art. 9, Annex II UNCLOS, which punctuates that the actions of the CLCS do not in any way affect matters relating to the delimitation of boundaries between states. Those provisions are further strengthened by Art. 134 (4), which provides that nothing in Part XI "affects the establishment of the outer limits of the continental shelf in accordance with Part VI". Challenges to the work of the Commission are multiple and shall be discussed in the following item.

3.3.2 The Commission's Arduous Way Ahead

3.3.2.1 Interpreting the Convention

As approached above, the Commission is competent to interpret the Convention to the extent needed for it to fulfill its tasks, that is, the Commission has competence to interpret UNCLOS.[74] However, such competence goes not without criticism from coastal states, some of which see the Commission in its main role, that of a technical nature, responsible exclusively for implementing the Convention. There is and there will always be a *fundamental tension* between states and international organizations, and the relationship between the CLCS and submitting states is no different.

---

[72] *Id.* 27.

[73] In fact, the Commission is far from the status of an international court; it does not act on behalf of state parties to UNCLOS, neither is it an organ of the Meeting of the State Parties. Analyses of the CLCS often include terms such as "unique" and "autonomous", what allows for a qualification of the Commission as a *sui generis* body. For a similar conclusion, *see* McDorman (2013), p. 93. For some scholars, the Commission is a technical body in a political world. For other, it is a body that combines technical and legal tasks, including the possibility to interpret UNCLOS, as far as feasible without distorting neither the *mens legis* nor the *mens legislatoris* of the Convention.

[74] This view is espoused by the ILA (2004), pp. 5–6.

International law remains rooted in state consent as the basis for its existence. After all, states are the main subjects creating organizations.[75] And even the organizations mandated to participate in the creation of other organization, e.g. the European Community as a member of the Helsinki Convention, are themselves the fruit of state consent. Strains between state sovereignty and international institutions are inherent given the current legal framework upon which international law is based, particularly so in the case of the law of the sea, where institutions such as the CLCS or the ISA stand out for being technical bodies in a political world.[76] One could not expect the relationship between those organizations and states to be entirely peaceful and devoid of noise.

The continental shelf, although originally a physical concept, is principally a legal or artificial concept that developed to suit the interests of sovereign states. The 350-mile limit does not correspond on a one-to-one basis to the geological nature of the continental shelf. As such, the CLCS explores permanently new ground, as every submission presents a plethora of possible approaches to terms enshrined in Art. 76. In a sense, only by enabling a *flexible interpretation* of rules and regulations, in full respect of both the letter and the spirit of the Convention, are international organizations to give a long life to ambitious and pioneers creations such as the outer continental shelf.

That is not to say that tensions are inherently vicious for the development of international law. In fact, practice of international organizations has repeatedly shown that the exigencies of real life may create alternative implementation routes where none existed before, ultimately contributing to the overall implementation of international law. In other words, *el camino se hace caminando*, and that is what the Commission has done in the past, for instance, when it adopted its Rules of Procedures, namely Rule 46,[77] which interprets UNCLOS provisions requiring the Commission's actions not to prejudice boundary delimitations between states.

A reasonable solution to the question of how far the Commission may interpret the Convention is to limit the hermeneutic maneuver room of its members, subjecting the act of interpreting to the fulfillment of certain requirements. First of all, the hermeneutic activity may only relate to the understanding of Art. 76 and other pertinent articles of the Convention indispensable for the exercise of the

[75]The clash between the international organization and its members mirrors ultimately the dichotomy between state sovereignty and community interests in international law, if one takes IOs as representatives of those interests. Up to now, the existence of international organizations has altered the relevance of state sovereignty in international law, but not vanished it. *See* Klabbers (2009), p. 5.

[76]McDorman reaches the conclusion that the CLCS is a technical body in a political world, aiding the act of delineating boundaries, i.e. an eminently political matter. That author is of the view that the CLCS role in the delineation process could become more significant, not via adoption of stricter proof standards, but via flexibility in the acceptance of reasonable and credible data—what the author calls the prevalence of the "politician" facet of the Commission over its "scientist" one. *See* McDorman (2002), p. 324.

[77]Rule of Procedure no. 46, on the "submissions in case of a dispute between States with opposite or adjacent coasts or in other cases of unresolved land or maritime disputes".

Commission's mandate. Secondly, no interpretation may amplify obligations to coastal states beyond those assigned by UNCLOS. Thirdly, such legal competence of the Commission does not exclude the competence of state parties to interpret the Convention themselves. In other words, the CLCS should be open for reasonable interpretations of Art. 76 made by coastal states in their submissions.[78] In cases where the Commission's mandate be unclear, states must refer to the firm principle of international law that only a tribunal of international law is deemed to know what this law is.[79] Although it seems clear to common sense, it is never too much to remind that the Commission is not a tribunal.

A rather critical view of the Commission's performance of this competence is formulated by Andrew Serdy, to whom the commissioners have shown a "disturbing propensity to legislate" through the introduction of new requirements for states, which are either not supported by Art. 76, or by qualifying rights specified in Art. 76.[80] That would amount to a violation of the Commission's mandate, the result of which would be to deprive states of areas of legal continental shelf to which a reasonable interpretation of Art. 76 entitles them. Similarly, ITLOS Judge Vladimir Golitsyn denies, in principle, an interpretative mandate to the Commission. For the Judge, interpretation of Art. 76 is an exclusive prerogative of states parties to UNCLOS and competent international adjudicative bodies, amongst which ITLOS.[81]

Another challenge to the work of the Commission has been the constant activation of the clause of *ongoing maritime delimitation dispute* within submissions, a measure that halts indefinitely the Commission. According to the Virginia Commentaries, the Commission "is not to function in determining, or to influence negotiations on, the continental shelf boundary between states with overlapping claims (assuming the boundary in question is beyond 200 nautical miles)".[82] However, difficulty in defining the term "dispute" has impeded the Commission's work in a number of occasions. There is no word on Annex I of the Rules of Procedure hinting how the CLCS shall proceed when states differ over the question whether a dispute in relation to a submission exists. It seems to flow logically from the wording of the relevant provisions that the CLCS must conduct an assessment on the *prima facie* existence of a dispute—low threshold. If it finds that a dispute exists, paragraph 5 of Annex I to the CLCS Rules of Procedure provides that the Commission only will examine a submission in an area under dispute with the prior consent of all the

[78]ILA (2004), p. 6.

[79]PCIJ *Brazilian Loans Case*, Judgement, Rep. 1929, Ser. A, 124.

[80]For instance, the Commission has shown a tendency to overlook the depth constraint in favor of that based on distance, not only in the media but also surprisingly in academic writing. *See* Serdy (2011), p. 356.

[81]Golitsyn (2009), p. 406.

[82]Nordquist et al. (2002), p. 1017.

States that are parties to such a dispute. The wording is clear, a positivist would have to bend to that wording, or call for an amendment to the Rules of Procedure.[83]

Examples are the cases of South West Africa and the case between Palau and Philippines, where a mere objection was depicted as a dispute. The fear by CLCS members rests on a "serious misunderstanding of the non-prejudice clauses in LOSC Art. 76, paragraph 10 and Annex II, Art. 9". Provided the CLCS does not stray beyond its technical task, by definition nothing it does is capable of bringing about such prejudice [of influencing ongoing delimitation disputes].[84] Here, the Commission has shown what authors have termed a "counterproductive oversensitivity to disputes",[85] that is, it has repeatedly granted third states *veto power* over the examination of a submission by simply notifying a dispute. It would be more reasonable for the Commission to consider only opposing claims of an advanced nature as "disputes", instead of mere overlapping claims for areas where no bilateral negotiations have started. A similar view was espoused some years ago by the ILA, according to which Art. 76 (10) UNCLOS represented a "safeguarding clause", which impeded overlapping claims to be invoked by a state as an obstacle to the functioning of the Commission with respect to a submission on the disputed area.[86]

3.3.2.2 Composition and Integrity of CLCS Members

Already during UNCLOS' negotiations, there were fears that the provisions determining the CLCS composition were unsatisfactory in that they based election to the commission entirely on the principle of equitable geographical distribution.[87] That would not preclude the possibility of the Commission being *dominated by nationals of the broad-margin states* and those sympathetic to their views. Hence, a major concern was to have nationals of relevant interest groups should be fairly represented in the Commission, so as to ensure that its integrity was not open to question.[88]

Twenty years into the creation of the Commission, one could fairly say that the worries as to legitimacy of its composition have *partially* materialized. On the fears of a Commission dominated by experts of industrialized states, it is certainly not the

[83]Alex Elferink and Constance Johnson are of the view that the CLCS Rules should not be read in isolation from the relevant UNCLOS provisions, a combined reading of which would lead to the conclusion that the Commission needs not to halt considerations of a submission of a state that raises issues of delimitation of the continental shelf. The consideration by the Commission does not prejudice the rights of coastal states with overlapping claims over the continental shelf. *See* Oude Elferink and Johnson (2006), p. 485.

[84]Serdy (2011), p. 364.

[85]*Id.* 362.

[86]ILA (2004), p. 27.

[87]Carrera (2017).

[88]Such fears were espoused by Singapore. See A/CONF.62/SR.125 125th Plenary meeting Extract from the Official Records of the Third United Nations Conference on the Law of the Sea, Volume XIII, para. 3.

case in its current composition (2017–2020), in which approximately two thirds of its members are representatives of developing countries, such as Angola, Brazil, Madagascar, Oman, and others. However, when it comes to the presence of nationals from broad-margin states, a quick look into the Commission's composition shows that the *only* representative of a narrow-margin state that has no submission pending before the Commission is Chilean.[89] In other words, twenty out of twenty-one seats of the Commission are occupied by experts from broad-margin states, a number that could raise some eyebrows as to the impartiality of the Commission's recommendations.

3.3.2.3 Transparency and Confidentiality: A Classical Trade-Off

By now, it should come with no novelty that the procedure for delineating the outer limits of a continental shelf be somehow opaque, firstly due to the complex criteria accommodated in Art. 76 UNCLOS.[90] Secondly, given the exceptionally delicate information about submitting states at stake, such as geodesic and bathymetric data of the ocean floor, which may hint at the existence of mineral and hydrocarbon resources within national jurisdiction; thirdly, the lack of adequate regulation in the Convention as to the matter of publicity of CLCS recommendations.[91] The latter attracts most of the criticisms against the opacity of the delineation process, a situation that could theoretically impair the overall *credibility* of the process, resulting in permanent skepticism as to Commission's trustworthiness by the international community.

For the Commission's recommendations to fulfill their task, it is necessary for them to be made public. Should that not happen, other states would be left in the dark, having no other means of assessing whether certain outer limits were determined indeed on the basis of the recommendations.[92] Hence, if other states cannot defend their legitimate interests before an international body, the likelihood of compliance with the recommendations of that same body is limited. This could even put a question mark as to the "final and binding" nature of the CLCS

[89]Data available at the Commission's website.

[90]Specialists have identified ambiguity in several provisions of Art. 76, such as the test of appurtenance of the continental shelf to the land territory (via morphological and geological review); determining the foot of the continental slope; applying the formulae of Art. 76; and determining the cutoff limits. All those steps in the procedure of delineating the outer limits are subject to questions by scientists, what would allegedly make the procedure ambiguous and somewhat blurred. *See* Macnab (2004), pp. 3–11.

[91]According to the 2006 ILA Report on the outer limits of the continental shelf, "the Convention does not address the publication of information concerning the submission of a coastal State or the recommendations issued by the Commission". *See* ILA (2006), p. 23.

[92]It is the case of Macnab (2004), p. 1.

recommendations.[93] Such *modus operandi* is advisable, as it would enable coastal states an improved understanding of Commission's practice, pave the way for future submissions, and adjust state's expectations.

Nonetheless, a strict reading of the Convention will reveal that the coastal state has the final word regarding publicity. Art. 6, paragraph 3, Annex II UNCLOS requires the recommendations be submitted in writing to the coastal state and to the Secretary-General of the United Nations, but Art. 76 (9) UNCLOS demands charts only (with the outer limits adopted in accordance with the recommendations) to be given publicity by the UN Secretary-General. In fact, "desirable though transparency is, there is nothing in LOSC [Law of the Sea Convention] Art. 76 that requires States to make recommendations public".[94] A submitting state may prioritize the confidentiality of recommendations to the detriment of a more transparent and legitimate procedure before the international community.

A balance to the power of coastal states is struck with the prerogative of third states to obtain additional information, in order to confirm that the outer limits are established on the basis of the CLCS recommendations and in consistency with Art. 76. Thus, one possible interpretation would say that coastal states which have made a submission may be required to allow access to relevant information concerning its proposed outer limits. Such conclusion follows from Rule 54, paragraph 3, which stipulates that the CLCS shall give due publicity to the summary of recommendations adopted by the sub-commission in charge, taking into account the confidentiality of certain data submitted by the coastal state.[95] According to that rule,

> the recommendations prepared by the sub-commission shall include a summary thereof, and such summary shall not contain information which might be of a confidential nature and/or which might violate the proprietary rights of the coastal State over the data and information provided in the submission (emphasis added).

At the end of the day, the Commission accepts it is not about disclosing confidential information on resource potential of a given state, but making public the rationale followed by the CLCS members, be the recommendations favorable to the submitting state or not.

A suggestion to overcome the transparency issue would be, thus, to require states to disclose fully and publicly the rationale and the information from which their proposed outer limits are derived. Here, the delineation process could simultaneously determine the world's maritime boundaries and advance scientific knowledge of the ocean floor.[96] Such quest for transparency, however, should not come at

---

[93]That is also the opinion of Judge Vladimir Golitsyn, to whom "the Commission should make its reasoning accessible to the international community" after every recommendation. *See* Golitsyn (2009), p. 408.

[94]Serdy (2011), p. 381.

[95]Rules of Procedure, CLCS, rule 54, paragraph 3.

[96]Such optimism clashes, nonetheless, with a realistic view of international relations. Firstly, the main reasons why states spend hundreds of millions of dollars on data collection missions that support official submissions are of economic and geopolitical natures. There is no reason to believe

the expense of the coastal state's right to uphold relevant data which may be intimately connected to national sovereignty and security considerations. The issue is so politically complex and delicate that the Commission's Committee on Confidentiality has been faced with submitting states' denial of access to classified documents to some Commission members, let alone making those documents public to the whole planet. Additionally, it could also be the case to institute a clear and straightforward procedure before the CLCS whereby affected states could seek clarification of the reasons for a state's proposed outer limits, under the risk of a considerable increase in the workload of the Commission, thereby retarding even longer the recommendations awaited by over 50 submitting states.

These are but some of the challenges ahead of a body that is inherently limited in its mandate and strained to its limit with a massive workload, legally complex and politically sensitive issues under its evaluation, added to a *pro bono* work scheme of its members. Other issues raised by CLCS members include: lack of secure means of online communication among members during and between sessions, so as to facilitate the work of the Commission; delay of state parties to nominate members to the Commission in light of a vacancy, thereby cumulating the workload of remaining members and increasing the chance of lack of quorum for important decisions; "significant risk for health-related incidents during their CLCS members' stay in New York, compounded by the fact that the members are placed in a situation of important responsibility and associated stress"; elevated out-of-pocket costs for medical expenses while performing Commission duties, due to lack of proper insurance of Commission's members and limited funds in the Trust Fund for members from developing countries; loss of income, benefits or career opportunities experienced by half of the Commission's members.[97]

That much could be said on the work of the CLCS in the procedure of delineating outer limits of continental shelves. Nonetheless, the Commission is not mandated to perform in cases where a maritime border dispute takes place. It is, thus, the case to assess the relevance of international courts and tribunals in delimiting outer continental shelves under dispute.

that data collection projects would include information other than bathymetric and seismic ones that's are strictly necessary to fulfill Art. 76 criteria and, in parallel, identify potential natural resources in the seabed and subsoil of the floor under their national jurisdiction. Secondly, even information about ecosystems is collected, such as samples of genetic resources, studies of fauna and flora density farther away offshore, frailty of marine living species in the continental shelf within and beyond 200 nm, such info is top-secret, as it contains direct and sensitive state interests.

[97] *Letter dated 2 April 2018 from the Chair of the Commission on the Limits of the Continental Shelf addressed to the President of the twenty-eighth Meeting of States Parties*, SPLOS/319, 2 April 2018.

3.4 Delimiting and Delineating: The International Tribunal for the Law of the Sea

Flawed as it may be, the CLCS is certainly a key institution in outer continental shelf delineation processes. Yet, it is not the only one. The question now is to understand what the role of other UNCLOS-based bodies is, in the delineation and delimitation of continental shelves beyond 200 nm, i.e. whether the ITLOS (or arbitral tribunals) and the ISA have a say in such processes. Lawyers will boast that the Tribunal, empowered as it is to settle international UNCLOS-related controversies, may entertain disputes regarding the delimitation of adjacent or opposing outer continental shelves.[98] However, does the Tribunal have jurisdiction to assess whether a particular coastal state has delineated its outer limits in full compliance with CLCS recommendations? More, does ITLOS have jurisdiction to *judge the validity* of those recommendations, if proven that Art. 76 of the Convention was disrespected? Finally, it should be clarified what role remains to the ISA in outer continental shelf questions, given the intersection between the rules applicable to the outer continental shelf and the Area.

Starting with international tribunals and arbitration courts, it is not novel that they enjoy jurisdiction to analyze and decide on a concrete case with binding force. Since recently, international law has been conferring on states freedom to choose among several dispute settlement mechanisms, including more recently the avenue of compulsory resolution procedures.[99] International courts and tribunals, previously unknown to mankind, quickly take the spotlight in the twentieth century, the reason for that being their strength to advance international law by filling in legal lacunae and dispersing ambiguities—*combler les lacunes et éclaicir les ambiguités*.[100] The fundament of international adjudication, on a quick note, dates back to the legal contributions by followers of Wilsonian and Lauterpachtian traditions to international law.[101]

---

[98]Much could be written about the possibility given to states by international law to delimit opposing maritime boundaries beyond 200 nm through bi- or multilateral agreements. Thus far, 15 such agreements have been concluded, both before and after the CLCS had made recommendations on the outer limits of the continental shelf of one of the parties to those agreements. However, it escapes the purpose of this work to dive into this option, as it would offer limited contribution to the book's main arguments, on the environmental jurisdiction of coastal states on the outer continental shelf. For a more detailed analysis of those treaties, *see* Magnússon (2017), p. 208.

[99]Regarding compulsory jurisdiction of international tribunals, a pertinent case is the ITLOS and the Chamber of Marine Funds, which were recognized compulsory jurisdiction over specific issues related to the Law of the Sea, as described in UNCLOS, Part XV, Section 1.

[100]Ford (1994), p. 35.

[101]It is not meant here that all international lawyers share the same premise that international tribunals advance international law or are key to the functional of the international legal system. A critical school would dismiss such relevance, due to the fetishism or even messianism inherent to the judicial activity. For more on the criticisms to judicial fetishism, *see* D'Aspremont (2015), pp. 1–6.

During the "golden twenties", US President Woodrow Wilson famously pronounced the 14 points, or requirements, for achieving permanent peace, a doctrine that relied heavily on the respect for the rule of law in international relations. In such a pulverized and decentralized ambience as that of interstate affairs, the rule of law was reserved a pivotal role in the quest for long-lasting peace (just like open and frank diplomacy between nations). The former President considered the "negotiation of open covenants of peace", as well as the "enforcement of international covenants" crucial steps in the path towards good mutual understanding in the international stage.[102]

Another theoretical cornerstone, amongst others, in the consolidation of the rule of international law as a key principle to foreign relations was Hersch Lauterpacht, for whom there was no distinction between legal and political questions. Everything is legal and therefore justiciable, i.e. susceptible of being brought to court.[103] In a system with weak legislativeity, such as the international one, the centrality of judges was the solution found by Lauterpacht to tackle the problem of ineffectiveness of international provisions. In light with that centrality, he did not admit the *non liquet* as an a priori legal principle in international law—in other words, judges must realize social peace even in light of lacunae in the law.[104] International courts should not fail to decide the merits of a case for whatever reason. Such a powerful defense of the international rule of law influenced generations of internationalists, by attaching great importance to the judiciary and international judges in the study of discipline. For Lauterpacht, the expansion of the judiciary's activities would lead to peace, progress, justice and social order at the international level.[105]

That was the macro-context of a move towards the *internationalization of institutions*, mainly from 1945 onwards, with the creation of the United Nations, a glorious moment for the institutionalist school in international relations theory.[106] Within such trend, came the formulation of specialized courts and tribunals, such as the European Court of Justice and the European Court of Human Rights, Inter-American Court of Human Rights, Andean Court, Permanent Court of Appeal of the MERCOSUR, Caribbean Court of Justice, amongst others.

In that context, some of the core reasons which explain the enlargement of international adjudicative institutions are: (i) faith in the international rule of law

[102]Woodrow Wilson, *14 points, Speech to the US Congress*, points I and II, 8 January 1918. Available online.

[103]Galindo (2014), p. 397.

[104]Lauterpacht (1933), pp. 71–72.

[105]Lauterpacht's views influenced greatly the international legal system adopted after World War II, with the creation of the ICJ and the drafting of Art. 38 of the Court's Statute, which included "general principles of law" as sources of international law, therefore, prohibiting *non liquet* in international law.

[106]Two of the most known and quoted institutionalists worldwide are Joseph Nye and Robert Keohane, whose theoretical constructs on the power of institutions in shaping international relations have inspired several other institutionalist theories and schools. *See*, generally, Keohane and Nye (1977).

for solving conflicts, as was the case of Lauterpacht; (ii) the insufficiency of pre-existing international jurisdictions, namely the Permanent Court of International Justice (PCIJ); (iii) the regionalization of international law, with the creation of economic and political regional blocs;[107] and (iv) the growing complexity of trans-national problems and conflicts, a sum of factors that have led to the creation of tribunals with universal aspirations. The resulting phenomenon was the *jurisdicionalization* of the international society, fully legitimized by the will of sovereign states. Offspring of that phenomenon were the Dispute Settlement Body of the World Trade Organization, in 1994, the International Criminal Court, in 2004, and the centerpiece of this section, the ITLOS, in 1996.

Following that *institutional boom*, time had come to implement the rule of law in international affairs, a herculean task which is still undoubtedly a "work in progress".[108] Yet, the effectiveness of the international rule of law has certainly gained momentum in past decades. Take the case of the law of the sea, for instance, where international courts and tribunals have played an increasingly relevant role, due mostly to the entry into force of UNCLOS in 1994, but to the burgeoning uses of the oceans. In this field of international law, UNCLOS was awarded a robust part devoted exclusively to the settlement of disputes, including the pioneering compulsory procedures entailing binding decisions on the parties.[109]

Already in the first sessions of the Third Conference, negotiating parties admitted the need for a specific dispute settlement system for ocean-related controversies.[110] Most states anticipated an increase in conflicts related to the rights and duties exercisable by each party in the newly created maritime spaces, which gave birth to the plurality of legal regimes in the law of the sea. Particularly worrisome were three points: the extension of the territorial sea, the creation of the EEZ and the delimitation of the continental shelf vis-à-vis the Area. Hence, "where there had previously been a single jurisdiction there would be a plurality of powers, giving rise to new conflicts".[111]

[107]Karagiannis (2003), p. 15.

[108]Oxman (2011), p. 437.

[109]It should be born in mind that a "dispute" amounts to the disagreement on a point of law or fact, the conflict of interests or views, or the objective opposition by a party to the claims/interests of another party.

[110]During UNCLOS negotiations, both formal and informal, two sets of countries would emerge in relation to a dispute settlement mechanism. The so-called "maximalists" and the "minimalists". The former demanded an internationally binding adjudicating body to solve legal oceanic disputes, whereas the minimalists rejected wide compulsory jurisdiction to an international tribunal. *See* Noyes (1999), p. 116. Brazil is one of the countries that expressly rejected a wide compulsory jurisdiction to the Tribunal. Reason for that may be the reluctance to cede sovereignty in matters considered to be politically sensitive, such as economic rights over natural resources offshore or even increase in geopolitical influence over the South Atlantic Ocean. See *Statement of the Brazilian Delegation*, 62nd Plenary meeting Extract from the Official Records of the Third United Nations Conference on the Law of the Sea, Volume V, A/CONF.62/SR.62.

[111]*See* 59th Plenary meeting Extract from the Official Records of the Third United Nations Conference on the Law of the Sea, Volume V, A/CONF.62/SR.59, Note of the Chairman.

According to a study by Philippe Gautier, Registrar of the ITLOS, there has been a surge in the number of law of the sea-related cases referred to ITLOS since 1994. In the pre-UNCLOS era, only as much as 12 cases affiliated to boundary delimitation, navigation and fisheries had been brought either to the ICJ or to international arbitration. Between the entry into force of the Convention and 2011, a total of 35 ocean-related disputes had been brought to international adjudication, of which 18 landed at ITLOS docket. At the time of writing, the number of cases decided by the Tribunal has risen to 25, a significant one compared to the *status quo ante* UNCLOS.[112] Such growth corroborates the key role of international courts and tribunals in settling ocean-related disputes and contributing to a law-based public order of the oceans.

The ITLOS was acknowledged the purest form of jurisdiction, i.e. to interpret and apply the treaty from which it was born, in pursuance of Art. 288 (1) of the Convention and Art. 21 of the Statute of the Tribunal.[113] The Tribunal has, thus, jurisdiction over a vast array of disputes related to the content of the Convention, such as maritime delimitation claims, especially of boundaries involving the territorial sea, the exclusive economic zone and the continental shelf. Yet, the aim of the current item is to assess the Tribunal's competence to entertain both delineation and delimitation issues; the former, in which no competing entitlements are at stake, but solely the actions by the CLCS and coastal states, upon excessive or abusive determination of the outer limits of their continental shelves; the latter, in which translucent antagonistic claims exist.

3.4.1 Maritime Delimitation of Continental Shelves Beyond 200 nm

The ITLOS and other international courts face a legal challenge when delimiting continental shelves beyond 200 nm, which is to determine jurisdiction, where the distance criterion may play no role at all, and scientific and technical intricacies will come to the spotlight. That could be the case of outer limits to be established through the 2500-meter isobath, of Art. 76 (4) (a) (ii) UNCLOS. While it is a task for the judicial or arbitral forum, competent in such disputes, to determine the geographical extent of entitlements in maritime disputes within 200 nm, the situation with regard to the continental shelf beyond such limit is slightly different.

An analysis of this issue must ineluctably refer to the most paradigmatic case of maritime delimitation beyond 200 nm from the baselines that has made it to the ITLOS jurisprudence. In the Bay of Bengal case, between Bangladesh and Myanmar, the parties disagreed on the Tribunal's jurisdiction to delimit the continental

[112]Gautier (2014), p. 574.

[113]Under Art. 288, paragraph 2, UNCLOS, the Tribunal has also been given jurisdiction over any dispute concerning the interpretation or application of other agreements.

shelf beyond 200 nm. Myanmar contested such jurisdiction under the argument that, although ITLOS *could* have jurisdiction, as a matter of principle, to delimit the continental shelf beyond 200 nm, it would not be *appropriate* to exercise jurisdiction over that specific case.[114] Bangladesh contended that UNCLOS made no distinction between inner and outer continental shelf, what empowered the judges to decide upon the entirety of the continental shelf, as allowed by Art. 83 of the Convention.[115]

Amongst the claims contrary to ITLOS jurisdiction, two were particularly eye-catching. Firstly, that delimiting the outer continental shelf could encroach upon the Area and, therefore, harm rights of the international community. Any decisions by the Tribunal "might prejudice the rights of third parties and also those relating to the international seabed area".[116] Secondly, that a judicial verdict would infringe upon the preeminence of the CLCS as the most appropriate locus for the determination of the outer limits of continental shelves. Given that the Commission's recommendations are a prerequisite for legal and binding outer limits, no international court or tribunal could determine a boundary line without knowing the precise trajectory of those outer limits.

Some reflections on the abovementioned arguments are called for. The interpretation of Art. 288 (1) UNCLOS, combined with Art. 21 of the Tribunal's Statute, leaves no controversy as to the fact that "the jurisdiction of the Tribunal comprises *all* disputes and *all* application submitted to it in accordance with the Convention" (emphasis added).[117] If a dispute relates to the interpretation and application of UNCLOS provisions, as is the case with Art. 76 and other pertinent provisions governing the continental shelf regime, it must be concluded that the ITLOS has jurisdiction to entertain such dispute.

In addition to that, ITLOS found jurisdiction to delimit the continental shelf in its entirety, as the Convention does not divide between inner and outer continental shelf, thereby giving reason to Bangladesh. Crystal clear jurisprudence on the singularity of continental shelf was set by the Arbitral Tribunal in the Arbitration between Barbados and Trinidad and Tobago, which stated that "there is in law only a single 'continental shelf' rather than an inner continental shelf and a separate extended or outer continental shelf".[118]

Contesting the argument that potential overlapping claims by third states would deprive the Tribunal's jurisdiction was the easiest part. It is not only a well-established principle of international law, but it is also inscribed into the Tribunal's Statutes, Art. 33, that an international judgement shall produce effects to the parties

[114] ITLOS *Dispute concerning delimitation of the maritime boundary between Bangladesh and Myanmar in the Bay of Bengal (Bangladesh/Myanmar)* para 45.

[115] *Id.* para 350.

[116] *Id.* para 344.

[117] *Dispute concerning delimitation of the maritime boundary between Bangladesh and Myanmar in the Bay of Bengal (Bangladesh/Myanmar)* para 48.

[118] PCA *Arbitration between Barbados and the Republic of Trinidad and Tobago, relating to the delimitation of the exclusive economic zone and the continental shelf between them*, Vol. XXVII, 11 April 2006, 165, para 213.

to the dispute alone, thereby not binding third states.[119] Besides, the rights of the international community (concerning the Area) are not involved in the dispute. The Tribunal, in order to demonstrate that a judgement would not harm the rights of the international community by encroaching upon the Area, analyzed both parties' submissions to the CLCS. That analysis confirmed that the continental shelf beyond 200 nm under dispute between the parties rested far from the international seabed area.[120]

Now to the alleged conflict of competences between the Tribunal and the CLCS, it should be noted that the Convention states nowhere that the delimitation of maritime boundaries curbs the work of the Commission. In fact, UNCLOS contains a carefully crafted institutional framework composed of ITLOS, CLCS and ISA that can only implement the Convention via *complementary work.* Provisions for such complementarity abound in the wording of the Convention. Besides, the Convention clearly separates the activities of delineating the outer limits of the continental shelf, under Art. 76, and delimiting the continental shelf, under Art. 83. A thorough reading of Art. 76 (10) leads to the unequivocal conclusion that rules governing the delineation of outer limits of the continental shelf shall not prejudice "the question of the delimitation of the continental shelf between states opposite or adjacent coasts".[121]

On the top of that, there can be no conflict between the ITLOS and the Commission in maritime boundary disputes, as the CLCS is blocked from making recommendations until the dispute has been judicially settled. In fact, the Commission has halted the consideration of submissions by Myanmar and Bangladesh upon request of the latter.[122] So, if the Tribunal waives for the Commission, the practical result is that the Tribunal will not act at all, thereby creating "circularity" and an endless loop in disputes over maritime boundaries beyond 200 nm.[123] The Tribunal has not only the jurisdiction, but the *obligation* to adjudicate, leaving aside the question whether it was appropriate to exercise jurisdiction or not. So, the ITLOS went on to determine the *entitlements* of the parties to the continental shelf beyond 200 nm, a legal construct that does not depend on any procedural requirements—Art.

[119]Art. 33, paragraph 2, ITLOS Statute, on the right to intervene in cases of interpretation and application.

[120]ITLOS *Dispute concerning delimitation of the maritime boundary between Bangladesh and Myanmar in the Bay of Bengal (Bangladesh/Myanmar)* para 368.

[121]In its judgement, the ITLOS found that "The absence of established outer limits of a maritime zone does not preclude delimitation of that zone". *Id.* para. 370.

[122]Statement by the Chairman of the Commission on the progress of work in the Commission, CLCS/72 of 16 September 2011, 7, para 22.

[123]To decide that, the ITLOS had to confront a past decision by the ICJ, in the *Nicaragua v. Honduras* case, 2009, in which the ICJ abstained from delimiting the outer continental shelf, deferring to the CLCS. For McDorman (2013), p. 97, "what other courts and tribunals may have done and said respecting the role of the Commission is confined to the facts of those cases".

77 (1) UNCLOS. In fact, to establish entitlement in those cases is a predominantly legal task, not a technical one.[124]

The Bay of Bengal case and ITLOS' decision "has not diminished or otherwise changed the role of the Commission in the process of the establishment by a coastal State of its outer limits of the continental shelf".[125] It is up to the state parties and to the adjudicative body of the Convention, ITLOS, "to determine whether or not the wording or application of wording in Art. 76 is subject to legal or scientific interpretation", whereas the mandate of the CLCS is extremely limited.[126]

3.4.2 *Delineation: Compulsory Judicial Accountability of the Commission*

Other sensitive issues surrounding ITLOS' role in outer continental delineation relate to: (i) the legality of applying UNCLOS compulsory settlement mechanism to coastal states which have delineated their outer limits in disrespect to the Commission's recommendations; and (ii) the judicial control of CLCS recommendations. In other words, may ITLOS be provoked, in those situations, based on UNCLOS Part XV, Section 2? Those are two different questions that merit analysis in the coming paragraphs.

Firstly, on the international judicial intervention in cases of excessive outer continental shelf limits, imagine the following hypothetical scenario: State A declares its extended continental shelf limits beyond those recommended by the CLCS. Sure, coastal states are the sole competent to delineate their outer limits, due to sovereignty over the landmass and the inherent right exercised over the shelf. However, those limits will only be final and binding, i.e. opposable to other states of the international community, provided they implement Art. 76 criteria and follow the CLCS recommendations to the letter.[127] A variation from those recommendations would, thus, most likely amount to an illegal encroachment on the Area, thereby curtailing the common heritage principle, a structural principle for the international seabed regime, and violating the basic principle of non-appropriation of the international seabed.[128] In such a scenario, the rights of the international community as a

[124]*Bay of Bengal Case*, para 413.

[125]McDorman (2013), p. 102.

[126]Schofield *et al.* sketched a similar argument, noting that the delimitation of the continental shelf seaward of the 200-nm limit did not constitute an encroachment on the functions of the CLCS as was without prejudice to the establishment of the outer limits of the continental shelf. *See* Schofield et al. (2013), p. 372.

[127]*See* ILA (2006), p. 28. That is also the view shared by Oystein Jensen, to whom there must be identity between the outer limits established by the coastal state and the CLCS recommendations. Thus, the state is left with no margin of discretion, if the fixed outer limits are to be "final and binding", and opposable to the international community. *See* Oystein (2013), p. 277.

[128]Art. 137, paragraph 1, UNCLOS, on the legal status of the Area and its resources.

whole—addressee of the *res communis* beyond national jurisdiction—would be under siege, a situation that would legitimize each and every state party to the Convention to seek judicial relief in face of such a breach to the regime of the Area.

Hence, in that scenario, a State B is entitled to take legal action, due to its interest in the case, an interest to be found in the illegal advancement of State A over the Area. The expected judgement would bear consequences only for the parties to the dispute, which would potentially include the obligation to make a revised or new submission to the CLCS, in full consistency with the judgment. It would not be too bold to assert that the violating state may be required to compensate the international community for eventual damages caused to what was actually the Area, and not the state's outer continental shelf.[129]

Now, *even if* the coastal state followed the Commission's recommendations, the delineation of the outer limits of the continental shelf by a coastal state is open to compulsory adjudication.[130] It is so due to the fact that *all* unilateral acts of states may be challenged by third states, no distinction looming over outer limits' delineation. In fact, Art. 76 (8) of the Convention does not exclude recourse to dispute settlement regarding the delineation procedure, and according to the principle of legality in international (criminal) law, if a behavior is not forbidden, then it is allowed—*nullum crimen sine lege*. Assuming that the parties to UNCLOS have adopted the ITLOS as their default litigation forum, the dispute may be unilaterally brought to that Tribunal.[131] Such a view has been endorsed and further developed by the ILA, which held that "a dispute over the question whether the outer limit has been established 'on the basis' of the recommendations of the CLCS can be settled in accordance with Section 2 of Part XV of the Convention".[132] At the end of the day, it is not about creating a hierarchy between UNCLOS-based institutions, but safeguarding the right of sovereign states to seek relief for an alleged violation of law before an international adjudicating body.[133]

Secondly, Tribunal may be required to exercise *judicial control over the actions of the Commission*, a mandate which is not entirely clear from UNCLOS provisions.[134] It would be the case of State B challenging the recommendations of the

[129]Details on this position would be too complex to handle within this section and would, besides, escape the main purpose of the work.

[130]Of the same view, Marotta Rangel, to whom "judicial and arbitral control are admissible even after the Commission's recommendation". *See* Rangel (2006), p. 362.

[131]If the parties opted for different mechanisms, the legal dispute may be submitted unilaterally to arbitration. See Wolfrum (2008), p. 9.

[132]ILA (2002), p. 6.

[133]In the view of Rüdiger Wolfrum, ITLOS judgement in such a case could even strengthen the Commission's recommendations, instead of crippling the authority of the Commission. *See* Wolfrum (2008), p. 12.

[134]Authors such as Marotta Rangel point out the need for "judicial control over the Commission's actions", based on the obligation falling upon the Commission to make recommendations in accordance with UNCLOS Art. 76. The ITLOS is the body responsible for interpreting and settling disputes related to the enforcement of the Convention. *See* Rangel (2006), p. 359.

Commission, its validity, its material consistency with UNCLOS, and its procedural correctness. Here, it seems that ruling out the possibility of a judicial institution examining the validity of the actions of another international body would prejudice the intrinsic function of international courts and tribunals—that of settling controversies and pacifying society. Not in vain, the general rule in international law is that "a court or tribunal is not excluded from exercising its jurisdiction in contentious case between two States in which the validity of a decision of an international body is being impugned".[135]

In this case, the CLCS cannot be a party to the proceedings and shall not be bound by the final decision, given that the judgement effects solely the disputing parties, even though it would be advisable for the Commission to do so. A control of this kind is necessary for the coherent implementations of UNCLOS' provisions and does not amount to a violation of the functions and mandate of the Commission. In other words, as long as it is provoked (for a tribunal could never initiate such control *ex officio*), a court or tribunal may indeed entertain such a case and find that a CLCS recommendation is invalid, in case the Commission acted beyond the limits of its legal mandate.[136]

Intervention by the Tribunal in those borderline situations, though beneficial for the upholding of international law as it may be, raises questions on the multifaceted *interaction between law and science* on the interpretation of Art. 76.[137] In the quest for tackling a recommendation by the CLCS, which was allegedly rendered after extensive scientific and technical debates, the Tribunal ought to anchor its judgement on the most accurate scientific knowledge available. Conscious of such a challenge ahead of the international judge, UNCLOS negotiators have provided for the designation of scientific experts in both delineation and delimitation cases beyond 200 nm.[138] In fact, Art. 289 of the Convention is an important innovation in international law.

Yet, neither ITLOS nor arbitral tribunals have invoked it so far in their decisions. Instead, they have resorted only moderately to experts, as in the Southern Bluefin Tuna and Land Reclamation cases,[139] with the so-called "cross-examination" procedure by the other party. A possible reason for reluctance, according to Judge Tullio Treves, could be the skepticism of parties to as dispute as to the independence of experts, since they are chosen upon consultations.[140] The fact is that, the need to

[135]ILA (2002), p. 10.

[136]ILA (2006), p. 27.

[137]Magnússon (2017), pp. 260–274.

[138]On the benefits of having international courts and tribunals resorting to scientific experts in complex cases, *see* Rosenne (2007), p. 250.

[139]See ITLOS *Southern Blue Fin Tuna case*, Order of Provisional Measures, 27 August 1999, paras 21 and 25. See also ITLOS *Case Concerning Land Reclamation by Singapore in and around the Straits of Johor*, Order of Provisional Measures, 8 October 2003, para 86, on the Tribunal's request that a scientific study by independent experts be conducted by the disputing parties.

[140]For more on the use of scientific experts by international courts and tribunals, *see* Treves (2012), p. 483. Relevance of defining the outer limits of the continental shelf. *See* Brown (1971), p. 3.

evaluate complex scientific and technical information, a challenge as it may be, does not in any degree curb international courts and tribunals' jurisdiction to adjudicate in continental shelf delimitation cases.

In the context of continental shelf delimitation, international courts and tribunals have, thus, basically three roles. First, to settle disputes on delineation and delimitation issues pursuant to the applicable law; second, to guarantee the "holistic interpretation" of international law, preventing it from the threat of fragmentation; third, to contribute to substantive law-making.[141] Concerning the record of ITLOS in particular, it is undeniable the complementary role of the Tribunal in developing international law.[142] Overall, despite some rightful criticisms to its work, the Tribunal has made justice to that complementary role, thereby developing international law in the (limited) cases brought before it until now.

3.5 Benefits of Delineating the Outer Limits of the Continental Shelf

In light of the coastal state's inherent right over the continental shelf, the procedure to delineate the portion of the shelf beyond 200 nm assumes a *declaratory nature*. The delineation of outer limits does *not* constitute new boundary lines. Here, the fundamental principle is that the lines which result from the delineation are taken as pre-existing, the rights of the coastal state therein not depending on CLCS recommendations.[143]

For that reason, there is no real "expansion" of the continental shelf at the end of the delineation procedure, since the shelf had been there all along. "To expand" would imply an increase in size, whereas "to extend" would mean an increase in distance/length.[144] What is there is the international validation of the precise area of the seafloor where the coastal state may exercise sovereign rights. At the end of the day, this is a less relevant semantic question. Perhaps, some scholars would favor the "extension" over the "expansion" of the continental shelf, given the sovereignty connotations that an "expansion" may carry, such as the expansion of an empire, a territory.

Back to the benefits, given the declaratory nature of the delineation procedure, the CLCS recommendations lack the legal ability to impede coastal states from exercising sovereign rights over their claimed outer continental shelf. Coastal states have a right to explore their resources before the limits become final and binding, *provided that* Art. 76 requirements have been respected, the best way to assess such

[141] *See* Magnússon (2017), p. 277.

[142] Lowe (2013), p. 35.

[143] Kunoy (2013), p. 5.

[144] The authoritative Virginia Commentaries on UNCLOS refer to "extension", as in Nordquist et al. (2002), p. 879.

compliance being the delineation procedure before the CLCS.[145] For that, coastal states must be aware that any unlawful exercise of right in an area that turns out not be part of their outer continental shelf will trigger international responsibility.[146] Then what are the benefits for the coastal state of delineating the outer limits of the continental shelf?

First of all, gradual delineation in accordance with UNCLOS provisions and on the basis of CLCS recommendations contributes to the determination of maritime boundaries worldwide, especially between coastal states' shelves, and between coastal states and the international *res communis*, the Area. That is a condition *sine qua non* for investments in and further exploration of the world's oceans. In this regard, UNCLOS achieved the great deed of defining all maritime zones and establishing scientific criteria for the definition of what is perhaps the most complicated zone to define: the continental shelf. As attested by Brown back in 1971, "a definite boundary cannot but contribute to a dispute-free climate for submarine research and development and exploitation of the resources of the seabed".[147] Here, without definite and legally certain boundaries, discussions on the regimes applicable to the continental shelf and the Area could easily be taken for pointless.

Secondly, legal certainty can only be obtained via coastal state compliance with the procedure set forward at Art. 76 UNCLOS. Only then the internationally recognized outer limits of the continental shelf form the state's maritime boundaries.[148] Once the maritime borders are known, orderly development of natural resources within and beyond national jurisdiction, in pursuance with UNCLOS pertinent provisions, will be made possible. Thus far, there is no reason to question the orderly and peaceful implementation of Art. 76, with coastal states drawing the outer limits of their continental shelves on the basis of the Commission's recommendations.[149]

States know it is in their best interest to follow UNCLOS with regard to continental shelf jurisdictional assertions and have done so with laudable regularity thus far. Such widespread acceptance of Art. 76 has prompted the International

[145]Of a similar view, *see* Armas-Pfirter (2010), p. 493.

[146]For a detailed analysis on coastal states rights over the outer continental shelf prior to CLCS recommendations, *see* Churchill (2016), p. 137.

[147]Brown (1971), p. 3.

[148]To say that is not equivalent to defending that the maritime zone of the continental shelf equals the state's territory. Here, on must make use of a rather restrictive concept of territory, that is, the physical medium in which the state exercises full sovereignty, and not merely functional jurisdiction. That is not, however, what the Brazilian Navy has been doing. According to that institution, delineating the outer limits of the continental shelf is setting the final border of the "Brazilian territory", as in the Navy-edited book "Brazilian Blue Amazon: the last frontier of Brazilian territory". *See* generally Marinha do Brasil (2013). The Navy establishes an analogy between the delimitation of terrestrial boundaries in the Amazon tropical forest and the delineation of maritime boundaries in the "Brazilian Blue Amazon". Legally, it wrong to refer to the Blue Amazon both as "Brazilian territory" and "Brazilian sea" or "seas belonging to Brazil". In the waters beyond 12nm, the coastal States has neither full imperium (power to rule) nor dominium (ownership).

[149]Koivurova (2011), p. 221.

Court of Justice to confirm the first paragraph of that provision, on the definition of the outer limits of the continental shelf, as "part of customary international law".[150] It does not mean, however, that the entirety of Art. 76 has achieved a recognized customary nature, as the delineation process, its nuances and details are still a debated topic. Tullio Treves, for instance, holds that "the procedures to be followed before the CLCS are binding for States parties to UNCLOS even in the context of a dispute with a non-party",[151] a view which seems to have been confirmed before the ICJ, namely in the dispute between Nicaragua and Colombia, as the latter is not a party to the Convention, but still took measures to abide by the procedural provisions of Art. 76.

On the one hand, coastal states have massively resorted to that provision and made submissions to the CLCS, abiding by the procedure established by the Convention. On the other, the process of delineating has seen *differing views* embraced by coastal states with active submission at the CLCS concerning technical provisions and the interpretation of specific terms of the Convention. For that reason, the opinion on the customary nature of Art. 76 and the delineation procedure has not been consensual, as some authors question the opinion juris element of the practice, based on the view that states have differing interpretation of Art. 76 concepts and requirements.[152] With *data venia* to the scholars embracing this latter view, it seems evident by resort to state practice and international jurisprudence that large portions of Art. 76 and its procedures have been internalized by the international society as law. It is, thus, consentaneous to international law to claim that the delineation procedure has acquired a customary nature, which ought to be recognized including by non-parties to UNCLOS.

3.6 Partial Conclusions

Broad-margin coastal states have managed to include the continental shelf beyond 200 nm into the wording of UNCLOS, yet not in an absolute manner. The acceptance of extended coastal state jurisdiction over the seafloor came along several compromises, including the limitation of the outer limits to 350 nm or 100 nm from the 2500-meter depth isobath. In order to protect their rights, broad-margin states made sure the Convention would *not* admit reservations concerning the delineation

[150]ICJ *Territorial and Maritime Dispute (Nicaragua v. Colombia)*, Judgment, ICJ Reports 2012 (II), para 126.

[151]Treves (2017), p. 539.

[152]For more on the denial of customary nature to the process of delineating the outer limits of the continental shelf, *see* Tassin (2013), p. 22.

and delimitation of outer continental shelves, therefore, instituting a sort of iron-clad clause in the treaty.[153]

More than 30 years into the adoption of the Convention, provisions regarding the delineation and delimitation of the outer limits of the continental shelf have enjoyed tremendous adherence. Given the widespread abeyance to the rules set forward in Art. 76 UNCLOS, some authors claim that the procedure to delineate the outer continental shelf has acquired a *customary nature*, both requisites for custom would be present, namely reiterated practice and opinion juris.[154] This opinion has not been consensual, as some authors question the opinion juris element of the practice, based on the view that states have differing interpretation of Art. 76 concepts and requirements, concerning the definition procedure.[155]

There is wide acceptance in international law to the view that the delimitation of the continental shelf is a unilateral act of the coastal state, but its *validity* in relation to other states depends on its consistency with public international law.[156] That calls for the work of the CLCS in entertaining submissions for outer continental shelf limits and ITLOS, for settling disputes. Both institutions created by the Convention to aid and monitor the delineation and delimitation of outer continental shelf lines have performed satisfactorily thus far. However, the job is far from over, and the road ahead seems a rather bumpy one.

On the Commission's trench, the main challenge concerns the massive workload in front, with most optimistic estimates shooting at 40 more years until the last outer continental shelf has been delineated. Reasons for that are the gigantesque amount of data under analysis in every submission, added to the limited number of members of the Commission, and the far-from-optimal working conditions. Besides, complexities of a technical nature and high costs of gathering high quality data are factors that will postpone the recommendations of the CLCS and the adoption of the recommendation by coastal states.

On the ITLOS trench, the Tribunal has faced questions regarding its jurisdiction to delimit and delineate outer continental shelves, apart from speculations as to the relation between the Tribunal and the CLCS. In its jurisdiction, ITLOS has asserted jurisdiction to delimit the continental shelf in its entirety, within and beyond 200 nm, particularly due to the concept of a single continental shelf embodies by Art. 76 UNCLOS. The Tribunal has also carved a distinction between delimitation of opposing continental shelves beyond 200 nm the delineation of its outer limits. Besides, the judges have also crafted the notion of "grey area", in which a State exerts sovereign rights over the seabed and the other over the superjacent EEZ. On the relationship between the Tribunal and the Commission, it should be noted that

---

[153] Art. 309 UNCLOS stipulates that "no reservation or exceptions may be made to this Convention unless expressly permitted by other articles of this Convention".

[154] Rangel (2006), p. 350.

[155] Tassin (2013), p. 20.

[156] Rangel (2006), p. 347.

each actor has a clear and precise role in what can be seen as the coherent system of the international law of the sea.

In light of recently announced exploratory activities for hydrocarbon development off the outer continental shelves of Canada and Norway, it is to be expected that exploitation on areas beyond 200 nm will soon follow suit. Oil prices are again on a surge, from a bottom low in July 2017, and states increasingly consume hydrocarbons to keep their respective economies running. In such a scenario, there is a need to clarify the interactions between different regimes of neighboring and overlapping maritime areas, namely continental shelf beyond 200 nm, the high seas and the Area. In addition to that, lawyers are required to identify the exact jurisdiction of the coastal state over the continental shelf, with a focus on the environmental jurisdiction, and the implications of the delineation of the outer limits of the continental shelf to that environmental jurisdiction.

References

Armas-Pfirter F (2010) Submissions on the outer limit of the continental shelf: practice to date and some issues of debate. In: Vidas D (ed) Law, technology and science for the oceans in globalization. Nijhoff, Leiden, pp 477–498

Brown ED (1971) The legal regime of hydrospace. Steven & Sons, London

Busch JM (1993) Oceanopolítica: una alternativa para el desarrollo. Andres Bello Editorial, Santiago

Carrera G (2017) 20 Years of the Commission on the Limits of the Continental Shelf: achievements, challenges and way ahead. Keynote Speech presented at the Open Event of the International Foundation for the Law of the Sea (IFLOS), Hamburg, 4 August, 2017

CCSM (2013) Amazônia azul: última fronteira. Centro de Comunicação Social da Marinha, Brasília

Churchill R (2016) The exercise of coastal state rights on the outer continental shelf pending establishment of its outer limit. In: Law of the sea: UNCLOS as a living treaty. BIICL, London, pp 137–163

Churchill R, Lowe V (1999) The law of the sea. Manchester University Press, Manchester

D'Aspremont J (2015) If international judges say so, it must be true: empiricism or fetishism? Eur J Int Law Talk 4(9):1–6

Donoghue D (2012) Statement of the US Chamber of Commerce. US Senate Foreign Relations Committee. 28 June 2012

Ford CA (1994) Judicial discretion in international jurisprudence: Art. 38(1)(c) and general principles of law. Duke J Comp Int Law 5:35–86

Galindo GRB (2014) Hersch Lauterpacht. In: A formação da ciência do Direito Internacional. Unijuí, Ijuí, pp 387–425

Gautier P (2014) The settlement of disputes. In: Attard D (ed) The IMLI manual of international maritime law, vol I. Oxford University Press, Oxford, pp 533–576

Gena K (2013) Deep sea mining of submarine hydrothermal deposits and its possible environmental impact in Manus Basin, Papua New Guinea. Proc Earth Planet Sci 6:226–233

Golitsyn V (2009) Continental shelf claims in the arctic ocean: a commentary. Int J Mar Coast Law 24:401–408

Hedberg HD (1972) National-International jurisdictional boundary on the ocean floor. Law of the Sea Institute, University of Rhode Island, Occasional Paper no. 16, Kingston, Rhode Island

Horta PA et al (2016) Rhodoliths in Brazil: current knowledge and potential impacts of climate change. Braz J Oceanogr 64(2):117–136

Jayakumar S (2013) The continental shelf regime under UNCLOS. In: The regulation of continental shelf development: rethinking international standards. Nijhoff, Leiden, pp 1–12
Karagiannis S (2003) La multiplication des jurisdictions internationales: un systeme anarchique? In: La jurisdictionnalisation du Droit International, Colloque de Lille, SFDI. Pedone, Paris, p 71
Kelly PL (2004) Deepwater oil resources: the expanding frontier. In: Nordquist MH et al (eds) Legal and scientific aspects of continental shelf limits. Nijhoff, Leiden, p 414
Keohane RO, Nye JS (1977) Power and interdependence: world politics in transition. Little Brown & Co, Boston
Klabbers J (2009) An introduction to international institutional law, 2nd edn. Cambridge University Press, New York
Klare MT (2012) The race for what's left: the global scramble for the world's last resources. Metropolitan, New York
Koivurova T (2011) The actions of the arctic states respecting the continental shelf: a reflective essay. Ocean Dev Int Law 42(3):211–226
Koskenniemi M (2012) Hegemonic regimes. In: Regime interaction in international law. Cambridge University Press, Cambridge, pp 305–324
Kunoy B (2011) Establishment of the outer limits of the continental shelf: is crossing boundaries trespassing? Int J Mar Coast Law 26(2):313–334
Kunoy B (2012) The terms of reference of the commission on the limits of the continental shelf: a creeping legal mandate. Leiden J Int Law 25(1):109–130
Kunoy B (2013) The delimitation of an indicative area of overlapping entitlement to the outer continental shelf. Br Yearb Int Law 83:61–81
Kwiatkowska B (2013) Submissions to the UN Commission on the limits of the continental shelf: the practice of developing states in cases of disputed and unresolved maritime boundary delimitations or other land or maritime disputes, part one. Int J Mar Coast Law 28(2):219–341
Lauterpacht H (1933) The function of law in the international community. Clarendon Press, Oxford, pp 71–72
Lowe V (2013) The complementary role of ITLOS in the development of Ocean law. In: Schreiber H, Paik JH (eds) Regions, institutions, and law of the sea: studies in Ocean governance. Nijhoff, Leiden, pp 29–36
Macnab R (2004) The case for transparency in the delimitation of the outer continental shelf in accordance with UNCLOS Art. 76. Ocean Dev Int Law 35:1–17
Magnússon BM (2017) The continental shelf beyond 200 nautical miles: delineation, delimitation and dispute settlement. Int J Mar Coast Law 32:603
McDorman TL (2002) The role of the Commission on the limits of the continental shelf: a technical body in a political world. Int J Mar Coast Law 17(3):301–324
McDorman TL (2013) The continental shelf beyond 200 nm: a first look at the Bay of Bengal (Bangladesh/Myanmar) case. In: Nordquist MH et al (eds) The regulation of continental shelf development. Brill, Leiden, pp 89–103
Morgenthau HJ (1948) Politics among nations: the struggle for power and peace. Alfred Knopf, New York
Murton BJ, Parson LM, Hunter P, Miles P (2001) Global non-living resources on the extended continental shelf: prospects at the year 2000. Report to the International Seabed Authority, United Nations. ISA, Kingston, Jamaica
Nordquist MH, Grandy NR, Nandan SN, Rosenne S (eds) (2002) United Nations Convention on the law of the sea 1982: a commentary, vol II. Nijhoff, The Hague
Noyes JE (1999) The International tribunal for the law of the sea. Cornell Int Law J 32:109–182
Oude Elferink AG, Johnson C (2006) Outer limits of the continental shelf and "disputed areas": state practice concerning article 76(10) of the LOS Convention. Int J Mar Coast Law 21 (4):461–487
Oxman BH (2011) Idealism and the study of international law, Collected Courses of the Hague Academy of International Law. Brill, Nijhoff

Oystein J (2013) The commission on the limits of the continental shelf: law and legitimacy. Nijhoff, Leiden
Poll R, Schofield C (2010) A seabed scramble: a global overview of extended continental shelf submissions. In: Proceedings of the Advisory Board on the Law of the Sea (ABLOS) conference on Contentious Issues in UNCLOS – Surely Not? ABLOS, Monaco, pp 1–11
Rangel VM (2006) Settlement of disputes relating to the delimitation of the outer continental shelf: the role of international courts and arbitral tribunals. Int J Mar Coast Law 21(3):347–362
Rosenne S (2007) Fact-finding before the International Court of Justice. In: Rosenne S (ed) Essays on international law and practice. Nijhoff, Leiden, p 235
Sale R, Potapov E (2009) The scramble for the Arctic: ownership, exploitation and conflict in the far north. Frances Lincoln, London
Schofield C (2012) Parting the waves: claims to maritime jurisdiction and the division of ocean space. Penn State J Law Int Aff:40–58
Schofield C, Telesetsky A, Lee S (2013) A tribunal navigating complex waters: implications of the Bay of Bengal case. Ocean Dev Int Law 44(4):363–388
Serdy A (2011) The Commission on the limits of the continental shelf and its disturbing propensity to legislate. Int J Mar Coast Law 26(3):355–383
Soares LFM (2014) O Brasil e as negociações sobre Direito do Mar. In: Reflexões sobre a Convenção do Direito do Mar. FUNAG, Brasília, pp 255–312
Suarez SV (2008) The outer limits of the continental shelf. Beiträge Zum Ausländischen Öffentlichen Recht Und Völkerrecht, 199. Springer, Berlin
Tassin VJM (2013) Les défis de l'extension du plateau continental: la consécration d'un nouveau rapport de l'État à son territoire. Pedone, Paris
Treves T (2012) Law and science in the interpretation of the Law of the Sea Convention: Art. 76 between the law of the sea tribunal and the Commission on the limits of the continental shelf. J Int Dispute Settlement 3(3):483–491
Treves T (2017) Evolution and present problems of the law of the sea. In: Boletim da Sociedade Brasileira de Direito Internacional, vol 103. SBDI, Rio de Janeiro, pp 533–542
Wilson W (1918) Fourteen points speech to the US Congress, 8 January
Wolfrum R (2008) The outer continental shelf: some considerations concerning applications and the potential role of the International Tribunal for the Law of the Sea. In: Statement by the President of ITLOS (2008) 73rd Conference of the International Law Association, Rio de Janeiro

Resolutions

A/CONF.62/SR.59 (1976) 59th Plenary meeting Extract from the Official Records of the Third United Nations Conference on the Law of the Sea, Volume V, Note of the Chairman
A/CONF.62/SR.62 (1976) Statement of the Brazilian Delegation, 62nd Plenary meeting Extract from the Official Records of the Third United Nations Conference on the Law of the Sea, Volume V
A/CONF.62/SR.125 (1980) 125th Plenary meeting Extract from the Official Records of the Third United Nations Conference on the Law of the Sea, Volume XIII, para. 3
A/CONF.62/SR.65 (1982) 65th Plenary meeting Extract from the Official Records of the Third United Nations Conference on the Law of the Sea, Volume V
A/CONF.62/121 (1982) Final Act of the United Nations Conference on the Law of the Sea. Annex II, Official Records XVII
UNGA Res2574 A (1969) Question of the reservation for exclusively peaceful purposes of the sea-bed and the ocean floor, and the sub-soil thereof, underlying the high seas beyond the limits of present national jurisdiction and the use of their resources in the use of mankind. Vol. I, 169

United Nations General Assembly, Resolution 2574 A, "Question of the reservation for exclusively peaceful purposes of the sea-bed and the ocean floor, and the sub-soil thereof, underlying the high seas beyond the limits of present national jurisdiction and the use of their resources in the use of mankind" of 15 December 1969, Vol. I, 169

Final Act of the United Nations Conference on the Law of the Sea, A/CONF.62/121, 27 October 1982, Annex II, Official Records XVII

A/CONF.62/SR.65 65th Plenary meeting Extract from the Official Records of the Third United Nations Conference on the Law of the Sea, Volume V

A/CONF.62/SR.125 125th Plenary meeting Extract from the Official Records of the Third United Nations Conference on the Law of the Sea, Volume XIII, para. 3

Statement of the Brazilian Delegation, 62nd Plenary meeting Extract from the Official Records of the Third United Nations Conference on the Law of the Sea, Volume V, A/CONF.62/SR.62

59th Plenary meeting Extract from the Official Records of the Third United Nations Conference on the Law of the Sea, Volume V, A/CONF.62/SR.59, Note of the Chairman

Reports

ECORYS (2014) Study to investigate the state of knowledge of Deep Sea Mining. Final Report under FWC MARE/2012/06 - SC E1/2013/04, drafted by for the European Commission, 28 August 2014. Rotterdam/Brussels

ILA (2002) Preliminary Report of the Committee on the Legal Issues of the Outer Continental Shelf. International Law Association, New Delhi

ILA (2004) Legal Issues of the Outer Continental Shelf. International Law Association, Berlin

ILA (2006) Legal Issues of the Outer Continental Shelf. 72nd Conference of the ILA. International Law Association, Toronto

NAUTILUS MINERALS (2016) Annual Report 2015. NAUTILUS Minerals, Toronto

UN (1999) Scientific and Technical Guidelines of the Commission on the Limits off the Continental Shelf, Doc. CLCS/11. 13 May 1999. United Nations, New York

Jurisprudence

ICJ (2012) Territorial and Maritime Dispute (Nicaragua v. Colombia), Judgment, ICJ Reports 2012

ITLOS (2012) Dispute Concerning Delimitation of the Maritime Boundary Between Bangladesh and Myanmar in the Bay of Bengal (Bangladesh/Myanmar). Judgement of 14 March 2012, ITLOS Reports

ITLOS (2003) Case Concerning Land Reclamation by Singapore in and around the Straits of Johor (Malaysia v. Singapore), Order of 8 October 2003. ITLOS Reports

ITLOS (1999) Southern Bluefin Tuna Cases (New Zealand v. Japan; Australia v. Japan), Order of 27 August 1999. ITLOS Reports

PCA (2006) Arbitration between Barbados and the Republic of Trinidad and Tobago, relating to the delimitation of the exclusive economic zone and the continental shelf between them. Decision of 11 April 2006. In: Reports of International Arbitral Awards, Vol. XXVII, UN, New York

PCIJ (1929) Brazilian Loans Case, PCIJ Report

Chapter 4
Sovereignty and Jurisdiction in the Law of the Sea

UNCLOS' contributions to the stability and certainty of the international legal system are numerous and have rightfully deserved the praising of lawyers from all over the world.[1] One of the categories of provisions that has levered that recognition is that allocating jurisdictional rights and duties to the different actors currently engaged in ocean-related activities, i.e. coastal, port, flag states, amongst others. Throughout its 320 provisions, the Convention has regulated conflicting uses of the ocean and codified a delicate system of multiple maritime zones, in which progressive territorial jurisdiction applies. In other words, coastal states are granted varying jurisdiction over different zones offshore, in a system that may have the undesired outcome of complexifying the already complicated relations between states concerning the oceans.

It is imperious to analyze the relevant UNCLOS provisions on jurisdiction, particularly vis-à-vis the continental shelf, both within and beyond 200 nm. The first items offer a detailed view on sovereignty and jurisdiction both in general international law and the international law of the sea. Those are crucial concepts to the conveyance of this thesis and have deserved a specific chapter. Moreover, as one of the resolutions of this work is to map out the rights and duties attributable to coastal states on their respective continental shelves, particularly in light of the delineation of the outer limits of the continental shelf beyond 200 nm, the final part of the chapter will depict how the concept of "functional jurisdiction" applies to the EEZ and continental shelf of coastal states.

[1] It is not the same as to claim the Convention would still be up-to-date and perfectly suited for tackling, at least in the legal arena, current problems and challenges posed to the world's oceans. Issues such as climate change and sea-level rise would in theory call for amendment procedures, based on Art. 300 UNCLOS, a strategy that is immediately dismissed an unrealistic by both lawyers and politicians, due to the difficulties entangled in amending such a carefully and hard-fought package-deal as UNCLOS.

V. Alencar Mayer Feitosa Ventura, *Environmental Jurisdiction in the Law of the Sea*,
https://doi.org/10.1007/978-3-030-50543-1_4

Subsequently, an attempt is made in Chap. 5 to critically assess whether pre- and post-UNCLOS jurisdictional assertions by coastal states, also regarding continental shelf activities, is reason strong enough for "sounding the sirens" of the international community against the practice of the so-called "creeping jurisdiction". Finally, that chapter also entertains the question as to what extent the legal possibility of delineating the outer limits of the continental shelf beyond 200 nm would be in itself an exercise of excessive jurisdiction.

There has been a minimal number of works on the inventory of coastal states' jurisdictional rights on the outer continental shelf,[2] which have begun to lay down a most needed picture of the delicate balance between coastal state and flag state jurisdiction in the continental shelf area. The added value of this book is, therefore, to (i) problematize the current regulatory maneuver room of coastal states in terms of prescribing and enforcing enhanced environmental protective legislation on the continental shelf; and (ii) to link the exercise of jurisdiction by coastal states on the continental shelf to the analysis of domestic legislation and policies of a relevant, but in recent times ignored global player in ocean affairs: Brazil.

The focus of this work lies on the legal analysis of the prescriptive and enforcement jurisdiction of coastal states and the way it affects the current balance between opposing uses of the oceans, in particular the opposition between navigational freedoms and the coastal state's right-duty to protect and preserve the marine environment. Before engaging with that specific issue, it is advisable to scrutinize the concept of jurisdiction in general international law and in the law of the sea, as this scrutiny will prove pivotal to the development of the argumentation to come, on the composition of an alleged "environmental jurisdiction" of coastal states over the continental shelf within and beyond 200 nm.

One may ask whether the answer to all questions regarding state jurisdiction on the continental shelf are not straightforwardly found in UNCLOS Part VI. The reply is naturally a negative one, as it is not simple as that. Large chunks of the Convention's provisions are built on the dichotomy between two grand principles: those of state jurisdiction and freedoms of the high seas.[3] Consequently, it is safe to affirm that several political and legal tensions arise out of such dichotomy. The apparent simplicity of the allocation of rights and duties over the continental shelf is deceptive, as UNCLOS does not specify the material extent of coastal states' jurisdiction to regulate and enforce domestic laws on the marine environmental protection in borderline cases, such as the regulation of fish-trawling or bioprospecting for marine scientific resources, or marine scientific research on the outer continental shelf for economic and ecological purposes. The objective of the following argumentation is to consider the Convention's weakest and potentially contradictory points, so as to facilitate domestic enforcement in accordance with the wording and the spirit of the legal text.

[2] *See* generally Mossop (2016).

[3] Tanaka (2012), pp. 16–20.

4.1 Sovereignty and Jurisdiction in International Law

Sovereignty and jurisdiction are two the most relevant concepts in international law, upon which the theoretical edifice of the discipline is construed. To understand the latter, one must first analyze the former. Thus, sovereignty consists of an abstract element that transforms an agglomeration of people in a specific territory into an *independent* entity to the eyes of the international community. In this sense, the Charter of the United Nations states that the Organization is based on the principle of *sovereign* equality of all its member states.[4] A reader of international legal works will, thus, be faced with several qualifiers to sovereignty, such as the doctrines of equality between states; self-determination; or independence from external unconsented intervention or interference. In addition, sovereignty usually transmits the idea of a *collection of rights, competences, and powers*,[5] although no specific substantive ones.

Often regarded as a principle of international law, sovereignty may be taken as the "basic constitutional doctrine of the law of nations",[6] which govern states that have *uniform legal personality* and, as such, can be said to be formally equal among themselves. It is "constitutional" in a sense that without the element of sovereignty attached to states there could hardly be any law of nations, since the relationship between non-sovereign and unequal states could not possibly be governed by law—the resulting scenery would be one of utter chaos, instability and unpredictability in interactions. It is so that Hobbes, in a theological analogy, considered sovereignty to be the substance of the Leviathan, that mystical and terrifying creature, but necessary for the sake of order and stability as opposed to the chaos and anarchy of life in the natural phase.[7] It is no wonder that the concept of sovereignty is closely connected to the ideas of formal equality and non-intervention in the domestic affairs of other states.

Jean Bodin, together with Nicollo Machiavelli,[8] initiated the age of political modernity, after centuries of relative scarcity of attempts to systematize the field of politics. In spite of the initial concern with politics, Antiquity lost the focus of the theoretical construction and systematization of this field of knowledge, which had the interactions of states and other independent political entities as one of its main

---

[4]United Nations, *Charter of the United Nations*, 24 October 1945, 1 UNTS XVI, Article 2 (1).

[5]The term "powers" is not used with the same meaning as in the field of international relations, to which power is the ability to influence the behavior of others in order to achieve a desired outcome. In this regard, it is advisable to understand the work of Joseph Nye, creator of the concept of "soft power" as the intangible influence of a country amongst other nations in fields such education, media, financial institutions, sports or entertainment. *See* Nye (1990), p. 153. Power, here, is used in the same sense as Hohfeld, to whom power represents the control of a specific legal relation by a subject against another. Power is, thus, a legal entitlement to modify a particular legal relation in face of other legal subjects. *See* Hohfeld (1913), p. 16.

[6]Crawford (2012), p. 449.

[7]Hobbes (1651) ch. XXXI.

[8]Machiavelli (1515).

convergent points. In the context of the rebirth of political science, Jean Bodin analyzed the political phenomena in his work "The Six Books of the Commonwealth" in another recognized attempt to systematize the domestic and international politics.[9] It diffused the sovereignty of the state, as *supreme potestas*, having, from that study, arrived at a concept of sovereignty mainly linked to the ruler, which makes Bodin one of the philosophers of the Absolutist period. For the French philosopher, political power has no competitors, being superior to the other social powers, both in the internal order and in the international order.[10]

Sovereignty has been for more than five centuries intimately linked to the ideas of power, a trend that initiated with Jean Bodin. Currently, another element has been added to the notion of sovereignty, particularly regarding the interaction of states in the international stage: *consent.*[11] Whenever states opt to exercise some sort of power, that action will be *conditioned* by international law. In this sense, international law embodies also the role of limiting state's arbitrary and abusive exercise of power on the international stage. For that reason, sovereignty may be also seen as "discretionary power within areas delimited by the law".[12] On the other hand, states owe compliance exclusively to the limitations to which they have consented. By the wonders of sovereignty, states are both limited in their discretion to act and entitled to influence the development of the international legal system at any given time, albeit not all states with the same intensity.

Of the main characteristics of the principle, one could remark that sovereignty is *indivisible, inalienable and imprescriptible*. In other words, it cannot be broken into different concepts or separated without losing its meaning,[13] cannot be sold or given away by the State and is not subject to being taken away by lapse of time. Since the Roman period, one of the few things the sovereign could not do was to destroy its own sovereignty, and act that could bring about impoverishment of centralized power and consequently political instability.

The principle of sovereignty as we understand it today is corollary of the Post-Westphalian world, as before that agreement there were no clear bases for national

[9]Bodin (1955).

[10]For Bodin, the state is described first of all in term of power, *puissance souveraine*, which was necessarily perpetual and absolute. The Commonwealth, or Republic, can be defined as "the rightly ordered government of a number of families and of those things which are their common concern, by a sovereign power".

[11]It is beyond the purpose of this work to deepen the study usually conducted by legal sociologists and international political scientists on the intricate relationship between international legal norms and power. Major references in the connection of critical sociology and international law analyses are Pierre Bourdieu and Michel Foucault. Yet, it is inevitable to resort to the category of power when developing ideas and systems of thought in the international law realm. *See* D'Aspremont (2015), p. 4.

[12]Crawford (2012), pp. 447–448.

[13]Not even in the cases of supranational blocks, such as the European Union, does a "division" of sovereignty occur. In those cases, there is a voluntary cession of specific rights and powers to determine a member-state's own domestic policies and laws. Sovereignty is, therefore, not divided but made flexible and limited to the new political and economic reality.

self-determination. The Treaties of Westphalia (1648),[14] which ended the Thirty Years War, threw the cornerstone of a new political order in central Europe based on the notion of peaceful co-existence of sovereign states. Each sovereign entity consented to refrain from interfering in another state's internal matters, where the latter exercised supreme authority over its territory. Since then, for the past centuries, the main behavioral pattern in the relationship between states has been one of either peaceful coexistence or conflict of sovereignties.[15]

The history of the concept is far from linear, as there have been shifts in its understanding.[16] Throughout time, sovereignty has been more or less "plastic", having served many purposes and justification strategies throughout the history of international relations.[17] A critical view of international law will credit to the idea of sovereignty, amongst others, the perverse colonialist rule of Western European powers over large portions of the world. As the European states were the only ones truly sovereign (independent externally and supreme internally), the rule of non-interference applied only among themselves, and consequently excluded the colonies and their peoples. By that time, the "civilizing mission" embraced by the religiously backed European sovereigns functioned as a moral justifier for practically any sort of colonialism.[18]

As decolonization intensified in the second half of the twentieth century, for a variety of reasons, a plethora of erstwhile colonies joined the international society as sovereign entities. One by one, they became members of the United Nations and expected to be protected by the doctrine of non-interference by sovereign states in the international affairs of each other. Again, to a critical school of international law and politics, what followed was far from the end of arbitrary interventionism in other state's businesses. For that, the old Christian-based justification of the higher civilizing mission could not offer the moral ground for further interference and control.

The alternative did not take long to be molded. In the aftermath of WWII, "the rhetorical language shifted to a concept that came to have new meaning and strength

[14]The Treaties were negotiated upon and signed in the cities of Münster and Osnabrück, and the principle of peaceful co-existence between sovereign states can be said to have shaped the order of today's Europe.

[15]Pursuant to the premise of rational choice theoreticians, states are *rational* actors which act to pursue identifiable self-interests. *See* Goldsmith and Posner (2005), p. 5.

[16]The classical of Jean Bodin marks the maturity of the debate on sovereignty. According to the French scholar, sovereignty would represent simultaneously the *suprema potestas* of state entities within their territory, and independence in face of other states in the international community.

[17]Koskenniemi (1998), pp. 240–245.

[18]From the conquer of the Indigenous empires in America by Spaniards and Portuguese to the subdue of the Indian subcontinent by the English, the "civilizing mission" fulfilled a powerful role in justifying the colonial model of spoliation. Such "mission" consisted of forcing, by religious and military means, an allegedly virtuous process of enlightening the barbaric and noncivilized people, but it did not go unquestioned. For a staunch critique against the flawed arguments of Western colonial powers, particularly Spain, enabling the conquest by force, *see* de Las Casas (1552).

in this post-colonial era: human rights".[19] Direct interventions in Africa and Asia were grounded on the argument that the governments under intervention had violated humanitarian values. Intervenors claimed to act in a way compatible with the maximization of justice, what made the intervention "morally justified in natural law, if not legally justified in international law".[20] Hence, sovereignty continued to be a plastic concept, to be invoked in propagandistic and instrumental ways whenever one version or the other would suit the invoking part.

Despite the controversies surrounding the concept of sovereignty, which has been referred to as plastic, or "organized hypocrisy",[21] it is still resilient. It is a *fait-accompli* that states cannot simply close themselves to the scrutiny of the rest of the world in thorny issues such as the protection of human and minority rights or the increasing role of international financial institutions, and that has led to a certain erosion of the original concept. However, sovereignty, albeit weakened, is far from being moribund. The *consent-based conception* of the relationship between sovereign states and between them and international organizations "precludes the argument that state sovereignty is under threat of some form of overarching 'world government'".[22] Instead, it has been through changes and adaptations, to the point that, nowadays, a modern notion of sovereignty can mean *interdependence* of states in the global context.

Nowadays, sovereignty corresponds in essence to the collection of rights held by a state both as a powerful entity within a given territory and as an independent entity on the international sphere. The current view equates sovereignty to *competences* and makes it possible for the international lawyer to refer to jurisdiction by the terms of "sovereignty" and "sovereign rights". At the end of the day, sovereignty depicts states' powers, which originate from legal custom and do not depend on consent of any other state, but the sovereign state itself.

---

[19] *See* Wallerstein (2006), p. 12.

[20] *Id.* 15. The author brings as examples of human-rights based interventions the Entebbe Operation (by Israel in Uganda) in 1976, the Vietnamese overthrow of the Khmer Rouge in Cambodia in 1978 and the Tanzanian counterattack of Idi Amin's Ugandan troops, which led to overthrow of Idi Amin and the installation of a new president in Uganda, also in 1978.

[21] The idea behind the provoking affirmation is that despite longstanding and internationally acknowledged, norms containing the meaning of sovereignty (such as non-interference in domestic affairs) have been systematically violated. This "organized hypocrisy" has been, thus, an enduring attribute of international relations since many centuries. *See* Krasner (1999), p. 2.

[22] Crawford mentions the erosion of the concept of "domestic jurisdiction", understood as the "reserved domain" of topics under exclusive discretion of states. Since the adoption of the UN Charter, article 2 (7) has been given an interpretation that permits UN intervention in "matters which are essentially within the domestic jurisdiction of any state", the exact contrary of that article's original intent. Thus, UN bodies have acted in several occasions on topics related to the relationship between governments and their own people, as in the case of human rights violations. As an example, one may refer to Resolution 1973, of 2011, passed by UN Security Council, authorizing "all necessary measures" to protect civilians in Libya, which resulted in the death of former Libyan *Staatschef*, Muammar Gaddafi. For more information on this process of "erosion", *see* Crawford (2012), p. 454.

From the multifaceted notion of sovereignty, states derive certain abilities, such as plain internal *jurisdiction* to prescribe and enforce laws, immunity from other states' own jurisdiction and freedom from other states' intervention on their territory. Indeed, one the most prominent corollaries of the principle of sovereignty is jurisdiction, a concept that operationalizes that of sovereignty, the focus of the following item.

4.2 From Sovereignty to Jurisdiction in International Law: Bases of Jurisdiction

As observable by now, sovereignty consists of a broad concept and is often taken as a principle of international law, key feature of the current world-system for international relations theories. Jurisdiction, on the other hand, will be a rather operational notion, usually considered a consequence of the sovereignty and equality of states, alongside a duty of non-intervention in internal affairs of fellow states, and the prevalence of consent in order for a sovereign state to be bound by international obligations.[23] Originating from the juxtaposition of the Latin expressions "*iuris*" and "*dictio*", jurisdiction relates to the power to "say the law" or, in other words, to the competences or the administrative domain over which a legal authority extends.[24]

In international law, jurisdiction typically links a situation or event to the competence of a state to regulate such situation, which may relate to any of the branches of government: legislative, executive and judicial. It is often defined in a negative fashion, as an ensemble of rules and principles that serve the purpose of *limiting legal competences* of a state to regulate the conduct of natural and juridical persons in certain situations and to enforce measures in the wake of that conduct.[25] As a consequence, the so-called law of jurisdiction represents a fundamental step in the pursuit for a (relatively) peaceful coexistence in the international arena, providing rules that have the main characteristic of allocating competences to regulate daily life between states and international organizations. In this sense, jurisdiction becomes a major concern of international law inasmuch as it attempts to prevent sovereignty-based assertions of interest by one state from unduly encroaching upon the rights and freedoms of other states.[26] That powerful states shall not legislate and regulate activities taking place in the territory of other states has become a widely accepted principle of international law, of noninterference, and is the result of allocating jurisdiction in the international sphere.

---

[23]This classification is adopted by James Crawford (2012), p. 449.

[24]Entry "Jurisdiction", Online Etymology Dictionary.

[25]Staker (2014), p. 309.

[26]Ryngaert (2015), p. 6.

International law of jurisdiction determines how far, *ratione loci* and *ratione materiae*, the laws and rules of a state may reach.[27] One of the main goals of that is to enable a peaceful coexistence between sovereign state in the international arena via creating obstacles to excessive and unbalanced exercises of power.[28] Limiting the state's coercive powers is, therefore, one much celebrated feature of jurisdiction, particularly if one understands jurisdiction as a source not only of rights, but also of *duties*.[29] States are not free to do whatever they want, nor to exercise authority unrestrictedly. There must be "linking points", or *bases of jurisdiction*.[30] When analyzing the manifestations of jurisdiction, international lawyers include territoriality, nationality, universality and the protective principle.[31] Those bases require a brief explanation on their content and scope.

International jurisdiction is historically informed by the concepts of *territoriality and nationality*. A key presumption to the study of the topic is that the regulatory authority of the state is essentially territorial and relative to its own nationals. The primary source is territoriality, according to which states exercise power over persons, things or events within their territories.[32] The argument in favor of territoriality is reinforced by the domestic legal presumption against the extraterritorial application of legislation—which is valid in several national legal orders worldwide. A bit of the problematic exercise of extraterritorial jurisdiction and the problems involved in the (sometimes) tense relationship between international and national law are further addressed below.

Another basis of jurisdiction is *nationality*, i.e., the personal identity of the parties. In these cases, power can travel beyond borders and remains intimately connected to people. These two "linking points" between state and regulatory power

[27]Article 2 (1), UN Charter and the principle of "one state, one vote"—famous expression of sovereign equality in the international sphere, albeit from a formal perspective.

[28]Blakesley ponders that international law on jurisdiction is less developed than the domestic law on jurisdiction, or in other words, that the advance of the law on jurisdiction has been promoted in the past decades mostly by domestic court decisions. International law in this sense has given a limited contribution. See Blakesley (1999), p. 37. An interesting query would be to assess the causes for this *Distanzierung* of international law from issues relating to state jurisdiction.

[29]For more on the shift from the traditional view that conceived jurisdiction as ascribing mainly rights to states, to an understanding of international jurisdiction that focuses increasingly on individual rights, and therefore, increasingly levies duties on states, *see* Mills (2014), p. 230. For the purpose of this work, to analyze the environmental jurisdiction of coastal states in the law of the sea, there seems to be little relevance of the emerging influence of rights and powers of individuals to the overall functioning of the law of the sea, as the main actors continue to be sovereign states and international organizations.

[30]Most common basis for the exercise of extraterritorial jurisdiction are treaties, in which states agree to cooperate and secure the effective subjection of offenses to the law. *See* Staker (2014), p. 315.

[31]Ryngaert (2015), p. 114.

[32]*See* Staker (2014), p. 317. A controversy lies on the claim that states have regulatory powers over the events that were not triggered nor finished, but merely produced "effects" within their territories.

enable the possibility of overlap between two or more states' jurisdiction.[33] Thus, the generally accepted rule is that jurisdiction may not be exercised extraterritorially, except for situations in which there is a clearly identifiable link between the object of jurisdiction and the "reasonable interests" of the state in question.[34] It is, therefore, inevitable that situations of multiple jurisdictional competence occur on the international stage, and the new law of the sea is prodigious in such sort of overlaps.

4.2.1 *Forms of Jurisdiction: Prescriptive, of Enforcement and Adjudicative*

The concept of jurisdiction is twofold, for it may regard *form* and *content*. In contemporary literature, there are few types of formal jurisdiction, which relate to all branches of government: (i) to establish *rules*: legislative jurisdiction or prescriptive competence; (ii) to establish *procedures*: judicial jurisdiction or adjudicative competence; and (iii) to impose *consequences*: enforcement jurisdiction.[35] Prescriptive, adjudicative and enforcement jurisdiction are independent among themselves, but deeply intertwined. In other words, although a treaty provision may contain competence to enact legislation without the corresponding enforcement powers, it is reasonable to expect that state parties will take enforcement measures to implement

[33]In cases of conflict, states could resort to some general principles, such as the principle of reasonableness—not widespread recognized as a principle of international law. Lawyers must also investigate special agreements between the states involved in an eventual overlap of regulatory powers.

[34]Crawford (2012), p. 457. The term "extraterritoriality" is per se confusing, as it could imply that a state exercises jurisdiction in a certain situation without any territorial link, although the expression is used for cases in which states have some territorial link. According to Ryngaert (2015), p. 7, "the term "extraterritorial jurisdiction" is only accurate if it refers to assertions of jurisdiction over persons, property, or activities which have no territorial nexus whatsoever with the regulating State". If most, that sort of jurisdiction would be a "not exclusively territorial" one. Due to the misconceptions that the expression may cause, the author suggests legal operators to avoid using the term extraterritorial jurisdiction.

[35]Oxman (2007) online. On the adjudicative jurisdiction, it suffices to say that it relates to the jurisdiction of courts. Sometimes though, international courts exercise a counterintuitive prescriptive role, as in those cases where the wording of a treaty is not clear. Here, tribunals may conjure up the *mens legislatoris*, or the intent of the legislator, in particularly complex cases. In the realm of the law of the sea, the ITLOS has been called to determine the precise content of the expression "reasonable bonds", to be paid by flag states who had their vessels and crew arrested, in cases of prompt release. Art. 73 (2) UNCLOS refers only to the obligation of flag states to post a "reasonable bond or other security" prior to the prompt release of arrested vessels. The Tribunal's role was to define criteria for a bond to meet the qualifier of *reasonability*, such as: gravity of offenses; penalties imposable by the law of the detaining State; value of the detained vessel; value of cargo seized. See *The "Monte Confurco" Case*, (Seychelles v. France), Order of 27 November 2000, ITLOS Reports 2000, 80, paras 73 ff.

its laws.[36] It is one of the most relevant attributes of international law to determine which state has jurisdiction and in which respect.

Of those formal categories, *prescriptive jurisdiction* corresponds to the competence to make the laws and rules of a state applicable to activities, relations or status of persons, be via ordinary legislation, administrative regulation, or executive order. For the early political thinkers of modern time, particularly Jean Bodin, the peculiar and essential mark of sovereignty was the right to make law—then understood as the sheer command of the sovereign.[37] That idea has stood the test of time and, until nowadays, the power to command is still an essential mark of sovereignty. Commands in modern democracies are usually expressed in terms of laws that are passed by the legislative branch of a certain territory, in an attempt to shape behavior of the governed citizens. Questions of prescriptive jurisdiction regularly relate to the geographical reach of a state's laws, where those laws may be expected to produce effects.[38]

States may well exercise abusive prescriptive jurisdiction concerning a plethora of issues. Take, for instance, the case in which a state would pass legislation enabling the exercise of criminal power by its authorities in another state's territory. That state prescribing jurisdiction to act extraterritorially would certainly be faced with heated protests in the international community. However, the mere passing of legislation unilaterally extending jurisdiction over other territories and peoples is unlikely to generate right to compensation or to trigger any substantive legal action. To merely enact abusive legislation is not the same as to enforce such legislation. However, if that abusive rule is enforced, then it is safe enough to say that the enforcing state will have most likely committed an international wrong, which may generate consequences on the international level.[39]

Enforcement jurisdiction, on the other hand, means the power

> to enforce or compel compliance or to punish non-compliance with its laws or regulations, whether through the courts or by use of executive, administrative, police, or other nonjudicial action.[40]

To enforce, from old French *enforcier*, based on the Latin expression *in fortis*, which meant "to drive by physical force".[41] The concept's current meaning amongst

---

[36]An example, to refer to the law of the sea, is jurisdiction of the coastal state in the contiguous zone. According to Art. 133 UNCLOS, the coastal state may only "exercise control" necessary to prevent and punish violations of domestic legislation related to customs, taxation, immigration and sanitation. Even though the Convention does not expressly mention the prescriptive competence (to legislate), in practice the domestic laws enacted by the coastal state may be enforced in accordance with UNCLOS, what would indirectly amount to a jurisdiction to legislate in the contiguous zone. For a different view, *see* Tanaka (2012).

[37]Tooley (1952), p. 24.

[38]Ryngaert (2015), p. 9.

[39]Crawford (2012), p. 477.

[40]*SS Lotus*, PCIJ Reports, Series A, No 10, 1927, 18–19.

[41]Online Etymology Dictionary. *Enforce*. Available at: http://www.etymonline.com/index.php?term=enforce. Accessed 07 April 2020.

lawyers is that of compelling obedience to a norm. Enforcement of laws on the international stage must be conducted with absolute caution and respect for the rule of law. A state may not take action on the territory of another state without the consent of the latter. States are not entitled to enforce nationally prescribed rules over another state's territory, unless there exists cooperation treaties and agreements between the interested sovereign entities calling for such an interference.[42] *Extra-territorial enforcement* is, thus, the exception rather than the rule.

Although the concepts of prescriptive and enforcement jurisdiction are logically independent, they are *intertwined* in practice.[43] It is reasonable to expect that once a state has enacted certain regulations on a concrete matter, that same state will undertake all efforts to compel compliance to those rules. If the regulations are supposed to apply extraterritorially, the affected states (or the entirety of the international community) may then expect measures in order to enforce a given provision. Given the potential for conflicts arising of reiterated and multiple assertions of extraterritorial jurisdiction to the world order, states should aim at lending the international arena predictability and cohesion, enabling the resolution of *différends* within the toolbox offered by the international rule of law.

4.2.2 Content of Jurisdiction: Civil, Criminal and Environmental

Having assessed the different forms of international jurisdiction and some of the most controversial issues around them, the next logical step is to clarify the possible content of jurisdiction. In other words, the matters in relation to which sovereign states possess power to prescribe rules and to establish procedures and sanctions. Such content is traditionally subsumed to the fields of criminal and civil law. In a wider perspective, however, there can be potentially as many types of jurisdiction content-wise as the special subfields of legal system. One could speak of an administrative, economic, environmental, or labor jurisdiction, amongst others, apart from the civil and criminal macro-branches. The study of each of these types of jurisdiction *rationae materiae* is conducted by their respective epistemic communities, which specialize in analyzing and pushing towards increased implementation of their respective fields.[44]

For the purposes of this work, the three main categories of jurisdiction concerning content are criminal, civil and *environmental*. It is possible, and even advisable, that civil and criminal jurisdiction interact and be applied concomitantly with environmental provisions, or rules concerning the protection and preservation of the marine

---

[42] It is the case of the North Atlantic Treaty provisions, concerning the status of the forces integrating the alliance. See NATO Treaty, 199 UNTS 67, article VII, 1951.

[43] O'Keefe (2004), p. 735.

[44] On this view of how international law operates, *see* D'Aspremont (2015), p. 14.

environment. In fact, the ensemble of rights and duties exercisable by coastal states over their adjacent continental shelves can be broken down to those three categories. In other words, this work entertains legal questions relating to the exercise by coastal states of environmental, criminal, and civil jurisdiction, both on the prescriptive and enforcement levels, over the continental shelf. It should also be borne in mind that it deals exclusively with territorial jurisdiction of coastal states over maritime zones adjacent to their shores.

Although UNCLOS mentions no "environmental jurisdiction", it contains provisions disciplining environmental jurisdiction of coastal states, for instance, on the EEZ. In accordance with Art. 56 (1) (b) (iii), in that zone the coastal state has jurisdiction with regard to "the protection and preservation of the marine environment". That is the case of a provision that awards civil and criminal jurisdiction on environmental matters to the coastal state. Based on that article, combined with other provisions of the Convention, coastal states may enact legislation and enforce domestic measures within their EEZ.

The content of UNCLOS' jurisdictional clauses is mostly civil, seldom criminal. One of the few provisions that regulate criminal jurisdiction over a particular maritime zone is Art. 27 (1), which determines that "the criminal jurisdiction of the coastal State should not be exercised on board a foreign ship passing through the territorial sea to arrest any person or to conduct any investigation in connection with any crime committed on board the ship during its [innocent] passage", except for a handful of situations, which enable the coastal state to exercise criminal enforcement jurisdiction over foreign vessels on transiting on their territorial waters.

Apart from Art. 27, the word "crime" is nowhere else in the Convention, neither is the phrase "sanction". The Convention makes scarce references to other vocabulary that indicate existence of criminal jurisdiction: (i) "wrongful acts" in Art. 22 of Annex III, concerning the liability of the contractor for any damage arising out of "wrongful acts" in the conduct of its operations in the Area; (ii), "illicit", in two provisions relating to the criminal jurisdiction of coastal states to enforce measures within their territorial sea against a foreign vessel suspected of illicitly trafficking narcotic drugs;[45] or the international obligation to "cooperate in the suppression of illicit traffic of narcotics on the high seas.[46] It follows that UNCLOS is not the most adequate reference for the discussion of criminal jurisdiction over distinct maritime zones. That was not the main goal of negotiators and the jurisprudence of the ITLOS shows how delicate a topic such as criminal jurisdiction on the contiguous zone can be, as an analysis of the *Enrica Lexie* case may evidence.[47]

[45]Art. 27 (1) (d) UNCLOS.

[46]Art. 108 (1) UNCLOS.

[47]That dispute stems from an incident which occurred on February 15, 2012, approximately 20.5 nautical miles off the West coast of India, thus in the Indian EEZ, involving the M/V *Enrica Lexie*, an Italian-flagged tanker, and the ship *St. Anthony*, of Indian nationality. The incident is complex and involves the murder of two Indian citizens by two Italian citizens who fired from an Italian flagged vessel and produced the death effect on an Indian-flagged vessel, in the EEZ of India. The core of the dispute relates to which party has jurisdiction to trial the Italian marines. The case was

State practice following the *Lotus* case (1927) evidenced a shift from the prohibitive to a permissive approach to jurisdiction in international law. In other words, extraterritorial prescriptive jurisdiction is prohibited, lest a permissive rule allows the jurisdictional assertion. That new approach, also labelled "permissive principles approach" primarily links sovereignty with territoriality—or "territorial sovereignty"—in which a state is independent and, therefore, not bound to alien legislation that attempts to regulate the conduct of individuals in other countries. Said differently, a state may not exercise jurisdiction in cases where it has no basis of jurisdiction or when it is not affected by an activity.

A relevant cornerstone in this shift towards the permissive principles approach was laid by UNCLOS. In fact, the Convention relies heavily on the principle of territoriality, particularly in relation to the law applicable in the different maritime zones off the coast of states.[48] Territoriality, as implemented at UNCLOS, serves two main purposes: it prevents other states from encroaching on coastal states' jurisdictional zones, and it prevents coastal states from unlawfully attacking other states' sovereignty and jurisdiction.

4.3 From Sovereignty to Progressive Jurisdiction in the New Law of the Sea

A systematic reading of UNCLOS allows for the identification of three main actors that are granted jurisdiction in oceanic affairs: coastal, flag and port states. Adding to that variety of actors, the new law of sea divides the ocean into maritime zones in which different legal regimes apply. An inevitable consequence of such plurality is the phenomenon of *concurrent or conflicting jurisdictions* between these zones. Concurrent jurisdiction may, in certain cases, deem the basic principles of territoriality and nationality not very helpful in tackling disputes. In this context, the analysis of jurisdiction, if taken to level of details, turns into a complex and challenging endeavor, as disputes and clashes of rights within those different maritime zones may be governed by diverse rules on both prescriptive and enforcement jurisdiction.

The concepts of sovereignty and jurisdiction play out in a rather interesting way in the law of the sea, whose origins could be summed up to the ancient and opposing

brought by the parties to an Annex VII Arbitral Tribunal, while, pending the composition of the tribunal, Italy applied for provisional measures before the ITLOS, pursuant to Art. 290 (5), UNCLOS. The case was so thorny, that the ITLOS abstained from granting the provisional measures sought by Italy prior to the ascertainment of the exact criminal jurisdiction to trial by Arbitral Tribunal. For more, *see The "Enrica Lexie" Incident (Italy v. India), Provisional Measures*, Order of 24 August 2015, ITLOS Reports 2015.

[48] The codification of a 12 nm territorial sea, also known as "territorial waters", Article 2 ff., is a sign of the territorialist approach enshrined at UNCLOS. The Convention has also accommodated differing interests of coastal and flag states and expanded the maritime zones over which the formers exercise some degree of authority.

doctrines of "open seas" (*mare liberum*) and "closed seas" (*mare clausum*).[49] In fact, the law of the sea has been "made, changed, challenged and remade" on the grounds on that fundamental dichotomy.[50] Each doctrine gives birth to different principles and different ways to see the ocean. On the one hand, the *mare liberum* thesis is supported by the freedom of the seas principle, which had in Hugo Grotius its main defender.[51] On the other, the *mare clausum* relies on the possibility of territorial dominance over the seas by specific countries and was defended by authors such as William Welwood.[52]

In the early ages of the law of the sea as a discipline, one could perceive the intimate interplay between the notions of *imperium*, the power to legislate and to rule, and *dominium*, ownership. Since the 1700s, both concepts have been linked, at least in the law of the sea.[53] One could only exercise the power to legislate and to enforce if one had the rights of an owner. Hugo Grotius and Emmerich de Vattel have pioneered in dedicating reflections to oceanic matters. While Grotius laid the basis of the freedom of the seas' principle, de Vattel presented the modern concept of territorial seas, defined as jurisdictional waters, which form the territory of a state.[54]

In the acclaimed works of Ulpian, the Dutch author built his central argument that the seas are by nature "open to all", and not just to citizens of a single state. For there is an abyssal distinction between conceptions of the sea as a "common good", as opposed to the seas as "public good". Given that the seas were common from its first origin, it is obvious that it cannot become entirely the property of anyone by nature. The cornerstone of four coming centuries of legal treatment of the oceans was laid, and the principle of freedom of navigation was immediately acclaimed as the key norm of the law of the sea.

De Vattel represented likewise a powerful voice against the ownership of the "open seas". In his words, "no nation has a right to take possession of the open seas or claim the sole use of it, to the exclusion of the others". Centuries onwards, maritime powers such as Portugal, Spain, The Netherlands, France, England, Canada, Russia, the United States, among others, sailed the seas with absolute

[49]The two mains opposing principles may be resumed to the following: one grants state sovereignty over a certain sea strip along the shore, and the other restricts such sovereignty and concedes freedom of use of the high seas. The long-standing opposition between those principles prompted a permanent balancing of interests between maritime powers and coastal nations, thus reflecting the struggle for exercising ever greater and exclusive powers over the oceans.

[50]*See* Pirtle (2000), p. 31.

[51]Grotius (2004), p. 95.

[52]The theory of the sovereignty of the sea was advanced by William Welwood, in a response to Grotius. According to the English author, sovereignty represents a power composed of two rights: to navigation and to fisheries. *See* Welwood (1613). Other authors that advanced the idea of the seas as territory of the coastal states that could exercise authority over them were John Selden, from Britain; Paolo Scarpi, from Venice; and Serafim Freitas, from Portugal.

[53]Part of that logic still applies nowadays to the legal status of vessels in the law of the sea, according to which coastal States shall not, in principle, exercise jurisdiction over foreign-flagged vessels outside of the costal state's boundaries.

[54]De Vattel (1863).

freedom, trading with peoples from all parts of the world. Davor Vidas and Peter Schei see in the *mare liberum* theory the ideological foundation of the law of the sea, and postulate that freedom of the seas "facilitated the emergence of the forces that led to the Industrial Revolution".[55] The distinction between open seas and territorial waters marked the legal beginning of dualism between two distinct zones of the ocean.

On the other side of the equation, coastal states that for centuries have watched the harvest of their natural resources by merchant fleets of developed countries were gradually claiming exclusivity to marine resources offshore. Consequently, after World War I traditional maritime states witnessed a stark decline in their powers within the international arena. Equally noteworthy was the increasing jurisdictional claims of developing states to secure ocean resources, mainly fisheries, which responded for a burgeoning part of their economic activity. Dissatisfaction with the then world ocean order increased in the twentieth century. One was by then faced with a sort of "tug-of-war" between coastal States and maritime powers around the allocation of territorial sovereignty and navigation freedoms, respectively. Such an opposition played out in every single part of UNCLOS. This opposition, and the contribution of Latin American states in shaping the "new law of the sea" will be analyzed in a subitem on the phenomenon of "creeping jurisdiction". Important to note is that the current status of the historical dichotomy points towards a renewed balance between both principles, with greater weight attributed to the principle of "respect for sovereignty and jurisdiction".[56]

4.3.1 Coastal State Sovereignty in the Territorial Sea

Coastal states exercise *authority* and jurisdiction not only over their internal or archipelagic waters, but also in waters beyond their land territory. The basis for exercising such jurisdiction is still, nonetheless, the territory. In fact, "authority flows automatically from the sovereignty exercised over the land territory and so all coastal States do in fact have a territorial sea",[57] and comprises competences to prescribe, adjudicate and enforce domestic laws. The jurisdiction of the coastal State over seaward maritime areas remains "nothing less that the projection of State sovereignty onto the sea".[58] The territoriality of the State influences all maritime zones, from the internal waters, through the territorial sea, reaching up to the exclusive economic zones and the continental shelf. Yet, jurisdiction exercised by coastal States over the ocean is not identical to that exercised on land—case in point is the right of innocent passage, a pillar of UNCLOS, but non-existent on land.

---

[55]Vidas and Schei (2010), p. 6.

[56]Article 118 (1) UNCLOS, on the promotion of international cooperation.

[57]Evans (2014), p. 657.

[58]Gavouneli (2007), p. 39.

After the adoption of UNCLOS, the single case of comprehensive *sovereignty* and not of jurisdictional competences, in a specific maritime zone is the territorial sea, which extends seaward up to 12 nm from the coastal states' baselines. In fact, UNCLOS Art. 2 (1) posits that "the sovereignty of a coastal State extends, beyond its land territory and internal waters to an adjacent belt of sea, described as the territorial sea". In addition to the waters, coastal states also exercise sovereignty over the air space and the seabed within the 12 nm. That same treatment applies to archipelagic states, whose sovereignty extends to the waters enclosed by the archipelagic baselines, regardless of their depth and distance from the coast.[59] Even in the territorial sea (or archipelagic waters), however, coastal states have their sovereignties restricted, from the moment they are obliged to observe the fundamental right of innocent passage, inasmuch as the passage be truly innocent.[60]

Even though coastal states' sovereignty over their territorial sea is reassured in various parts of UNCLOS, as in Art. 211 (4),[61] it would be technically wrong to refer to that ensemble of powers exercisable by the coastal states over the territorial sea as "full sovereignty" (in contrast with lighter variants exercised in maritime zones farther away offshore, such as the contiguous zone, the EEZ or the continental shelf). As seen above, sovereignty over the territorial sea is limited in certain occasions, what prevent one from asserting "full sovereignty".[62] That kind of complete and plain power is exercisable only over the internal waters and port facilities of the coastal state, which receive the same legal treatment of the land territory.[63] Overall, the Convention explicitly recognizes the sovereignty of coastal state over the territorial waters, but does impose limits in the exercise of that sovereignty, for the sake of safeguarding navigational rights, without which international maritime trade would be at risk.

[59] Article 49 (1) UNCLOS.

[60] The passage of a foreign vessel through the territorial sea shall be expeditious and continuous, and not prejudicial to the peace, good order and security of the coastal state. UNCLOS Articles 18 and 19. Overall, UNCLOS is coherent in prohibiting any foreign vessel of engaging in activities within the territorial sea that may be regarded as a threat against the sovereignty of coastal states and states bordering international straits. *See* also UNCLOS Article 39 (1), on the duties of ships and aircraft during transit passage through an international strait.

[61] Article 211 (4) UNCLOS, according to which coastal States may, "*in the exercise of their sovereignty* within their territorial sea, adopt laws and regulations for the prevention, reduction and control of marine pollution from foreign vessels".

[62] UNCLOS mentions "full sovereignty" solely in reference to the powers of transit states over their *land* territory, in cases where freedom of transit exists between a land-locked state and a transit state. See UNCLOS, Article 125 (3).

[63] UNCLOS, Article 8, on internal waters.

4.3.2 States' Authority in the Area: Limitations Imposed by the Common Heritage of Mankind Principle

Only recently has a *third major principle* come into play in the law of the sea, one that equally regulates issues of sovereignty, but this time over the deep seabed beyond national jurisdiction, or the Area. The common heritage of mankind principle, enshrined in Art. 137, UNCLOS, represented a paradigmatic shift in the way parcels of the ocean beyond national jurisdiction are to be managed.[64] Prior to the adoption of the Convention, humankind was at a rather embryonic stage of exploration of the deep seabed and its resources.[65] Given the inaccessibility of those zones at the time, no legal treatment had been dedicated to it, until the discovery of massive mineral deposit concentrations in depths earlier unknown to humanity.[66] Once the minerals were there, interest was due to awake in many nations of the world, particularly those with technological requirements for the hardcore task of extracting minerals from such extreme conditions.

In order to prevent the unilateral exercise of sovereignty over the pristine deep seabed and an oligarchic exploitation of riches located beyond every country's jurisdiction, the international community has opted for a legal regime that keeps deep-sea minerals outside the unilateral appropriation by individual states. The political motor for that option is believed to be the speech of Arvid Pardo before the United Nations General Assembly in 1967, when Malta's ambassador to the UN urged states to declare the seabed beyond national jurisdiction as common heritage of mankind (CHM).[67]

---

[64]The principle of common heritage of mankind is also considered by some scholars as a "status", which is attributed to the seabed beyond national jurisdiction and its resources by UNCLOS. In the law of the sea there is plenty of room for different wordings and term combinations, each of which will have different meanings and scopes. In the case of the common heritage of mankind, as a "status".

[65]Scientists believe the international society is now venturing into a second phase of deep ocean exploration. The first phase took place during the 1950s and 1960s, when Jacques Piccard designed a submersible vehicle with financial support of the United States Navy, and dove into the depths of the Challenger Deep, the deepest hole known in the world's oceans, in 1960. In that occasion, the submersible *Trieste* descended 11.000 meters until the very bottom of the sea. See *First Trip to the Deepest Part of the Ocean*. Available at: http://geology.com/records/bathyscaphe-trieste.shtml. Accessed 07 April 2020.

[66]One of the most promising industries of the deep-sea is perhaps the mining of the deep ocean floor for massive mineral deposits, including the so-called "polymetallic nodules", "polymetallic sulfide deposits", "manganese nodules" and "cobalt crusts". For further information on every mineral compound, refer to the ISA homepage. Available at: https://www.isa.org.jm/mineral-resources/55. Accessed 07 April 2020.

[67]Common space areas are regarded as regions owned by no one, though hypothetically managed by everyone. On the gender-related issue, it should be noted that, although some reports prefer the gender-neutral equivalent "common heritage of humankind", the expression is widely quoted as "of mankind", and so will it be used on this book.

In the view of Ted McDorman, Pardo sought to halt the political trend of "creeping jurisdictionalism" over the seas.[68] With due respect, such a statement does not resume the complexity of the context in which the common heritage principle was proposed. While Pardo may have sought to halt the expansion of territorialist intentions, he did so by suggesting a communitarian approach that would simultaneously keep sovereign states from appropriating portions of the deep-sea and its incalculable riches, and contribute to a fairer world economic order, via a revenue-sharing mechanism.

As such, the activities in the deep seabed were to be carried out for the benefit of humankind as a whole, meaning that states would seek for an equitable sharing of financial and economic gains derived from activities therein.[69] There is, thus, a fundamental difference between the "creeping jurisdictionalism" that Pardo was fighting (appropriation of natural resources by wealthy states who already had practically the vastness of the oceans under the reach of their fleets) and the move of coastal states towards the exercise of unilateral jurisdiction over the waters immediately adjacent to their shore in order to prevent colonial-like spoliation of marine natural resources therein. This issue will be addressed further below, in the item on "creeping jurisdiction".

Hence, UNCLOS was adopted with the Part XI and its 58 articles dedicated to the regulation of the Area and to creating the institutional machinery responsible for implementing the newly agreed upon principle, which made direct exploitation of the deep seabed and its incalculable riches unreachable to States, and restricted autonomy and authority of those States over a part of the ocean that would otherwise belong to nobody—*res nullius*—until someone encloses a particular slot and sinks a flag therein. Instead, the principle represents a vibrant option of the international community for the orderly management of the Area according to a *res communis* approach, in which the seafloor beyond national powers belongs to everyone and, as such, shall only be exploited in the benefit of humankind.[70] The implementation of the common heritage principle is a task for the ISA, who has the legal mandate to exercise prescriptive and enforcement jurisdiction over the deep seabed and its resources.[71] The creation of the Authority thus symbolized a severe restriction of

[68]One of the main purposes of the common heritage principle is to protect areas beyond national jurisdiction or, when necessary, to allow exploitation in a way that enhanced the common benefit of humankind. For a detailed narrative on this principle, *see* generally Galindo (2006).

[69]This feature of the common heritage principle is enshrined in Art. 140 (2), UNCLOS, on the use of the Area of the benefit of mankind.

[70]Due to its revenue-sharing mechanism, Peter Bautista Poyoyo highlights crucial role the common heritage principle may play in dealing with world inequality and promoting sustainable development. *See* generally Poyoyo (1997).

[71]The prescriptive jurisdiction of the Authority is exemplified in the adoption of the "Mining Code" and other Regulations on the Exploration and Exploitation of seabed resources, as well as on the environmental protection of the deep-sea environment, as confirmed by UNCLOS Art. 137 (2). The enforcement jurisdiction is exercised every time the ISA adopts measures to control pollution and other hazards to the marine environment, in line with Art. 145 (a) an (b).

state's discretion to harvest the riches of the deep-sea, albeit while preserving freedom of the high seas over the superjacent waters and the airspace above them.[72]

After having faced initial resistance on behalf of the traditional scholarship of international, it became clear that the fundaments of the CHM principle could not be sought in traditional doctrines of international law, but in new, equitable and moral doctrines. As such, the common heritage principle "not only symbolized the interests and aspirations of the developing countries, but had been endorsed by all the developed countries, including the United States".[73] That endorsement did not last long after the signature of the Convention, when some states performed significant opposition to specific provisions of Part XI. As a consequence, the international society worked on an Implementing Agreement to Part XI, which sought to give flexibility to some clauses relating to the legal regime of the Area and, thus, attract more support from staunchest objectors, in particular the United States.

The Agreement was adopted in 1994[74] and is considered by some scholars a mutilation of the common heritage principle.[75] Amongst the most relevant modifications in the original content of Part XI, provisions compelling the transfer of seabed mining technology were dropped, as was the provision for large annual fees that miners were to pay prior to commercial production. In practice, the distortion of the original meaning of the principle may amount to vested disregard of the "needs and interests of the weaker members of the international community".[76] As interesting as it may sound, this work is not centered on the CHM principle, but on the analysis of the interplay between the two early principles of the law of the sea, freedom of navigation and territorial sovereignty, due to their complex interaction in maritime zones within national jurisdiction.

4.3.3 Progressive and Functional Jurisdiction in the Exclusive Economic Zone and Continental Shelf

UNCLOS instituted a balance between the *mare liberum* and the principle of territorial sovereignty through a carefully crafted system of "*progression*" or "gradation" from stronger to weaker forms of jurisdiction over maritime zones. The Convention drafters, during almost a decade-long negotiation, have sought for a balance of rights between different and sometimes conflicting uses of the ocean. At the end of negotiations, the international community signed a treaty that

---

[72]Art. 135 UNCLOS, on the legal status of the superjacent waters and air space.

[73]Anand (2004), p. 182.

[74]*Agreement Relating to the Implementation of Part XI of the UNCLOS*, UNGA, A/RES/48/263, 17.08.1994.

[75]Anand (2004), p. 182, is of the view that the common heritage principle had its original nature and intent overtly assailed by powerful states.

[76]*Id.* 196.

simultaneously awarded increased jurisdictional rights to coastal states, in comparison to the pre-UNCLOS era, and established ceilings to the exercise of those rights, as part of what has been called "graduated approach to coastal State intervention".[77]

If, on the one hand, the notion of "progressive jurisdiction" seems quite intuitive, the same does not hold true to the phrase "functional jurisdiction", on the other. In fact, UNCLOS has adopted a multiple zonal approach to the world oceans and divided them into several maritime zones, each of which regulated by specific sets of rules and, most importantly, to a progressive (or regressive) territorial jurisdiction based on the geographical location of each zone. As an example, the territorial sea, being the sea belt closest to the shore, is under the sovereignty of the coastal state. There, coastal states are allowed to adopt laws and regulations on varied matters (prescriptive jurisdiction, such as regulations on the safety of navigation or the protection of navigational facilities)[78] and to take appropriate measures to enforce domestic and international legislation.

Adjacent to the 12 nm territorial sea lies the contiguous zone, which has a breadth of 12 nm and may not extend beyond 24 nm from the baselines.[79] Coastal state jurisdiction in the contiguous zone is limited to the exercise of control strictly necessary to prevent and punish infringement of its customs, fiscal, immigration or sanitary laws. The progressive character of the jurisdictional rights exercisable by the coastal state in the two aforementioned marine spaces remains clear, as in the latter (contiguous zone), enforcement jurisdiction exists solely regarding specific purposes—customs, taxation, immigration, and sanitation. The development of contiguous zone albeit a complicated one,[80] can be considered already a concession of maritime states to the long-lasting claims of coastal states for more control over sensitive issues in distances not so far from the shore, but also not as close as within the territorial sea.

A similar progressive reduction of jurisdictional rights occurs between the contiguous zone and the EEZ, where the coastal state exercises prescriptive and enforcement jurisdiction for limited issues provided by UNCLOS. The normative logic supporting the LOS is, thus, one in which coastal States' rights progressively diminish in each successive zone seaward.[81] Concerning the qualifier of "functionality" to jurisdiction, Maria Gavouneli postulates that "functional" means that the

[77]Gavouneli (2007), p. 19, on the treaty obligation of coastal states to have due regard to the rights and duties of other states in the maritime zones under coastal states' jurisdiction while exercising its rights under the Convention.

[78]Art. 21 (1) (a) to (h) UNCLOS, on the laws and regulations of the coastal State relating to innocent passage.

[79]Art. 33 (1) and (2) UNCLOS, on the contiguous zone.

[80]There is some controversy as to the origin of the concept of a contiguous zone, whether it dates back to the Hovering Acts passed by Great Britain in the eighteenth century or not. *See* Tanaka (2012), p. 121. However, codification of the contiguous zone occurred only in 1958, with the adoption of the Geneva Convention on the Territorial Sea and the Contiguous Zone, UNTS, vol 516, 205.

[81]Kreca (2002), p. 1208.

competences of the coastal state respect an *inherent economic purpose* and do not infringe upon the rights and duties of other states in the same zone.[82] In this sense, some authors refer also to "resource jurisdiction" when discussing the continental shelf and EEZ regimes, in a rather clear reference to the economics behind the competences of coastal states in those spaces.[83]

This "functional" character allows for coastal states to select specific functions they wish to exercise within the default 200 nm, examples being the Ecological Protection Zone, Fisheries Protection Zone, Exclusive Fisheries Zones or the full Economic Exclusive Zone.[84] From the analysis of the EEZs in the Mediterranean Sea, Gavouneli concluded that the concept of the EEZ has acquired a certain *flexibility* concerning spatial delimitation (the exact length of the zone may vary from state to state, never exceeding 200 nm)[85] and substantive content.[86] That flexibility enables states to claim jurisdiction relating either to fisheries, or to ecological protection, or to the entirety of rights awarded by the Convention in that zone. It is not the case with the continental shelf regime, which is (i) geographically more limited than the EEZ and (ii) rather rigorous in the sort of jurisdiction exercisable over the seabed, according to Art. 77 (1), UNCLOS.

In the EEZ and on the continental shelf adjacent to the territorial sea, coastal states has authority over certain activities, notably with respect to the management, exploration and exploitation of natural resources therein. The jurisdiction, in this case, is *not strictly territorial*.[87] Coastal states do not have unlimited jurisdiction over resources and foreign persons, ships and activities, but merely a tempered jurisdiction to regulate activities directly affecting the seafloor, in the case of the continental shelf. In this sense, the continental shelf is not to be considered as territory of the coastal state, but a maritime space where the state exercises limited rights and is bound by specific duties. An interesting, although legally questionable opinion is formulated by Virginie Tassin, to whom the continental shelf may be considered an "accessory territory" of the coastal state.[88]

Finally, it should be reminded that sovereign rights and jurisdiction must be expressly attributed by international law.[89] This is a legalist approach to jurisdiction in the international law of the sea, according to which states (and other subjects) may only act in certain maritime zones where a provision permits action. In this regard, states are guided by the principle of administrative legality, as applied in domestic

[82]Gavouneli (2007), p. 68.

[83]Kaye (2006), p. 347.

[84]For further details on the different functional zones within 200 nm, *see* Gavouneli (2007), pp. 93–96.

[85]The Kingdom of Spain, for instance, declared a 37nm-long Fisheries Protection Zone in 1997. Real Decreto 1.315 de 1 agosto 1997, BOE no. 204 de 26 agosto 1997.

[86]Gavouneli (2007), p. 93.

[87]Oxman (2007) online.

[88]Tassin (2013), p. 31.

[89]Molenaar (2015), p. 297.

law, according to which an action that is not expressly allowed is prohibited. As a direct consequence, difficulties emerge because of the framework (and generalist) nature of a treaty with the magnitude of UNCLOS. The Convention as such does not, and could not, prescribe every possible jurisdiction for its state parties in particularly complex and overlapping zones. The exercise of environmental jurisdiction over continental shelf activities is a case in point, inasmuch as it confronts four different regimes: the continental shelf, EEZ, high seas, and the Area.

4.4 Partial Conclusions

Sovereignty and jurisdiction are interrelated concepts, both of which having shaped the law of the sea for a long time. Understood as a constitutive element of statehood, sovereignty usually transmits the idea of independence of a people in a territory vis-à-vis other states. In addition to that, sovereignty also conveys the meaning of a *collection of rights, competences, and powers* applicable within a certain territory. Its corollary, jurisdiction, is an instrumental concept that stems from sovereignty and consists of the competence to determine the administrative domain over which a legal authority extends.

A modern conception of jurisdiction comprises not only rights, but also duties. In this sense, to say that a coastal state has jurisdiction implies also in saying that it is bound by specific obligations. This remark, though not novel, is a fundamental premise of this work, especially in light of the task announced in the introduction and initial titles to map the environmental rights and duties of coastal states over the continental shelf.

Moreover, as new maritime spaces made their way into positive international law, the distribution of jurisdiction in the new law of the sea became more complex than ever, having nothing to compare with its predecessor, the dual-division of the seas. Hence, from the perspective of coastal states, what started as a black-and-white opposition between sovereignty and non-sovereignty (marginal sea of 3 nm and the high seas), shifted into a multicolored scheme of sovereignty, functional jurisdiction, and non-sovereignty. The very concept of "sovereign rights" embodies this nuanced approach to sovereignty and jurisdiction in the law of the sea, as seen in Chap. 2. Such innovative system was grounded on the principle of progression from stronger to weaker forms of authority over different maritime zones: the farther away offshore, the less powers a coastal state has.

Yet, upon the adoption of UNCLOS, the international community witnessed the phenomenon of *concurrent or conflicting jurisdictions* between the new zones, in particular the continental shelf, EEZ, high seas and the Area. Chapter 5 addresses the sometimes tumultuous legal and geographical overlaps between those zones, to situate the debate on coastal states' jurisdiction over the continental shelf in a broader picture. The main question, there, remains how to balance coastal states' jurisdiction with freedoms of the high seas and the obligation of due regard for the rights of other states. The next step will, then, consist of the analysis of coastal states' jurisdictional expansion in the second half of the last century, followed by a critique on the specialized literature that overemphasizes the aspect of illegality and abusiveness of coastal states' jurisdictional claims seawards.

References

Anand R (2004) Studies in international law and history. Springer, Dordrecht

Blakesley CL (1999) Extraterritorial jurisdiction. In: International criminal law II: procedural and enforcement mechanisms, 2nd edn. Transnational Publishers

Bodin J (1955) Six books of the commonwealth (trans: Tooley MJ). Alden Press, Oxford

Crawford J (2012) Brownlie's principles of public international law. Oxford University Press, Oxford

D'Aspremont J (2015) Epistemic forces in international law: foundational doctrines and techniques of international legal argumentation. Edward Elgar, Cheltenham

de Las Casas B (1552) The devastation of the indies: a brief account. Johns Hopkins University Press

de Vattel E (1863) The Law of Nations: or principles of the law of nature applied to the conduct and affairs of nations and sovereigns. Law Nook Sellers, Philadelphia

Evans M D (2014) The law of the sea. In: International law. Oxford University Press, Oxford

Galindo GRB (2006) Quem diz humanidade, pretende enganar? internacionalistas e os usos da noção de patrimônio comum da humanidade aplicada aos fundos marinhos (1967–1994). PhD Dissertation, Universidade de Brasília

Gavouneli M (2007) Functional jurisdiction in the law of the sea. Publications on ocean development, vol 62. Nijhoff, Leiden

Goldsmith JL, Posner EA (2005) The limits of international law. Oxford University Press, Oxford

Grotius H (2004) The free sea. Liberty Fund, Indianapolis

Hobbes T (1651) Leviathan: or the matter, form and power of a commonwealth ecclesiastical and civil Ch. XXXI, on the Kingdom of God by Nature

Hohfeld W (1913) Some fundamental legal conceptions as applied in judicial reasoning. Yale Law J 23(1):16–59

Kaye S (2006) Freedom of navigation in a post 9/11 world: security and creeping jurisdiction. In: Law of the sea: progress and prospects. Oxford University Press, Oxford, pp 347–364

Koskenniemi M (1998) From apology to utopia: the structure of international legal argument. CUP, Cambridge

Krasner SD (1999) Sovereignty: organized hypocrisy. Princeton University Press, Princeton

Kreca M (2002) A few remarks on the theoretical basis of the new law of the sea. In: Liber Amicorum Judge Shigeru Oda, vol II. Nijhoff, Leiden, pp 1207–1216

Machiavelli N (1515) The Prince (trans: Marriott WK)

Mills A (2014) Rethinking jurisdiction in international law. Br Yearb Int Law 841:187–239

Molenaar EJ (2015) Port and coastal states. In: The Oxford handbook of the law of the sea. Oxford University Press, Oxford, pp 280–303

Mossop J (2016) The continental shelf beyond 200 nautical miles: rights and responsibilities. Oxford University Press, Oxford

Nye JS (1990) Soft power. Foreign Policy 80:153–171

O'Keefe R (2004) Universal jurisdiction: clarifying the basic concept. J Int Crim Just 2

Oxman BH (2007) Jurisdiction of states. In: Max Planck Encyclopedia of Public International Law

Pirtle CE (2000) Military uses of ocean space and the law of the sea in the new millennium. Ocean Dev Int Law 31(1–2):7–45

Poyoyo PB (1997) Cries of the sea: world inequality, sustainable development and the common heritage of humanity, vol 33. Publications on Ocean Development. Nijhoff, Leiden

Ryngaert C (2015) Oxford monographs in international law. In: Jurisdiction in international law, 2nd edn. Oxford University Press, Oxford
Staker C (2014) Jurisdiction. In: Evans MD (ed) International law, 4th edn. Oxford University Press, Oxford
Tanaka Y (2012) The international law of the sea. Cambridge University Press, Cambridge
Tassin VJM (2013) Les défis de l'extension du plateau continental: la consécration d'un nouveau rapport de l'état à son territoire. Pedone, Paris
Tooley MJ (1952) The argument of the six books of the commonwealth. Oxford University Press, Oxford
Vidas D, Schei P (eds) (2010) Law, technology and science for oceans in globalisation. Nijhoff, Leiden
Wallerstein I (2006) European universalism: the rhetoric of power. The New Press, New York
Welwood W (1613) An abridgement of all sea-lawes. London

Resolutions

A/RES/48/263 (1994) Agreement Relating to the Implementation of Part XI of the UNCLOS

Jurisprudence

ITLOS (2000) The "Monte Confurco" Case, (Seychelles v. France), Order of 27 November 2000. ITLOS Reports
ITLOS (2015) The "Enrica Lexie" Incident (Italy v. India), Provisional Measures, Order of 24 August 2015. ITLOS Reports
PCIJ (1927) SS "Lotus" (France vs. Turkey), Series A, No 10. PCIJ Reports

Chapter 5
Jurisdictional Intersections Between the Continental Shelf and Other Maritime Spaces: Exclusive Economic Zone, High Seas and the Area

The emergence of the outer continental shelf has brought along difficulties regarding the interaction between regimes governing other maritime areas, in particular the EEZ, the high seas and the Area. For instance, it is relevant to assess the extent to which the coastal state may exercise rights over the water column above the continental shelf, having in mind that those superjacent waters enjoy the legal status of high seas. Also, to determine what rules overlap in the seafloor between the outer continental shelf and the Area and how does UNCLOS fend off possible jurisdictional conflicts therein. Those are intriguing questions, the answers to which shall level the ground for the discussion on coastal state environmental jurisdiction over the continental shelf.

Each of the zones mentioned supra owns a particular set of rules that defines their legal statuses, the rights and duties exercisable in each, apart from other relevant provisions, both for coastal states and the international community at large. In order to understand the specificities of the continental shelf regime, one must grasp the ways in which UNCLOS has provided for a coherent intersection between differing but overlapping maritime spaces, so that these crossings between maritime zones do not challenge the overall stability and cohesion of the Treaty.

V. Alencar Mayer Feitosa Ventura, *Environmental Jurisdiction in the Law of the Sea*, https://doi.org/10.1007/978-3-030-50543-1_5

5.1 The Continental Shelf and the EEZ: Parallelism and Integration

In the new law of the sea, the origins of the EEZ dates back to the wide variety of fisheries zones established by the Latin American states in the late 1940s and 1950s, mostly as a response to the 1945 Truman Proclamations.[1] At the time, despite international community's *resistance* to the suggested notion of "exclusive fisheries zone",[2] the idea of a maritime zone where coastal states could explore and exploit natural resources with *exclusivity* gained momentum.[3] The speed with which the concept gathered support was portrayed by Judge Oda, to whom "throughout the history of international law, scarcely any other major concept has ever stood at the threshold of acceptance within such a short period".[4] Perhaps due to that rapidness, questions abounded as to whether the EEZ regime came to life at the expenses of the continental shelf or the high seas.

The EEZ embodies a maritime space for which a tailor-cut regime had to be designed, in order to conciliate opposing interests of coastal and flag states. The creation of this zone occurred in a time when a simple and reducing dichotomic view of the oceans (sovereignty/non-sovereignty) was questioned by coastal states worldwide. A new demand was on the negotiating table: to shift from a dichotomic to a trichotomous structure of the law of the sea, i.e. to a scheme of *sovereignty/semi-sovereignty/non-sovereignty* over a plurality of zones.[5] The semi-sovereignty level was inserted in the new law of the sea upon the creation and codification of the EEZ, a hybrid zone where the coastal state does not exercise full sovereignty but only

[1]One hypothesis for the provenance of the celebrated 200-nm limit was the adoption of this distance in a map in a paper discussing the Panama Declaration of 1939, in which the United Kingdom and the United States agreed to establish a zone of security and neutrality around the American continents in order to prevent the resupplying of Axis ships in South American ports. The map showed the width of the neutrality zone off the Chilean coast to be about 200 miles. This became the basis for the 200-nm limit. *See* Ben-Yami (2017) Available at: http://www.worldfishing.net/news101/Comment/ben-yami/the-200-mile-limits-origin. Accessed 08 April 2020.

[2]Maria Gavouneli mentions the "the proliferation of 'fisheries zones', 'pollution-protection zones' or 'ecological-protection zones'", a phenomenon that contributed to the *cacophony* surrounding the EEZ. In those zones, coastal states have opted for "different combinations of jurisdictional powers", in different distances from the baselines. *See* Gavouneli (2007), p. 92.

[3]It could also be claimed that the term EEZ could be *per se* misleading, as coastal states would not enjoy "exclusive", but rather "preferential" rights over the natural resources therein. An illustration of that would be Art. 61 of the Convention and the idea of a "total allowable catch" within the zone. This is, however, courtliness and would relate solely to the fisheries' aspect of the Zone. To the contrary, the expression "sovereign rights" over the EEZ suggests that the coastal state enjoys exclusiveness, and not preferential rights over natural resources of the zone, including conservation and protection of marine resources, an authority that the states exercises on an exclusive, not preferential basis. For a similar view, *see* Beckman and Davenport (2012), p. 7.

[4]ICJ *Case Concerning the Continental Shelf (Tunisia/Libya)*, Judgement of 24 February 1982, dissenting opinion of Judge Shigeru Oda, ICJ Rep. 1982, para. 120.

[5]Kreca (2002), p. 1215.

limited rights, and where third parties cannot expect to exercise certain economic freedoms. That can also be said of the continental shelf.

Hence, it is paramount to understand that the EEZ is a sui generis and *multifunctional* zone. Art. 55 of the Convention defines it as the "area beyond and adjacent to the territorial sea, subject to the specific legal regime established in this Part", in which both the rights and jurisdiction of the coastal state and some of the freedoms of the high seas shall apply.[6] Moreover, Art. 58, paragraph 1 UNCLOS establishes that all states enjoy freedoms of navigation, overflight, laying of submarine cables and pipelines, and "other internationally lawful uses of the sea related to these freedoms". Both provisions clearly posit the overlapping nature of the EEZ as a zone marked by the combination of rules from different maritime spaces, what renders the conciliation of powers between coastal and other states necessary.

The multifunctional feature of the EEZ relates to the possibility acknowledged to coastal states to determine the rights and competences they will exercise within the 200 nm, a characteristic that renders the EEZ rather plastic in comparison to the continental shelf.[7] "Plastic" here means that the state is given discretion to opt for the bundle of powers (or functions) it will exercise over the zone. International practice thus far has shown a plurality of different functions claimed over the EEZ ranging from powers over fisheries, to energy sources within the zone, or just competences to protect and preserve the marine environment therein. Whether the coastal state will exercise authority over fisheries alone, or over the ecological protection of the marine environment, it remains entirely up to that state to decide.

Despite the commonalities shared between both zones, differences exist. The first considerable one relates to the conditions for the exercise of rights in each space. Whereas "the rights of the coastal state over the continental shelf do not depend on occupation, effective or notional, or on any express proclamation",[8] the EEZ must be expressly proclaimed by coastal states. Thus, where a coastal state has no EEZ, Part VI provisions apply only to the submerged areas from the 12-mile territorial sea until

[6] Apart from the maritime zone known as the EEZ, coastal states may also proclaim other types of 200 nm zones, despite the fact that such zones are not expressly in UNCLOS. It is the case of Exclusive Fishery Zones (EFZ), which preceded the EEZ during the 1960s, claimed by the Netherlands, Norway and others; Fisheries Protection Zones (FPZ), claimed by Norway, Spain, Libya and others); Ecological Protection Zones (EPZ), claimed by Italy and Slovenia, among others; Ecological and Fisheries Protection Zone (EFPZ), as claimed by Croatia. Such 200 nm functional zones are in principle consist with UNCLOS as long as coastal states do not claim more sovereign rights and jurisdiction than that granted by the Convention. *See* Molenaar (2015), p. 299.

[7] The concept of "function" adopted in this book is akin to that used by Maria Gavouneli, which refers to the different categories of themes *ratione materiae* that the coastal state may regulate. Examples of functions in the law of the sea are: environment; resource exploration and exploitation; customs, immigration, and health regulation, among others. *See* Gavouneli (2007), p. 10. The term "functional jurisdiction", however, was not coined by Gavouneli. Already in 1984, María Teresa Infante posits that "the Convention makes distinctions on a *ratione materiae* basis, according to which functional jurisdiction are introduced". *See* Infante (1984), p. 169.

[8] Art. 77, paragraph 3, UNCLOS.

the outer limits of the continental shelf, as defined by Art. 76, paragraphs 4 to 8 UNCLOS.

Moreover, the size of both areas may vary. The EEZ regime applies until 200 nm from the baselines, also for the sake of natural resources eventually present on and below the seafloor, such as precious minerals, biodiversity ecosystems populating hydrothermal vents, among others. Where the continental margin *extends beyond* 200 nm, coastal states may delineate the outer limits of their continental shelves, as analyzed before, and will be subject to the regime set forward in Part VI UNCLOS.

Another aspect which separates both regimes concerns the jurisdictional powers attributed to coastal states in each zone. UNCLOS guarantees coastal states sovereign rights to explore, exploit, *conserve and manage* natural resources in the EEZ.[9] Jurisdiction to conserve and manage natural resources are not expressly mentioned in the continental shelf regime, what would theoretically restrict the environmental powers of coastal states over the continental shelf extending beyond EEZ limits, i.e. the outer continental shelf.

Coastal states have, thus, a relatively *narrow* scope of rights over natural resources of the continental shelf, if compared to the array of sovereign rights exercisable within the EEZ. However, regardless of the limitations inherent to the concept of sovereign rights, it should be noted that coastal states still enjoy the necessary rights to "control *resource development* within the exclusive economic zone and on the continental shelf".[10] The coexistence between both EEZ and continental shelf regimes is the corollary of a fundamental idea underpinning the Convention, the "plurality of regimes", as an attempt to contemplate opposing claims and interests by a variety of states.[11] Negotiators meant the regimes to coexist with as little normative conflict as possible, despite the unavoidable overlaps of rights and duties. As a result, one could say that the Convention comprises a number of new zones governed by specific rules under a framework that sought simultaneously for parallelism and harmony between legal regimes.

The theory of *parallelism* between the EEZ and continental shelf regimes is to be found in the work of Barbara Kwiatkowska. In a study about the degree of harmony between EEZ and continental shelf rules with respect to rights and jurisdiction, the Dutch scholar defended that the EEZ regime is aligned to that of the continental shelf, but does not encompass it, nor does it render the continental shelf a mere appendix to the EEZ.[12] Such parallelism is twofold: within 200 nm, rights and duties over the continental shelf are similar to the EEZ, where coastal states exercise *extra* sovereign rights over economic resources of the water column and other

[9]ITLOS *"Virginia G" case, Panama v. Guinea Bissau*, ITLOS Reports 2015, judgment of 14 April 2014.

[10]Townsend-Gault (2014), p. 70.

[11]Garcia-Amador (1974), pp. 33–37.

[12]For Kwiatkowska, that parallelism between the EEZ and the continental shelf within 200 nm as two distinct, but coexisting regimes has entered the realm of general international law. Kwiatkowska (1989), p. xvi. Confirming that theory, *see* also Stoll (2008) para 6.

competences not contemplated by the continental shelf regime;[13] in the continental shelf extending beyond 200 nm, the rights and duties of the coastal states are practically the same as within that distance, with two relevant exceptions, namely the revenue-sharing mechanism and the marine scientific research clause, which will be analyzed in detail in the following item.

Due to the overlap between the EEZ and the continental shelf regime until 200 nm, some speculation existed whether the continental shelf regime held autonomy, or whether it had been absorbed by EEZ rules. One could say, however, that the continental shelf regime is autonomous, not dependent on, but complementary to the EEZ regime. The Convention granted each zone not only its own rights and duties, but has attributed the continental shelf a "special character", which gives provisions on the continental shelf preeminence over those of the EEZ, a reading that flows from Art. 77, paragraph 3 UNCLOS.[14]

The *harmony* element animating the differing regimes within UNCLOS lives in the provisions bridging both, adopted in order to prevent confusion between them. It is the case of Art. 56, paragraph 3, which orders EEZ provisions to be exercised in accordance with continental shelf rights. Or articles 60 and 80, on artificial islands; Art. 58, paragraph 1, on the rights and duties of other states in the EEZ; Art. 77, paragraph 4, on the rights of coastal states over the natural resources of the continental shelf, amongst others.

Summing up, the EEZ is ought to be seen as a sui generis zone, neither residual continental shelf, nor residual high seas. This view is crucial for the limitation of coastal state's jurisdiction on the EEZ, but also certain freedoms of the high seas.[15] The EEZ is also *not* to be considered an extension of the legal regime of the territorial sea, but a strip of ocean where two different regimes apply simultaneously, as UNCLOS provisions stipulate that the rights with respect to the seabed and the subsoil within the EEZ are to be exercised in accordance with the provisions on the continental shelf.[16] That this work speaks of the need for harmonization between both regimes until the 200-nm limit is evidence of the differences between both spaces. Now, to the intersections in the space beyond 200 nm between the continental shelf and another regime, namely the high seas.

---

[13] Art. 56 (1) (a), UNCLOS.

[14] For a similar understanding, *see* Leanza and Caracciolo (2014), p. 209.

[15] Orrego Vicuña (1984), p. 3.

[16] Leanza and Caracciolo (2014), p. 208.

5.2 The Continental Shelf and the High Seas: The Superjacent Waters of the Continental Shelf Beyond 200 nm

One of the concerns most commonly shared by international lawyers regards the possible threats posed by the delineation and management of the outer continental shelf to the freedoms of other states on the high seas. It is uncontroversial that coastal states enjoy sovereign rights over natural resources within 200 nm, be it in the air and water column, seabed, or subsoil. In other words, where the continental shelf coincides with the EEZ, states have rights over energy resources of the air column (wind energy), fisheries, sedentary species and minerals (on the seafloor), hydrocarbons in the subsoil, among others. Yet, the same is not true to the area beyond 200 nm, where coastal states enjoy solely sovereign rights over the resources of the shelf and subsoil,[17] leaving the superjacent waters and airspace under the regime of the high seas and its respective freedoms to fish, navigate, conduct marine scientific research, lay cables and pipelines, and to overflight.[18]

In fact, UNCLOS Articles 86 ff. on the high seas provide a definition of the high seas, as well as the principles and mechanisms governing the interaction with the continental shelf regime, in order to prevent mutual violations or encroachments into one another. Upfront, the Convention provides a *negative* definition of the high seas, taken as those areas not included in the EEZ, territorial sea and internal waters of coastal states. Then, Art. 87 UNCLOS crystalizes the famous freedom of the seas' principle, while balancing it with the duty of flag states to have due regard respect the interests and rights of other states in the high seas. On the one hand, it enunciates the freedoms reigning on and in the high seas, i.e. of navigation, overflight, fishing, to lay submarine cables and pipelines, to construct artificial islands and installations not prohibited by international law, and to conduct scientific research. On the other, it reinforces one of the most relevant provisions concerning the high seas, the obligation to have *due regard* to the interests of other states and to the provisions governing the Area.[19] The core idea embedded in those provisions alludes to the *mare liberum* principle, as famously defended by Grotius.

Since the creation of the continental shelf, however, *geographical and functional limitation* of the principle of freedom of the seas followed suit. The high seas have shifted from an area where freedoms may be exercised in an absolute manner to a "managed common area".[20] In fact, international developments have pushed for the reappraisal of the traditional meaning of "freedoms" of the high seas, in order to condition such freedoms to the respect of other states' rights. An example, among

---

[17] Art. 78, paragraph 1, UNCLOS.

[18] A non-exhaustive list of freedoms of the high seas is to be found in Art. 87, UNCLOS.

[19] Art. 87, paragraph 2, UNCLOS, on the obligation to exercise freedoms of the high seas with due regard to the interests of other states and the rights applicable to activities in the Area.

[20] This expression is used by Rothwell and Stephens (2016) chap. 7.

many, is the creation of regional fisheries management organizations (RFMO), which have restricted the once unregulated freedom to fish, as an attempt to tackle the depletion of fish stocks and loss of marine biodiversity worldwide.[21]

Limitations to freedom of the seas, however, have not been enough to threaten the principle. Instead, UNCLOS has struck a carefully crafted balance between traditional freedoms and the rather recent sovereignty ambitions of coastal states, thereby, proving it possible to preserve the core of the *mare liberum* without jeopardizing attempts by coastal states to exercise exclusive jurisdiction over natural resources off their coast not ignoring wake-up calls of the international community for better regulating of the uses of the oceans.

Questions remain as to the managerial maneuver room available for coastal states over the outer continental shelf, particularly in terms of environmental protection efforts. Take, for instance, the hypothetical case of national measures taken to prevent deep-sea bottom trawling above the outer continental shelf; or the stricter regulation of marine scientific research above that area—issues that will be tackled later in this work. This is one of the reasons why the interaction between the high seas regime and the continental shelf is so delicate. In fact, we may stand in the wake of a shift in mentality, but will it weight heavier towards the high seas regime or the continental shelf one?

More recently, it became clearer the long road ahead of coastal states and the international community with regard to the sustainable management of the extended continental shelf areas. Securing rights over that area farther away offshore is but a first step, one that ought to be followed by decided environmental action regarding the management and governance of these remote, subsurface seabed areas under national jurisdiction.[22] Following such concerns, part of the law of the sea literature has called for a *new ethos* for the principle of freedom of the high seas, according to which "an appreciation of the context and arguments advanced by Grotius should, at least, soften the views that states hold on the principle of freedom".[23] Similar well-founded concerns have been expressed with regard to the intricated intersection between the outer continental shelf and the seabed beyond national jurisdiction, or the Area.

[21]The RFMOs are present in Art. 118, UNCLOS, on the cooperation of states in the conservation and management of living resources.

[22]Schofield et al. (2010), p. 575.

[23]In line with the suggested "new *ethos*" for the principle of the high seas, Michaela Young claims that the establishment of a regime to govern biodiversity beyond national jurisdiction be a "next logical step" in the evolution of the rules governing the high seas. *See* Young (2016), p. 180.

5.3 The Outer Continental Shelf and the Area

The continental shelf regime arose from the dichotomy between the founding principles of freedom of the seas and territorial sovereignty, which have traditionally opposed coastal and flag states. Nonetheless, the delineation of outer continental shelf limits does not concern exclusively those parties, nor does it concern solely the coastal state and the CLCS. In fact, it interests the international community at large, since outer continental shelf limits shall define the boundary between the seafloor under national jurisdiction and the Area. It pertains to a new actor in the law of the sea chess table: humanity.[24]

Recent developments in the law of the sea brought to life another core principle in order to safeguard the interests of humanity, which rendered the relationship between the continental shelf and the ocean floor beyond national jurisdiction all the more complicated. The traditional principle of *mare liberum* is now faced not only with its centuries-old contender, but with the *common heritage of mankind principle*,[25] applicable to the maritime zone of the Area. No matter how convoluted the previously analyzed interaction between the regimes of the continental shelf regime, EEZ and the high seas is, the knottiest interaction between regimes of UNCLOS is that of the continental shelf and Area.

Consequently, overlapping rules and distinct legal nuances as to the rights and duties of the coastal states in the intersection between those two maritime zones, added to the indeterminacy of their concrete boundaries worldwide will likely raise legal uncertainty as to the applicable regime, namely in borderline cases. Examples of those delicate nuances is the relation between the application of the common heritage principle in the Area[26] and the consequences for the delineation of outer continental shelf limits; or the institution of a revenue-sharing system for commercial activities occurring on the continental shelf beyond 200 nm, pursuant to Art. 82 UNCLOS. These issues are further analyzed below, alongside the topic of boundary indeterminacy and the environmental protection standards applicable in the Area and the on outer continental shelf.

As experts in the field have confirmed, the legal relationship between the outer continental shelf and the Area remains understudied.[27] In this juncture, it is still valid to ask whether peaceful coexistence between norms of the outer continental shelf and the Area will exist.[28] In fact, there was plenty of tension between the common

[24]Yu and Ji-Lu (2011), p. 318.

[25]Art. 136, UNCLOS. For more on the metaphoric "battle" between the principles in the law of the sea, refer to Brown (1982), p. 521.

[26]Art. 136, UNCLOS, on the principles governing the Area.

[27]Chircop (2011), p. 307.

[28]The tension between both regimes was captured by McDorman, to whom the emergence of the common heritage principle and the will to establish a just international regime for the areas beyond national jurisdiction, based on the sharing of benefits, has been but a "blip in the law-of-the-sea radar". *See* McDorman (2015), p. 202.

heritage principle and the principle of territorial sovereignty upon the birth of the continental shelf beyond 200 nm, what makes one still wonder if the continental shelf regime somehow poses a threat to the definition and management of the Area.

5.3.1 Relationship Between the Common Heritage of Mankind Principle and the Definition of the Outer Limits of the Continental Shelf

A combined reading of Part XI UNCLOS, the Convention's *travaux preparatoires* and the original notion devised by Arvid Pardo suggests that the common heritage of mankind encompasses both the Area (as a physical medium) and the natural non-living resources therein.[29] As defined in the Convention, the "Area" is the seabed, ocean floor and subsoil thereof beyond the limits of national jurisdiction,[30] while "resources" are solely the "solid, liquid or gaseous *in situ* in the Area at or beneath the seabed", i.e. non-living resources alone.[31] Altogether, the common heritage of mankind is beyond state appropriation and beyond any claims of sovereignty.[32]

International lawyers, in general, recognize the common heritage of mankind as a key principle of general international law, applicable initially to space law and the law of the sea, but nowadays to other fields, such as international environmental law. That new principle, one the most innovative legal constructs of the last century, is at the core of the establishment of an international administration for areas open to the use of all states, or as some scholars name it, the *international commons*, such as the deep-sea, outer space bodies or elements of the Antarctic environment.

One of the principle's main features is to embrace *humankind* as the main recipient of rights valid in the Area, as well the beneficiary of activities happening in the seabed and subsoil beyond national jurisdiction.[33] The use of that concept does raise, however, questions. Whether the phrase "humankind" possesses any legal meaning, or whether it is purely political is one of the difficulties related to the emergence of mankind as an addressee of rights under UNCLOS. Since the adoption of the Convention, scholars have debated whether a new subject of international law was brewed, one distinct from states and from the international community. In this regard, Rüdiger Wolfrum notes that the Convention expressly mentions the *peoples*

[29] Art. 136, UNCLOS, on the common heritage of mankind.

[30] Art. 1, paragraph 1(a), UNCLOS, on the use of terms and scope of the Convention.

[31] Art. 133 (a) UNCLOS, on the use of terms of Part XI, the Area.

[32] Art. 137, paragraph 1, UNCLOS, on the legal status of the Area and its resources.

[33] Art. 137, paragraph 2, UNCLOS states that "all rights in the resources of the Area are vested in *mankind* as a whole, on whose behalf the Authority shall act" (emphasis added).

who have not attained full independence or other self-governing status as beneficiaries to the exploitation of the seabed.[34]

As a consequence, it would be unproblematic to claim that "humankind" encompasses more than the notion of sovereign states recognized by international law, what means that the application of the common heritage principle shall bear in mind peoples not unanimously recognized as states, as the Palestinians. Interestingly, some third world approaches to international law could also claim that social movements (or civil society movements) be taken as composing particles of that "humankind", as a means to foster increased participation of civil society representatives within the ocean and deep-sea governance schemes, thereby adding transparency, legitimacy and crafting an international law informed by inputs from those "below"—in a sort of bottom-up dynamics.[35] Regardless of how beneficial such a hypothesis would be, it escapes the purpose of this work to scrutinize it any deeper; it suffices to recognize sovereign states as the ultimate effective *participants* in the legal and economic regime governing the Area and the implementers of the common heritage principle, alongside the ISA.

The main issue at discussion here is the interaction between rules applicable to the outer continental shelf and those rules governing the seabed, an analysis that rests on the scope and implementation of the common heritage principle. As rightfully put by Barbara Kwiatkowska and other scholars, the materialization of Art. 76 UNCLOS and the extended continental shelf is "closely tied to the concept of the common heritage of mankind".[36] Despite the fact that the principle *per se* is not applicable to maritime zones within national jurisdiction, the common heritage's content produces a "spillover effect" over the continental shelf regime, as analyzed below. As such, one ought to understand the common heritage principle, so as to grasp the legal overlaps alive between the regimes of the Area and the continental shelf. It is, thus paramount to shed some light on the emergence of the principle at stake, followed by an analysis of the content of that novel legal construct.

The rise of the common heritage principle results from a push to internationalize the deep seabed and meant a restriction on coastal states' territorial ambitions towards submarine areas of the globe. Once again, the 1945 Truman Proclamation and the 1958 CSC can be seen as the paradigmatic events which triggered international reaction against two potential threats to the public order of the oceans: firstly, the likelihood of coastal states placing larger portion of the ocean floor under national jurisdiction; and secondly, pressure by maritime powers towards pre preservation of freedoms of the seas worldwide, namely freedom to exploit the seabed beyond national jurisdiction. Heated debates followed those two events during the 1960s, time in which the common heritage of mankind embryo began to mature, showing that the principle should not be regarded as an unpredicted creation, a

[34]*See* Wolfrum (1983), p. 318.

[35]For more on resistance to traditional views of state-centered international law, *see* generally Rajagopal (2003).

[36]Kwiatkowska (1991), p. 157.

"lightning in a blue sky". To the contrary, it embodies values, discussions and trends of that time.

Juridically, the principle had its cornerstone a tick earlier, in the 1958 CSC—in a quite paradoxical way. Art. 1 of the CSC defined continental shelf as the submarine areas "to a *depth* of 200 meters or, beyond that limit, to where the depth of the superjacent waters *admits the exploitation* of the natural resources of the said areas", only to enter history as one of the most disastrous provisions ever to be inserted in a treaty that vital to humankind.[37] In fact, the provision allowed coastal states to place potentially *all* submarine areas of the globe under some sort of coastal state jurisdiction—a move that triggered stark criticisms from the international community of states.[38] Such dual criteria for the designation of the continental shelf (depth and exploitability) was the reason both for the timid acceptance of the treaty and the appearance of the idea of a "common heritage of mankind", albeit not with those terms.[39]

It was understandable, thus, that the decade following the adoption of the CSC witnessed discussions between *universalism and particularism* in the jurisdictional division of the ocean. In the United States, the debate acquired greater proportions for the development of the law of the sea. Following the Truman Proclamations, the country was the stage of a fiery debate between opponents of a larger continental shelf and those sympathetic to larger jurisdiction over the seafloor. Rivaling a larger shelf, and siding with a doctrine of universalism in the division of the oceans, Louis Henkin; supporting an expansion of the shelf as the advancement of particular American interests, Luke Finley.[40] The controversy was at the core of the debate between extending the continental shelf beyond geological criteria and internationalizing the deep seabed.

At that point, on the political level, US President Lyndon Johnson formulates a call for an internationally negotiated solution to the potential race for the unchecked appropriation of the deep seabed. In Johnson's words, the international community must "ensure that the deep seas and the ocean bottoms are, and remain, the legacy of all human beings".[41] To that goal, international cooperation would be key in preventing deep-sea mineral riches from enticing a "new form of colonial competition among the maritime nations".[42]

The semantic power of the phrase "common heritage of mankind", which points to the idea that international resources should be a "legacy to all human beings", combined with the tense international relations in the wake of the decolonization

[37]Friedmann (1971), p. 759.

[38]Judge Shigeru Oda was among the first ones to alert to the possibility of such a radical interpretation of Art. 1 CSC. *See* Oda (1968), p. 10.

[39]Galindo (2006), p. 107.

[40]For more on the debate, *see* Henkin (1969) and Finley (1969).

[41]President Lyndon B. Johnson, 2 *Weekly Compilation of Presidential Documents*, 930, July 13, 1966.

[42]*Idem.*

wave of the 1960s had the pendulum swing towards a law of the sea informed by principles of peaceful uses and political cooperation, and not by particularist appropriation logics valid for the "law of the land".[43] In this context, creative and bold formulations surfaced, such as that of Robert Creamer, who postulated that the UN should be given *ownership* of the deep seabed, i.e. jurisdiction and control, but not sovereignty.[44]

Nonetheless, the proposal that deserved international acclamation was the one forwarded by Arvid Pardo, on 18 August 1967, which advised the adoption of a declaration and a treaty "concerning the reservation exclusively for peaceful purposes of the seabed and ocean floor, underlying the seas beyond the limits of present national jurisdiction, and the use of their resources in the interest of mankind". That was the first time when the principle was formally voiced.[45] Pardo's proposal opposed vehemently the utilization of the traditional principles underpinning the law of the sea: sovereignty and freedom of the seas. On the one hand, it objected the concept of sovereignty for the deep seabed, a position noted in the negative valuation of national appropriation of larger portions of continental shelf.[46] On the other hand, it countered the application of an absolute freedom of the seas to the deep seabed, which could lead to unequal access by states and unregulated exploitation.[47] The international context was one of a *move to institutions*, in which the institutionalist matrix enjoyed relative prestige in comparison to realist approaches.[48]

The UNGA discussed the Maltese proposal and adopted Resolution 2749,[49] next challenge being to incorporate the principle into a binding treaty, so as to prevent both the national appropriation of the world's ocean floor and an irresponsible race to natural resources of the deep seabed. With these goals in mind, it was paramount to halt coastal states' increasing jurisdiction seawards by determining with sufficient clarity the limits of the continental shelf and, thus, repairing the disastrous definition of the Art. 1 CSC. In sum, the perfect stage for the Third Conference.

During the Conference's negotiations, tensions between international seabed and continental shelf rules arose several times, usually countering broad- and

---

[43]The divergence between law of the sea and law of the land was a recurrent topic in the work of Elisabeth Borgese. *See* generally Borgese (1968).

[44]Creamer (1968), pp. 225–228.

[45]*See* item 3 of the *note verbale* of the Permanent Mission of Malta to the United Nations addressed to the Secretary-General to the United Nations, A/6695, 18 August 1967. In the note, Malta requested the inclusion of a supplementary item in the agenda of the 22nd session of the UNGA.

[46]"It is feared that [...] the seabed and the ocean floor, underlying seas beyond present national jurisdiction, will become progressively and competitively to national appropriation and use". *See* item 2 of the Maltese *note verbale*.

[47]"The financial benefits derived from the use and exploitation of the seabed and of the ocean floor shall be used primarily to promote the development of poor countries". *See* item 3 (c) of the Maltese *note verbale*.

[48]*See* generally Keohane and Nye (1977).

[49]UN Resolution 2749, New York, 17 December 1970. The approval of the Declaration was followed by heated debates on a moratorium on all activities on the deep seabed.

short-margin states. On the one corner, countries such as Brazil, Argentina, Australia, Canada and others sided for a continental shelf extending beyond 200 nm, based on the principle of sovereignty over the landmass that shares sediment affinity with the submerged areas offshore. On the other corner, African and Arab countries, along with land-locked and geographically disadvantaged states opposed vehemently an extended continental shelf on several grounds.

Short-margin countries rejected proposals of an outer shelf on the ground that Art. 76 and its complex formulae attributed "too large a portion of the sea-bed to coastal States, to the detriment of the international sea-bed area, thus depriving mankind of the extensive maritime space which should be part of its common heritage".[50] In other words, any extension of the national jurisdiction of the coastal state with respect to the exploitation and exploration of the natural resources of the continental shelf beyond 200 nm effectively reduced the common heritage of mankind.[51] For those countries, two conditions were quintessential to the approval of an outer continental shelf regime: first, the Convention should stipulate a "common heritage fund", with a mandate to assist third world development, to protect the marine environment, to foster the transfer of marine technology, amongst other purposes; secondly, the outer limits of the continental shelf should be determined by a clear, simple and unambiguous formula—not the ones approved in Art. 76.[52]

Moreover, opposition to the outer continental shelf insisted that Art. 82, providing for payments and contributions with respect to the exploitation of the continental shelf beyond 200 nm, seemed to indicate a certain *guilty conscience*. If the parties would endorse the outer continental shelf, not even the revenue-sharing arrangements would compensate for the large losses of the international community.[53] As such, not even unilateral action taken by certain countries to exploit seabed resources beyond the limits of national jurisdiction was extremely serious, despite the assurances that such exploitation would not begin before the entry into force of the Convention.[54]

An illustrative list of states opposing the outer continental shelf includes Zaire,[55] Swaziland, to whom Art. 76 "severely truncated the concept of the common heritage

[50]Sweden, A/CONF.62/SR.105 105th Plenary meeting, para 63.

[51]Nepal, A/CONF.62/SR.125 125th Plenary meeting Extract from the Official Records of the Third United Nations Conference on the Law of the Sea, Volume XIII, para 10. Malta also who claimed for more safeguards against the "shrinkage of the common heritage of mankind". See A/CONF.62/SR.105 105th Plenary meeting, para 36.

[52]To Bulgaria, the formulae contained in Art. 76 tended to "accentuate inequalities" and to affirm a doctrine of appropriation based on geopolitical advantages". *See* A/CONF.62/SR.103, 103rd Plenary meeting, para. 56.

[53]Position defended by the Romanian delegation, A/CONF.62/SR.125, 125th Plenary meeting, para 26.

[54]A/CONF.62/SR.140, 140th Plenary meeting Extract from the Official Records of the Third United Nations Conference on the Law of the Sea, Volume XIV, para 12.

[55]A/CONF.62/SR.138, 138th Plenary meeting Extract from the Official Records of the Third United Nations Conference on the Law of the Sea, Volume XIV, para 92.

of mankind, which was already limited in scope by the 200-mile exclusive economic zone",[56] Syria,[57] Bulgaria, to whom the outer continental shelf implied an "appropriation of the ocean space",[58] Libya,[59] Algeria,[60] Ghana,[61] among others.[62] Despite the organized aversion to the outer continental shelf and the push towards setting a greater portion of the seafloor beyond national appropriation, compromises were struck. The arm wrestling came to an end with the creation of a pioneering maritime zone, the Area, to be governed by an avantguardiste legal construct, the common heritage principle.

The key tripod of the common heritage principle applicable to that novel zone would, thus, be: *non-appropriation, peaceful uses, common benefit.* The first foot of the tripod defines a specific *status* for the Area and its resources, rendering the deep-sea resources beyond national jurisdiction as *res communis* and turning mankind into the addressee of all rights over the resources of the Area.[63] It is, nonetheless, false to refer to a legal private relationship of *ownership* in this case, as mankind (as a collective and unidentifiable subject) shall not dispose nor alienate the resources. In civil law, the *res communis* is precisely a good that cannot be subject to private ownership, the usual example being the air we breathe. There is, thus, no a priori ownership relation between mankind and the resources of the Area, except for the relationships that come to exist in pursuance of the provisions and regulations of Part XI UNCLOS. The difficult task of managing the Area and its resources on behalf of mankind is attributed to the ISA.

Another key feature of the common heritage principle is to restrict utilization exclusively for *peaceful purposes*, which forbids the "threat or use of force against

[56]A/CONF.62/SR.138, 138th Plenary meeting Extract from the Official Records of the Third United Nations Conference on the Law of the Sea, Volume XIV, para 131.

[57]A/CONF.62/SR.139, 139th Plenary meeting, para 172.

[58]A/CONF.62/SR.103, 103rd Plenary meeting Extract from the Official Records of the Third United Nations Conference on the Law of the Sea, Volume IX, para 56.

[59]According to the Libyan position, if the proposed international sea-bed authority was to have due competence and to be able to explore and exploit efficiently the resources of such areas, the continental shelf must not extend beyond the 200-mile limit. See A/CONF.62/SR.104, 104th Plenary meeting, para 66.

[60]The Algerian delegation fully supported the position of the Arab group, which would place a limit on the prolongation of the continental shelf. Otherwise, the concept of the common heritage of mankind would be infringed. Any formula which would have the effect of reducing the common heritage of mankind could not be supported. *Id.* para 74.

[61]To Ghana, it was essential that the outer limit of the continental shelf should not exceed 200 nautical miles if activities on the sea-bed beyond the limits of national jurisdiction were to be regulated for the benefit of mankind as a whole, in accordance with the concept of the common heritage of mankind. *See* A/CONF.62/SR.105, 105th Plenary meeting, para 26.

[62]Such a view was shared by scholars to whom the extension of maritime zones under national jurisdiction deprived the common heritage principle of its primary content and rendered it a mere political slogan. *See* Vitzthum (1979), p. 769.

[63]Art. 137, paragraph 2, UNCLOS, on the legal status of the Area and its resources.

the territorial integrity or political independence of any State",[64] or other aggressive activities in line with Art. 2 (4) of the UN Charter. It means that whereas military exercises and maneuvers with nuclear weapons and weapons of mass destruction in the Area are prohibited, it cannot be said that the deployment of regular weapons therein are a priori forbidden. States should, nonetheless, refrain from deploying any kind of military artillery over the deep seabed, given the still undetermined losses in terms of biodiversity and overall ecosystem balance such drills may cause. In this sense, it is different from the continental shelf regime, where coastal states may conduct military exercises, having in mind the limitations imposed by domestic environmental rules, internationally recognized standards, as well as the rights and freedoms of other states.[65]

An additional element of the common heritage principle is that the seabed shall be used in a manner consistent with the *protection of deep-sea marine environment*, in line with Art. 145 UNCLOS. Such a feature approximates both regimes of the Area and the continental shelf, as coastal states are also bound by the obligation to protect and preserve the marine environment within national jurisdiction. A chapter of this volume is dedicated to the analysis of the environmental powers and duties of coastal states over the continental shelf beyond 200 nm, a moment in which the intersections between the regimes of the Area and the continental shelf shall be studied in further detail.

Finally, the "common benefit and equal participation" aspect of the principle embraces the logic that deep seabed mining and its profits should not be monopolized by developed and industrially advanced states, and parties should prevent discrimination (both formal and material) in the right to access natural resources of the Area.[66] Activities in the Area should be carried out in the benefit of humanity *as a whole*. A possible way to achieve this sharing of benefits would be the sharing of benefits obtained through deep seabed mining.[67] A justification for this was formulated by the so-called "compensation" school of thought: use of resources was open to all states; however, several states lacked technological advancements to access those resources; thus, in order to uphold UNCLOS-given right of access to resources, the distribution of benefits would constitute a sort of "indirect participation" in the use of the Area. In short, the right of access could only be materialized

[64]Art. 301, UNCLOS, on the peaceful uses of the seas.

[65]A limitation to the military use of the continental shelf is imposed by the so-called "Seabed Arms Control Treaty", or the Treaty on the Prohibition of the Emplacement of Nuclear Weapons and Other Weapons of Mass Destruction on the Seabed and the Ocean Floor and in the Subsoil Thereof, signed 1971.

[66]Art. 140, UNCLOS, on the benefit of mankind.

[67]A way to implement *de facto* participation of all states in deep seabed mining was to create an international institution mandated with managing the activities of exploring and exploiting the seabed, but also receiving financial contributions from exploiting states and distributing those contribution among the international community—that is precisely the mandate of the ISA.

through the receipt of a share of revenues derived from the exploitation of deep seabed resources.[68]

Adjacency between the two zones may breed unexpected issues concerning the extension of jurisdictional powers and duties of states parties to UNCLOS over each zone. For an analysis of the interaction between both regimes of the Area and the continental shelf, the combined interpretation of Parts VI and XI provides an initial framework, which covers some of the most controversial topics, such as implementation of the revenue-sharing mechanism of Art. 82, titularity of natural resources shared between the outer continental shelf and the Area, adoption of environmental standards by coastal states in the extended shelf which are softer or stricter than the standards adopted by the ISA concerning the Area, among others.

Upfront, it should be made clear that UNCLOS contains no legal prohibition on the exploitation of outer continental shelf resources by coastal states *prior* to the recommendations of the CLCS. However, it is high advisable that those states refrain from doing so, particularly in portions of the seafloor that may be considered the Area. If a State exploits a part of the seabed that turns out to be the Area, the state will have breached UNCLOS provisions and may be held liable for that. The only way to achieve certainty as to the exact area of legitimate action by the coastal state's offshore sector is through delineation of the outer limits of the continental shelf in pursuance with CLCS recommendations.

In addition to that, it should be noted that the common heritage principle does not apply to the outer continental shelf, but some of its key features analyzed supra found their way into the core of the continental shelf regime. Firstly, the principle is at the core of the obligation imposed on coastal states to *share the benefits* of the commercial development of outer continental shelf resources with the international community.[69] Secondly, the principle permeates the outer continental shelf regime by restricting the discretion of coastal states to withhold consent for the conduct of marine scientific research on the continental shelf beyond 200 nm.[70]

Intersections between regimes are also due to the fact that coastal states will necessarily interact with the ISA for the management of the outer continental shelf. Indeed, coastal states are expected to dialogue with the ISA concerning strategies for implementing the Convention's mechanism for sharing benefits of international seabed exploitation. It is so due to the ISA status as the international organization entrusted by UNCLOS to manage the resources of the Area on behalf of humanity. The Authority, nonetheless, exercises no hierarchy over the coastal state, the lack of which is noted on the issues of management of bordering resources and the definition of environmental standards for the Area and for the outer continental shelf.

---

[68]Wolfrum (1983), p. 321.

[69]Obligation contained in Art. 82 UNCLOS, on the payments and contributions with respect to theexploitation of the continental shelf beyond 200 nautical miles.

[70]Art. 246, paragraph 6, UNCLOS, on the marine scientific research on the continental shelf beyond 200 nm. Disputed issues connected to the jurisdiction to conduct marine scientific research on the outer continental shelf will be analyzed in Chaps. 7 and 8.

A potential conflict may arise in the case of natural resources lying across limits of national jurisdiction, i.e. bordering both maritime spaces of the continental shelf and the Area. Art. 142 UNCLOS specifies that "activities in the Area, with respect to resource deposits in the Area which lie across limits of national jurisdiction, shall be conducted with *due regard* to the rights and legitimate interests of any coastal State across whose jurisdiction such deposits lie".[71] In such scenarios, the Convention would favor coastal states, not the international community. This is the view espoused by the authoritative Virginia Commentaries to UNCLOS, according to which coastal state rights and jurisdiction over the resources of the continental shelf have *primacy* over those of the Area.[72] That problem would only exist in the case of shared reservoirs of hydrocarbons, which occur beneath the seabed and generally respect no artificial boundaries, whereas minerals such as polymetallic nodules or sulfides occur on the ocean floor and allow for a more accurate division prior to exploitation.

On the issue of *environmental protection* standards, although the standards to be adopted by the ISA may be used as parameters for coastal states, nothing in the Convention impedes coastal states from adopting stricter standards for authorizing and monitoring exploitation of outer continental shelf resources. The question is, however, whether coastal states can adopt less protective standards to the outer continental shelf than those in place for the Area. These questions are answered on a superficial manner in this item, as a following chapter will dwell into the specificities of coastal state jurisdiction over the outer continental shelf.

In case an *environmental damage* originates from activities in the Area, the coastal state may seek compensation, but not from the ISA, as it enjoys immunity from legal process in the territory of parties to the Convention.[73] The respondent will likely be the contractors operating the mining field, and, under specific circumstances, the respective sponsoring states. The latter have the obligation of due diligence to ensure compliance by sponsored contractors with the terms of the contract and the provisions of the Convention, among which environmental protection rules of Parts XI and XII. Liability emerges for the sponsoring state provided it failed to fulfill its duties under the Convention, namely the obligation to take national measures to supervise and enforce the activities of sponsored contractors.[74] On their side, contractors assume the risks of deep-sea operations and are the first in line for compensation in the aftermath of an environmental harm.

[71]Art. 142, UNCLOS, on the rights and legitimate interests of coastal states.

[72]Nordquist et al. (2002), p. 947.

[73]Art. 177, UNCLOS, on the privileges and immunities of the Authority, stipulates that "to enable the Authority to exercise its functions, it shall enjoy in the territory of each State Party the privileges and immunities set forth in this subsection". Among the immunities held by the ISA in face of states parties is the *immunity from legal process*, as affirmed by Art. 178 UNCLOS.

[74]ITLOS *Responsibilities and obligations of States sponsoring persons and entities with respect to activities in the Area (Request for Advisory Opinion submitted to the Seabed Disputes Chamber)*, Advisory Opinion, 1 February 2011, ITLOS Reports 2011, at 11, para. 242.

When it comes to environmental risks and harms from operation in deep waters, the coastal state is usually thought to be the party with most at stake.[75] For that reason, compensation may be sought, in order to relief the usually tragic consequences of an environmental disruption offshore. This is partially true in light of the possible development of hydrocarbons in the seafloor beyond coastal state jurisdiction, as seems to be the case off the Canadian coast. For the other activities, in particular deep-sea mining, there cannot be traditional "oil spills", but ecosystem alterations and eventual biodiversity losses, which would not affect a particular state, but the entire international community. Hence, it is not against international law to conclude that coastal states with potential deep-sea resources may adopt stricter regulations for their exploitation than the standards applicable by the ISA.

5.3.2 Controversies Regarding the Size of the Area and the Emergence of the Continental Shelf beyond 200 nm

The Area is defined in Art. 1 (1) (1) UNCLOS as the "seabed and ocean floor and subsoil thereof, beyond the limits of national jurisdiction". A key element of that definition is the phrase "beyond national jurisdiction", indicating the definition's negative (or *a contrario*) nature and emphasizing the need for coastal states to delineate their precise outer continental shelves, so that the exact size of the Area may be one day plainly determined. Combined with Art. 134 (3), the outer limits of the continental shelf, delineated in accordance with Art. 76 criteria and on the basis of the CLCS' recommendations, will establish the boundary between the seafloor within and beyond national jurisdictions.

On this regard, two factors complicate the assessment of the Area's size: the possible indefinite protraction in time of outer limits' delineation, and the ISA incapacity to interfere in that process. On the first complication, the literal wording of Art. 8, Annex II of the Convention suggests that the process of delineation could extend indefinitely in time, as the CLCS may reject the outer limits claimed by a coastal state, and the coastal state may submit revised submissions *ad eternum*.[76] In this sense, the extent of the Area gets particularly arduous to assert, in comparison to other maritime zones, such as the high seas or the EEZ, for it depends on the delineation of all outer limits of the continental shelves of the world.

---

[75] Chircop (2011), p. 193.

[76] Art. 8, Annex II UNCLOS reads: "In the case of disagreement by the coastal State with the recommendations of the Commission, the coastal State shall, *within a reasonable time*, make a revised or new submission to the Commission". This provision has been entirely absorbed by the CLCS Rules of Procedure, Rule 53, paragraph 3, without adding any restrictions on the amount of revised submissions a coastal state may forward the Commission.

The second complication refers to the considerably limited role of the ISA in outer continental shelf delineations. It has been suggested that the Authority, taken as a representative of the international community, would have no other choice but to passively watch the entire process and accept it.[77] After all, despite having been granted legal personality by the Convention, the Authority would have no power to protest a national delineation of outer limits before an international adjudicative body.[78] The lack of an express mandate to deal with issues related to the size or geographical extension of the Area, nor to protest judicially against excessive unilateral delineations of outer limits by coastal states would be regrettable.[79] Ultimately, such ill-equipment of the ISA could contribute to the "tragedy of the common heritage of mankind" (in a cross-reference to the famous work of Garrett Hardin) which stems from the overall weak status of both the common heritage principle and the international community to tackle abusive outer continental shelf claims.[80]

These remarks on the limited role of the Authority in defining the size of the Area reflect, however, a deeper concern which is shared by several international lawyers: the threat of the so-called "creeping jurisdiction" of coastal states against the common heritage of mankind and, consequently, the international community. It spreads the perception that coastal states' expected aggressiveness in asserting jurisdiction over the outer continental shelf, via constant attempts to place as much ocean floor under national jurisdiction as possible, symbolizes a decline of the common heritage principle.

As abominable as national excessive claims may be, there seems to be an exaggerated emphasis on the imminence of conflictive scenarios between coastal states and the international community in the process of outer continental shelf delineation. By doing so, international lawyers seem to attempt to justify their existence as problem-solvers. Even if allegedly well-intentioned, such alarmism against coastal states' jurisdictional expansion, depicted as one of the greatest threats to the common heritage principle, is in fact prejudicial to a precise analysis of the interactions between the legal regimes of Area and the continental shelf. Ultimately, some hyperbolic criticisms may pose risks to the consolidation of the continental shelf regime, in particular the portion extending beyond 200 nm.

[77]"As the coastal states are in the positive position in determining the outer limits of the continental shelf, it seems that the international community can only accept passively the limits as the boundary of the Area." *See* Yu and Ji-Lu (2011), p. 320.

[78]Pursuant to Art. 176, UNCLOS, the Authority has "international legal personality and such legal capacity as may be necessary for the exercise of its functions and the fulfillment of its purposes". However, it has "no impact upon this delineation process for the outer continental shelf and equally has no possibility later to challenge the delineation issues by the coastal State concerned". *Id.* 321. Similarly, Wolfrum (2008), p. 3.

[79]Erik Franckx is of the view that "it is to be regretted that the body supposed to act on behalf of mankind of a whole, *i.e.*, the ISA, did not receive the competence necessary to institute legal proceedings on its behalf". *See* Franckx (2010), p. 563.

[80]*Id.* 566.

For instance, Ted McDorman, when commenting on the efforts and the "untold millions" spent by coastal states to collect data of the seafloor adjacent to their coasts and elaborate a submission to the CLCS, makes the following statement: "the ethos of the 1970s, when there was the international political will to accept the Common Heritage concept and a degree of global sharing increasingly appears to have been a blip on the historic law-of-the-sea radar".[81] That is a quite polemic affirmation, to say the least. How can the communal ethos of the 1970s (provided there is such an abstract phenomenon as the ethos of a decade) be challenged by coastal states' efforts to operationalize a right of theirs, a right which was sculpted into the Convention at the same time as the common heritage principle?

The author seems to romanticize the decade of UNCLOS negotiations, blurred by the subjective perception that the general ethos of the time was one of prevalence of the common heritage, as if the struggles to extend coastal state jurisdiction seawards would not constitute part of the same ethos. Well, the push for internationalizing the seabed was never unanimous, it came to life alongside pressure to expand coastal state powers over natural resources offshore. Finally, the sentence seems to disregard the fact that "a degree of global sharing" will also occur in the case of exploitation beyond 200 nm, as the revenue-sharing mechanism enshrined in Art. 82 of the Convention confirms. In sum, McDorman's statement delivers the undesired effect of pitting the outer continental shelf against the common heritage of mankind, as if both concepts would have been bred and raised in a permanent tug-of-war.

Other criticisms have the unwanted impact of boiling down to one single cause all the practical problems immanent to the implementation of the common heritage principle: the territorial temptation of coastal states and the encroachments over the Area. In a paper on the ISA and the common heritage on mankind, Erik Franckx mentions only *en vole d'oiseau* the 1994 Implementing Agreement and the subsequent devastation to the principle's hard core,[82] opting instead for crediting practical challenges to the principle's implementation mostly on the ill-equipment of the Authority to tackle coastal states' abusive intrusions in the Area.

The road to implementation of the common heritage principle, up to now, has surely been a bumpy one. Coastal states may have a share on this, but a key development in the law of the sea that deserves attention was the adoption of the Implementing Agreement to Part XI in 1994.[83] In fact, changes brought about by that instrument have diminished Third World countries' ability to access both research results and financial benefits obtained in the Area. That is due partially to the fact that contractors have gained permission for free and corporate access to seabed, i.e. unbound by the once existing obligation to transfer technology. Such an alteration results partly from changes in world politics during the 1990s. On the one

[81] McDorman (2015), p. 202.

[82] Limitations such as the dropping of the obligation upon miners to pay fees prior to the commercial extraction of mineral, or the dropping of technology transfer clauses have impaired the very essence of the common heritage principle, as devised by Arvid Pardo.

[83] Agreement relating to the Implementation of Part XI of UNCLOS, New York, 28 July 1994.

hand, the 1970s witness the cooling of the Cold War, the reinforcement of multilateralism as a way to accommodate conflicting views, and the containment of the American power—features which have undeniably benefited the negotiation and adoption of UNCLOS. On the other hand, the early 1990s were rather influenced by commercial ultraliberalism and the prevalence of hegemonic interests in the making of a regime for the use of the ocean floor.[84]

One of the voices critical to the attack on the original meaning of the common heritage principle is R. P. Anand, to whom the concept was left as good as "mutilated". To that scholar, the modifications effected by the 1994 Agreement shall lead to the exploitation of the deep seabed in "commercial terms, irrespective of the needs and interests of the weaker members of the international community".[85] From a critical perspective, such changes may be interpreted as having effectively amended Part XI and core features of the common heritage principle, in violation of Art. 311 (6) of the Convention (despite efforts by negotiating parties to conveniently sell the move as an "implementing" effort).[86] By loosening the obligation to transfer technology, deregulating deep-sea exploitation, and flirting with liberal and free trade ideals, the adoption of the 1994 Agreement has shown how much international lawyers in general, with a few exceptions, were subservient to political interests, acting in order to justify the 1994 Agreement.[87]

Regardless of the critiques to the loosening of the common heritage principle, it would be exaggerated to dismiss efforts to create an international regime for the submerged spaces beyond national jurisdiction as a failure. For Loureiro Bastos, there is a strong international regime for the Area in place, which has gained a *de facto prevalence* due to the customary nature of its rules, thereby producing conventional effects in relation to third states.[88] This prevalence, so Bastos, stems from the fact that the majority of states especially interested in the use of mineral resources of the Area are currently parties to UNCLOS and have been orderly complying the Conventions stipulations on access to the common heritage of mankind.[89]

Besides, the insistence in portraying coastal states' jurisdictional ambitions as the source of evil in the law of the sea does not help assess the difficulties ahead of the international community regarding the application of the common heritage principle.

---

[84]*See* Moreira and Silva (2010), p. 13.

[85]Anand (2004), p. 196.

[86]Art. 311, paragraph 6, UNCLOS stipulates that "States Parties agree that there shall be no amendments to the basic principle relating to the common heritage of mankind set forth in Art. 136".

[87]Opinion embraced, among others, by Galindo (2006), p. 384.

[88]Bastos (2012), p. 141.

[89]A consequence of this claim would be that even non-parties to Convention would be obliged to respect the international legal regime contained in Part XI. For Bastos, "coastal states cannot interpret 'sovereignty and 'sovereign rights' granted to them for the exploitation of mineral resources in the submerged areas under their sovereignty or jurisdiction using the perspective of the pursuing of strictly individual interests"—it is a restriction established by Art. 193 UNCLOS. *See* Bastos (2012), p. 143.

That a pattern of argumentation is to be found with relative frequency in specialized literature of the field, according to which the increase of coastal state's competences over larger maritime spaces offshore leads to less stability in the *ordre publique océanique*, therefore posing greater hazard to principles dear to the law of the sea, such as the very common heritage of mankind, the protection of the marine environment, among others. A critique to such scare-mongering against the jurisdictional assertions of coastal states is formulated in Chap. 6.

Finally, specialized literature occasionally depicts an excessively impotent Authority and an equally powerless international community, when criticizing the current governance edifice of the Area.[90] Sure, the ISA is not mandated to intervene in delineation processes between coastal states and the CLCS. It has also been said to have no legal capacity to question judicially excessive national claims for outer continental shelves. And yes, the Authority was given no explicit *locus standi* before adjudication bodies as specified by the dispute settlement rules of the Convention's Part XV.

However, UNCLOS does attribute to the ISA the major responsibility for safeguarding the common heritage of mankind,[91] a duty which comprises insurgence against abusive unilateral encroachment on the Area. To protect the community commons of the Area and the natural resources thereof is one of the main purposes of the Authority, acting on behalf of humankind. A possible avenue for legal action would, thus, be the to provoke the Seabed Disputes Chamber, in its contentious jurisdiction, to decide upon conflicts involving the Area.[92] That Chamber operates within the structure of the ITLOS and has jurisdiction, among others, over disputes with respect to "acts or omissions of the Authority or of a State Party alleged to be in violation of this Part or the Annexes relating thereto or of rules, regulations and procedures of the Authority adopted in accordance therewith" (emphasis added).[93] Such a dispute may be referred to the Chamber by the ISA Council, as UNCLOS grants the Council powers to "institute proceedings on behalf of the Authority before the Seabed Disputes Chamber in cases of non-compliance".[94] As such, an eventual encroachment upon the Area could be judicially questioned before that Chamber of the ITLOS.

In addition to that, even assuming that the Authority (and its Council) has its hands entirely tied, and the alternative suggested above would not be accepted before an international tribunal, individual states are still legally entitled to defend

---

[90]Vicente Marotta Rangel, for instance, considered it deplorable that "la Convention n'est pas accordé à l'Autorité (des fonds marins) le pouvoir de négocier avec l'État côtier leurs frontières communes". *See* Rangel (1985), p. 364.

[91]Art. 137, paragraph 2 of the Convention.

[92]Vicente Marotta Rangel had raised that possibility a while ago. For the Brazilian scholar, "under Part XI it would be able to accede to the Sea-Bed Disputes Chamber, to its contentious and advisory jurisdiction, since some conditions specified in the LOSC, Arts. 187 (b) (i) and 191 are effectively met". *See* Marotta Rangel (2006), p. 362.

[93]Art. 187 (b) (i), UNCLOS, on the jurisdiction of the Seabed Disputes Chamber.

[94]Art. 162, paragraph 2 (u), UNCLOS, on the powers of the ISA Council.

their interests over the Area by bringing up a case against other states before an international adjudicating body. On the power of third states to question the delineation of outer limits, Rüdiger Wolfrum dismisses the argument that legal action by any other coastal state party to the Convention would amount to an "actio popularis", which is traditionally non-accepted in international law. For the former ITLOS Judge, potential mining states or states sponsoring contractors engaged in deep seabed mining activities "have not only a general but also an *individual interest* in potential mining sites not being taken from the Area" (emphasis added).[95] The road for encroaching on the Area can be, thus, made a lot more difficult than some of the criticisms analyzed supra may suggest.

In sum, the common heritage of mankind is an ambitious principle and, precisely because of that, a difficult one to implement. It restricts both principles of freedoms of the seas and territorial sovereignty of states, but ultimately leaves states plenty of maneuver room as to *how* to implement the "benefit of mankind as a whole" clause.[96] In order address some of the issues highlighted above, the international community will necessitate *new types of cooperation schemes*, particularly between the Authority and coastal states with an outer continental shelf.[97] As seen above, part of the common heritage principle regulates a core provision of UNCLOS continental shelf regime, namely the duty incumbent upon coastal states to share the financial benefits of deep-sea mineral exploitation on the shelf beyond 200 nm. That intersection between the Area, the common heritage principle and the outer continental shelf is the topic of the following item.

5.3.3 Revenue-Sharing Mechanism of the Outer Continental Shelf

An important part of the intersection between the legal regimes established at UNCLOS Part VI and Part XI is materialized in the obligation of coastal states to share revenues deriving from the exploitation of non-living resources of the continental shelf beyond 200 nm—the so-called *revenue-sharing mechanism*. In fact, Art. 82 UNCLOS requires coastal states to make payments or contributions in kind in respect of the exploitation of the non-living resources of the continental shelf beyond 200 nm, exempting only developing states who are net importers of the resources in question from paying contributions to the Authority. This provision serves the cause of protecting the common heritage principle and, as such, is believed to be a legal tool against the "maritime expansionism of broad-margin states".[98] Such a claim is

---

[95]Wolfrum (2008), p. 13.

[96]Art. 140, paragraph 1, UNCLOS, on the benefit of mankind.

[97]Position held by Chircop (2011), p. 182.

[98]Kwiatkowska (1991), p. 157.

analyzed below, alongside a discussion on the impacts of the birth of the common heritage principle to the continental shelf regime.

It is uncontroversial that Arts. 82 and 76 UNCLOS have more in common than the sheer blackletter of the law may suggest. The drafting history of the Convention indicates that the revenue-sharing mechanism was a sort of *quid pro quo* for the outer continental shelf beyond 200 nm.[99] Such revenue-sharing system consubstantiates the second half of the compromise reached between broad-margin states and states opposing the expansion of coastal state jurisdiction, together with the very possibility of exercising jurisdiction over the shelf beyond 200 nm. In other words, the approval of Art. 76 was only made possible via concessions by broad-margin states in return, agreeing to the equitable distribution of financial benefits of outer continental shelf exploitation, pursuant to Art. 160 (2) (f) (i) UNCLOS.[100]

One of the reasons grounding the need for a compromise was the argument by narrow-margin countries that the outer continental shelf would come to life at the expense of the Area and the common heritage of mankind[101]—under the reasoning that the outer continental shelf is no purely geological concept, having been given a legal treatment via the formulae enshrined in Art. 76 (4) to (6) UNCLOS. Hence, Art. 82 became a response in form of *compensation* to criticisms that the enlargement of the continental shelf beyond 200 nm would imply a reduction in size of the common heritage of mankind.[102] This impression is consistent with several pronunciations made during the III UNCLOS. Thus, broad-margin states have agreed (i) to "compensate" the international community for diminishing the potential size of the Area;[103] and (ii) to contribute to the sharing of benefits from deep-sea mining.

---

[99]ISA (2009), p. xv.

[100]During negotiations, even liberal countries such as the United States considered that the payment of royalties would be reasonable in light of the massiveness of natural resources that would be placed under American jurisdiction with the approval of the Convention. As an analyst has put it, "These royalty rates were negotiated by the U.S. Government with extensive input from U.S. oil and natural gas interests. As oil and natural gas companies have recognized, the royalties are reasonable in view of the immense value of the resources that would be made subject to the United States' exclusive sovereign jurisdiction. The oil and natural gas companies—and the U.S. Treasury—would be able to retain much more than the U.S. would be required to pay to the Seabed Authority. Notwithstanding the required payments to the Seabed Authority, joining the Convention would be overwhelmingly beneficial to U.S. economy and the U.S. Treasury." Donoghue (2012), p. 5.

[101]The revenue-sharing mechanism has also been interpreted as *materializing* the common heritage principle, even if the application would take place within the coastal state's jurisdiction and not in the Area. It was the case of Shigeru Oda, to whom Art. 82 was "instituted in such a manner that the concept of the common heritage of mankind plays a role in controlling over-expansion of the exclusive interests of coastal States in their continental shelves". *See* Oda (1989), p. xxxii. That view, however, is discarded by the ISA, on the basis that Art. 82 UNCLOS was not meant by the negotiating parties to be an implementation of the common heritage principle. What occurs is merely the sharing of revenues, which is but one of the multiple facets of the principle.

[102]This view is espoused, among others, by Galindo (2006), p. 266.

[103]On the issue of a potential continental shelf "encroachment" over the Area, it could also be sustained that there was no such intrusion, for two reasons. Firstly, both regimes were born at the same time, with the signature of UNCLOS. Secondly, the geological continental margin has always

The revenue-sharing mechanism became a "new rule of equity in the form of a unique royalty in international law".[104]

UNCLOS disciplined the revenue-sharing mechanism and governed the particulars of that system of payments and contributions. Firstly, the coastal state is given discretion as to the modality, whether it opts for payment or contribution in kind. Secondly, payments are due after 5 years of production at an extraction site, in a sort of "grace period", with respect to the *entirety* of production.[105] For the period between the sixth and twelfth year of production, the Convention set up a system of gradual increase in the rate of payment or contribution, starting at 1% of the value or volume of production in the sixth year. Then, "the rate shall increase by 1 per cent for each subsequent year until the twelfth year and shall remain at 7 per cent thereafter", as stated in paragraph 2, Art. 82. Refusal to make payments or contributions will amount to an international illicit and may trigger judicial proceedings by *any* other state, given the individual states' legitimate interests in the well-functioning of Part XI. Parallelly, the ISA may start proceedings before ITLOS.[106]

Despite the creation of a revenue-sharing system, the management, protection and exploitation of outer continental shelf resources is subject to the national jurisdiction of the coastal state. The Convention imposes upon them the obligation to share revenues, but the loose wording leaves plenty of maneuver room as to how each state will raise and transfer the cash to the Authority. Hence, the resolution of issues and problems emerging from the implementation of Art. 82 is primarily a *responsibility* of the coastal state and, although the ISA is not obliged to advise the coastal state in that regard, coastal states are expected to interact with the Authority in tackling practical implementation difficulties.

Coastal states will pursue exploration efforts of continental shelf resources, aiming at an exploitation that may come to life sooner than expected. The likelihood of exploration and exploitation of outer continental shelf resources can be attested in two particular episodes, one of which of direct interest for this work: the assumption by the ISA of potential mineral and hydrocarbon resources on the Brazilian outer continental shelf, and the recent (and rather concrete) Norwegian oil and gas discoveries off the Canadian coast beyond 200 nm.

Firstly, the Norwegian state petroleum company, Statoil, has recently reported both the discovery of oil and gas reservoirs off the Canadian east coast beyond 200 nm and the intention to implement Art. 82.[107] Thus far, Norway and the United

---

been there. What the coastal state did was merely claim jurisdiction over a submarine portion of its land territory.

[104]Chircop (2011), p. 183.

[105]Art. 82, paragraph 2, UNCLOS, on the sharing of revenues.

[106]Art. 20, paragraph 2, Annex VI, UNCLOS.

[107]This information has been obtained via e-mail interview with Dr. Wiley Spicer, one of the authors of the ISA Technical Study no. 15, on the key expressions of Art. 82 UNCLOS, an absolute authority worldwide on the topic. When enquired no the existence of any ongoing exploitation projects on the continental shelf beyond 200 nm, Spicer confirmed that Statoil has a discovery off the Canadian coast beyond that threshold. Regarding the implementation of Art. 82, Spicer

States have apparently been the only ones discussing strategies to operationalize the revenue-sharing mechanism. In fact, the Norwegian government has released plans to design a model in which taxpayers and not oil companies would pay the royalties, so as to foster prospection in areas father away from land. Costs in connection to the royalties due to the ISA Fund would be, thus, deducted in the final calculation of the petroleum tax in Norway.[108] Despite the fact that this is the only case, up to now, in which exploitation beyond 200 nm is expected to take place, thus far, it is not ludicrous to expect other states to reach farther out offshore for petroleum and gas.

Secondly, the potential for non-living resource exploitation is also present off the Brazilian coast, as highlighted in the ISA Technical Study no. 5. Pursuant to that report, "with sediment thickness in excess of 5 km in water depths between 2,000m and 4,500m, Brazil has a very real potential of hydrocarbon exploitation in its outer continental shelf."[109] In addition to that, the methodologies used suggest that "more than a third of the Brazilian continental shelf beyond 200 nm offers, in theory, potential and accessibility for hydrocarbon exploitation". Were it not enough, the study also reports potential for polymetallic sulfides around the hot-spot volcanic Trindade and Martin Vaz Islands. Further details on Brazilian national assessments of non-living resources of the outer continental, and a comparison with the ISA expectations is drawn in Chap. 10.

Given the expectancy of further exploration and potential exploitation of outer continental shelf resources worldwide, a multitude of issues may arise in close connection to the *environmental regulation* of activities on and above the outer continental shelf. As such, it is urgent to systematize the bulk of coastal state's powers and duties within the outer continental shelf, as well as the influence of stricter regulations and standards approved, for instance, by the ISA into coastal states outer continental shelf activities. Much of the discussed above merit further scrutiny, a task reserved for the appropriate chapter on the coastal state's environmental jurisdiction over the continental shelf and the interfaces with the high seas and the Area.

---

categorically emphasized that the resolution of unexpected issues during the implementation of Art. 82 is primarily the responsibility of coastal states, the ISA having no a priori role. That does not prohibit the state from seeking the Authority for advice.

[108] Alister Doyle and Nerijus Adomaitis. "Norway plans tax breaks for remotest Arctic oilfields". In *Reuters*, Environment Section, September 5 2017. Available at: https://www.reuters.com/Art./us-energy-norway-exclusive/exclusive-norway-plans-tax-breaks-for-remotest-arctic-oilfields-letters-idUSKCN1BG2CE. Accessed 08 April 2020.

[109] ISA (2010), p. 46.

5.4 Partial Conclusions

This section was but an appetizer to the discussion concerning the environmental jurisdiction of coastal states over the outer continental shelf and the regulatory maneuver room enjoyed by those states in the seafloor beyond 200 nm. As a pre-requisite to that discussion, it was paramount to shed light on the legal regime applicable to the portion of the continental shelf extending beyond 200 nm.

The continental shelf regime is marked by a plurality of intersections and overlaps with those regimes of other maritime spaces, which characterized the emergence of the new law of the sea. Regarding the interaction between the continental shelf and the EEZ regimes, it was said above that, despite the merging of provisions for both zones in the Convention, as in the case of Art. 60 and 80, on artificial islands, installations and structures, the relationship between continental shelf and EEZ rules is marked by *autonomy* and *parallelism*. Both zones have upheld slightly differing rules, which run, however, in parallel to each other. They are zones in which coastal states exercise differing competences in differing degrees, as is the case of jurisdiction to manage and conserve natural resources, a power explicitly acknowledged to them over the EEZ, but not over the continental shelf.[110] For instance, jurisdiction to conserve and manage natural resources are not expressly mentioned in the continental shelf regime, what could theoretically restrict the environmental powers of coastal states over the continental shelf extending beyond EEZ limits, i.e. the outer continental shelf. This remark will be questioned and debunked in coming chapters, reason why it was necessary to bring it to light in this part.

The intersection between continental shelf and high seas rules is a rather complex and delicate one. Here, it was shown that the powers exercisable by the coastal state over the outer continental shelf relate *exclusively* to the seafloor, as UNCLOS preserved the legal status of the superjacent waters beyond the 200 nm as high seas. The exact *jurisdictional maneuver room* left for coastal states over the outer continental shelf are analyzed in Chaps. 7 and 8.

Another intersection with great potential for conflict is between the continental shelf and the Area, governed by the common heritage of mankind. The current item showed how the need to determine the exact size of the international deep seabed was a powerful driver for the adoption of precise formulae to delineate the outer limits of the continental shelf—Art. 76. In the light of the indeterminacy of Art. 1 CSC, it was pressing to reinforce the idea that continental shelves had limits, and so did the drafters of UNCLOS.

In addition, the creation of the common heritage of mankind principle added another pint of salt to the complex interaction between the Area and the outer continental shelf. That principle is, by all means, an extremely relevant norm for the management of the world's oceans. Indeed, part of the literature takes the common heritage principle as *ius cogens* of international law, due to the fact that

[110] Art. 56, paragraph 1 (a) UNCLOS, on the rights, jurisdiction and duties of the coastal states in the exclusive economic zone.

signatories to UNCLOS are not allowed to make reservations nor amendments to the principle.[111]

There is a problematic perception among international lawyers that coastal states' expected aggressiveness in asserting jurisdiction over the outer continental shelf, via constant attempts to place as much ocean floor under national jurisdiction as possible, symbolizes a decline of the common heritage principle. This chapter identified a certain insistence among scholars in portraying coastal states' jurisdictional ambitions as the source of evil in the law of the sea, a move that does not help assess the difficulties ahead of the international community regarding the application of the common heritage principle.

Finally, it was discussed the extent to which the common heritage principle has influence the regime of resource exploitation of the continental shelf beyond 200 nm and the practical challenges ahead of the implementation the revenue-sharing mechanism contained in Art. 82 UNCLOS. Overall, despite the challenges analyzed supra, concerted efforts to create an international regime for the submerged spaces beyond national jurisdiction have been successful. In view of overlapping norms from different regimes of distinct maritime spaces, it is urgent to identify the coastal states rights to regulate environmental issues on the outer continental shelf, a task in which UNCLOS only partially helps. Given the environmental factor, and the interconnectedness of international legal subsystems,[112] resorting to international environmental law instruments is advisable.

Finally, it became clear the existence of a confrontation between calls for a "renewed ethos" for the *mare liberum* doctrine, in which environmental rights are better placed in the relationship with traditional freedoms of the seas, *as opposed to* calls for a detachment from the "territorial mentality" that allegedly purports more losses than gains to a holistic marine environmental ocean governance. Both forces press against each other and the space of the outer continental shelf corresponds to the optimal battlefield for both, given the confluence of elements of high seas freedoms and territorial mentality governing the zone. Chapter 6 discusses those opposing calls and takes a stance towards the better placement of environmental rights and duties in the relationship with the traditional freedoms of the seas, for the reasons and motives exposed therein.

References

Anand RP (2004) Studies in international law and history. Springer, Dordrecht

Bastos FL (2012) Setting the field for future 'mineral rushes': some reflections on the international regime for the exploration and exploitation of marine minerals. In: Ribeiro MC (ed) 30 years

[111]For Rüdiger Wolfrum, however, the common heritage principle does not impede deep seabed mining by states not party to UNCLOS. *See* Wolfrum (1983), p. 313.

[112]On the interaction between especial legal regimes and general international law, *see* Simma and Pulkowski (2006), p. 483.

after the signature of the United Nations Convention on the law of the sea: the protection of the environment and the future of the law of the sea. Coimbra Editora, Coimbra

Beckman R, Davenport T (2012) The EEZ regime: reflections after 30 years. In: Proceedings from the LOSI-KIOST Conference on Securing the Ocean for the Next Generation, pp 1–41

Ben-Yami M (2017) The 200-mile limit's origins. World Fishing and Aquaculture, 29 August 2017. https://www.worldfishing.net/news101/Comment/ben-yami/the-200-mile-limits-origin. Accessed 13 Apr 2020

Borgese EM (1968) The ocean regime: a suggested statute for the peaceful uses of the high seas and the sea-bed beyond the limits of national jurisdiction. A Center Occasional Paper vol 1, no. 5. Center for the Study of Democratic Institutions, Santa Barbara, California

Brown ED (1982) Freedom of the high seas versus the common heritage of mankind: fundamental principles in conflict. San Diego Law Rev 20:521–560

Chircop A (2011) Managing adjacency: some legal aspects of the relationship between the extended continental shelf and the international seabed Area. Ocean Dev Int Law 42(4):307–316

Creamer R (1968) Title to the deep seabed: prospects for the future. Harv Int Law J 9:205–231

Donoghue T (2012) Statement of Thomas J. Donoghue: The Law of the Sea Convention: Perspectives from Business and Industry. Testimony before the Senate Foreign Relations Committee, 28 June

Finley LW (1969) The outer limit of the continental shelf: a rejoinder to professor Louis Henkin. Am J Int Law 64(1):42–61

Franckx E (2010) The international seabed authority and the common heritage of mankind: the need for states to establish the outer limits of their continental shelf. Int J Mar Coast Law 25 (4):543–567

Friedmann W (1971) Selden redivivus: towards a partition of the seas? Am J Int Law 65 (5):757–770

Galindo GRB (2006) Quem diz humanidade, pretende enganar? Internacionalistas e os usos da noção de patrimônio comum da humanidade aplicada aos fundos marinhos (1967–1994). PhD Dissertation, Universidade de Brasília

Garcia-Amador FV (1974) The Latin American contribution to the development of the law of the sea. Am J Int Law 68(1):33–50

Gavouneli M (2007) Functional jurisdiction in the law of the sea. Publications on ocean development, vol 62. Nijhoff, Leiden

Henkin L (1969) International law and 'the interests': the law of the seabed. Am J Int Law 63 (3):504–510

Infante MT (1984) The settlement of disputes regarding the law of the sea and its bearing on the legal nature of the exclusive economic zone. In: Vicuña FO (ed) The exclusive economic zone: a Latin American perspective. Taylor and Francis Group, pp 166–167

Johnson LB (1966) 2 Weekly Compilation of Presidential Documents, 13 July

Keohane RO, Nye JS (1977) Power and interdependence: world politics in transition. Little Brown & Co, Boston

Kreca M (2002) A few remarks on the theoretical basis of the new law of the sea. In: Liber Amicorum Judge Shigeru Oda, vol II. Nijhoff, Leiden, pp 1207–1216

Kwiatkowska B (1989) The 200-mile exclusive economic zone in the new law of the sea. Nijhoff, Dordrecht

Kwiatkowska B (1991) Creeping jurisdiction beyond 200 miles in the light of the 1982 law of the sea convention and state practice. Ocean Dev Int Law 22(2):153–187

Leanza U, Caracciolo M C (2014) The exclusive economic zone. In: Attard D, Fitzmaurice M, Martinez NA (eds) The IMLI manual on international maritime law, vol I: the law of the sea. Oxford University Press, Oxford

McDorman TL (2015) The continental shelf. In: The Oxford handbook of the law of the sea. Oxford University Press, Oxford

Molenaar EJ (2015) Port and coastal states. In: The Oxford handbook of the law of the sea. Oxford University Press, Oxford, pp 280–303

Moreira FK, Silva DV (2010) A exploração dos fundos marinho: de patrimônio comum da humanidade à administração condominial. In: Estudos de Direito Internacional vol XIX. Juruá, Curitiba
Nordquist MH, Grandy NR, Nandan SN, Rosenne S (eds) (2002) United Nations Convention on the law of the sea 1982: a commentary. Nijhoff, The Hague
Oda S (1968) Proposals for revising the convention on the continental shelf. Columbia J Transnatl Law 7:1–31
Oda S (1989) International control of sea resources. Nijhoff, Dordrecht
Rajagopal B (2003) International law and social movements: challenges of theorizing resistance. Columbia J Transnatl Law 41(2):397–433
Rangel MV (1985) Le plateau continental dans La Convention de 1982 sur le Droit de la Mer. Coll Courses Hague Acad Int Law 194:269–428
Rangel MV (2006) Settlement of disputes relating to the delimitation of the outer continental shelf: the role of international courts and arbitral tribunals. Int J Mar Coast Law 21(3):347–362
Rothwell D, Stephens T (2016) The international law of the sea. Bloomsbury, London
Schofield C, Arsana A, Poll R (2010) The outer continental shelf in the Asia-Pacific Region: progress and prospects. In: Vidas D, Schei PJ (eds) Law, technology and science for oceans in globalisation. Nijhoff, Leiden, pp 539–576
Simma B, Pulkowski D (2006) Of planets and the universe: self-contained regimes in international law. Eur J Int Law 17(3):483–529
Stoll PT (2008) Continental shelf. In: Max Planck Encyclopedia of Public International Law [MPEPIL]
Townsend-Gault I (2014) The 'territorialization' of the exclusive economic zone: a requiem for the remnant of the freedom of the seas? In: The limits of Maritime Jurisdiction. Nijhoff, Leiden, pp 65–78
Vicuña FO (1984) The exclusive economic zone: a Latin American perspective, vol 1, the foreign relations of the third world series. Westview Press, Boulder
Vitzthum WG (1979) A new international economic order and a new global maritime regime. Law State 19:7–24
Wolfrum R (1983) The principle of the common heritage of mankind. ZaöRV 43(2):312–337
Wolfrum R (2008) The outer continental shelf: some considerations concerning applications and the potential role of the international tribunal for the law of the Sea. Statement presented at the 73rd ILA Conference, Rio de Janeiro, 21 August 21
Young M (2016) Then and now: reappraising freedom of the seas in modern law of the sea. Ocean Dev Int Law 47(2):165–185
Yu J, Ji-Lu W (2011) The outer continental shelf of coastal states and the common heritage of mankind. Ocean Dev Int Law 42(4):317–328

Resolutions

A/RES/2749(XXV) (1970) Declaration of Principles governing the Sea-Bed and the Ocean Floor, and the Subsoil Thereof, beyond the Limits of Nations Jurisdiction, 17 December 1970

Reports

ISA (2009) Issues Associated with the Implementation of Article 82 of the United Nations Convention on the Law of the Sea. Technical Study N. 4. International Seabed Authority, Kingston

ISA (2010) Non-Living Resources of the Continental Shelf beyond 200 Nautical Miles: Speculations on the Implementation of Article 82 of the United Nations Convention on the Law of the Sea. Technical Study N. 5. International Seabed Authority, Kingston

Jurisprudence

ICJ (1982) Case Concerning the Continental Shelf (Tunisia/Libya), Judgement of 24 February 1982. ICJ Reports

ITLOS (2011) Responsibilities and obligations of States sponsoring persons and entities with respect to activities in the Area (Request for Advisory Opinion submitted to the Seabed Disputes Chamber), Advisory Opinion, 1 February 2011, ITLOS Reports

ITLOS (2014) The M/V "Virginia G" Case (Panama/Guinea-Bissau). Panama v. Guinea Bissau, Judgment of 14 April 2014. ITLOS Reports

Chapter 6
Creeping Jurisdiction in the Law of the Sea: Threat to Navigational Freedoms or Stand Against "*Spoliative* Jurisdiction"?

Despite increasing environmental awareness regarding ocean affairs, the law of the sea is comprised of rules which embody the attempt to prioritize economic interests of states, in vague and general terms.[1] Prevailing rule is "abstention from unjustifiable interferences" on the rights of other states, the underpinning philosophy of freedom of the seas. In this context, this book dedicates an item to discuss the long-established customary and treaty norms which praise navigational freedoms as unshakable, fully aware that the affirmation of coastal states' right to protect the marine environment in areas within national jurisdiction (to the detriment of freedom of the seas) is likely to face some degree of rejection by parcels of the international community. Should the book provoke questions marks on the current balance of rights and duties between coastal and other states on the continental shelf, it will have achieved its intention.

However, this work is not ignorant of a need to guarantee a more realistic and effective protection of the environment, not the ideal one. The regime of the continental shelf within and particularly beyond 200 nm must have in mind the contingencies of current-day law of the sea. One should, thus, foster the creative and innovative use of UNCLOS and environmental legal treaties and soft law instruments, with the objective of strengthening the possibilities of coastal state action in face of traditional freedoms of the seas on the continental shelf, always bearing in mind UNCLOS Art. 78 (1) and (2), on the obligation of due regard to the rights and freedoms of other states. This is an exercise of attempting at harmonizing contrary

[1] The preeminence of the economic rationale can be observed in Arts. 56 (2) and 58 (1) UNCLOS, on the economic facet of the EEZ; Art. 78 (1), on the preservation of high seas freedoms above the continental shelf, seen as indispensable to international commerce; and Art. 194 (4), on coastal states' duty to refrain from unjustifiable interference on activities of other states when taking measures to prevent, reduce and control pollution of the marine environment.

V. Alencar Mayer Feitosa Ventura, *Environmental Jurisdiction in the Law of the Sea*, https://doi.org/10.1007/978-3-030-50543-1_6

values, based on the premise that coastal states represent "trustees" of common concerns of mankind, such as the oceans and marine environmental protection.[2]

This work does not intend to exhaust reflections on this topic, but merely to provide an arena for the exchange of ideas on the development of the law of the sea. The ultimate goal is to make the scholarship of this fascinating field of international law permeable to critiques, inputs and insights from all distant corners of the world. With that end in mind, this part analyzes the concept of "creeping jurisdiction" both in the pre- and post-UNCLOS eras, in relation to the extension of coastal state jurisdiction not only on security, but also on marine environmental matters. In the first part, this title defines and identifies the context in which the expression "creeping jurisdiction" is coined and spread. Then, it goes on to analyze state practice prior to and after the adoption of UNCLOS, in order to answer to the question whether there is serious ground for raising alarms against an alleged enclosure of the oceans.[3]

6.1 Context of the Practice Known as "Creeping Jurisdiction"

The law of the sea has been shaped by the not always peaceful opposition of interests between sovereign states. On the one hand, the maritime powers, on the other, developing coastal states.[4] Maritime states, or dominant naval powers, usually acted on an individual basis, advancing interests that usually broke down to preserving freedom of navigation throughout the world oceans.[5] Take, for instance, the past two hegemonic maritime powers in history, the United Kingdom and the United States. During the glory days of the British Empire, in the first half of the nineteenth century, the so-called *Pax Britannica*, the Royal Navy had 335 warships navigating every inch of the world.[6] More recently, the United States Navy sailed 274 vessels as part of its battle force fleet as of December 2016, including ten aircraft carriers,

---

[2]Ribeiro (2013), p. 64.

[3]Part of this chapter was published in the Brazilian Journal of International Law, in a thematic issue dedicated to the "Southern narrative of international law". *See* Ventura (2018), p. 161.

[4]A similar classification between states has been used in other law of the sea works. *See* Valencia (1987), p. 541.

[5]Marta Chantal Ribeiro refers to "states most prone to commercial interests". *See* Ribeiro (2013), p. 64.

[6]In 1810, the Royal Navy had 183 cruisers (then known as "frigates") and 152 battleships. Those are solely large warships and exclude a plethora of sloops, brigs and corvettes flying the ensign of King George III. *See* generally Fenton (2007).

eighty-four large surface combat ships (such as destroyers and cruisers) and twelve nuclear-powered attack submarines.[7]

With the United States Navy's announced plan of achieving a force structure of 355 warships,[8] what would be the use of a mighty navy without legal certainty to navigate and demonstrate power in as many corners of the world oceans as possible? Apart from deterrent power, maritime states possess large and well-equipped fishing fleets, as well as enough technical development to drill down several kilometers of the seabed and subsoil in search of hydrocarbons, no matter how harsh the climate conditions at the water surface, nor the geological ruggedness. Due to commercial interests, such countries favor the limitation of coastal state jurisdiction to the least geographical and material scope possible—which is, as a matter of fact, an unannounced purpose of Freedom of Navigation Operations (FON).[9]

While all maritime powers are coastal states, the reverse does not hold true. In fact, littoral states exercising little influence in ocean geopolitics respond for most of the international community. Coastal states from Europe, Latin America, Southeast Asia, and Africa (particularly after the decolonization wave of the 1960s), have long been excluded from the selected category of maritime powers. Precisely those states acted either individually,[10] or on a concerted basis,[11] and were the main drivers of a sea-change in the traditional dual-jurisdiction division of the oceans that took place in the second half of the twentieth century.

The category of coastal states has never been homogeneous, and so were not the main interests behind the remodeling of the division of the oceans in the pre-UNCLOS era. On the one hand, there were Western European states, endowed with better economic conditions. On the other, developing and least developed states. Both had economic-based interests in forwarding jurisdictional assertions to larger maritime spaces, but non-European developing coastal states also wielded the overarching objective to impede the perpetuation of a system based on the deprivation of coastal state's power over natural resources off their shores. Were it not for the centuries old "marginal sea" of 3 nm, the principle of freedom of the seas would have been absolute, be it to navigate, explore or exploit.

If freedom prevails, some could say, all coastal states alike may enjoy it and the international community as whole would profit from it. In this regard, it is interesting

---

[7]O'Rourke (2017), p. 19.

[8]*Id.* 19.

[9]Regarding the tension between freedom of the seas and sovereignty claims of third world countries towards the ocean, noteworthy is the Freedom of Navigation Program (FON) of the United States Navy. In force since 1979, a few years before UNCLOS III was open for signature, this program has the main goal of highlighting "navigation provisions of the LOS Convention to further the recognition of the vital national need to protect maritime rights throughout the world". Available at: http://www.state.gov/e/oes/ocns/opa/maritimesecurity/. Accessed 08 April 2020.

[10]It is the case of Norway and Denmark, which claimed a territorial sea of 4 nm, and Italy, with claims of a 6 nm territorial sea, in the period anteceding the 1930 League of Nations Conference.

[11]It is the case of Latin American states, which joined efforts to validate jurisdiction expansion with international declarations on the topic.

to note that "freedom" is a relative capacity, i.e. only those financially powerful and technologically advanced had the choice to navigate large parcels of the world oceans, explore and exploit its natural resources. Without significant funds nor socioeconomic development, freedom was but a catch phrase—and that was the reality of several developing coastal states.

In the juncture of dissatisfaction with the pre-UNCLOS dual-division of the oceans, the likelihood of conflicts led delegates of 47 states to meet in The Hague in 1930 with the arduous task of codifying and developing international law in several fronts, not only in oceanic matters. The Conference was organized by the League of Nations, who formed a Committee of Experts for the Progressive Codification of International Law in order to represent "the main forms of civilization and the principal legal systems of the world".[12] Three topics were at the table, amongst which the codification of territorial waters, its geographical limits, and the rights and duties valid therein.

Already then, during the first half of the twentieth century, the international community had identified pressing issues connected to ocean uses, in special the degree of coastal state powers offshore and the over-exploitation of high seas fisheries, both intimately intertwined. At the time, a few suggestions made it to the headlines, such as the creation of an international bureau endowed with the task of maintaining a registry of rights beyond certain nautical limits,[13] or even the adoption of uniform rules of living resources exploitation, including the designation of reserved zones and seasonal restrictions to high seas fishing.[14] Despite such creative proposals, the Conference was unable to adopt any final binding document on that topic. The terms of the debate on maritime jurisdiction were set, yet it would take states another half a century to negotiate solutions under an encompassing international convention.

The result of inaction was that state practice with regard to territorial waters continued to vary extensively. As Henry Fraser wrote in 1926, "one country will claim three miles, another four miles, another six miles", with such diversity resulting in harmful effects to international trade and political relations. That author anticipated suggestions that would be later codified in the 1958 Geneva Conventions and, after that, in the 1982 UNCLOS, such as the proposition to establish two distinct zones under the *influence* of littoral states: the "marginal sea", where they would exercise all powers of sovereignty; and a zone beyond that, with a fixed maximum limit, "up to which a state, if it chose, might exercise jurisdiction for the three or four special purposes for which each of the said maximum limits would be provided".[15] Back at the day, however, it was taken for certain that "the nations will hardly consent to enlarging the marginal sea". So did the Experts Committee of the 1930

[12]League of Nations, *Official Journal, Special Supplement*, no. 21, 10.

[13]Proposal by Walther Schücking, 1925 Meeting of the League of Nations Committee of Experts for the Progressive Codification of International Law, as commented upon by Vicuña (1999), p. 18.

[14]Suarez (1926), p. 231.

[15]Fraser (1925), p. 457.

Conference proceed, working with a tentative draft of a 3 nm marginal sea that ultimately did not yield consensus.

Continued failure to delimit the breadth of territorial waters and the material extent of control over marine resources stirred a move by the President of the United States, which further promoted the division of the oceans. The Truman Proclamations of 1945, one on fisheries and another on the continental shelf, secured "property rights" over resources on the seabed and water column of the United States' continental shelf, and came as a model to be followed.[16] Back then, several Latin American states took the same course of action and declared jurisdiction over their contiguous seas, triggering a phenomenon that Ted McDorman named as "the great expansion of coastal state jurisdiction."[17]

Less than 30 years later, the expansion of coastal state jurisdiction was codified at the closing of the III United Nations Conference for the Law of the Sea. A most relevant factor during the negotiations were the newly politically independent African and Asian states, which held a point of view differing significantly from those of their colonial predecessors. It was clear that the developing countries of the third world, sympathetic to the political orientation of the so-called "Group of 77",[18] played an important role in UNCLOS III negotiations. Against this background, the Conference can be associated to the phenomenon of the *rise of coastal states*, having fulfilled old demands of exclusive jurisdiction over marine resources and codified jurisdictional assertions over the oceans. The next item shed light on the definition of creeping jurisdiction consist and the extent to which it has influenced the current continental shelf regime.

---

[16]U.S. Presidential Proclamations no. 2667, *Policy of the United States with Respect to the Natural Resources of the Subsoil of the Seabed and the Continental Shelf*, and no. 2668, *Policy of the United States with Respect to Coastal Fisheries in Certain Areas of the High Seas*, done at Washington, 28 September 1945, 10 FR 12303. Even though the Truman Proclamation is probably the most known episode of territorial expansion seaward, it was not the first move to advance claims to maritime areas beyond the territorial sea. Prior developments in this regard include the 1942 Treaty between the UK and Venezuela Relating to the Submarine Areas of the Gulf of Paria, which divided the seabed and the subsoil beyond respective territorial seas at the Gulf of Paria, signed at Caracas, 26 February 1942, 205 LNTS 122, and terminated on 23 July 1991. The Treaty was the first one in the world to delimit the seabed. Another example is the Argentinian Continental Shelf Decree of 1944.

[17]McDorman (1981), p. 2.

[18]The Group of 77 advocated a more radical form of the CHM principle, based on the ideology underpinning the so-called "New International Economic Order", designed to rebalance economic relations between industrialized countries of the North and poorly developed states of the South.

6.2 Definition of "Creeping Jurisdiction"

Creeping jurisdiction, for the purposes of the law of the sea,[19] is usually referred to as the practice by sovereign states of seeking to extend territorial jurisdiction over maritime spaces beyond what is permitted by international customary or treaty law. In so doing, walk a thin line between legality, when for instance adopting ampliative or restrictive interpretation of treaty provisions,[20] and illegality, via open disdain for unwanted restrictions. It would the case of a coastal state's declaration not to admit unauthorized military maneuvers by foreign warships in that state's EEZ, an interpretation that is not *prima facie* at UNCLOS and that creates much confusion up to present days. Or when states unilaterally expand jurisdiction over lengths farther away than the 200-nm zone established at UNCLOS, such as the Chinese Nine Dash-Line claim.[21]

In temporal terms, creeping jurisdiction is a relatively recent phenomenon, if one takes the long history of the law of the sea into account. This phenomenon has been analyzed in specialized literature since the first half of the twentieth century, although some authors refer to "creeping jurisdiction" only regarding coastal states' abusive behavior following the Montego Bay Convention, from 1982 onwards.[22] Others, such as Stuart Kaye, refer to that practice as having occurred "through the course of the twentieth century".[23] This work deals with criticisms to the concept that stretch back to pre-UNCLOS times and influence the main narrative in the traditional law of the sea doctrine, which sees the expansion of coastal state's power as a vicious development, equal to the enclosure and private appropriation of the oceans.

---

[19]In general, one could refer to the quest for enhanced power and authority as an inherent and essential feature of sovereign states, being that one of the reasons for the existence of international law, as a limiting tool to state expansionism in different ambits of international relations.

[20]In the view of Maria Gavouneli, the majority of claims of creeping jurisdiction "are not set in regulatory language but are rather based on construing new ways to read the provisions establishing the existing maritime zones". *See* Gavouneli (2007), p. 59. In other words, states nowadays do not unilaterally declare that a certain maritime zone is under their jurisdiction, but rather interpret the UNCLOS provisions in an expansive fashion in order to legitimate expansive claims towards the ocean. Several coastal states do so on political, rather than juridical grounds, with the final aim of restricting the intensity of foreign activities off their coasts, Brazil and its non-acceptance of unauthorized military maneuvers in the EEZ being a case in point.

[21]The Chinese Nine-Dash Line consists of a territorial claim by Chinese authorities which effectively places most of the South China Sea under Chinese jurisdiction, thus inflating uproar among its maritime neighbors. The case was brought to arbitration under Annex VII UNCLOS by the Philippines, and the arbitral award deemed the Chinese claims as excessive and inconsistent with the Convention. For more, access the final award. PCA *The South China Sea Arbitration (Philippines v. China)*, Award of 12 July 2016.

[22]Ribeiro (2013), p. 621.

[23]Kaye (2006), p. 347.

The practice of creeping jurisdiction is usually attributed to coastal states[24] and amounts to the "extension of municipal jurisdiction seaward along the seabed and from thence to the vertical column above and the souterrain below".[25] Similarly, creeping jurisdiction has been defined as the "*gradual extension* of State jurisdiction offshore", with a focus on the steadiness of jurisdictional expansionism towards the high seas.[26] In short, creeping jurisdiction would be the power unilaterally revendicated by coastal states in violation of UNCLOS legal edifice, beyond either the maritime limits established therein or the competences exercisable in each zone.

Key elements of the concept are, accordingly, the *unilaterality* of claims, and the *violation* of a valid international legal rule.[27] For that reason, specialized literature refer also to "excessive claims" on behalf of states in pre-UNCLOS times and even after the adoption of the Convention. Concerning the first element, the practice is unilateral in the sense that it consists of an action performed by one state involved in a concrete situation without the agreement of other fellow states. The phenomenon has been inserted in a broader movement of *unilateralism*, which comprise coastal states' struggle to increase real power and authority over adjacent waters offshore, in order not only to reap the economic benefits of marine resources with exclusivity, but also to keep other maritime powers (sometimes perceived as threats) away from their areas of geopolitical influence.[28]

In this sense, it could be also labeled *exclusivism*, amid plenty of others possible tags, depending on the political ideology of the analyst. This element of unilaterality, particularly when it concerns assertions older than UNCLOS, goes not without controversy and will be analyzed in the next subitem. As to the second element, to "creep on" jurisdiction is widely believed to entail the breaching of a legal norm enshrined either in customary or treaty law. Thus, the practice of creeping jurisdiction is taken by the law of the sea literature as inherently vicious and threatening to the stability of the international rule of law in oceanic affairs, to the extent of being

---

[24]In theory, states creeping on jurisdiction could be both flag states and coastal states, as both could seek to exercise extended powers over the oceans. However, there are no records of unilateral declarations by flag states asserting jurisdictional rights (such as fishing rights) within maritime zones of coastal states—when such practices happen, they are usually carried on in the shadows. Thus, for this work, precedence will be given to jurisdictional claims of coastal states.

[25]As referred by John Craven, once Chief Scientist of the United States Navy. For that reason, the practice of creeping jurisdiction is also known as "Craven's Law", in line with Burke (1970), p. 195.

[26]Kaye (2006), p. 347.

[27]The expression "creeping", to Erik Franckx, "includes the idea of *unilateral* action directed at *upsetting a legal framework* adhered to by the *majority* of other States" (emphasis added). *See* Franckx (2005), p. 136.

[28]*See* generally Kraska (2011).

referred to as "parcellation",[29] "propertization",[30] and "territorialization of the oceans" via unilateral declaration of "psycho-legal boundaries at sea".[31]

Most law of the sea scholars share two grounding premises for the viciousness of creeping jurisdiction: firstly, that *freedom of navigation* is a right that precedes all others,[32] an overriding principle,[33] the long-standing heart of the law of the sea; secondly, that coastal states are *inherently attracted* to increased power and authority[34] and, as such, doomed to always pursue enlarged jurisdiction overseas. For the literature grounded on the first premise, freedom is the core element in the law of the sea. In fact, according to David Anderson,

> freedom of the high seas are freedoms under the law. They should be viewed increasingly as no different from other fundamental rights of States under international law. [...] The particular term 'freedom' is perhaps most relevant in the context of the non-exhaustive nature of the list of freedoms of the high seas.[35]

As to the second general premise, the "old problem of creeping jurisdiction" is considered dangerous due to coastal states' "tendency to expand the reach of their regulations beyond 200 nautical miles".[36] The argument according to which states are fueled by desire for wealth and power is not novel to international relations theories. Hence, the practice of creeping on jurisdiction would be the result of an almost insatiable *temptation* to additional powers and competences over waters adjacent to the coast. As analyzed by Richard Bilder, "any coastal state extension of jurisdiction into the contiguous high seas, even if functionally limited, tends over time to expand to include more claims, until it becomes the functional equivalent of a territorial sea, in substance if not in name".[37]

The concept of creeping jurisdiction may be divided in two, according to the *nature* of the expansion, whether geographical or in regulatory powers. There have been distinctions between CJ, associated with the *geographical* enlargement seawards, and "thickening jurisdiction", an increase in the activities regulated by a coastal States within a particular maritime zone.[38] The latter would be equally old and worrisome, as coastal states' can be expected to permanently aim at asserting

---

[29]Brown (1973), p. 157.

[30]Gary Knight uses this expression in the context of discussions on the most adequate regime to deep-sea mining, so as to make a point that a system of free enterprise and minimal regulation would be best tailored for the exploitation of deep seabed minerals. In so doing, states would rely on the "propertization" of the seabed to develop a regime that would recognize property rights over seabed resources. *See* Knight (1981), p. 13.

[31]Booth (1983), p. 373.

[32]Lagoni (2003), p. 157.

[33]Becker (2005), p. 132.

[34]Gavouneli refers to coastal state's "tendency to expand seawards". *See* Gavouneli (2007), p. 59.

[35]Anderson (2006), p. 345.

[36]Türk (2012), p. 159.

[37]Bilder (1973), p. 104.

[38]Wayne (1996), p. 103.

extra rights over maritime zones under national jurisdiction by incrementing the range of activities falling under domestic regulation, without consultation and/or agreement of other states.

Besides, the phenomenon of creeping jurisdiction may be also seen as operating in two different directions: in favor of coastal states or the international community. Erik Franckx labels the latter "creeping common heritage",[39] which occurred when sovereignty over the Area, which corresponds to extremely large portions of the ocean, was forbidden to individual states by UNCLOS Art. 137 (1), on the legal status of the Area and its resources. In a rather poetical sense, it could be said that mankind has crept on jurisdiction over the deep seabed through the adoption of the common heritage principle, analyzed supra, so as to prevent the exclusive appropriation of the seabed by technically developed states.

Ex positis, one may righteously repudiate unilateral excessive claims in the law of the sea, having, nonetheless, in mind that not all jurisdictional assertions over the ocean are the same, nor can they be subsumed to the criteria above. In fact, there are some problems with the way in which literature examines the issue of creeping jurisdiction: (1) all kinds of jurisdictional assertions in confrontation with customary or treaty law are analyzed with the same negative lenses, what could lead to prejudices on coastal states' role in promoting environmental protection on the continental shelf within and beyond 200 nm; (2) jurisdictional assertions pre- and post-UNCLOS are condemned under the same standards, for being unilateral violations of existing law; (3) jurisdictional claims are seen as an insatiable and uncontrollable temptation for more territory or even as an irrational reaction against the ocean policies of state A or B—a view that fails to grasp the complexity of the practice.[40]

6.3 Reasons for Alarm?

In international law, there is radical opposition to coastal state's jurisdictional expansionism oceanward (or the *territorialization* of the seas), according to whom both creeping and thickening jurisdiction represent an immediate danger to the stability of the public order of the oceans. The layout of flag states' powers in the high seas, pursuant to UNCLOS, would be imperiled, amongst other reasons, because coastal states have increasingly challenged those powers and claimed additional rights, such as that of granting permit for foreign navy vessels to enter their EEZ, the prohibition of military exercises in the coastal state's EEZ without

[39]Franckx (2005), p. 119.

[40]During UNCLOS negotiations, there was even room for an absurd view that "Latin-American countries moved towards 200 nm territorial seas more because of the United States stubborn opposition to the 200 nm limit, than out of true national self-interest". Loring (1971), p. 446. That view falls short of a frontal insult to Latin American states' ability to determine and pursue their own strategic interests on the international stage.

consent, or the control of marine hydrographic surveying in the EEZ. In the light of the grounding premises underlined previously, alarmist law of the sea practitioners fear that the material balance of rights struck for the regimes of the EEZ and the continental shelf within and beyond 200 nm be progressively eroded to a point in which traditional freedoms of the seas become "mere exceptions to coastal state sovereignty".[41]

As early as 1956, Josef Kunz heavily criticized the so-called "doctrine and practice of the continental shelf", understood as the combination of different claims in character and substance to the seafloor, which purportedly led to a situation of confusion and abuse by coastal states. Kunz was of the opinion that unilateral proclamations of sovereignty over the seafloor and (sometimes) superjacent waters, sounded the death knell on freedom of the seas.[42] In line with that argument, the author criticized what he labeled the "triumphant upsurge of national sovereignty" against the long-established customary principle of freedom of the high seas. Kunz's view may have been defeated in the international arena, as the 1958 CSC codified coastal state jurisdiction over continental shelf resources and activities, but it has nonetheless influenced subsequent generations of international lawyers, more worried with securing navigational freedoms than building a system of fair access to natural oceanic riches. It is now imperative to examine state practice in pre- and post-UNCLOS days, in order to determine whether the expansion of coastal state's jurisdiction is as nefarious as doomed and whether there have been reasons for alarm or not.

6.3.1 Pre-UNCLOS State Practice

Such an opposition was sponsored by both developed and developing countries, who anticipated benefits from exclusive access to marine natural resources in their shore vicinities. Nonetheless, differing intensities of rejection (or of "jurisdictional crept") occurred. Whilst maritime states, such as the United States, proclaimed exclusive jurisdiction over natural resources of the seabed and subsoil of continental shelf up to a depth of 600 ft (approximately 182 m),[43] several developing coastal states went a step further and claimed jurisdiction over marine resources of the seafloor, subsoil, water column, and airspace up to 200 nm from the baselines.

The practice of Latin American states in this regard merits a detailed analysis.[44] In fact, the systematic opposition of Latin American countries to the 3 nm territorial

[41]Türk (2012), p. 161.

[42]Kunz (1958), p. 829.

[43]Harry S. Truman, Proclamation 2667—Policy of the United States with Respect to the Natural Resources of the Subsoil and Sea Bed of the Continental Shelf, September 28, 1945.

[44]Outside the Latin American scope, to quote but one example, the cod wars between the UK and Iceland, between 1958 and 1975, symbolized the battle between David and Goliath, coastal and

waters has seen no parallel in no other region of the world, with the region staging the largest organic movement to enlarge territorial jurisdiction seawards that the law of the sea had ever seen.[45] Initially, those states reacted to the 1945 Truman Proclamations and formulated claims to expand *specialized* and *functional jurisdiction* over the seas, with a few exceptional claims to full sovereignty. The rights asserted in the region were such, that the Truman Proclamation on the continental shelf appears modest along their side, as explained below.

Upon analyzing the behavior of Latin American states prior and during UNCLOS negotiations, Garcia-Amador identified two distinct phases of jurisdictional expansionism. In a moment, some states sought exclusive access to living and non-living resources, and paid little attention to delimiting the distance up to which exclusive jurisdiction would be exercised. They affirmed jurisdiction to legislate and control overfishing beyond the territorial sea adjacent to their shores. To start with, the Declaration of Mexico on the Continental Shelf of 1945, claimed the right to take unilateral measures to conserve the *living resources* in zones of the high seas.[46] Following Mexico, other countries claimed exclusive protective jurisdiction over natural resources outside the territorial sea.[47] Argentina claimed the "Epicontinental Sea" in 1946[48] and Honduras passed instruments that placed both continental shelf and water column above under national jurisdiction in 1950 and 1951.[49]

A second phase was characterized by far-reaching assertions over a clearly defined 200-nm adjacent zone. In this context, postulations by Chile (1947)[50] and Peru (1947), the latter having proclaimed "national sovereignty and jurisdiction" over submarine areas whatever their depth or extension, as well as over the adjacent waters to the extent necessary "to preserve, protect, maintain, and utilize natural

maritime states. Showed how relevant for a nation's interests exclusive fishing rights were. Iceland were successful in extending the EEZ to a breadth that is currently internationally accepted. In 1958, Iceland unilaterally extended their EEZ to 12 nm, in order to suppress the overexploitation of their fisheries. The breadth of the economic zone was then pushed to 50 nm seaward in 1972 and to 200 nm in 1976. This classical example of creeping on jurisdiction has certainly upset the United Kingdom and damaged English and Scotch ports, fishermen, and shore-based laborers. However, the absence of exclusive rights for the coastal state (Iceland) would have meant limited management maneuver room in terms of exploitation rhythm and conservation measures, as well as the unilateral harvesting of natural resources close to the shore by well-equipped fishing fleets from economically advanced countries. See Icelandic Ministry of Fisheries and Agriculture, Available at: https://www.government.is/topics/business-and-industry/fisheries-in-iceland/history-of-fisheries/. Accessed 10 April 2020.

[45]*See* generally Garcia-Amador (1974).

[46]Declaration of the President of Mexico claiming the resources of the Continental Shelf off the coasts of the Republic. El Universal, Mexico City, 30 October 1945.

[47]Garcia-Amador (1974), p. 34.

[48]Republic of Argentina, Decree no 14.708, 11 October 1946, Arts. 1 and 2.

[49]Republic of Honduras, Legislative Decree No. 25, 17 January 1951.

[50]Declaration by the President of the Republic of Chile, regarding Chilean Territorial Claims, President Gabriel Videla, 23 June 1947.

resources and wealth".[51] The Chilean and Peruvian claims were unisonous in stating that both declarations did not affect freedom of navigation on the high seas. Following those proclamations, it was Costa Rica's turn to assert "the protection and control of the state" over a 200-nm zone offshore.[52] Similarly, the El Salvadorian Constitution of 1950, Art. 7, prescribes the country's territory as including "the adjacent sea within a distance of 200 marine miles measured from the line of lowest tide, and it embraces the air space above, the subsoil, and the corresponding continental shelf".[53] Those were individual actions taken without open consultation with neighboring states.

The first concerted effort at the international level was headed by Chile, Ecuador and Peru, and resulted in the 1952 Declarations of Santiago.[54] In the first Declaration on fishing issues in the South Pacific, all parties showed consternation with the "lack of protection which endangers the conservation of fishing resources" and the "serious threat of exhaustion" of those resources offshore. By acknowledging an *urge* to exercise prescriptive and enforcement jurisdiction relating to the conservation of fisheries, the parties to the Declaration set off to "ensure a better yield for the benefit of national food supplies and economics".[55] Impressively, that was an inchoate attempt to exercise exclusive economic jurisdiction over a marine resource sited in a blurred zone, both within and beyond national jurisdiction, which is the case of migratory fish stocks, supported by arguments of an environmental background.

The Second Declaration, this time on the maritime zone, expressly deemed the traditional length of territorial seas and contiguous zones *inadequate* for the purposes of "conservation, development and exploitation" of marine natural resources, due to both geographical and biological factors.[56] As a consequence, all parties proclaimed that each possess "exclusive *sovereignty* and *jurisdiction* over the sea along the coasts of their respective countries to a *minimum* distance of 200 nautical miles from these coasts". Such exclusive sovereignty and jurisdiction were not limited to the water column, but encompassed the seabed and subsoil thereof.[57]

The Santiago Declarations represent an outstanding effort of international cooperation with the objective to safeguard fisheries and subsoil minerals for the peoples and interests of the mobilized countries. They have reverberated in the region and enthused waves of territorial seas declarations that aimed at re-balancing rights and duties in a new phase of the law of the sea. That does not mean, however, that those

[51] Peruvian Supreme Decree no 781, 11 August 1947.

[52] Costa Rican Decree-Law no 116, 27 July 1954.

[53] Constitution of the Republic of El Salvador, Art. 7, 1950.

[54] Joint Declaration Concerning Fishing Problems in the South Pacific, Santiago, 18 August 1952, UNTS 1006, 318–319.

[55] *Id.*

[56] A geographical motive would be the proximity of the traditional limits to the littoral of coastal states, whereas a biological one was the migratory nature of several fish species. *See* Declaration on the Maritime Zone, Santiago, 18 August 1952, UNTS 1006, 326–327.

[57] *Id.* item III.

instruments have shown contempt for traditional principles. In fact, esteem for principle of freedom of navigation featured each of the Declarations, which were to be interpreted without prejudice to the innocent passage for ships of all nations. As such, the signatory states asserted jurisdiction over a specific economic aspect of the 200-nm zone, without intention to restrict navigation, nor innocent passage therein. The documents represented a "controlled detonation" of previous customary rules on the high seas and gave a clear sign of change in the political dynamics in the international stage.

Overall, the purposes of the first 200-nm claims were not to exert *sovereignty* in all its capacity over the stretched zone—despite the use of phrases such as "exclusive sovereignty" in some of the afore analyzed declarations. An encompassing and detailed interpretation of the philosophy and interests underpinning the abovementioned instruments shows that the objective has been *to affirm exclusive rights for specific purposes*—a special economic and environmental jurisdiction over a wider maritime zone. In fact, none of those claims expressly assail freedom of navigation. They were excessive in relation to customary norms of the time, but Latin American states lent the claims a legal clothing, in a sign of appreciation to the internationally recognized navigational rights. The declarations reassured respect for navigational freedom, as coastal states understood the relevance of such principle to the economic development via international trade, and to healthy interstate relations. What they attempted to limit were the economic freedoms, represented by unlimited access to marine living and non-living resources beyond the 3 nm territorial sea, thereby preventing, on the one hand, the perpetuation of an unequal economic order, and, on the other, the occurrence of the "tragedy of the commons".[58]

In this context, equally important is the 1970 Montevideo Declaration on the Law of the Sea,[59] signed by nine Latin American states in a combined effort to promote acceptance of their 200-nm claims by creating a *regional consensus* on the matter.[60] The document perceives an international law in progressive evolution, which admits the *legitimate priority of littoral states* to benefit from maritime resources, based on geographic, economic and social ties that bind sea, land and the men who inhabit it. In order to justify the "crept" on jurisdiction, state parties resorted to a vibrant economic and moral reasoning. Economically, the jurisdictional expansion is viewed as paramount to increasing life standards of their peoples. Morally, rules on sovereignty and jurisdiction over the sea are understood to be fair solely when mindful of special economic and social needs of less developed states.[61] Besides, enhanced jurisdiction would also advantage humankind, because of the resulting rational use

[58] *See* generally Hardin (1968).

[59] The Declaration of Montevideo on the Law of the Sea, 9 ILM, no. 5, ASIL, 1081–1083, 8 May 1970.

[60] Argentina, Brazil, Chile, Ecuador, El Salvador, Nicaragua, Panama, Peru, and Uruguay signed the Montevideo Declaration on the Law of the Sea.

[61] 1970 Declaration of Montevideo on the Law of the Sea, 1082.

of resources and augmented economic development, particularly in light of hazards posed by abusive extractive practices and ecological disturbances.

Regarding substance, the Montevideo Declaration contains provisions asserting a variety of rights to coastal states over the 200-nm zone. Firstly, a provision affirming power to enforce and to exercise *control* over natural resources of the adjacent seas. Secondly, a paragraph on jurisdiction to legislate and to *enact regulatory measures* to achieve the goals of conservation and prudent use of resources. Thirdly, the right to delimit their maritime sovereignty and jurisdiction in conformity with their own geographic and geological characteristics. Finally, the right to explore, conserve and exploit living and non-living resources of the water column and continental shelf. Despite the jurisdictional enlargement effected in the Declaration, there are not enough elements to permit the conclusion that countries such as Argentina, Brazil or Chile interpreted the Montevideo Declaration in order to restrict freedom of navigation of other states to that enjoyed within the territorial sea, i.e. right of innocent passage. In fact, the exercise of such expanded jurisdiction was to be "without prejudice to freedom of navigation by ships and overflying by aircraft of any flag".[62] Similarly to the 1952 Santiago Declaration, the Montevideo Declaration consisted not of a projection of full territoriality over the oceans, but an attempt to exercise exclusive jurisdiction over some aspects of seas adjacent to the coast.

A bolder move was undertaken by some Latin American countries that unilaterally declared a *200-nm territorial sea*, possibly encouraged by the sub-regional concertation on the topic of territorial waters. It was the case of Ecuador,[63] Panama,[64] and Brazil,[65] who established a territorial sea *strictu sensu*, i.e. for all legal purposes. In the Brazilian case, the state understood that the special interest of coastal states in maintaining productivity of living resources in maritime zones adjacent to their coasts could only be effectively protected by exercising sovereignty, and that each state had competence to delimit its territorial sea, particularly in the absence of an internationally agreed treaty on maritime jurisdiction. Thus, in the deceased Decree-Law, the Brazilian state was given exclusive right to regulate fisheries and activities related to marine research and exploration, both in the water column and the continental shelf.[66] Those were unquestionably excessive claims, due to the intention to regulate every possible use of the 200-nm belt adjacent to the coast, not just a specific economic or ecologic use, and the potential legal uncertainties for international navigation and trade.

Other types of 200-nm claims were headed by Nicaragua, Argentina, Uruguay, and Costa Rica, albeit with little in common between each other. Nicaragua claimed solely a 200-nm "national fishing zone",[67] whereas Argentina asserted sovereignty

---

[62]*Id.* 1083.

[63]Republic of Ecuador, Decree no 1542, 10 November 1966.

[64]Republic of Panama, Act no 31, 02 February 1967.

[65]Federative Republic of Brazil, Decree-Law no 1.098, 25 March 1970.

[66]Art. 4 of the repealed Decree-Law no 1.098, 1970.

[67]Executive Decree no 1-L, 05 April 1965.

in the sea adjacent to its territory, safeguarding, nonetheless, freedom of navigation and overflight.[68] Similarly, Uruguay also extended sovereignty over the 200-nm limit, respecting free navigation and overflight.[69] Slightly different was the move by Costa Rica, which proclaimed a *patrimonial sea* with a breadth of 200 nm, measured from the low tide mark along its coast, which would encompass (but stretch further seawards) the territorial sea.[70] That sea was also explicitly not intended to impair freedom of navigation nor overflight.

The concept of patrimonial sea, which gives a clear hint to the prevailing economic aspect in those waters, was brought by Costa Rica to the sub-regional level. Thus, in 1972, eleven Caribbean states[71] signed the Declaration of Santo Domingo, the result of unified efforts to adopt a common maritime policy to the region and consensus on the issue of maritime sovereignty and jurisdiction.[72] The signatories expressly recognized that the sovereignty of a state is exercisable solely in territorial waters, which would have a breadth of up to 12 nm. The Declaration already used the phrase "sovereign rights" to refer to rights over natural resources within the "patrimonial sea", adjacent to the territorial sea. In the patrimonial sea, some freedoms would not be as intense as in the high seas, a case in point being the conduct of marine scientific research by other states. Coastal states, in line with the 1972 Declaration, would have the duty to promote and the right to regulate scientific research within the patrimonial sea. Finally, the document underscored the prevalence of an international agreement over national declarations by coastal states, in the absence of which signatory parties were entitled to claim a 200-nm zone consisting of territorial and patrimonial sea.[73] As usual in previous initiatives of the kind, ships and aircrafts were acknowledged freedom of navigation and overflight within the patrimonial sea.

The plurality of instruments supra evidences a concerted opposition by Latin American states to the traditional dual-division of the ocean into territorial sea and high seas. While the earlier Latin American claims of the 1940s and 1950s were vague,[74] the newer claims were sturdier in favor of a 200-nm special zone.[75] A marking feature of those assertions was their fundament on the right of the coastal

---

[68]Act no 17.094, 29 December 1966.

[69]Act no 13.833, 29 December 1969.

[70]Decree no 2204-RE, 10 February 1970, Art. 3.

[71]The 1972 Declaration of Santo Domingo was signed by Colombia, Costa Rica, Guatemala, Haiti, Honduras, Mexico, Nicaragua, Dominican Republic, Trinidad and Tobago, and Venezuela.

[72]Declaration of Santo Domingo. Specialized Conference of Caribbean Countries Concerning the Problems of the Sea. AJIL 66 (5), 1972, 918–920.

[73]*Id.* 919.

[74]To Ian Townsend-Gault, in 1958, "state practice with respect to claims to offshore jurisdiction beyond the limits of the territorial sea did not really display the requisite degree of consistency and uniformity required for the identification of a rule of customary international law". One claim was widely shared though: that coastal states' rights seaward extend beyond the then applicable 3-nm limit. *See* Townsend-Gault (2014), p. 71.

[75]Garcia-Amador (1974), p. 45.

state to unilaterally determine the breadth of the zone or zones to which the extension of jurisdiction applies. Some of the main aspects standing out of the pre-UNCLOS Latin American contribution were, on the one hand, coastal states' central interest in exploiting marine resources in larger areas for the purposes of domestic socioeconomic development, and, on the other, the subsequent decision to push jurisdiction seawards to the amount necessary for coastal states to achieve those objectives.[76]

While it would be inappropriate to refer to a united Latin American stance, it would not be entirely wrong to refer to a *systematic regional disapproval* of the classical allocation of jurisdictional rights over the oceans. According to Garcia-Amador, the trend to "move away from the legal regime which has traditionally governed the territorial sea reflects a concept of 'plurality of regimes' for that area."[77] A broader collective signal was being issued, one grounded on the idea that littoral states should be entitled to exercise exclusive jurisdiction over renewable and nonrenewable natural resources in the waters, seabed, and subsoil of maritime spaces adjacent to the coast. Such expansionist message was, thus, not interrupted by UNCLOS I and II, which committed the gravest sin of not hearing the voices of newly independent states.[78] In fact, that message was to impregnate negotiations during the Third Conference.

6.3.2 Post-UNCLOS State Practice

One of the goals of several states upon the signature of UNCLOS was the disruption of burgeoning unilateral assertions of jurisdiction over the high seas,[79] thereby halting the process of "territorial expansion of coastal States sovereignty, sovereign rights and jurisdiction" seaward.[80] There was a sense of need to impose strict limits on the extent of state jurisdiction over maritime areas.[81] Particularly with regard to the EEZ and the continental shelf, negotiating parties sought to make sure that those are not zones *of* national jurisdiction, but zones *with some degree of* national jurisdiction,[82] the essence of which lies in the substantive balance between rights of coastal States and rights of the international community. A balance that had been struck not by repressing coastal states' territorialist demands prior to UNCLOS, but by incorporating several of those demands in a new equilibrium between state sovereignty and freedom of the seas.

---

[76]*Id.* 50.

[77]*Id.* 46.

[78]Between 1943 and 1969, sixty-nine countries declared independence. Of those, fifty-five were coastal states.

[79]Knauss (1985), p. 209.

[80]Türk (2012), p. 159.

[81]Townsend-Gault (2014), p. 84.

[82]Türk (2012), p. 161.

Despite the Convention's restriction of coastal state claims to a few competences, some authors alert to the still reining *temptation* to claim excessive rights in the EEZ and continental shelf which are not present in the Convention.[83] The adoption of UNCLOS was, thus, not enough to suppress unwarranted enhanced jurisdiction of coastal states seaward, a possible reason for which could be the *insufficient precision* and deliberate vagueness of UNCLOS' provisions, which have been providing a "springboard for coastal States to expand the prerogatives given to them over parts of the sea".[84] In this sense, Selden's *mare clausum* would continue to haunt the law of the sea. Whether motivated by the plastic wording of the Convention or by pursuing domestic interests, such as security and economic growth, state practice post-UNCLOS includes some examples of jurisdictional assertion over natural resources beyond the 200-nm limit.[85] The most symbolic illustrations of current-day creeping jurisdiction will be categorized below according to the maritime space they take place, whether the EEZ or the continental shelf.[86]

In general, there have been criticisms against the obstacles posed by the conception of the EEZ in terms of limiting the common heritage principle and emptying freedom of scientific research in the high seas. In addition, emphasis has also been laid on three common situations in which the EEZ and the Exclusive Fisheries Zone (EFZ) has been extended beyond the 200-nm limit, in a kind of creeping jurisdiction by coastal states: (i) extension of certain coastal state rights and interests related to *fisheries*; (ii) extension of the coastal state right of intervention in cases of maritime casualties and the liability regime for *oil pollution* damage; and (iii) extension resulting from retreat of baselines due to sea level change or to man-made intervention in the shore, in the case of pier and port constructions.[87]

Concerning the first criticism, and the role of creeping jurisdiction in the conformation of the new architecture of the law of the sea, it certainly is intriguing to face a critique by Milenko Kreca to the creation of that zone. According to the author, the emergence of the EEZ harmed the principle of common heritage of mankind by emptying (on practical terms) the relevance of the principle to the international seabed area, since most valuable living and non-living resources would come under national jurisdiction upon the materialization of the zone.[88] In a sense, the creation of the EEZ does shrink the size of the Area. However, the argument as a whole is difficult to defend. Firstly, because the main causative agent of such

---

[83]Oxman (2007), p. 830.

[84]Kreca (2002), p. 1210.

[85]For more on the "creeping unilateralism beyond the 200-nm limit", *see* Scovazzi (2000), p. 133.

[86]Recently, there have been records of coastal states' claims to straight baselines in cases where normal baselines could apply, a situation which resembles a jurisdiction crept and may amount to a potential breach of UNCLOS. The most notable cases are Japan—protested by South Korea and China; and Myanmar—protested by Bangladesh. It should be noted upfront that such cases of straight baselines are not the crux of this work and have not, for that reason, been scrutinized here in detail.

[87]Kwiatkowska (1991), p. 167.

[88]Kreca (2002), p. 1213.

reduction is the continental shelf regime, which regulates the seafloor and had been in place way before the emergence of the EEZ, since the Truman Proclamations. Secondly, the regime for the Area does not relate to living resources, but solely to non-living ones. And finally, the deep seabed beyond 200 nm is likely have most of deep-sea minerals.[89] Therefore, in our view, it is rather unlikely that the creation of the EEZ affected the common heritage principle (both in theory and practice) in a significant way.[90]

Scholars have also expressed uneasiness with undue restrictions to scientific research in maritime zones under coastal state jurisdiction, which renders the planning and execution of research projects therein more problematic and expensive.[91] The practice of creeping jurisdiction would be, thus, especially nefarious with regard to scientific projects aiming at enhanced knowledge of the world oceans. In the opinion of Helmut Türk, "the domestic legislation of certain States does not reflect the balance achieved with respect to marine scientific research between the interests of coastal and other States in UNCLOS".[92] The problem with this argument is that it equates interests of researched and researching states, and assumes all scientific research conducted in other countries' EEZ would be pure and unrelated to commercial intents, but the interests at stake are not the same. The bulk of scientific research conducted worldwide is commercially-oriented and it is natural that coastal states interpret the Convention so as to shield themselves against foreign surveys which aim at assessing the resource potential within those coastal states' maritime zones. If it were not for some restriction on researching rights, in commercially-oriented investigations, the law of the sea would have perpetuated the unfair pattern of colonial spoliation in place in many regions of the world at least until 1970s, by further guaranteeing privileged knowledge of the seabed to technically advanced states.[93]

---

[89]Apart from the Pacific Ocean, where deep-sea minerals abound within EEZ of island states, the remaining mineral deposits occur beyond national jurisdictions. *See* German Marine Research Consortium, *Resource Assessment of Marine Mineral Deposits*, online. Available at: http://www.deutsche-meeresforschung.de/en/sg_mineral_resources. Accessed 10 April 2020.

[90]That meant a much stronger blow to the common heritage principle was the adoption of the 1994 Implementing Agreement, which was crafted to satisfy demands and needs of a few developed countries, particularly the United States. The instrument made the principle more flexible than its original design, without having resulted in the adherence by the United States to UNCLOS, nor to the deep-sea mining regime. For a similar view, *see* Anand (2004), p. 196.

[91]Türk (2012), p. 163.

[92]*Id.* 163.

[93]To some authors, the colonial nature of International Law is still there a key feature in the discipline. It is the case of scholars affiliated to the so-called Third World Approaches to International Law (TWAIL), such as Anthony Anghie, Balakrishnan Rajagopal, B.S. Chimni, R.P. Anand, G. Galindo, amongst others. When it comes to the law of the sea, it is inevitable to attach the uses of the oceans to the traditional unequal distribution of world riches. Thus, the new law of sea is usually connected to the New International Economic Order (NIEO), which aimed at surpassing such inequality and granting by legal terms more access to world's riches, in which the rights and duties of *all* the actors are fully protected. On the NIEO, *see* generally Makarczyk (1988).

In general, the main "villains" that continued to creep on (or thicken) jurisdiction after the signature of UNCLOS are the following. Firstly, Chile and its policy of *mar presencial* advanced in 1990,[94] which would mean in practice the affirmation of undue rights far beyond the 200-nm zone, thereby posing a threat to the careful balance struck at UNCLOS. Such a view could not have been more distant from reality, as the *mar presencial* is merely a space of special interest to Chile, due to the economic and security activities that may play out within the zone. It is no claim to exclusive jurisdiction, but a geopolitical (or *oceanopolítico*, in Spanish) concept, which sought to foster efforts against predatory fishing by foreign fleets in the waters adjacent to the Chilean EEZ. The concept, crafted by the Admiral of the Chilean Navy, Jorge Martínez Busch,[95] in a time prior to the 1995 UNFSA,[96] intended to supplement UNCLOS' serious deficiencies in surmounting abusive extraction of straddling and highly migratory fish species. Interestingly, the notion of "presential sea" is at the roots of the year-long political and legal battle between Chile and the European Union regarding the exploitation of swordfish stocks in the South-Eastern Pacific Ocean.[97]

Another excessive claimant was Canada, a developed state that passed municipal legislation to conserve fish stock in the Grand Banks of the coast of Newfoundland—the Canadian Coastal Fisheries Protection Act, amended in 1994. The main problem was that the statute, after the amendment, asserted jurisdiction over specific parts of the Grand Banks, known as "nose" and "tail", which lie beyond the 200-nm limit. Enforcement of the abovementioned legislation resulted in the boarding and seizure of the Spanish fishing vessel *Estai* approximately 245 nm off the Canadian coast, i.e. beyond the Canadian EEZ. According to Canada, the newly reformed legislation extended the area of application of the Act in order to include the Regulatory Area of the Northwest Atlantic Fisheries Organization (NAFO).[98] The case, also known as the "Turbot war", was brought by Spain to the ICJ, which in its judgment of 4 December 1998 decided that it had no jurisdiction to hear the case.

---

[94]For further details on the *mar presencial, see* generally Vicuña (1993).

[95]The concept of *mar presencial* was presented in a lecture at Viñas del Mar on 4 May 1990. *See* Yturriaga (1990), p. 228.

[96]Agreement for the Implementation of the Provisions of the United Nations Convention on the Law of the Sea of 10 December 1982 relating to the Conservation and Management of Straddling Fish Stocks and Highly Migratory Fish Stocks, UNTS 2167, New York, 4 August 1995.

[97]*Case Concerning the Conservation and Sustainable Exploitation of Swordfish Stocks in the South-Eastern Pacific Ocean* (Chile/European Community), International Tribunal for the Law of the Sea, 15 March 2001.

[98]Concerning the admission of the case before the ICJ, Canada stated that the Court had compulsory jurisdiction "over all disputes other than disputes arising out of or concerning conservation and management measures taken by Canada with respect to vessels fishing in the [Northwest Atlantic Fisheries Organization's] Regulatory Area and the enforcement of such measures". That had been the reservation made by Canada on 10 May 1994, excluding the Court's jurisdiction. The Canadian delegation argued that the dispute referred to in the Spanish Application concerned matters covered by the reservation, and this thesis was ultimately adopted by the Bench.

On the multilateral level, coastal states have engaged in claims that equally restrict access by other states to living resources beyond the 200 nm limit. Frankcx identifies two particular situations on this regard. Firstly, the creation of "pockets of high seas", surrounded by the maritime zones of coastal states. For instance, the "Donut hole" in the Bering Sea, the Peanut hole in the Sea of Okhotsk, and the Loophole in the Barents Sea. In all "holes", the relevant coastal states have reached arrangements to settle the dispute. Secondly, the signature of agreements on straddling and highly migratory fish stock by a larger number of states that expressly place additional competences on coastal states.

A case in point is the "Galapagos Agreement" concluded between Chile, Colombia, Ecuador and Peru, aiming at the protection and conservation of high seas fisheries of the Southeast Pacific Ocean.[99] The basis for that agreement was the 1952 Santiago Declaration, which recognized the coastal state's obligation to prevent excessive exploitation of natural resources even "outside the reach of their national jurisdiction". The rationale behind the Agreement is that:

> The uncontrolled exploitation of living marine resources in high seas areas adjacent to zones under national jurisdiction represents a threat to the conservation and sustainable use of said resources, as well as to fish populations dependent on or associated with them, and it may undermine the effectiveness of measures adopted by the coastal States with respect to the same species, within their 200-mile zones.[100]

There have also been pledges that the 1995 UNFSA has crept on jurisdiction of the high seas by allocating extra powers to coastal states, namely with respect to straddling and highly migratory fish populations. Such powers were not in accordance with UNCLOS provision on the issue.[101] Besides, for some scholars, the adoption of the 2001 Convention on the Protection of the Underwater Cultural Heritage[102] would have further confirmed the continuous "territorial expansion" of coastal states by granting them the right to prohibit or authorize any activity on underwater cultural heritage located on its EEZ or continental shelf.[103] The fact such a right is nowhere present at UNCLOS worries parcel of the international legal scholarship.[104]

---

[99]2000 Framework Agreement for the Conservation of the Living Marine Resources of the High Seas of the South Pacific. The Agreement is not in force.

[100]Galapagos Agreement, 2000, Preamble.

[101]*See* Zumwalt (1997), p. 35.

[102]Convention on the Protection of the Underwater Cultural Heritage, UNTS 2562, signed in Paris, 2 November 2001. Brazil is not a party to the Convention.

[103]Art. 2 (2) of the 2001 UNESCO Convention, on Protection of underwater cultural heritage in the exclusive economic zone and on the continental shelf.

[104]The alarm had already been sounded by Barbara Kwiatkowska, according to whom there were several risks stemming from creeping jurisdiction over underwater cultural and archaeological heritage found on the coastal State's continental shelf within and beyond 200 nm. Claims made by Cape Verde, Australia, Ireland, Spain, Norway and the Seychelles were a clear confrontation with UNCLOS Art. 303 (2). According to this provision, removal of archaeological objects located on a coastal State's contiguous zone without approval by the affected State would amount to a

Finally, the latest episode of creeping jurisdiction on the EEZ was performed by developed states, in which Portugal, Spain and France, following the *Prestige* incident, took unilateral action in order to ban single-hull oil tankers from entering their EEZs. Those are certainly some of the most discussed measures in the recent history of the law of the sea, and it escapes the aim this book to provide a thorough description of the incident's minutiae.[105] In short, the single-hulled tanker *Prestige* sent a distress call offshore the region of Galicia, Spain, carrying 77,000 metric tons of heavy fuel oil. Spanish authorities denied refuge to the tanker, who was towed away to some 130 miles off the Spanish coast, where it broke apart and sank, causing disastrous harm to peoples, businesses and the marine environment of the countries by the Bay of Biscay. The decision to ban old single-hull tankers was faced with opposition by international shipping associations and parcel of academia.[106]

The primary consequence of that oil slick was the adoption of the regional Málaga Agreement in 2002, containing preventive measures of a "not in my backyard" nature. The affected states banned single-hull tankers over 15 years-old and claimed the right to escort out from their respective EEZs all vessels transporting hydrocarbons that did not abide by international rules, including ships in transit.[107] Enforcement of those prescriptions was ruthless,[108] having met opposition both of the international community, due to its inconsistency with UNCLOS, and international legal scholars,[109] to whom the decision would not lead to improved environmental protection.[110]

With regard to excessive jurisdictional assertions to the *continental shelf*, risks presented by the "territorial temptation" are apparently manifold and stem from a variety of claims. Barbara Kwiatkowska alerted against the potential "erosion of UNCLOS' balanced system", should the creeping of jurisdiction over the high seas prevail.[111] In particular, that delicate balance was put at stake the moment coastal states decided to claim rights over the *territory* of the continental margin, instead of

breach of laws and regulations referred to in the part of the Convention that deals with the contiguous zone. Those states claimed to have jurisdiction to decide also on heritage found on the continental shelf, i.e. beyond 24 nm. See generally Kwiatkowska (1991).

[105]A detailed account of the *Prestige* incident can be read at Nordquist (2007).

[106]Galiano (2003), p. 113.

[107]*See* Frank (2005), p. 9.

[108]According to the Lloyd's List (05 June 2003, p. 1), in the six months following the *Prestige* accident a total of 81 ships were expelled from the French and Spanish EEZs.

[109]For Galiano, the ban would hardly represent a major advance in tackling oil spills. In fact, it would not be as effective as better inspection and maintenance would. Apart from that, there were also criticisms to the unilateral banning of single-hull tankers without previous consultation before the International Maritime Organization (IMO), since navigation-related measures beyond 12 nm must be grounded on scientific and technical evidence and, above all, approved by the IMO Plenary body. *See* Galiano (2003), p. 123.

[110]Concerning the negative repercussion of the measure, *see* Losa et al. (2003), p. 52.

[111]Kwiatkowska (1991), p. 163.

the natural resources therein.[112] Moreover, Kwiatkowska points out to claims by developing states to "*full and exclusive* sovereign rights" over all continental shelf resources, such as India, Mauritius, Pakistan, Seychelles, and Guyana, and worry that such phrase could empower an ampliative interpretation that would, in its turn, define the continental shelf as territory of those states—an understanding hardly in accordance with UNCLOS.

Another risk would be illustrated by jurisdictional assertions over all types of artificial islands, installations, and structures, without exception, whatever their nature or purpose.[113] The deployment of military installations and devices on the continental shelf would, thus, be subject to prior coastal state consent, a move that represents a stark drawback against powerful military navies worldwide. In this regard, Brazil assumed a leading role in seeking the expansion of coastal state powers over the maritime zones under national jurisdiction. For that reason, the country is labelled by Kwiatkowska as *leader of the territorialists* since the early 1970s, when it placed military activities on its EEZ and continental shelf under a previous requirement of consent.[114] The territorialist approach should raise, thus, concern as to the possibility of "further proliferation of such a practice".[115]

Brazil struck once again, following the 1988 United Nations Convention against Illicit Traffic in Narcotic Drugs and Psychotropic Substances,[116] when it argued that *permission* should be requested not only to the flag state but also *to the coastal state*, in order for other states to take measures under Art. 17 (on the repression of illicit traffic by sea) against a foreign ship assumed of illegal trafficking drugs in the EEZ of the coastal state.[117] Brazil made a declaration to this effect, in relation to Art. 17 (11), and faced staunch objection by member states of the European Community, who cried that the Brazilian declaration would go further than the rights accorded to

---

[112]*Id.* 161.

[113]Item V, *Brazilian Declaration upon Signature of the UNCLOS*, Montego Bay, 10 December 1982.

[114]The Brazilian Government understands that the provisions of the Convention *do not authorize other States to carry out in the exclusive economic zone military exercises or maneuvers*, in particular those that imply the use of weapons or explosives, without the consent of the coastal State. Item IV, *Brazilian Declaration upon Signature of the UNCLOS*, Montego Bay, 10 December 1982.

[115]Kwiatkowska (1991), p. 162.

[116]United Nations Convention against Illicit Traffic in Narcotic Drugs and Psychotropic Substances, UNTS 1582, 95, Vienna, 20 December 1988.

[117]Brazil staged yet another "jurisdictional crept", regarding freedom of overflight above the EEZ and the continental shelf, an instance of pressure endangering this accommodation. The country requested the International Civil Aviation Organization (ICAO) to subject overflight above the EEZ and the CS to the same conditions as those applicable not to the high seas, but to land territory and the territorial sea. The proposal was rejected by ICAO as flagrantly contradicting UNCLOS, which allows high seas overflight freedom for air navigation over the EEZ and the CS, Arts. 58 (1) and 78. *See* ICAO Doc LC/26-WP/5-1, 4 February 1987, 26.

coastal states by international law.[118] Finally, an example of inconsistency with UNCLOS could be seen in claims by India, Pakistan, Mauritius and Seychelles to specific areas within their EEZs and the continental shelves, where these states may take measures regarding *nearly all activities* that are subject to their jurisdiction and control within these spaces.[119]

Thus far, this book has outlined powerful critiques both on coastal states' insurrection against the pre-UNCLOS dual-division of the oceans and coastal states' challenging of the jurisdiction edifice erected after 1982. The lines below are dedicated to highlighting some of the main theses that lie implicit or explicit from scholarly reactions contrary to all kinds of jurisdictional crept, in particular the assertion of prescriptive and enforcement jurisdiction on environmental grounds. This time, from a coastal state's and an environmental perspective.

6.4 Coastal States' Jurisdictional Expansion from an Environmental Perspective: Creeping Jurisdiction or Valid Attempt at Raising the Bar?

The abovementioned critiques on the practice of creeping jurisdiction, or on the "territorial temptation" of coastal states in the law of the sea, allow for a few conclusions on the dominant theses in specialized literature. Firstly, most analyses give priority to the principle of freedom of navigation, the unofficial overriding principle, and to the detriment of territorial sovereignty and environmental conservation. Secondly, the practice of creeping jurisdiction is depicted as consisting of excessive unilateral claims of jurisdiction seaward held both *before and after* the adoption of UNCLOS, without distinguishing between time-periods. In other words, to creep on jurisdiction is considered illegal and undesired in every scenario and, therefore, damaging to the maintenance of peace and order in the world oceans.[120] The early claims have violated customary law and newer claims have infringed UNCLOS provisions.

Thirdly, there is widespread concern that an excessive jurisdictional assertion may open the gate for many assertions more, thereby stimulating the indefinite territorialization of the seas and triggering a downward spiral adverse to the stability of the world's oceans. Finally, acts of creeping jurisdiction disguised with an environmental clothing may be a sort of *Trojan horse* that could implode the carefully sewed balance between territorial sovereignty and freedom of navigation within UNCLOS. Hence, bold assertions of environmental jurisdiction over the EEZ and continental shelf are to be fought against to the hilt.

[118]For the Brazilian Declaration, see *Multilateral Treaties Deposited with the Secretary-General*, UN Doc. ST/LEG/SER.E/8 (New York: United Nations, 1990), 283–284.

[119]Kwiatkowska (1991), p. 164.

[120]*See*, for instance, Burke (1970).

Those assertions merit some questioning, particularly the last one, concerning the allegedly cloaked and deceiving nature of jurisdictional claims aimed at preserving and protecting the marine environment. With the intention of offering a plausible counterpoint to those claims and advancing the study of environmental jurisdiction in the law of the sea, this work puts forwards the following theses: the wholesale use of the phrase "creeping jurisdiction" to refer to every jurisdictional assertion over the sea should be avoided by international lawyers; secondly, the assertion of enlarged jurisdiction seawards, if done on a systematic and collective basis, may amount to a call for change in the international rules; thirdly, while the exercise of increased environmental powers in areas within national jurisdiction may be interpreted as inconsistent with UNCLOS, such a practice should not be dismissed as illegal *a priori*. Those theses are further detailed below.

6.4.1 Avoiding the Wholesale Use of the Phrase "Creeping Jurisdiction"

To being with, the widespread phrase known as "creeping jurisdiction" does not neutrally depict the expansionist claims staged by coastal states *prior* to the adoption of UNCLOS. That concept is value-laden and describes an inherently wicked practice, which may not be the case with the systematic opposition to the *ordre publique* of the oceans before 1982. Anne Peters, in a sharp critique against the once fashionable alarmism amongst internationalists as to the "fragmentation" of international law, pondered that

> the term 'fragmentation' is inevitably descriptive-evaluative, and thus loaded. 'Fragmentation' has a predominantly negative connotation, it is a pejorative term (rather than diversity, specialization, or pluralism). Finally, it is a term which describes not only a legal process in the real world of law but has also been a label for the accompanying discourse (mostly among academics, less among judges, and even less among political law-making actors).[121]

Replace the phrase "fragmentation" by "creeping jurisdiction" and the resulting text makes as much sense as the original one. In fact, the notion of creeping jurisdiction is descriptive-evaluative, assuming a rather negative connotation. It is a term that describes not just a behavior by coastal states, but has been used as a label to raise awareness to an allegedly disorder-creating movement in the law of the sea—a critique that took the pre-UNCLOS order for valid and agreed upon by the international community in its entirety, which was by far not the case. In fact, the verb "to creep" in the language of Shakespeare means "to enter or advance gradually so as to be *almost unnoticed*". As an adjective, it means "advancing by slow, imperceptible degrees".[122] A similar meaning includes "happening very slowly so

[121]Peters (2016), p. 4.

[122]Merriam-Webster. Entry "Creeping".

that people *do not notice*",[123] which emphasizes the surreptitious way in which the jurisdictional assertions by coastal states would occur. It would perhaps make sense to describe some excessive claims effected after the adoption of UNCLOS, as analyzed supra, but it fails to comprehend the systematic opposition of coastal states to the dual division of the oceans prior to 1982.

It is no novelty that states performing the staunchest objection to creeping jurisdiction are mainly located in Europe and North America.[124] Coincidently, authors criticizing the movement of creeping on jurisdiction prior and after UNCLOS originate or have been trained in those regions. It lies beyond the purpose of this work to assess whether such protestation would be the reflex of a hegemonic narrative, in which a particular actor "seeks to make its particular project or interest or pursuit seem the general project or interest".[125] It does seem nonetheless plausible that a phenomenon of "universalizing" freedom of navigation and demonizing creeping jurisdiction without distinction between pre- and post-UNCLOS eras indicates the defense of a particular political order of the oceans. In other words, powerful proponents invoke universal values or posit to act on behalf of the entire "international community", thereby equating all jurisdictional assertions, a common strategy observed throughout the history of international law.

Ironically, the creator of the expression "creeping jurisdiction" was an American. When John Craven coined the expression during the 1960s, the United States Navy revealed profound concern with jurisdictional assertions by coastal states to rights not just over the seafloor and subsoils of the continental shelf, but the water column. Only then, the alarm was sounded. In other words, as long as the unilateral expansion seawards was limited to the seabed, there was little reason to bother—particularly because the Americans are credited to having set the square one in shaping a new division of the oceans with the Truman Proclamations. However, once territorialization meant potential restrictions to freedom of navigation (only *potential*), the phenomenon triggered uneasiness amongst some countries.

In this case, perhaps the expression "universalization vocabulary", by Martti Koskenniemi, could help analyze the reiterate use of the expression "creeping jurisdiction" in law of the sea books and manuals. Could it be a universalized vocabulary, with which maritime powers have sought to describe their own social items and values as universal characteristics or objectives of the law?[126] Maritime powers have been claiming even after the adoption of the Montego Bay Convention to have the correct understanding of significance and scope of functional jurisdiction

---

[123]MacMillan Dictionary. Entry "Creeping".

[124]The United Kingdom and The Netherlands, for instance, oppose the interpretation of UNCLOS according to which coastal states may forbid military exercises on their EEZs. On another level, the United States were the only country to present a *note verbale* to the CLCS pending the analysis of the Brazilian submission for delineating the outer limits of the continental shelf. Such objection shows concerns by the naval superpower with potential extended territorial jurisdiction of the Brazilian state over the South Atlantic Ocean.

[125]Koskenniemi (2005), p. 115.

[126]Koskenniemi (2012), p. 311.

rules in the law of the sea. Such understating is expected to be universal, as it derives from human nature and human reason—in a dangerous process of naturalizing legal norms. This view is authoritarian, as it denies the plurality of *topoi* based on which international legal argumentation is made possible.[127] One of the problems lie, thus, on the judgmental nature of the writings and legal analyses about Latin American leadership in "creeping" on jurisdiction in the law of the sea. This view ignores that international law has always been and will continue to be, in essence, a battlefield for competing understandings and opposing interpretations of certain rules—functional jurisdiction in the law of the sea being no exception.

6.4.2 *Asserting Jurisdiction as a Means of Pushing for Changes in the Law*

Secondly, in no sense is the individual violation of international norms seen as regular means to realize state's particular self-interests. However, if states systematically and on a collective basis object specific treaty provisions or customary rules, then the behavior acquires a broader meaning—that of a call for renewed balance between powers, rights and duties on the international stage.[128] With this in mind, the opposition staged by several countries (various Latin American amongst them) against the traditional 3 nm territorial sea between the 1940s and the adoption of UNCLOS amounts to a violation that is not at the same level of other punctual breaches effected post-UNCLOS. There is a difference, if not in legal, at least in moral terms, between the "expansionist movement" prior to 1982 and recent individual, excessive jurisdictional claims. First, the pre-UNCLOS opposition does not

[127]A rhetorical reading of international law sees moral values and judgments behind the pretended assertiveness of positive law and focuses on the study of the so-called *topoi*, or places, or cultural (relative) elements, which influence the perception of law that a nation builds. On the legal level, Rhetoric as a methodology originates from the *rethorical turn*, in light of the limitations faced by the Kelsenian objectivist theory of law. At that time, Theodor Viehweg emerged as one of the main exponents of the argumentative theory, conceiving Jurisprudence, object of legal science, as a procedure for discussing problems. For the rhetorical reasoning, the starting line is no longer the blackletter of the law, but the controversial principles, or *topoi*, that directly influence legal interpretation. This makes Rhetoric known for operating in the field of legitimacy (not of positive legality), in which it seeks the acceptance of certain world views. Viehweg's considerations do not assume a cogent nature, as it happens with the legal positivism, since they are located in the domain of *dubium*, the uncertain. According to Viehweg, Topics would be a technique of thinking for problems, inspired and developed by rhetoric. *See* Viehweg (2007), p. 149.

[128]For Goldsmith and Posner, "every state act that is inconsistent with existing international law is open to two interpretations. First, the act might be said to be a violation of international law by a state that intends only to take advantage of other, compliant states. Second, the act might be said to be a proposal for revision of existing international law; the state acts inconsistently with international law in an effort to change it, to stimulate a new equilibrium that better serves its interests and, in the usual case, the interests of other states that have sufficient power and influence." *See* Goldsmith and Posner (2005), p. 197.

deserve the pejorative label of "creeping jurisdiction", for it was justified in the light of general objectives of international law—amongst which the shaping of a politically fair and economically just order. Secondly, not all jurisdictional claims post-UNCLOS fall under the same category of "excessiveness", and due to their isolated and not uniform occurrence cannot be designated as an "expansionist movement".

One way to tell the story of the law of the sea development is to confuse the pre-UNCLOS expansionist movement with contemporary attempts by coastal states to restrict freedoms of the high seas beyond the 200-nm line after the Convention. Recent attempts are considered particularly harmful to the international ocean order when they constrain freedom to access living resources in the water column beyond that limit—a practice inconsistent with the blackletter of UNCLOS Art. 87 (1) (e). Such a "creep" on jurisdiction is in the roots of the *Estai* incident between Canada and Spain during the 1990s, or the Chilean geopolitical concept of *mar presencial* in the adjacent waters of its EEZ. In that version, some coastal states are described as the causative agents of disorder in the *ordre publique océanique*.[129] Those subscribing to excessive claims beyond the limits imposed at UNCLOS are accused of touting anarchy in international law, as if before UNCLOS order and stability in the oceans would reign. For Michael Becker, there are still non-navigational practices which promote and sustain disorder, including "unilateral, excessive claims over the extent of the territorial sea or the continental shelf".[130]

There again, the problem emerges when the disorder created by the practice of asserting jurisdiction to change the legal division of the oceans prior to UNCLOS is equated to individual excessive jurisdictional claims post-UNCLOS. When analyzing breaches of the international legal-oceanic system, one ought to take into account that disorder is not necessarily bad, as it could mean the push for a revised, new order—one more in line with the demands of a certain time. In this sense, it helps to enquire on the *fairness* of international interactions before UNCLOS and the so-called "jurisdictional creep" by coastal states, when there was no internationally codified EEZ, and exclusive resource-jurisdiction was continuously questioned by maritime powers. In short, before the creation of the EEZ, developing coastal states considered that international law allowed developed countries to "appropriate the lion's share because only developed countries would have the capability of harvesting such resources on a commercial scale".[131]

The kind of disorder that comes to promote general fairness and justice is justifiable, and the pre-UNCLOS legal regime of absolute prevalence of freedom of the seas over territorial sovereignty of coastal states was all but fair. Indeed, customary law disciplining access to natural marine resources did not take into account the special needs of developing and least developed coastal states. General dissatisfaction with the ruling order was such that negotiating parties to the Third

---

[129] "Since the end of the Cold War, disorder on the oceans appears resurgent". *See* Langewiesche (2003), p. 63.

[130] Becker (2005), p. 132.

[131] Fidler (2003), p. 43.

Conference dedicated a paragraph of the Convention's Preamble to highlight state parties' commitment to the "maintenance of peace, *justice and progress* for all peoples of the world".[132] The Convention was negotiated on the widely shared assumption that the pre-UNCLOS economic (and oceanic) order was inadequate, what made a just and equitable international economic order due.[133] Needless to say, the new order ought to take particular note of the special interests and needs of developing countries.

In this sense, territorialization and disorder in the pre-UNCLOS ocean order arose so as to defy the previous model of colonial spoliation which inspired customary international law of the sea. The opposite of the so-called creeping jurisdiction would be a *spoliative jurisdiction*, one that connotes the colonialist origins of international law as legal system that favored technologically advanced coastal states through overwhelming prestige to freedom of the seas in detriment of technical deficits and economic needs of developing coastal states. Such prestige was none other than the direct result of a "primary role" played by maritime states in shaping the public order of the oceans over the course of history.[134] Privileges to developed nations would have been exacerbated in the deep seabed regime, were it not for Arvid Pardo's proposal of a common heritage principle. In fact, under the freedoms of the high seas principle, "the developed States of the West, which alone could muster the necessary investment and technology, would be the main beneficiaries of sea-bed mining".[135] To assert jurisdiction over those resources was the alternative found by developing states to the inherent unfairness in previous rules of international law. If this was a "crept of jurisdiction", then it was justified.

It has been suggested, albeit without any practical evidence, that the phenomenon could be applied in revert as well. Hence, flag states could opt for exploiting living resources within coastal states' unilaterally declared maritime zones.[136] This legalist argument inadequately simplifies the problem of creeping jurisdiction, by basically focusing on the element of breaching of an international rule, without taking into account the context in which such violation occurs. In some cases, the practice of creeping on jurisdiction seawards was a political response to the politically agreed system of laws that instituted a jurisdiction to plunder. Furthermore, it equals all kinds of creeping jurisdiction, from maritime powers to least developed coastal

[132]"Prompted by the desire to settle, in a spirit of mutual understanding and cooperation, all issues relating to the law of the sea and aware of the historic significance of this Convention as an important contribution to the maintenance of peace, justice and progress for all peoples of the world." UNCLOS, *Preamble*.

[133]"Bearing in mind that the achievement of these goals will contribute to the realization of a just and equitable international economic order which takes into account the interests and needs of mankind as a whole and, in particular, the special interests and needs of developing countries, whether coastal or land-locked". *Id.*

[134]According to Becker, "over the course of history, powerful maritime states have played the primary role in shaping the public order of the oceans". *See* Becker (2005), p. 131.

[135]Churchill and Lowe (1999), p. 157.

[136]Franckx (2005), p. 139.

states, in a move that further deepens the abyss existent in the international society, leaving it some steps farther from fairness and justice.[137] The reverse of creeping coastal state jurisdiction would be the continuation, and perhaps even deepening, of the once spoliative jurisdiction.

Concerning the practice of creeping and thickening jurisdiction after the signature UNCLOS, there were fears during the 1990s that the 200-nm limit would be wiped out in favor of coastal states' increasing powers, specifically concerning access to straddling and highly migratory fish populations.[138] However, that prophecy did not materialize and the 200-nm limit stood the test of state practice—according to some authors, due to the entry into force of the Convention. In fact, some authors are of the view that, "for States, it still constitutes a sound policy to become party to the 1982 Convention in order to protect themselves against the attacks of creeping jurisdiction".[139]

Apparently, evidence shows that coastal states' unilateral assertions did not continue significantly after the adoption of UNCLOS.[140] Instead, there is a limited state practice inconsistent with the Convention that cannot be considered customary law, neither does it set new trends in the law of the sea, being therefore essentially different from the concerted rejection of the pre-UNCLOS ocean order. Whether states advancing excessive claims could be held liable for acting in disregard of UNCLOS provisions is a more complicated issue,[141] one that will be tackled in coming chapters.

Overall, the balance between the rights and interests of flag and coastal states achieved at UNCLOS is not at risk and "remains essentially unchanged today".[142] There may be isolated threats to freedom of navigation, but on a limited scale and not able to shake the entire edifice built after 1982. Isolated state practice inconsistent with UNCLOS is, thus, devoid of power to question the overall functioning of law of the sea dynamics, such as normative implementation and institutional work. Such practice would be, therefore, no reason for sounding alerts of an alleged growing "territorial temptation" by coastal states, a movement that ceased to exist since the adoption of the Convention.

---

[137]For a thorough notion of "fairness" as adopted in this work, one based on sustainable development and serious fight against poverty, *see* Tourme-Jouannet (2013), p. 88. The French author analyzes fairness in the context of international economic law and considers fairness to be a "general principle for creating or revising the legal norm". When inquiring onto the fairness, the internationalist aims at correcting "classical international development law which, by a tragic paradox in its effects, may perhaps only ever have perpetuated the dependence and underdevelopment of the poor nations as it is unable to rectify the deep-rooted unfairness of the global system".

[138]Kwiatkowska (1991), pp. 166–170.

[139]Franckx (2005), p. 149.

[140]Molenaar (2015), p. 302.

[141]For instance, one could ask whether a coastal state, such as Brazil, could be held internationally liable for impeding the realization of an unconsented marine military exercise in its EEZ.

[142]Molenaar (2015), p. 303.

The text adopted in 1982 and signed by 167 parties will stand the test of time as long as its provisions are perceived as fair and its regimes, just, by the majority of the international community. The *effectiveness* of UNCLOS is a process in constant need of reassessment and intimately connected to the fairness of its provisions and justice of the regimes it creates. The balance of powers needs to be recurrently checked, regardless of the herculean efforts required for that. For now, the greatest dilemma for the law of the sea in the twenty first century seems to be how to conciliate the principle of non-interference in navigational freedoms and the need to promote ecological conservation and socioeconomic well-being in coastal states. If advancement of the latter is inflicting disorder and instability into the façade of UNCLOS, then it may be time to effect changes in the Convention or in admissible state practice, so that international community profits from state-of-the-art marine ecological policies.

From international legal scholars, it is expected a critical understanding of the power struggles in international law when referring to the issue of jurisdictional claims beyond what is in the Convention. It is not enough to simply read the blackletter of the law (UNCLOS and related international treaties) and reach the conclusion that every jurisdictional claim apparently inconsistent with or unregulated by the Convention amounts to creeping jurisdiction, being therefore an illegal and undesirable behavior in international law. In the case of stricter environmental regulations, international lawyers ought not to depart from the presumption of prevalence of an almost absolute freedom of navigation, but from the prevalence of marine environmental health and good conditions of the world oceans.

The current maritime context is one in which jurisdiction has evolved from an exclusive to an *inclusive model of enforcement*, one performed in unity and combination with other interested states.[143] Lawyers ought to forward a project of public order that prevents fallback into chaos, while mirroring power struggles and social values of current days. Developing coastal states, the majority of the international community, will not take pendants in exchange for precious metals any longer, and that must be present in every international legal analysis attempting to sound any sort of alarm. Besides, international scholars ought to embrace the complexity of the current UNCLOS structure of *complementary and competing jurisdictional* models. For a fact, this plurality of regimes will sometimes translate into difficult and blurred relationships, uncertainty of applicable rights in overlapping zones, need for balancing conflicting principles on an *ad hoc* basis, for every delicate situation. The times of a straightforward and easy-to-grasp dual jurisdictional division of the oceans are unquestionably gone.

[143]The wording "inclusive model of enforcement" is formulated by Michael Becker, on considerations by McDougal and Burke on the risks of arbitrary unilateral enforcement action against foreign vessels on the high seas to the "freedom of access". *See* Becker (2005), p. 135.

6.4.3 Exercising Increased Powers to Protect the Marine Environment

The exercise of environmental powers over maritime spaces under national jurisdiction for ecological purposes may consist of borderline cases, but such a practice is not indefensible *a priori*. While it may amount to a behavior inconsistent with UNCLOS, it may be sometimes justified in the coastal state's quest for fulfilling its right-duty to preserve and protect the marine environment.[144] Effectively, coastal states are the mainly interested parties in maintain the health of adjacent seas to their shores, and are in fact obliged to do so.[145] They are also the main interested parties in securing peaceful uses of the waters off their littoral. Finally, coastal states, taken as rational players, are not interested in disrupting merchant navigational freedom on adjacent waters as the nefarious socioeconomic consequence of such disruption would be felt immediately on the domestic level.

More than three decades after the signature of UNCLOS, it rests clear that the principle of freedom of the seas is eroding. Nowadays, to postulate that freedoms of the seas and correlated rights of other states are untouchable[146] is to annihilate coastal states' expectations of securing ecologically correct uses of the oceans and to impede actions towards the protection of marine biodiversity.[147] UNCLOS itself contains provisions that demand the reassessment of the theory of untouchability of freedom of the seas, especially in light of renewed environmental sensitivities. Besides, the righteous consequences of a jurisdictional crept for environmental conservation purposes ought not to be neglected. Unilateral action, when based on reasonable and convincing reasons, may trigger a *virtuous process* of developing new and/or supplementing existing instruments which regulate a particular use of the oceans. Hence, isolated action inconsistent with the Convention may be justified by the objectives aimed therewith.

Regarding the conservation of living resources in the EEZ, unilateral Canadian action in the *Estai* incident has virtues that ought not to be underestimated. According to Ribeiro, such action denounced the artificiality of legal borders crafted by the law of the sea, with regard to the dynamics of fish stocks and the reality of specific ecosystems.[148] Coastal states have undertaken action to protect and conserve fish stocks that may amount to a light jurisdictional crept. That action has triggered the adoption of an Implementing Agreement to UNCLOS on fisheries—the 1995 UNFSA, whose provisions create an exception to the principle of exclusive

---

[144]The expression "right-duty" is used by Marta Chantal Ribeiro, to whom the protection of the marine environment is both a power and a duty granted to coastal states by several UNCLOS provision, not only of Part XII (on the protection of the marine environment). *See* Ribeiro (2013), p. 618.

[145]Art. 192 UNCLOS.

[146]*See* Lagoni (2003), p. 167.

[147]Ribeiro (2013), p. 626.

[148]*Id.* 636.

jurisdiction of the flag state—coastal states may board and inspect foreign vessels.[149] Besides, Art. 8 stipulates that coastal states may control particular maritime areas through management agreements.

Concerning the protection of living resources of the continental shelf beyond 200 nm, it is indispensable to listen to the voices postulating stronger coastal state's powers for the protection of marine species directly connected to their continental shelves. Such voices can be read in a report of the UN Informal Open-ended Working Group on the Protection of Biodiversity in Areas Beyond National Jurisdiction, in which some delegations emphasized coastal state's right to adopt conservation measures that it considers necessary in order to protect sedentary species on the continental shelf.[150] It is the case of imposing restrictive measures on fisheries above the continental shelf, both within and beyond 200 nm.[151] In the same report, some delegations emphasize the complex and sensitive nature of seamounts, hydrothermal vents and cold-water reefs, formations that may host valuable ecosystems while having a seat on the outer continental shelf of any giver coastal state.

To take but one example, the Portuguese declaration upon ratification of UNCLOS is yet another voice favoring coastal state's enlarged environmental jurisdiction over the continental shelf. In that instrument, Portugal reserves itself the right to exercise, based on international cooperation and the implementation of the precautionary principle, *inspecting activities beyond 200 nm.*[152] Actions ought to be praised, that enlarge the normative powers of coastal states over the water column

---

[149] Arts. 21 and 22 of the United Nations Agreement for the Implementation of the Provisions of the United Nations Convention on the Law of the Sea, relating to the Conservation and Management of Straddling Fish Stocks and Highly Migratory Fish Stocks (UNFSA), 34 ILM 1542 (*1995*), 2167 *UNTS* 88.

[150] According to the Report, some delegations have stated that "in conformity with the Convention, the coastal State was fully entitled to adopt *any* conservation and management measures it deemed necessary to protect its sedentary species on the continental shelf. Those may include the possibility of imposing restrictive measures on fishing activities in the high seas over its continental shelf, including on fishing practices that were deemed to have a negative impact on sedentary species. *See* Report of the Ad Hoc Open-Ended Informal Working Group to Study Issues Relating to the Conservation and Sustainable Use of Marine Biological Diversity beyond Areas of National Jurisdiction (New York: United Nations, 20 March 2006), para 22.

[151] Some authors have suggested that coastal states may take measures to enforce their sovereign rights over sedentary species beyond 200 nm, what may include visiting, inspecting and seizing a fishing vessel on the high seas above the extended shelf. Restrictions of navigational rights in the water column above the outer continental shelf are not a priori excluded. However, every measure ought to be taken after consultation with the IMO and in line with its specific instruments. *See* Owen and Chambers (2006), p. 40. Erik Molenaar disagrees with this view. *See* Molenaar (2007), p. 89.

[152] Item 9 of the Portuguese declaration upon ratification of UNCLOS states that "bearing in mind the available scientific information and with a view to the protection of the environment and the sustained growth of economic activities based on the sea, Portugal will, preferably through international cooperation and taking into account the precautionary principle, *carry out control activities beyond the areas under national jurisdiction*". Portuguese Declaration upon Ratification of UNCLOS, available online, 3 November 1997.

above the extended continental shelf, for the purposes of conserving sedentary species inhabiting that shelf.

Vessel-source pollution in the EEZ and continental shelf is yet another dimension where coastal states have reasons to bargain for expanded environmental jurisdiction, particularly hydrocarbon pollution and oil slicks. The incidents of Erika and Prestige, as seen supra, have prompted inflamed reactions by the affected coastal states and the proliferation of arguments to increase their inspecting powers to the detriment of freedom of navigation.[153] Here, coastal states are faced with complex matters of (i) implementing CDEM standards (construction, design, equipment and manning) of oil tankers and (ii) deficient inspection and monitoring of vessel by several flag states—and the discussions on the so-called "open registries". In the EEZ, the Convention permits coastal states solely to take *reactive* measures, once the harm has already occurred.[154] Marta Ribeiro sees with little surprise the reaction of Portugal, Spain and France to the *Prestige* disaster, which the author considers a valid objection to the "(un)balance of interests" sanctioned by UNCLOS.[155]

Indignation was also shown by Myron Nordquist, to whom international law had to do better in the aftermath of a major oil spill, with stronger emphasis on the need to reform the current liability regime following a maritime catastrophe. That regime is flawed shelters "flags of convenience, single hull tankers, sham corporations, marginal operators, shadowy owners and totally inadequate caps on liability for the actual damages".[156] In light of these flaws, it should come with little awe that coastal states adopt stricter environmental regulations in relation to vessels carrying pollutants and noxious substances. Erika and Prestige were not isolated cases. Several countries focus on their environmental protective powers and disregard UNCLOS provisions, openly or in a camouflaged manner, in order to achieve internally agreed goals. Maritime powers and coastal states alike.[157] Canada, Spain, US, France, Poland, Indonesia claim the right to exercise preventive control prior to the entrance of a foreign vessel in their EEZ. Regarding environmental regulation and protection, maritime powers are the ones to creep on jurisdiction, what makes the traditional dichotomy *developing vs developed states* a pitfall. The European Union (EU) is equally an influential international actor that has adopted largely restrictive regimes in favor of the marine environment.

In the decades to come, the affirmation of *environmental security jurisdiction* is due to increase, as the size of vessels grow, the world gets further interdependent, and knowledge of marine ecosystems functioning surge.[158] A case in point are

[153]Frank (2005), p. 7.

[154]Art. 221 UNCLOS, on measures to avoid pollution arising from maritime casualties.

[155]Frank (2005), p. 63.

[156]Nordquist (2007), p. 503.

[157]Losa et al. (2003), p. 52.

[158]In the case *overlapping jurisdiction*, in which more than one state make claims to regulate the conduct in question (grounded on valid legal bases for jurisdiction), there is a matter of *priority*. States are encouraged to act in accordance to UNCLOS and to solve their disputes in a peaceful and

coastal states which unilaterally assert the right to deny passage to vessels carrying ultra-hazardous cargoes, not only through their territorial sea, but also EEZ.[159] The environmental security jurisdiction is heavily grounded on a greatly sensitive interest of coastal states (safety from ecological dangers), what makes it unsurprising that approximately one third of the international community attempts to impose restrictions to navigation based on ecological security interests.[160]

This sort of jurisdictional assertion, known as *environmental security jurisdiction*, has come to stay. Coastal states will increasingly face the dilemma between protecting marine environmental health off their shores and securing international shipping and trade. That is, enacting environmentally protective legislation and taking enforcement measures in order to minimize risks and dangers of marine pollution that may occur from vessels and installations (foreign and national) which do not match the highest available environmental standards—both domestically and internationally, and looking for alternatives to the plain restriction of navigation rights in their EEZs and continental shelves. However, the legal possibility to adopt restrictive measures aimed at preserving a particularly sensitive area needs to be "on the table", in case the coastal state can make a decent case, based on justified restrictions to the rights of other states. The exercise of environmental (security) jurisdiction should not be considered a priori nefarious to the legal order of the oceans, merely because it may interfere with the overriding freedom to navigate. To the contrary, coastal states are to be given regulatory maneuver room for uses of the waters adjacent to their littoral, for security and ecological purposes.

6.4.4 Reducing Tensions Between Military Security Interests and the Protection of the Marine Environment

Historically, the law of the sea has been shaped by the fundamental tension between freedom to navigate and sovereignty claims, in which naval powers, while prioritizing mobility and accessibility, opposed any move by coastal states to exercise jurisdiction over larger portions of the oceans. From the perspective of a state equipped with powerful military and/or merchant fleets, waters untouched by any sort of national jurisdiction should optimally be as large as possible. It has been so for centuries, until the adoption of the Montego Bay Convention, when the already

negotiated way. In that case, it is uncontroversial in international law literature burden of proof lies with the state that claims to have jurisdiction, not with the ones that object. These questions related to the extension of coastal state's environmental jurisdiction and issues arising therefrom are the at the core of Chap. 7. *See* Staker (2014), p. 315.

[159]Kaye contests that attempts aimed at expanding jurisdiction on the EEZ are not expressly backed by UNCLOS, which does not anticipate any restriction on navigation in the EEZ based upon the nature of the cargo. *See* generally Kaye (2006).

[160]From South America alone, one can identify Argentina, Brazil, Chile, Colombia, Peru and Venezuela. A table with the precise states can be found at Kaye (2006), p. 362.

mentioned "rise" of coastal states shifted the balance from the principle of freedom of the sea to the principle of territorial sovereignty.

As international relations changed and adapted to current power dynamics and values shared by different peoples of the world, in particular environmental conservation, that centuries-old opposition made way to a new kind of tension: security and trade interests vs. environmental concerns.[161] It would not be accurate to depict the relation between both categories as a dichotomy, as security and environmental concerns may come hand-in-hand, in the case of measures taken to repress illegal fishing or human trafficking by sea. However, it is undeniable that a tension between them exists, a tension which is ultimately informed by the traditional binary between freedom and sovereignty.

For that reason, it is widely disseminated worldwide that territorial practices (or "jurisdictional crept") towards the EEZ and the continental shelf, while generating benefits for the coastal states, "negatively impacts the maritime and security interests of naval powers".[162] If, in the past, territorialism often dressed up as blunt jurisdictional assertions, such as the unilateral measures by coastal states decreeing exclusive uses to a 200-nm zone,[163] which led to the emergence of the EEZ, nowadays naval powers worry substantially that territorialism may camouflage as environment-based measures. Admittedly, actions justified as seeking and implementing increased marine environmental health standards enjoy more persuasive power before the international community, having thus become coastal states'

[161]The tension between environment and trade has been exhaustively discussed by scholars in the field of international trade law, in particular the relationship between Art. XX of the General Agreement on Tariffs and Trade (GATT) and impacts on world trade. Art. XX GATT beefed up environmental clauses allowing for discrimination against products which may harm the environment, having been claimed in different occasions by members of the World Trade Organization (WTO), such as Brazil in the "Brazil Tires Case". This section of the work focuses rather on the opposition between military and environmental considerations pertaining to the oceans.

[162]Ikeshima (2011), p. 6.

[163]State practice related to maritime security considerations which allegedly amount to excessive claims, so James Kraska, is provided by states such as Brazil, Bangladesh, India, and Pakistan, among others. For instance, Bangladesh has declared upon the ratification of UNCLOS that "The Government of the People's Republic of Bangladesh understands that the provisions of the Convention do not authorize other States to carry out in the exclusive economic zone and on the continental shelf military exercise or maneuvers, in particular, those involving the use of weapons or explosives, without the consent of the coastal State", in 27 July 2001. India deposited a similar declaration upon ratification on 29 June 1995, and so did Pakistan, on 26 February 1997. The staunchest opposers to that interpretation have been the United States, the Netherlands and the United Kingdom, among other developed countries. The latter has declared that "declarations and statements not in conformity with Arts. 309 and 310 include, inter alia, the following: those which are not in conformity with the provisions of the Convention relating to the exclusive economic zone or the continental shelf, including those which claim coastal state jurisdiction over all installations and structures in the exclusive economic zone or on the continental shelf, and those which purport to require consent for exercises or maneuvers (including weapons exercises) in those areas. *See* The United Kingdom Interpretative Declaration upon Accession, on 25 July 1997.

favorite strategy when advancing special and particular interests to the detriment of established norms and customs.

Hence, it is often complained that stricter rules on marine environmental protection are becoming deterrents to both long-distance trade and military security.[164] A most pertinent illustration of such complaint can be drawn from the pronouncement of Jay Johnson, United States Navy Admiral, to the American Senate. In the communication, the Admiral remarks that:

> During my tenure, I have witnessed the *jurisdictional creep* of coastal states, often with the direct support of non-governmental organizations (NGOs) contrary to the law of the sea as codified in the Convention. These claims of regional and coastal state jurisdiction and authority are invoked to the *detriment of navigational freedoms* to further a wide range of special interests, including *enhanced environmental protection*, total nuclear disarmament, world health, limitations on measures to combat transnational crime and illegal migration, and management and allocation of the radio frequency spectrum. During the past decade, coastal states and regional groups of coastal states have continued their efforts to extend jurisdiction beyond that which is recognized and permitted under the Convention (emphases added).[165]

Military security is part of the general concept of maritime security, a select group of concerns that seems reluctant to accept marine environmental security issues as a member. A traditional definition of security itself is limited to *military* responsibilities, scenarios in which the armed forced would be called into action, in a way that renders "maritime security" identical to "military security" in practice.

A significant flaw in that debate, however, is to equal environmental concerns with purely ecological issues, in a radical biocentric approach to the content and scope of those concerns.[166] Such an identification between maritime and military security is mostly likely unproductive for analyses of contemporary environmental threats and possible answers to them.[167] Sure, environmental preoccupations do have the intention to increase the overall quality of the world's oceans, a reason why they made their way into Part XII of the Convention, among other provisions sparsely spread in the treaty, such as Art. 19 (2) (h), on the prohibition of willful pollution acts while transit through the territorial sea of a coastal state; or Art. 240 (d), on the duty to comply ecological regulations while conducting marine scientific research, to name but a few. However, environmental concerns *are also marine security concerns*, which are broader than traditional maritime concerns (such as piracy, drug and human-trafficking at sea, armed robbery at sea, and other threats to shipping and navigation).

---

[164]Ikeshima (2011), p. 8.

[165]Letter from Chief of Naval Operations, Admiral Jay Johnson, to Senator Jesse Helms, Chairman, Senate Foreign Relations Committee, 29 June 2000.

[166]Some authors reveal skepticism as to the utility of a concept of "environmental security threats", based on the expectation that such broadly defined threats would tend to transform environmental security into "security for the environment *per se*", in an exclusively biocentric view that disregards military, political, societal and economic considerations. *See* Buzan (1991), p. 5.

[167]*See* Calley et al. (2015), p. 512.

Calley, Hulme and Ong advocate for the more encompassing phrase "marine security" to discuss contemporary threats posed to the marine environment, not necessarily limited to the military universe or to the intervention of armed forces, but which do impact the levels of individuality, community, globality that a security threat requires. Examples of marine security threats include ocean acidity in the context of climate change, geoengineering, illegal, unreported and unregulated (IUU) fishing, and dumping of hazardous wastes offshore, to name but a few. In light of these global-scale challenges, the very conception of the sovereign state as the sole provider of security is antiquated. It makes more sense from a political and legal perspective to embrace a broader understanding of "marine (environmental) security", so as to steer international *multi-player initiatives* towards minimizing all sorts of harms to the world oceans, not just traditional military threats, before large-scale destruction of marine habitats, ecosystems and resources reach a point of no return to human lives planetwide.

One ought to admit that environment-based measures that allegedly foster marine security efforts may disguise other interests. It has been so in the realm of international trade law, and others. However, a realist would claim that such practice is not an exclusivity of environment-based measures; it has also been common in military security-based strategies in the past, which have dressed up as security action, when in fact they cloaked fundamental economic and geopolitical interests. The "humanitarian" intervention in Iraq by the United States in 2003 could be summoned as an example of such disguise, one that has not hampered governments worldwide to design and implement further military actions to tackle traditional threats.[168] That well-intentioned and well-marketed state actions may disguise individual interests is a truism in international law and politics, but the advancement of such interests must occur within the boundaries of existing rules and in light of a ponderation of applicable legal principles.

To dismiss every coastal state measure which reasonably limits certain freedoms of the high seas for the sake of promoting environmental protection based on scientific evidence and best-available data would be to declare the premature failure of UNCLOS. For one, because the Convention anticipated a few environmental threats to the ocean, namely pollution and depletion of living resources, thus elevating at a pioneering moment the ocean protection as an important legal good to be safeguarded—albeit from an anthropocentric perspective.[169] That a aprioristic

[168] A philosophical critique to the military interventions effected in Iraq, Afghanistan and in other parts of the world is advanced by Danilo Zolo (2010), chap. 27.

[169] Contemporary theories on the environment usually refer to two possible ethics towards the environment. The historically dominant one is anthropocentrism or homocentrism, which sees society as superior to nature, thus instrumentalizing natural elements to enable a better life for human collectivities. The other ethics is known as "biocentric" or ecocentric, which as the name suggests, focuses on nature and postulates that all living and non-living resources have intrinsic value. Such resources are not means to an end, but ought to be conserved for their role in the overall smooth functioning of nature systems that enable human life on the planet. Basically, those ethics underpin the action of individuals, institutions, governmental agencies and other societal actors. As

dismissal would contradict the conception of the Treaty as a "living organism".[170] To interpret UNCLOS as a living organism is particularly relevant in light of current challenges, as it seems to offer the only viable solution for the Convention's frequent silences and vagueness on complex environmental issues. An extreme dogmatic approach to UNCLOS, as the one espoused by the United States Navy, may show pertinent concerns with certain developments in the law of the sea, but will not admit that the approach is already an interpretation of the Convention; and that every international treaty may have its provisions interpreted and, if necessary, adapted to the needs and demands of the current time.

Besides, maritime security considerations vary from country to country, as do the methods for facing them. Thus, the United States Navy may consider the "enclosure" of open seas as a priority threat to maritime security worldwide and, then, enforce the famous FON operations to reinstall respect for the law of the sea. Yet, that may not be the same priority of a West-African state, for instance. As illustrated by this example, maritime security considerations also reflect special self-interests, which relate to the political and economic agendas of nations that rely more heavily on high seas freedoms to sustain economic leadership and that wish to project power capacities to the ocean. The rhetorical and argumentative strategy to disguise such self-interested action is to formulate special interests of naval powers as "rights of the international community".[171] In this context, why do only environmental concerns camouflage illegal jurisdictional expansionism, while maritime security interests are not considered to veil maritime hegemonisms over the oceans?

Finally, it should be born in mind that one of the key philosophies underpinning UNCLOS (as there is not a single philosophy) is to acknowledge the coastal state as part of the solution to marine environmental pressures, not just the problem. In times of greater marine environmental awareness, it would be a mistake to disregard coastal states' role as necessary actors in tackling marine threats. They are certainly not the panacea to all problems, but are no less relevant than flag states, particularly in light of the problematic record of "open registries" which indirectly contribute to a state of disdain for the oceans. To include coastal states in the equation for better marine ecological protection is not just relevant from a moral perspective but is legally grounded on several provisions of the Convention. In fact, UNCLOS has granted coastal states room for the exercise of a *multifunctional jurisdiction* over maritime spaces under national jurisdiction,[172] including the continental shelf,

---

most of solutions for complex problems, the solution for the environmental degradation would lie on a middle ground, as a radical biocentrism could render every economic activity detrimental to the environment and nefarious to the intrinsic value of nature's elements, a consequence which would ultimately benefit no one. For more on the different environmental ethics, *see* Leff (1998), p. 72. *See* also Merchant (1998), p. 463.

[170] *See* generally Barrett and Barnes (2016).

[171] Kraska (2011), p. 8.

[172] Art. 56 (1) (a) UNCLOS. The expression "multifunctional jurisdiction" is based on the idea of a "functional jurisdiction", but seems to better reflect coastal states' plural competences in areas under national jurisdiction.

i.e. not just sovereign rights over the exploration and exploitation of natural resources (an economically oriented and applied jurisdiction), but also rights to enact and enforce environmental regulations concerning the use those resources.

In this sense, there should be mutual understanding on behalf of both naval powers and coastal states, so as to assess on a *casuistic basis* the measures taken by the latter to foster ecological protection and tackle marine environmental threats. Coastal states may (and sometimes must, depending on UNCLOS provisions supporting the action) adopt environmental measures through relevant agreements, measures which are not deeply incompatible with freedom of the high seas enjoyed by third states or parties.[173] Should the measures be incompatible with such freedoms, it will be the case to assess the context in which they are enacted, as in the case of the array of national legislation adopted by European states affected by the Erika and Prestige oil spills.

In order to prevent confrontation and unjustifiable violations of navigational freedoms, clear communication, reasonableness and proportionality from the involved parties must be. As pointed out by Ikeshima,

> coastal states should refrain from stepping too far in search for environmental protection (even if genuinely meant, and not a sort of security strategy dressed up as ecologically friendly); and naval powers should accept the fact that the current era is shaped not exclusively by military considerations anymore, but also by marine environmental concerns. Although military issues remain "high politics", they are not the only ones at the table and must now share attention and prominence with ecological awareness.[174]

The era in which military might and economic thrill alone mattered is over. For some time now, institutionalists, environmentalists, idealists (you name it) have faced the rather simplistic way of understanding the world, which set aside other preoccupations as less relevant in relation to those two. Considerations of a socio-environmental nature inspire international politics and international law more and more, making it thus impossible for military interests to rule alone. For that reason, the modern law of the sea has consecrated marine environmental concerns, sometimes in opposition to traditional freedoms.

Thirty-five years into the adoption of UNCLOS, pressing ecological threats to the marine environment have been offering arguments to those voices calling for a revision of the long-established idea of navigational freedom as an absolute and unconditioned right. As some authors have righteously pointed out, the umbrella agreed upon in 1982 is likely not be the same as the umbrella states are currently willing to accept.[175] Biodiversity protection, for instance, is not within UNCLOS' list of priorities, but this does not mean it cannot become an issue of primary concern

---

[173] Ikeshima (2011), p. 25.

[174] *Id.* 25.

[175] Franckx (1998), p. 324. Despite not calling for a revision of freedom of the seas, Tullio Scovazzi sees a "natural process of erosion" of that principle, sponsored in the twentieth century by the creation of legal concepts in the law of the sea, such as EEZ and continental shelf. It is, however, difficult to conceive such erosion as "natural", but deeply conditioned by the actions and interests of coastal states over the world's oceans. *See* Scovazzi (2015), p. 63.

for states. Indeed, lately there have been shifts in power struggles on the international stage, raising awareness towards complex matters such as environmental protection, climate change, ocean acidification etc.

Despite the current trend towards the consolidation of marine environmental jurisdiction (both prescriptive and to enforce), the goal has never been to attack freedom of navigation as a general legal principle. Ribeiro, therefore, denies the version that environmental jurisdiction may represent a Trojan horse against the freedom-centered normative structure of UNCLOS.[176] In this regard, the international community is faced with the need to strike a *renewed balance* that makes justice for both most interested categories of states, that is between the prerogatives and expectations of flag-states and the legal possibility for coastal states to defend the marine environment off their shores.[177] Even though coastal states pursue marine environmental defense in their own interests, such action should imply benefits to all humankind.

That trend does not entail a complete reversion in trajectory of the law of the sea thus far, but simply an adaptation, with the contribution of representatives from maritime and coastal states alike. Current state practice on enlarging environmental jurisdiction may ensure the formation of customary rules in opposition of certain UNCLOS provisions. Hence, the international community would have to opt between amending the Convention or accepting the partial revoking of its provisions due to disuse. Either the Convention internalizes this "dynamics of territorialization" or faces its partial revoking.[178]

While it is true that individual coastal state initiatives have been condemned and often frustrated whereas multilateral action has proven to be more effective, the "threat of unilateralism seems to have become both the weapon of choice and the *best available means* to reach a mutually acceptable solution on the global level".[179] Ultimately, all interested parties realize that universal problems, such as the marine environment-related ones, require universal solutions. On the one hand, coastal states are aware they are not expected to act on a unilateral manner. On the other, they know the bargaining power that such action (or indication of action) exercises over other states in the international community, particularly if the action is well-grounded on an environmental *rationale*.

Finally, the clash between the principle of freedom of the seas and territorial sovereignty is due to continue. In the universe of law, it is reasonable to expect that coastal states reach diverse interpretations of UNCLOS jurisdictional provisions, or

[176]Ribeiro (2013), p. 803 ff.

[177]In this renewed balance, the practice of some degree of creeping jurisdiction is almost inevitable. Chiefly in the case of MPAs in the EEZ and continental shelf, the protected areas have "vocation" to be agents of creeping jurisdiction. The international community has acquiesced to some controlling powers of coastal states over maritime zones under some degree of their jurisdiction. Hence, Ribeiro claims that, at least in the case of the regime of MPAs beyond the territorial sea, the balance between coastal state powers and third state rights must be reassessed and updated. *Id.* 805 ff.

[178]Losa et al. (2003), p. 71.

[179]*See* generally Gavouneli (2006).

attempt to supplement the Convention whenever sensitive interests are not being adequately protected by positive law. The international community, and scholars, should listen to those attempts and ask whether they can be inserted in a bigger picture, a bigger movement towards the strengthening of a particular set of provisions, such as the ecology-oriented ones, instead of simply dismissing them as abusive. That would be an exercise of trying to grasp the complex relationship between the political sphere and the legal universe that plays out in the law of the sea.

Freedoms of the seas are no longer absolute rights, and not all restrictions to those freedoms are necessarily wicked.[180] In the case of fishing in the high seas, Art. 116 UNCLOS makes it clear that freedom to fish is conditioned, amongst others, to the rights, duties and interests of coastal states.[181] Concerning freedom of navigation, coastal states have sought cooperation to adopt international rules and standards governing vessel-source pollution and aiming at increasing the environmental quality of the world oceans, even if such measure may restrict navigational freedoms. Examples of such efforts have been crystalized in instruments such as MARPOL, the IMO's resolutions, widespread designation of PSSAs. Combined with the declaration of MPAs in EEZs, and unilateral restrictions (France, Spain and Portugal after the *Prestige* incident), those efforts may be welcomed as benefits to general ocean's health.

Besides, creeping on jurisdiction may be morally justified in some cases, especially if one take into account that the available tools for balancing the different uses of the seas are not enough and especially not in favor of coastal states. In light of current oceanic challenges, coastal states ought to have greater power to influence the balance of opposing interests and uses of the waters adjacent to the shore. Maria Gavouneli even mentions a "powerful urge of the coastal State to break the procedural constraints the world community has placed upon its actions".[182] The answer to those constraints remains unilateralism, namely in cases where consensual multilateral action or conventional amendments are expected to be costly and lengthy.[183]

The current shape of jurisdictional regimes and zones, albeit relatively stable, is *not permanent and final*. Nothing in the universe of law is final. The maritime zones as they stand will certainly not last forever, but there does seem to be enough evidence to assume that the current division of the oceans will last for a while, despite the tension between the three core principles of the discipline.[184] When reading some of the critiques which attempt to raise awareness to the destructive power of jurisdictional claims to the architecture of UNCLOS, one may be confronted with the feeling that the current *ordre publique* of the oceans would be

[180] Freestone (2012), p. 200.

[181] Art. 116 UNCLOS, on the right to fish in the high seas.

[182] Gavouneli (2006), p. 82.

[183] That is why, weeks following the Prestige disaster, the respective ministers of France and Spain have agreed to unilaterally adopt a new (and much wider) interpretation of their rights and duties in their respective EEZs.

[184] The three cores are freedom of the seas, territorial sovereignty and common heritage of mankind.

on the verge of a profound shift. This is by no means the case. The jurisdictional division of the seas achieved at UNCLOS is a remarkable piece of art, which has conciliated several opposing interests. However, it is inevitable that the law of the sea and UNCLOS, as products of social change and relative power distributions in the international stage, eventually change, in order to internalize newer inputs. Social change is an intrinsic feature of all legal systems, the international one being no exception.

As key variables for the ocean legal regime change, so does the equilibrium of forces in the international arena. Indeed, modifications in the availability of natural resources, status of technological advancement, knowledge of ocean services, functioning and dynamics, level of ocean pollution, and data on ecosystem interaction, amongst others, change etc.), can be expected to trigger renewed pressures on the holy balance sewed during the 1970s. In other words, the edifice created by UNCLOS is solid, but ought to be flexible enough to resist to strain, when needed, but also to adapt to tensions in specific cases. Despite the relative stability of the current maritime political map of the world, the issue of "creeping coastal jurisdiction" is expected not only to remain,[185] but to increase as a tool for operating transformations in the public order of the oceans, especially in our world primarily marked by scarcity and deficient distribution of natural resources.

6.5 Partial Conclusions

A renewed balance between territorial sovereignty and freedom of navigation gives a handful of prestige to the former, with the consolidation of the principle of "respect for sovereignty and jurisdiction" of states, as well as the physical expansion of the areas under coastal state's sovereignty (territorial sea from 3 to 12 nm) and jurisdiction (creation of the EEZ and possibility of expanding jurisdiction over the continental shelf beyond 200 nm). Overall, jurisdiction in international law is used as synonym for *competence, power or authority* of states over their people and within their territory. Rules on jurisdiction flow from the acceptance by the state of limits to their regulatory activity, in a way that even when restricting its powers, states are exercising sovereignty. However, one should bear in mind that jurisdiction does not break down to regulatory authority; it is more than just the power to regulate.

Traditionally, jurisdiction has been taken solely as a matter of rights and powers of the state. However, there is more to that, as the concept encompasses gradually the notion of duties and obligations. A more up-to-date view on the concept of jurisdictions suggests that it is not solely a matter of rights to prescribe and enforce, but also an issue of *duties and obligations*.[186] Jurisdiction should, hence, be conceived not only as a "ceiling" to state powers, but also as a "floor", containing the minimum

[185]Schofield et al. (2014), p. 57.

[186]Mills (2014), p. 188.

requirements for the exercise of regulatory powers. The core of this discussion is international criminal law, in which states have recognized jurisdiction more as a matter of duty than of right.[187]

Aware of the complexity of the concept of sovereignty and jurisdiction, this part has, nonetheless, attempted at facilitating the understanding of the relationship and the differences between both.[188] Jurisdiction (domestic and internationally) is the operationalization of the principle of sovereignty. International jurisdiction, attributed to states by treaties, represent the expression of sovereignty by means of state consent. Besides, there is not an absolute jurisdiction (prescriptive, adjudicative and of enforcement), i.e. the state cannot exercise power in absolute and unlimited ways. Secondly, jurisdiction is determined in order to prevent the state from exercise abusive powers over its own or foreign individuals. Grasping this will be of use for the analyses of the problems set out at the introduction of this paper with regard to the law of the sea.

Sovereignty and jurisdiction are there to stay, despite the temptation to believe that internationalism will prevail and that the international body of rules will render the concept of territoriality, extraterritoriality and nationality obsolete. Even if a global administrative law emerges,[189] individual states will continue to be key actors in global governance schemes and the international regulation of activities. The matter is, thus, one of delineating jurisdiction with clarity, so as to achieve as much legal security and predictability as possible in the international relations.

Unilateral and excessive exercise of jurisdiction by states or international organizations can be problematic, especially if one considers that global problems usually call for collectively worked solutions, to be cast in local terms and tackled locally. In this context, unilateralism may lead to political and economic abuse, as well as regulatory anarchy, a situation which benefits just a few. A solution to that problem could be a rule of reason and, as with every issue in international law, compromise between conflicting interests, the law of the sea and "territorial pressures" from coastal states being no different. Unilateral assertion of powers over larger maritime areas offshore are also widespread known in the law of the sea literature as "creeping jurisdiction". In short, this practice would amount to "ocean enclosure movement"[190] in which coastal states have unlawfully expanded territorial jurisdiction to the detriment of the overriding principle of freedom of the seas.

---

[187] *Id.* 211.

[188] A most interesting case that points out to the distinction between sovereignty and jurisdiction is the Lease Agreement of 1903 for the Guantanamo Naval Base in Cuba to the United States. The agreement confers the United States "complete jurisdiction and control" over the Base, but retains Cuban sovereignty over the territory where the Base is located. In the *Rasul v. Bush* case, the United States Supreme Court decided that the detention of prisoners in the Guantánamo Base was legal and, due to the Lease Agreement, US federal courts had jurisdiction to entertain cases concerning the Base.

[189] For further reading on the concept of global administrative law, *see* generally Krisch (2010).

[190] Alexander (1983), p. 561.

Yet, one should not feel tempted to rule out *a priori* any jurisdictional assertion that takes place in the international stage as "creeping jurisdiction" and, therefore, nefarious to the world's order. As explained above, the phrases "creeping jurisdiction" or "ocean enclosure" can be misleading. Besides, a common feature in legal analyses of creeping jurisdiction is to equate all actions that somehow expand territorial competences over any maritime space throughout history, from maritime powers and coastal states alike. In such analyses, focus lies on the element of unilaterality and illegality of the action, in breach of established international law. While respect for the international rule of law is certainly the ultimate goal of internationalists, one should not neglect the element of politics that inspire this discipline, nor the fact that law is primarily a cultural construct, international law included.

With the erosion of the dogmatic view of freedom of the seas an untouchable principle, sovereign rights of coastal states are enlarging, and the question remains whether this enlargement implies greater prescriptive and enforcement powers of the coastal states relating to environmental regulations. That question is all the more relevant in gray areas that embody the sovereign ambition of coastal states, such as the outer continental shelf.[191] It is therefore urgent to define the environmental regime applicable, so as to promote a principled management of the continental shelf beyond 200 nm. The problem has already been raised by Barry Dubner, when analyzing the interplay of international law of the sea and the prevention of maritime pollution. In so doing, the author highlighted the *virtue of certain reasonable and well-grounded unilateral state actions* "in order to achieve national and international legal congruity, depending on the urgency of the danger".[192]

At the end of the day, there has not been enough reason to raise alarms against an allegedly excessive territorial expansion of coastal states seawards. Likewise, there has not been a systematic breach of the 1982 Convention, i.e. provisions on the jurisdiction of coastal states have not been modified by subsequent state practice. In fact, state practice has not been enough to outdo UNCLOS, mainly due to the Convention's functioning system of checks and balances for every maritime zone, in which opposing interests are brought to an equilibrium. As such, jurisdiction ought not to be approached as a matter exclusively of territorial control, but also as a question of duties and obligations falling upon the entity exercising jurisdiction.

An inevitable (though undesired) consequence of the expansion of coastal state's jurisdiction over the oceans is the *accumulative number of overlapping claims* and the potential for disputes and conflicts. This rose the need for states to delimit maritime boundaries between each other, a process not always consensual and peaceful. To prevent the emergence of conflicts, interested states should have the

---

[191]The possibility of expanding gained momentum after the scientific discovery of immense hydrocarbons reserves in the deep sea, in areas beyond the tradition 200 nm EEZ. In Brazil, the oil field "Garoupa" was discovered in 1974, that is during the negotiations of UNCLOS, and possibly reinforce the country's territorial vocation.

[192]Dubner (1998), p. 137.

means to address problems as to provide fairness to the international community. For that to happen, some authors will claim, there ought to be a process of "mutual recognition" between states and their respective interests, i.e. states should have empathy for the interests and needs of other states.[193] That would be ideal, yet history and the record of international relations have shown that one cannot rely on empathy (not even comity) in international law, and the open critique by powerful states directed against littoral states that crept on jurisdiction in the past is a proof of that.

Against this backdrop, it is mandatory to assess the precise environmental jurisdiction of coastal states over the continental shelf. In other words, to identify the rights and duties relating to the regulation of the marine environment that fall upon coastal states and find answer to the question of the precise regulatory maneuver room of coastal states concerning the prescriptive, judicial and, above all, enforcement jurisdiction over the continental shelf. The answer to that enquiry will prove particularly relevant to the study of the specific case of the Brazilian continental shelf regulations and practice.

References

Alexander LM (1983) The ocean enclosure movement: inventory and prospect. San Diego Law Rev 20(3):561–594

Anand R (2004) Studies in international law and history. Springer, Dordrecht

Anderson D (2006) Freedom of the high seas in the modern law of the sea. In: The law of the sea: progress and prospects. Oxford University Press, Oxford, pp 327–346

Barrett J, Barnes R (eds) (2016) Law of the sea: UNCLOS as a living treaty. British Institute of International and Comparative Law, London

Becker MA (2005) Shifting public order of the oceans: interdiction of ships at sea. Yale Law Rev 46:131–230

Bilder R (1973) The Anglo-Icelandic fisheries dispute. Wisconsin Law Rev 37:37–132

Booth K (1983) Naval strategy and the spread of psycho-legal boundaries at sea. Int J 38 (3):373–396

Brown ED (1973) Maritime zones: a survey of claims. In: New directions in the law of the sea. The Eastern Press, London

Burke WT (1970) Law, science, and the ocean. Nat Resour Law 3

Buzan B (1991) People, states and fear: an agenda for international security studies in the post-cold war era, 2nd edn. L. Rienner Publishers

Calley D, Hulme K, Ong D (2015) New maritime security threats. In: The IMLI manual on international maritime law, vol III. Oxford University Press, Oxford

Churchill R, Lowe V (1999) The law of the sea. Manchester University Press, Manchester

Dubner B (1998) On the interplay of international law of the sea and the prevention of maritime pollution: how far can a state proceed in protecting itself from conflicting norms in international law. Georgetown Int Environ Law Rev (GIELR) 11(1)

[193] *See* generally Ryngaert (2015).

Fenton B (2007) How Britannia was allowed to rule the waves. "The Telegraph" Newspaper. http://www.telegraph.co.uk/news/uknews/1538569/How-Britannia-was-allowed-to-rule-the-waves.html. Accessed 10 Apr 2020
Fidler DP (2003) Revolt against or from within the West? TWAIL, the developing world, and the future direction of international law. Chin J Int Law 2:29–76
Franckx E (1998) Regional marine environment protection regimes in the context of UNCLOS. Int J Mar Coast Law 13(3):307–324
Franckx E (2005) The 200-mile limit: between creeping jurisdiction and creeping common heritage. Germ Yearb Int Law 48:117–149
Frank V (2005) Consequences of the prestige sinking for European and international law. Int J Mar Coast Law 20:1–64
Fraser HS (1925) Extent and delimitation of territorial waters. Cornell Law Q 11:455–480
Freestone D (2012) International governance, responsibility and management of areas beyond national jurisdiction. Int J Mar Coast Law 27(2):191–204
Galiano E (2003) In the wake of the Prestige disaster: is an earlier phase-out of single-hulled oil tankers the answer? Tulane Marit Law J 28:113–133
Garcia-Amador FV (1974) The Latin American contribution to the development of the law of the sea. AJIL 68(1):33–50
Gavouneli M (2006) From uniformity to fragmentation: the ability of the UN convention on the Law of the Sea to accommodate new uses and challenges. In: Unresolved issues and new challenges to the Law of the Sea: time before and time after. Nijhoff, Leiden
Gavouneli M (2007) Functional jurisdiction in the law of the sea. Publications on Ocean Development, vol 62. Nijhoff, Leiden
Goldsmith JL, Posner EA (2005) The limits of international law. Oxford University Press, Oxford
Hardin G (1968) Tragedy of the commons. Science 162(3859):1243–1248
Ikeshima T (2011) Is the freedom of the high seas under threat from marine protected areas? Environmental protection versus security interests under international law. Waseda Global Forum 8:5–30
Kaye S (2006) Freedom of navigation in a post 9/11 world: security and creeping jurisdiction. In: Law of the sea: progress and prospects. Oxford University Press, Oxford, pp 347–364
Knauss JA (1985) Creeping jurisdiction and customary international law. Ocean Dev Int Law J 15 (2):209–216
Knight G (1981) Legal aspects of current United States Law of the Sea Policy. Paper presented to American Enterprise Institute Conference on United States Interests in the Law of the Sea, 19 October 1981
Koskenniemi M (2005) International law in Europe: between tradition and renewal. Eur J Int Law 16:113–124
Koskenniemi M (2012) Hegemonic regimes. In: Regime interaction in international law. Cambridge University Press, Cambridge, pp 305–324
Kraska J (2011) Maritime power and the law of the sea: expeditionary operations in world politics. Oxford University Press, Oxford
Kreca M (2002) A few remarks on the theoretical basis of the new law of the sea. In: Liber Amicorum Judge Shigeru Oda, Nijhoff, Leiden, vol II, pp 1207–1216
Krisch N (2010) Global administrative law and the constitutional ambition. In: Dobner P, Loughlin M (eds) The twilight of constitutionalism. Oxford University Press, Oxford
Kunz LJ (1958) Continental shelf and international law: confusion and abuse. AJIL 50(4):828–853
Kwiatkowska B (1991) Creeping jurisdiction beyond 200 miles in the light of the 1982 Law of the Sea Convention and State Practice. Ocean Dev Int Law 22(2):153–187
Lagoni R (2003) Marine protected areas in the exclusive economic zone. In: International Marine Environmental Law: Institutions, Implementation and Innovations Kluwer Law, Leiden
Langewiesche W (2003) Anarchy at sea. The Atlantic Monthly, September, 50–80
Leff E (1998) Saber ambiental: sustentabilidad, racionalidad, conplejidad, Poder. Siglo Veintiuno Editores, Mexico

Loring D (1971) The United States-Peruvian 'Fisheries' dispute. Stanford Law Rev 23:446–447
Losa JP, Delgado IL, Urbina JJ (2003) En torno a la revision del regimen juridico internacional de seguridad martima y proteccion del medio marino a la luz del accidente del Presitge. Revista Española de Derecho Internacional 55:43–78
Makarczyk J (1988) Principles of a new international economic order: a study in international law-making. Nijhoff, Boston
McDorman TL (1981) The marine environment and the Caracas Convention on the law of the sea: a study of the Third United Nations Conference on the law of the sea and other related marine environmental activities. Dalhousie University, Halifax
Merchant C (1998) Green versus gold: tools for an ecosystem approach to conservation: Sources in California's Environmental History. Island Press, Washington DC
Mills A (2014) Rethinking jurisdiction in international law. Br Yearb Int Law 84:187–239
Molenaar EJ (2007) Managing biodiversity in areas beyond national jurisdiction. Int J Mar Coast Law 22:89–124
Molenaar EJ (2015) Port and coastal states. In: The Oxford handbook of the law of the sea. Oxford University Press, Oxford, pp 280–303
Nordquist MH (2007) International Law governing places of refuge for tankers threatening pollution of coastal environments. In: Mensah TA et al (eds) Law of the sea, environmental law and settlement of disputes: Liber Amicorum Judge Thomas A. Mensah. Nijhoff, Leiden
O'Rourke R (2017) Navy force structure and shipbuilding plans: background and issues for Congress. In: Congressional research service. Library of Congress, Washington DC
Owen D, Chambers F (2006) The powers of the OSPAR Commission and coastal state parties to the OSPAR Convention to manage marine protected areas on the seabed beyond 200 nm from the baseline. WWF Germany, Frankfurt am Main
Oxman BH (2007) The territorial temptation: a siren song at sea. Am J Int Law 100(4):830–851
Peters A (2016) The refinement of international law: from fragmentation to regime interaction and politicization. MPIL Research Paper Series 2016–2019:1–29
Ribeiro MC (2013) A protecção da biodiversidade marinha através de áreas protegidas nos espaços marítimos sob soberania ou jurisdição do estado: discussões e soluções jurídicas contemporâneas: o caso português. Coimbra Editora, Coimbra
Ryngaert C (2015) Jurisdiction in international law, 2nd edn. Oxford Monographs in International Law. Oxford University Press, Oxford
Schofield CH, Yi S, Kwon MS (eds) (2014) The limits of maritime jurisdiction. Nijhoff, Leiden
Scovazzi T (2000) The evolution of international law of the sea: new issues, new challenges, vol 286, Collected Courses of the Hague Academy of International Law. Nijhoff, Leiden
Scovazzi T (2015) The origin of the theory of sovereignty of the sea. In: Law of the sea: from Grotius to the international tribunal for the law of the sea. Liber Amicorum Judge Hugo Caminos. Nijhoff, Leiden, pp 48–63
Staker C (2014) Jurisdiction. In: Evans M (ed) International law, 4th edn. Oxford University Press, Oxford
Suarez JL (1926) Exploitation of the resources of the sea. Report to the League of Nations Committee of Experts for the Progressive Codification of International Law. Am J Int Law, 20
Tourme-Jouannet E (2013) What is a fair international society? International law between development and recognition. French studies in international law, vol 5. Hart, Oxford
Townsend-Gault I (2014) The 'territorialization' of the exclusive economic zone: a requiem for the remnant of the freedom of the seas? In: The limits of Maritime Jurisdiction. Nijhoff, Leiden, pp 65–78
Türk H (2012) The waning freedom of the seas: reflections on the contemporary law of the sea. Nijhoff, Leiden
Valencia MJ (1987) Law of the Sea in transition: navigational nightmare for the maritime powers. J Marit Law Commer 18:541

Ventura VAMF (2018) Revisiting the critique against territorialism in the law of the sea: Brazilian state practice in light of the concepts of creeping jurisdiction and spoliative jurisdiction. Braz J Int Law 15:161–179
Vicuña FO (1993) The 'presential sea': defining coastal states' special interests in high seas fisheries and other activities. Germ Yearb Int Law 35:264–292
Vicuña FO (1999) The changing international law of high seas fisheries. Cambridge University Press, Cambridge
Viehweg T (2007) Topica y jurisprudencia, 2nd edn. Civitas, Madrid
Wayne B (1996) The old grey, mare, national enclosure of the oceans. Ocean Dev Int Law 27:97–124
Yturriaga JA (1990) The international regime of fisheries: from UNCLOS 1982 to the presential sea. Viñas del Mar, Lectures
Zolo D (2010) Humanitarian militarism? In: Besson S, Tasioulas J (eds) The philosophy of international law. Oxford University Press, Oxford, pp 549–568
Zumwalt A (1997) Straddling stock spawn fish war on the high seas. Univ Calif Davis J Int Law Policy 3:35–56

Jurisprudence

ICJ (1998) International Court of Justice, Case Concerning Fisheries Jurisdiction, Spain v. Canada, Judgement of 4 December 1998. ICJ Reports
ITLOS (2001) Case Concerning the Conservation and Sustainable Exploitation of Swordfish Stocks in the South-Eastern Pacific Ocean (Chile/European Union). Order of 15 March 2001. ITLOS Reports
PCA (2016) The South China Sea Arbitration, Philippines v. China, Award of 12 July 2016

Chapter 7
Legal Basis of Coastal States' Environmental Jurisdiction on the Continental Shelf

> I have always had difficulties in accepting the Convention in mere legal terms. As an incurable romantic, I see it as a statement of human aspiration, as a carefully-negotiated compromise among unequals, as a series of commandments for the rational use of man's last frontier.[1]—Edgar Gold

The resource potential of the continental shelf, particularly in areas beyond 200 nm, triggers concerns as to the ecological impact of activities is such remote areas. Wherever there is commercial exploitation, there is to a smaller or greater degree environmental damage, the challenge being to limit risks of concrete harm, so as to simultaneously enable economic prosperity and minimize the destructive footprint of offshore activities. To that end, UNCLOS offers a comprehensive and pioneering legal framework regarding marine environmental regulation, having contributed to the awakening of an environmental consciousness sea-wise, but having also exhibited the limitations of a treaty negotiated in the 1970s, when little was known about current deep-sea activities and their corresponding ecological threats. Despite having been praised as "the strongest comprehensive environmental treaty now in existence or likely to emerge for quite some time",[2] it is undeniable that UNCLOS is a product of its epoch and has daunting challenges ahead of it. For instance, the Convention is silent on the precise extent of coastal states' environmental regulatory powers on the continental shelf, particularly beyond 200 nm. Whether on bioprospection for marine genetic resources or conservation of species

[1]Gold (1987), p. 449.

[2]Stevenson and Oxman (1994), p. 496. In fact, UNCLOS incorporates environmental concerns at a moment prior to the dissemination of the idea of "sustainable development", formulated in 1986 within the Report "Our Common Future", UN World Commission on Environment and Development, also known as *Brundtland Report*, A/42/427, 1986.

V. Alencar Mayer Feitosa Ventura, *Environmental Jurisdiction in the Law of the Sea*,
https://doi.org/10.1007/978-3-030-50543-1_7

and habitats of the outer shelf,[3] to give but two examples, UNCLOS' *insufficiency* to regulate continental shelf activities will become evident.

The Convention's limitations are aggravated by the problem of *uncertainties* as to the exact size of the outer continental shelf and, consequently, the extension of coastal states' powers and duties over the seafloor beyond 200 nm.[4] Besides the *physical* uncertainty, the *material* uncertainty regarding coastal state powers over the continental shelf following the final and binding delineation of outer limits may trigger legal questions in the foreseeable future. Sure, the traditional maxim of the "new" law of the sea prays that the farther away offshore, the lesser jurisdiction coastal states will exercise. It is, nonetheless, paramount to assess the precise environmental regulatory powers of coastal states over a maritime space as farther offshore as the outer continental shelf, as well as the situations in which the state may exercise increased jurisdiction, if the area is to be exploited with legal certainty and some degree of predictability.

The focus of this section is to analyze coastal states' environmental jurisdiction regarding the specific maritime zone of the continental shelf, namely the parcel beyond 200 nm. The focus of this work on the jurisdiction granted to *states*, and not to other subjects of international law.[5] As any work in the field of legal sciences, political views of the author influence the analysis of the work's main arguments and its findings. It does not mean that this work disconnects from law and dives into political sciences, as it also does not mean that the arguments herein are equivalent to political pamphleteering alien to legal methodology. These lines are not intended to display political-environmental activism, but to provide an as equidistant as possible analysis of the implications of continental shelf extension in terms of environmental rights and duties to coastal states. Eventually, in the act of pondering principles and values intrinsic to the new law of the sea[6] more weight will be given to contemporary environmental considerations than to traditional principles which have governed the *ordre publique océanique*.

Emphasis on environmental concerns are justified by the fact that pristine and fragile deep-water species and habitats are found on outer continental shelves worldwide, ecosystems whose dynamics and functioning are still poorly understood

[3]Environmental legal scholars have identified the need to develop new legal principles (apart from the common heritage of mankind and the notion of "common concern"), as well as to conclude more bilateral, regional and global regulatory agreements that precisely define "conservation" and prescribe appropriate measures. To date, there is no accepted international definition of the term. *See* Birnie et al. (2009), p. 600.

[4]For Clive Schofield (2011), p. 665, due to ongoing outer continental shelf submissions, "less than half of the potential maritime boundaries around the world have been delimited".

[5]States are still the main actors in the international negotiation of environmental commitments, the onus of protecting the oceans falling with special weight upon them. As put by Benedict Sage-Fuller, "the onus to protect the oceans from degradation remains on States, acting individually and collectively, on the basis of national jurisdiction. The limited effectiveness of marine environmental law in preventing degradation is therefore imputable to States". Sage-Fuller (2015), p. 310.

[6]The technique of pondering values in legal hermeneutics has been explained by Ronald Dworkin in his master-piece "Taking rights seriously". *See* generally Dworkin (1978).

by scientists, let alone by jurists.[7] There is a clear need for more attention to deep-water ecosystems, in particular hydrothermal vents, which are known to occur in great quantities throughout the Area, as enough evidence suggests that such vents host plural marine ecosystems.[8] Besides, the ocean is an interconnected whole, in which an alteration in a particular ecosystem can stir changes of incalculable proportions in several other ecosystems. Thirdly, it remains a coastal state duty according to international law to protect and preserve the marine environment, both within and beyond national jurisdiction. Those are reasons strong enough for coastal states to take protective measures off their coasts. Finally, due to the need for greater and more detailed understanding of the exact regulatory maneuver room of coastal states on issues related to the protection of the marine environment—so as to delimit the scope of environmental prescription and enforcement over the continental shelf, particularly beyond 200 nm. Such clarity is paramount for broad-margin states to grasp what is expected from them upon the delineation of outer continental shelf limits and how far their national legislations may reach in the protection of the marine environment without damaging uncontested rights and duties of other states.

Unilateral action by a state member to UNCLOS on a remote area such as the outer continental shelf may spark controversies concerning the rights and interests of other states in overlapping and neighboring maritime zones. In fact, controversies in the law of the sea are inevitable, particularly in light of the permanent *trichotomy* between the core principles of territorial sovereignty, freedom of the seas and common heritage of mankind. Consequently, national measures aimed at protecting the marine environment that somehow restrict high seas freedoms (such as fishing or researching) may be both perceived as laudable initiatives towards increased marine ecological conservation (Art. 192 UNCLOS) and, paradoxically, as violations of the principle of freedom of the seas (Art. 87 (1) UNCLOS). For no less, it has been said that "the balance between the freedom of navigation and the protection of the environment is not always easy to achieve and often does not meet current environmental challenges".[9] As explained throughout this chapter, the blackletter of the Convention does not sufficiently safeguard that balance, due among others to the option made by the Treaty's drafters for broadness and comprehensiveness—the so-called package deal approach.

In early 1990s, there were signs of strain in the Convention's compromises on environmental jurisdiction, at a time when the text had not even entered into force. At stake were provisions regarding the enforcement of vessel-source pollution rules by coastal and port states, and the apparent conflict with freedom of navigation.[10]

[7] It can be said with relative security that fragile ecosystems, such as coral reefs, are expected to occur close to the baselines of coastal states, continental or island nations. There are known cases of reefs in the EEZ, but "it is expected that these are proportionally far fewer than those that lie within and straddle the boundaries between internal waters and territorial seas". *See* Goodwin (2011), p. 59.

[8] Van Dover (2014), p. 60.

[9] Ribeiro (2014), p. 457.

[10] *See* Bodansky (1991), p. 720.

Since then, technological advancements and a changing morality from an almost purely navigation-oriented to an environment-friendly one, have been gradually unveiling further inconsistencies of the Convention. For instance, as coastal states strive to protect the environment from marine pollution incidents offshore, national measures are met with reluctance, skepticism and protests—as was the case of the domestic measures following the Erika and Prestige oil spills.

In this context, the outer continental shelf seems the perfect stage, and the coastal state, a perfect contender in the ongoing "battle of ethos" and values in the law of the sea. The outer continental shelf accentuates the traditional opposition between state sovereignty and community interests, and reveals the difficulties of adding certainty to international legal rules.[11] In current legal oceanic literature, there is a clear confrontation between calls for a "renewed *mare liberum* ethos",[12] one in which environmental considerations are better placed in the relationship between traditional freedoms of the seas and coastal states' environmental rights and obligations; and calls for a detachment from the "territorial mentality" that allegedly purports more losses than gains to a holistic marine environmental ocean governance.[13] If, on the one hand, by international law's very nature, unilateral action by coastal states "remains a potent yet unwieldy weapon at the hands of the coastal State" in the strive for a balance of interests between users of the sea; on the other, coastal states' actions ought to be me within international legal parameters and in line with valid rules, so as not to lead to systemic instability in oceanic relations.[14] This part takes a side and attempts at assessing the environmental regulatory power of coastal states on the continental shelf within and beyond 200 nm, while attributing increased focus on environmental rules and principles which are inscribed not only in UNCLOS, but also in other international law provisions pertinent to the oceans.

[11]For more on the opposition between state sovereignty and community interests, *see* Klabbers (2009), p. 4.

[12]Ground for such a call is the realization that coastal states have enjoyed over the centuries an unlimited right to exploit marine resources of the high seas. *See* Burke (1994), p. 83.

[13]*See* generally Oxman (2006) and Tassin (2013).

[14]Gavouneli (2014) chap. 1.

7.1 The Role of Law in Protecting Nature: Birth of an Obligation to Protect and Preserve the Marine Environment

It is not novel that the oceans are under strain due to anthropocentric causes.[15] A 2016 Report by the World Wide Fund for Nature shows an overall decline of 36% in biodiversity between 1970 and 2012, and stresses that the most common threats for marine species are overexploitation and loss or degradation of habitat.[16] The world ocean is threatened in its roles as "climate regulator, carbon sink, source of marine biodiversity, and as key provider of food and nutrition, ecosystem services, maritime trade and transportation, and as an engine for sustainable economic development and growth".[17] In sum, the quality of the marine environment is not improving; to the contrary, the outlook for marine biodiversity is rated as "poor and alarming".[18] For instance, hydrothermal vents, submarine mounts and cold-water corals are amongst deep-sea habitats and ecosystems threatened by man-made interference.[19]

Such a scenario of diffuse and human-led marine damage could eventually suggest the absence of political and legal efforts to halt ecological aggressions to the oceans—as if damages occurred with the connivance of public authorities. However, that is not the case, as the international community has been resorting to law- and policy-making to devise strategies aimed at decreasing marine pollution. Evidence of that is the fact that marine environmental protection has gained, in the past decades, the status of "common concern of humankind", following the realization that ecological deterioration extrapolates the jurisdiction of multiple states and threatens the well-being of several peoples.[20] To tackle a common concern, the

[15]Coastal pollution, heavy metal and radioactivity pollution, degraded wetlands, coastal and marine nutrients over-enrichment, eutrophication, acidification, decline and decimations of fisheries, destroyed coral reefs, marine litter, sedimentation, beach erosion, loss of marine mammal populations, red tides, industrial and shipping pollution are but some of the environmental concerns related to the sea. For the purposes of this work, marine environmental pollution is the phenomenon described in Art. 1 (4) UNCLOS as the "introduction by man, directly or indirectly, of substances or energy into the marine environment, including estuaries, which results or is likely to result in such deleterious effects as harm to living resources and marine life, hazards to human health, hindrance to marine activities, including fishing and other legitimate uses of the sea, impairment of quality for use of sea water and reduction of amenities".

[16]The WWF adopts a methodology named "Living Planet Index" (LPI), which measures biodiversity by gathering population data of various vertebrate species and calculating an average change in abundance over time. The global LPI is based on scientific data from 14,152 monitored populations of 3,706 vertebrate species (mammals, birds, fishes, amphibians, reptiles) from around the world. *See* WWF (2016), p. 6.

[17]Zero Draft of the Call for Action "Our Ocean. Our Future", 10 April 2017.

[18]*See* UNEP (2010)5.

[19]*See* OSPAR *List of Threatened and/or Declining Species and Habitats* (Reference Number: 2008-6). See also *Descriptions of habitats on the OSPAR list of threatened and/or declining species and habitats* (Reference Number: 2008-07).

[20]Harrison (2017), p. 2.

subjects of the international community ought to cooperate in several fronts and define rules and standards that nudge behavior towards the rational management of the marine environment.

For decades, law has served a number of functions in protecting environmental goods,[21] among which: a *distributive function*, in which law allocates ownership over or access to marine resources; a *conservatory* one, in which legal norms leave specific resources untouched or allows only for a limited and non-predatory exploitation; a *proscriptive*, as law stimulates or prohibits particular methods and forms of exploitation of a given resource; and a *judicial function*, which offers the possibility of referring disputes on abusive or wrongful state behavior to competent international courts and tribunals.[22]

Belief in law's contribution to the protection of nature was corollary to the birth and rapid maturation of an *environmental awareness* that changed the way in which industrialized societies valued risks to the (marine) environment. This shift paved the way for a normative boom of environment-related soft- and hard law instruments. In fact, the *prise de conscience environmentale*[23] prompted the emergence of new ethics and ethos towards the environment, a turn especially felt from the 1972 Stockholm Declaration on the Human Environment and the creation of the United Nations Environmental Programme (UNEP).[24]

International collective efforts to tackle ecosystem degradation followed suit with a specific change in the *modus operandi* of international negotiations. Sovereign states were deprived from monopoly in deliberating and deciding on environmentally sensitive matters, as civil society movements became increasingly interested in the outcomes of such negotiations—classical examples of which are the creation of the World-Wide Fund for Nature (WWF) in 1961, Switzerland; and the Greenpeace, founded in 1971 in Canada. Hence, the public international sphere of debate witnessed an enlargement of its participants: international organizations, non-governmental organizations and local communities were, to a greater or lesser

---

[21] A major problem, though, is that law usually comes as a reaction to events perceived and valued as negative by a certain society in a specific time. For instance, interest in protecting marine natural resources, particularly fisheries, was only perceived to be relevant once there were alarming levels of overexploitation, failure of stocks and concrete danger of extinction. It was so with salmon and whales. Until the red light started to blink, overexploitation was not socially constructed as problem and, therefore, did not deserve conservation efforts on the international stage. In the case of whales, the most relevant treaties to initiate this trend, and show that uni- or bilateral regulating efforts were not sufficient to effectively conserve the migratory mammals, were the 1882 North Sea Overfishing Convention, and the 1885 Convention for the Uniform Regulation of Fishing in the Rhine. *See* Marine Mammal Commission, *Compendium of Selected Treaties*, 2nd update, 475. There followed several conventions and non-binding documents aiming at regulating abusive fishing practices and conserving particular threatened stocks, so that all those who fish may prolong access to such resources.

[22] Birnie et al. (2009), p. 594.

[23] Kiss (2005), p. 115.

[24] Declaration of the United Nations Conference on the Human Environment, 11 ILM 1416, 1972.

degree, brought to the decision-making table.[25] Public pressure became responsible for a paradigmatic change from the traditional principle of permanent sovereignty over natural resources,[26] which stimulated careless exploitation of living and non-living resources, towards the adoption of legal obligations to conserve and protect the environment, thus balancing economic growth with societal and ecological well-being. In legal terms, such a shift was formulated in the following way: states have rights over their natural resources but shall not harm the environment in exercising those rights.[27]

In the period spanning from the 1970s to the 1990s, several binding and non-binding instruments were agreed upon, which to a greater or lesser extent inserted environmental goods under international legal protection. At that historical moment, UNCLOS was signed, and followed by documents of the 1992 Rio Conference on Development and the Environment: the Rio Declaration;[28] the Agenda 21 (and the call to protect and preserve "rare or fragile ecosystems", such as coral reefs); the UN Framework Convention on Climate Change (UNFCCC)[29] and, most relevantly for the topic of biodiversity conservation, the Convention on Biological Diversity (CBD).[30]

Such a legislative boom, also depicted as the "transversalization" of environmental matters throughout treaties of multiple international legal regimes, quickly raised questions as to the overall coherence of environmental concepts employed in those treaties. Concerns with the normative inflation in environmental matters prompted authors to ask whether "*trop de loi tue la loi*".[31] Plurality and lack of harmony among the thousands of provisions and hundreds of obligations within bi- and multilateral environmental treaties, coupled with terminological ambiguity, cast doubts on the effectiveness of environmental protection, especially of oceans. Yet, despite those issues, the mainstreaming of environmental concerns has brought along numerous benefits to the cause of protecting the marine ecosystems, and prompted a better overture and permeability of law of the sea instruments to environmental norms, as the next item shows.

---

[25]For the purposes of this argument, resort is made to Habermas' theory of rationalization of "public sphere", adapted to the international arena, in line with which the decision-making process profits from the ampliation of its participants. See Habermas (1973), p. 61.

[26]The principle of permanent sovereignty over natural resources under national jurisdiction evolved during the postwar period and was explicitly recognized in United Nations General Assembly Resolution 1803 (XVII), 1982, as well as in other international documents. According to the original meaning of this principle, states had the right to dispose freely of their resources, in an approach that Nele Matz-Lück and Johannes Fuchs label as "rights-based approach". Upon the maturing of ecological arguments, the principle was restricted, as rights were associated to duties and obligations of an environmental matrix. *See* Matz-Lück and Fuchs (2015), p. 491.

[27]Sands and Peel (2012), p. 235.

[28]Rio Declaration on Environment and Development, 31 ILM 874, 1992.

[29]United Nations Framework Convention on Climate Change, A/RES/48/189, 20 January 1994.

[30]The Convention on Biological Diversity, 1760 UNTS 69, 5 June 1992.

[31]Kiss (2005), p. 115.

7.1.1 *Historical Track of the International Obligation to Protect and Preserve the Marine Environment*

UNCLOS is a powerful source of substantive rules on the protection of the marine environment. With the adoption of the Convention, the obligation to protect and preserve the *marine* environment was, for the first time in history, inserted into a multilateral treaty with binding force.[32] If, in its initial provisions, UNCLOS prioritizes self-interests of the states, subsequently the Convention codifies *diffuse and collective interests*, as is the case of environmental protection, regulation of marine scientific research, development and transfer of marine technology, and settlement of disputes. Even though the focus of negotiations was not on the diffuse and environmental aspects, but on the allocation of competences on well-defined maritime spaces, in order to ensure the peaceful use of the oceans, UNCLOS has undoubtedly innovated by codifying *erga omnes* interests from Part XII onwards.[33]

In this sense, it would be possible to refer to insertion of a new category of "trans-individual interests" of a diffuse and collective nature into the Convention, with a particular reference to environment-related concerns. If, as some scholars claim, UNCLOS has assumed the core anxieties which inspired the 1972 Stockholm Declaration,[34] then a core part of the Convention must have been dedicated to trans-individual environmental interests. Such interests belong to no isolated person, but refer to an abstract and indiscriminate chain of peoples—any injury is against the whole community. In short, those are interests to an indivisible good.[35] In this sense, it is pertinent to apply the Convention to the environmental aspects of the seas, whenever legal provisions allow for that.

In so doing, negotiating parties had to strike balances and compromises, in order to fit the nascent topic of marine environmental protection into the new treaty without jeopardizing traditional freedoms of the seas. As noted by Alexander Yankov, Chairman of the Third Negotiating Committee of the Convention,

> [e]fforts had been made to keep a viable balance between ecological considerations and the legitimate demands of expanding international navigation, between national legislation and enforcement measures on the one hand, and the international rules, standards and regulations

---

[32]By marine environment, it is understood not only the physical medium where underwater life thrives, but also life itself.

[33]The expression "*erga omnes* interests", to describe the object of UNCLOS' Parts XII, is employed by Beirão (2014), p. 132.

[34]This view is advanced by Maria Helena Rolim, to whom UNCLOS implicitly confirmed the 1972 Stockholm Declaration by codifying several of the environmental legal principles of the Declaration, amongst which: (i) the prohibition of cross-border pollution and the duty of prior notification and exchange of information; (ii) international cooperation; (iii) technical assistance, via training of personnel and granting assistance to developing states; and the international responsibility of the state, as in UNCLOS Art. 235. *See* Rolim (2014), p. 349.

[35]*Id.* 364.

on the other, between the jurisdiction of the coastal State and that of the flag State, between the interests of developed maritime powers and those of developing countries.[36]

In a sense, UNCLOS can be seen as a set of legal norms that raise the health of the marine environment to the level of a legal good, therefore, worth tutelage. The Convention is the first multilateral binding instrument to legislate on general marine environmental protection, instead of on the conservation of particular species. In fact, several of the Convention' provisions fit into each of law's functions to protect the environment, as depicted supra. There are *distributive* provisions, which determine who has the right to exploit with exclusivity natural marine resources, to what extent, and where—articles on the rights and competences in each maritime space, such as Art. 56 on the EEZ or Art. 77 on the continental shelf; *conservatory* provisions, such as the ones obliging the protection of the marine environment from vessel-source pollution—*vide* Art. 194 (1); and *proscriptive* provisions, such as the determination of a total allowable catch in relation to fisheries within national jurisdiction—Art. 61 (1), or the obligation to promote the "optimum utilization" of the living resources of the EEZ without prejudice to the total allowable catch—Art. 62 (1).

Nevertheless, the Convention has done so in a fragmented and incomplete way.[37] Fragmented, because it treated conservation and management of living resources differently than prevention, reduction and control of marine pollution, in separated sections and subject to different rules. Incomplete, because it did not elaborate on delicate issues such as bioprospecting, the material extent of coastal state's environmental powers on the outer continental shelf, and the exploration and exploitation of living resources in areas beyond national jurisdiction. Those are matters which still provoke disagreement among states on the international arena.

Besides, the international obligation to protect and preserve the marine environment was still at an inchoate stage during UNCLOS' negotiations. In the Convention, such obligation is incipient and rather general, as noticed from Art. 192, according to which "States have the obligation to protect and preserve the marine environment"; or Art. 194 (1), in which "States shall take all measures necessary to prevent, reduce and control pollution of the marine environment". After all, the Convention is a product of its time, and it is no environmental treaty in essence. It is, thus, illogical to expect a pact negotiated during the 1970s and aiming at regulating the uses of the oceans to assume a prevalent ecological stand. Quite to the contrary, UNCLOS embraces an *exploitation-oriented approach* to marine living resources, however tempered by environmental considerations, particularly concerning marine pollution.[38]

[36]*See* Bulgaria, A/CONF.62/SR.99, 99th Plenary meeting, para 4 and 5.

[37]Sands and Peel (2012), p. 344.

[38]Concerning UNCLOS' environmental facet, Robin Churchill engages in the interesting hypothetical exercise of comparing UNCLOS with an "ideal contemporary marine environmental treaty". At the end of the comparison, the scholar finds the Convention's environmental provisions to be encrusted with *normative deficiencies*, namely: lack of substantive norms of its own (as in

The underpinning philosophy inscribed into UNCLOS as to the protection of marine living resources is one of facilitating access, while calling for respect to rates of self-reproduction. In this sense, the international community agreed on concepts such as "maximum sustainable yield", "optimal utilization", "sustainable use", "rational management", among others, which have also been included into several international environmental law instruments. In the maritime realm, UNCLOS adopts a complex web of balancing provisions between exploitation and conservation, which nonetheless amounts to a logic of appropriation of the oceans. On the one hand, it grants exclusive access to marine resources located up to 200 nm from coastal baselines, while stipulating the need for coastal states to assess the maximal catch levels of living resources; on the one hand, the Convention sustains the freedom to fish in the high seas, while subjecting it to quotas and ratios to be determined by the relevant regional fisheries organizations, the Regional Fisheries Management Organizations (RFMOs).[39] As one can see, despite UNCLOS' pioneering efforts towards conservation, it is not a purely environmental treaty, nor was it intended to be.

That said, it is still a crucial instrument in assessing states' powers and responsibilities in ocean-related matters, despite all criticism, reason for which the bulk of the current examination relies on UNCLOS' provisions on the marine environment. The Convention dedicates an entire part with 46 provisions to elaborate on the protection and preservation of the marine environment in terms of: cooperation; technical assistance; systematic control and ecological assessment; international rules and national legislation to prevent, reduce and control pollution in the marine environment; implementation of standards; guarantees; and responsibility.[40] Cooperation is effected at the global and regional level by the states, either directly or through international organizations, and comprise measures such as notification of damages, development of combined research programs, exchange of information, etc. States, either directly or through organizations, are required to provide scientific and technical assistance to developing countries, apart from conducting systematic monitoring and ecological assessment of the risks or impacts of pollution, publishing reports and evaluating potential consequences of human activities in the marine environment.

In sum, international law in general and the law of the sea in particular have played a significant role in reaffirming mechanisms to protect nature, by turning the

---

marine pollution, due to the plethora of existing treaties prior to the adoption of the Convention); or, when UNCLOS has substantive norms, they are too imprecise and ambiguous to be effective (as in the case of provisions on the conservation of marine biodiversity and protection of habitats). Churchill believes the one of the possible ways to address such flaws would be to adopt an implementing agreement governing the protection of biodiversity in areas beyond national jurisdiction. *See* Churchill (2015), p. 30.

[39] Art. 118 UNCLOS, on the cooperation of states in the conservation and management of living resources.

[40] Agustín Blanco-Bazán used the phrase "environmental UNCLOS", to refer to the bulk of ecology-oriented provisions within the Convention. *See* Blanco-Bazán (2003), p. 31.

terrestrial and marine environment into legal goods worthy of safeguarding. Law, taken as a behavior-shaping tool, is an important motivating variable to shape human action.[41] Regardless of its limitations, UNCLOS has contributed to marine environmental protection by establishing a jurisdictional framework for the enactment and implementation of national measures aimed at protecting the marine environment, thus helping to raise awareness towards marine environmental issues. As noted by the Canadian delegation approaching the closure of the Third Conference,

> [t]he Third Committee had registered a signal achievement of historic importance. At the beginning of the Conference, there had been no international law on the marine environment but, as a result of the Committee's work, the *principle of the preservation of the marine environment* had been accepted and a number of practical draft provisions prepared (emphasis added).[42]

7.1.2 *Marine Environmental Protection and the Consolidation of the Ecosystem Approach*

States, international organizations, NGOs and other stakeholders have realized that ocean-use regulation is not straightforward nor linear. The interdependence between numerous marine ecosystems and functions, if not taken into account during national planning and decision-making processes, may render national measures useless or even worse to the overall management and quality of the oceans. In other words, stakeholders have learned that the relations between ocean management/regulation and human interactions is most complex and instable, in such a way that measures aimed at protecting a specific threatened species may cause a disbalance in the food chain of the ecosystem of the protected species, that protective measures may unjustifiably interfere with other human uses of the oceans. Possible consequences and different scenarios need be weighed and thoroughly debated prior to the domestic decision-making.[43] To this comprehensive, integrated management of human activities based on best scientific evidences available about the ecosystems and their dynamics,[44] international scholarship refers as "ecosystem approach".

---

[41]Such conception of law as a shaping tool is formulated, among others, by Anne van Aaken in her critique to Posner and Goldsmith's work on the limits of international law. According to van Aaken, law both reflects and shapes the values and interests of those it governs. *See* Van Aaken (2006), p. 291. A rather skeptical view on the extent of UNCLOS' influence in shaping states' behavior towards the environment is held by Robin Churchill, to whom such an influence is not clear. *See* Churchill (2015), p. 30.

[42]A/CONF.62/SR.113, 113th Plenary meeting, para 35.

[43]Public participation in decision-making processes is, in fact, a fundamental principle of public policies' studies and public administrative theories. For more on public participation, the expansion of the public sphere and the communicative action between governments and citizens. *See* generally Habermas (1981).

[44]Official Statement of the First Joint Ministerial Meeting of the Helsinki and OSPAR Commissions, Bremen, 25–26 June 2003.

Marine environmental governance, here understood as international, regional and national regulatory efforts aimed at protecting and managing the marine environment, has been a constant experimental process. States and civil society stakeholders have gradually uncovered the mysteries surrounding the functioning of the marine environment, even though much is still unknown. In this sense, marine governance and regulation has been transitioning from an initial culture/belief of adopting isolated protective measures directed at specific animals or habitats, towards an integrated and holistic understanding of oceanic systems. Single-sector decisions are gradually being replaced by multi-level cooperation between pertinent agencies, with participation of affected stakeholders, as in the case of the IMO or the NEAFC (North Atlantic Fisheries Commission).

Classic examples of the previous approach are the binding instruments aimed at protecting marine mammals, such as seals and whales.[45] On the other side, an embryonic illustration of a treaty with a predominant ecosystem approach is the Convention on the Conservation of Antarctic Living Resources (CCAMLR), signed in 1980. In addition to that, international commitment to implement an ecosystem approach made its way to the CBD, at the COP 05,[46] as well as to regional instruments, such as the Helsinki and OSPAR Conventions. Nowadays, the ecosystem approach may be linked to three main areas of ocean regulation, i.e. fisheries management, pollution prevention and species and habitat protection, of which two directly relate to the management of the continental shelf, core of this study. As such, the ecosystem approach may be considered a brick in the construction of a legal obligation to protect and preserve the marine environment, thus inserting values as relevant as multi-sectoral cooperation and enhanced coordination between agencies and stakeholders into the traditional, rather unstable edifice of ocean management.

Despite the binding character of the obligation to conserve and protect the marine environment, its exact scope is still controversial in international law, particularly so in the law of the sea. One of the main reasons for that is the fear that, relying on the exercise of environmental jurisdiction, coastal states may foster excessive claims and violate rights and freedoms of the high seas. As contended by Bernard Oxman, "even though yielding to the territorial temptation with respect to a particular environmental problem may promise some short-term or tactical benefit, doing so may augment the difficulties of achieving a desired level of international regulation on environmental problems in that area".[47] For the reason listed above, it is necessary to discuss the definition, content and scope of coastal state's environmental jurisdiction, with a particular look at UNCLOS and the CBD.

---

[45]Remember the 1946 International Convention for the Regulation of Whaling, which set out catch limits for commercial whaling.

[46]CBD, Fifth Ordinary Meeting of the Conference of the Parties, COP 05, Nairobi, Decision V/6, 2000, on the ecosystem approach.

[47]Oxman (2006), p. 845.

7.2 Coastal States' Environmental Jurisdiction in the Law of the Sea: Seeing Beyond Part XII UNCLOS

The study of the "environmental UNCLOS"[48] and the Convention's impact on the management and protection of the marine environment are not new.[49] However, few works have been dedicated to compiling the bulk of environmental powers owned by coastal states on and beneath the continental shelf. Apart from belonging to such restricted group, this book also confronts some well-established premises in literature, according to which coastal states have a very limited environmental jurisdiction on the continental shelf, especially so on the portion beyond 200 nm. As the analysis below will show, such jurisdiction is rather considerable, and should be so, if the international community is to stand a chance in coping with ocean's deterioration worldwide. The applicable law for the assessment of coastal states' environmental jurisdiction over continental shelf activities can be extracted from different sources. First and foremost, it can be found in international customary law;[50] also, in a joint reading of UNCLOS' relevant provisions and the MEAs which eventually apply to the marine realm, such as the CBD.

The premise underpinning this item is that, in the new law of the sea, coastal states have been entrusted with legislative and enforcement powers on behalf of the international community and charged with the challenging task of protecting and preserving the marine environment. If glanced from this perspective, coastal states may be considered to have been imposed colossal responsibilities, namely the greater role in tackling transnationally-caused degradation of the seas, a degradation which has reached levels that could not have been foreseen during UNCLOS negotiations back in the 1970s. In a sense, coastal states have been attributed the role of "keepers" of common, diffuse and collective concerns, particularly the protection and preservation of the marine environment.[51]

As the international community realized the magnitude of the problem described as the "tragedy of the commons", states took steps towards "privatizing" some of those common goods provided by the ocean and conditioning their use to the respect of internationally agreed principles and practices.[52] That change in approach, so as to

[48]Expression employed by Blanco-Bazán (2003), p. 31.

[49]For instance, *see* generally Bodansky (1991) and Molenaar (1998).

[50]It has been claimed by none other than the United States government that *most* of UNCLOS provisions concerning the protection of the marine environment reflect customary international law, a claim far from unanimous. *See* United States, *Restatement of Foreign Relations Law of the United States*, 1987, 102. This view is criticized by William Burke, to whom there was at the time no evidence that some principles of UNCLOS reflected international custom. Burke (1989), p. 508.

[51]Tassin (2013), p. 20.

[52]An example of such principles is the rational and sustainable use of marine resources. Within UNCLOS, the rational use of living resources can be found in provisions such as Arts. 62 and 64, on the conservation of living resources, among others.

tackle the "tragedy" at least in waters adjacent to the coast, is accurately described by Nilufer Oral, to whom

> [t]he common thread in extending the reach of national jurisdiction was to give coastal states *greater control to conserve and manage* valuable resources of the seas and to protect the marine environment from the increasing threats caused by human activities. [. . .] Reliance on flag state jurisdiction to protect the marine environment of the high seas has not proven effective (emphasis added).[53]

Such a shift in environmental awareness has inspired the birth of not just international obligations, but also rights to all states, in a sense that measures may be taken within the domestic order limiting or conditioning the rights and freedoms of other states. From that shift emerged the already cited Arts. 56 (1) (a), 61, 62, 192 and 194 UNCLOS, which have guaranteed all states rights and duties umbilically connected to the protection and conservation of the marine environment. From a combined reading of those provisions emerges an enlarged spectrum of powers and duties falling upon states, to be exercised with due regard to the rights of freedoms of other interested parties.

Should the interests of the international community as whole not matter in the determination of coastal states' and other states' rights and duties in the EEZ, the Convention would not have expressly cared for it in Art. 59. If jurisdictional conflicts emerge, resolution should privilege a ponderation between the rights and duties of coastal and other states and the interests of the international community at large. Thus, in cases in which

> a conflict arises between the interests of the coastal State and any other State or States, the conflict should be resolved on the basis of equity and in the light of all the relevant circumstances, taking into account the *respective importance of the interests involved to the parties as well as to the international community as a whole* (emphasis added).

It seems reasonable to claim that no other consideration appeals to "the international community as a whole" more than the protection of the marine environment and the well-functioning of ocean ecosystems, which enables life on the planet. Other interests such as trade and communications sure matter, but ought to converge to a use of the seas that is not harmful.

Methodologically, this section will propose and defend the concept of a "right-duty to manage the marine environment" as the ground for an interpretation of UNCLOS jurisdictional provisions which favors enhanced coastal state environmental powers. Then, this work will analyze the main activities which may take place on the continental shelf, namely beyond 200 nm, such as oil and gas exploitation, deep-sea mining, bottom-sea fishing, and marine scientific research, thus assessing the most relevant categories of jurisdictional competences, i.e. *prescriptive* and *enforcement* environmental jurisdiction. Finally, this section will attempt at answering whether there are any implications of delineating the outer

[53] Oral (2012), p. 403.

limits of the continental shelf for the environmental powers of the coastal state beyond 200 nm.

7.2.1 Definition of Environmental Jurisdiction in International Law

The concept of jurisdiction comprises both *rights and obligations* held by sovereign states in a given legal framework.[54] Applied to the protection and preservation of the world's oceans, those rights and obligations form what some scholars have named as "marine environmental state jurisdiction".[55] This work sides with the Canadian conception of "environmental jurisdiction", employed as early as 1986, in that country's Memorial in the Gulf of Maine case before the ICJ. For Canada, delimiting a physical boundary enables states to allocate jurisdiction for environmental purposes within the EEZ, such as pollution control or regulation of oil and gas operations. What is more, "as a general proposition, States have a legitimate interest in the exercise of this jurisdiction in areas that are nearer to their coasts than to the coasts of a neighboring State".[56]

When it comes to analyses of marine environmental issues, one should take into consideration provisions from within UNCLOS, but also from outside the strict realm of the law of the sea, in particular principles and rules set out in multilateral environmental agreements (MEAs) and, occasionally, in international human rights instruments. Sure, assessing coastal states' environmental jurisdiction in a given maritime zone is a task which demands a holistic reading of UNCLOS, its implementing agreements and its preparatory works. Yet, marine environmental matters extrapolate UNCLOS, peering into the domain of other special subsystems of public international law. Such a *diagonal regime interaction* is in line with a unifying approach to international law, one that prioritizes a coherent application of the discipline, instead of focusing on fragmentated parts and the tensions permeating inter-regime relations.[57]

For instance, states have obligations under diverse human rights treaties to protect the fundamental rights to life, to physical integrity, to health, as well as the right to a healthy and sane environment.[58] In order to protect those rights, states are required to

[54]This view has been defended in previous sections of this work.

[55]Sage-Fuller (2015), p. 310.

[56]ICJ *Case Concerning Delimitation of the Maritime Boundary in The Gulf of Maine Area (Canada/United States)*, Memorial of Canada, 27 September 1982.

[57]For more on the need for focus on regime interaction and unity, rather than on fragmentation of international law, *see* generally Peters (2016) and Young (2012).

[58]This author has claimed in a previous publication that certain human rights, particularly the right to life and the right to health, could be interpreted in a way that the environment would also be safeguarded. It is the case of human rights established in the American Convention on Human

comply with *general and particular environmental obligations*, so as to prevent violations from occurring within their territories and, in case they occur, to prevent them from trespassing borders. There is, here, a salutary dynamic of interaction and complementarity between rules and obligations of both regimes.

The environmental obligations, both of a substantive and procedural nature, may be grouped in two categories: general and specific. The general obligations consist of *obligations of due diligence* and include: the obligation of prevention;[59] the precautionary principle;[60] the duty to cooperate;[61] procedural obligations connected to the duty to protect the environment, among others.[62] They are general due not only to their rather broad and vague content, but also because they are to be upheld by states whatever the activity, geographical area or component of the environment affected.

Parallelly to general obligations, there are a multitude of *specific environmental obligations* that, for example, refer to the type of damages, such as conventions, agreements and protocols on oil spills, the handling of toxic substances, climate change or the emission of toxic gases.[63] Particular obligations may relate either to a single activity, such as maritime and fluvial transportation, hydrocarbons exploitation or deep seabed mining; or to an element of the environment to be protected, such as biological diversity and protection of habitats and ecosystems, or the conservation of precise species.[64] Both sets of obligations concerning the protection of the continental shelf's marine environment are the focus of next sections.

Rights (1969), the European Convention on Human Rights (1950), and the African Convention on the Rights of Peoples (1981). *See* Ventura (2013), p. 89.

[59]The obligation to prevent harm does not imply an abstract ban on all harm, but the duty falling upon states to take measures to prevent activities under national jurisdiction from causing significant harm to the environment. This duty is expressed in the Rio Documents: Principle 17 of the Rio Declaration; Chapter 22 of Agenda 21; and Art. 14 (1) (a) and (b) of the CBD.

[60]The much spoken-about precautionary principle consists of a legal norm, gradually developed in the past 40 years, that essentially imposes an obligation to take preventative measures in case of risk to the environment and human health. Such principle may be invoked whenever a phenomenon, product, process or activity may have a dangerous impact, identified by a scientific and objective evaluation. It has been codified within the CBD, both in principle during its original drafting, and also directly referred to in the 2003 resolutions of the Cartagena Protocol, which has now been ratified by 170 states. Additionally, the precautionary principle was included as a part of the 1995 UN Fish Stocks Agreement (83 signatories), and in regional agreements such as the Maastricht Treaty formulating the European Union, and the OSPAR Convention, among many others. For further references on the international legal instruments embodying the precautionary principle, *see* Trouwborst (2007), p. 186.

[61]Art. 197 UNCLOS, on the duty cooperate on a global and regional basis; and Art. 283 UNCLOS, on the obligation to exchange views, to name but a few provisions which codify the duty to cooperate in the international normative framework of the oceans.

[62]The Inter-American Court of Human Rights has advised in that direction before. *See* Advisory Opinion 23/17, Requested by Colombia, published in 2018, para 125.

[63]Art. 1, MARPOL Convention.

[64]The obligation to protect habitats and ecosystems can be found in provisions of the CBD (Art. 8, paragraph d), UNCLOS (Art. 194, paragraph 5); RAMSAR Convention (Art. 4, paragraph 2), among other international instruments.

7.2.2 Environmental Jurisdiction on the Continental Shelf

UNCLOS has codified environmental concerns at an early stage of international discussions on ecological protection, in moment prior even to the dissemination of the idea of sustainable development. While the concept of sustainable development was brought to life in 1987 by the Brundtland Report, a nonbinding instrument,[65] already in 1982, 5 years earlier, Part XII of the Convention pioneered an attempt to offer a global response to the increasingly perceived problem of marine pollution, thus turning some of the soft law environmental provisions of the time into binding norms.[66]

Hence, the Convention has built upon existing soft norms and contributed to the consolidation of a body of international environmental legislation, in a dynamics in which both regimes (of sea and environmental law) permanently inform each other. In the one direction, early environmental preoccupations with pollution and deep-sea mining had shaped the law of the sea even before the kickstart of UNCLOS negotiations.[67] In the other, UNCLOS principles form a concrete part of international environmental law, to the point of references to an "environmental law of the sea"[68] or "marine environmental law"[69] being summoned rather frequently in the specialized literature. Inter-regime porosity is undeniable and ought to be at the core of current-day interpretations of law of the sea provisions.

The attribution of environmental rights and obligations to coastal, port, landlocked and flag states conforms, thus, a part of UNCLOS. In so doing, the Treaty is informed by the quest of striking the famously recognized balance between different uses of the world oceans and conflicting views as to the allocation of jurisdiction on ocean spaces. In reality, when dealing with the distribution of "maritime jurisdiction", UNCLOS has struck two key balances for a peaceful and sound use of the oceans: on the one hand, the equilibrium between coastal states' sovereign rights and freedoms of the seas; on the other, the balance between safeguarding the *mare liberum* principle while advancing marine environmental protection initiatives.[70] As it will be analyzed below, striking balances is easier said than done, as environmental concerns may serve as excuses for unduly interferences on traditional rights and freedoms of other states, while international skepticism towards the environmental motivation of domestic measures may deter coastal states from embracing higher environmental standards within their waters.

---

[65] Report of the World Commission on Environment and Development: Our Common Future, 1987.

[66] McConnell and Gold (1991), p. 83.

[67] Remember the UN Resolution 2749 (XXV), on the Declaration of Principles Governing the Sea-Bed and the Ocean Floor, and the Subsoil Thereof, beyond the Limits of National Jurisdiction, A/RES/25/2749, 1970.

[68] McConnell and Gold (1991), p. 99.

[69] *See* generally Kirchner (2003).

[70] *See* generally Nelson (2010).

The interrelation between ocean and environmental law is particularly noted with regard to the continental shelf, perhaps due to recent scientific interest on the seafloor, thereby dismissing the traditional view of the continental shelf as a place devoid of marine biodiversity and, therefore, of environmental concern. In fact, the submersed areas adjacent to the coast have been depicted as "the most geologically diverse component of the seafloor, providing diverse habitats for living resources",[71] an affirmation particularly true with regard to the continental shelf beyond 200 nm, whose biological resources include rare and understudied species, such as hydrothermal vents and cold seeps.[72] Biodiversity riches and the "perceived value of the resources of the continental shelf"[73] are one of the coastal states' main reasons for seeking the extension of their continental shelves and *regulating* activities taking place thereon—together with the projection of power seawards, which an outer continental shelf delineation entails.

As mentioned supra, it would be illogical to pursue an all-embracing regulation of continental shelf activities exclusively within the realm of the law of the sea, reason for which the main legal text inspiring this analysis is UNCLOS, as complemented by other international environmental treaties.[74] The legal framework informing environmental jurisdiction on the continental shelf must rely, at the very least, on: UNCLOS Parts V, VI, XI, XII and XIII;[75] MEAs, in particular the CBD and obligations to take measures to protect marine biodiversity;[76] customary international law, namely the obligation not to cause transboundary harm, the obligation to act with precaution, the obligation to exercise due diligence, the obligation to conduct Environmental Impact Assessments (EIA); and, finally, nonbinding instruments, such as, *inter alia*, resolutions, recommendations, guidelines, and codes of conduct by international organizations.

In that context, UNCLOS' edifice on continental shelf environmental jurisdiction rests on two main philosophies. Firstly, that coastal states shall not have environmental competencies that unjustifiably violate the freedom of navigation of other states. Secondly, the "environmental jurisdiction forms an inherent part of the *control over natural resources*",[77] a control that was entrusted to coastal states after decades of spoliation overlooked by the traditional law of the sea. In other words, the power to take measures aimed at protecting the marine environment is a

---

[71]Ramirez-Llodra et al. (2010), p. 2857.

[72]Some organisms found in hydrothermal vent sites have a high degree on endemism and cannot be found anywhere else.

[73]Mossop (2016), p. 180.

[74]For the relation between the CBD and UNCLOS, refer to Art. 22 CBD, and Art. 311 UNCLOS. *See* Birnie et al. (2009), p. 750.

[75]In UNCLOS' scope, the most pertinent provisions for the debate stem from Part V, on the EEZ, which informs specific provisions on the continental shelf as well; Part VI, on the continental shelf; Part XII, on the protection and preservation of the marine environment; and Part XIII, on marine scientific research.

[76]Arts. 5 and 8, CBD.

[77]Kwiatkowska (1991), p. 160.

corollary of natural resources' control, which undeniably recognized by international scholarship. Therefore, if a state has control over natural resources, it has environmental jurisdiction (rights and duties) to manage those resources in the least degrading way to the marine environment.

On the first assertion, knowing that coastal states may feel tempted to camouflage excessive jurisdictional claims as environmentally sound practices,[78] the drafters of the Convention codified the traditional "gradual approach" to coastal state jurisdiction seaward, or "progressive jurisdiction", according to which the intensity of rights and duties over adjacent areas to the shore is not uniform and will be directly proportional to the proximity to the shore—the closer, the stronger.[79] This premise has rendered coastal states' powers beyond the territorial sea traditionally limited,[80] as on the continental shelf, where coastal state jurisdiction is less than its authority over internal waters and the territorial sea.

Directly embedded into such a gradual approach are concerns by naval and maritime powers of losing navigational and other high seas freedoms to special interests of coastal and port states.[81] Of particular relevance to the debate between increased environmental protection and freedom of navigation are the so-called maritime and military security concerns. Policy-makers and strategists of maritime states consider that an enhanced environmental jurisdiction could serve as an alibi for curtailing navigational rights of both military and merchant fleets, thereby leaving threats such as piracy, terrorism, human and drug-trafficking by sea unaccounted for. The fundamental tension between military security interests and environmental concerns will be analyzed in a specific section below, so as to tackle the traditional view of maritime security considerations as justifying restrained environmental powers by coastal states.

The second premise, that marine resource control is the cradle of coastal state environmental jurisdiction on the continental shelf, the reason why coastal states are entitled environmental powers in the place, will also be scrutinized in detail, as a fundamental step in assessing the nature and scope of those powers. In fact, it flows logically that marine resources and life are part of the environment—a key ITLOS

---

[78]Maria Gavouneli considers that "the affirmation of State power within the prescribed limits does not preclude further, often unilateral, attempts not to affirm its already established jurisdiction but rather to exclude other users of the seas". *See* Gavouneli (2014), p. 14.

[79]Remember the principle according to which coastal states' powers over maritime ones derives from sovereignty over the land. "The land is the legal source of the power which a State may exercise over territorial extensions to seaward". See *North Sea Continental Shelf cases (Federal Republic of Germany v Denmark, Federal Republic of Germany v the Netherlands)*, para 96.

[80]In this sense, this book shares the opinion of Bodansky (1991), p. 755.

[81]James Kraska claims that the liberal ocean order, as he calls it, "faces widespread acceptance as well as concerted challenge and preserving broad and permissive understanding of high seas freedoms in the EEZ requires more effective engagement in the ongoing struggle to interpret and shape the international law of the sea". *See* Kraska (2011), p. 9.

finding in the Southern Bluefin Tuna cases.[82] Yet, environmental jurisdiction on the continental shelf is not identical to control over natural resources, as coastal states are granted rights and duties to protect and preserve the marine environment which extrapolate the sheer conservation of marine resources.

Finally, the rights and duties codified at UNCLOS, in particular Arts. 77, 194 and 208 indicate that coastal states' sovereign rights over EEZ and continental shelf resources mean the power to *legislate* and *enforce* protective measures upon those very resources. A considerable share of coastal state's environmental jurisdiction in the EEZ and on the continental shelf emerged out of the need for enhanced conditions to tackle environmental disasters off their coasts—a claim inspired by tragic maritime casualties, such as the Torrey Canon or the Amoco Cadiz incidents. So, the rights and duties contained in Art. 77 UNCLOS are not restricted to legislating but extend to enforcement measures; and not only with regard to the exploration of the continental shelf and the exploitation of its resources, but the management of those resources, which also comprises conservation and protection schemes. Every single one of the issues raised above will now be tackled in detailed, starting by the traditional opposition between military security interests and environmental concerns in the law of the sea.

7.2.3 The Right-Duty to Manage the Continental Shelf

Based on the increasing environmental awareness of the time, and attentive to calls for a global answer to ecological stresses to the world oceans, the drafters of the Convention have arduously negotiated *general and specific* environmental norms to states parties. Coastal, port, flag states, and others, postulated different intensities to rights and duties, depending on the maritime space in question. In 1982, after striking the necessary compromises, those states were attributed *prescriptive* and *enforcement* powers, in order to tackle marine pollution from a variety of sources: land (Art. 207), ships (Art. 211), seabed activities (Art. 208), and dumping (Art. 209), to name but a few. For the purposes of this work, focus is laid on coastal states and with regard to the continental shelf.

The general environmental provision *par excellence* in UNCLOS is the dual-edged *right-duty to manage the marine environment under national jurisdiction*—a postulation that ground the analysis of coastal states' environmental jurisdiction on the continental shelf. The right-duty is dual-edged in the sense that it comprises simultaneously rights and duties, endowing coastal states not only the right to explore and exploit marine resources under their authority in a sustainable fashion,

[82] ITLOS *Southern Bluefin Tuna Cases*, New Zealand v. Japan; Australia v. Japan, Order of 27 August 1999, para 70.

but the duty to adopt and enforce legislation aiming at conserving those same resources and general marine health in jurisdictional spaces.[83]

That the right to conserve and manage natural resources extrapolates the strict meaning of conservation, was already pointed out by the ITLOS, in the *Virginia G* case:

> the use of the terms 'conserving' and 'managing' in article 56 of the Convention indicates that the rights of coastal States go beyond conservation in its strict sense. The fact that conservation and management cover different aspects is supported by article 61 of the Convention, which addresses the issue of conservation as its title indicates, whereas article 62 of the Convention deals with both conservation and management.[84]

However, the Tribunal has found that management and conservation measures must be directly connected to *fishing*, what could lead one to believe that activities other than fishing, but which also impact on the marine environment, would fall beyond coastal states' environmental jurisdiction.[85] That conclusion could not be more wrong. It is the scope of this work to emphasize that it is possible, legal and reasonable to extract a reading of UNCLOS, in which environmental powers to conserve and manage living resources other that those "fished" are comprised by the right-duty of coastal states to manage resources. It is not just about protecting fisheries but taking measures towards protecting living organisms, including genetic resources, and their habitats.[86]

The concept of a "right-duty" is widely employed in Brazilian legal doctrine, namely in constitutional studies, to refer to a category of rights, in a sense of formulation containing a subjective *Anspruch* to a particular good, which is simultaneously an obligation to act or behave on a particular way.[87] An illustration of this legal formula in practice is the Brazilian right-duty to vote, which is concurrently a subjective power and a duty in Brazil, where voting is mandatory.[88] Applied to the law of the sea, the right-duty to manage the continental shelf contains, on the one hand, the right to explore and exploit, thus pursuing national developmental policies and the welfare of its people, and the duty to protect and conserve the marine space under the coastal state's jurisdiction, by enacting and enforcing national laws and

[83] In a similar view, Joanna Mossop writes that "the right to explore and exploit the ocean resources is accompanied by the responsibility to consider the environmental impacts of such activity". *See* Mossop (2013), p. 183.

[84] ITLOS *The M/V Virginia G Case, Panama/Guinea-Bissau*, para 212.

[85] *Id.* para 215.

[86] By habitat conservation, one understands the adoption and enforcement of rules which does not directly connect to fishing stocks, but only in an indirect manner. The reasoning for this claim is developed throughout the current item.

[87] For more on the idea of a "*direito-dever*" in the Brazilian legal order, *see* Andrade Neto (2018), p. 212.

[88] In Brazil, voting is mandatory for citizens aged between 18 and 70 years-old, with but a few exceptions, and the penalty for not voting is a fine of a symbolic value (approx. four Reais, or less than one Euro, exchange rate of November 2018). Compulsory voting is regulated by Federal Act no. 4.737/90.

regulations consistent with international customary and treaty law on marine environmental conservation.[89]

An important note on the nature of a right-duty is needed, particularly considering possible criticisms as to its (dis)service in grounding excessive jurisdictional claims over increasing maritime zones. The right-duty postulated in this work should in no circumstance be confused with claims to "ownership" over the areas under some degree of national jurisdiction, but solely a particular set of rights and obligations applicable to those areas. In fact, when Art. 56 UNCLOS mentions sovereign rights "for the purpose of", it makes clear that those rights are not associated with the EEZ "in a spatial sense, but are mainly related to its *economic potential*".[90] It is the case to ensure that no "sense of ownership" over spaces under national jurisdiction prevail. Such a concern is formulated by James Kraska, to whom

> [t]he EEZ has acquired an undeniable psychological and emotional importance as an element of homeland security, national "sovereignty," and nationalism. Sovereign rights over the living and non-living resources inevitably morph into a sense of not just entitlement to the resources, but ownership over the area—including the water column and the airspace.[91]

Another concern relates to the extension *ratione materiae* of coastal states' powers over the natural resources of the continental shelf. Admittedly, Art. 77 (1) UNCLOS grants coastal states sovereign rights to explore and exploit natural resources, no mention made to "conservation" or "management", as in Art. 56 (1) (a) on the EEZ. Does it mean that coastal states exercise no other sovereign rights over the continental shelf than those connected exclusively with the "exploration" and "exploitation" of natural resources?

A dogmatic reading of Part VI of the Convention would certainly indicate so, especially if such a reading be deliberately isolated from other provisions of the Convention that complement the regime of the continental shelf. In fact, sovereign rights over natural resources of the continental shelf are not limited to exploration and exploitation. They also include management and conservation measures, the kind of measures that may restrict navigational freedoms and generate the impression that coastal states believe themselves to own the waters within 200 miles from the shore.

Coastal states enjoy not only sovereign rights over natural *resources* of the continental shelf, but also a more comprehensive jurisdiction over continental shelf *activities*, as well as a jurisdiction to protect and preserve the marine

---

[89]Examples of customary environmental rules include some procedural obligations, such as the principle of preventive action, conduction of EIAs or the duty to cooperate before, during and after any actions that might adversely impact the marine environment. For more on customary environmental rules, *see* Sands and Peel (2012), pp. 111, 187.

[90]According to Proelss, the phrase "for the purpose of" "requires that a direct connection exist between the activity concerned and the fields mentioned in Art. 56 (1) (a)" so that the coastal state may be entitled to sovereign rights. *See* Proelss (2017), p. 425, mn 11.

[91]Kraska (2011), p. 7.

environment within that zone.[92] Such a position flows from taking the obligations enshrined in Arts. 192, 194, and 208 UNCLOS seriously.

Thus, referring to a right-duty to manage the marine environment, in this context, should offer legal ground for basically two purposes, two broad sets of state actions: firstly, the regulation of activities which may interfere with the exploration and exploitation of marine resources subject to national jurisdiction; and the regulation of activities which may pose a serious risk to the marine environment (fauna, flora, ecosystems' functioning etc.) of the continental shelf, such as marine pollution or other forms of direct, physical interference with those ecosystems. In this sense, the right-duty does not apply exclusively to natural resources, for it is not identical to the sovereign rights prescribed in Art. 77 (1) UNCLOS. It also governs activities which do not directly interfere with natural resources, but which may pose harm to the marine environment. In other words, the right-duty to manage goes a step further than sovereign rights in providing international legal contours for coastal states' domestic environmental powers.

Moreover, note that regulating uses of the ocean which may degrade the marine environment is not just a right of coastal states, but essentially a duty. Based on that general right-duty to manage claimed here, coastal states are entitled with the *right to regulate* activities potentially interfering with marine resources and the marine environment under national jurisdiction, thereby limiting rights and freedoms of other states. Yet, at the same time, coastal states are bound to a general environmental duty to take domestic action in consistency with the remainder of UNCLOS provisions. No paraphrasing can ever replace the wording of Art. 194:

1. States shall take, individually or jointly as appropriate, all measures consistent with this Convention that are necessary to prevent, reduce and control pollution of the marine environment from any source, using for this purpose the best practicable means at their disposal and in accordance with their capabilities, and they shall endeavour to harmonize their policies in this connection.
2. States shall take all measures necessary to ensure that activities under their jurisdiction or control are so conducted as not to cause damage by pollution to other States and their environment, and that pollution arising from incidents or activities under their jurisdiction or control does not spread beyond the areas where they exercise sovereign rights in accordance with this Convention.

According to the provisions supra, states are explicitly bound. They "shall take all measures" necessary to prevent, reduce and control pollution of the marine environment, as well as not to cause damage by pollution to other states and their environment. The significance and extent of such wording was accurately grasped by Alan Boyle, to whom it provides "the foundation for a much more complex and *wide-ranging structure of powers and duties* covering the control of pollution, the adoption and enforcement of laws and regulations, global and regional cooperation

[92]In the EEZ, the Convention dedicates simultaneously an item to the allocation of sovereign rights to coastal states, Art. 56 (1) (a), and another item for the allocation of jurisdiction with regard to the protection and preservation of the marine environment, Art. 56 (1) (b) (iii) UNCLOS.

and assistance, monitoring and environmental assessment, notification and intervention, and state responsibility".[93]

To adapt Boyle's words, a general right-duty to manage natural resources would function as an umbrella-principle, under which a "complex and wide-ranging structure of powers and duties" of an environmental nature interact. In short, coastal states' rights range from having the prerogative to *legislate* on the uses of the waters under national jurisdiction—taking into account the specificities of every context and the precise goals of every national society, in line with Art. 193 (1) UNCLOS, to *enforcing* domestic legislation, so as to prevent unlawful uses of marine resources and the degradation of the submersed environment under national jurisdiction. Such rights, as applied to continental shelf regulation, deserve to be analyzed in a specific item, due to the intricacy of legal questions arising from the exercise of prescriptive and enforcement powers in the law of the sea.

Onto the particular environmental duties covered by the general right-duty to manage the marine environment of the continental shelf, an analysis of four particular obligations suffices for the purposes of this work. Firstly, one could allude to the *duty not to cause damage by pollution to the environment of other states*, Art. 194 (2) UNCLOS. The straightforward phrasing of that provision has been praised as containing a stronger obligation than the one usually found in international customary law, which often relates to the duty not to cause *significant* transboundary harm, as reinforced by the ICJ in the Pulp Mills case.[94] This duty has also been confirmed by the ITLOS in the 2011 Advisory Opinion on the responsibility of sponsoring states and private entities with respect to activities in the Area.[95] In international jurisprudence, the obligation to prevent has been defined as an obligation of means, not of result; an obligation of *due diligence*, in which states are not required to guarantee a certain result but must prove to have taken all the necessary measures domestically to prevent environmental harm.[96]

Similarly, the Convention crystalizes the *duty not to transfer damage or hazards* from one area to another or to transform one type of pollution into another, so Art. 195 UNCLOS.[97] In essence, these duties limit coastal states' powers when adopting measures to prevent, reduce and control pollution to the marine environment, by clarifying that pollution must be fought at its sources, and not surreptitiously transferred to another area—neither of other states nor the high seas. This duty is credited with partially anticipating the integrative and ecosystem-oriented approach

---

[93] Boyle (1985), p. 350.

[94] ICJ, *Pulp Mills on the River Uruguay (Argentina v. Uruguay)*, para 101.

[95] ITLOS, *Responsibilities and obligations of States with respect to activities in the Area*, para 148.

[96] According to Mossop, this category of legal obligation requires states to "adopt appropriate rules and measures to ensure the outcome, but also to monitor activities". *See* Mossop (2018), p. 446.

[97] The duty not to transfer pollution is also enshrined in Principle 14 of the Rio Declaration: "States should effectively co-operate to discourage or prevent the *relocation* and *transfer* to other States of any activities and substances that cause severe environmental degradation or are found to be harmful to human health" (emphasis added). The Rio Declaration on Environment and Development, Rio de Janeiro, 1992.

to ocean management,[98] apart from bonding with another famous environmental law principle, the "polluter-pays" one. The 1992 Rio Declaration defined the "polluter-pays approach" as one in which the polluter should "bear the cost of pollution, with due regard to the public interest and without distorting international trade and investment", thereby obliging the polluter to act quickly and on-site. The duty not to transfer harm has also been praised for blocking "existing loopholes that enabled states to get rid of pollution easily",[99] perhaps an exaggeration of the practical meaning of Art. 195 UNCLOS, but in no means a wrong assertion.

Then, UNCLOS imposes on coastal states the *duty to monitor risks and effects* of all sources of pollution to the marine environment, as well as the *duty to assess the potential effects of activities* which may cause substantial pollution of or significant and harmful changes to the marine environment, pursuant to Arts. 204 and 206 UNCLOS. Both provisions prematurely consubstantiate the procedural obligation to conduct Environmental Impact Assessments (EIA), an international customary norm most cherished by environmentalists.[100] Yet, the use of vague adjectives such as "substantial pollution" and "significant changes" indicate intention to raise the threshold of application. Ultimately, such terms mirror the battle behind the adoption of both provisions and the concerns by maritime powers as to the risks that environmental considerations posed to traditional freedoms of the seas.

Thirdly, coastal states parties to the CBD are obliged to *regulate, enforce and monitor measures towards the preservation of marine biodiversity*, pursuant to Arts. 5 to 8 CBD; to exercise due diligence upon implementation of environmental duties, such as the establishment of contingency plans;[101] to implement the precautionary principle (or, in the wording of the Seabed Disputes Chamber of the ITLOS, the precautionary approach);[102] to take steps to protect vulnerable marine ecosystems,[103] or to "take measures to protect and preserve rare or fragile ecosystems as well as the habitat of depleted, threatened or endangered species and other forms of life", so Art. 194 (5) UNCLOS.

Finally, and in line with the previous obligations, states are compelled by the *duty to promote the sustainable development of marine natural resources*, an obligation which may be extracted not only from UNCLOS provisions, but also from key environmental treaties. Within the law of the sea, of particular pertinence are Art. 56 (1) (a), on the rights and duties of coastal states on the EEZ; Art. 61, on the conservation of living resources of that zone; and Arts. 63 and 64, on the

---

[98]Czybulka (2017), p. 1319, mn 17.

[99]*Id.* 1319, mn 18.

[100]Shortly after the UNCLOS adoption, the UNEP adopted a series of goals and principles governing the conduction of environmental impact assessments. *See* UNEP, *Environmental Guidelines and Principles* (1987), p. 536.

[101]IACHR, *Advisory Opinion 23/17*, 2018, para 174.

[102]ITLOS, *Responsibilities and obligations of States with respect to activities in the Area*, para 125–135.

[103]UNGA, *Sustainable fisheries*, A/RES/61/105, 6 March 2007, 4.

management of straddling stocks and highly migrant fisheries. Based on these provisions and in line with the theory of UNCLOS as a "living treaty",[104] a treaty that constantly adapts to current cries from the seas, it is reasonable to envisage within the Convention a duty to develop marine resources in a sustainable fashion.

Beyond the law of the sea, efforts to strike a balance between economic growth and environmental conservation have also been undertaken by other special sub-systems of international law, particularly international environmental law. Such a balance is the backbone of the concept of sustainable development, as enshrined into the CBD, according to which states shall use finite natural resources "in a way and at a rate that does not lead to the long-term decline of biological diversity", so as to "meet the needs and aspirations of present and future generations".[105] In other words, economic prosperity is relevant, but it only makes sense if ecological conservation and societal development are simultaneously met during the prosperity pathway. The idea of sustainable development implies likewise that the right to exploit natural resources under national jurisdiction is not absolute and must be in tune with the duty to use natural resources in a rational fashion.

In sum, the relevance of emphasizing the existence of such a right-duty to manage within UNCLOS' edifice lies on the fact that a literary reading of Art. 77 (1) of the Convention could eventually lead to the understanding that coastal states exercise sovereign rights over continental shelf resources for the exclusive purpose of *exploring* and *exploiting* those resources, nothing else. The deliberate absence of expressions such as "management" or "protect and preserve", or "marine environment" in Part VI of the Convention could, thus, lead to stricter interpretations on the extent of jurisdictional powers enjoyed by coastal states in that specific maritime space. Such a literal interpretation would not survive a thorough legal analysis, based also on the evolutive and purpose-oriented hermeneutics suggested at the Art. 31 (1) of the Vienna Convention on the Law of Treaties.[106] In this sense, the idea of that right-duty to manage permits ampliative interpretations upon assessing coastal states' environmental jurisdiction on the continental shelf.

This is not to say, however, that this work believes so blindly on the capacity of individual nation-states to solve trans-individual issues, that it neglects contemporary calls for collective action, for a global and concerted strategy, or for enhanced cooperation to tackle the deterioration of the world's oceans. The idea of a right-duty to manage the continental shelf, falling upon coastal states, aims exclusively at clarifying the regulatory maneuver room left to those states, so that municipal measures which announce increased protection of the marine environment within national jurisdiction not be dismissed as abusive based on a dogmatic and

---

[104] Barrett and Barnes (2016), p. 2.

[105] Art. 2, CBD, on the definition of *sustainable use*: "use of components of biological diversity in a way and at a rate that does not lead to the long-term decline of biological diversity, thereby maintaining its potential to meet the needs and aspirations of present and future generations".

[106] Art. 31, paragraph 1, VCLT: A treaty shall be interpreted in good faith in accordance with the ordinary meaning to be given to the terms of the treaty in their context and in the light of its object and purpose.

traditionalist reading of UNCLOS. The purpose of that suggested legal construct is to offer collective action and cooperation a powerful complement, that of coastal states' domestic action, given those states' immediate susceptibility to marine environmental harms and, thus, their direct interest in the overall quality of the seas washing their shores.

7.3 Partial Conclusions

This section has shown that UNCLOS represented a giant leap towards the regulation of the marine environment, albeit in a fragmented and incomplete way. The Convention was drafted at a time of profound "*prise de conscience environmentale*", in which the value of environmental conservation gains the hearts and minds of populations across the globe, thus prompting organized pressure from social (environmentalist) movements towards enhanced legal protection of species, habitats and ecosystems. In this context, the Convention has pioneeringly codified two dimensions of environmental concerns that caught the attention of the international community by the time of negotiations: the conservation of living resources and prevention, reduction and control of marine pollution from different sources. The way in which the Convention has codified the obligation to preserve and protect the marine environment, by indissociably coupling it with the sovereign rights to conserve and manage marine living resources, allows for the drawing of a general, overriding *right-duty* to manage the marine environment within national jurisdiction.

However, the Convention is a product of its time and, as such, has met its limits throughout the last decades. For one, it only vaguely contains provision on the prescriptive and enforcement powers of coastal states on the continental shelf within and beyond 200 nm. This work has dealt with the most complex issues of managing biodiversity (including genetic resources) on the outer continental shelf, and the conflicts that could potentially arise from coastal states' conservation measures on that maritime space. It was concluded that coastal states' sovereign rights and jurisdiction over the continental shelf are far from absolute, but so are the traditional freedoms of the seas enshrined in Art. 87 UNCLOS. That is the so-called "mutual due regard", which falls upon both coastal state other states. In current days, the balance between rights and obligations of coastal states and other states over the continental shelf necessarily involves taking environmental considerations seriously.

Currently, there is a "battle of ethos" for UNCLOS, which is amidst calls for detachment from a logic of appropriation of the oceans (via territorial claims, which are allegedly cloaked by hyper-protective environmental measures), and calls for an increased sensitivity to ocean ecological issues, such as species' depletion and habitat destruction. The latter would, thus, insist on an environment-oriented interpretation of UNCLOS provisions, and the combined application of the Convention and the CBD in areas within national jurisdiction. This work identifies itself with the latter call and has attempted to draft possible legal tools and concepts, so that increased environmental conservation efforts may emerge from purpose- and context-oriented interpretations.

In this task, the theory of UNCLOS as a "living treaty" has greatly inspired the vies defended in this work. In line with that theory, UNCLOS is "a living instrument, capable both of change in order to accommodate new challenges and of construing novel associations of existing provisions, both in the text itself and in other international conventions, to support the evolving needs of the international community."[107] It is undeniable that the international law of the sea, as any branch of law, undergoes a permanent process of evolution and progressive development that is linked to states' practice and to institutional and academic interpretation of UNCLOS provisions—a typical case of evolutionary interpretation of treaties, a method of interpretation firmly situated in Arts. 31 to 33 of the VLCT.

A correct evolutionary interpretation of a given treaty necessarily combines considerations of evolution (intertemporal) and intention of the parties at the time of adoption. In other words, it calls for the interpreter to take into account the changing needs of the objects protected by the treaty and the objective determination of the parties' intention while drafting the treaty, or the *mens legislatoris*.[108] While there can be divergence as to the "objective" intention of UNCLOS negotiators regarding the marine environment, one should repeatedly refer to the Convention's Preamble and drafting history, in order to extract the intention of establishing a legal order for the seas that will promote the conservation of living resources and protection and preservation of the marine environment.[109] And when it comes to the intertemporal aspect of the law of the sea, we join Tullio Scovazzi in his opinion that "the present challenges of international law of the sea are to be found in the practical capacity of States to adapt and change old principles to conform with new needs".[110]

Coastal states' jurisdiction on the outer continental shelf is not a matter of black and white, but rather of different shades of grey. As long as the protection of the environment be regarded as the Trojan horse of coastal states for advancing national jurisdiction seawards, thus violating the *ordre publique océanique*, the health of the world's oceans can be expected to decrease in coming years. And may coastal states not be tempted to take abusive and unjustified unilateral measures, for every push towards an expansion of sovereignty or jurisdiction over greater portions of maritime zones comes an equally powerful reaction from the international community. In this sense, it is risky and costly for coastal states to advance self-interests disguised as the protection of global commons (such as the marine environment), particularly in the current moment, when the international community accepts that universal problems require universal and negotiated solutions.

---

[107]Gavouneli (2007), p. 146.

[108]For more on evolutionary interpretation, *see* Bjorge (2014), p. 9.

[109]UNCLOS, Preamble.

[110]Scovazzi (2000), p. 232.

References

Andrade Neto J (2018) O voto nulo e seus efeitos: um ensaio sobre a (falta de) lucidez da jurisprudência do TSE. In: Tratado de Direito Eleitoral, 1° Fórum, Belo Horizonte, pp. 209–238
Barrett J, Barnes R (eds) (2016) Law of the sea: UNCLOS as a living treaty. British Institute of International and Comparative Law, London
Beirão AP (2014) Segurança no mar: que segurança? In: Reflexões Sobre a Convenção de Direito do Mar. FUNAG, Brasília, pp 127–166
Birnie P, Boyle A, Redgwell C (2009) International law and the environment. Oxford University Press, Oxford
Bjorge E (2014) The evolutionary interpretation of treaties. Oxford University Press, Oxford
Blanco-Bazán A (2003) The environmental UNCLOS and the work of IMO in the field of prevention of pollution from vessels. In: Kirchner A (ed) International marine environmental law: institutions, implementation and innovations. Kluwer Law International, London, pp 31–47
Bodansky D (1991) Protecting the marine environment from vessel-source pollution: UNCLOS III and beyond. Ecol Law Q 18(4):719–777
Boyle A (1985) Marine pollution under the law of the sea convention. Am J Int Law 79(2):347–372
Burke WT (1989) Customary law of the sea: advocacy or disinterested scholarship? Yale J Int Law 14(2):508–527
Burke WT (1994) The new international law of fisheries: UNCLOS, 1982 and beyond. Oxford University Press, Oxford
Churchill R (2015) The LOSC regime for protection of the marine environment: fit for the twenty-first century? In: Rayfuse R (ed) Research handbook on international marine environmental law. Edward Elgar Publishing, pp 3–30
Czybulka D (2017) Article 195. In: Proelss A (ed) United Nations Convention on the law of the sea: UNCLOS: a commentary. C.H. Beck/Hart/Nomos, Munich, pp 1315–1318
Dworkin R (1978) Taking rights seriously. Harvard University Press, Harvard
Gavouneli M (2007) Functional jurisdiction in the law of the sea. Publications on ocean development, vol 62. Nijhoff, Leiden
Gavouneli M (2014) State jurisdiction in relation to the protection and preservation of the marine environment. In: Attard DJ et al (eds) The IMLI manual on international maritime law, 1st edn. Oxford University Press, Oxford
Gold E (1987) Mare liberum? mare clausum? mare nostrum? can we really have it all? In: The international implications of extended maritime jurisdiction in the Pacific. The Law of the Sea Institute, Honolulu
Goodwin EJ (2011) International environmental law and the conservation of coral reefs. Routledge Research in International Environmental Law, Routledge
Habermas J (1973) Öffentlichkeit (Ein Lexikonartikel). In: Kultur Und Kritik. Suhrkamp, Frankfurt am Main, pp 61–69
Habermas J (1981) The theory of communicative action. Beacon Press, Boston
Harrison J (2017) Saving the oceans through law: the international legal framework for the protection of the marine environment. Oxford University Press, Oxford
Kirchner A (ed) (2003) International marine environmental law, institutions, implementation and innovations. Kluwer Law
Kiss A (2005) Réflexions sur l'interêt general de l'humanité. In: Liber Amicorum Judge Cançado Trindade. Sérgio Antônio Fabris Editor, Porto Alegre
Klabbers J (2009) An introduction to international institutional law, 2nd edn. Cambridge University Press, Cambridge
Kraska J (2011) Maritime power and the law of the sea: expeditionary operations in world politics. Oxford University Press, New York
Kwiatkowska B (1991) Creeping jurisdiction beyond 200 miles in the light of the 1982 law of the sea convention and state practice. ODIL 22(2):153–187

Matz-Lück N, Fuchs J (2015) Marine living resources. In: The Oxford handbook of the law of the sea. Oxford University Press, Oxford, pp 491–515
McConnell ML, Gold E (1991) The modern law of the sea: framework for the protection and preservation of the marine environment. Case West Reserv J Int Law 23:83–105
Molenaar EJ (1998) Coastal state jurisdiction over vessel-source pollution. Kluwer Law
Mossop J (2013) Legal framework for the regulation of safety and environmental issues on the outer continental shelf. In: The regulation of the continental shelf development: rethinking international standards. Nijhoff, Leiden, pp 179–194
Mossop J (2016) The continental shelf beyond 200 nautical miles: rights and responsibilities. Oxford University Press, Oxford
Mossop J (2018) The relationship between the continental shelf regime and a new international instrument for protecting marine biodiversity in areas beyond national jurisdiction. ICES J Mar Sci 75:444–450
Nelson D (2010) Maritime jurisdiction. In: Max Planck Encyclopedia of public international law. Oxford University Press, Oxford
Oral N (2012) 1982 UNCLOS +30: confronting new complexities in the protection of biodiversity and marine living resources in the high seas. Proc Ann Meet (ASIL) 106:403–406
Oxman BH (2006) The territorial temptation: a siren song at sea. Am J Int Law 100(4):830–851
Peters A (2016) The refinement of international law: from fragmentation to regime interaction and politicization. MPIL Research Paper Series 2016–2019:1–29
Proelss A (2017) Article 56. In: United Nations Convention on the law of the sea: a commentary. C.H. Beck/Hart/Nomos, Baden-Baden
Ramirez-Llodra E et al (2010) Deep, diverse and definitely different: unique attributes of the world's largest ecosystems. Biogeosciences 7(9):2851–2899
Ribeiro MC (ed) (2014) 30 years after the signature of the UN Convention on the law of the sea: the protection of the environment and the future of the law of the sea. Coimbra Editora, Coimbra
Rolim MHF d S (2014) A CONVEMAR e a proteção do meio ambiente marinho: impacto na evolução e codificação do direito do mar – as ações implementadas pelo brasil e seus reflexos no direito nacional. In: Reflexões Sobre a Convenção de Direito Do Mar. FUNAG, Brasília, pp 347–372
Sage-Fuller B (2015) A jurisprudential reflection on marine environmental state jurisdiction. In: Legal regimes for environmental protection. Brill, pp 310–323
Sands P, Peel J (2012) Principles of international environmental law, 3rd edn. Cambridge University Press, Cambridge
Schofield C (2011) The delimitation of maritime boundaries: an incomplete mosaic. In: Wastl-Walter D (ed) The Ashgate research companion to border studies. Ashgate, Farnham, pp 665–681
Scovazzi T (2000) The evolution of international law of the sea: new issues, new challenges. Collected Courses of the Hague Academy of International Law. Nijhoff, Leiden
Stevenson JR, Oxman BH (1994) The future of the UN Convention on the law of the sea. Am J Int Law 88:488–499
Tassin VJM (2013) Les défis de l'extension du plateau continental: la consécration d'un nouveau rapport de l'état à son territoire. Pedone, Paris
Trouwborst A (2007) The precautionary principle in general international law: combating the Babylonian confusion. Rev Eur Commun Int Environ Law 16:185–195
UNEP (1987) Environmental impact assessment. Environmental law guidelines and principles. UNEP, Nairobi
UNEP (2010) Global synthesis. A report from the Regional Seas Conventions and action plans for the marine biodiversity assessment and outlook. UNEP, Nairobi
van Aaken A (2006) To do away with international law? Some limits to 'the limits of international law'. Eur J Int Law 17:289–308
Van Dover C (2014) Impacts of anthropogenic disturbances at deep-sea hydrothermal vent ecosystems: a review. Mar Environ Res 102:59–72

Ventura VAMF (2013) Direito humano ao meio ambiente sadio: afirmação histórica e crítica jurídica. In: Direitos humanos de solidariedade: avanços e impasses. Appris, Curitiba, pp 89–138
WWF (2016) The living planet report. WWF International, Gland, Switzerland
Young MA (ed) (2012) Regime interaction in international law: facing fragmentation. Cambridge University Press, Cambridge

Jurisprudence

IACHR (2018) Advisory Opinion OC no 23/17
ICJ (1982) Delimitation of the Maritime Boundary in The Gulf of Maine Area (Canada/United States of America). ICJ Reports
ICJ (2010) Pulp Mills on the River Uruguay (Argentina v. Uruguay). Judgment of 20 April 2010, ICJ Reports
ITLOS (1999) Southern Bluefin Tuna Cases (New Zealand v. Japan; Australia v. Japan), Order of 27 August 1999. ITLOS Reports
ITLOS (2011) Responsibilities and obligations of States sponsoring persons and entities with respect to activities in the Area (Request for Advisory Opinion submitted to the Seabed Disputes Chamber), Advisory Opinion, 1 February 2011, ITLOS Reports
ITLOS (2014) The M/V "Virginia G" Case (Panama/Guinea-Bissau). Panama v. Guinea Bissau, Judgment of 14 April 2014. ITLOS Reports

Chapter 8
Material Extent of Coastal States' Environmental Jurisdiction on the Continental Shelf

The previous chapter dealt, in general terms, with coastal states' environmental jurisdiction to take measures to manage and conserve living resources of the continental shelf, to tackle seabed marine pollution and, in general, to protect the seafloor's environment. Whenever the concept of "environmental marine jurisdiction" appears in this work, it is to be conceived as comprising both rights and duties, for those rights (powers) and duties (responsibilities) interact with each other in a Siamese way, as two sides of the same coin. The allocation of these rights and duties within the framework of UNCLOS and the CBD is just the first step in the "three-step approach" to environmental law implementation, as formulated by Gerhard Hafner.[1] This chapter deepens the understanding of the two remaining steps, i.e. the exercise of *prescriptive* and *enforcement* jurisdiction over activities taking place on the continental shelf which may deteriorate the marine environment.

This work classifies UNCLOS' ecological provisions in two layers. The first layer relates to the material content of those provisions, and basically encompasses two normative groups:[2] *conservation of marine biodiversity*, including the protection of species and habitats; and prevention, reduction and control of *marine pollution*.[3]

---

[1]Hafner (2006), pp. 347, 367.

[2]One taxonomic possibility would be to include the *study* of the marine environment, materialized by environmental regulations on the conduct of marine scientific research, as a distinct dimension of the protection of the marine environment. For the purposes of this work, however, it has been considered that the Convention emphasizes the two dimensions analyzed herein.

[3]Other studies on UNCLOS' adequateness to address modern environmental challenges have also included a separate dimension of *climate change*. *See* Churchill (2015), p. 6. Concerning UNCLOS' contributions to mitigating the threat of climate change, Catherine Redgwell has rightfully reasoned that the Convention has limited tools to fight the root causes of climate change (such as greenhouse gases emissions), but that, in compensation, UNCLOS offers legal ground for increased "emphasis on the restoration, maintenance, and enhancement of certain habitats as (blue) carbon sinks", such as mangroves and seagrass beds. *See* Redgwell (2012), p. 409. For the purposes of this work, little attention will be given to climate change, as the main mitigation techniques aimed at tackling the

V. Alencar Mayer Feitosa Ventura, *Environmental Jurisdiction in the Law of the Sea*, https://doi.org/10.1007/978-3-030-50543-1_8

One must not lose sight of the epoch in which the treaty was negotiated, a time when environmental concerns were just beginning to be taken seriously at the global level, and the marine environmental issues *par excellence* were overfishing and ocean pollution from vessels and land. Still, the Convention is certainly to praise for its avant-gardist philosophies and pioneering provisions on ecological matters, namely the motivation to establish a legal order for the seas and oceans which will facilitate the conservation of living resources and the study, protection and preservation of the marine environment. It is claimed here that every continental shelf activity match either one or both of the supra-mentioned dimensions of marine environmental considerations.

The second layer relates to the procedural nature of powers and duties allocated to states, so that conservation of living resources and control of marine pollution may happen, i.e. legislative and enforcement powers. Given that international instruments *per se* are of limited help in shaping state behavior, the Convention contains several provisions ascribing rights and duties to states, especially linked with the incorporation of UNCLOS and its obligations into the domestic order. In other words, the drafters expected the signing-parties not only to ratify the text, but also to undertake efforts to equip the municipal legal order in a way adequate to fulfilling the Convention's goals. For that, states are granted *prescriptive* and *enforcement* jurisdiction domestically, so as to arrive at the desired state behavior and fulfillment of such goals.[4]

Thus, the following investigation of the rights and duties of coastal states on the continental shelf takes those two layers into account, in order to: assess the prescriptive *and* enforcement jurisdiction of coastal states both with respect to the conservation of marine biodiversity *and* the prevention, reduction and control of marine pollution of the seabed under national jurisdiction.

problem (such as geoengineering methods, as ocean iron fertilization) take place and affect primarily the water column and not the seafloor.

[4]The aspect of rights is undoubtedly more relevant than that of duty. States perceive the negotiation of international standards and adoption of domestic legislation allegedly as part of their right to do so granted by the Convention, not a normative duty. For that reason, it is questionable whether the duty to adopt standards or to enact municipal legislation has played a relevant role in configuring current rules on, say, pollution from offshore oil and gas extraction. Robin Churchill considers with skepticism that "there is little evidence that the LOSC has had much influence on their adoption". *See* Churchill (2015), p. 30. A laudable exception to Churchill's skepticism relates to the autonomous development of environmental regulations for mining the Area (Part XI UNCLOS), i.e., regulations which came from within the Convention and by its normative thrust.

8.1 Environmental Jurisdiction to Prescribe

On the initial question, i.e. the material extent of coastal state environmental powers on the continental shelf, it is mandatory to examine these powers on a systematized manner. Firstly, this section will cover the prescriptive environmental jurisdiction allocated to coastal states for regulating continental shelf uses within 200 nm. The same section will also skim the most relevant activities which may take place on or in connection with the continental shelf, so as to determine the legislative maneuver room of coastal states with regard to those activities. Aware of the industry inherent to such an analysis, it will suffice, for the purposes of this work, to provide an overview of the main seabed activities and coastal states' regulatory maneuver room with regard to the conversation of living resources and the prevention, reduction and control of marine pollution.

8.1.1 First Dimension: Conservation of Marine Living Resources

The conservation of living resources of the continental shelf refers expressly to the sedentary species, i.e. those living organisms that are either immobile on or under the seabed or are unable to move except in constant physical contact with the seafloor.[5] Such species may occur in shallow and deeper waters, the latter being known for hosting deep-sea ecosystems below 400 m. In general, the scientific community lacks detailed data on deep-sea species, but a broad consensus exists on the high biodiversity rates of the deep seafloor, as well as on the chief threats to bottom-sea ecosystems.[6] The greatest threats are posed by destructive fishing practices as bottom trawling, or bottom fishing on deep-sea habitats.

In spite of this work being on the continental shelf, a valid starting point for an analysis of jurisdiction to conserve living resources is to glance at the regime applicable to the EEZ. Up to 200 nm, the EEZ and the continental shelf regimes, although independent from each other, form an *integral whole*, inasmuch as coastal states have proclaimed an EEZ for their own.[7] Environmental rights and duties falling upon coastal states are basically the same until 200 nm, be them with respect to the water column or the seabed. Hence, Art. 56 (1) (a) provides for coastal states' sovereign rights over natural resources of the EEZ, for the purposes of exploring, exploiting, managing and conserving those resources. That provision comprises both prescriptive and enforcement jurisdiction to do so.

[5]Art. 77, paragraph 4, UNCLOS, on the rights of the coastal state on the continental shelf.

[6]Sands and Peel (2012), p. 439.

[7]Proelss (2017), p. 436, mn 34.

The sovereign rights set out in Art. 56 which relate to the seabed and subsoil shall be exercised *in accordance with* Part VI, pursuant to paragraph 3 of that article. Note that the expression used is "in accordance with" and not "subject to", which emphasizes that both regimes of the EEZ and continental shelf are independent but connected in the new law of the sea.[8] Alexander Proelss even speaks of an "overarching regime" applicable to the 200-nm zone, where "a closer analysis of the history and the *ratio* of the EEZ arguably militates in favor of accepting a 'shift of emphasis in favor of the coastal state'".[9] The same can be said, in rough terms, with regard to the continental shelf, despite the slight decrease in favoritism over the seafloor beyond 200 nm.

Upfront, a controversy emerges as to coastal states' rights over living resources of the continental shelf: unlike in Art. 56 (1) (a), no express mention to "manage" or "conserve" is made in Part VI to the seafloor. A strict and literal reading of the Convention would, therefore, conclude that sovereign rights to manage and conserve natural resources would apply solely to the EEZ, thus excluding living organisms of the outer continental shelf from management or conservation measures by coastal states. Within the EEZ, the conservation and management of living seabed organisms that do not qualify as sedentary species is governed by Art. 56 (1), while sedentary species are governed by Art. 77, Part VI.[10]

However, the terminology of the Convention in this regard is not unambiguous. For instance, Art. 61 (3) links conservation and management measures to the attainment of a "maximum sustainable yield", which is to mirror economic and *environmental* factors, including the economic needs of *fishing* communities and specific *fishing* patterns. A connection could be, thus, established between conservation measures and environmental considerations, regardless of the locus where such measures take place. Likewise, Art. 65 is directed specifically at marine mammals and enables coastal states to adopt conservation measures stricter than those provided for in Part V, as long as they are aimed at mammals in general, and cetaceans in particular. In this sense, a traditional interpretation could claim that "conservation" and "management" rights refer exclusively to the specific category of fisheries and marine mammals. Nonetheless, it seems reasonable to claim that the

[8]Such interconnection has been highlighted by the ICJ already in 1985 and went undisputed ever since. In the Continental Shelf case between Libya and Malta, the bench pondered that "even though the present case relates only to the delimitation of the continental shelf and not to that of the exclusive economic zone, the principles and rules underlying the latter concept cannot be left out of consideration. As the 1982 Convention demonstrates, the two institutions—continental shelf and exclusive economic zone—*are linked together in modern law*" (emphasis added). *See* ICJ, *Continental Shelf (Libya v. Malta)*, 1985 ICJ 13, para 33.

[9]Proelss (2017), p. 433, mn 28.

[10]The inclusion of "sedentary species" in the continental shelf doctrine has historical roots and results from diplomatic quarrels. According to Shirley Scott, Australia's commitment to promote the inclusion of sedentary species in that regime, which was primarily based on its goal to remove the threat posed by Japanese pearl fisheries off the Australian coast, turned out to be successful in 1953. *See* Scott (1992), p. 800.

phrase "living natural resources", within the EEZ, refers not only to fishes, but to marine flora and genetic organisms inhabiting the seabed and the subsoil.[11]

Regardless of UNCLOS' terminological ambiguity, one consideration is clear: provisions on living resources of the EEZ *do not apply* to sedentary species as defined in Art. 77 (4) UNCLOS; and the only living resources upon which coastal states exercise sovereign rights on the shelf beyond 200 nm are the sedentary species. In part, because the normative extent of management and conservation powers is enshrined and listed (albeit not in an exhaustive fashion) in Arts. 61 to 67 UNCLOS, applicable to the EEZ, which comprise measures such as: the determination by coastal states of the "total allowable catch" of living resources (Art. 62 (2)); the obligation to promote the "optimum utilization" of natural resources (Art. 62(1)); the duty to give other states the surplus of allowable catch, in case the coastal state does not have the capacity to harvest the entirety of it (Art. 62(3)), among others. In part, because nothing in the Convention enables such provisions to apply to the continental shelf; quite the contrary, the wording of UNCLOS could not be more vibrant in ruling the regime of sedentary species out of Part V. So, could Part V provisions on the conservation of marine living resources be applied to sedentary species of the outer continental shelf by means of legal analogy? The answer is an eloquent "no", due to the different nature of the EEZ and continental shelf regimes.[12] Beyond the EEZ, the concept of "living organisms" is expressly limited to sedentary species of Art. 77 (4) UNCLOS, thus not including general benthic fauna such as fishes that just eventually touch the seafloor.

Consequently, a glance at UNCLOS leads to the conclusion that management and conservation of sedentary species of the outer continental shelf are left outside coastal states' sovereign rights. In line with this understanding, coastal states would not be entitled to take measures aimed at managing or conserving living resources of the continental shelf beyond 200 nm. The practical consequences of such a view are that coastal states may only explore and exploit, but not manage in any sense, nor adopt conservation measures to sedentary species beyond the EEZ. Such a strict interpretation of the Convention does not take into coastal state's environmental powers and obligations seriously. It seems illogical that provisions applicable to sedentary species within the 200-nm zone not be valid for the continental shelf beyond 200 nm—even if the Convention does not expressly endorse such an interpretation.[13]

Even realizing that Parts V and VI do not communicate between each other with regard to living seabed organisms, other provisions within UNCLOS and other

[11]Proelss (2017), p. 427, mn 14.

[12]The inappropriateness of resorting to analogy in this case was also discussed by Rüdiger Wolfrum and Nele Matz-Lück, to whom the clear distinction between the EEZ and continental shelf regimes must be respected. *See* Matz-Lück and Wolfrum (2000), p. 452.

[13]In the same direction, Joanna Mossop is of the view that "it would seem a logical step to say that the flag state also has an obligation to comply with coastal state conservation measures enacted in respect of sedentary species", even if UNCLOS has not explicitly referred to management and conservation of living organisms of the continental shelf. *See* Mossop (2018), p. 446.

environmental treaties may offer legal ground for the exercise of environmental powers by coastal states over the continental shelf, including its sedentary species. In fact, the category of "sovereign rights" contained in Art. 56 UNCLOS, which includes exploration, exploitation, management and conservation, refers simply to natural resources and not to a physical medium, such as the water column or the seafloor. Those sovereign rights may assume the scope of environmental rights (as in the case of management and conservation measures, confirmed by the ITLOS in the Southern Bluefin Tuna case as measures aimed at the protection of the marine environment).[14] Yet, together with those rights, coastal states also enjoy an environmental jurisdiction, which does not relate purely to natural resources and whose object is the quality and health of the marine environment at large—the second dimension of the environmental powers of coastal states over areas within national jurisdiction, analyzed below. That is also the opinion of Joanna Mossop, to whom

> Coastal states have legal obligations to protect the biodiversity on their continental shelves. Part VI of UNCLOS imposes no obligation to protect sedentary species, compared with Part V relating to the EEZ, which imposes obligations on coastal states to ensure the sustainable utilization of the living resources of the EEZ. However, Part XII of UNCLOS imposes a number of environmental obligations on all states, including coastal states. In addition, other treaties and customary international law impose separate obligations.[15]

The same holds true with respect to the duty of "mutual due regard" between flag and coastal states in the EEZ. Even though the Convention has not expressly bound flag states to give "due regard" to coastal state rights on the continental shelf, such a duty is to be read in light of the history of the 1958 CSC, which inspired Part VI UNCLOS. It is not entirely inconceivable that, on specific occasions, high seas rights be abridged to promote coastal states' ecological interests.

Regarding fisheries' regulation, for instance, whenever living resources exist under the jurisdiction of the coastal state, there is municipal jurisdiction to protect, preserve and stimulate the sustainable and rational use of those resources. That is essentially an environmental power. This claim follows from a holistic interpretation of UNCLOS Part XII, on the protection and preservation of the marine environment, the right of permanent sovereignty over domestic natural resources (UNCLOS Art. 193), and conventional obligations towards the defense of the environment present in other binding instruments.

Also, provisions of the CBD could be read in such way as to impose conservation obligations vis-à-vis sedentary species, inasmuch as the CBD provisions be

---

[14]The Tribunal has also found that Art. 192, together with Art. 58 (3), reinforce the obligation of flag states to ensure that vessels flying their flag neither their nationals are engaged in IUU fishing activities, thus confirming the intimate connection between protection and preservation of the marine environment and management and conservation of living resources. See ITLOS, *Request for Advisory Opinion submitted by the Sub-Regional Fisheries Commission*, Advisory Opinion, 2 April 2015, ITLOS Reports 2015, para 124.

[15]Mossop (2018), p. 446.

consistent with the rights and obligations of states under the law of the sea.[16] For instance, Art. 4 (a) of the CBD delimits the scope of the Convention and determines that its provisions apply "in the case of components of biological diversity, in areas within national jurisdiction". Well, it is beyond doubt that sedentary species consist of elements of biological diversity, and that the outer continental shelf is an area within national jurisdiction. Furthermore, Art. 6 CBD imposes on states the obligation to "develop national strategies, plans or programs for the conservation and sustainable use of biological diversity", sedentary species clearly being a part of this provision. Finally, in abiding by such obligation, coastal states may resort to *in-situ* and *ex-situ* measures to conserve marine biodiversity within national jurisdiction. One of such measures is the establishment, as far as possible and as appropriate, of a system of protected areas where special measures need to be taken to conserve biological diversity. That is no other than the blackletter of the Convention, which has been ratified by 196 parties, with the notable exceptions of the United States and the Holy See. When dealing with an international binding instrument, it is never too much to remember that "failure by parties to abide by conservation measures in treaties results in the breach of an international obligation and gives rise to international legal responsibility for harm".[17]

8.1.1.1 Environmental Jurisdiction Over Genetic Resources of the Outer Continental Shelf

When it comes to defining coastal states' environmental powers with respect to marine genetic resources of the continental shelf, the international legal framework turns even cloudier. Neither UNCLOS nor the CBD live up to the challenges arising from new marine research techniques and legal/technical questions which only now emerge, almost 40 years into the adoption of UNCLOS. Here, a confusion which should not occur is the one between the concepts of biodiversity, sedentary species and marine genetic resources. As the law of the sea navigates through different areas of knowledge and has in its essence the print of interdisciplinarity, lawyers usually have to leave their "comfort zones" and venture deep into topics seemingly unrelated to law, yet only at a first glance.

From the outset, it should rest clear that biological diversity is a broad concept initially adopted by ecological advocates and then incorporated into international instruments, so as escape the traditional species-based conservation approach (as in the case of seals, whales and other marine mammals and fishes). As such, biodiversity includes all living organisms from all sources, "including, *inter alia,* terrestrial, marine and other aquatic ecosystems and the ecological complexes of which they are

[16]That is the wording of Art. 22, paragraph 2, CBD, which governs the relationship between CBD and UNCLOS.

[17]*See* Borg (2014), p. 359.

part: this includes diversity within species, between species and of ecosystems".[18] This umbrella concept comprises both large and microbial elements of marine life, such as whales, crabs and genetic resources.

However, sedentary species are *not* the same as genetic resources. According to the definition encrusted in Art. 77 (4) UNCLOS, sedentary species are *specific* natural resources, not be confused with the broader concept of biodiversity, nor that of resources of genetic material. In fact, the definition of sedentary species as organisms which are at a "harvestable stage" focuses on the resource to be exploited, thereby mirroring the overwhelming logics of appropriation entrenched in the law of the sea Convention. No references to "ecosystems" are present throughout the treaty, solely to single sedentary species, an ascertainment that creates major challenges to the protection and preservation of the marine environment under national jurisdiction.

The first identifiable challenge emerges from the fact the concept of sedentary species "has little or no relationship to biological taxonomy".[19] This makes it difficult for states to reach consensus on what species are "sedentary" or not, with state practice varying drastically on the issue, according to each state's economic and political interests.[20] In other words, there is no consensus as to the (relatively) straightforward question of which living organisms are unable to move except in constant physical contact with the seabed, as determined by Art. 77 (4) UNCLOS. The second challenge lies on borderline cases of deep-sea marine ecosystems where both sedentary and non-sedentary organisms live, and whether the two categories ought to be subject to different legal regimes. A coastal state would have legal rights and obligations in respect of sedentary species but not others, which nonetheless inhabit the very same ecosystem. This understanding would go against the CBD definition of ecosystem as a "dynamic concept of plant, animal and micro-organism communities and their non-living environment interacting as a *functional unit*". The problem is particularly acute with regard to the portion of the continental shelf beyond 200 nm.

Should one apply the single-regime approach to both species on the *outer continental shelf*, in the case of hydrothermal vent sites, either active or inactive, coastal states would have sovereign rights in relation to worms and microbes which move in permanent connection to the tubes, but not shrimps and other species that live in the same ecosystem. Such an approach does not seem compatible to current environmental and ecosystem-oriented interpretations in international law. It is clearly a case in which UNCLOS reveals itself as product of its time: avantguardiste

[18] Art. 2 CBD, on the use of terms.

[19] *See* Allen (2001), p. 563.

[20] *See* the Brazilian Lobster War (1963) or, more recently, the snow crab case in the Barents Sea or the Scallups off the coast of Canada. Those animals can be said to move without need for permanent contact with the seafloor, yet they have been repeatedly considered as sedentary species by coastal states.

in certain aspects, but necessarily limited in others, namely in light of the legislative boom experienced by the fields of environmental and sustainable development law.

Hence, while every sedentary species is composed of genetic resources, not all marine genetic resources equate sedentary species. In fact, such genetic resources also consist of eggs and larvae of species that will float in the water column until occlusion. Pursuant to the CBD, Art. 2, "genetic material" means any material of plant, animal, microbial or other origin containing functional units of heredity; and "genetic resources" means genetic material of actual or potential value. Understanding such resources is indispensable for the purposes of regulating bioprospection, which necessarily involves genetic resources. A third challenge is, thus, how to fit new scientific researching techniques into traditional and anachronical legal categories and regimes. It is the case of the technique of "environmental prospecting", in which researchers collect genetic material from environmental DNA, instead of aiming for samples of specific species. Such genetic material may include "skin, feces, mucus, and other matter that is in the water".[21] By using such technique, genetic material of sedentary species can be sampled without the need for collecting the organism *per se*, or even physically touching the seafloor.[22]

In light of such questions, the combined resort to UNCLOS and CBD provisions for the assessment of coastal states' environmental jurisdiction over living resources within national jurisdiction is not uncontroversial, especially with respect to marine genetic resources. On the one hand, it has been praised, given that UNCLOS does not regulate generic resources directly and that law of the sea rules on living resources are not entirely adequate for the specificity of genetic resources. In such a scenario, it would make little sense have UNCLOS always side kick the CBD. Indeed, according to Matz-Lück and Wolfrum "the two regimes exist in parallel and supplement and reinforce each other", and only in cases when the CBD does violate the rights of other states, should UNCLOS provisions be given precedence.[23]

On the other, resort to the CBD to govern genetic resources of the outer continental shelf has been ruled out as essentially "political" and "ideological". For Alexander Proelss, coastal states' management and conservation rights regarding activities on the continental shelf, including marine scientific research, ought to be governed exclusively by law of the sea and intellectual property rights' provisions, as "rules contained in UNCLOS are better suited to achieve a *fair balancing of conflicting interests* involved in such research than those of the CBD".[24] For that scholar, Art. 246 UNCLOS supersedes the CBD, due to Art. 22 (2) CBD itself, and thus limits coastal states' regulatory maneuver room regarding marine research in the EEZ and on the continental shelf. Hence, in line with UNCLOS Part XIII, coastal states exercise limited prescriptive and enforcement rights to discipline marine

---

[21] *See* Barnes and Turner (2016), p. 3.

[22] *See* generally Mossop (2017).

[23] Matz-Lück and Wolfrum (2000), p. 476.

[24] Proelss (2008), p. 442.

scientific research, within national jurisdiction, subject to the "implied consensus rule" of Art. 252 UNCLOS.[25]

This book takes side with the view that does not rule out the application of the CBD to the management and conservation of marine living resources within national jurisdiction, including genetic resources. In fact, the CBD concepts of "ecosystem" and "functional unit", mentioned supra, are of particular relevance in determining the living resources of the outer continental shelf over which coastal states will exercise environmental jurisdiction. Thus, coastal states have rights and duties not only over sedentary species *stricto sensu*, but over the functional unit of living resources of a given ecosystem of the outer shelf. That is particularly relevant for the fragile and pristine ecosystems of hydrothermal vents.

8.1.1.2 Genetic Resources in Areas Beyond National Jurisdiction

In the EEZ alone, the regulation of bioprospection for marine genetic resources is considerably clearer, as the all-encompassing notion of "sovereign rights" over natural resources accommodates all marine life until 200 nm from the baselines, which may have a potential commercial value. For that reason, the largest discussion in terms of bioprospecting for genetic resources refers to both the outer continental shelf and the areas beyond national jurisdiction (ABNJ). The relationship between UNCLOS and CBD is much discussed in recent publications, but almost exclusively with respect to the protection of biodiversity in areas beyond national jurisdiction. In fact, the protection of biodiversity in ABNJ is the "hot topic" of the day, a star whose shine is all the more potentialized by the ongoing negotiations on the adoption of an implementing agreement to UNCLOS on that regard.

Chances of reaching consensus on the topic are extremely low, due to staunch mutual opposition between developing and developed states as to the applicability of the common heritage of mankind principle to high seas genetic material, which would mean the insertion of such resources into the legal regime of access and benefit-sharing of the Area. Research states oppose such proposal and stick to freedom of the high seas, including of research (Art. 87 UNCLOS), while developing states with little technical capabilities pray the submission of bioprospection in the high seas to the common heritage principle.

For Alexander Proelss, given that the odds of such implementing agreement coming to life are rather low, the solution would be to consider MGR as living organisms of the high seas beyond national jurisdiction and expand the mandate of RFMOs to deal with them. Thus, RFMOs would manage hydrothermal vent sites beyond the national jurisdiction of coastal states, and an argument in favor of such a

---

[25]The first part of Art. 252 UNCLOS stipulates that "States or competent international organizations may proceed with a marine scientific research project six months after the date upon which the information required pursuant to article 248 was provided to the coastal State". Then, the provision clarifies some exceptions to the implied consent mechanism.

suggestion would be, so Proelss, the constructive practice of the North-East Atlantic Fisheries Commission (NEAFC) in fighting bottom trawling and designating high seas MPAs. In this sense, the solution for high seas genetic resources would pass far from discussing benefit sharing, but by conserving genetic resources *per se*.[26]

With due respect to Proelss' view, the suggestion gives little relevance to the core claims of developing states, which are (i) to limit access to genetic resources by developed countries and (ii) to create an access and benefit sharing regime that grant developing nations a share of the direct (and indirect) benefits of such genetic and extremely valuable resources. Any solution that neglects such demands is, thus, doomed to fail.[27]

8.1.2 Second Dimension: Prevention, Reduction and Control of Marine Pollution

The second dimension of coastal states' environmental powers on the continental shelf concerns the prevention, reduction and control *marine pollution* from seabed activities, for the analysis of which, mandatory reference to Part XII UNCLOS is due. The concept of seabed activities, used here, may comprise the continental shelf and the Area, thus making it necessary to emphasize the application of the following thoughts and ideas exclusively to pollution originating from continental shelf activities. Upfront, it should be noted that the regulatory scenario for pollution from seabed activities within national jurisdiction does not look bright. Perhaps because it responds for about one per cent of degradation of the marine environment,[28] such sort of pollution is regulated only in general terms within UNCLOS, which sets out the elementary framework for general commitments to be established in regional seas agreements and other specific regional treaties on the issue.

In line with the "three-step implementation" approach,[29] UNCLOS initially outlines states' *general obligation* to protect and preserve the marine environment and defines the obligation to take all measures consistent with the Convention that are necessary to prevent, reduce and control pollution of the marine environment—Arts. 192 and 194. Then, as a second step, Art. 208 establishes states' jurisdiction to *prescribe* laws and regulations for combatting marine pollution from all sources,

---

[26]*Id.* 444.

[27]A counter argument to Proelss' position can also be found in the work of Tullio Treves, to whom international law does *not* address marine genetic resources beyond national jurisdiction. It would be, thus, the case to deal with new a problem through new law. For Treves, "their natural peculiarity, the difficulty to adopt general assumptions as to whether they belong to the seabed or to the water column, the fact that in most cases only samples are needed for subsequent research, and that huge investments are often required to develop potential applications, explain how difficult it is to determine the law of the sea rules applicable to them". See Treves (2017), p. 540.

[28]Sands and Peel (2012), p. 387.

[29]*See* Hafner (2006), note supra.

thereby elaborating on the general obligations laid down previously. Finally, Art. 214 closes the implementation cycle by granting coastal states the right to *enforce* the laws and regulations adopted in accordance with the two previous steps. The last "step" of the approach is scrutinized in the next item.

States (coastal and flag ones alike) do not have an absolute power to legislate on the control of marine pollution, neither a freedom to pollute without being held accountable. States are subject to a "framework based on obligations of control, regulation, enforcement, cooperation and responsibility",[30] all of which are covered in general terms by Part XII UNCLOS. Hence, upon disciplining coastal states' powers and duties regarding pollution from continental shelf activities, the object of this work, Art. 208 UNCLOS must be read in combination with Arts. 192 and 194. In particular with paragraph 4, Art. 194, which prohibits unjustifiable interferences with lawful activities carried out by other states in the exercise of their rights.

Article 208 UNCLOS reads:

1. Coastal States shall adopt laws and regulations to prevent, reduce and control pollution of the marine environment arising from or in connection with seabed activities subject to their jurisdiction and from artificial islands, installations and structures under their jurisdiction, pursuant to articles 60 and 80.
2. States shall take other measures as may be necessary to prevent, reduce and control such pollution.
3. Such laws, regulations and measures shall be no less effective than international rules, standards and recommended practices and procedures.
4. States shall endeavor to harmonize their policies in this connection at the appropriate regional level.
5. States, acting especially through competent international organizations or diplomatic conference, shall establish global and regional rules, standards and recommended practices and procedures to prevent, reduce and control pollution of the marine environment referred to in paragraph 1. Such rules, standards and recommended practices and procedures shall be re-examined from time to time as necessary.

That provision governs coastal states' legislative jurisdiction with regard to pollution *from* or *in connection with* seabed activities,[31] or pollution that does not come from the seabed, but that is generated by *man-made objects* employed to explore or exploit continental shelf resources, such as flowline end terminations—in offshore drilling processes—or remotely operated rovers—in the case of deep-sea mining. In this regard, it is beyond doubt that some continental shelf ecosystems will fall into such a category of pollution.[32] Pursuant to Art. 208, all coastal states have the right-duty to adopt, as may be necessary and in conformity with the Convention,

[30] Boyle (1985), p. 351.

[31] For the purposes of this work, the phrase "seabed activities" is used interchangeably with continental shelf activities, given that the drafters of the Convention meant Art. 208 to apply exclusively to areas within national jurisdiction. Environmental jurisdiction concerning pollution in the Area is regulated by the next article in line, in the Convention.

[32] Mossop (2018), p. 446.

national binding and non-binding instruments, such as recommendations, guidelines, codes of conduct, among others.[33]

When enacting legislation, states have a limited margin of discretion. If, on the one hand, they are given a certain degree of flexibility, which can be extracted from the phrase "as may be necessary", on the other, they are bound by *minimum standards*, meaning that domestic instruments must be equally or more effective than international practices and recommendations concerning pollution from seabed activities.[34] Such minimum standards may be found in international instruments other than UNCLOS, to which states are bound even if they did not consent to, unless they actively dissent. That argument is rightfully advanced by Frank Wacht, to whom states parties to UNCLOS can be said to have voluntarily agreed with UNCLOS provisions relating to *other* treaties, pursuant to Art. 311 of the Convention.[35] It is the case, for instance, of the CBD and the 1972 London Convention, among others.[36] That possibility does not violate the *pacta tertiis* rule of international law, given states' voluntary adherence to UNCLOS. The minimum standards imposed by this "no-less-effective" clause of Art. 208 (3), are to be established on a global and regional level through cooperation between states and international organizations.

Noteworthy is also that the "no-less-effective" rule is to be read in combination with another duty, enshrined in Art. 208 (4), which calls states to endeavor to harmonize domestic environmental policies with neighboring countries, in order to generate a coherent regional body of regulations on pollution from seabed activities. In international legal language, "endeavor" clearly weakens the duty to harmonize policies at the appropriate regional level, rendering it no more than a duty to use best efforts to achieve a goal. Once again, the wording of the Convention is vague and left open for interpretation, since no specific set of requirements is provided.

In Brazil, the Constitutional Complementary Act no. 97/1999, which provides for the general norms on the organization, preparation and employment of the Armed Forces, specifies the duties of the Brazilian Navy. Art. 17 (4) of that Act specifies the Navy attribution to implement and enforce compliance with laws and regulations, at sea and inland waters, in coordination with other executive, federal or state agencies, when necessary. Besides, the "Oil Act", no. 9.966/2000, governs the issue. As far as

---

[33]This obligation falls upon all states, including land-locked ones, given that they are also granted freedoms of the high seas prescribed by Art. 87 UNCLOS.

[34]Art. 208, paragraph 3 UNCLOS.

[35]*See* Wacht (2017), p. 1397, mn 12. Such a view can also be based by official interpretations, such as the authoritative United States Restatement of Foreign Relations Law, according to which "some multilateral agreements may come to be law for non-parties that do not actively dissent. That may be the effect where a multilateral agreement is designed for adherence by states generally, is widely accepted, and is not rejected by a significant number of important states". *See* also United States, *Restatement of the Law, Third, Foreign Relations Law of the United States*, American Law Institute, 1987, Comment "i", 5.

[36]*Convention on the Prevention of Marine Pollution by Dumping of Wastes and Other Matter*, 1046 UNTS 120, 1972. The London Convention was updated by the *1996 Protocol*, 36 ILM 1, 1997.

this study could find out, Brazil has undertaken timid regional harmonization efforts on marine pollution with its South American and South Atlantic neighbors.[37] For instance, there is no regional binding treaty on marine pollution for the western share of the South Atlantic Ocean, whereas multiple conventions have been adopted in the Caribbean, the North-East Atlantic, the Mediterranean, the Baltic Sea and the Black Sea, the Red Sea, the Arab Gulf, Western and Central Africa, the Southeast Pacific, and the South Pacific.

Finally, states are also obliged to adopt global and regional rules, standards and recommended practices and procedures, pursuant to Art. 208 (5) (1) UNCLOS. Note that the Convention does not require states to "endeavor" to adopt such standards (as it does in Art. 208, paragraph 4), but binds states to do so without any qualifiers. Even though there is *no* global treaty governing liability and pollution from seabed activities,[38] the international community has adopted important instruments in the past decades in that regard, namely the 1990 Convention on Oil Preparedness and its 2000 Protocol to Pollution Incidents by Hazardous and Noxious Substances.[39] Besides, one ought also to rely on the several IMO nonbinding codes and guidelines on that issue.

The third step of the implementation cycle of Part XII provisions on marine pollution is to enforce international and national provisions locally. For that, the next item will scrutinize what it means in practice for coastal states to have prescriptive environmental jurisdiction with regard to continental shelf activities. In other words, it will complete the *in abstracto* examination of that jurisdiction with a focus on the most controversial aspect of enforcement by coastal states of international norms and domestic environmental legislation regarding the continental shelf.

[37]In general terms, Brazil and the European Union, together with South Africa, have announced intentions to strengthen efforts towards a *Transatlantic Ocean Research Alliance* by designing enhanced regional cooperation projects on marine science, research and innovation within the framework of the 2017 Belém Statement. One of the purposes of the Partnership is to tackle scientific challenges of the Atlantic Ocean, namely the effects of emerging pollutants. See *Belém Statement on Atlantic Research and Innovation Cooperation*, Conference in Lisbon, July 2017, 2.

[38]International literature has warned over and over on the need for a clearer international legal framework for the environmental regulation of the offshore oil and gas industry. Current regulatory gaps of the international regime relate to environmental safety of operations offshore, and liability and compensation in cases of accidents. There still abound debates on the sustainability of the current international regulatory framework for offshore oil and gas activities, be it in the continental shelf within or beyond 200 nm. For more, *see* Rochette et al. (2014), p. 9.

[39]*International Convention on Oil Pollution Preparedness, Response and Co-operation*, London, IMO, 13 May 1995.

8.2 Environmental Jurisdiction to Enforce

In legal theory, most of the time, the enacted must be enforced.[40] Prescriptive and enforcement jurisdiction are two sides of the same coin, key to the idea of a right-duty to manage marine resources. Of those, prescription is relatively easier to grasp, as legal complications arising from enacting abusive laws and regulations turn out fairly easy to avoid. However, the prescription of rules alone rarely suffices in shaping human behavior, which is the ultimate goal of legal rules. For nor less, enforcement is a crucial element in any legal order, one of the main pillars of the notion of "law" itself. In a poetic sense, it is the "soul" that sustains the "body" of Themis. When applied to international law, enforcement jurisdiction is governed by a fundamental principle, that of territoriality, according to which the enforcement jurisdiction may not be exercised in the territory of any other state without the consent of that state. Still, the exercise of enforcement is not always consensual—and it is no different with the law of the sea.

With respect to coastal states' environmental enforcement powers, it is useful to split once again the analysis of the material extent of such jurisdiction into the two relevant dimensions of environmental protection: management and conservation of marine living resources; and prevention, reduction and control of marine pollution.

As to the biodiversity conservation, bottom trawling and marine scientific research, or more specifically, bioprospecting for marine genetic resources are key activities taking place on or in connection with the continental shelf which relate to the management and conservation of marine living resources. In general, coastal states have the right to take enforcement measures aimed at implementing their prescriptive jurisdiction against activities which may harm living resources of their continental shelves, especially within, but also beyond 200 nm, pursuant to UNCLOS Arts. 73 and 77.

On to the second dimension of environmental powers, regarding the combat of marine pollution, drafters of UNCLOS have dedicated an entire Section to the topic of enforcement.[41] Of all provisions of Section 6, Part XII UNCLOS, particular interest is given here to the ones directly related to the seabed and subsoil subject

[40]Following Hart's concept of Law, there can be, however, primary norms which do not need a secondary norm to ensure its implementation. It is especially the case in the domestic order, in which a (administrative) rule establishes, for instance, the capital city of a certain state. *See* generally Hart (2012).

[41]Section 6 UNCLOS deals with enforcement regarding a plethora of different situations and activities, such as enforcement with respect to pollution from land-based sources (Art. 213); enforcement with respect to pollution from seabed activities (Art. 214); enforcement with respect to pollution from activities in the Area (Art. 215); enforcement with respect to pollution by dumping (Art. 216); enforcement by flag States (Art. 217); enforcement by port States (Art. 218); enforcement of measures relating to seaworthiness of vessels to avoid pollution (Art. 219); enforcement by coastal States (Art. 220); enforcement of measures to avoid pollution arising from maritime casualties (Art. 221); and finally, enforcement with respect to pollution from or through the atmosphere (Art. 222).

to national jurisdiction, i.e. Arts. 208, 210 and 214. Together with Art. 208, Art. 214 UNCLOS is the other side of the coin of environmental jurisdiction over continental shelf activities, as it contains provisions on coastal states' enforcement rights therein.[42] It reads as follows:

> States shall enforce their laws and regulations adopted in accordance with article 208 and adopt laws and regulations and take other measures necessary to implement applicable international rules and standards established through competent international organizations or diplomatic conference to prevent, reduce and control pollution of the marine environment arising from or in connection with seabed activities subject to their jurisdiction and from artificial islands, installations and structures under their jurisdiction, pursuant to articles 60 and 80.

Similarly, coastal states' discretion to implement laws and regulations against pollution from continental shelf activities is limited, as the standards adopted shall be no less effective than international standards, rules, recommendations and procedures.

Another provision governing the topic is Art. 220, on coastal states' enforcement powers over vessels. Following pollution incidents in jurisdictional waters, UNCLOS grants coastal states the right—not duty—to exercise plain enforcement authority, including *in loco* inspection and detention of a vessel—one of the most intrusive enforcement measures in the law of the sea, in cases "where the evidence so warrants"[43] and clear ground exists for believing that the vessel has violated laws and regulations of the coastal state.[44] Those provisions reflect what Maria Gavouneli calls the "graduated approach to coastal state intervention"[45] and form he bulk of legal rules underpinning the current item of this book.

Note, however, that Art. 220 applies only to vessels navigating the territorial sea and the EEZ; not a single reference is made to the seabed. In other words, wherever an overlap exists between EEZ and continental shelf, that provision shall subsidize coastal states' enforcement actions, whereas the same may not be held true for the outer continental shelf. There, Art. 220 does not apply for a simple reason: the waters above the outer continental shelf are considered as high seas, so navigation which does not engage in continental shelf activities falls beyond the bulk of activities upon which coastal states may exercise prescriptive and enforcement rights. Thus, a vessel which is suspected of having discharged pollutant in waters above the outer continental shelf may not be subject to coastal states' enforcement powers from Art.

[42] Article 214 UNCLOS relates not only to coastal states, but to flag states which have ship flying their flag engaged in seabed activities, such the FPSOs, ships used for towing, offshore storage and transportation or other sorts of vessels used in connection with seabed activities. *See* König (2017), p. 1460, mn 6.

[43] Article 220, paragraph 2 UNCLOS.

[44] Art. 220, paragraphs 3 to 6 UNCLOS, on enforcement by coastal states.

[45] Gavouneli (2014), p. 19.

220, but should be held accountable by its flag state for breaching provisions of the MARPOL Convention, or others, where applicable.[46]

Yet, the exercise of enforcement powers by coastal states *regarding the continental shelf* has not been uncontroversial.[47] The much-praised balance between coastal and flag state enforcement rights, achieved by UNCLOS, has been put to test in some occasions, as coastal states have asserted increased powers for environmental purposes in areas within national jurisdiction. Such practices (also described as "thickening jurisdiction") are taken by some countries as excessive maritime claims, what confirms their elevated conflict potential. It is, thus, mandatory for coastal states with strong marine environmental agendas to be aware of the legal limits of their regulatory maneuver room, as well as to ponder permanently the reasonableness and proportionality of every enforcement measure aimed at protecting the marine environment of the continental shelf.[48]

One can think of arguments *against* enforcement rights of coastal states on the continental shelf, particularly based on the blackletter of the Convention. Such an argument would claim that no explicit provision at UNCLOS recognizes enforcement rights on the continental shelf, as the Convention does on other zones such as the territorial sea and the EEZ. Concerning the territorial sea, Arts. 25 and 33 allow coastal states to "take the necessary steps" to prevent passage that is not innocent, and in the EEZ, Art. 73 crystalizes coastal states' rights to enforce laws and regulations. As seen above, the hall of enforcement measures includes boarding, inspection, arrest, detention and the institution of civil and criminal proceedings, as may be necessary to ensure compliance with the laws and regulations adopted by it in conformity with the Convention.[49]

Indeed, there is no reference in Part VI to the words "enforce", "enforcement", "take measure", nor "ensure compliance", as in the provisions applicable to other zones. Quite the contrary, Art. 78 (2) UNCLOS restricts coastal state authority that may unjustifiably interfere with high seas freedoms: "[t]he exercise of the rights of the coastal State over the continental shelf must not infringe or result in any unjustifiable interference with navigation and other rights and freedoms of other States as provided for in this Convention". According to this view, it would be inadmissible for a coastal state's guard vessel to board and inspect a foreign ship based on claims that it is violating its sovereign rights over continental shelf resources, unless the foreign vessel would *directly* interfere with consecrated rights

---

[46]*Protocol of 1978 relating to the International Convention for the Prevention of Pollution from Ships*, 1340 UNTS 184, 1978.

[47]In the late 1960s, Zdenek Slouka pointed out that the issue of enforcement jurisdiction is one of considerable legal uncertainty. *See* Slouka (1968), p. 168.

[48]Gavouneli (2014), p. 16.

[49]Art. 73 UNCLOS is limited to activities relating to living resources, since the article explicitly mentions those resources (and excludes the non-living ones). Such a view is confirmed by the *travaux préparatoires* of the Convention and the Virginia Commentaries (Vol. II, 794). Art. 73 also does not apply to enforcement actions over installations and marine scientific research, although other articles do confer the coastal state such authority.

of the coastal state. Indirect interference would not allow for such a drastic measure by the coastal state.

In spite of that blackletter argument against enforcement powers, there are arguments in abundance in favor of an enforcement jurisdiction of the coastal state. Firstly, wherever the continental shelf length matches the EEZ of a state, the rule of enforcement contained in Art. 73 *supra* applies to ships engaged in or interfering with seabed activities. With regard to enforcement powers over foreign vessels in the waters above the outer continental shelf, coastal states may exercise authority *in some circumstances*, a detailed examination of which will follow suit.

Another argument *pro*-enforcement was formulated by the ILC commentaries to the 1958 CSC, designed to give clarity to that Convention's ambiguity concerning coastal states' prerogative to exercise control over continental shelf activities. In that document, coastal states are conferred "all rights necessary for and connected with the exploration and exploitation of the natural resources of the continental shelf. Such rights include *jurisdiction in connection with the prevention and punishment* of violations of the law" (emphasis added).[50] In other words, the Commission has recognized civil and criminal, prescriptive and enforcement jurisdiction to coastal states for the regulation of the exploration of the continental shelf and exploitation of its resources.

Despite the ambiguity of the 1958 CSC, it has been suggested that, as a matter of *analogy*, the Convention on the Territorial Sea and the Contiguous Zone, of the same year, recognized coastal states control powers to prevent violations of their rights. Here, the definition of "control" consists of two elements, one of prevention and another of punishment. In the opinion of Edward Brown, for the purpose of prevention, "control means a power rather than a right to stop and search vessels in the Contiguous Zone but not to arrest them or escort them to the port". For the purpose of punishment, "control means the power to arrest vessels in the contiguous zone and take them into port for proceedings under its penal legislation".[51] Such an interpretation prioritizes the effective achievement of coastal states' sovereign rights and functional jurisdiction over the continental shelf, without extending such rights *ratione loci* to the superjacent waters. As rightfully noted by Brown, "a limited degree of jurisdiction and control over foreign vessels on the high seas above the shelf must be admitted".[52]

All in all, the right to implement domestic laws and regulation in areas of national jurisdiction exists and is protected by international law. The exercise of such rights, however, is subject to the *obligation of due regard* when taking measures, both to manage and conserve biodiversity and to prevent, reduce and control marine pollution, so Arts. 78 and 194 (4) UNCLOS. In fact, the Convention expressly prohibits "unjustifiable interferences" to the rights and freedoms of other states in the maritime spaces under coastal states' national jurisdiction and calls for a reasonable balancing

---

[50] ILC (1956), p. 297.

[51] Brown (1973), p. 95.

[52] *Id.* 94.

of interests between conflicting interests. At the end of the day, the measures taken must not be disproportionate to the protection of the interests at stake nor hurt the freedom of other states in an unnecessary way. Such criterion (of not interfering with other rights in an unjustifiable manner) has been considered vague, but according to Joanna Mossop it is "all there is".[53] Hence, border-line cases involving environmental measures with interfering potential may only be evaluated on a casuistic basis, so as to assess whether the measures were justified or not. Despite of the conflictive potential of environmental measures in zones of functional jurisdiction, such as the EEZ and the continental shelf, "a rebuttable presumption of competency in favor of the coastal state should be applied".[54]

The limited state practice under the 1958 CSC confirmed the view that coastal states claimed enforcement jurisdiction over activities directed at living and non-living resources of the continental shelf.[55] The United States, despite having a domestic law acknowledging enforcement jurisdiction over foreign vessels fishing for sedentary species on the continental shelf, has preferred not to seize any foreign ships for doing so—not a single one had been seized by 1974. The Soviet Union and Australia also had provisions on enforcement powers in national legislations, powers considered legal and reasonable due to their connection with the right to *control* sedentary species of the continental shelf.[56]

To refer to the case study of this work, Brazilian enforcement powers in superjacent waters of the continental shelf were implicit in national legislation.[57] Of particular relevance for that time were the Decree-Law no. 44/1966, signed during the military regime, which enlarged the limits of the Brazilian territorial sea from 3 to 6 nm, apart from creating a contiguous zone of extra 6 nm, where the country exercised exclusive fishing rights.[58] That decree was to be "enforced accordingly", so the original Portuguese text—Art. 4 Decree-Law no. 44. In addition to that, Decree-Law no. 553/1969, Art. 2, extended the Brazilian territorial sea to 12 nm and contained a provision on enforcement identical to the previous Decree-Law no. 44.

The later Decree-Law no. 1.098/1970, declaring a territorial sea of 200 nm in length, determined that foreign vessels must respect domestic regulations aimed at preventing water pollution and damage to marine resources within the 200-nm zone, so Art. 3 (2). Likewise, the Statute stipulated that foreign vessels fishing within areas allowed by the legislation could only carry out their activities when duly registered

---

[53]Mossop (2013), p. 193.

[54]Czybulka (2017), p. 1309, mn 28.

[55]Mossop (2016), p. 208.

[56]For details on national legislations of the United States, Australia and the Soviet Union, *id.* 208.

[57]Brazilian legislation analyzed includes: Decree 28.840/1950, which declared the "submarine shelf" an integral part of the national territory and subject to the jurisdiction of the Federal State; the 1967 Federal Constitution, which included the "submarine shelf" as property of the Federal State. A detailed study on those laws follows in Chaps. 9 and 10.

[58]Arts. 2 and 3, Decree-Law no. 44, 18 November 1966.

and under an obligation to comply with Brazilian regulations.[59] Pursuant to Regulatory Decree no. 68.459/1971, which detailed the Decree-Law no. 1098/1970, enforcement measures were to be exercised by the Ministry of the Navy and included the arrest of vessels as well as imprisonment of perpetrators—a measure that would frontally breach current UNCLOS Art. 73 (3), which prohibits the incarceration or any form of corporal punishments for violation of fisheries laws.[60]

Due to their complexity and conflict-creating potential, legal questions concerning enforcement have made it to international jurisprudence in several occasions. When it comes to international tribunals' contribution to the clarification of the issue in general, and not just related to environmental concerns, the ITLOS has contributed with valuable inputs. In fact, the Tribunal has decided, for instance, that the use of force in the law of the sea must be avoided as far as possible, and that enforcement powers must not go beyond what is reasonable and necessary in the circumstances, as determined in the *M/V Saiga* case.[61] In another paradigmatic case, the *Virginia G*, the Tribunal decided that coastal states have sovereign rights in their EEZ to adopt regulations concerning exploration, exploitation, conservation and management of natural resources, including, *inter alia*, the right to "take the necessary enforcement measures" for the implementation of national legislation. According to the decision,

> Article 56 of the Convention refers to sovereign rights for the purpose of exploring and exploiting, conserving and managing natural resources. The term "sovereign rights" in the view of the Tribunal encompasses all rights necessary for and connected with the exploration, exploitation, conservation and management of the natural resources, including the right to take the necessary enforcement measures.[62]

International jurisprudence has confirmed coastal states' limited enforcement powers, as in the emblematic *Arctic Sunrise* case, which landed at the ITLOS docket in 2012. The case opposed Netherlands and Russia, following the arrest of Greenpeace's vessel "Arctic Sunrise", flying the Dutch flag, by Russian authorities, after an alleged violation of Russian sovereignty during a peaceful protest at an oil rig within the Russian EEZ. Following the arrest, the Dutch initiated a compulsory procedure before the ITLOS, requesting for provisional measures under Art. 290 (5) UNCLOS, while simultaneously starting arbitral proceedings against Russia in accordance with Annex VII UNCLOS. Despite Russia's "no show" in both procedures, a conduct heavily criticized in the international sphere, the ITLOS found that enough evidence supported the granting of provisional measures to immediately release the vessel and its crew, upon the posting of a bond by the Dutch government.[63] Subsequently, and the arbitral tribunal found that the Russian

---

[59] Art. 4, paragraph 2, Decree-Law no. 1098/1970.

[60] Art. 11, paragraph 3, Regulatory Decree no. 68.459/1971, Brazil.

[61] ITLOS, *The M/V Saiga (Saint Vincent and the Grenadines v. Guinea), Prompt release, Judgment, ITLOS Reports* 1997, at 16, para 155.

[62] *Id. The Virginia G case*, para 211.

[63] *Id. The Artic Sunrise case*, para 105 (1) (a).

arrest had violated freedom of navigation and manifestation enjoyed by vessels sailing within the EZZ.[64]

In a dissenting opinion, however, Judge Vladimir Golitsyn reasoned that laws and regulations passed by the coastal state would be "meaningless if the coastal State did not have the authority to ensure their enforcement". As a logical consequence, coastal states would have the right, pursuant to Art. 60 (2) UNCLOS, to enforce domestic rules governing artificial islands, installations and structures.[65] The overall content of the Arctic Sunrise case is rather complex and escapes the purpose of this book. Nonetheless, it is noteworthy that, in the merits of the case, the Arbitral Tribunal found that Russia did not have enforcement rights over the vessel, because the country has no right to enforce violations to domestic laws beyond the 500-meter safety zones around oil platforms, unless it had met the criteria for hot pursuit—which the Tribunal asserted Russia did not.[66] In any case, it remains beyond doubt in both decisions that coastal states do enjoy enforcement rights in the circumstances provided for in the Convention.

The Arbitral Tribunal also stated that coastal states have the right to enforce domestic laws relating to non-living resources in the EEZ, but it did not elaborate on the extent of the right. In line with the ILC Commentaries to the 1958 CSC (or ILC draft articles), enforcement is an integral part of sovereign rights. With regard to enforcement rights over vessels outside of safety zones surrounding oil installations and structures, the Convention is supposed to be applied to that area alone, not to the whole EEZ or continental shelf. Otherwise, it would have made no sense for UNCLOS drafters to make express references to safety zones in Art. 60 (4).[67]

Note, thus, that the legal reasoning employed by the Arbitral Tribunal also applies to the relationship between navigation freedoms and coastal states' rights on the continental shelf within and beyond 200 nm. Measures taken by coastal states must be *reasonable, necessary and proportionate*.[68] In the Arctic Sunrise case, there was

---

[64]PCA, *The Arctic Sunrise Arbitration* (The Netherlands v. Russian Federation), Award on the Merits, 14 August 2015, para 401 (c).

[65]Judge Vladimir Golitsyn, Dissenting opinion, *The Arctic Sunrise case*, ITLOS, para 23.

[66]PCA, *The Arctic Sunrise Arbitration*, 2015, para 229.

[67]Such was the understanding of Judges Rüdiger Wolfrum and Elsa Kelly in the Arctic Sunrise case, to whom "as far as enforcement actions in the exclusive zone in general are concerned the enforcement jurisdiction of the coastal State is limited if it is not legitimized by one of the exceptions mentioned above. It is for the flag State to take the enforcement actions not entrusted to the coastal State by the Convention on the Law of the Sea". Para 13. Still according to the judges, "this division of enforcement functions between the coastal State and the flag State should have been of relevance in formulating the provisional measures since such provisional measures should have taken into account that the Russian Federation enjoys enforcement functions in respect of the protection of the platform within the safety zone whereas it has no such right in its exclusive economic zone *vis-à-vis* the *Arctic Sunrise* as the facts present themselves at the moment". See *The Arctic Sunrise Case (Kingdom of Netherlands v. Russian Federation), Provisional Measures*, Order of 22 November 2013, ITLOS Reports, *Separate Opinion*, Judges Rüdiger Wolfrum and Elsa Kelly, para 14.

[68]PCA, *The Arctic Sunrise Arbitration*, 2015, para 326.

no evidence that, at the time of detention, the vessel was unjustifiably interfering with the operation of the platform, and enforcement jurisdiction may only be exercised provided there is threat of undue interference with a coastal state's sovereign rights over the continental shelf.

The Arbitral Tribunal's adding of a temporal element to qualify the right to enforce national laws by the coastal states seems to have created yet another legal conflict with the Convention. The Tribunal's view seems to severely restrict the power of the coastal state to actually exercise its enforcement rights against foreign vessels engaged in breaches to domestic laws and regulations. In this sense, the Tribunal went a tick too far and may have created an enormous barrier to the exercise of enforcement jurisdiction by coastal states. The decision has faced criticism by the specialized literature, to whom the interpretation given by the Tribunal to Art. 73 UNCLOS restricts coastal states' enforcement rights "in such a way would be a serious limitation on the ability of a coastal State to protect its rights and does not reflect the reality of enforcement in remote parts of the ocean".[69] In this sense, a reasonable and dogmatic interpretation of the Convention would acknowledge coastal states enforcement rights, even over violations which occurred in the recent past.

Existing case law has centered, thus far, on the exercise of jurisdiction in the EEZ and not on the continental shelf. Nevertheless, the decisions have to a lesser or greater extent confirmed coastal state's prescriptive and enforcement jurisdiction in the EEZ. Given the existing parallelism between the Zone and the continental shelf, it is logical de deduce that coastal states also enjoy prescriptive and implementing powers on the continental shelf, as mentioned supra. A most delicate part of a study on coastal state environmental jurisdiction on the continental shelf surfaces once one looks at the portion of the seabed extending beyond 200 nm from the baselines.

Hence, coastal states must exercise environmental jurisdiction over the outer shelf with due regard to the rights and freedoms of other states and respecting the high seas status of the superjacent waters. They are expected to exercise environmental powers within the material limits of Art. 78 UNCLOS ("must not infringe or result in any unjustifiable interference" with navigation and other rights of other states). Yet, "unjustifiable" is a term passive of different interpretations, especially as time passes and new values inspire the international community. When France, Spain and Portugal decided to unilaterally ban the access of single-hull tankers from their EEZ, such a measure was considered by many as "unjustifiable" at the time, but certainly is not so nowadays. Thus, borderline cases in which coastal states restrain rights and freedoms of high seas of other states, while exercising environmental jurisdiction above the outer continental shelf a should be analyzed on a case-by-case basis.

There may be occasions, however, when coastal states' interests in protecting living resources and habitats of the outer continental shelf are provenly significant. In those situations, coastal states may adopt rules and enforcement measures that

[69]This criticism, which this work sides with, is formulated by Mossop (2016), p. 214.

upset other states' rights in the high seas. The most important criteria that coastal states must obey when exercising such "enlarged" environmental jurisdiction on the continental shelf, especially beyond 200 nm, are the tripod: reasonability, necessity and proportionality. In light of those criteria, every coastal state, before prescribing or enforcing a rule, should meet a number of requirements, so that conflicts be prevented.

A potentially useful tool is the methodology developed by Joanna Mossop for coastal states who are looking into environmentally protective measures on their outer continental shelves, in order to prevent conflicts with other states navigating the superjacent waters or engaged in some sort of activity in connection with the seabed.[70] According to Mossop, a coastal state must (i) prove the scientific foundation of the measure, backed by evidences of likely environmental harm; (ii) the value of the goods to be protected, in terms of conservation impact; (iii) the special circumstances of each case, such as the parties involved, the economic and social relevance of the activity to be limited, the costs of finding alternative activities, etc.; (iv) the degree of proportionality between the good under protection and the restricted freedom(s); and (v) that the interference with the high seas freedoms is as minimal as possible.

In practical terms, via employing such a methodology, it is lawful for coastal states to adopt and enforce several measures on the outer continental shelf, especially so regarding the protection of living resources thereof. For instance, coastal states may enact rules and to enforce their sovereign right to explore sedentary species, such as corals, sponges, clams, crabs, lobsters and scallops on an exclusive basis. A massive problem is posed by the recent increasing bioprospection and sampling of sedentary species for industrial screening, practices that makes coastal states' life much harder, as cutting-edge technologies—like the environmental genetic screening mentioned supra—allow for the researching state to sample genetic resources of the continental shelf without interfering with the sedentary species nor touching upon the seabed. Here, coastal states have the right to establish *non-harvest zones* on the outer continental shelf to protect vulnerable marine ecosystems, with access denial extendable even to scientific research projects.[71]

Also, coastal states may refuse permission to marine scientific research if there is well-founded fear that the research will result in harm to the marine resources, particularly in the case of by-catch of sedentary species in scientific missions, which originally aim at non-sedentary species. As rightfully put by Joanna Mossop, in those occurrences, "coastal state regulations may seek to have an impact on activities that, strictly speaking, relate to the high-seas regime".[72]

Despite the legal and political sensibility of the situations referred to supra, cases involving the exercise of enforcement jurisdiction over foreign vessels above the outer continental shelf are even more delicate. Still, it is possible to read UNCLOS in

---

[70]For more on that methodology, *see* Mossop (2010), p. 325.

[71]*Id.* 323.

[72]*Id.* 325.

such a way as to grant legal ground to coastal states' exercising of enforcement jurisdiction over vessels in the waters above the outer shelf. In fact, two circumstances come to mind: enforcement over ships that violate the safety zones around artificial islands, installations and structures above the outer shelf, pursuant to Art. 80 UNCLOS; and the right of hot pursuit for violations on the extended continental shelf, as allowed by Art. 111 (2) UNCLOS. Likewise, fishing vessels engaged in destructive bottom-sea techniques that have the potential to harm habitats and sedentary species of the continental shelf beyond 200 nm may also be targeted by coastal states' environmental jurisdiction.

Those are but a few concrete scenarios in which coastal states may exercise environmental jurisdiction on the outer continental shelf. Regardless of their right to do so, coastal states are permanently bound by the obligation to act in good faith, as prescribed by Art. 300 UNCLOS. In addition to that, it is always advisable that coastal states engage in previous consultations with affected states (such as researching or flag sates) prior to enacting legislation or enforcing environmental rules which may negatively impact on certain high seas freedoms. After all, jurisdiction in the maritime context has changed from an exclusive to an *inclusive model of enforcement*, one performed in combination with other interested states, with the utmost goal of upholding an *ordre publique océanique* grounded on healthy oceans.

8.3 Partial Conclusions

A common problem with global treaties, such as UNCLOS, is the high level of compromise in negotiations, which results in the adoption of the lowest common denominator. In the case of Part VI and the provisions on the extended continental shelf, the international community could not have anticipated the possibility of legal conflicts stemming from the delineation of outer continental shelves and the conflicting uses of that area, enabled by rapid technological development. The result was the adoption of rather general provisions on the continental shelf (as a single unit), despite the possibility of conflicts relating to the rights of the coastal state over the seafloor beyond 200 nm. A case in point is the regulation of activities above the shelf on environmental grounds. Or the potential for conflict between clauses on the protection of biodiversity beyond areas of national jurisdiction and the rights of coastal states over the shelf lying below waters that are already beyond national jurisdiction. Potential for overlap is there, as shown throughout the chapter.

Although excesses and abuses in coastal state actions may exist, such as camouflaging encroachments on other state's rights and interests as environment-friendly measures, not every restriction to high seas freedoms will amount to a violation of the Convention. UNCLOS leaves enough maneuver room for a ponderation of values and principles, and the protection of the marine environment is certainly one quite high in that moral and conventional ranking. Besides, every measure that restricts freedoms of the high seas may contested at the international level—such is the spirit of international relations and the underpinning philosophy of the international Rule of Law. Hence, in order to prevent unnecessary tensions, coastal states are advised to seek cooperation and international dialogue with its counter-parts prior to enacting any measure that may raise wariness in the international community. In this sense, the functional environmental jurisdiction exercised by coastal states over the outer continental shelf may be more easily questioned by other states, particularly naval powers with interests in preserving freedom of navigation as a steady (yet eroding) pillar in the international law of the sea.

With those thoughts in mind, the next chapters materialize a case study on the state practice of Brazil with regard to the domestic environmental regulation of the so-called "Brazilian Blue Amazon", with particular regard to the continental shelf within and beyond 200 nm under the jurisdiction of the Brazilian state. As a global player with maritime and geopolitical ambitions and one of the most biodiverse countries in the planet, including in terms of marine life, it is the case to assess the extent of Brazilian environmental regulation employed in the management of the Blue Amazon; the adequateness of the national legal framework for tackling conservation challenges; the domestic institutional design for marine ocean conservation; and the overall maneuver room available for the country in its efforts to manage the Blue Amazon in consonance with international and national law.

References

Allen CH (2001) Protecting the oceanic gardens of Eden: international law issues in deep-sea vent resource conservation and management. Georgetown Int Environ Law Rev 13:563–660

Barnes MA, Turner CR (2016) The ecology of environmental DNA and implications for conservation genetics. Conserv Genet 17:1–17

Borg S (2014) The conservation of marine living resources under international law. In: Attard D et al (eds) The IMLI manual on international maritime law, vol 1. Oxford University Press, p 347

Boyle A (1985) Marine pollution under the law of the sea convention. AJIL 79(2):347–372

Brown ED (1973) The legal regime of hydrospace. Steven and Sons, London

Churchill R (2015) The LOSC regime for protection of the marine environment – fit for the twenty-first century? In: Rayfuse R (ed) Research handbook on international marine environmental law. Edward Elgar Publishing, pp 3–30

Czybulka D (2017) Article 195. In: Proelss A (ed) United Nations convention on the law of the sea: UNCLOS: a commentary. C.H. Beck-Hart-Nomos, Munich, pp 1315–1318

Gavouneli M (2014) State jurisdiction in relation to the protection and preservation of the marine environment. In: The IMLI manual on international maritime law. Oxford University Press, Oxford

Hafner G (2006) Meeresumwelt, Meeresforschung und Technologietransfer. In: Handbuch des Seerechts. Beck, Munich, pp 355–462

Hart H (2012) The concept of law, 3rd edn. Oxford University Press, Oxford

ILC (1956) Articles concerning the law of the sea with commentaries. In: Yearbook of the International Law Commission II, pp 265–301

König D (2017) Article 214. In: United Nations Convention on the law of the sea: a commentary. C.H. Beck/Hart/Nomos, Munich

Matz-Lück N, Wolfrum R (2000) The interplay of the United Nations Convention on the law of the sea and the United Nations Convention on biological diversity. Max Planck UNYB 4:445–480

Mossop J (2010) Regulating the uses of marine biodiversity on the outer continental shelf. In: Law, technology and science for the oceans in globalization: IUU fishing, oil pollution, bioprospecting, outer continental shelf. Nijhoff, Leiden, pp 319–337
Mossop J (2013) Legal framework for the regulation of safety and environmental issues on the outer continental shelf. In: The regulation of the continental shelf development: rethinking international standards. Nijhoff, Leiden, pp 179–194
Mossop J (2016) The continental shelf beyond 200 nautical miles: rights and responsibilities. Oxford University Press, Oxford
Mossop J (2017) Marine genetic resources and the need for an integrated approach to the seabed and water column. In: Biodiversity beyond national jurisdiction: a navigating guide through the new implementing agreement to UNCLOS. D'Plácido, Belo Horizonte
Mossop J (2018) The relationship between the continental shelf regime and a new international instrument for protecting marine biodiversity in areas beyond national jurisdiction. ICES J Mar Sci 75:444–450
Proelss A (2008) Marine genetic resources under UNCLOS and the CBD. German Yearb Int Law 51:417–446
Proelss A (2017) Article 56. In: United Nations Convention on the law of the sea: a commentary. C.H. Beck/Hart/Nomos, Baden-Baden
Redgwell C (2012) UNCLOS and climate change. ASIL Proc 106:406
Rochette J et al (2014) Seeing beyond the horizon for deepwater oil and gas: strengthening the international regulation of offshore exploration and exploitation. Institut du développement durable et des relations internationales, Paris, p 38
Sands P, Peel J (2012) Principles of international environmental law, 3rd edn. CUP, Cambridge
Scott SV (1992) The inclusion of sedentary fisheries within the continental shelf doctrine. Int Comp Law Q 41:788–807
Slouka ZJ (1968) International custom and the continental shelf: a study in the dynamics of customary rules of International Law. Springer, Dordrecht
Treves T (2017) Evolution and present problems of the law of the sea. Boletim Da Sociedade Brasileira de Direito Internacional 103:533–542
Wacht F (2017) Article 208. In: United Nations Convention on the law of the sea: a commentary. C.H. Beck/Hart/Nomos, Munich

Jurisprudence

Belém Statement on Atlantic Research and Innovation Cooperation, Conference in Lisbon, July 2017
ICJ (1985) Continental Shelf (Libyan Arab Jamahiriya/Malta). Judgment of 3 June 1985 ICJ Reports
ITLOS (1997) The M/V Saiga (Saint Vincent and the Grenadines v. Guinea), Prompt release, Judgment, ITLOS Reports
ITLOS (2015) Request for Advisory Opinion submitted by the Sub-Regional Fisheries Commission, Advisory Opinion, 2 April 2015, ITLOS Reports
PCA (2015) The Arctic Sunrise Arbitration (Netherlands v. Russia). Award on the Merits, 14 August 2015
UN (1987) Restatement of the Law, Third, Foreign Relations Law of the United States. American Law Institute

Chapter 9
The Environmental Dimension of the "Brazilian Blue Amazon": Environmental Rights and Duties on the Continental Shelf

> The 'Blue Amazon' is not intended to create a sort of dispute with the Green Amazon. [...] What we intend is to draw attention of the Brazilian society to another immense area for which we also have an obligation to care, and which deserves similar concern, given its strategic and economic importance.[1]—Roberto de Guimarães Carvalho

Up to now, this work has raised questions ranging from the possibility of legally delineating the outer limits of the continental shelf, to the legal conflicts which may arise from the extension of a coastal state's marine environmental jurisdiction over the seafloor. To states delineating their outer continental shelves, an extended maritime area implies not only prospects of wealth and enlarged sovereign rights, but also increased responsibilities over those areas. A reasonable next step, in line with the original research plan, is to scrutinize a particular state's legal and institutional framework in place for the management of the maritime spaces under national jurisdiction. That state is Brazil, and the maritime zones under examination are the domestically labelled "Brazilian Blue Amazon", with stark emphasis on the continental shelf within and beyond 200 nm.

Hence, this part is dedicated to analyzing Brazilian domestic *substantial* and *procedural* obligations concerning the management and conservation of the marine environment in face of continental shelf activities. The main goal of which is to assess (i) the domestic legislative framework's consistency with international law, and (ii) the country's legal and institutional preparedness to conduct a sustainable exploration and exploitation of natural resources of the seabed under national control. In the Brazilian case, despite the absence of disputed maritime areas or neighboring conflicts, it is unequivocal that the expansion of the continental shelf

[1] "A Amazônia Azul não tem como propósito criar uma espécie de disputa com a Amazônia verde [. . .] O que pretendemos é chamar a atenção da sociedade brasileira para uma outra imensa área pela qual também temos obrigação de zelar e que deveria merecer os mesmos cuidados e preocupações, tal a sua importância estratégica e econômica". Roberto de Guimarães Carvalho, 'A "Amazônia Azul"', *Folha de São Paulo* (São Paulo, 11 May 2005), section Debates. Free translation.

V. Alencar Mayer Feitosa Ventura, *Environmental Jurisdiction in the Law of the Sea*,
https://doi.org/10.1007/978-3-030-50543-1_9

may trigger legal questions, especially environment-related ones. Brazil is known for its "territorialist" stances towards the sea, as seen previously. For that, it is paramount to assess the Brazilian legislative and institutional adequateness to manage the extended zone, a study which has not yet been thoroughly conducted neither in Brazil, nor abroad, and which would serve not only as legal guidelines to Brazilian future regulations on the field, by highlighting international duties, but also identify domestic lacunae in terms of marine environmental legislation and policies.

Within Brazilian academic circles, publications on the Blue Amazon initially focused on international relations and politics and were dedicated to the strategical/defense element of the Brazilian maritime space.[2] References to the societal and environmental challenges arising from the delineation of the outer limits of the continental shelf do exist, yet *en passant*.[3] This book engages, thus, with the governance and regulation of the marine environment of the continental shelf, a pioneering approach on this specific maritime space in Brazil, with the intention to contribute to more effective ocean governance schemes domestically, as well as to more updated legislations, or regulations caring for the marine environment.

This work does not aim at exhausting the comprehension of possible conflicts and lacunae concerning the whole of the marine environment. To the contrary, it aims at offering a detailed examination of the legal environmental treatment given to one maritime zone within Brazil: the continental shelf.[4] Such a focus connects with the initial inspiration to conduct this research, i.e. to assess the legal (environmental) implications of the delineation of the outer continental shelf limits, and the potential normative conflicts which could emerge from such extension of economic and environmental jurisdiction seawards.

In short, this is a qualitative research, grounded on geopolitical, institutional and legal analyses, with resort to official and officious documents, both primary and secondary sources. The *methodology* employed for that end is the case study research. Thus far, this work has laid the theoretical and factual foundations for detailed analysis of a specific country and its normative and institutional framework. Following up on the previous considerations, this chapter is devoted to the "intensive

[2]Note that the concept of "maritime space" has different meanings in legal and international political studies. In legal terms, "maritime spaces" are usually employed to depict the maritime zones created by UNCLOS (territorial sea, contiguous zone, EEZ, continental shelf, high seas, the Area, etc.), whereas in international relations' papers the concept seems to acquire a broader meaning, that of a physical medium composed of water where power relations develop. In this sense, the "South Atlantic Ocean" is often analyzed as a relevant maritime space to be studied and understood, and whether it may be construed as a "region" in international political terms or not. For an example, *see* Hoffmann and Marcondes (2017), p. 234.

[3]*See* generally Silva (2013), Oliveira et al. (2018) and Machado (2015).

[4]This work understands that the marine environment is complex and that its regulation should adopt a holistic and integrated perspective, and precisely this vastness and complexity calls for the specification of the object under scrutiny, if the research is to succeed in conducting analyses and reaching credible conclusions. In fact, every scientific study is narrowed down to the analysis of a particular aspect of a broader whole, which does not mean it denies the need for integrated solutions to problems affecting that particular universe.

study of a single case which draws on observational data and promises to shed light on a larger population of cases".[5] The Brazilian Blue Amazon case comprises the phenomena that the argument seeks to make, the argument that without a domestic legal and institutional framework consistent with international law (namely UNCLOS and the CBD), the expansion of the continental shelf may reinforce suspicions against the detrimental effects of an enhanced territorial temptation of coastal broad-margin states.

It is a highly focused research, which has chosen depth over breadth. It scrutinizes the Brazilian domestic legal and policy framework on marine environmental protection of the continental shelf, but seeks to serve as a platform for understanding domestic constraints to effective marine governance and regulation, which may be shared by other developing and developed coastal countries, thus making it possible to resort to this study and its conclusions into a larger context. The research is observational, "an observational form of analysis", aimed at a "causal inference". In this sense, the research is predominantly empirical, drawing on the theoretical ground built in previous chapters, as well as in the below-explained mixture of political agendas, laws, action plans and governmental programs—those are the fundamental primary documents which feed the analyses made herein. Incidentally, this part will be informed by cross-case comparisons, to add credibility to the research, e.g. marine rules and institutional arrangements held in Portugal.

Still on the methodological page, one must justify the option for a specific case in a case study research, i.e., why Brazil and its Blue Amazon. Despite claims within Brazil that the country has never experimented an "economic maritime era",[6] Brazil has undoubtedly been a major player in international ocean negotiations and law-making. To start with, reference ought to be done to the country's participation in international talks for current binding and non-binding oceanic instruments. Here, Brazil has been playing a proactive role in shaping the contemporary law of the sea, particularly in the second half of the twentieth century. The great number of international maritime treaties and conventions signed and ratified by the Brazilian state suggests the country's dedication to the international rule of law applied to oceans.

Examples of those instruments on the protection of the marine environment include: the 1946 Convention for the Regulation of Whaling;[7] the 1959 Antarctic Treaty;[8] the 1966 Convention on the Conservation of Tuna and Related Fish of the

---

[5]Gerring (2017), p. 28. John Gerring calls this sort of highly specialized study a "small-C study", as it deals with either one or very few cases.

[6]To the East, Brazil had its extremely long coast, the open seas without international straits nor opposing neighbors. To the West, the vast, unexplored and unoccupied territory, which grounded fears of territorial losses and sovereignty weakness. Historically, there was no stimulus to navigational adventures, nor the longing for maritime sovereignty. That view is embraced by Soares (2014), p. 259.

[7]Promulgated by Decree no. 73.497, 17 January 1974.

[8]Ratified by Brazil on 16 May 1975.

Atlantic;[9] the 1969 Convention on Civil Liability for Damage Caused by Oil Pollution (OILPOL);[10] the 1972 London Dumping Convention;[11] the 1973 Convention for the Prevention of Pollution Caused by Ships (MARPOL) and its respective 1978 Protocol;[12] the 1980 Convention on the Conservation of Antarctic Marine Living Resources (CCALMR);[13] the 1989 Basel Convention on the Control of Transboundary Movements of Hazardous Wastes and their Disposal;[14] the 1990 International Convention on Oil Pollution Preparedness, Response and Cooperation (OPRC);[15] the 1992 Convention on Biological Diversity,[16] among others.

In addition to that, Brazil participated in the First Conference on Law of the Sea (1958) and signed its four Conventions and Optional Protocol; the Second Conference and, finally, joined the Third Conference, from 1973 until 1982.[17] As confirmed from this list, Brazilian commitment to developing the international law of the sea has been consistent and constant, even if the country's practice may have experimented changes through time. In fact, as the international society changes, countries adapt and postulate new parameters for the behavior of international actors, Brazil being no exception.

Yet, Brazilian stances have not always enjoyed peaceful international head-nods, and that is precisely another reason for studying Brazil: the country's record of controversial attitudes. In fact, Brazil's practice regarding coastal state's jurisdiction on the continental shelf has been contentious, with the country becoming notorious in the past for pushing coastal states' authority over adjacent waters beyond the acceptable by naval powers. It was the case of Decree 1.087/1970, which established a 200 nm territorial sea just years prior to the kickstart of the Third Conference, as well as the country's prominent role during those tough negotiating years.

Despite Brazil's past of participation in international oceanic negotiations, the challenges ahead are monstrous. In light of the country's grandiose narrative of the Blue Amazon and the need to exercise sovereignty and jurisdiction thereon, one ought to examine the Brazilian legal and institutional preparedness to address questions arising from the management of its maritime spaces. It is, thus, the case to review the country's marine environmental legislation and assess whether normative and institutional conflicts may be hampering the principled governance of Brazilian maritime spaces. For instance, one ought to assess the consistency of domestic instruments, such as Resolution 003/2010 of the Interministerial

---

9Promulgated by Decree no. 65.026, 20 August 1969.

10Promulgated by Decree no. 79.437, 28 March 1977.

11Promulgated by Decree no. 87.566, 16 September 1982. The 1996 Protocol to the London Dumping Convention has not been ratified by Brazil.

12Approved by Legislative Decree no. 4, 1987.

13Ratified by Brazil on 28 January 1986.

14Promulgated by Decree no. 875, 19 July de 1993.

15Promulgated by Decree no. 2.870, 10 December 1998.

16Promulgated by Decree no. 2.519, 16 March 1998.

17UNCLOS was promulgated in Brazil by Decree no. 99.165/1990.

Commission for Marine Resources (CIRM),[18] subjecting scientific research on the claimed outer continental shelf to previous authorization by the coastal state, with international obligations voluntarily seized by Brazil. Similarly, it is the case to assess the extent of Brazil's jurisdiction on the continental shelf to pursue environmental crimes, namely those related to oil spills.[19]

This investigation consists of an *empirical axis* of the book, in which the "Brazilian Blue Amazon" will be scrutinized. After a careful analysis of that concept and its objectives, the work will determine whether the Brazilian state has adopted laws and regulations relating to the sustainable exploitation of the continental shelf, and whether those statutes lie in harmony with international environmental and oceanic provisions. Moreover, an analysis of Brazil's legal and institutional capabilities to comply with environmental obligations plays a central role in this work—goal achieved via resort to interviewing techniques conducted during a field research in Brasília, in November 2016. Finally, is there a principled management of the seabed currently in place in for the Brazilian Blue Amazon, or is there a need for legal and institutional improvement?

This chapter examines the domestic marine environmental governance architecture in place for the management of the Brazilian Blue Amazon, in particular Brazil's continental shelf. For that, it tackles the definition, objectives, geopolitical implications and legal status of the Brazilian Blue Amazon; then, it offers a view on the Brazilian efforts to delineate its outer continental shelf. In so doing, it is expected that the bases for the examination of the legal framework applicable to the marine environment of the continental shelf be adequately laid.

9.1 Marine Environmental Governance in Brazil: Policies and Institutions

A legal study on the environmental facet of the Brazilian Blue Amazon encompasses the marine environmental *governance structure* and *regulatory framework* regarding continental shelf activities. Broadly, the expression "governance" relates to the norms and agencies that provide standards of acceptable public behavior in the international system,[20] and encompasses the participation of all stakeholders involved in the activity to be governed. Building on that concept, it could be said

[18]The precise content of CIRM Resolution 003/2010, as well as its polemics, are discussed in Chap. 10.

[19]The next chapter will assess the Brazilian environmental jurisdiction, following the domestic confusion between Brazilian courts as to which instance had competence to entertain the criminal prosecution of Chevron operators that participated in an oil spill off the Rio de Janeiro coast in 2014.

[20]*See* generally Nye and Donaghue (2000), introduction.

that marine environmental governance deals with the policies, institutions and stakeholders that actively participate in governing activities linked to the ocean. Those activities may include management, conservation, protection, exploration, research, exploitation etc. In this sense, "governance" is associated with policy-making and planning, as well as with law-making and law-enforcement of marine environmental norms.

Thus, a study on the domestic legal framework for the marine environment of the continental shelf could not start without first the analysis of the status of marine environmental policies in Brazil, documents which set out the most basic norms for marine environmental protection. The study of Brazilian policies, institutions and actors managing maritime regions should pave the way for the discussion on the consistency of the Brazilian legal framework with international rules, as well as the adequateness (and completeness) of that body of national laws to manage the continental shelf, its environment and resources in a sustainable manner.

To start with, some facts on the Brazilian maritime spaces are due, despite the risk of having the reader bored. The Brazilian coastline is exceptionally long, stretching out for over 7491 km along the South Atlantic Ocean.[21] If the deeply indented features of that coast are considered, it then extends to more than 9000 km long, washing no less than 17 (out 27) Brazilian states.[22] It is a convex coast, without maritime boundary delimitation disputes with neighboring countries [Uruguay and France], neither adjacent nor opposing. Overall, the country enjoys approximately 3.5 million km^2 of maritime spaces within national jurisdiction, numbers which, together with Brazil's geographic position, grant the country an important political and strategic status in the South Atlantic region, if one can speak of the South Atlantic as a "region".[23]

The maritime spaces under national jurisdiction are given immense economic, geopolitical, scientific and environmental relevance. Maritime trade is responsible for over 90% of the Brazilian commercial balance and the ocean represents hope for oil and gas self-sufficiency, as well as socioeconomic development.[24] Offshore

---

[21]CIA, The World Fact Book, entry *Coastlines*.

[22]*See* generally Short and Klein (2016).

[23]The adoption of a *functional* definition of 'South Atlantic Ocean' takes into account that the geographical definition does not match with the geo-strategic comprehension of the region. Note that there are two possible uses of the expression "South Atlantic Ocean", especially in international political studies: the geographic and the geo-strategic notion. The geographic one is provided by the IOC, International Oceanographic Organization, according to whom the coastal states bordering the South Atlantic Ocean are, in geographical descending order: Brazil, Uruguay and Argentina, from the American continent, and Gabon, Congo (Brazzaville), the Democratic Republic of Congo (Kinshasa), Angola, Namibia and South Africa, from the African continent. The geostrategic concept is based on geographical proximity, cultural affinities, socio-economic patterns, institutional characteristics and political comprehension. It equals the "central Atlantic", between tropic of Cancer and the Ecuador Line, and the South Atlantic *strictu sensu*. For more, *see* Ribeiro (2017), p. 740.

[24]From 2007, when petroleum and natural gas were discovered in the pre-salt layers, until 2010, a set of laws proposed by the Lula da Silva presidency imposed a stricter system of oil exploitation:

hydrocarbon sites corresponded to a staggering 96.7% of the entire oil production in Brazil in February 2020, while production in the pre-salt layer alone (deep-sea wells located at approximately 7000 m below the water surface) corresponded to 66.0% of the total.[25] For the abovementioned reasons, Brazil faces gigantic challenges of raising popular awareness to the country's dependency on the ocean, while simultaneously adopting domestic measures to foster the sustainable management of those maritime areas.

Given such dependency, it comes with little surprise that Brazil has been an active actor—together with other Latin American neighbors—in stimulating the development of the law of the sea. From a foreign policy perspective, Brazil is an original signatory to UNCLOS and has exercised a prominent in the realm of oceans debates within the UN System. In addition, since 1967, the country has been permanently re-elected to the Council of the International Maritime Organization (IMO) and hosts the Regional Office of one of the most relevant programs of the International Oceanographic Organization (IOC), the Global Ocean Observing System (GOOS), in Rio de Janeiro. Brazil has also been consolidating its leadership role in the South Atlantic in recent years through cooperation initiatives on marine issues in various regional fora, such as the South Atlantic Zone of Peace and Cooperation (ZOPACAS),[26] the Community of Portuguese Speaking Countries (CPLP), and the India, Brazil and South Africa Dialogue Forum (IBSA). The country was the second state to forward to the CLCS a submission for the delineation of the outer limits its continental shelf, as early as 2004. Regarding the Area, or the international seabed, Brazil implemented in 2009 the Program for the Prospection and Exploration of Mineral Resources of the International South Atlantic and Equatorial Area (PROAREA) and, after an official request to the ISA, has been granted a slot for prospecting and exploring mineral potentialities thereof.

Such an emphatic international projection of interest over the oceans has been accompanied by domestic ocean-related policies and legislation. Brazil has had interests in ocean policies and regulations during the twentieth century, when international discussions on the depletion of fish stocks, the endangerment of certain species of marine mammals, as well as on a fairer oceanic order were at the

---

the sharing regime, in which the coastal state is the final owner of the oil exploited by private contractors. Besides, a "social fund" was created by the Federal Act 12.351/2010, charged with collecting and directing royalties of exploitation in the pre-salt layer to health and education programs internally. Those rules were believed to instrumentalize the offshore oil sector towards domestic socioeconomic development.

[25]Latest data published by the National Oil Agency (ANP), *Boletim Mensal da Produção de Petróleo e Gás Natural,* February 2020.

[26]In the last years of the Dilma Rousseff government (2010–2016), the ZOPACAS initiative experienced a boost from regional partners, including Brazil. The 2013 Montevideo Declaration emphasizes the plans for enhanced cooperation in the South Atlantic region, namely on matters such as mapping and exploration of the seabed; maritime environment; air and maritime transportation and port security; maritime safety and security; coastal defense and peacekeeping operations; public security and combating transnational organized crime; and capacity-building in trade, culture, science and technology. *See* Duarte (2016), p. 99.

spotlight.[27] Yet, as this is no book on the history of Brazilian municipal law, it suffices to analyze Brazil's *recent* domestic policy and institutional architecture ocean-wise. By recent, it is meant the official decisions and measures taken since the beginning of UNCLOS negotiations, a treaty that attempted at managing all recognized dimensions to the oceans (surface, airspace, depth, and subsoil), thus setting a paradigmatic landmark in the history of the law of the sea.

One should keep in mind that the formulation of ocean public policies is a rather recent phenomenon, as witnessed by the practice of states.[28] In other words, domestic attention to the oceans is only a few decades old, as a result of the needs and self-interests of coastal states, but also of international pressure via diplomatic conferences and concerted calls from international organizations and NGOs for stricter environmental protective standards to certain activities. Hence, considerable analytical weight will be given to marine environmental governance in Brazil since the early 1970s, in order to draw a picture of the Brazilian policy and institutional panorama on the marine environment—a sort of "Brazilian Ocean Strategy", similar to the strategies adopted by other coastal states, such as Portugal.[29] Brazil's official policies regarding the marine environment can be traced back to 1973, when the Special Secretariat for the Environment was established under the auspices of the Ministry for Internal Affairs,[30] as a direct consequence of the 1972 Stockholm Declaration and the already mentioned "*prise de conscience environmentale*" in motion since the late 1960s. The combined work of the Secretariat and other organs charged with the management of the oceans has produced a series of governmental policies, plans and specific actions.

Public policies are usually the subject-matter of investigations in the fields of political science, economics and public administration. In short, a public policy emerges from concrete societal demands, or from the perception of a problem to be solved by the governmental highest circles. The government then translates its actions into plans and programs, which are in turn expected to produce enhancements for the citizens' lives.[31] These results should be subsequently measured and evaluated, so that the system can be permanently fed back and improved.[32] In practically every definition of "public policy", the elements "government", "plan", "program", "actions", "choices", "results" and "citizens" are to be found.[33]

[27]It was the case of the (failed) 1930 Hague Conference on the Territorial Sea, for the purpose of determining an enlarged length for territorial waters, or the 1946 International Convention for the Regulation of Whaling, to name but two examples of international discussions on the governance of the seas.

[28]Franckx (2009), p. 9.

[29]*See* Ministério da Defesa Nacional, *Estratégia Nacional Para o Mar*, Portugal, 2006.

[30]The Secretariat of the Commission was created by Decree no. 73.030/1973.

[31]Souza (2006), p. 24.

[32]The phases of "public policy cycle" are: identification of the problem, agenda setting, formulation, implementation, and policy evaluation. For more, *see* Serafim and Dias (2012), p. 128.

[33]Souza (2006), p. 29.

Setting out the political agenda consists of picking the societal problems to be tackled, a practice embedded in tension between political actors, social networks, pressure groups and their respective power to influence the selection of those problems. In Brazil, after consultations with civil society groups at large and political articulations within the Parliament, public policies are enacted by a national law. Socially shared values and strategic governmental interests inform public policies, which are usually specified into more concrete "plans" or "programs", each accommodating detailed measures to be taken by public authorities, in order to achieve specific objectives. For that reason, broader policies related to the marine environment are analyzed first, to then examine the concrete plans and actions adopted to implement the terms of the wider policies. Finally, this part scrutinizes the main institutional actors which participate both in setting the marine environmental agenda and in enforcing the policies, plans and actions on that regard.

When it comes to managing the marine environment, the Brazilian domestic network of policies is not particularly straightforward. To the contrary, the country has crafted a complex network of different governmental policies, plans, programs, and actions connected to different activities, maritime zones, and objectives. Despite such a complexity, the individual elements of that network can be said to complement themselves and to cover, in a fairly decent manner, the most relevant aspects of marine environmental governance.[34] Three chief national policies inform the management—in the sense of conservation and exploitation—of the Brazilian seas and marine resources: the 1994 National Maritime Policy, the 1981 National Environmental Policy, and the 1980 National Policy for Marine Resources. Note that the policies are not listed in a chronological order, but on an order of increasing administrative relevance for the purpose of ocean governance. Those three documents are at the origin of pluriannual plans of action and programs, the ensemble of which conforming what could be labelled a "Brazilian ocean strategy".

9.1.1 National Marine Environmental Policies at the Federal Level

The *1994 National Maritime Policy* (PMN) followed UNCLOS' footprint, which had just entered into force, and included key objectives into a strategy aimed at the integrated management of Brazilian maritime areas and activities.[35] For the purposes

[34]One possible parameter for such "relevancy" are the annual reports drafted by UN DOALOS, in which debates on up-to-date marine issues are brought to the forefront of appreciation by the international community. The last report dates from September 2019 (A/79/250) and handles issues related to the human dimension of oceans (migration by sea and labor at sea), whereas the 2018 Report dealt closely with underwater noise and its implications to marine life. The ultimate goal being that of implementing Sustainable Development Goal 14 of the 2030 Agenda for Sustainable Development and its 10 targets.

[35]Instituted by Decree no. 1.265/1994.

of the Policy, "maritime activities" are defined as those related not only to the sea, but also to navigable rivers, lakes and lagoons—granting the policy a broader scope than the documents which exclusively govern marine resources. The PMN is the highest-ranking national policy for maritime activities, one that should be taken into account by other national policies, plans and programs—sectorial and interministerial policies and measures shall respect the terms of the PMN.

The Policy is underpinned by the general objective to inform the development of maritime activities in Brazil in an integrated and harmonious way, aiming at the effective, rational and optimal utilization of the sea and internal waterways, in accordance with national interests. Complementing that major goal, the specific objectives include: the development of a national maritime mentality; the research, exploration and rational exploitation of living resources—in particular fisheries—and non-living resources of the bed and subsoil of the sea, rivers, lagoons and navigable lakes; finally, the *protection of the environment* in areas where maritime activities take place.[36]

In order to implement such objectives, the PMN lists concrete actions, which were grouped in seven different axes, such as naval construction, security, maritime research and development, and others. Relevant issues to the PMN are Brazil's commitment to international rules, the quality of port services in the country, incentives to cabotage navigation, to shipbuilding, to research and development of national maritime technology, professional training to maritime activities, the levels of safety of navigation and maritime traffic, among others.[37]

One of the strategic axes governed by the PMN is "marine resources" (*recursos do mar*),[38] which deals mainly with growing Brazilian nationals' participation in marine fisheries, as well as with increasing Brazilian exploration of non-living resources of the Area and the sustainable exploitation of marine resources in areas under Brazilian jurisdiction. "Action 2" on marine resources relates directly to the management of the continental shelf, by setting out the goal to *intensify activities of prospecting, exploring and exploiting mineral resources of the Brazilian continental shelf*, especially those which may contribute to minimizing the net import of strategic minerals. Overall, the PMN worries little with the conservation of marine environment and aims clearly at governing maritime activities which may foster socioeconomic development. Not much is elaborated on marine environmental concerns, such as measures to protect oceanic ecosystems, prevent marine pollution or else—just the general and cliché-wise employment of key terms, such as "sustainable exploitation".

[36]National Maritime Policy, Chapter 2, available online.

[37]The main participants of the PMN are the Ministries of the Navy (nowadays, Ministry of Defense), Foreign Affairs, Finance, Transportation, Agriculture, Education, Labor, Industry and Commerce, Mining and Energy, Regional Integration, Justice, Science and Technology and Environment, and the Secretariats of Planning, Strategic Affairs and Federal Administration.

[38]National Maritime Policy, Introduction, at 3.

Concerns on the marine environment were the *ratione materiae* of the *1981 National Policy for the Environment* (PNMA),[39] which aims to preserve, improve and recover the environmental quality conducive to life, in accordance with the principle of rationalization of land, subsoil, water and air use. In the Policy's text, ports and marinas, as well as the transportation and commercialization of dangerous cargoes, oil, gas and derivates are classified as activities with a *high* risk of environmental pollution—thus demanding particular attention from all involved stakeholders.[40] Even though the Policy did not explicitly prescribe principles or practices to the oceans, but solely to the environmental in general (a broader concept which undoubtedly comprises the seas), it represented an important, albeit not the first, step in the arduous path towards environmentally sound and sustainable activities. Importantly, the Environmental Policy created National Council for the Environment (CONAMA), a proactive governmental agency that regulates the uses of the oceans.

The 1981 PNMA certainly is pertinent to the management and conservation of the marine environment. Yet, the most relevant document for that end is a national policy approved before both the Maritime and the Environmental Policy. As early as 1980, a year before the adoption of the Environmental Policy, Brazil approved its first *National Policy for Marine Resources* (PNRM), which underwent a thorough update in 2005 under the Lula da Silva presidency, in order to face the considerable modifications witnessed by the international community since the early 1980s.[41] The "new" policy for marine resources reiterated several principles, key pillars and objectives of its predecessor, thus aiming at governing the development of maritime activities focused on the effective use, exploration and exploitation of living, mineral and energy resources of the Brazilian maritime spaces, in a *rational and sustainable* way, in accordance with national interests and towards the socioeconomic development of the country.[42]

The 2005 PNRM is fundamentally informed by the 1994 PMN and the 1981 PNMA, although it consists itself of an umbrella framework with principles and objectives that influence the preparation of further government plans, programs and actions—keep the "complex web" of policies description in mind. Among these *principles*, some have a direct connection to marine environmental governance, namely: resort to the precautionary principle in the exploitation of marine resources; the protection and conservation of biodiversity and genetic heritage in marine areas under national jurisdiction; and, lastly, the respect for the internationally accepted

[39]Act no. 6.938/1981.

[40]Annex VIII to Act 6.938/81, incorporated by Act no. 10,165, 27 December 2000, on potentially polluting activities.

[41]Taking into account the historical moment when this policy entered into force, the 1980s, it can be considered a valuable mechanism for the protection of the Brazilian coastal area. "major advance in terms of standardization of multiple uses of the coastal and marine zone of Brazil". *See* Marroni (2014), p. 165.

[42]Art. 2, on the objectives of the PNRM, Decree no. 5.377/2005.

commitments by the Brazilian state.[43] The Marine Resources Policy must be compatible with other maritime and environmental policies and is entrusted with creating and coordinating the following Plans: quinquennial *Sectorial Plans for Marine Resources* (PSRM); the National Coastal Management Plan (PNGC);[44] and the Brazilian Continental Shelf Survey Plan (LEPLAC)—as examined below.

The quinquennial *Sectorial Plans for Marine Resources* are one of the outcomes of the Marine Resources Policy, whose objectives are to assess the economic, scientific and environmental potential of the seas, as well as to monitor the living and oceanographic phenomena and climate elements of marine areas under jurisdiction.[45] Each Sectorial Plan is a long-term document, profoundly informed by the three strategic objectives of the that Policy, namely: training of human resources; research development, marine science and technology; and encouraging the exploitation and sustainable use of marine resources. In order to fulfill such objectives, the PSRMs unfold into a variety of specific *actions*, some of which have fulfilled their objectives and did not make it to the following Plan; some which are still ongoing and, therefore, continuously make it into the next Plan. Each subsequent plan engages in continuing the efforts of previous plans, deepening actions which may be deemed more urgent, and perfecting implementation techniques and methodologies.[46]

From an operational perspective, each Sectorial Plan is coordinated by the Interministerial Commission on Marine Resources and executed by a Committee composed, among others, of the Ministry for the Environment and the Brazilian Institute for the Environment and Renewable Natural Resources (IBAMA). Ultimately, the Plans have been inspired by the goals to manage and use marine resources in a sustainable fashion, as well as guaranteeing the fair and equitable distribution of the benefits derived from their use at the national level. The first PSRM was adopted in 1982, while the current one—the ninth—is valid from 2016 until 2019.

The Plans' early editions focused on generating knowledge on the marine environment, so that a sustainable use of marine riches could be possible. In line with the national policy which informs the plans' actions and measures, the initial PSRMs

[43] Art. 4, PNRM.

[44] In 1988, Brazil drafted and approved the National Coastal Management Plan (PNGC), Act no. 7.661/1988, a direct outcome of the National Policy for Marine Resources and the National Environmental Policy. Due to the absence of references within the Plan to the continental shelf, core of this study, it does not deserve a detailed analysis. For more information of the concrete measures and actions included in the Plan, see Maria Luiza Machado Granziera and et al., *Os Desafios Ambientais Da Zona Costeira* (Essential Idea, 2014).

[45] List of quinquennial Sectorial Plans for Marine Resources thus far: I PSRM (1982–1985); II PSRM (1986–1990); III PSRM (1990–1994); IV PSRM (1994–1998); V PSRM (1999–2003); VI (2005–2008); VII (2008–2011); VIII (2012–2015); IX (2016–2019). As of April 2020, there had been no news on the adoption of PSRM X.

[46] In public policy studies, this feature would be described as an "*incremental process*", in which plans and actions are cumulative, usually not departing from scratch. *See* Souza (2006), p. 29.

were inspired by the search for an *integrated management* of coastal and marine ecosystems, as well as the need for amplified participation of different stakeholders. The rationale behind such an integration was that, without the incorporation of all interested parties, effectiveness will be harder to reach. In addition to the integrated management and the participatory drafting and execution of the plans' actions, they are also inspired by a precautionary approach to the exploration and exploitation of the oceans.[47]

The IX PSRM built on the previous ones and maintains the integrated and participatory management model between Ministries, development agencies, academic and scientific communities and the private sector, who eventually collaborated to the Plan's elaboration and shall cooperate in the execution of joint, comprehensive actions. Among the topics of interest to the IX Sectorial Plan, "sustainability" occupied a privileged spot in practically every paragraph, alongside marine conservation efforts. Among the Plan's objectives, one can quickly spot (i) the monitoring of living marine resources and their *conservation*, *sustainable* exploration and exploitation; (ii) the exploration of coastal and marine biodiversity, with a view to its *conservation*; (iii) the research of non-living resources and their economic potential, both in areas within and beyond national jurisdiction; (iv) the environmental research and monitoring of the deep sea.[48] Overall, marine environment-related concerns of the current and previous Plans have focused on ensuring the *quality* of the marine environment; reducing the vulnerability and risks of extreme events and climate change; expanding and disseminating knowledge on the global role of oceans; developing and applying national technologies for the *sustainable* use of marine resources; and promoting innovation in products, services and processes related to the sustainable use of marine resources.[49]

Of the several *actions* implemented by each Sectorial Plan for Marine Resources, only those concerning the marine environment of the continental shelf are of interest to this study. It is the case to mention the 1994 REVIZEE, 1997 REMPLAC, and the 2005 REVIMAR.

The *1994 Program for the Assessment of the Sustainable Potential of EEZ Living Resources* (REVIZEE) resulted from the IV PSRM (1994–1998) and was implemented by the Brazilian Environmental Institute, IBAMA. The Program addressed the fisheries sector and aimed at identifying the living resources of the EEZ and the environmental conditions of their occurrence. Subsequently, authorities

---

[47]The VIII Sectorial Plan, for instance, focused on the relationship between "Sea, Coastal Zone and Antarctica", thus embracing concerns with natural resources of the coastal zone—not directly the topic of this work.

[48]IX PSRM, CIRM Resolution 191/4, 2016, 5.

[49]Pursuant to Decree no. 6.678/2008, which instituted the VII PSRM, valid from 2008 to 2011. Concerning the continental shelf, two objectives called attention: (f) to investigate the mineral potential of the continental shelf and the international seabed, also aiming at acquiring the right of exploitation and mineral exploitation in the Area; and (k) to promote studies and suggest the updating of Brazilian legislation with a view to its application in all aspects concerning the resources of the sea.

set out to determine the biomass of such resources and the pertinent *sustainable yield*, pursuant to UNCLOS Art. 60. Noteworthy is that the results of the REVIZEE Program are, however, not limited to warnings about the availability and status quo of key living resources of the country's EEZ. Knowledge on marine biodiversity, including in deep waters—demersal and benthic species, witnessed a great expansion, as scientific researches on the ecosystems of the continental slope up to 2000 m deep provided information and empirical subsidies to the management of fisheries off the Brazilian shore.[50] Among the main findings of the Program was that coastal and marine areas contain numerous species endemic to Brazilian waters, some of which severely threatened with depletion.[51]

Alongside the REVIZEE, other actions stemmed from later sectorial plans for marine resources. Yet, unlike the REVIZEE, the following actions and programs are still on-going. It is the case of the *1997 Program for the Assessment of the Mineral Potential of the Brazilian Legal Continental Shelf* (REMPLAC), designed by the Interministerial Commission for Marine Resources via Resolution no. 004/1997. The Program's general objective is to evaluate the mineral potential of the Brazilian continental shelf, while simultaneously (i) depicting the physical environment of that continental shelf; (ii) identifying and detailing areas of relevant mineral potential; (iii) collecting basic geological information for the management and integrated management of the shelf and the adjacent coastal zone; (iv) implementing a georeferenced digital database for use by the scientific community, government agencies and Brazilian companies;[52] (v) proposing a methodology and standards for the execution of marine scientific research on the shelf; and, finally, (vi) fostering research that aims advancing and innovating techniques and equipment employed in the exploitation of continental shelf mineral resources.[53]

The REMPLAC's main purpose is to elaborate a geological and geophysical model for the evaluation of mineral resources in the continental shelf, so as to assess the mineral potential of at least 8% of the entirety of that area.[54] It is ongoing, albeit on a rather slow rhythm, what suggests a lack of priority by the CIRM and national stakeholders to surveying the mineral potential of the Brazilian shelf. The time gap between the end of the VII and the approval of the IX Plan, as well as the extremely

---

[50]The REVIZEE produced several reports on the status of fisheries in the Brazilian EEZ, all of which unfortunately only in Portuguese. For more, visit: https://www.marinha.mil.br/secirm/revizee. Accessed 11 April 2020.

[51]The Final Executive Report of the REVIZEE Program, delivered in 2006, identified at least ten endemic species within the Brazilian EEZ that risk depletion. The species belong to rays, sharks, sawfishes and others. For a complete list of the endangered species in Portuguese and Latin, *see* MMA (2006), p. 64.

[52]A result of the such objective was the crafting of an online Geographic Atlas of the Brazilian Coastal and Marine Regions, by the Brazilian Institute of Geography and Statistics. Available at: http://www.atlasmar.ibge.gov.br/. Accessed 11 April 2020.

[53]For more on the REMPLAC, *see* Longo (2014), p. 97.

[54]Those objectives can be accessed at the CIRM's website, at: https://www.marinha.mil.br/secirm/remplac. Accessed 11 April 2020.

low speed in which concrete measures were met to implement specific objectives of the Program indicate it lags behind in the priority scale of the Brazilian authorities. In other words, it is unlikely that mineral exploitation of deep-sea areas under national jurisdiction will start anytime soon, what does not speak for the exploitation of hydrocarbons. The latter is likely to happen in the near future, as the key Brazilian oil production company has shown interest in carrying on activities in slots farther away from offshore.

The IX PSRM (2016–2019) reiterates the REMPLAC project, but this time on a different methodology. Where the surveying of the continental shelf potential has traditionally been rather generic/ample, future research shall be detailed and focus on specific minerals. According to the Plan, the REMPLAC shall concentrate on detailing specific potential mining sites along the Brazilian continental shelf, limiting itself to surveying specific minerals, such as aggregates employed in civil construction and materials used as soil correctives, such as marine bioclasts, necessary for the development of agriculture.[55] The "renewed" REMPLAC also contains the identification and evaluation of the biotechnological potential associated with the mineral resources of the continental shelf. The economic logics behind the REMPLAC stands out, with little being said and done with respect to the marine environment of the continental shelf.

Of the actions designed within the PSRMs, the one most directly governing the management of the Brazilian marine environment is the *2005 Action for the Assessment, Monitoring and Conservation of Marine Biodiversity* (REVIMAR), coordinated by the Ministry for the Environment. Its goals are to evaluate, monitor and promote the conservation of marine biodiversity, with an *ecosystem approach.* Broadly, the REVIMAR sets out to ensure the monitoring and conservation of existing ecosystems in coastal and marine areas. Based on the conclusions and scientific data obtained by the REVIZEE Program, the REVIMAR Action aims to establish scientific bases and integrated actions capable of subsidizing measures towards the shared management of the Brazilian marine biodiversity, as well as the conservation and sustainable use of living resources under national jurisdiction.

The specific goals of the REVIMAR regard directly the management of the Brazilian continental shelf: to continuously evaluate five protected areas of reef ecosystems offshore—no reports available online; to continuously evaluate the conservation status of marine species, aiming to subsidize conservation policies including updating the lists of endangered species; to implement at least 70% of the actions of the Actions and Programs of previous PSRMs regarding threatened ecosystems—no reports available online; to develop and implement recovery plans for at least 75% of endangered marine species—no reports available online; and,

[55]IX PSRM (2016) 21. Due to the above-mentioned methodological "adaptation", the index of progress associated to the individual actions of the REMPLAC has dropped to zero. It is as if a new phase of the Program was about to start, one which expects to raise detailed material on the mineral potential of only three specific portions of the Brazilian continental shelf.

finally, to increase the total number of marine protected areas to 4% of the territorial sea and EEZ (3.5 million km^2)—this is the only goal which was objectively fulfilled.

Apart from public policies and strategies for the maritime spaces under national jurisdiction, Brazil has also devised the *2009 Program for the Prospection and Exploration of Mineral Resources of the International South Atlantic and Equatorial Area* (PROAREA).[56] This action resulted from the VII PSRM, with the objectives of expanding Brazilian strategic presence in the South Atlantic and Equatorial Oceans (considered by the Navy as zones of natural Brazilian influence); collecting data to support future Brazilian requests for mineral exploration before the ISA; obtaining technical, economic and environmental information; preparing and qualifying human resources to implement activities in the Area. Given that the PROAREA does not relate to the Brazilian Blue Amazon, in that it focuses exclusively on the Area, it lays beyond the scope of this study.

9.1.2 Core Institutional Actors at the Federal Level

Charged with the implementation of the multiple actions and measures examined supra is an equally complex net of institutional actors. They participate in setting the agenda, debating approaches to the implementation of specific actions, and evaluating the overall compliance to the plans and programs' objectives. Depending on the problem to be solved, they may be the legislature, government leaders, technicians from ministries and various public administration bodies, political parties, non-governmental organizations, interest groups, unions, academia, others.

The first and crucial governmental body tasked with the coordination of the Actions referred to supra is the *Interministerial Commission for Marine Resources* (CIRM). The Commission was created in 1974,[57] just a year after the creation of the Brazilian Secretariat for the Environment, as a result of the bureaucracy's awareness of the importance of the marine environment in whichever national development strategies. The Commission's main task is to coordinate the 2005 National Marine Resources Policy, as well to oversee the implementation of the National Coastal Management Plan and other programs and actions stemming from the quinquennial PSRMs. As the name itself suggests, the Commission is composed of representatives of several ministries, but coordinated by the Navy Commander—also known as "Maritime Authority".[58] In its almost 40 years of existence, the CIRM presents a

[56]For more on the Program, its guidelines and objectives, see *Executive Summary of the PROAREA Program* (Brasília: Comissão Interministerial para os Recursos do Mar, September 2009), 34.

[57]The CIRM was instituted by Decree no. 74.557/1974 and regulated by Decree no. 3.939/2001.

[58]In its composition, the CIRM has representatives from: Civil Cabinet of the Presidency; Defense Ministry; Ministry of Foreign Affairs; Ministry of Transport; Ministry of Agriculture, Livestock and Supply; Ministry of Education; Ministry of Health; Ministry of Development, Industry and Foreign Trade; Ministry of Mines and Energy; Ministry of Planning, Budget and Management; Ministry of Science, Technology and Innovation; Ministry for the Environment; Ministry for

truly impressive service sheet, seeking to fill the institutional vacuum in the Brazilian maritime space—an ambition it achieves to a large extent.[59]

Another key institutional actor in the management of the Brazilian maritime spaces is the *Brazilian Navy*, who holds a tradition not only of defending, but also *managing* the areas under Brazilian national jurisdiction.[60] The first Minister of the Navy and Overseas Domains was appointed in 1808, upon arrival of the Portuguese crown in Brazil, escaping the Napoleonic conquer of the Iberian Peninsula that same year. Since those times, the Navy has had its headquarters in Rio de Janeiro, where the core of the Brazilian fleet is located.

In its vision of the future, the Brazilian Navy strives to be a modern and balanced force, equipped with adequate means for the political-strategic insertion of Brazil in the international scenario. Thus, the marine force should be permanently ready to act both offshore and within internal waters, singularly or jointly, in order to fulfill its constitutional purposes.[61] Interestingly, fundamental tensions arise within the Navy with respect to the balance between sovereignty considerations and environment conservation goals.[62] Despite the Navy's awareness of its broader institutional role of not only shielding Brazilian waters and mainland, but also caring for the conservation of the marine environment, the latter is not the Navy's primary role, nor concern. Enforcement of marine environment-related regulations falls under the responsibilities of the Brazilian Environmental Institute, IBAMA, a situation which could potentially trigger institutional conflicts between both, due to the overlap of tasks, and makes one wonder whether a shared prominence between these two institutions exists.

The *Brazilian Institute for the Environment and Renewable Natural Resources* (IBAMA) is a federal entity endowed with legal personality, administrative and financial autonomy and linked to the Ministry for the Environment.[63] The Institute has the power of environmental police within Brazil's jurisdiction and is charged with (i) carrying out actions of the national environmental policies related to environmental licensing, environmental quality control, authorization of the use of natural resources and *environmental monitoring and control*, observing the guidelines issued by the Ministry for the Environment; and (ii) conducting supplementary actions of the competence of the Union, in accordance with the domestic environmental legislation.[64] Such responsibilities are aimed at several strategical objectives,

Sports; Ministry of Tourism; Ministry of National Integration; Ministry of Fisheries and Aquaculture; and, finally, the Secretariat of Ports of the Presidency of the Republic.

[59]For more on the services and achievements of the CIRM, *see* Soares (2014), p. 302.

[60]That is the essence of the Brazilian Navy's official slogan, which goes: "protecting our riches; caring for our people".

[61]The announced "vision" and "mission" of the Brazilian Navy is to be consulted online, at: https://www.marinha.mil.br/content/missao-e-visao-de-futuro-da-marinha. Accessed 11 April 2020.

[62]For more info on this tension, refer to Chap. 6, on the false dichotomy between marine security and marine conservation initiatives.

[63]IBAMA was created by the Act no. 7.735/1989.

[64]Art. 5, Act no. 7.735/1989.

of which two are particularly eye-catching: promoting and improving laws and regulations on environmental matters, as well as providing environmental data and information.

Similar to IBAMA, another Institute shares the power of environmental police within Brazilian national jurisdiction, yet solely with regard to protected areas. The *Chico Mendes Institute for Biodiversity Conservation* (ICMBio)[65] is a special federal autarchy linked to the Ministry for the Environment responsible for effecting management and conservation actions within the National System of Conservation Units, as well as supervising and monitoring protected areas designed by the Union. It also falls upon it to promote and execute programs aimed at researching and conserving biodiversity, both within terrestrial and marine protected areas.

Both IBAMA and ICMBio consist of *enforcement* agencies linked to the *Ministry for the Environment* (MMA), an organ which displays repeated concern with the Brazilian coast side, but little attention to the rest of the marine environment. That conclusion is possible from analysis of the Ministry's official reports—revised for the purposes of this work—and the structure of the Ministry's website. After exploring the website for hours, should one look for information on "coastal zone and oceans", under the macro-topic of "water" in that website, the only available info relates to "coastal management"—that is as much details on oceans as one will find on the official website.[66]

Regarding coastal management, the Ministry develops a couple of projects on the conservation of marine biodiversity. Firstly, the Project *TerraMar* monitors and manages two MPAs (*Costa dos Corais* and *Abrolhos*), totaling 400 ha. That project aims at enforcing conservation measures in the two above-mentioned biodiversity sanctuaries and is funded by the German Ministry for the Environment (BMUB) and the German Society for International Cooperation (GIZ). Secondly, the Project *GEF-Mar* seeks to support the establishment, expansion and implementation of a globally significant, representative and effective System of Marine and Coastal Protected Areas in Brazil, apart from identifying tools for their financial continuity, in order to reduce the loss of coastal biodiversity. This system integrates different categories of protected areas and other area-based conservation measures under different management strategies. It is a Federal project, created and implemented in partnership with the private sector and civil society, aimed at increasing the amount of MPAs in Brazilian waters, as well as designing and implementing at least two financial

[65]ICMBio was created by the Act no. 11.516/2007.

[66]Information is also available on yet another Program of the MMA, namely the National Program for the Conservation of the Brazilian Coast Line (PROCOSTA), launched in 2018 by the Decree 76/2018. The Program should ensure the monitoring, management and conservation of the country's coastal region in order to minimize damages and preserve the environmental characteristics and services provided by that area. The initiative also integrates coastal management into actions to mitigate and adapt to climate change.

mechanisms capable of contributing to the long-term sustainability of coastal and marine protected areas.[67]

While the relevance of such projects should never be underestimated, by virtue of the concentrated conservation efforts towards those fragile MPAs, it seems also reasonable to disapprove the Ministry for not having broader programs in place, nor concerns with the conservation of the Brazilian marine environment from threats such as pollution from continental shelf activities, dumping of waste and other sorts of substances on the seafloor, among others. For instance, the Ministry adopted a national strategy for monitoring Brazilian biomes in 2007, and, worryingly, the document does *not* mention the marine biome. Only by late 2018 has a bill for a national policy for the conservation of the marine biome been proposed before the Brazilian National Parliament—the PNCMAR, mentioned elsewhere.

To close the cycle of environmental agencies, one must mention the *National Council for the Environment* (CONAMA), chaired by the Ministry of Environment. CONAMA has representatives from ministries, state governments and the Federal District, municipalities, NGOs and industry, commerce and agriculture class entities.

9.1.3 The Struggle for Coherence in Domestic Ocean Policy-Making

In light of the plethora of different (although complementing) values, policies, programs, plans, and actions, several challenges emerge to the Brazilian authorities. One related to the general *coherence* of the national ocean management system; another one connected with the *effectiveness* of such policies.

Different views can be expressed on the quest for coherence. For Erik Franckx, for instance, striving for coherence means reducing *fragmentation* in policy-making, understood here as the tendency of having different sectors and stakeholders overlap in domestic ocean decision-making spheres. For that author, coherence would correspond to "harmonization" between national ocean policies, so that efforts are not wasted in different directions, when not plainly annulated by conflicting measures. For that, local authorities would be demanded to achieve an "improved operational process in order to balance sectoral interests and coordinate action and goals in accordance with sustainability principles".[68]

Even if one would share the underlying concern with coherence expressed by Franckx, the association built by that author between coherence and *unity*—or the fight against fragmentation—stems from a rather idealistic conception. A quick glimpse at the policies, programs, actions and institutions participating in the Brazilian ocean governance reveals the complexity of such a process in the historic

[67]Information available online at the MMA website: http://www.mma.gov.br/areas-protegidas/programas-e-projetos/projeto-gef-mar. Accessed 11 April 2020.

[68]Franckx (2009), p. 14.

era that scientists have agreed to refer to as the "Anthropocene".[69] The intricacy of regulating and disciplining the management of the ocean emanates from the plurality of activities involved (such as navigating, fishing, mining, researching, etc.), as well as the emergence of new stakeholders in the past decades (environmental groups and an increased amount of people negatively impacted by ocean uses), all that within a context of economic and technological asymmetries between countries worldwide.[70]

The complexity inherent to drawing and implementing ocean policies under those circumstances could not logically result in simple, plain and straightforward documents. In this sense, fragmentation of marine environmental governance seems to be an inevitable reality both internationally and domestically, as the work by Boyes and Elliott depicts. Upon examining the international, European and English legislation safeguarding the marine environment, the authors have come up with a map that synthetizes the intricacy of policies, rules, programs and agencies that interact for that purpose—such a map (or the chaotic overlap of policies and rules that it portrays) was suggestively labelled "the ultimate *horrendogram*".[71] In this context, to strive for a centralized or unified marine governance edifice is not only utopic, but also undesirable, as decision-makers and stakeholders ought to embrace the ocean as a complex set of different regimes to be governed. The old-school "top-down approach" to ocean regulation has proven insufficient in the past and does not allow for the effective implementation of agreed goals.

To acknowledge that is not equivalent, by no means, to defending that domestic legal and policy frameworks be unnecessarily labyrinthine. A too complex ocean governance system is likely to lead to internal conflicts of formal competence, as well as to material contradiction, consequences which are to be avoided by every policy- and law-maker. As it does not mean that public authorities should not aim at harmonizing policies and plans for the marine environment. To the contrary, it means that expecting a handful of documents to regulate all uses of the oceans may not be consonant with reality. Admitting the inherent complicatedness of the process, due to the multiplicity of opposing interests at stake and the great variety of stakeholders, is a first step towards the drawing of effective strategies for the oceans.

In the Brazilian case, when confronted with the question whether the Brazilian "ocean strategy" is coherent, harmonic and uniform, the answer is: partially. For one, Brazil does not pay lip service to those requirements, simply by mentioning them at the beginning of each document containing a policy, plan or program.[72] The country concretely attempts at intertwining key strategic priorities into the policies mentioned supra (PMN, PNMA, PNRM), while sharing general and specific objectives, as analyzed above. In this sense, the key topics and objectives of the National Policy on Marine Resources informs the Programs and Plans designed after it, as well as the

[69]Vidas et al. (2014), p. 23.

[70]Barros-Platiau et al. (2015), p. 158.

[71]Boyes and Elliott (2014), p. 43.

[72]Harmonization with other plans and policies is considered a "basic principle" by the Marine Resources Policy, Art. 4.

practical actions put in motion to fulfill specific objectives, to some degree of success thus far, as in the case of the REVIZEE. Furthermore, a multi-stakeholder organization (CIRM) coordinates the policies and supervises several of those Plans and Actions, while communicating with other agencies that are charged with implementing parallel Actions, as the Ministry for the Environment and the task of assessing the biodiversity and genetic potential of Brazilian waters (REVIMAR).

For that reason, credence should be given to Ana Paula Barros-Platiau in her claim that national ocean planning needs to be discussed *in light of fragmentation*, taking into account the porosity and circulation of international, regional, national and local standards, apart from involving local actors into the process, i.e. academic researchers, fishing communities, and others affected by regulations. All that, despite the well-known financial and logistic difficulties of such a broad participation. That approach amounts to the so-called "integrated management" of maritime areas, a doctrine which seems to enjoy widespread acceptability within Brazilian academia, with growing literature on this topic being registered in Brazil.[73]

Out of comparison—on a superficial tone, as this work is not intended to compare different legal realities as preconized by the field of international comparative law—the Portuguese "National Strategy for the Oceans" may strike at first sight as a cohesive and coherent document, limited to the essentials of ocean governance.[74] Yet, one should never forget that such strategy is inserted in a complex web of policy papers, plans and programs both at the national, regional and international levels—the notorious "horrendogram". With that in mind, it is noteworthy that Portugal's strategy embraces key environmental legal principles, such as the integrated management of ocean issues; the principle of sustainable development; the precautionary principle, namely with respect to risk management; and the ecosystem approach, as a methodology and framework for the integrated management of terrestrial and aquatic ecosystems and their resources, with a view to their conservation and sustainable use. But then again, one should not lose sight of the document's essence: a programmatic and strategical declaration of intentions, which envisages whereto the country wishes to head in the future.

Three strategic cornerstones in the Portuguese strategy include ocean knowledge; marine spatial planning and regulation; and the promotion of national interests. Here, the Brazilian Marine Resources Policy is similar by focusing on the training of human resources in ocean sciences; the intensification of MSR and the sustainable exploitation of marine resources. Regarding the marine environment, the Portuguese strategy emphasizes the action to protect and recover marine ecosystems, establishing a national network of marine protected areas, and maintaining marine habitats in a favorable condition, apart from monitoring the overall health status of the Portuguese marine zones, in which it turns out to be rather more detailed than the Brazilian PNRM. The macro-objective sought after through the implementation of those core principles is rather straightforward: to turn the Portuguese seas into a

[73]Barros-Platiau et al. (2015), p. 162.

[74]"National Strategy for the Oceans", Portugal, note supra.

national project,[75] i.e. to implement action plans capable of mobilizing stakeholders around crucial questions pertaining to the management of Portuguese maritime spaces. Such a clear objective is not easily extractable from the Brazilian marine governance edifice—and this shows how a decentralized web of policies, plans and actions may blur essential goals. Brazil could certainly benefit from such a symbolism of raising the Brazilian seas to the status of a "national project", instead of a destiny, some sort of fate and predestination.

Noteworthy is that, in the Portuguese strategy, little is discussed in terms of national defense and security, with but specific measures on the need to promote the national interest in matters of national defense, security and alertness, both domestically and in relation to the international sphere.[76] Even so, references to "security and national defense" are often accompanied by preoccupation with equipping the Portuguese ocean-related agencies to monitor the seas, prepare for natural hazards, and combat marine pollution, as in this section:

> No national strategy for the sea can be effectively implemented without an efficient integrated *surveillance, security and national defense system* that has the means to enable effective and coordinated maritime surveillance, safeguarding against natural hazards and combating pollution.[77]

Such a relative freedom from national defense considerations is, perhaps, due to the relative restrain or political clout of the national Navies in each context. In the Portuguese case, it is not farfetched to picture a Navy that avoids the spotlight and exercising pressure on other stakeholders when the issue is marine conservation policies. One of the consequences of such a balance between interested parties is a refreshed national strategy that focuses less on security and defense issues, being given ample maneuver room to regulate issues on innovation, technology, impulses to the blue economy, marine environmental conservation, and others, not necessarily subject to a militaristic viewpoint. Brazil, on the other side, has been criticized by literature for designing its national ocean policy from a stark military perspective.[78] This issue, on the role of Navies is shaping national ocean policies and legislation, would render another investigation of its own, and falls beyond the scope of this chapter.

On to the second challenge identified above, the difficulties of *implementing* the "integrated ocean management" plans should not be underestimated. Obstacles exist, which hinder the much-needed leap from academic awareness of the virtues of the

[75]Ministério da Defesa Nacional, Portugal, 7.

[76]*Id.* 13, 22, 23, 29. Interestingly, "safety" and "security" are represented by the same word in Portuguese: "segurança". Hence, for the purposes of the analysis in the current item, concerns such as "safety of navigation" are disregarded in favor of "national defense and security" considerations, even though both relate, in Portuguese, to the same concern: "segurança".

[77]Id. 23. All that even though the National Strategy for the Oceans was published by the "Mission Structure for Maritime Affairs", a body under the purview of the Ministry for National Defense.

[78]According to Erik Franckx, Brazil's military inputs in domestic ocean policies are not as stark as in Russia but do still inform plenty of the measures and goals therein. For more on this particular criticism, *see* Franckx (2009), p. 15.

integrated management approach, to the inclusion of integrated management measures in concrete domestic decision-making procedures. In Brazil, to date, the comprehensive package of laws and policies formally integrating all levels of government (regional, state and federal) has been met with incipient implementation. In a detailed study on the effectiveness of the Brazilian domestic marine environmental policies, Jablonski and Filet have found that the more incisive laws in relation to ocean and coastal management are in the form of resolutions and not of decrees or acts, thus hinting at the presumption of a weak system by those required to abide by the resolutions and recommendations.[79]

Besides, the Brazilian ocean strategy has been criticized thus far for being excessively concentrated in the Executive branch of government, which does not facilitate the effective regulation of marine issues at the national level.[80] Besides, *insufficient dialogue* at the national level usually jeopardizes the selection of national interests which will make it to oceans policies—not interests picked in hermitically isolated offices in the Brazilian capital, located more than 1000 km away from the coast, by technicians with little contact to the populations affected by governmental measures. After all, "if one does not know where one is sailing, no wind is favorable".

In addition to that, effectiveness of marine governance is questioned by the deficient flow of financial resources to ground-force agencies, so as to keep an integrated ocean policy functioning with decent results.[81] Finally, the current institutional marine governance architecture tasked with implementing the national policies, programs, plans and actions is considered unfit for the job. Scholars have urged for immediate institutional reforms, in order to reduce number of leaderships that unnecessarily bureaucratize the entire process, as well as to the update the tasks of certain institutions towards more dialogue and better coordination between authorities responsible for the ocean governance.

That panoramic insight onto the Brazilian marine environmental governance (its policies, plans, programs, actions and institutions/agencies) paves the way for a closer look at the Brazilian plan to delineate the outer limits of its continental shelf and how such a plan is deeply informed by the rather recent concept of "Brazilian Blue Amazon", or the Brazilian maritime regions. An important part of this "Amazon" is composed of the seabed under national jurisdiction, and a considerable focus of the "rhetorics" of the Blue Amazon was directed at raising awareness to the plan

[79]Jablonski and Filet (2008), p. 541.

[80]Barros-Platiau et al. (2015), p. 162.

[81]Just as an example of the underfunding of domestic enforcement agencies and the monitoring of protected areas, Brazil invests the least in Conservation Units (R$ 4.43/ha) in a comparison with other biodiverse-rich countries. In the UNEP Report "Contribution of Brazilian Conservation Units to the National Economy", carried out in 2011, investments per hectare were analyzed in the maintenance of protected area systems in: The United States, New Zealand, South Africa, Australia, Canada, Mexico, Costa Rica, Argentina and Brazil. Of those, Argentina, the second-worst ranked, displayed an investment almost five times bigger than that of Brazil in the maintenance of protected areas (R$ 21.37/ha). *See* Medeiros et al. (2011), p. 10.

to delineate the outer continental shelf limits. Ultimately, it is the view adopted in this work that to study the Brazilian environmental regulatory maneuver on the continental shelf is to study the broader policy and legislative stances adopted by Brazilian authorities with respect to the regulation of the maritime spaces under national jurisdiction—i.e. the Blue Amazon.

9.2 The Brazilian Extended Continental Shelf: A Larger Blue Amazon

Brazil's strategic interests on the continental shelf date back to 1950, when Act no. 28.840 incorporated the continental shelf to the national "territory". After that, several constitutional and ordinary laws regulated the continental shelf, including the notorious Decree no. 1.078/1970, which expanded Brazilian sovereignty seaward up to 200 nm, including on the continental shelf. By then, it had become clear to national strategists that the seabed is as relevant to economic prosperity as the other dimensions of the ocean. The 1970 "Sovereignty" Act

> had among other objectives to establish unequivocally that the country sovereignty over the seabed and its subsoil extends until at least the distance of 200 nautical miles. This distance goes far beyond where the depth 200 meters from the Brazilian shore. In other hand, the adoption of the 200 miles did not implied the renunciation to the continental margin areas (or the continental shelf, in the proper sense), which has proven to extend beyond this limit.[82]

The next legislative step was to adopt the 1988 Federal Constitution and to promulgate UNCLOS domestically via Act no. 8.617/93, whose Art. 11 specifically disciplines the continental shelf regime—provisions which will be examined further below.

Such strategic interest attributed to the continental shelf is not unfounded. Its riches lie not only on the *economic* potential of non-living resources, mainly hydrocarbons and minerals—as confirmed by the REMPLAC Action, mentioned supra, but also on the *biodiversity* universe to be unveiled thereon. It is no novelty that massive hydrocarbon reserves exist in the so-called "pre-salt" area, which extends beyond 200 nm. In 2005, the Brazilian oil state company, Petrobras, published the first evidences of oil and gas in the pre-salt fields, namely in the Santos Basin (*Tupi* Field). In 2008, production *in situ* kicked off and the first oil barrel from the pre-salt was sucked up from the Campos Basin—off the coast of Rio.[83]

---

[82]Castro (1989), p. 20.

[83]*See* Section "Facts and Info" of the Petrobras website. From the first oil extracted in the pre-salt in September 2008 to the volume of 2.07 million barrels-per-day achieved in April 2020, results have been largely positive. There has been a surge since late 2018, when production reached 1.5 million bpd. Available at: https://petrobras.com.br/fatos-e-dados/. Accessed 11 April 2020.

From a *biodiversity* perspective, the Brazilian continental shelf thrives with life. There are records of rhodolith beds consisting of a diversity of living organisms in both steep and shallow areas of the shelf.[84] Furthermore, recent scientific discoveries of corals off the Amazon coast, in 2016,[85] and extremely biodiverse seamounts off the coast of the Martim Vaz and Trindade islands, in 2017,[86] have dragged attention to the biodiversity potential of the Brazilian continental shelf and the risks ran in case such marine life rest unregulated and unprotected.

Still, of the vast amount of seafloor constituting the Brazilian continental shelf—approximately 4.5 mi km^2, little has been explored, a conclusion reached by the IX PSRM, both in terms of biodiversity and non-living resources' potential. Given that marine scientific research has only to a limited extent impregnated the Brazilian political and scientific agenda, it is difficult to list the species of deep-water marine life populating the Brazilian outer continental shelf and where precisely those ensembles of marine fauna and flora ought to be found. Despite such restrictions, progress has been made in mapping out the seafloor, both in terms of economic resources and overall fauna and flora, with a significant role played by the Action REMPLAC and the independent Plan LEPLAC, to map out the Brazilian shelf and ground the submission for outer limits, conjointly implemented by the Brazilian Navy and the Petrobras.

9.2.1 The Brazilian Continental Shelf Survey Plan: LEPLAC

As early as 1978, Brazil had evidences that its continental margin would exceed the 200 nm limit at some points. The country produced at the time more than half of its petroleum offshore and understood the strategic value of having an extended continental shelf. In 1986, the Brazilian Government initiated a project to survey the outer limits of the Brazilian continental shelf beyond 200 nm, based on Art. 76 UNCLOS, which produced the first results a year later,[87] at a moment when UNCLOS was not

---

[84]Rhodoliths are colorful, unattached, branching, crustose benthic marine red algae. The surface morphology of rhodoliths presents variations regulated by depth, hydrodynamic bioerosive processes and taxonomy. For more, *see* Horta et al. (2016), p. 117.

[85]The Amazon coral reefs are tacked away on the bottom of the Atlantic Ocean, at a depth which varies from 70 to 200 m. Worryingly, the corals are located in an area that could at any time be released for oil exploration. The discovery was made by Brazilian researchers aboard the ship Esperanza, donated by Greenpeace to the scientific mission.

[86]The seamounts around the Islands of Trindade and Martin Vaz hold one of the highest rates of biodiversity among all Atlantic islands. In addition, there is a high diversity of open sea and deep-sea species, including those of commercial importance, all found around the seamounts and the oceanic islands of the Chain. The area where the seamounts have been registered has been declared an MPA in March 2018. Federal Decree no. 9.312/2018, MMA, 2018.

[87]In June 1987, the oceanographic ship *Almirante Câmara*, of the National Hydrographic Directorate, of the Brazilian Navy (DHN) held the first survey mission of the Brazilian continental shelf. Information available at LEPLAC page of the Brazilian Navy's website.

yet in force, nor had been domestically ratified in Brazil. During the first phase of data collection, about 330,000 km of multi-channel, bathymetric, magnetic and gravity seismic data were collected along the entire length of the Brazilian continental margin.[88]

Those events preceded the adoption of the *Brazilian Continental Shelf Survey Plan* (LEPLAC), as part of the II Marine Resources Plan, in order to collect geodesic and bathymetric data for the delineation of the outer limits of the Brazilian shelf.[89] LEPLAC emphasized the importance of surveying the outer edge of the Brazilian continental margin as a way to integrate living and non-living resources to Brazil's socioeconomic reality, to increase knowledge on them and to promote their rational use. The Survey Plan was also praised as a means to enhance the Brazilian influence over the South Atlantic Ocean through a pioneering activity that could serve as a cooperation tool with other countries washed by that ocean.[90]

Working within LEPLAC were the Navy, Petrobras, the National Department of Mineral Production, Higher Graduate Schools on Geology and Marine Geophysics, as well as members of the scientific community. In fact, the Decree no. 98.145/1989 had the Survey Plan stimulate the employment of Brazilian researchers and the private sector in surveying activities. LEPLAC's initial field-work lasted for about 10 years and gathered data over more than 350,000 km of the Brazilian seafloor. During the twenty expeditions of its initial phase, bathymetric, seismic, gravimetric and magnetometry data were collected on a gigantic scale, the costs of which have been estimated in over US$ 40 million, conjointly spent by the Navy (with ship employment and project execution) and Petrobras (acquisition and processing of geophysical data).[91]

In short, the Survey Plan represented the possibility for Brazil not only to gather the data needed for a formal submission on the outer limits of its continental shelf to the CLCS, but also to increase national knowledge on the marine environment thereon. The delineation of the outer limit of the continental shelf is considered a fundamental legacy for future generations in Brazil, as it enables increased possibilities of new petroleum fields farther away offshore, the exploitation of biotechnology and biogenetics, as well as the exploitation of non-living resources at depths not yet commercially viable. The technology for that is there, as Petrobras proves to be one of the most advanced companies worldwide with technical skills and know-how to conduct such hardcore exploitation. The legacy is also related to the international

[88]Marinha do Brasil. LEPLAC—*O Brasil além das 200 milhas*. Apresentação da Região Sul nas Nações Unidas. Sep 2017.

[89]The first LEPLAC was approved by Decree no. 95.787/1988, which was revoked by Decree no. 98.145/1989 one year later.

[90]LEPLAC underscored its usefulness in meeting one of the essential objectives of Brazil's foreign policy in relation to the South Atlantic, to foster the development of the potential of the countries of the region through a cooperative effort among them, without interference by foreign powers.

[91]Marinha do Brasil. Diretoria de Hidrografia e Navegação. *LEPLAC*—Plano de Levantamento da Plataforma Continental Brasileira. Available online at: https://www.mar.mil.br/dhn/dhn/quadros/ass_leplac.html. Accessed 11 April 2020.

cooperation made possible by LEPLAC, as Brazil gained unique technical training regarding the delineation of outer limits, thus clearing prospects for international technical cooperation with neighboring coastal states on that regard.

Thus far, Brazil has forwarded *three submissions* for outer continental shelf limits to the CLCS.[92] The first submission dates from 2004, well within the 10-year limit established at the SPLOS,[93] claiming sovereign rights over approximately 911,000 km^2 of extended continental shelf. The submission was followed by revised partial submissions in 2015, 2017 and 2018.[94] The fact that the Brazilian submission was presented within the 10-year limit has been praised as demonstrating the country's "compliance in good faith with Article 76 UNCLOS".[95] Following deliberations on the initial submission, the CLCS formalized recommendations in April 2007, according to which Brazil was acknowledged approximately 765,000 km^2 of the claimed limits, which corresponded to approximately 79% of the initially required area. The remaining 21% were not initially acknowledged, mostly due to insufficient data supporting the submissions. Yet, in 2019 the Commission approved the recommendations regarding the partial revised submission made by Brazil in respect of the Brazilian Southern Region.[96]

Hence, the Brazilian government persisted with LEPLAC activities, with a view to preparing revised proposals, in order to have the Commission greenlight the rest of the area initially requested. The entire extension requested by Brazil corresponds to five areas: Amazonas Cone, Northern Chain, Vitória e Trindade Chain, Southern Continental Margin, and São Paulo Plateau.[97]

The *Amazonas Cone*—one of the largest submarine sedimentary cones in the world—is formed by the successive depositions of sediments brought from the mouth of the Amazon River. The Amazon cone has the largest sedimentary thicknesses of the Brazilian continental margin.[98] The cone is often described as an "anomalous sedimentary accumulation",[99] with its own peculiarities, in which sedimentary accumulation occurs on the continental geomorphological platform, thus making it extremely difficult to assess the exact foots of continental slope,

---

[92]The Commission on the Limits of the Continental Shelf established by the Convention had granted a period of up to 10 years from the date of entry into force of the Convention for the delineation of the outer limits beyond 200 nm. That limit was later amended.

[93]Meeting of the State Parties to the UN Convention on the Law of the Sea, *SPLOS/72*, which determined the commencement of the 10-year period as 13 May 1999.

[94]*See* Brazilian Executive Summaries of Submission, available online at the CLCS website.

[95]Silva (2012), p. 299.

[96]CLCS/108, *Progress of work in the Commission on the Limits of the Continental Shelf*, Forty-ninth session New York, 28 January–15 March 2019.

[97]For a detailed chart, elaborated by the Hydrographic Department of the Brazilian Navy and Petrobras, *see* Brazilian Summary, CLCS. Available at: https://www.un.org/Depts/los/clcs_new/submissions_files/submission_bra.htm. Accessed 11 April 2020.

[98]Mohriak (2003), p. 89.

[99]Figueirôa (2014), p. 61.

according to the typical models of Art. 76 UNCLOS. Its marking feature is the smooth and low-gradient slope into the ocean floor.

The *Northern Chain* begins East of the Amazon cone and is associated with the Equatorial Fracture Zone, which formed upon the separation between Northeastern Brazil and Equatorial Africa. The Chain illustrates ongoing tectonism, in which continental plates slid side by side in opposite directions, forming marginal chains relatively parallel to the coast on the fracture zones. The Northern Brazilian Chain acts as a natural barrier to sediment deposition on the continental margin, thus rendering the margin rather short in comparison with other parts—an area where Brazil has less bold claims to outer limits.[100]

Southwards, the continental margin of Brazil has once again a broader width. The *Vitória-Trindade Chain*, formed by a linear sequence of hills that extend along the coast of Espírito Santo stands out in this area, linked geologically and geomorphologically to the bank of Abrolhos. It covers about thirty seamounts and is 950 km in length. At its far East are the islands of Trindade and Martim Vaz, around which the frequency of the seamounts increases, which suggests intense magnetism associated with them

The *São Paulo Plateau* consists of another enlargement of the Brazilian continental margin, with a formation associated to the rupture of the Gondwana paleocontinent. Largest marginal plateau of the Brazilian coast, the São Paulo Plateau interrupts the continental slope, standing between it and the continental rise, and has sediments that can reach up to 4 km in depth, covering the sedimentary basins of Campos, Santos and Paraná—precisely where most of the oil production in Brazil and all the pre-salt reserves are.

To the south of the São Paulo Plateau, the continental margin slides down until Brazil's maritime border with Uruguay. The *Southern Continental Margin* has characteristics of a margin heavily modified by the magmatism that led to the Gondwana separation. Within that margin are the Santa Catarina Plateau and the Rio Grande Cone, which share with the Amazon Cone the characteristic of a smooth and relatively constant slope, since the continental shelf and into the ocean floor, without the classic slope and steep divisions.[101] Brazil's claim towards the Southern Margin was approved by the CLCS in March 2019.

Thus far, only the executive summaries of the Brazilian submissions have been made public, as part of the strategy chosen by the Brazilian delegation, pursuant to Rules 48 and 49 of the CLCS, in order to safeguard sensitive information on the Brazilian submarine areas from the eyes of third states. As explained in Chap. 3, such a behavior has raised criticisms from international specialized literature, due to the act that secrecy prevent other states from assessing the lawfulness of the Brazilian claims, thus adding to the opacity of the delineation procedure and to cuts of overall legitimacy.[102] The issue of secrecy has also raised much uproar in the case of the

[100]Milani et al. (2000), p. 360.

[101]Torres et al. (2008), p. 2.

[102]Egede (2006), p. 42. *See* also Macnab (2004), p. 11.

Russian submission, when responses from Denmark, Japan, Canada and the United States have emphasized the impossibility of the affected neighboring states to confirm the lawfulness of the Russian claims and its consistency with the criteria set out in Art. 76 UNCLOS.

Upon knowledge that UNCLOS would permit the delineation of outer continental shelf limits beyond the default length of 200 nm, Brazil did not waste time and created LEPLAC almost simultaneously with domestic ratification of the Convention, thus portraying the relevance of the continental shelf to the Brazilian interests. The operationalization of the continental shelf Plan also emphasized Brazil's determinacy in asserting jurisdiction far offshore in the South Atlantic Ocean. Ultimately, the measure was inspired by a mix of geopolitical ambitions and the prospect of future economic benefits.[103] LEPLAC mirrored a country zealous of its authority seawards, even if it did not stand at its best moment in economic and financial terms—the 1980s are known in Brazilian political science literature as the "lost decade", given the successive economic crises, hyperinflation and several emergency changes of currency.

Still in the international arena, Brazilian expertise acquired while collecting scientific data and preparing its CLCS submissions has been shared with other neighbors in the South Atlantic Ocean. One such country is Namibia, which has counted on consultancy from Brazilian experts to draft its own proposal.[104] Such a conduct is the outcome of the Brazilian Decree establishing LEPLAC, which refers to "intrinsic relevance of knowledge gained throughout the procedure of data collection".[105] During the Lula da Silva presidency, Brazil was keen on stimulating the development of regional potentialities, by offering help to neighboring countries in following a similar path—a cooperative posture that sought to repulse the undesired interference of foreign naval powers in the South Atlantic Ocean.

9.2.2 *Status of the Brazilian Submissions*

Phase II LEPLAC began in 2008 and collected approximately 440,000 km of geophysical data. After the CLCS's denial of 21% of the country's initial submission, Brazil opted for drafting and submitting three partial revised submissions. On 10 April 2015, the *Subpart of the Southern Region* was submitted to the CLCS, upon five meetings with the Commission's Subcommittee responsible for entertaining the Brazilian submission, made up of experts from Angola, Chile, South Korea, Denmark, Japan and Nigeria. On 8 September 2017, the Subpart of the *Brazilian Equatorial Margin* followed suit,[106] a move confirmed by the 2018 letter of the

[103]This opinion is shared by Zanella (2017), p. 411.

[104]Namibia's submission to the CLCS, 13 May 2009. *See* Moller (2003), p. 248.

[105]Marinha do Brasil, *LEPLAC*, 11.

[106]The second Brazilian revised submission contains: an introduction to the physiography of the Equatorial Margin, a detailed description of the regional morphology, the methodologies applied to

CLCS Chair to the 28th SPLOS, in which the Commission assured the hearing of "presentations on new, amended or revised submissions made by several States since the previous Meeting of States Parties, namely, Brazil, in respect of the Brazilian equatorial margin (partial revised submission)". Finally, on 7 December 2018, the Brazilian delegation ledged the third partial revised submission, related to the Brazilian Oriental and Meridional Margin. As of April 2020, the Commission had approved recommendations concerning the first Brazilian revised submission, on the Southern Continental Margin.

The Brazilian strategy seems to be one of slicing the revised submissions in parts, so as to increase the likelihood of obtaining positive recommendations by adapting posterior partial revisions to the approach adopted by the CLCS during the analysis of the previous ones. An inherent risk of walking this path is to end up in an endless "ping-pong" match with the Commission, given the amount of Brazilian partial revised submissions and the lack of a formal restriction on states resubmitting infinite revised applications for outer continental shelf limits to the CLCS.[107]

9.2.3 *The Brazilian Blue Amazon: A Political Concept with Legal Implications*

The ocean has been occupying a crucial place in Brazilian history since colonial times. Yet, only in the second half of the Twentieth century did the country start nurturing special interests in maintaining a certain level of geopolitical influence over the South Atlantic Ocean, in order to keep the region secure and untroubled by Northern maritime powers. Episodes such as the "Lobster War" against France—a Northern naval power—over the fishing rights of lobsters and other crustaceans on the Brazilian continental shelf, in 1963, highlight the relevance attributed by Brazilian authorities to the country's maritime aspirations—which sometimes took the shape of unilateral jurisdictional assertions.[108]

Moreover, Brazil's active participation in the Third Conference, as one of the leaders of the Group of 77—which then rendered Brazil the fame of "leader of territorialists", is also an emphatical evidence of the value that the country attributed to a new order for the oceans. Prioritizing negotiations over shows of force and "gunboat diplomacy" has been historically a means for weaker countries to advance an agenda favorable to their interests at the international stage. For that reason,

---

the implementation of the provisions of Article 76 UNCLOS, as well as three appendices on the data obtained by LEPLAC Phase 2, the description of the foot of the continental slope points and the description of the points with 1% sedimentary thickness used when defining the outer limits. *See* Brazilian Executive Summary, "*Continental Shelf and UNCLOS*", presented to the CLCS, 8 September 2017.

[107]That risk was highlighted, among others, by Silva (2012), p. 117.

[108]Azzam (1964), p. 1453.

perhaps, Latin American diplomats and intellectuals have stood at the forefront of some renowned doctrines in international law, such as the Calvo and Drago doctrines.[109]

Yet, the greatest challenges for Brazil's interests offshore have just emerged, namely upon the discovery of the massive hydrocarbons reserves of the pre-salt layer, off the Brazilian South-East coast. Despite the existence of such mineral and ecological riches; the geopolitical relevance of the ocean for the Brazilian economy; and the fact that more than 80% of the Brazilian population live near the coast, ocean-related matters are still relatively unknown to large portions of the Brazilian population. According to a comprehensive report by the Brazilian Excellence Cluster for the Seas (CEMBRA), while 73% of the Brazilians who participated in the study attributed large relevance to the sea, they perceived the sea almost exclusively as a source of food and leisure. In addition, UNCLOS was known to only 22% of the Brazilian population and, concerningly, only 8% of the population was aware that the territorial sea stretches up to 12 nm from the baselines.[110] Compared to oceans, forests—in particular the Amazon—seem to enjoy greater importance, awareness and consciousness among Brazilians.

The lack of a "maritime mentality" can be explained in terms of the dichotomy between *maritimity*—or maritime dimension—and *continentality*, i.e. the focus of a certain population on the role played by the seas or the mainland on their well-being. Paradoxically, while the Brazilian delegation negotiated UNCLOS, Brazilian military generals grappled with the issue of terrestrial sovereignty in the farthest corners of the country. Stimulating the economic development of Brazil's inland and upholding national sovereignty over land boundaries and natural resources were key strategies of different governments in Brazil during the second half of the last century. The construction of Brasília in 1960, by President Juscelino Kubitshek, and the "March to the West" of the 1970s and 1980s stimulated by the military regimes aimed at asserting Brazilian populational presence over the land territory, especially those areas with least demographic density around the Amazon forest.[111] Those efforts can be said to have aroused a certain continentality among Brazilians, even those who live at the littoral.

The monstrous challenges facing the management of the Amazon forest remain, especially in light of the recent renewal of alarming deforestation rates within the

[109]For more on both doctrines, see Hershey (1907), p. 27.

[110]CEMBRA (2012), p. 466.

[111]Such policies were not uncontroversial, but it can be said that they brought more benefits than evils to the country's overall economic, social and political situation. If, on the one hand, they may have generated negative outcomes, particularly the farming pressure towards the Amazon forest that claimed record levels of deforestation during the late 1980s and 1990s, on the other, he marches fulfilled the goal of occupying larger portions of the mainland, prompted the birth of one of the most competitive and efficient agricultural sectors of the world, and dispelled fears of the "internationalization" of the Amazon forest and foreign military interventions in the region. For a resounding critique against the calls for "internationalizing" the Amazon forest, *see* generally Buarque (2004).

Brazilian territory,[112] as do also challenges to assert of sovereignty and public power in Brazil's terrestrial boundaries. Still, public authorities, decision-makers and armed forces have also come to realize that the attention dedicated to the land territory had rendered another border "neglected", and it is not an irrelevant one. Brazil's international efforts to assert jurisdiction seaward and to protect riches adjacent to the shore met a timid effort domestically to create legal and institutional conditions for such arduously acquired rights and duties in the international sphere to be implemented.

That scenario slowly began to change in the late 1980s, upon the domestic ratification of UNCLOS in 1988, as well as the decision to kickstart LEPLAC. Internationally, the country negotiated with fellow states sharing the South Atlantic Ocean the transformation of the area into a nuclear free and peaceful-uses only ocean, and creating an organization and military alliance, the so-called South Atlantic Peace and Cooperation Zone (ZOPACAS) in 1986.[113] Subsequently, in the 1990s, public policies and acts aimed at governing the oceans were enacted, such as the Ocean Act no. 8.617/1993; the 1994 National Maritime Policy; the Marine Scientific Research Decree no. 96.000/1988, among others.

Despite those steps, not enough attention had been dedicated to reverse the context of decades of overlook of the oceans and the Brazilian Navy—unable to secure and protect the vastness of the Brazilian marine spaces. In parallel, some authors warned to the possible "race to carve up the seabed"[114] upon the adoption of UNCLOS, a move which steered national measures worldwide towards increased investments in ocean exploration and exploitation technologies, namely in the field of biogenetic resources and deep-sea mining.

In this context, Navy Admiral Roberto de Guimarães Carvalho coined the phrase "Brazilian Blue Amazon" in 2004, not per coincidence in the same year of the first Brazilian submission for an outer continental shelf before the CLCS.[115] By creating and spreading the idea of a "Blue Amazon", with its slight poetic touch, the Brazilian Navy placed itself as an actor to be heard in the domestic political debate, thus proposing policies and highlighting the need for a well-equipped naval force to safeguard not only the country's interests in the adjacent waters but also the "ocean destiny" neglected by Brazil for decades, according to doctrines fed within the Navy.[116] As the future of humanity is expected to depend on the riches of the sea,

---

[112] According to the *Brazilian National Institute for Space Research* (INPE), deforestation rate of the Brazilian Legal Amazon was 9762 km^2, from August 2018 to July 2019. This value represents an increase of 29.5% in relation to the deforestation rate of the previous year, which was 7536 km^2. That is the highest rate since 2008, and may well represent a trend for the Jair Bolsonaro presidency, for reasons explained below. Available at: http://www.inpe.br/ Accessed 12 April 2020.

[113] UNGA Resolution A/RES/41/11, *Declaration of a Zone of Peace and Co-operation in the South Atlantic* (ZOPACAS), 16 October 1986.

[114] Cavnar (2009), p. 391.

[115] Carvalho (2004), online.

[116] The 2012 CEMBRA Report emphasizes, in a rather grandiloquent fashion, that "Brazil's maritime destiny is a birthmark". *See* CEMBRA (2012), p. 174.

the Brazilian Navy considers it paramount for Brazil to pursue its *destiny* by enforcing its maritime awareness, "so that the Brazilian sea is protected from environmental degradation and from international interests".[117]

The Blue Amazon may be understood as an all-embracing concept which integrates all maritime zones under some degree of Brazilian jurisdiction which quickly became a key geopolitical concept with profound legal implications. The idea of a Blue Amazon now informs actions and plans of the Navy, environmental protection agencies, research centers and institutes, among others. In 2010, the phrase was registered as a trademark, and in 2013, Brazil founded the *Blue Amazon Defense Technologies Corporation* (AMAZUL), a public corporation charged with modernizing the Brazilian naval fleet—an indispensable tool for monitoring such an immense area.[118] In order to understand Brazilian ocean policies and laws, it is paramount to study the concept of the "Blue Amazon" in its multifaceted-nature.

As such, there are two possible dimensions of the "Blue Amazon" concept, two ways in which it can be defined: the physical area and the extension of maritime spaces comprised by the expression—definition *ratione loci*; and the uses and activities in those maritime spaces, including the respective challenges of governing the areas within national jurisdiction on a principle manner—definition *ratione materiae*.

Ratione loci, the Blue Amazon consists of the ensemble of territorial sea, EEZ and continental shelf off the Brazilian coast, i.e. the physical medium delimited in accordance with the pertinent UNCLOS provisions. That comprises a surface of 3,539,919 km^2, which remains, nonetheless, unsettled in light of Brazil's partial submissions to the CLCS for the delineation of continental shelf outer limits. If approved, Brazilian claims will grant the country jurisdiction over an extended area of about 911,000 km^2 seaward to the EEZ, rendering the Brazilian continental shelf approximately 4.5 million km^2 in total.[119]

The frenzy with the new concept steered a plethora of domestic publications on the Blue Amazon, its definition, objectives and practical implications for the Brazilian authorities. Somewhat regrettably, Brazilian scholars have misleadingly referred to the Blue Amazon as the "Brazilian maritime territory"[120] or the "Brazilian jurisdictional waters",[121] references that deserve immediate clarification. Firstly, it is

---

[117]According to former Brazilian President Juscelino Kubitschek, Brazil was "an ocean-facing nation, and shipping is, and will be, for a long time, the truly national communications system of our extensive coastal strip, where the main centers of economic activity in the country and most of its population". *See* Juscelino Kubitschek, Diário Oficial da União, 18 February 1959, 77, para. 187. Also, on the awareness page, in order to raise awareness to the relevance of the concept and the projects and visions of country behind it, Brazil instituted the *National Blue Amazon Day*, celebrated on 16 November, day of UNCLOS' ratification in Brazil.

[118]The Amazul S.A. was instituted by Federal Act no. 12.706/2012.

[119]As of April 2020, the CLCS had received 85 submissions, some from the same state who chose to separate its claims.

[120]Martins (2007), p. 266.

[121]Marques (2007), p. 143.

not "territory", because territory in international law is a stark concept with clear definition; it is the physical medium where a state exercises sovereignty.[122] In this sense, only the internal waters and the territorial sea, and not the EEZ nor the continental shelf of coastal states are to be considered as territory. Given that the notion of "Blue Amazon" concretely encompasses the Brazilian EEZ and continental shelf, it would be misleading to label it as "territory" belonging Brazil, even if the qualifier "maritime" is added to the phrase. The same holds true for any references to "jurisdictional waters", as the continental shelf beyond 200 nm does not comprise Brazilian waters, but solely the seabed and subsoil thereof. Scholars should, thus, favor the use of maritime "space" or "areas", and refrain from making references to "territory" or "jurisdictional waters", as the adequate legal phraseology for referring to the Brazilian Blue Amazon.

Ratione materiae, the Blue Amazon concerns the governance and regulation of ocean uses, such as the rational management of living resources, the ecological operation of ports, the sustainable exploitation of the pre-salt hydrocarbon reserves, the prospects of mineral resources, among other challenges. The concept of a Blue Amazon takes into account that the ocean is an endless source of resources; has incalculable natural assets; and has a precious biodiversity—further reasons for the analogy with the Amazon forest.[123] Those are motives enough to envisage the concept as more than just the sum of maritime spaces where Brazil exercises either sovereignty or the right-duty to manage natural resources and the marine environment: it comprises the governance challenges ahead of Brazilian authorities, especially in terms of environmental protection, marine security, and sustainable development. It informs the objectives of efficiently managing the maritime zones under Brazilian jurisdiction, be it jurisdictional waters or the seabed. By adding the adjective "blue" to the heavy-loaded word "Amazon", the Brazilian Navy intended a link not only with the element of the ocean's color—as in the other well-known concepts of "blue planet" or "blue economy", but mainly to raise awareness to the *potentialities* and *challenges* of managing the Brazilian maritime space.[124] Yet, it should always be kept in mind, for methodological and clarity purposes, that the focus of this chapter lies on the domestic environmental powers over continental shelf activities—even if the Blue Amazon refers to the totality of the marine zones.

[122]For more on the criteria of statehood according to international law, and a definition of territory, *see* Crawford (1977), p. 93.

[123]Information available at the homepage of the Brazilian Navy, Section on the Blue Amazon: https://www.marinha.mil.br/content/amazonia-azul. Accessed 12 April 2020.

[124]The analogy between blue and green economies, as in the case of blue and green Amazons, is explained in the Concept Paper drafted by the UNEP, according to which "the Blue Economy espouses the same desired outcome as the Rio +20 Green Economy initiative namely: *"improved human well-being and social equity, while significantly reducing environmental risks and ecological scarcities"* and it endorses the same principles of *low carbon, resource efficiency and social inclusion*, but it is grounded in a developing world context and fashioned to reflect the circumstances and needs of countries whose future resource base is *marine*". *See* UNEP, "Blue Economy Concept Paper", 2012, online.

A mesh of theories has shaped the concept of a Blue Amazon, particularly in the field of international relations and geopolitical studies.[125] Currently, it seems to be consensual in academia that three main pillars support the theoretic edifice of the Blue Amazon. Firstly, the strong association between the Blue Amazon and *oceanopolitics*—understood as geopolitical studies centered on the oceans—which attributes great relevance to the management and defense of the Blue Amazon in line with UNCLOS.[126] Secondly, the consideration that only an efficient management of the Blue Amazon will pave the way for economic prosperity and the defense of Brazilian sovereignty.[127] Thirdly, the categorization of the Blue Amazon in four main dimensions—or major areas of interest of the Brazilian state: assurance of sovereignty national defense, via exercising politico-strategical influence in the South Atlantic Ocean; economic prosperity; scientific and technological innovation; and, finally, environmental conservation.

Beginning by that last theoretical "pillar", or the dimensions of the Blue Amazon, one should clarify upfront that a hierarchy exists between them. In most states' strategic calculations, considerations of an economic, political, and sovereignty nature occupy a more privileged place than environmental ones in national long-term planning and decision-making. To use a term borrowed from international relations theory, the economic, political and sovereignty realms could be equaled to topics pertaining to "high politics", whereas environmental considerations are rarely given such a centrality, being usually relegated to the field of "low politics".[128]

9.2.3.1 Sovereignty and Defense Dimension

Stark emphasis is laid on the dimension of sovereignty and national defense of the Brazilian Blue Amazon concept. Tor the Brazilian naval strategists, reflections on the South Atlantic Ocean relate to matters of geopolitical influence through the sea towards other states. The South Atlantic represents the most accessible medium for Brazilian regional power projection, but its importance has not been linearly assessed throughout the country's history. An important landmark in the theorizing of the South Atlantic Ocean as a key platform for the projection of Brazilian geopolitical influence can be found in the 1996 First National Defense Policy, according to which, "the conception of regional space extrapolates the South American continental mass and also includes the South Atlantic Ocean".[129]

---

[125]Several texts and publications dedicated to analyzing different facets of the Blue Amazon concept are authored by officials of the Brazilian Navy or have been bred within the premises of the Brazilian Naval War College. It is the case of publications by Barbosa Júnior and More (2012).

[126]More (2012), p. 247.

[127]Marinha do Brasil (2013), p. 10.

[128]For a critical view on the distinction between "low" and "high politics" in international relations theory, *see* Olsen (2017), p. 638.

[129]Ministério da Defesa do Brasil (1996) *1° Plano Nacional de Defesa.*

The conception of the South Atlantic Ocean as an acute defense concern for the Brazilian authorities gained momentum over the 2000s. In 2008, the National Defense Strategy (EDN)[130] a document discussed between government, military forces and civil society, declared both the Blue and Green Amazons the *crux* of defense apprehensions for the Brazilian armed forces. The document was then updated in 2012, under the Rousseff Presidency, in order to crystallize the main pillars of the Brazilian strategic naval thinking, contemplated by a mostly deterrent policy: denial of the use of the sea, control of adjacent maritime areas and projection of power regionally. Following the 2012 EDN, Brazilian strategists have coined the phrase "Brazilian strategic contour" (*entorno estratégico brasileiro*) to refer to most sensitive areas surrounding Brazil in terms of defense considerations, a crucial part of which is the South Atlantic Ocean. According to the Brazilian Navy, key strategic and defense maritime areas for the country, in descending order of priority, are the "*vital area*", or the Blue Amazon; the "*primary area*", which covers the South Atlantic Ocean, defined as the part comprised between the 16° N parallel, the west coast of Africa, Antarctica, eastern South America and the eastern Lesser Antilles (excluding the Caribbean); and, finally, the "*secondary area*", encompassing the Caribbean Sea and the South Pacific Ocean. In sum, the so-called "Brazilian strategic contour" comprises the "vital area" and the "primary area", including the South Atlantic Ocean, the West African coast and Antarctica.[131]

The successful narrative created by the Brazilian Navy on the sovereignty dimension of the Blue Amazon has leveraged the Navy to the spotlight of domestic political debates, thus granting the Navy increased funding for strategic projects, as well as greater awareness as to the need for a well-equipped force, capable to protect the Brazilian Blue Amazon. In fact, the sovereignty and defense elements of the Blue Amazon have in the Brazilian Navy their main guardian, which is bound by the constitutional duty to defend the country from external threats, as well as to safeguard the constitutional order domestically.[132] In its mission to dissuade traditional and modern marine threats off the Brazilian coast, which range from terrorism, drug, arms and people trafficking, piracy, as well as climate change, ocean structural modifications, marine pollution and biodiversity death, the Navy ought to be equipped with trained personnel, best means and cutting-edge technology. If any

[130] Ministério da Defesa do Brasil (2008), p. 4. Despite the relevance attributed to the defense of the South Atlantic Ocean, due to Brazil's marine resources and geopolitical interests therein, the 2008 Defense Strategy makes no reference to "Blue Amazon".

[131] Estratégia Nacional de Defesa (2012), pp. 19, 23. In addition to that, for further detail on each strategic maritime area, *see* generally Pesce (2008).

[132] To protect the Brazilian Blue Amazon, the Navy lays priority on denying potential enemy forces access and use of Brazilian waters, pursuant to international law. Navy actions are informed by strategic objectives delineated in the 2012 EDN, namely: protection of oil rigs, naval and port facilities, archipelagos and oceanic islands within Brazilian jurisdictional waters; readiness to respond to any threat to maritime trade routes, by state or unconventional, criminal forces, and ability to join international peace operations, outside Brazilian jurisdictional waters, under the aegis of the United Nations or multilateral organizations in the region. *See* Estratégia Nacional de Defesa (2012), p. 69.

country in the world wishes to effectively combat such threats, it is indispensable to structure themselves appropriately, with a management and monitoring system strengthened by partnerships, information sharing and cooperation with other institutions and the Navy.

A list of concrete outcomes of the political pressure exerted by the Blue Amazon concept domestically include the negotiations to purchase 36 *Grippen* fighter jets from the Swedish company SAAB;[133] and the founding of the AMAZUL S.A., the public company established to promote, develop, transfer and maintain technologies sensitive to the Brazilian Marine Nuclear Program (PNM), the Submarine Development Program (PROSUB), and the Brazilian Nuclear Program (PNB). In this context, AMAZUL's primary mission is to support the development of a nuclear-propelled submarine, a technological advancement taken as essential by Brazilian strategists for the monitoring of Blue Amazon. In order to execute its projects and offer technological services, the company has sought to attract qualified human resources, a massive challenge in a developing economy which undergoes a severe political and economic crisis.[134]

The sovereignty and defense dimension of the Blue Amazon concept also informs *politico-strategic considerations* for the South Atlantic Ocean. In fact, the concept itself is essentially politico-strategic, both for international and domestic purposes, as it locates maritime spaces in a decisive position for the dynamics of international relations and the well-being of the Brazilian population. In a broader scenario, the entire philosophy behind the narrative of a "Blue Amazon" points towards the use of the oceans for national development and international cooperation. For that reason, the Brazilian Navy equals the preparedness to defend the Blue Amazon as a prerequisite for the country to exert geopolitical influence in the South Atlantic Ocean, while attaining economic prosperity and social development. To those goals, strategic projects of the Brazilian Navy have sought for a strong synergy with academic, industrial and business sectors.

Regarding the international cooperation objective, *capacity-building* programs have been designed and implemented, so as to stimulate cooperation with countries such as South Africa, Namibia and others. The idea behind the curtains is to train highly-qualified specialists in different fields of knowledge, as well as to foster coordination between the navies of the countries involved. In fact,

---

[133]The Brazilian Air Force signed a contract in 2014 with the Swedish company SAAB to acquire 36 *Grippen NG* fighter jets, in a total investment of approximately US$ 4.05 billion. The first aircraft was delivered in 2019, and the last one should occur in 2026. The contract involves the training of Brazilian pilots and mechanics in Sweden, logistical support and the transfer of technology to Brazilian industries, as part of the country's policy to surveil the Blue Amazon.

[134]The political and economic crises referred to here has been triggered by the Impeachment of former President Dilma Rousseff, in 2016, which paved the way for her Vice-President to rule the country, imposing austerity measures that have deepened the symptoms of political turbulence and economic backlash. Despite minor recovery signs, the overall scenario for the Brazilian economy and political arena, at the time of writing is devastating. For more on the causes for the crises, *see* Malamud (2017), p. 150.

> Brazil intends to support an emerging South Atlantic system of maritime traffic by expanding its own data platforms (SISTRAM). These already integrate Uruguay and Argentina via Regional Centre of Maritime Traffic of South Atlantic Area (CRT-AMAS). An ultimate stage of surveillance and control of Brazil's coasts is the Blue Amazon Management System (SISGAAZ). This involves a more comprehensive multi-platform surveillance system (vessels, radars, satellites and drones) and an integrated data processing and communication capability.[135]

In so doing, the country expects to exercise a prominent geopolitical influence in the region, thus keeping the South Atlantic Ocean undisturbed by maritime powers. For instance, the country realizes the massive influence and impact of the British presence in the South Atlantic—through a "belt" of several islands in that Ocean—a situation which has been prompting Brazilian concentrated efforts to reaffirm itself as a regional reference in terms of cooperation for the states bordering the South Atlantic, so that this Ocean remain free from the presence of "the North"—or at least that this presence "does not jeopardize the interests of the South in general and of Brazil in particular".[136]

Nonetheless, from an international relations perspective, the Brazilian efforts towards increased South-South cooperation do not go unquestioned or uncriticized—no matter how romantic such intentions may sound. Thus far, some limitations have hindered the process of designing unisonous cooperation schemes and common defense strategies for the South Atlantic Ocean. A possible reason explaining such difficulties is the *unilaterality* of the Brazilian narrative on the relevance of the South Atlantic Ocean, which at some point could be mistaken for the attempt to impose a hegemonic will in the entire region. In this sense, scholars have identified the need to hear West African and South American states' perceptions on the South Atlantic Ocean,[137] to ensure the pursue of a more or less uniform strategy by those coastal states. Only so could Brazil exercise real geopolitical influence in the region and keep other maritime powers quiet in nudging the region without amounting to a traditional hegemon that holds secretive self-interests and abuses its regional partners to achieve such goals.

9.2.3.2 Economic Dimension

On the economic dimension, it should be clear upfront that the Blue Amazon has living and non-living resource potentialities which have gone unexploited thus far. The living resources may be summed up to natural offshore fisheries, such as the Mullet or the Southern Atlantic Tuna off the Brazilian coast.[138] Fishing activities are of great importance for local seaside communities, but the practice lacks in public surveillance and control. That renders necessary the daily struggle against predatory

[135]Duarte (2016), p. 105.

[136]Wiesebron (2013), p. 118.

[137]Such a claim is formulated by Pedro Seabra (2017), p. 325.

[138]*See* Executive Report of the REVIZEE Program (2006) note supra.

practices and IUU fishing by national and foreign vessels with high technology, which disrespects environmental standards and inflicts economic social damages to the country.

The economic potential of the Blue Amazon is not restricted to living resources. Analyses of shipping industry data and the transportation of goods through the seas shows that only 3% of maritime trade in Brazil is operated by the Brazilian merchant shipping. Such a low number suggests the need for investments in this sector, so as to reduce a dependency on foreign ship owners that exercises a negative weight on Brazil's trade balance. Substantial investments are also needed in the modernization of Brazilian ports. For the national economy, dependency on the South Atlantic Ocean is enormous and growing, in light of the expected exploitation of natural resources lying on the adjacent ocean floor.

In fact, Brazil is currently exploiting hydrocarbon reserves of the pre-salt area, in order to meet the demand of the domestic market and guarantee the export of surpluses. That is an undeniable reality, despite traditional skepticism inside Brazil as to the ability of the state-owned petroleum company, Petrobras, to lead the most challenging exploitation of oil in ultra-deep waters. Apart from that, Petrobras developed activities in Africa, including offshore reserves in Namibia.[139] The expansion of the Brazilian continental shelf requires the carrying out of researches capable of endorsing the prospect, exploration and commercialization of these natural resources, which are economically relevant, but also ecological, for the world.

Some publications on Brazilian geopolitical and strategical calculations see the Blue Amazon as the prospect of achieving economic development through technological advancements and innovation.[140] In other words, the Brazilian maritime zones would form a "Brazilian oceanic complex" with the following main axes: (a) security and defense; (b) aquaculture and fisheries; (c) recreational and leisure activities; (d) renewable energies and offshore exploration; (e) maritime transport; and (f) marine sciences.[141] In order to achieve socioeconomic development, Brazil would thus need specific public policies, especially the industrialization of the ocean technology sector, capable of providing long-lasting ground for a developmental standard based on investments on marine sciences and the sustainable use of marine

[139]Information available at Petrobras' website. Available at: http://201.77.217.135/en/countries/namibia/namibia.htm. Accessed 12 April 2020.

[140]In Brazilian strategic studies, one can find references to the need to overcome the oil-dependency, via materialization of a "Brazilian Oceanic State" (*Estado Oceânico Brasileiro*). That multi-faceted objective is grounded on the belief that Brazil should not repeat the same mistakes from the past and, thus, take the oceans into account when drafting development plans for the future. That Brazilian Ocean State ought to be aware of the risks of turning to the East (i.e. to the ocean) with the same mindset that inspired the occupation of the Green Amazon—illegal granting of lands and lack of monitoring, which nowadays is responsible for alarming rates of deforestation. The occupation of Brazil last economic frontier, the Blue Amazon, must be, above all, *sustainable* in the traditional sense of the word. *See* More (2012), p. 248.

[141]Cruz Júnior (2012), p. 115.

resources.[142] Such policies would have the power to turn Brazil into an "ocean developmental state", a topic that connects the economic dimension of the Blue Amazon with that of science and technology.

9.2.3.3 Scientific and Technological Dimension

On the scientific and technological side, knowledge of the waters under Brazilian jurisdiction is still limited, regardless of the perspective one looks at this dimension. Despite the national policies, programs, plans and actions examined supra (such as the REVIZEE), biodiversity within the Brazilian maritime spaces is poorly researched and recorded, in comparison with other maritime states. The recent discoveries of deep-sea corals thriving in the Amazon basin, Northern part of Brazil, and extremely biodiverse and rich seamount around the volcanic islands of Trindade and Martin Vaz, have called public authorities' attention to the need to map out and inventory the marine life off the Brazilian coast and its role in promoting national socioeconomic development. When it comes to non-living resources, with the growing demand for metals and minerals and rising prices for these materials, interest in knowing more about the resources in the deep sea and explore what is economically viable is surging.[143]

The 2005 Marine Resources Policy was the embryo for the scientific programs associated with the exercise of Brazilian jurisdiction at sea. The set of policies, programs and actions coordinated by CIRM—analyzed supra—benefits, mainly, scientific knowledge of the marine environment, its preservation, the rational use of its resources and the training of qualified human resources. Of the groups of actions and plans set in motion under the Marine Resources Policy framework, two have not been mentioned thus far, which relate intimately to scientific research and an enhanced comprehension of the Brazilian waters: the projects for managing the São Pedro and São Paulo Archipelago—PROARQUIPÉLGAGO—and the Archipelago of Trindade and Martin Vaz—PROTRINDADE.

Both Archipelagoes are of a volcanic nature and were uninhabited until the launching of the aforementioned projects, the objectives of which are to inhabit key islands in both Archipelagoes for the purpose of enhancing scientific research in the Atlantic region. Parallelly, the projects are also meant to adjust both island formations to the regime of islands prescribed in Art. 121 UNCLOS.[144] In the PROARQUIPELAGO, for instance, the CIRM initiated in 1996 a scientific project aimed at keeping permanently at least four Brazilian researchers in a research station on the Belmonte Island, so as to enable those scientists an *in-situ* lab for researching, sampling, analyzing marine fauna and flora, as well as currents patterns, oceanic

[142] *Id.* 106.

[143] Martins (2007), p. 267.

[144] For more on the legal status of the São Pedro and São Paulo Archipelago, *see* generally Ventura and Mello Filho (2020) Forthcoming.

strain factors, etc. Up to now, the Actions PROARQUIPELAGO and PROTRINDADE have achieved, in view of the Brazilian authorities, considerable scientific data production with significant results and direct impacts on the sustainable optimization of food supply chains, generation of employment and elevated income in various segments of the Brazilian society. In addition to that, the Actions are also credited with having developed technological know-how on system-building in inhospitable areas, as well as on clean energy production and logistic support capacity for long distances.[145]

Those are but a few examples of how the principled management of the Blue Amazon, with a focus on instrumentalizing the region towards the technological advancement of Brazil and the enlarged understanding of ocean dynamics, can prove beneficial to the country. The question remains, though, whether such instrumentalization of the Blue Amazon respects internationally accepted environmental standards and rules or whether local excitement with the benefits of the immense ocean obfuscate the quest for a truly sustainable, in the sense of environment-friendly, management of the zone.

9.2.3.4 Environmental Dimension

Hence, on the environmental dimension, it is the case to assess whether Brazil is making use of its "right-duty" to manage continental shelf resources in accordance to UNCLOS and other internationally assumed commitments on the conservation of marine spaces under national jurisdiction. Key strategic topics of Brazilian ocean policies usually include, at least in paper, (i) *maintaining* biological diversity; (ii) *reconciling* competing interests in marine and coastal areas; (iii) *investing* in sustainable activities; and (iv) *sharing* benefits from the use of marine genetic resources in a fair manner, all that through cooperation with other countries and multilateral forums. Furthermore, the environmental conservation dimension of the Blue Amazon is not left aside in theorization efforts embraced by Brazilian political strategists, though it is also not given much of a relevance either.

In addition to the defense and economic facets of the "Brazilian seas", the *Marinha do Brasil* also highlights the biodiversity richness of the Blue Amazon. High-ranking Navy officials appraise the "Brazilian marine territory"[146] as critical for climate regulation, absorption and gradual release of heat, process of nutrients, thus contemplating a wide range of services, mineral reserves and food that benefit a large part of the coastal population. A possible reason for such concern is that, for the Brazilian Navy, both environmental and security considerations go hand-in-hand.

---

[145]Viana et al. (2009), p. 22.

[146]Letter of Admiral Ilques Barbosa Júnior, as to the festivities of the National Day of the Brazilian Blue Amazon, 16 November 2017, available online. As mentioned elsewhere, the expression is misleading from a strictly legal perspective, but is employed in the context of international relations' documents and writing of the Brazilian Navy officials.

The phenomenon of combining defense and environmental preoccupations under one roof has been studied by Ikeshima, to whom the BRICS countries (Brazil, Russia, India, China and South Africa) have awaken to a sense of maritime security, while looking after the sustainable exploitation of marine resources.[147]

In Brazil, an illustration of such combined efforts is the design of the *Blue Amazon Management System* (SISGAAZ), for the permanent monitoring of waters under national jurisdiction for all sorts of purposes, including defense and environmental conservation ones.[148] The SISGAAZ was created by Decree no. 12.598/2012. Although the Program's name includes the phrase "Blue Amazon", the SISGAAZ covers the Brazilian jurisdictional waters and the international waters under the country's responsibility for search and rescue operations. However, the system experienced significant hindrances, mainly related to investment cuts, which prevents forecasts of an implementation date. In fact, up to now, only the stage of designing the Program was concluded, with the remaining two stages—contracting and developing the system—halted until further ado. Another example are the country's marine protected areas, which can also be designed to serve both ways, thus keeping maritime powers away from conservation zones.[149]

Yet, until now, most of the programs and plans for the integrated management of coastal and marine environments have been directed mainly to the prevention of degradation of strictly coastal environments.[150] It is undeniable that coastal ecosystems, such as mangroves and shallow reef corals, are under significant stress due to pressure from multiple sources like land- and port-based pollution, excessive tourism, continental shelf mining and exploitation activities. Those are reasons strong enough for having conservation efforts of coastal areas given priority, what does not mean, however, that the rest of the marine environment under national jurisdiction, namely deep-sea ones, should be neglected. Integrated management policies and laws for the ocean owe their effectiveness to the holistic thinking of the marine environments, as has been highlighted in previous studies.[151] When it comes to deep-sea activities, the popular motto of "out of sight, out of mind" should be fought vehemently, as the continental shelf and the Area are prone to be the last frontiers of anthropogenic economic exploitation.

Another problem identified in this research refers to the link forced by the Brazilian Navy between safety of navigation measures and environmental conservation, a rationale according to which measures taken for increasing navigational

[147]Ikeshima (2011), p. 7.

[148]*See* Düring (2015) online.

[149]Further detail on the Brazilian marine protected areas in Chap. 10.

[150]The main environmental objectives within the Blue Amazon relate to: recovering the harmful effects of pollution, revitalizing marine urban areas, valuing the natural landscape, in order to develop new activities, such as ecotourism and environmental education, and to maintain high standards of marine environmental quality. *See* Marinha do Brasil, Amazônia Azul, Vertente Ambiental, available at: https://www.marinha.mil.br/content/vertente-ambiental. Accessed 12 April 2020.

[151]See generally Boyes and Elliott (2014).

safety in the Blue Amazon directly contribute to the environmental conservation of the area. Although that may be true, as measures adopted with respect to controlling vessel-source pollution may also be construed as increasing safety of navigation, one should first define the scope of "navigational safety measures". By doing so, it is intended to avoid a confusion between both objectives (safety and environmental protection) and worse, the cooptation of ecological concerns by the much specific commandment of navigational safety.[152] For instance, the Brazilian Navy's website which is dedicated to the environmental dimension of the Blue Amazon clearly emphasizes safety of navigation over any other criterion for the principled environmental management of the Blue Amazon—a somewhat misleading approach. No matter how relevant navigational safety measures may be for the peaceful use and management of the marine spaces under national jurisdiction, that element certainly does not exhaust environmental concerns over marine ecosystems. For that reason, considerations on safe navigation emerge only sporadically in this work, in connection with challenges for the environmental management of the Brazilian Blue Amazon.

Of the variety of maritime spaces calling for environmental protection, this work focuses on the regulation of the continental shelf in light of the expansion of domestic jurisdiction seaward. For Brazil, an extended continental shelf implies not only wealth and geopolitical clout, but also increased duties and responsibilities, what makes it reasonable for the attentive and concerned viewer to expect more conflicts of uses of Brazilian and international maritime zones. In the legal environmental field, attention should thus be paid to upholding substantive and procedural obligations related to the prevention of environmental damage, transboundary damage, preventive actions, protection of the marine and marine environment, precaution, pollution control due to several factors, among other topics, all of which examined in detail in Chap. 10.

Despite the hierarchy between the Blue Amazon's dimensions, the "lower" status of environmental considerations within the Brazilian interest's equation does not constitute a hindrance to the current study, but to the contrary, it is yet another motivation for grappling with this topic. In Brazilian academia, works proliferate on the security and geopolitical aspects of the that region, but reduced attention has been dedicated to assessing the adequateness of the Brazilian legal and institutional frameworks to tackle the massive challenge of managing the seafloor of the vast Blue Amazon, while respecting international environmental obligations set out in the law of the sea and environmental legal instruments.

[152]The *Prestige* disaster, in 2003, highlighted the interlink between the topics of safety of navigation and protection of vulnerable ecosystems.

9.2.4 Benefits and Risks of an Extended Blue Amazon

To assert jurisdiction over larger portions of the ocean floor, i.e. to expand the "Brazilian Blue Amazon" entails both benefits and risks. On the side of benefits, tangible *economic gains* probably stand out from the rest, given the (not yet fully known) exploitation potential of living and non-living resources of the outer continental shelf, namely deep seabed minerals, hydrocarbons, and sedentary species. One more benefit relates to *foreign policy achievements*, in terms of cooperation bonds with neighboring countries of the South Atlantic Ocean, stemming from the Brazilian ability and willingness to provide technical assistance and consultancy to states currently preparing submissions for the delineation of outer continental shelf limits.[153]

On the side of the risks, the most notable one, according to this work, is having the country ill-suited to manage the extended Blue Amazon both in legal and institutional terms. Usually, works in the field of international relations tend to dismiss legal risks arising from the continental shelf expansion, thus overemphasizing the political turbulence that might emerge from CLCS recommendations and the Brazilian state behavior. While there are certainly several political risks related to the delineation procedure, this work focuses rather on the legal risks and challenges falling upon the Brazilian state regard not the recommendations of the Commission, but the national regulations to manage the marine environment of the extended area.

Besides, weight is also given to the aspects of sovereignty and defense of the Blue Amazon within Brazilian strategical maritime thinking.[154] Even though one recognized dimension of the Blue Amazon concept be the marine environment, few in-depth studies have dwelled in the analysis of the environmental duties and responsibilities falling upon the coastal states with a broad continental shelf—so as to contemplate the "new" reality of having an internationally acknowledged outer continental shelf. Admittedly, a concept frequently employed by the Brazilian Navy to refer to ocean governance, that of "maritime mentality", binds together both sovereignty and environmental considerations, as it consists of the general

[153]Brazil has shown interest in the past in jointly exploiting continental shelf resources with its adjacent neighbors, Uruguay and Guyana. In Uruguay, for instance, Petrobras expressed interest in the exploration and exploitation of oil and gas on the Uruguayan continental shelf. In Guyana, an official visit of former President Lula indicated that the Brazil would have Petrobras work together with companies from that country to brainwash possibilities for joint operations in oil and gas exploration on the continental shelf. Concerning the French Guyana, Brazil's cooperation with France began even before the preparation of the proposal for French Guiana was completed. Following the beginning of the examination of the Brazilian proposal by the subcommittee, and taking into account the comments of some of its members, the Brazilian Government sought cooperation from France to establish the points of the foot of the slope in the region of the lateral border. In December 2004, the French authorities agreed to cede GUYAPLAC data, which were included in the addendum sent by Brazil to CLPC in March 2005. *See* Figueirôa (2014), p. 248.

[154]The reference work by Barbosa Júnior and More (2012) evidences the prominence of security considerations over environmental ones.

perception of the importance of the sea and the willingness to use its potential in a sustainable way, thus making such concerns blip on the Navy's radar. In this sense, IUU fishing in jurisdictional waters and marine environmental crimes—clear marine environment-related threats, have been identified as two of the greatest challenges to the Brazilian Navy.[155]

However, a maritime mentality alone may not be enough for the effective conservation or sustainable exploitation of marine resources, if the country in question has an ill-suited *legal* and *institutional* framework for implementing adequate environmental standards to the maritime zones under national jurisdiction. The environment-related threats listed by the Brazilian Navy as particularly challenging demand a clear legislative framework, suitable monitoring/enforcement powers and the need to promote increased cooperation between national agencies with some degree of ocean responsibility. For that reason, the next chapter investigates the marine environmental regulatory framework applicable in Brazil, with a focus on the continental shelf. The objective is to assess Brazil's legal adequateness to cater for the sustainable exploitation of the country's continental shelf, as well as the consistency of marine environmental domestic legislation with international binding instruments, particularly UNCLOS and the CBD.

The situation of Brazilian agencies engaged in marine conservation efforts did not look promising in the last years. Since 2014, a domestic political crisis has added to the unfavorable international context, thus shaking Brazilian economics and politics and throwing the country into a calamity that is referred to by scholars as the international "rollback" of Brazil.[156] According to an accurate analysis by Andres Malamoud,

> The rise of Vice President Michel Temer to the presidential office, which followed the ousting of Rousseff through congressional impeachment, was the last nail in the coffin of a twenty-year period of international prestige. Not only was Brazil nowhere to be seen when most of the Latin American presidents and several world leaders convened in Colombia to witness the signature of the peace agreement between the government and the FARC, but a few months later Temer declared that he would not attend the 2017 summit of the G20 in Germany due to domestic issues. On the international stage, Brazil no longer bites, nor does it kiss.[157]

More acutely, the impeachment of former president Dilma Rousseff, in 2016, and the shift towards an ultraliberal economic model lies also on the roots of the international rollback—the country's economy is in coma and current policies do not register much recovery. The Presidency of Michel Temer approved in Parliament a constitutional amendment to halt public spending to 2015 nominal amounts for the upcoming 20 years. The PEC 241 (Project of Constitutional Amendment) has already limited investment in social programs and cut funds to environmental agencies, taken as less relevant in light of the country's historic problem with

[155] Moreira (2017).
[156] Malamud (2017), p. 164.
[157] *Id.* 163.

urban violence. The Project, nicknamed in Brazil as the "PEC of the end of the world", was nonetheless approved in the Parliament. As of April 2020, domestic austerity measures and the looming economic crisis expected to follow the pandemic of COVID-19 do not allow for the anticipation of brighter days ahead. Such contingencies not only contribute to Brazil exercising a less relevant role in international fora, but also place enormous challenges to the country's marine policies.

9.3 Partial Conclusions

Brazil is entangled in a complex web of policies, plans, and concrete actions which enable the environmental governance of its maritime spaces. The general policies—National Maritime Policy; National Policy for the Environment; National Policy for Marine Resources—share common principles and objectives. With respect to marine resources, several other plans have been put in motion under the PNRM umbrella and the CIRM coordination: the quinquennial National Sectorial Plans for Marine Resources; the Brazilian Continental Shelf Survey Plan; and the National Coastal Management Plan. The bulk of those policies, plans and actions conform what could be called a decentralized "Brazilian ocean strategy".

The balance of those marine environmental governance efforts is a rather difficult one to make, as there are records of successfully implemented actions and neglected ones. Under the quinquennial Sectorial Plans, specific actions have been designed and effectively executed, such as REVIZEE and LEPLAC—the former mapped out the living resources of the Brazilian EEZ and published extensive reports with the main findings. The latter was responsible for collecting massive amounts of data on the Brazilian seabed morphology which grounded the country's submissions for outer continental shelf limits before the CLCS. Yet, not-so-successful actions also exist, such as REMPLAC—concerned with the detailed evaluation of the mineral potentiality of the continental shelf—a survey program with parallel capability to increase scientific knowledge on the marine environmental features and ecosystems of the Brazilian seabed. Insider information from CIRM members, obtained via interviews, hinted at the likelihood of Brazilian authorities relaunching REMPLAC. Now, under a different work methodology and taking into account the relevance of marine mineral resources to the Brazilian socioeconomic development.

This chapter stressed the relevance of recognizing the complexity inherent to the governance of the oceans. A quick glimpse at the policies, programs, actions and institutions participating in the Brazilian ocean governance reveals the complexity of such a process in the historic era that scientists have agreed to refer to as the "Anthropocene". Hence, complexity is expected to increase, as new policies are about to come to life, the case of the National Policy for the Conservation of the

Marine Biome (PNCMar).[158] To embrace complicity, in context, does not mean that domestic legal and policy frameworks should be unnecessarily tortuous. In fact, a certain degree of harmony among the policies and laws ought to exist, if the overall governance is to be effective. A too complex ocean governance system is likely to lead to internal conflicts of formal competence, as well as to material contradiction, consequences which are to be avoided by every policy- and law-maker.

Regarding the Brazilian Blue Amazon, environmental conservation efforts are not left aside in theorization efforts of Brazilian political strategists, though it is also not given much of a relevance either. Overall, there are praises and criticisms to be made to the "Brazilian ocean strategy". Predominantly, the national policies (in particular the PNRM) have been serving the interests of the Brazilian society. They are responsible for initiating an ongoing process which has lasted for almost 40 years, expected to continue for many years more. Much has been achieved, but there is still much work to be done.

Besides, there is strong need for Brazilian authorities to improve domestic *coordination* within such a complex web of plans and programs, which is expected to become difficult by the day, thus adding more pressure to the work of the CIRM. Another obstacle to effective policies is posed by recent budgetary cuts to environmental agencies, including those tasked with monitoring the oceans. Despite the afore-mentioned marine riches under Brazilian jurisdiction, it is hardly disputable that insufficient funds to marine scientific research will hamper increased knowledge of the shelf and harden the drafting of environmentally sound exploration and exploitation strategies.

In addition to that, one should warn against the lack of or insufficient follow-up reports on the actions and objectives set out in each Action set out in different PSRMs, as REMPLAC or REVIMAR. The CIRM's website is not updated, as of April 2020, and several Actions contain several years-old reports.[159] The same situation was identified at the IBAMA website with respect to statistics on fisheries off Brazilian waters, the latest having been published in 2007.[160] That situation is beyond worrisome, what brings to surface yet another challenge to Brazilian marine environmental governance efforts. Communication and dialogue between public

[158]The National Policy for the Conservation and Sustainable Use of the Brazilian Marine Biome is currently under discussion in the Brazilian Parliament, under the proposed Bill no. 6.969/2013. The draft bill recognizes that "the oceans are suffering the impact of human action, as overfishing, pollution and acidification" and closes with the objective of "providing the country the ability to respond to climate change and ocean acidification providing mitigation measures and adaptation". That document, if passed by the Parliament, will be proof of Brazil's concern with climate change impacts on the marine environment, and represents a significant step towards special legislation on key threats to ocean health off the Brazilian coast.

[159]Navigation on the CIRM website is far from intuitive, with important actions and plans (such as the REMPLAC, BIOMAR and others) lacking follow-up reports and info on results or impacts of each measure. Available at: https://www.marinha.mil.br/secirm/ Accessed 12 April 2020.

[160]The criticism formulated herein may be confirmed at the following webpage: https://www.ibama.gov.br/biodiversidade-aquatica/gestao-pesqueira/estatistica-pesqueira. Accessed 12 April 2020.

authorities and the population ought to be enhanced, especially if one is to inform stakeholders about the objectives, actions and the consequences of all policies. That is a major challenge, as the specialty and technicality of public discussions may drive out crucial stakeholders and the population at large, a consequence that would irreparably crack the objective of developing a "maritime mentality" in Brazil. Only when Brazilians learn to treasure domestic ocean policies, will public authorities prioritize the sustainable management and conservation of the oceans, thus enabling the federal and state administrations the means and the financial resources necessary to achieve it.

References

Azzam I (1964) The dispute between France and Brazil over lobster fishing in the Atlantic. Int Comp Law Q 13(4):1453–1459

Barbosa Júnior I, More RF (eds) (2012) Amazônia azul: política, estratégia e direito para o oceano do Brasil. FEMAR, Rio de Janeiro

Barros-Platiau AF et al (2015) Correndo para o mar no antropoceno: a complexidade da governança dos oceanos e a estratégia brasileira de gestão dos recursos marinhos. Revista de Direito Internacional 12(1)

Boyes SJ, Elliott M (2014) Marine legislation – the ultimate "horrendogram": international law, European directives & national implementation. Mar Pollut Bull 86(1):39–47

Buarque C (2004) Internationalize the Amazonia? Envío Jornal, 273

Carvalho RG (2004) A Amazônia azul, Defesa Net

Castro LAA (1989) O Brasil e o novo Direito do Mar: mar territorial e zona econômica exclusiva. FUNAG, Brasília

Cavnar A (2009) Accountability and the commission on the limits of the continental shelf: deciding who owns the ocean floor. Cornell Int Law J 42(3):388–440

Centro de Excelência para o Mar Brasileiro (2012) O Brasil e o mar no século XXI: Relatório aos tomadores de decisão do país. CEMBRA, Niterói

Crawford J (1977) The criteria for statehood in international law. Br Yearb Int Law 77:93–182

Cruz Júnior AS (2012) O Atlântico Sul como nova fronteira tecnológica e sua contribuição para o desenvolvimento do Brasil. In: Amazônia Azul: política estratégia e direito para o oceano do Brasil. FEMAR, Rio de Janeiro, pp 100–117

Duarte E (2016) Brazil, the blue economy and the maritime security of the South Atlantic. J Indian Ocean Reg 12(1):97–111

Düring N (2015) Blue amazon management system: Brazilian navy decides not to decide and program comes to a halt. DefesaNet, 4 November

Egede E (2006) Submission of Brazil and article 76 of the Law of the Sea Convention (LOSC) 1982. Int J Mar Coast Law 21(1):33–55

Figueirôa CSB (2014) Limites exteriores da plataforma continental do Brasil conforme o direito do mar. FUNAG, Coleção CAE, Brasília

Franckx E (2009) Challenges to ocean policy making. University of Lapland Printing Centre, Rovaniemi

Gerring J (2017) Case study research: principles and practices, strategies for social inquiry, 2nd edn. CUP, Cambridge

Hershey AS (1907) The Calvo and Drago doctrines. Am J Int Law 1(1)

Hoffmann AP, Marcondes D (2017) Maritime regions and the South Atlantic. Contexto Internacional 39(2):229–236

Horta PA et al (2016) Rhodoliths in Brazil: current knowledge and potential impacts of climate change. Braz J Oceanogr 64(2):117–136

Ikeshima T (2011) Is the freedom of the high seas under threat from marine protected areas? Environmental protection versus security interests under international law. Waseda Global Forum 8:5–30

Jablonski S, Filet M (2008) Coastal management in Brazil: a political riddle. Ocean Coast Manage 51(7):536–543

Longo AR (2014) Em busca do consenso: a Terceira Conferência Das Nações Unidas Sobre o Direito do Mar. SECIRM, Brasília

Machado LAF (2015) A plataforma continental brasileira e o Direito do Mar : considerações para uma ação política. FUNAG, Brasília

Macnab R (2004) The case for transparency in the delimitation of the outer continental shelf in accordance with UNCLOS Art. 76. Ocean Dev Int Law 35:1–17

Malamud A (2017) Foreign policy retreat: domestic and systemic causes of Brazil's international rollback. Rising Powers Q 2(2):149–168

Marinha do Brasil (2013) Amazônia azul: a última fronteira. Centro de Comunicação Social da Marinha. CCSM, Brasília

Marques AA (2007) Amazônia: pensamento e presença militar. Uunpublished PhD Dissertation, University of São Paulo

Marroni EV (2014) The importance of public policy for blue Amazon marine spatial planning. Dev Stud Res 1(1):161–167

Martins EMO (2007) Amazônia azul: limites e extensão das zonas marítimas sob soberania e jurisdição nacional no Brasil. Revista Meritum 2(2):265–279

Medeiros R, Young CEF, Pavese HB, Araújo FFS (eds) (2011) The contribution of Brazilian conservation units to the national economy: Executive Summary. UNEP-WCMC, Brasília

Milani EJ et al (2000) Petróleo na margem continental brasileira: geologia, exploração, resultados e perspectivas. Revista Brasileira de Geofísica 18(3):352–396

Ministério da Defesa do Brasil (1996) Plano Nacional de Defesa, 1ª ed, Brasília

Ministério da Defesa do Brasil (2008) Estratégia Nacional de Defesa, Brasília

Ministério da Defesa do Brasil (2012) Estratégia Nacional de Defesa. Brasília

Ministério do Meio Ambiente do Brasil (2006) Relatório executivo do programa REVIZEE, Brasília

Mohriak W (2003) Bacias sedimentares da margem continental brasileira. In: Geologia, tectônica e recursos minerais do Brasil. CPRM, Brasília

Moller LE (2003) The outstanding Namibian maritime boundaries with Angola and South Africa. Int J Mar Coast Law 18(2):241–260

More RF (2012) Reflexões sobre a formação de um pensamento oceanopolítico brasileiro. In: Amazônia azul: política, estratégia e direito para o oceano do Brasil. FEMAR, Rio de Janeiro, pp 232–248

Moreira WS (2017) A segurança e a defesa no Atlântico Sul: perspectiva brasileira. Unpublished, XV Curso de Extensão em Defesa Nacional, Brasília

Nye JS, Donaghue JD (2000) Governance in a globalizing world. Brookings Institution Press

Oliveira CC, Galindo GRB, Silva ST, Mont'alverne TCF (2018) Meio ambiente marinho e direito, vol II, A gestão sustentável da investigação, da exploração e da explotação dos recursos marinhos na zona costeira, na plataforma continental e nos fundos marinhos. Juruá Editora

Olsen N (2017) Blurring the distinction between "high" and "low" politics in international relations theory: drifting players in the logic of two-level games. Int Relat Dipl 5(10)

Pesce I (2008) Atlântico Sul: aumento da presença naval norte-americana? Revista Marítima Brasileira 128(7/9)

Ribeiro MC (2017) South Atlantic perspectives on the future international legally binding instrument under the LOSC on conservation and sustainable use of BBNJ. Int J Mar Coast Law 32 (4):733–764

Seabra P (2017) Stretching the limits? strengths and pitfalls of South Atlantic security regionalism. Contexto Internacional 39(2):305–327
Serafim MP, Dias RB (2012) Análise de política: uma revisão da literatura. Cadernos Gestão Social 3(1):121–134
Short AD, Klein AHF (2016) Brazilian beach systems. Springer, Berlin
Silva AP d (2012) Brasil e Canadá na Convenção das Nações Unidas Sobre o Direito do Mar: os esforços brasileiros e canadenses para aumentarem suas plataformas continentais. Política Hoje 21(1):291–325
Silva AP d (2013) O novo pleito brasileiro no mar: a plataforma continental estendida e o projeto Amazônia Azul. Revista Brasileira de Política Internacional 56(1)
Soares LFM (2014) O Brasil e as negociações sobre Direito do Mar. In: Reflexões sobre a Convenção do Direito do Mar. FUNAG, Brasília, pp 255–312
Souza C (2006) Políticas públicas: uma revisão da literatura. Sociologias 16:20–45
Torres LC et al (2008) Brazilian Southern Margin: an example of the identification of the base of the slope on a passive continental margin. Unpublished 5th Conference of the International Hydrographic Organization, Monaco
UNEP (2012) Blue Economy Concept Paper
Ventura VAMF, Mello Filho EC (2020) The legal status of the São Pedro and São Paulo Archipelago in light of article 121 UNCLOS and the South China Sea Arbitral Award: uncontested right to EEZ and continental shelf or Brazilian 'creeping jurisdiction'. In: Global challenges and the law of the sea. Springer, Berlin
Viana DL et al (2009) O Arquipélago de São Pedro e São Paulo: 10 anos de estação científica. SECIRM, Brasília
Vidas D et al (2014) What is the Anthropocene—and why is it relevant for International Law? Yearb Int Environ Law 55(1):3–23
Wiesebron ML (2013) Blue Amazon: thinking the defense of Brazilian maritime territory. Austral: Braz J Strateg Int Relat 2(3):101–124
Zanella TV (2017) Manual de Direito do Mar. D'Plácido, Belo Horizonte

Chapter 10
Brazilian Legal Framework Applicable to the Blue Amazon's Seabed: An Assessment of Consistency with International Law

While the previous chapter depicted the domestic policy and institutional panorama framing the management of Brazilian maritime spaces, the so-called "Blue Amazon", this part sets out to map the *national marine environmental laws and regulations on the continental shelf* and to assess their consistency with international law, in particular UNCLOS. As Brazil "enlarges" its Blue Amazon, through the delineation of outer continental shelf limits, it is the case to answer two core questions: (i) Is the Brazilian legal framework in accordance with general international law and the law of the sea, namely UNCLOS? (ii) Are there any legal-environmental implications arising from the process of delineating outer continental shelf limits for the Brazilian state?

Concerns with the exploitation model of Brazilian marine resources are not new. Already in 1989, the LEPLAC Decree urged the need to both "integrate" the outer continental shelf to the Brazilian marine space and achieve the "rational exploitation of the ocean".[1] Such dual justification for the Decree—enlarging maritime spaces and riches under national jurisdiction *plus* regulating the exploitation of the area, so that it be rational—is praiseworthy. Yet, the phrase "rational exploitation" alone, if unaccompanied by any other qualifier, can be subject to dual interpretations, especially so at the time of the Decree's approval. It may suggest, for instance, the most efficient exploitation from an economic perspective, thereby neglecting ecological concerns in its reasoning. Following the LEPLAC Decree, Brazil hosted the 1992 World Conference on Environment and Development, in which marine concerns came decisively to the fore, as in Principle 17 of Agenda 21, on the protection of the oceans and all kinds of seas.[2] Since then, the country had been actively negotiating

[1]Decree no. 98.145/1989, item II.

[2]Principle 17 of Agenda 21 suggested the adoption of the following program areas by states: (a) Integrated management and sustainable development of coastal areas, including exclusive economic zones; (b) Marine environmental protection; (c) Sustainable use and conservation of marine living resources of the high seas; (d) Sustainable use and conservation of marine living

V. Alencar Mayer Feitosa Ventura, *Environmental Jurisdiction in the Law of the Sea*,
https://doi.org/10.1007/978-3-030-50543-1_10

international environmental treaties and helping shape the international environmental rule of law.[3]

Recently, marine governance of the Brazilian continental shelf earned the spotlight in the wake of the CLCS recommendation acknowledging Brazilian sovereign rights over a large portion of the seabed beyond 200 nm. Such recognition has raised questions, *inter alia*, as to the knowledge owned by Brazilian authorities on deep-sea fauna and flora, as well as the adequateness of current domestic rules and regulations to manage—i.e. conserve and exploit—such submarine universe. As one of the maps produced by the Brazilian Institute for Geography and Statistics reveals, marine life abounds not only throughout the Vitória-Trindade Chain, but also on other spots of the Brazilian continental shelf.[4] Fragile ecosystems, as the seamounts neighboring the Atlantic islands of Trindade and Martim Vaz, or the coral reefs off the Amazon river delta, in the Northern cone of Brazil,[5] should inspire the need for the clear regulation of continental shelf uses, so that the national ecological patrimony does not vanish by virtue of inadequate domestic laws or deficient enforcement.

Another map of the same Atlas highlights the alarming scarcity of information and knowledge on the biological conservation status of several Blue Amazon spots, including large portions of the Brazilian EEZ—with the notable exception of waters adjacent to the Brazilian Southernmost state, Rio Grande do Sul.[6] Of the little which is known, the Brazilian Institute for Geography and Statistics has classified the biological relevance of the EEZ farther away offshore with the lowest level: it was labelled "high", in comparison to marine areas with a "very high" and "extremely high" biorelevance for the Brazilian coast system—an expected result, as coastal areas usually suffer from acuter anthropogenic pressures, such as land-based pollution, irresponsible tourism, port operations etc.[7]

---

resources under national jurisdiction; (e) Addressing critical uncertainties for the management of the marine environment and climate change; (f) Strengthening international, including regional, cooperation and coordination; (g) Sustainable development of small islands.

[3]Such a trend is of questionable continuity in light of the recently elected Brazilian President, Mr Jair Bolsonaro, for reasons previously highlighted in this work.

[4]The project *Atlas Mar*, of the Brazilian Institute for Geography and Statistics—IBGE—has pinned several entries of marine life around the seamounts of Martin Vaz e Trindade, as well as in the Vitoria-Trindade Chain and the Northern Amazonas Cone, portions of the seafloor that Brazil claims to pertain to the country's continental shelf, but which have been rejected by the CLCS following the first Brazilian submission. *See* IBGE, Atlas geográfico das zonas costeiras e oceânicas do Brasil.

[5]*See* Brady (2017) online. Available at: https://news.nationalgeographic.com/2017/01/photos-amazon-coral-reef-discovery-research-science/. Accessed 12 April 2020.

[6]One of the explanations for such concentration of information on the biological relevance within the Southern Brazilian EEZ is certainly the presence of well-equipped ocean-oriented research centers in the state of Rio Grande do Sul, such as the Federal University of Rio Grande do Sul (FURG).

[7]*See* Ministério do Meio Ambiente, *Portal Brasileiro sobre Biodiversidade*, 2010. Available at: https://portaldabiodiversidade.icmbio.gov.br/portal/. Accessed 12 April 2020.

Deficient information on the Brazilian marine environment, especially on seabed ecosystems, has sounded the alarm as to the country's precise environmental powers over the continental shelf. Not just that, questions and criticisms exist as to the suitability of the municipal legal and institutional framework for the management of the deep-sea marine environment under national jurisdiction.[8] Criticisms to the Brazilian marine environmental laws abound within Brazilian academia. On occasion, Ricardo Coutinho, researcher of the National Institute for Science and Technology, has emphasized the large number of existing laws regulating the Brazilian seas, which generates management instabilities and enforcement complications. For instance, on the issue of exploiting calcareous algae in international waters, Brazilian regulatory bodies are said not to know clearly what is allowed by international law and what is not. On another topic of interest, scholars consider the domestic ocean law-making process meagre in terms of public participation.[9] Those are but a few examples of the troubled Brazilian regulation of the Blue Amazon—further normative problems will be approached on an item-by-item basis below.

This leads to this chapter's main arguments, that Brazil could perform better to increase (i) overall domestic legislative coherence on marine environmental matters, and (ii) the consistency of domestic rules with international instruments on ocean and environmental law. Considering that the country is a federation, the domestic legal framework contemplated in this book is limited to federal acts, statutes, decrees, ordinances and others, thus leaving state- and city-level legislation aside—despite the concurrent prescriptive competence regarding the environment granted by Art. 24, sections VI and VII of the Brazilian Constitution to the Union, States, the Federal District and the Municipalities.[10] In fact, it would have been overambitious to examine specific state-level and city-level environmental legislation in the scope of this work. Besides, state- and city-level rules must always seek validation in the Federal Constitution, and may be stricter than federal acts, but never

[8]On the issue of insufficient information on the EEZ, the New Zealand EEZ Act (2012) may offer a reasonable parameter for decision-making when information on the risks and effects posed by a certain activity to the marine environment is undecisive. According to the Act, "the decision-making framework for the [EEZ] Act acknowledges that there is limited information about the EEZ and continental shelf environment and new technologies which may be employed there. Decision-makers are required to take into account the *best available information*, consider any uncertainty or insufficiency in the available information and exercise *caution* when information is *uncertain or insufficient*".

[9]It is the case of Ana Cláudia Farranha, professor at the University of Brasília. *See* Minutiae of the GERN Workshop held at the University of Brasília (UnB), 2014.

[10]Such an interpretation flows from the combined interpretation of Arts. 24 (VI) and (VIII) and Art. 30 (I) and (II) of the Brazilian Constitution. Art. 24 establishes that it is the responsibility of *Union, States and the Federal District* to legislate concurrently on: VI—forests, hunting, fishing, wildlife, nature conservation, soil and natural resources protection, environmental protection and pollution control; as well as on liability for damage to the environment. In parallel, Art. 30 stipulates that it is the responsibility of the *Municipalities*: I—to legislate on matters of local interest; II—to supplement federal and state-level legislation as appropriate.

softer—following the Kelsenian pyramidal hierarchy of legal norms.[11] Whereas the Union was granted competence to prescribe general rules on the protection of the environment, states and municipalities have mere supplementary legislative competence.

With that in mind, this chapter is structured in three parts. Firstly, it dwells into the Brazilian (federal) environmental regulatory powers on the continental shelf: "how far may Brazil go" section. Secondly, it assesses the domestic legislation in place which relates to the environmental regulation of activities on or in connection with the continental shelf: "how far has Brazil gone". This part equally contains an analysis of the Brazilian legislation's consistency with international law of the sea and environmental law, alongside a criticism against inconsistencies and insufficiencies of the laws and rules in place. Finally, the third part addresses the challenges ahead of the Brazilian state for striking a balance between jurisdictional assertions seawards and the corresponding domestic regulation of continental shelf uses, followed by the conclusions to this work.

10.1 How Far May Brazil Go?

One of the most exciting questions that triggered this work was the material and procedural extent of Brazilian legislation on the uses and management of the continental shelf. To that purpose, the phrase "activities on or in connection with the continental shelf"[12] means the activities which occur with physical contact with the continental shelf, either permanent or intermittent. It is the case of drilling, mining, collecting samples for MSR, dumping, bottom-trawling, submarine cabling, capturing and storing substances, i.e. activities that may threaten the ecological integrity of known—and unknown—deep-sea ecosystems of the continental shelf. The afore-mentioned activities are grouped in accordance with the two dimensions of marine environmental protection ascribed at UNCLOS, as identified previously in this work: (i) management and conservation of living resources of the seafloor under national jurisdiction; (ii) prevention, reduction and control of pollution from seabed activities; and (iii) the conduction of marine scientific research on the continental shelf.[13]

Needless to say, every classification is arbitrary and the act of classifying usually places the author in a difficult position before its peers, as the criteria employed may be questioned from a plethora of perspectives. The distinction between conservation

---

[11] *See* generally Jestaedt (2017).

[12] The meaning of the phrase "on or in connection with" has been discussed previously in this work and informs the continental shelf activities hand-picked for scrutiny in this chapter.

[13] This discussion has been handled, on a general level, in Chaps 7 and 8. The same which was discussed there applies to Brazil.

of living resources and prevention, reduction and control of pollution respects both the level of mediacy between such goals and the activities falling under them, as well as the categorization adopted by UNCLOS itself.

10.1.1 Conservation of Living Resources

This item deals with the regulation of activities that primarily affect continental shelf living resources' conservation, i.e. sedentary species, according to the interpretation of UNCLOS which defends the existence of right-duty of coastal States to manage fisheries and conserve biodiversity under national jurisdiction. That view follows from the application of Arts. 60 and 61 UNCLOS—on the right to manage and conserve living resources of the EEZ—to Part VI on the continental shelf, a procedure made possible by Art. 77 (1) and (4) UNCLOS, and the philosophy of conserving and rationally using marine resources, pursuant to the Convention's Preamble. Hence, crucial activities to be analyzed are bottom-sea trawling and marine spatial planning—and how the Brazilian legislation regulates them.

Upfront, and for the sake of clarifying the division between conservation marine living resources and the prevention, reduction and control of pollution adopted in this work, it is not intended here that activities such as oil and gas exploitation—placed under the category of control of marine pollution—do not cause harm to sedentary species. The distinction means solely that regulating bottom-sea trawling or marine spatial planning—rather than controlling marine pollution—immediately impacts the conservation of living resources.

10.1.1.1 Deep-Sea Fisheries on the Continental Shelf

Certain fishing activities may damage benthic communities on the continental shelf, both of a sedentary and non-sedentary nature, thus harming species under a coastal state's jurisdiction, or other jurisdictions. That is the case of bottom trawling, or bottom fishing on deep-sea habitats—which is not to be mistaken for "bottom fishing".[14] While the latter relates to sportive, non-industrial techniques to catch fish stocks that are found near the shallow seafloor, the former consists of an industrial fishing method where a trawl, or sizeable fishing net, is dragged across the seafloor in search for deep-sea pelagic stocks and sedentary species.[15] One does

[14]According to the online blog Fish Me, bottom fishing "can be done from a boat and also from the land using either handlines or rods. The main aim of this technique is to take the bait to the bottom of the sea and present it in a tempting way to the fish and to lure them into the hook". Available at: http://www.fishfishme.com/blog/bottom-fishing/. Accessed 12 April 2020.

[15]Some of the species targeted by bottom trawling are shrimp, cod, rockfish, sole and flounder, or seamount species, such as orange roughy. For the purposes of this work, a possible definition of deep-sea follows the depth criterion, i.e. seafloor deeper than 500 m. *See* ECORYS (2014), p. 21.

not need to be an environmentalist to grasp the environmental traumas that such a practice casts, especially if conducted in massive, Anthropocene-like scales. The main problems of bottom-trawling are the destruction of deep-sea habitats and ecosystems, damages to the structural elements of deep-sea ecosystems due to physical impact, and high rates of by-catch and untargeted fish, which are crucial species to the structure of benthic ecosystems are among.[16] Thus, the question: how far may coastal states reach when enforcing international and domestic legislation against destructive fishing, such as bottom trawling, in areas under national jurisdiction?

Bottom-trawling matters dearly for coastal states with outer continental shelves, as the legal regime applicable thereon must deal with an overlap between maritime zones. Above the outer shelf, states enjoy freedom to fish in the water column, according to Art. 87 UNCLOS, while coastal states have exclusive sovereign rights over the sedentary species lying on the seafloor within national jurisdiction, in line with Art. 77 (4) UNCLOS. The former is regulated by the high seas fisheries' regime, whereas the latter follows the continental shelf regime.

High seas fishing takes place beyond coastal states' exclusive economic zone and is governed by the 1995 United Nations Fish Stock Agreement (UNFSA), an implementing treaty to UNCLOS, adopted in order to reduce and control fishing in the high seas.[17] The trend initiated by the Implementing Agreement was confirmed by the 1995 Code of Conduct for Responsible Fisheries, as well as the 2008 International Guidelines for the Management of Deep-Sea Fisheries, both adopted under the auspices of the UN Food and Agriculture Organization (FAO). The current international legal regime governing fisheries attributes to coastal states a *significantly limited jurisdiction over high seas fishing*, as the activity is regulated by specific RFMOs and bi- or multilateral agreements—pursuant to UNCLOS Art. 116–119 and UNFSA Art. 10. An example of such RFMOs is the International Commission for the Conservation of Atlantic Tunas (ICCAT),[18] or the several

[16]For more on the environmental issues raised by bottom-sea trawling, *see* Stiles et al. (2010) online. Visit also the website of the Marine Conservation Institute, a Non-Governmental Organization based in the United States, at https://marine-conservation.org/. Accessed 12 April 2020.

[17]The 1995 UNFSA consolidated efforts for enhanced coordination and cooperation between coastal and flag states, who shall cooperate through international and regional bodies, such as the Regional Fisheries Management Organizations, or RFMOs. The legal regime created by the 1995, including the reliance on RFMOs, has been described as a "fine-tuned *mare clausum* in the limited context of fisheries regulation enforcement". See Türk (2012), p. 179. The Agreement also effects a sort of "encroachment" to freedom to fish in the high seas, a restriction which should be welcomed as necessary and beneficial to the conservation and management of endangered fishes, including straddling and highly migratory stocks. In fact, freedom to fish has "outlived its legitimacy", due to the mounting dangers of fish stock depletion. *See* Pendleton (2005), p. 514.

[18]The ICCAT aims at conserving more than 30 species of Atlantic Tuna and Tuna-like stocks. The Commission if the main body of the International 1966 Convention for the Conservation of Atlantic Tunas, signed in Rio de Janeiro. For more on the working of this specific RFMO, visit: https://www.iccat.int/en/. Accessed 12 April 2020.

bilateral Sustainable Fisheries Partnership Agreements between the European Union and developing countries, such as Morocco, Senegal and others.[19]

When it comes to the regulatory maneuver room of coastal states over deep-sea fisheries within national jurisdiction, it is unfortunate that international law does not regulate the issue specifically. No explicit rules on deep-sea fishing or bottom trawling within national jurisdiction are currently in place. Such a scenario has been confirmed by the FAO Report on the "Current Legal and Institutional Issues relating to the Conservation and Management of High-Seas Deep-Sea Fisheries", by Erik Molenaar, according to whom

> one of the most prominent gaps [in the governance of deep-sea fisheries] is the non-applicability of the Fish Stocks Agreement to discrete high seas fish stocks. Other relevant shortcomings relate to the regime for sedentary species, both on the continental shelves of coastal States and on the seabed beyond the limits of national jurisdiction (the Area).[20]

Yet, a combined reading of specific provisions and values behind pertinent treaties such as UNCLOS, the UNFSA and the CBD may offer guidance as to coastal states' jurisdiction on the issue. Particular obligations flow from those instruments, namely the requirement for states to assess the impact of fishing (including on the deep-sea), to minimize the impacts of fishing in ecosystems, to apply precaution and an ecosystem approach to new and exploratory fisheries.[21] Ultimately, within the EEZ—and, therefore, on the continental shelf up to 200 nm—coastal states are entitled to take a *vast range of measures to regulate fisheries domestically* and to enforce its fisheries laws and regulations.[22] Based on that, with respect to bottom-sea fisheries within national jurisdiction, it can be asserted that coastal states have a relatively broad *prescriptive jurisdiction*, as stipulated by UNCLOS Arts. 60, 61 combined with Arts. 192 to 194.

On to the *enforcement powers* within national jurisdiction, one must note that such powers are not as vast as the legislative ones. In short, enforcement measures in the EEZ, following whatever activities in violation of the domestic marine protective framework in place therein, may range from boarding, inspection, arrest and initiation of civil and criminal proceedings, pursuant to Art. 73 (1) UNCLOS. Here, the Convention only makes express reference to enforcement powers regarding management and conservation of living resources in Part V, without any express indications as to the continental shelf. It does not mean, however, that coastal states are expected not to enforce national legislation on sedentary species of the outer continental shelf. As discussed supra (on the environmental prescriptive jurisdiction), coastal states enjoy sovereign rights for the purpose of exploring and exploiting sedentary species of the continental shelf beyond 200 nm. Hence, it is

---

[19]European Commission. *SFPA Infographic*. Available at: https://ec.europa.eu/fisheries/sites/fisheries/files/docs/body/2015-sfpa_en.pdf. Accessed 12 April 2020.

[20]*See* Molenaar (2007), p. 113.

[21]*See* Gianni (2004), p. 67.

[22]*See* Nelson (2010) para 23.

reasonable to interpret the Convention as granting enforcement powers for the implementation of, at least, those two purposes. Yet, there is more to that story than a quick reading of UNCLOS could suggest, namely with respect to the environmental enforcement powers over the management and conservation of living resources of the continental shelf beyond 200 nm. As long as living resources abound within the jurisdiction of the coastal state, there is municipal environmental jurisdiction to manage and conserve those resources—a thesis advanced previously in this work, and contrary to what a literal reading of UNCLOS would suggest.

Traditionally, law of the sea scholars have focused on the aspect of *obligation* to manage and conserve living resources of the continental shelf, so as to conclude that coastal states "are not subject to the obligation to conserve them", thus claiming that the Convention's "exclusive focus on exploitation is also reflected in the key role accorded to the words 'harvestable stage' in the definition of sedentary species".[23] For Erik Molenaar, the wording of the Convention in ineluctable, though "defective" it may be for marine international environmental conservation efforts, with Part XII of UNCLOS doing little to resolve that defect.

The main argument of this work is that the question of conservation powers of coastal states in areas within national jurisdiction can be framed from the perspective of *rights*, and not just obligations, thus according coastal states the right to manage the deep-sea species of the continental shelf. Besides, the conservation of marine living resources is equally mandated by international binding instruments dealing with the preservation of biological diversity.[24] It is the case of the CBD and CITES (for the states simultaneously parties to them and UNCLOS), treaties with a clearer environmental scope than UNCLOS and which impose ecological obligations that can be interpreted as concerning sedentary species too.[25] Hence, "failure by parties to abide by conservation measures in those treaties may result in breach of international obligations of protect and conserve the marine environment, thus giving rise to international legal *responsibility* for environmental harm".[26]

The material extent of coastal states' environmental powers over continental shelf activities is not to be underestimated. Marta Chantal Ribeiro, for instance, is of the view that in cases of *illegal fishing of sedentary species* of the continental shelf within beyond 200 nm, regardless of who practices it, the coastal state is legitimated to act unilaterally.[27] In other words, coastal states were given (by UNCLOS)

[23]Molenaar (2007), p. 117.

[24]This view is shared by Wolfrum (2000), p. 251.

[25]Such position may be countered as being grounded on rather fragile arguments, as, it could be said, UNCLOS would rule out the application of Part V to sedentary species (while at the same time calling to coastal states to protect and preserve the marine environment under national jurisdiction); or that UNCLOS has priority over the CDB (Art. 22 CBD and Art. 311 UNCLOS)—which is true, but does not rule out resort to the CBD for matters related to marine biodiversity conservation. Those and other arguments have been countered previously in this book.

[26]*See* Nelson (2010) para 24.

[27]Ribeiro (2015), p. 63. In that view, the Portuguese scholar joins Owen and Chambers (2006), p. 40.

prescriptive and enforcement jurisdiction to repress illegal fishing beyond 200 nm, which may include measures such as boarding, inspection and arrest of fishing vessels engaged in the illicit activities. That is also the case for illegal fishing of other species which destroys the sedentary life and the ecological balance of the continental shelf beyond 200 nm.[28]

That seems a reasonable position, which is shared by this work. In general, it could be said that coastal states have *criminal jurisdiction* to persecute the illegal harvesting or exploration of sedentary species of the outer continental shelf. The application of domestic coastal state rules on fishing activities both on and above the outer continental shelf is also supported by the FAO Report on High-Seas Deep-Sea Fisheries, by Erik Molenaar. Not only does freedom to fish in the high seas above these outer continental shelves not apply to sedentary species, but fishing for other species can also be constrained by coastal State regulation in order to avoid or mitigate impacts on sedentary species.[29]

10.1.1.2 Marine Spatial Planning

The shared use of the marine environment in a planned and organized way is a great challenge for every coastal state in the world. Such a planning process is labelled "marine spatial planning"—sometimes also called "maritime" spatial planning, MSP—and presupposes the involvement and participation of the different stakeholders which depend on coastal and marine areas for their survival or the continuity of their activities. Its relevance is such, that it has been considered "a key planning tool for sustainable decision-making."[30] Of the tools available to public authorities when planning the uses of the marine environment, the most relevant ones for this section—due to their potential for conserving marine biodiversity—are the *area-based tools*, in particular the designation of marine protected areas within coastal states' national jurisdiction.

Drawing on the definition laid by the CBD, a marine protection area is a geographically defined maritime area "which is designated or regulated and managed to achieve specific conservation objectives".[31] When a coastal state establishes an MPA, it resorts to an *in situ* conservation measure, which means "the conservation of ecosystems and natural habitats and the maintenance and recovery of viable populations of species in their natural surroundings". The establishment of a representative and effective system of protected areas is part of the overall biodiversity conservation strategy and is agreed upon as a goal to be met by the CBD signatories.

[28] *See* Ribeiro (2015), p. 64. The scholar bases her point on the Portuguese legislative decree 28/2011/A, on the OSPAR MPAs beyond 200 nm, which she considerers an attack to the national "affirmation of sovereignty"—"manifestamente perigosa para a afirmação da soberania nacional".

[29] *See* Molenaar (2007), p. 117.

[30] *See* Long (2014), p. 712.

[31] Art. 2, CBD, on the use of terms.

Knowing that coastal states have discretion to specify the nature of the MPAs, whether entirely restrictive or allowing for the sustainable use of marine resources, the CBD Secretariat has insisted on organizing workshops to help states identify fragile marine ecosystems and ecologically significant marine areas (EBSA).

Within the realm of the law of the sea, such conservation measures are reinforced by pioneering provisions contained in UNCLOS, even though the Convention refrains from explicitly referring to "protected areas". Indeed, and pursuant to Art. 194 (5), "measures taken in accordance with this Part [XII] shall include those necessary to protect and preserve rare or fragile ecosystems as well as the habitat of depleted, threatened or endangered species and other forms of marine life".[32] That provision—which hints towards an "ecosystem approach" within UNCLOS—offers coastal states the necessary legal ground for exercising environmental prescriptive jurisdiction on their continental shelves.

Fact of great concern by coastal states is vessel-source pollution of ecologically sensitive marine areas, such as shallow coral reefs of deep-water cold corals. In that regard, it can be said that coastal states' power to pursue conservation strategies for shallow-water ecosystems, such as coral reefs, is relatively unconstrained by UNCLOS.[33] However, "obstacles posed by the freedoms of other states in marine waters do become more testing for coastal states as they move away from their baselines", as it is the case with the EEZ.[34] Prescriptive environmental jurisdiction in these cases is restricted by observation by foreign ship of internationally agreed standards. And if imposing limitations on navigation or other freedoms of the high seas is difficult in maritime zones where coastal states are entitled to clear environmental jurisdiction, let alone on outer continental shelves.

Enforcement jurisdiction on environment-related grounds are dealt with by Arts. 211 and 220 UNCLOS. The former concerns vessel-source pollution, which is likely to harm the overall health of marine life within a given coastal state's jurisdiction, on the other hand, is handled by Art. 211 (5) UNCLOS. According to that provision,

> Coastal States, for the purpose of enforcement as provided for in section 6, may in respect of their exclusive economic zones adopt laws and regulations for the prevention, reduction and control of pollution from vessels conforming to and giving effect to generally accepted international rules and standards established through the competent international organization or general diplomatic conference.

Such wording established a stricter threshold for coastal states to designate MPAs to prevent, reduce and control pollution from vessels, and to enforce environmental laws and regulations against transit vessels beyond their territorial seas, i.e. in the EEZ. This clause represents *per se* a major safeguard of freedom of navigation and an attempt to balance coastal states' environmental jurisdiction and the rightful exercise of navigation freedom by other states. In addition to that, UNCLOS Art. 211 (6) stipulates a complex system for designating MPAs in the EEZ, which

[32] Art. 194, paragraph 5 UNCLOS.

[33] Goodwin (2011), p. 54.

[34] *Id.* 54.

involve long consultations with affected flag states and resort to scientifically proven ecological and oceanographical conditions, a system which aims to safeguard navigation and other lawful uses of the ocean in the EEZ where coastal state wish to designate MPAs. The strictness of requirements under 211 (6) explain why not a single MPA has been designed in accordance with such provision up to now.[35]

Art. 220, on its turn, provides for coastal states' enforcement jurisdiction, which may not use excessive enforcement powers against vessels uncomplying protective measures established for an MPA within the EEZ. The wording of Art. 220 (6) is crystal clear:

> Where there is clear objective evidence that a vessel navigating in the exclusive economic zone or the territorial sea of a State has, in the exclusive economic zone, committed a violation referred to in paragraph 3 resulting in a discharge causing major damage or threat of major damage to the coastline or related interests of the coastal State, or to any resources of its territorial sea or exclusive economic zone, that State may, subject to section 7, provided that the evidence so warrants, institute proceedings, including detention of the vessel, in accordance with its laws.

Such a possibility of coastal states unilaterally establishing marine protected areas and enforcing national rules thereon raises issues on the traditional clash between freedoms of navigation and the right to protect and preserve the marine environment—thoroughly explored throughout this work. In this regard, Rainer Lagoni, once Professor at this University of Hamburg, is of the view that "the coastal State has no freewheeling jurisdiction to designate such areas [MPAs] unilaterally and to adopt binding measures vis-á-vis other States" in the EEZ. Lagoni goes a step further and claims that, given that area-based tools shall not affect other lawful uses of the oceans, any measure that affects navigation outside internal waters "can only be introduced with the agreement of IMO".[36] The author distinguishes between the obligation to prevent vessel-source pollution and the general obligation to protect marine ecosystems and habitats and considers Art. 194 (5) to provide a separate and independent obligation. This rationale is key to the author's conclusion that coastal states have (very) limited powers to establish MPAs for the purpose of protection of marine ecosystems and habitats beyond its internal waters.[37] Lagoni's radical conclusions, which disregard coastal states' environmental powers over both their

---

[35]Alternatives to classical MPAs under article 221 (6) are the Particularly Sensitive Sea Areas (PSSAs), relating to areas vulnerable to damage by maritime activities, as regulated by the 2005 IMO Revised Guidelines for the Identification and Designation of Particularly Sensitive Sea Areas. Overall, PSSAs offer a greater variety of measures to be adopted by the coastal State, but they do not apply to the seafloor. The designation of a PSSA "can affect navigation only by measures which are compatible with the Convention". *See* IMO, Resolution A.982(24), 01 December 2005. Such PSSAs, which can also be established over the continental shelf of coastal states, is praised as area-based management tools that have seen impressive use in the part years. One of the reasons for such success would allegedly be the PSSA's flexibility and lack of specific legal basis. *See* Gavouneli (2014), p. 20.

[36]Lagoni (2003), p. 167.

[37]*Id.* 160.

territorial seas are countered throughout this work, especially if one considers coastal states' environmental jurisdiction over their territorial seas and EEZ.

In fact, coastal states are allowed to designate, among others, a *zone de protection écologique* on their continental shelves. Nonetheless, only inasmuch as this zone do not infringe upon or result in an unjustifiable interference with the rights and freedoms of other states in the high seas above the shelf—Art. 78 (2) UNCLOS. By declaring such a zone, coastal states may limit freedom to fish in the high seas, as in the case of bottom-trawling. Yet, states are expected to adopt a pragmatic approach, i.e. to assess the relevance and environmental status of what needs formal and material protection. It is a priority to ascertain, scientifically, whether existing MPAs cover a number and extent of significant species and habitats by their uniqueness and sufficiently representative. Only so will coastal states avoid the trap of declaring ill-suited MPAs or protecting areas where little imminent risks or threats exist.

Coastal states may, thus, legislate domestically to designate MPAs and adopt measures to enforce such legislation. That is not only a right, but also an international obligation. The right to do so stems from the very nature of those area-based management tools: protecting and preserving the marine environment. As shown supra, coastal State's jurisdiction on the continental shelf include the adoption of measures towards marine ecosystems' protection. It is also an obligation, given the entry into force of Conventions and Agreements that rely on the establishment of networks of MPAs worldwide, so as to protect representative areas of the ecological regions and areas of particular relevance in terms of biological diversity. However, there exists great difference between designating area-based protective measures in the EEZ and on the continental shelf, in particular that portion extending beyond 200 nm.

Coastal States may resort to marine protected areas on the continental shelf as mechanisms towards short and long-term conservation of ocean nature—the so-called "seafloor MPAs". Given the global targets accorded by states in the last decades (of which the 1992 Agenda 21 and the 2010 Aichi Targets are but some examples), it is reasonable to expect that MPA may also be designated on the outer continental shelf. Scientifically, it makes sense to enact a network of MPAs on vast areas of the continental shelf, including beyond 200 nm, in order to protect representative areas of the marine environment.[38] A most interesting example is provided by Portugal, who had the Altair Sea Mount recognized as a high-seas protected area under the OSPAR Convention for the Protection of the marine environment of the North-East Atlantic and, after that, as a protected area within national jurisdiction on the basis of its claim on an extended continental shelf before the CLCS. In so doing, the country avoided the requirement of direct consent of involved parties—a valid and legal strategy.[39]

[38]For a scientific explanation of such a need, *see* generally Van Dover (2012).

[39]Marta Chantal de Ribeiro, drawing on the Portuguese practice on the topic, states that "the Menez Gwen field is located about 850 meters deep and the MPA occupies an area of 95.2 km^2. The Lucky

If the establishment of MPAs on the continental shelf is possible, one should determine the range of activities such protected zones will affect. In this sense, there is little controversy in the law of the sea on coastal states' authority over activities relating to the extraction of hydrocarbons and similar minerals from the seafloor and subsoil thereof—i.e. in direct physical contact with the ocean floor. Similarly, the regulation—and prohibition—of fishing for sedentary species of the continental shelf within and beyond 200 nm creates little confusion among specialized scholars and practitioners. Those activities affect straight the seafloor and, therefore, the natural prolongation of coastal states' land territory.

However, the matter of establishing MPAs on the outer continental shelf that could impact on activities taking place in the superjacent waters thereof raises a lot more of concern. Even if such activities are known for producing an impact on the benthic marine environment, i.e. the ecosystems in close contact with the seabed. A most polemic topic is the practice of bottom-trawling: may coastal states impede fishing boats flying other flags from bottom-trawling above the outer continental shelf even if the ships are not pursuing sedentary species? In those cases, there is a strong presumption in favor of protecting high seas freedom, and for coastal States to restrict those freedoms, they must consider several factors.

In this regard, Professor Joanna Mossop devised an appurtenance test capable of verifying whether a coastal state's legislation or law-enforcement measure is lawful and consistent with UNCLOS or not—thus abiding by Art. 78 (2) UNCLOS. After pondering the factors enumerated by the author, coastal states will, then, have arguably more elements to determine whether a municipal measure restricting the high seas freedoms is "justifiable" or not. Result is that, according to Mossop, "some forms of substantial interference with the high seas freedoms may be justifiable. Other forms of interference may be insignificant but yet unjustifiable".[40]

Hence, Art. 211 UNCLOS, regarding the designation of MPAs for the prevention of vessel-source pollution applies solely to the continental shelf within 200 nm, never to the outer shelf. Such designation is not conceivable in the waters above the outer continental shelf, since there is no reasonability in creating a specially protected area in the seabed that would restrict navigation on the water column some hundreds or thousands of meters above it. The activities carried on at the water surface must, thus, affect the seafloor of the coastal state for it to be entitled to environmental action.

Strike field is located at about 1.700 meters depth and the MPA occupies an area of 192 km^2. The Rainbow field is located between 2.270 and 2.320 meters depth and the MPA occupies an area of 250 × 60 m (1.5 km^2)". Then, Ribeiro concludes that the restriction of use or conditioning of activities in MPAs will have to be reconciled with the framework established by national and international legislation on the public maritime domain. *See* Ribeiro (2015), p. 83.

[40]Mossop (2015), p. 183.

10.1.2 Prevention, Reduction and Control of Pollution

The major source of pollution from continental shelf activities, or at least the source which attracts most public attention, is pollution from oil and gas exploitation. The entire continental shelf regime emerged because of states' economic interests in accessing offshore hydrocarbon riches with exclusivity—this is said nowhere but is mystery to no one. And the relevance of regulating offshore oil production lies on the fact that, according to Reports of the UN Environment Programme, sea-based pollution is responsible for twenty percent of all marine pollution, which is most often caused by ocean dumping or oil spills.[41] The environmental risks inherent to such operations are undeniable and there is a clear need to further develop the legal regime of the continental shelf, by virtue of, among others, relatively recent oil spill incidents involving exploitation on the continental shelf: the 2009 blow-out of the Montara Wellhead platform in the Timor Sea[42] and the 2010 bow-out of the Deepwater Horizon on the Gulf of Mexico.[43] As previously observed by Joanna Mossop, "in a global context, society is challenged to find an informed way of balancing between protection and tradeoffs in the often conflicting and accelerating uses of the continental shelves".[44]

Considering the particular case of Brazil, the country is known for its large deep-water market, and limited shallow-water activity. In February 2020, offshore oil and gas accounted for 96% of the national hydrocarbons production. In that month, the country pumped approximately 2.1 million barrels of oil equivalent per day, thus recording a growth in relation to previous years, due to deep water pre-salt discoveries off the South-East coast, Petrobras being the national oil company and major exploration and production player.[45]

Thus, the question: does UNCLOS offer a detailed framework within which the regulation of continental shelf activities can occur? The answer to that question is negative. Neither did UNCLOS enter in much detail, nor would it have been

---

[41] *See* UNEP website, available at: https://www.unenvironment.org/explore-topics/oceans-seas/what-we-do/working-regional-seas. Accessed 12 April 2020.

[42] The Montara Blowout took place 250 km north-west of the Western Australian coast, and almost 700 km from Darwin, on 21 August 2009. It occurred after a blowout and fire on the Montara wellhead platform, which caused oil to leak for 74 days, until an intervention on 3rd November was successful and mud was pumped in to "kill" the well. The Thai operator, PTTEP, estimated that the flow of oil may have been between 1000 and 1500 barrels/day in the early stages and declined to 400 barrels/day later. In total it is estimated that 30,000 barrels were spilled. For more, see Hart (2010) online.

[43] In early 2016, the non-governmental organization Oceana released a report entitled "Time for Action: Six Years after Deepwater Horizon", which compiled scientific studies about the ongoing impact of the oil leak on fauna, flora and residents of the Gulf. According to estimates, the loss of productivity from Gulf of Mexico fisheries will harm the local economy in $8.7 billion by 2020. Besides, more than 22,000 jobs were lost following the spill. *See* Sharpless (2016) online.

[44] Mossop (2016), p. 157.

[45] National Oil Agency (ANP), *Boletim Mensal da Produção de Petróleo e Gás Natural,* February 2020.

beneficial to marine conservation if the Convention had done so. In this sense, we agree with Jayakumar, to whom "the negotiators of UNCLOS intended to create an enduring framework to take into account future developments", including mechanisms to accommodate change and future developments of the law. An example of such intention is the obligation to adopt international rules, regulations and standards. Indeed, one must concede that the continental shelf is an area where "it was not possible or appropriate to establish detailed or highly technical regulations".[46]

Academic scholars have heavily criticized the international legal framework applicable to the protection of the marine environment against oil pollution. The legal regime governing offshore hydrocarbon activities has been said to be a "patchwork of international conventions, non-binding standards and guidelines, national legislation and industry practices".[47] Hence, the urgency to consolidate current provisions and reach consensus on a global international regime for the protection of the marine environment from offshore, deep-water oil and gas exploitation. Besides, there are still debates on the sustainability of the current international regulatory framework for offshore oil and gas activities, be it in the continental shelf within or beyond 200 nm.[48] Such a phenomenon causes domestic norms regulating offshore oil and gas activities to vary significantly, which is no news for lawyers.

When it comes to prescriptive jurisdiction, UNCLOS Art. 80 grants coastal states exclusive rights in relation to the construction, authorizations and regulation of installations and structures for the purposes of exploring and exploiting its natural resources, and artificial islands for all purposes. Coastal states are equally given the exclusive right to authorize and regulate drilling on the continental shelf *for all purposes*, an unequivocal wording. Whereas sovereign rights are limited in scope—case of Art. 77 UNCLOS, exclusive rights are not—they apply "for all purposes". Legal ground for coastal states' environmental prescriptive jurisdiction on oil and gas activities ought also to be extracted from Art. 194 (3) UNCLOS, in line with which states shall take measures to minimize to the fullest extent possible "pollution from installations and devices used in exploration or exploitation of the natural resources of the seabed".

Interestingly, the earliest obligation not to cause damage to the superjacent waters of the continental shelf emerged in the 1958 CSC, Art, 5, which expressly prohibited any "unjustifiable interference" by exploration and exploitation of the continental shelf with the "conservation of the living resources of the sea". Art. 5 (7) also mandated states to take "all appropriate measures for the protection of the living resources" from harmful agents around the installations. That was a timid attempt to impose an *environmental due diligence obligation* to states, but restricted to the 500 m safety zones. In addition to that, interference with activities which may have an *indirect impact* on the shelf resources were also considered illegal.

[46]Jayakumar (2013), p. 11.

[47]*Id.* 9.

[48]*See* generally Rochette et al. (2014).

Time passed and UNCLOS governed the issue differently, enlarging the hall of powers attributable to coastal states on the continental shelf. Still on the prescriptive jurisdiction to enact domestic rules on the prevention, reduction and control of seabed pollution—which may be caused by hydrocarbons exploitation and deep-sea mining, a most relevant section is Art. 208 UNCLOS. This provision supplements the general obligation of states under Art. 194 (3) (c), concerning the adoption of measures to prevent, reduce and control pollution of the marine environment from the exploration and exploitation of seabed and subsoil mineral resources.[49] The obligation contained in Art. 208 is stricter than that of Art. 207—on pollution from land-based sources, especially due to the "no-less-effective rule", according to which national legislation shall be no less effective that international rules on the matter.

On the enforcement jurisdiction of coastal states with respect to pollution from seabed activities, Art. 214 UNCLOS enables and obliges them to "adopt laws and regulations", as well as to take "other measures necessary" to reach that objective. As an attempt to prevent international conflicts and unnecessary tension between coastal states and flag states, UNCLOS calls enforcing states to implement "applicable international rules and standards established through competent organizations or diplomatic conference". Apart from the general obligation to protect and preserve the marine environment, coastal states are also granted the right to take reasonable measures for the "prevention, reduction and control of pollution from pipelines", as long as those measures do not effectively impede the laying and maintenance of those cables and pipelines. Such is the uncontroversial reading of Art. 79 (2) UNCLOS. That amounts to a clear indicative of the rights of the coastal State to care for the environmental sanity of its continental shelf and superjacent waters. The combination of those provisions applies for: hydrocarbon exploitation and laying of submarine cables and pipelines—even though the focus of this item was on the forms alone.

As one can see, coastal states have "a free hand in adopting laws and regulations to prevent, reduce and control pollution from seabed activities and artificial installations within its jurisdiction".[50] Continental shelf activities are radically different from shipping activities and, as such, merit a different legal treatment by UNCLOS, with McConnell and Gold rightfully claiming that coastal states have "*significant* regulatory autonomy in these areas".[51] A practical illustration of this sort of jurisdiction is the Directive 2013/30/EU—which regulates in a rather restrictive manner the complete life-cycle of offshore oil platforms in Europe. The positive externality of the Directive was to trigger a reaction by offshore oil and gas companies to adapt their operations worldwide to the relatively high European standards. The same restriction is not applicable to "offshore renewable energy facilities, the regulation of which would inevitably fall back into the full discretion of the coastal State and the

[49]Nordquist et al. (2002), p. 929.

[50]Gavouneli (2014), p. 18.

[51]McConnell and Gold (1991), p. 458.

general obligations it has under general environmental law".[52] Such a provision supports the relatively large environmental jurisdiction of coastal states—in this case, European ones—with regard to regulating seabed activities which may harm the marine environment.

10.1.3 Marine Scientific Research

The third axis of this analysis consists of the conduction of marine scientific research (MSR) on the continental shelf, a sort of activity which may impact on the overall health of the marine environment if not carried out properly. The complex interplay between law and science in the realm of the law of the sea is novelty to no one. In fact, several UNCLOS provisions rely on credible scientific information to be implemented, with illustrations ranging from the "maximum sustainable yield" formula to general and specific obligations ascribed in Part XII of the Convention.[53] With that in mind, MSR becomes the foundation for a sound ocean governance, given that credible data is achieved chiefly through scientific investigation. That is precisely one of the greatest challenges posed to humankind in its relationship with the seas: given that we now own the necessary technical means to access the oceanic depths, sufficient funding must be directed to research institutions, so that technology can be effectively put in place for an improved knowledge of the ocean and for the benefit of mankind.[54]

Scient of that, UNCLOS negotiators have destined an entire part of the Treaty to scientific research and agreed that all states and organizations have the right to conduct marine investigation on the basis of several core principles: realization with exclusively peaceful purposes; scientific methods consistent with the Convention; non-interference with other legitimate uses of the sea; and *respect for the protection of the marine environment*—Art. 240 (a) to (d) UNCLOS. The promotion and implementation of marine scientific research is regulated by the Convention with respect to the territorial sea, EEZ, continental shelf, high seas, and the Area. In the first three spaces, coastal states have the right to authorize research requests by other states, as a result of sovereign rights over natural resources within those spaces. In point of fact, placing and operating scientific research installations and equipment in the marine environment is legal, but ought to be carried out in a principled manner. For instance, research equipment and installations do not have the legal status of islands and do not affect the delimitation of the territorial sea, EEZ or continental

[52] Gavouneli (2014), p. 19.

[53] Tanaka (2015), p. 43.

[54] Edith Brown made the famous analogy between hydrospace and outer space, both of which shared vastness, inaccessibility and challenge to space-age technology; economic potential and strategic importance; difficult boundary problems. In her words, humankind ought to invest more in deep-sea research than outer space projects. For further details, *see* Brown (1973), p. 7.

shelf. Safety zones may be delineated surrounding those installations, with a width not larger than 500 m.[55] States and organizations may be held liable for any breaches, the disputes being settled directly by the parties or via resort to international tribunals of arbitration courts.

In general terms, and according to UNCLOS Preamble, states, by themselves or through organizations, shall promote the development and transfer of marine technology to all states concerned and developing countries in the exploration, exploitation, conservation and management of marine resources, the protection of the marine environment and *scientific research*. Forms of international cooperation include existing bilateral, regional or multilateral programs, expanded programs and new programs, including the establishment of national and regional centers for marine scientific and technological research.[56]

On the continental shelf specifically, the applicable law for scientific research lies within Part XIII UNCLOS, namely Art. 246. In fact, pursuant to paragraph 5 (b) of such provision, if the scientific research project envisages drilling of the seabed, including the portion beyond the 200 nm, the coastal state may withhold consent. Here, it is never too much to reinforce that Art. 81 UNCLOS grants coastal states the exclusive right to authorize and regulate drilling on the continental shelf *for all purposes*. In line with that provision, Article 246 (5) (b) applies, according to which if a research project involves drilling of the seafloor within national jurisdiction, the coastal state has discretion to withhold consent.

> Art. 246 (5): Coastal States *may* however in their discretion *withhold their consent* to the conduct of a marine scientific research project of another State or competent international organization in the exclusive economic zone or on the continental shelf of the coastal State if that project: (b) involves drilling into the continental shelf, the use of explosives or the introduction of harmful substances into the marine environment.

The wording used in Art. 246 UNCLOS differs from that Art. 245, which disciplines research in the territorial sea. On the one hand, Art. 245 stipulates that coastal state have the right to regulate, authorize and conduct marine scientific research in their territorial seas in the exercise of their sovereignty. Research projects in this area shall only be conducted with express consent of coastal states. On the other hand, Art. 246 grounds coastal states' rights on the exercise of *jurisdiction*—not sovereignty—which suggests a weaker degree of coastal state authority in the areas where it exercises "mere" jurisdiction. Such wording has led scholars to interpret UNCLOS as establishing a general freedom of MSR beyond the territorial

[55]Art. 260 UNCLOS, on the safety zones, states that "Safety zones of a reasonable breadth not exceeding a distance of 500 meters may be created around scientific research installations in accordance with the relevant provisions of this Convention. All States shall ensure that such safety zones are respected by their vessels".

[56]In joint scientific projects, international cooperation shall respect the sovereignty and jurisdiction of states, through information, through bilateral or multilateral agreements.

seas, especially in light of the provision according to which "coastal States shall, in normal circumstances, grant their consent"—Art. 246 (3) UNCLOS.[57]

Hence, for the inner continental shelf, coastal states have discretion to withhold consent to the conduct of researches of a resource-oriented nature, or which involve physical contact with the continental shelf, in line with UNCLOS Art. 246 (5) (a) to (d). For the outer portion, Art. 246 (6) dictates that coastal states may not withhold consent, *unless* in areas in which exploratory/exploitation activities are already going on or are expected to begin within a reasonable period of time (within the limits of good faith). States shall establish rules and procedures regarding this consent mechanism. Regardless of the area of the continental shelf were a proposed research should occur, UNCLOS embraces the rule of *implied consent*, Art. 252, a proposed research project may begin if the coastal state has not objected within 4 months. Then, 2 months after that—6 months in total, the project may start against the silence of the interested coastal state.

Interestingly, Plesmann and Röben consider that coastal states' consent "is not necessarily of material importance" and may be read as "notification", i.e. a requirement which would be satisfied by the notification of the coastal state in question of the scientific project ahead.[58] Furthermore, Art. 246 does not mention the need for *express* consent, leaving it open for the researching state, in the occasion of lack of reply by the coastal state, to interpret silence as consent—pursuant to Art. 252 UNCLOS. That is not, however, the most common state practice, and is certainly not how the Brazilian domestic legislation has regulated the issue of marine scientific research.

Still on matters of wording, which can broaden or restrict the scope on coastal states' powers on the continental shelf, the fact that UNCLOS adopts the phrase "*on* the continental shelf" has led commentators to claim that the article regulates only research that enters in physical contact with the seafloor.[59] The German Federal Mining Law, for instance, specifies that consent is required only when the investigation is conducted *on the spot*, that is, physically on the shelf.[60] Even though coastal states may interpret the Convention in such a way, it is not reasonable to require all other states to do so, as there is no evidence that negotiating parties meant to limit coastal state jurisdiction over the activities on the shelf by using the preposition "on". In fact, such a view is not consonant with UNCLOS, as research of the continental shelf can be conducted without any direct contact with the shelf, i.e. without being carried out *on* the seabed, as in the case of seismic studies that can

---

57 Plesmann and Röben (1991), p. 390.

58 *Id.* 391.

59 Churchill and Lowe (1999), p. 407. It should also be recalled that the 1958 Continental Shelf Convention, Art. 5 (8), was much clearer than UNCLOS in restricting the need for consent to activities which are directly undertaken on the continental shelf. According to the cited provision, "consent of the coastal State shall be obtained in respect of any research concerning the continental shelf *and undertaken there*".

60 Section 39, German Federal Mining Act (BBergG), 13 August 1980.

draw a map of the geological formation of the continental shelf and, therefore, the riches present therein.

Traditional and contemporary case law has confirmed such broader scope of the preposition "on" the continental shelf. In 1976, the ICJ decided in the Aegean continental shelf case that seismic exploration of the continental shelf of a state without consent is a breach of the coastal state's exclusive right to exploitation. However, Court declined to prescribe provisional measures, given that there was no risk of physical damage to the resources on the shelf, and that prejudice to Greece could be repaired at a later stage.[61] Similarly, in 2006, the Arbitral Tribunal in the Guyana v. Suriname case found that seismic tests were vested in an exploratory nature, with commercial ends, and not as pure research. Consequently, the parties were obliged to reach provisional arrangements of practical nature, according to Art. 74 (3) UNCLOS, to address the dispute on research projects over the continental shelf.[62] As such, UNCLOS Art. 246 applies to research concerned *with and about* the continental shelf, regardless of where they are based or whether they directly and physically contact the ocean floor or not.

Hence, from the discussed above it remains that scientific research activities carried out in the water column above the outer continental shelf may fall within coastal states' jurisdiction in some circumstances. However, states have traditionally exercised a rather limited jurisdiction there. In short, the generally agreed rules under the Convention stipulate that: consent is needed; application for consent must be submitted at least 6 months prior to estimated project commencement; "tacit coastal state consent" does not always prevail in practice, as researching states usually face silence as a negative answer from coastal states.

A whole different issue emerges with respect to scientific research on the outer shelf and the question of the dual legal regime for the same maritime space. In this regard, Art. 246 (6) embodies a compromise between freedom of research and the exercise of coastal state rights on the continental shelf. The marine scientific research regime on the continental shelf beyond 200 nm denies coastal states the discretion to withhold the consent they usually have under Art. 246 (5) (a).

Art. 246 (6) reads:

> Notwithstanding the provisions of paragraph 5, coastal States may *not* exercise their discretion to withhold consent under subparagraph (a) of that paragraph in respect of marine scientific research projects to be undertaken in accordance with the provisions of this Part on the continental shelf, beyond 200 nautical miles from the baselines from which the breadth of the territorial sea is measured, outside those *specific areas which coastal States may at any time publicly designate as areas in which exploitation or detailed exploratory operations* focused on those areas are occurring or will occur within a reasonable period of time. Coastal States shall give reasonable notice of the designation of such areas, as well as any modifications thereto, but shall not be obliged to give details of the operations therein.

---

[61] ICJ, *Aegean Continental Shelf case, Greece v. Turkey*, request for provisional measures, ICJ Reports, 1976.

[62] PCA, *Arbitration regarding the delimitation of the maritime boundary between Guyana and Suriname*, PCA Records, Award of 17 September 2007, para 468.

That provision entails a clear obligation to disclose information about exploitation or exploratory operations in the process of designation of specific areas of the continental shelf beyond 200 nm, thus granting research precedence but not entire exclusivity over the outer shelf to coastal states. Other interpretation issues on the wording of Art. 246 (6) are raised by Joanna Mossop, such as the definition of "detailed exploratory operations" and "reasonable period of time".[63]

The scientific research of *marine living resources* is much more problematic for coastal states than that aimed at non-living resources. The designation of an area for commercial fishing of sedentary species could trigger the closure of a portion of the outer shelf for research purposes. Here, coastal states enjoy different grounds for refusing consent to research projects by foreign states. The first one can be the coastal state's obligation to prevent "general environmental harm", which could be read in Art. 246 (5) (b) UNCLOS—such an argument applies for cases in which research is to be conducted with aggressive techniques or methods that can be proven to harm the deep marine environment. Secondly, coastal states may claim that the planned research could lead to valuable knowledge of genetic particles of its own biodiversity, which could lead to commercial production beyond the control of coastal states.[64]

In addition to that, Joanna Mossop identified two further avenues for the lawful refusal of consent to foreign research requests on the outer continental shelf. First, coastal states could refuse it based on an alleged interference with their sovereign rights, fowling Art. 246 (7) UNCLOS. Secondly, coastal states could designate a deep-sea area as MPA under article 246 (6), with the advantages that such designation would fall beyond the compulsory jurisdiction mechanism under Section II, Part XV UNCLOS. Such a designation would signal the coastal state's intention to the international community, thus preventing conflicts concerning research about the seabed demarked with an MPA in question.

In the soft and delicate balance between freedom of research and coastal states' jurisdiction, the latter must always bear the relevance of marine scientific research in mind, thus considering ways in which it could be stimulated, while simultaneously surround themselves of the necessary safeguards to prevent biopiracy by wealthier researching states. Coastal states are also bound by the obligation to act in good faith, therefore not declaring random MPAs under article 246 (6), but solely in areas where

---

[63]According to Mossop, "the negotiating history of article 246 (6) does not conclusively settle the matter of what activities will amount to 'detailed exploratory activities'". Reconnaissance works and broad prospecting, for instance, are not included. Besides, regarding the "reasonable period of time", almost no state has, as yet, incorporated details of article 246 (6) into their laws about marine scientific research—Brazil being no different. One exception is Russia: includes geological studies and prospection as activities that may trigger the closure of an area beyond 200 nm for MSR purposes. This provision is considered to be excessive in nature, violating the threshold of "detailed exploratory operations". Russia has interpreted article 246 (6) in a very broad manner, in order to claim maximum control over MSR done on its continental shelf. Apart from Russia, "Article 246 (6) has so far been incorporated in legislation of only one broad-margin state, namely, the marine scientific research regulations of Trinidad and Tobago". *See* Mossop (2016), p. 166.

[64]*Id.* 167.

vulnerable ecosystems exist. In this sense, an interesting Solomonic solution is suggested by Joanna Mossop, to whom "the coastal State can consider using conditions to ensure that its interests are protected, while also allowing for marine scientific research", for instance, requiring permission before samples are shared with researchers other than those originally involved in the sampling project.

Conscious of those difficulties, coastal states should take all precautions and obtain all relevant information about the research project prior to consent. In cases where no consent is needed, coastal states ought still to gather information on the purposes of the scientific project, situation in which a refusal by the researching state to share that information may give legal ground for the coastal state to take preventive environmental measures against a specific research project.

Yet, imposing environmental conditions on requests for MSR is a delicate borderline case. While it may be lawful in researches over which the coastal state has discretion to refuse consent, it may be unlawful in researches where the coastal state is obliged to give consent. State practice shows that coastal states have opted to impose environmental conditions to foreign research. However, concerning the coastal state jurisdiction to impose environmental obligations over researches on the outer continental shelf—where the state may not withhold consent, it has been argued that "imposing conditions to prevent undue harm to the marine environment is entirely consistent with States' general obligation to protect the marine environment", as in line with UNCLOS and customary international law".[65]

10.1.4 Bioprospection and Genetic Resources

The practice of bioprospecting disguises commercially-oriented "research and development, building on use of natural occurring compounds, all the way from first discovery, over patenting, benchmarking, improvement, development and commercialization".[66] In other words, and according to the CBD Secretariat, bioprospecting means the "exploration of biodiversity for commercially valuable genetic and biochemical resources, the process of gathering information from the biosphere on the molecular composition of genetic resources for the development of new commercial products".[67] In this regard, the combined application of UNCLOS and CBD is not only possible, but vital to the regulation of bioprospecting in maritime spaces under some degree of national jurisdiction. It is the case of Art. 7 CBD, on the obligation to monitor genetic resources in areas of national jurisdiction, under which

---

[65] *Id.* 171.

[66] International Expert Group convened by the Research Council of Norway, "Possibilities for a bioprospecting commitment in Norway 2008 – 2020", 2008, report available at www.forskningsradet.no. Accessed 12 April 2020.

[67] *See* Database maintained by the United Nations University—Institute of Advanced Studies atwww.bioprospector.org. Accessed 12 April 2020.

states are obliged to monitor the environmental effects of marine bioprospecting cruises conducted under their control, including in their EEZ.[68]

Generally, coastal states also have rights over the genetic resources of their continental shelves.[69] Yet, UNCLOS faces severe limitations concerning the regulation of bioprospecting. To start with, the definition of genetic resources. For instance, genetic material in microbial form can often be found suspended in the water column and on the seafloor. It would be the case to discuss which kind of microbial forms fall under coastal states' jurisdiction and which one not. Another nightmare is that of biocommunities inhabiting hydrothermal vent sites of outer continental shelves—situations in which the best interpretation would probably benefit coastal states' jurisdiction over the living organisms of the vent, given that it functions as an ecosystem, a macro biological unit where a multitude of endemic species thrive.[70] In light of the impossibility to differentiate between the organisms that touch the seabed and the ones that do not, coastal states are to be consulted prior to bioprospection and scientific research excursions to those hydrothermal vents.

10.2 How Far Has Brazil Gone?

Brazilian authorities claim to abide by international law—especially UNCLOS and the CBD—with but a few hermeneutic deviations from both Conventions' wording.[71] Yet, Brazilian legislation applicable to the continental shelf is extremely generalist and succinct, what suggests that the country gives relevance to asserting jurisdiction over continental shelf resources—e.g. dissuading other states from accessing the shelf—but falls short of transplanting such concerns into specific legislation for the continental shelf or the EEZ. Worryingly, public authorities

[68]Art. 7, CBD, according to which states shall "monitor, through sampling and other techniques, the components of biological diversity identified pursuant to subparagraph (a) above, paying particular attention to those requiring *urgent conservation measures* and those which offer the greatest potential for sustainable use".

[69]*See* Maggio (2017), p. 613, mn 26.

[70]*See* Warner (2008), p. 419.

[71]Concerning the CBD, the country was first to ratify sign the Convention and has endeavored to implement the commitments assumed therein via establishing a domestic network of national policies, action plans, institutions and competences. Cases in point are the 2002 National Biodiversity Policy, as well as the drafting of the National Biological Diversity Program, which concretizes the actions proposed by the National Policy. In addition, the technical body responsible for coordinating CBD implementation efforts domestically is the Secretariat of Biodiversity and Forests (SBF), through its Biodiversity Conservation Board. Among the biomes represented in the 2002 National Biodiversity Policy is the *coastal and marine* one, with specific actions devoted for minimizing marine biodiversity loss off the Brazilian coast. More information available at the website of the Brazilian Ministry for the Environment, Biodiversity section, at: www.mma.gov.br/biodiversidade. Accessed 12 April 2020.

seem satisfied with the domestic legislation in place, which is composed of acts and statutes that have instituted policies, sectorial plans, and specific programs.

In light the confusing mix of marine environmental public policies, plans and actions in place, increased coherence, cohesion, simplification and effectiveness could be achieved through the adoption of marine environmental legislation for different maritime zones. Cohesion in the early stages of drafting basic acts and rules, for instance, should lead to cohesion at the end of the process—upon designing policies, plans of action, and shaping the work of executive agencies. A "streamlined approach" to marine environmental management could offer better conditions for the country to tackle the problem of the existing multiple governmental bodies charged with marine protection (law-making, decision-making, and law-enforcing), each of which independently regulated, thus minimizing the potential for contradictory rules in disagreement with the legislation in force. Such a flaw hinders not only enforcement efforts and the overall effectiveness of the Brazilian marine environmental system, but also hampers investments in the country's blue economy.

The following items concentrate on the qualitative analysis of Brazilian legislation, respecting the three axes described before: conservation of biodiversity; prevention, reduction and control and pollution; and regulation of marine scientific research—all of them with respect to continental shelf activities. The examination of domestic legislation is structured from the most general to the more specific norms, i.e. from the general norms applicable to the continental shelf of the Brazilian Blue Amazon, to the ones applicable to particular seabed activities under Brazilian jurisdiction.

10.2.1 General Rules on the Continental Shelf

Following the Kelsenian pyramidal hierarchy of legal norms, the Brazilian legal order has the Federal Constitution at its vertex, followed by international treaties ratified by the Brazilian Congress, complementary laws to the Constitution, domestic ordinary legislation and, finally, decrees, resolutions and other sorts of administrative norms. Regarding the continental shelf in general, the Federal Constitution stipulates in Art. 20 (5) that the marine resources thereof are *property* of the Union. In light of the straightforwardness of that provision, there is little to dissect in it, but to affirm that it seems consonant with the rules and philosophy of Part VI UNCLOS. That is one of the two constitutional clauses which explicitly mention the continental shelf, the other one being of little use to this work.[72]

The Brazilian Constitution, which was drafter in 1988, incorporated the rising environmental conscience of the time and codified important environmental

[72]Art. 20 (1) of the Brazilian Federal Constitution dictates that states and municipalities where the exploitation of oil and gas from the continental shelf occur shall be financially compensated for the risks inherent to that activity.

principles. For instance, Art. 225 states that "everyone has the right to an ecologically balanced environment, a common use good of the people and essential to a healthy quality of life" and imposes on the different governments, economic actors and the community the duty to defend and preserve it for present and future generations.[73] In order to ensure the effectiveness of that broad right to an ecologically balanced environment, the Brazilian Magna Charta obliges the public administration to require a previous environmental impact assessment for the installation of construction works or activities which may cause significant degradation of the environment. As one can anticipate, several continental shelf activities fall invariably within that scope, and shall, thus, be controlled on constitutional (and infraconstituional) grounds.

Apart from the Constitution, Act 8.716/93, or "Ocean Act", has domestically regulated large portions of UNCLOS, namely the coastal state's powers and duties within diverse maritime zones. For instance, it revoked the infamous Decree-Law no. 1.098/70, thus replacing the former territorial sea of 200 nm by one of 12 nm, in line with Art. 3 UNCLOS. Materially, the Ocean Act dedicates four general clauses governing the coastal state's jurisdiction on the continental shelf, especially for the purposes of regulating: *marine scientific research*, *environmental protection*, and the construction, operation and use of artificial islands and installations on the continental shelf. The Act reads as follows:

> Article 11. The Brazilian continental shelf comprises the seabed and subsoil of submarine areas that extend beyond its territorial sea, throughout the natural extension of its land territory, to the outer edge of the continental margin, or to a distance of 200 nautical miles from the baselines from which the breadth of the territorial sea is measured, in cases where the outer edge of the continental margin does not reach that distance.
>
> Single paragraph. The outer limits of the continental shelf shall be fixed in accordance with the criteria established in Art. 76 of the United Nations Convention on the Law of the Sea, signed at Montego Bay on 10 December 1982.
>
> Article 12. Brazil exercises sovereign rights over the continental shelf for the purposes of exploiting natural resources.
>
> Single paragraph. The natural resources referred to in the caput are the mineral and other non-living resources of the seabed and subsoil, as well as the living organisms belonging to sedentary species, i.e. those which at a harvestable stage are on the seabed or in its subsoil, or which can only move in constant physical contact with the seabed or subsoil.
>
> Article 13. On the continental shelf, in the exercise of its jurisdiction, Brazil has the exclusive right to regulate marine scientific research, the protection and preservation of the marine environment, as well as the construction, operation and use of all types of artificial islands, facilities and structures.
>
> Paragraph 1. Marine scientific research on the continental shelf may only be conducted by other States with the prior consent of the Brazilian Government, in accordance with the legislation in force that regulates the matter.

[73] Art. 225, *caput*, Brazilian Federal Constitution.

> Paragraph 2. The Brazilian Government has the exclusive right to authorize and regulate drilling on the continental shelf, whatever its purpose.
>
> Article 14. All States are recognized the right to lay cables and pipelines on the continental shelf.
>
> Paragraph 1. The delineation of the course of such cables and pipelines on the continental shelf depends on the consent of the Brazilian Government.
>
> Paragraph 2. The Brazilian Government may establish conditions for the laying of cables and pipelines that enter its territory or its territorial sea.

A detained examination of the Act's wording allows for a few conclusions on its consonance with general international law at large and UNCLOS in particular. Firstly, Art. 11 supra depicts the definition of continental shelf in full accordance with Art. 76 UNCLOS. Also, Art. 12 and its single paragraph of the Brazilian Act are *ipsis litteris* incorporations of UNCLOS Art. 77 (1) on the coastal state's sovereign rights over the continental shelf for the purposes of exploring and exploiting natural resources thereon, as well as Art. 77 (4) UNCLOS on the specification of the natural resources of the shelf and the definition of sedentary species. Brazilian Art. 11 admits the future possibility of the country having both an inner and outer continental shelf, but falls short of making a distinction between the legal regimes to be applied to the seabed within 200 nm, and the portion beyond that distance.

The fact that the Brazilian Ocean Act makes no distinction between the continental shelf within and beyond 200 nm suggests the application of one single domestic regime for the entire shelf—thus in compliance with the *indivisibility* of the shelf and the *ipso facto* and *ab initio* doctrines on the appurtenance of the continental shelf to the coastal state. Somewhat worryingly, the provision is completely silent as to UNCLOS' revenue-sharing mechanism, which rules on the payment of contributions by the coastal state for exploitation of non-living resources of the seafloor beyond 200 nm.

Despite Brazil's interests on the outer continental shelf fueled by potential oil and gas reserves of the ultra-deep pre-salt layer, no reference to international revenue-sharing mechanism was found in internal documents, for instance, the current IX Sectorial Plan on Marine Resources (2016–2019)—which does not mean that the issue is not blipping in the radar of Brazilian decision-makers. Even if one considers that Art. 82 (3) UNCLOS exempts from such revenue-sharing rule those developing coastal states who are net importers of the natural resources to be extracted from the outer continental shelf, Brazil is certainly not a net importer of the most important resources of the continental shelf nowadays: oil and gas. As such, the country cannot escape from the obligation to discuss and enact domestic legislation regulating the revenue-sharing system domestically, prior to authorizing the commercial development of hydrocarbons fields beyond 200 nm from the baselines.[74]

---

[74]In Brazil, a paper by Karoline Souza has raised the pertinent question of the legality of levying two financial burdens on hydrocarbons exploitation beyond the 200 nm: an internal and an external *royalty*. Internal, in line with the Oil Act; external, pursuant to UNCLOS Art. 82. That could amount to double taxation, a practice prohibited in by Brazilian law. For more, *see* Souza (2015), p. 243. To

Back to the Ocean Act, Art. 13 lays out the general legal ground for Brazil's exclusive regulatory rights concerning the uses and *conservation* of the continental shelf, especially the regulation of marine scientific research; the protection and preservation of the marine environment; and the construction, operation and use of *all types* of artificial islands, facilities and structures. Here, important dissonances from UNCLOS' wording exist which deserve to be analyzed. Take, for instance, the affirmed jurisdiction to regulate the construction, operation and use of *all types* of artificial islands, facilities and structures on the continental shelf. Art. 80 UNCLOS, on the artificial islands, installations and structures of the continental shelf refers to the application, *mutatis mutandis*, of Art. 60—on the EEZ. Pursuant to the latter, coastal states have the right to construct and to authorize and regulate the construction, operation and use of artificial islands, installations and structures. However, on no occasion do any conventional provisions refer to "all types" of structures, as the Brazilian legislation does.

The inclusion of that phrase was already a bone of contention during the Third Conference and remained so after. In its Interpretative Declaration to the Convention, Brazil anticipated a rather ampliative understanding of that sovereign right and claimed Brazilian exclusivity to "construct, authorize and regulate the construction, operation and use of *all* types of installations and structures, *without exception*, whatever their nature or purpose".[75] In other words, the coastal state would have full discretion as to any artificial islands, installations and structures located in its EEZ and continental shelf. This comprehensive position may be construed by some as being in violation of UNCLOS Article 56 (1) (b) (i), which does not mention "all" islands, installations and structures.

Interpretations such as that have rendered Brazil the fame of "leader of territorialists", a jurisdictional creeper disrespectful of internationally established norms and customs. As posited in previous chapters, the widespread and thoughtless use of the expression "creeping jurisdiction" to refer to practices and interpretations adopted by countries such as Brazil, India, China and others, may be misleading, prejudiced and blurring of the way international relations concerning ocean topics function. Portraying Brazil as the leader of "territorialists" is not the problem *per se*. It becomes a problem when the quest for exclusive access to natural resources and, thus, to social, environmental and economic development, is associated with territorialism, understood as a corrosive practice to the stability of the public ocean order.[76]

In line with that argument, there seems to be little to worry with a coastal state claiming jurisdiction over artificial structures and installations within its EEZ and

---

counter the view that UNCLOS Art. 82 would lead to double taxation, Aldo Chirchop arguments that the concept of tribute is tied to the right of the sovereign state to impose charges to support public and governmental programs and services, in line with national legislation, which is not the case in the contribution outlined in Art. 82 UNCLOS. *See* Chircop (2004), p. 400.

[75]Paragraph V, *Brazilian Declaration Upon Signature of the UNCLOS*, Montego Bay, 10 December 1982.

[76]For more on that critique, *see* generally Ventura (2018).

continental shelf. For the artificial structures and installations which may have commercial and economic ends, coastal states exercise exclusive jurisdiction and have the right to authorize their construction and operation. In so doing, coastal states are expected to act with reasonableness and abide by the restrictions set out in Art. 60 UNCLOS, such as the establishment of reasonable safety zones around those installations or the duty to give due notice of the construction of any such installations.

With respect to the artificial structures and installations of the EEZ and continental shelf which are of proven pure, scientific purposes, this work considers of good tone to both inform the precise content of the research project and to request consent of the coastal state, as the coastal state cannot be expected to guess the intended use of the information collected and material sampled by researching states. Given the world's long history of colonial spoliation, biopiracy and unilateral resource exploitation by capitalisms' core countries,[77] developing coastal states who suspect any structures or installations off their shore are not to be blamed a priori, but the other way around: developed states which deploy such installations and structures without requesting for consent are.

That is the essence of Art. 13 (1) of the Brazilian Ocean Act, which asserts that marine scientific research on the continental shelf may only be conducted by other states with the *prior consent* of the Brazilian Government, in accordance with Act 96.000/1988, or "Marine Research Decree", whose analysis will follow suit. No reference is made in Art. 13 (1) to the dual-regime of scientific research of the continental shelf and the differential treatment applicable to the shelf within and beyond 200 nm, as established in Art. 246 UNCLOS. In general, Art. 246 (3) UNCLOS affirms that states have the exclusive right to regulate, authorize and conduct scientific research on their shelves, but limits it to the obligation of granting consent, in normal circumstances, to research projects designed "exclusively for peaceful purposes and in order to increase scientific knowledge of the marine environment for the benefit of all mankind"—the so-called "pure research", in contrast with "applied" or "resource-oriented" researches.[78] In cases of the latter, the coastal state is entirely discretionary, as explained in the previous item.[79] In cases where the coastal state remains silent over requests for scientific research, the "implied consent rule" of Art. 252 UNCLOS applies, even though the Brazilian legislation made no mention to such a rule, neither to the distinct treatment of scientific research on the outer continental shelf—the analysis of which lays at the core of a specific item below.

[77]The concepts of "core, semi-penpheric and peripheric countries" are key to Immanuel Wallerstein's World-System Theory and his critique to modern-day capitalism. For more, *see* generally Wallerstein (1974).

[78]UNCLOS Art. 246, paragraph 3, on marine scientific research in the exclusive economic zone and on the continental shelf.

[79]The expression "normal circumstances" means that only in scenarios of serious tensions and imminence of hostilities are states under abnormal circumstances. *See* Huh (2017), p. 1659, mn 23.

Whilst Art. 13 (1) of the Brazilian Ocean Act on marine scientific research deserves further discussion and scrutiny in the next item—upon the analysis of the national statute which regulated MSR domestically—it goes without controversies that Art. 13 (2), on drilling the continental shelf, rests in full accordance with UNCLOS provisions, namely Art. 81.

Finally, Art. 14 (1) and (2) of the Ocean Act acknowledges the Brazilian right to consent (or not) to the delineation course of submarine cables and pipelines on the continental shelf, as well as the right to set conditions on the laying of cables and pipelines which enter its territorial sea. A quick comparison between these provisions and UNCLOS shows that paragraph 1 of the Brazilian Ocean Act corresponds to Art. 79 (1) to (3) UNCLOS, while paragraph 2 matches Art. 79 (4) UNCLOS. Noteworthy, thus, the material consonance of the provisions of the Ocean Act on the laying of cables and pipelines on the continental shelf with the pertinent UNCLOS rules. While there is no mention to *enforcement* powers, a legislation that is not enforceable is pointless. Thus, it follows logically from the whole of the Brazilian legal order that the coastal state may exercise enforcement powers for the rights listed in Arts. 11 to 14, Act 8.617/93.

For the sake of a reference—another domestic legal order which could serve as parameter for the Brazilian one, let us resort to the "marine management regime" effected by New Zealand, one comprised of different acts: the 2012 EEZ Act, valid exclusively for the EEZ and the continental shelf within and beyond 200 nm; the 1991 Resource Management Act, valid for internal waters and the territorial seas; and the 1996 Fisheries Act. Of those, the New Zealander EEZ Act is of more interest to this work, as it regulates activities happening in the EEZ and continental shelf according to UNCLOS' provisions. In the regime instituted by the Act, the Minister for the Environment has regulatory powers, while the Environmental Protection Agency (EPA) has consenting power.

A key instrument of that Act is to classify activities in the EEZ, tagged as "permitted, discretionary or prohibited", according the level of environmental risk involved in the activity.[80] For instance, all offshore oil and gas activities need to be permitted or authorized, via an internal proceeding before the EPA for a "marine

[80]Sections 35 to 37, NZ EEZ Act, on types of activities. Regarding the level of risk involved in every marine activity within the NZ EEZ and outer continental shelf, a risk assessment report by the NZ National Institute of Water and Atmospheric Research indicated that "The number of activities assessed for an industry ranged from 7 for offshore ecotourism to 17 for mining of massive sulphide deposits, polymetalic crusts and polymetalic nodules and renewable marine energy. Four industries had between 3 and 7 activities we classified as posing an extreme risk to the environment. These industries were mining for phosphorite nodules, massive sulphides, polymetalic crusts, and polymetalic nodules. All industries had one or more activities that pose a high risk to the environment and 2–10 activities that pose a moderate risk. The industry with the highest percentage of activities in the low risk range was offshore aquaculture though there is a high risk in this industry to marine mammals from surface and sub-surface buoys, ropes and structures". Such indicators are key to every planning and environmental protection efforts offshore. *See* National Institute of Water & Atmospheric Research Ltd, *Expert Risk Assessment of Activities in the New Zealand Exclusive Economic Zone and Extended Continental Shelf* (Wellingston: NIWA, May 2012) 129.

consent".[81] The Act also comprises enforcement measures of the New Zealander state, such as enforcement orders,[82] as well as civil and criminal liability for a number of offenses related to the process of authorization for drilling in the EEZ and the continental shelf—it even comprises a provision for a term of imprisonment of up to 2 years for specific breaches, given the sensitivity of environmental degradation in those zones.[83] It applies to the owners and persons in charge of offshore installations within the EEZ.

In New Zealand, thus, specific legislation has been approved to regulate the uses and management of different maritime spaces. Whereas in Brazil a general Ocean Act confirmed several UNCLOS provisions, without dwelling into details, and adapting the national rules to the Brazilian interpretation of some UNCLOS sections, New Zealand drafted different Acts for different maritime spaces, covering different kinds of activities. One could call it a "zone-oriented regulation", whereas Brazil has opted for a "activity-oriented regulation".

Overall, it could be said that New Zealand has achieved an integrated regime, with three different acts regulating every possible use of the maritime spaces under New Zealander jurisdiction, in a demonstration of how a simplified legal framework could be drafted. Whether it has led to increased effectiveness, that is another question and remains to be seen. Taken individually though, the EEZ Act is proof of pioneerism in marine environmental protection efforts and the mirror of a country concerned with the principled management (conservation and exploitation) of the marine environment under national jurisdiction. In short, it is a streamlined and robust regulatory framework, which could perhaps offer valuable inputs to Brazilian authorities and decision-makers in ocean affairs.

Now that the Brazilian general norms regulating the continental shelf and their consistency with international law of the sea have been evaluated, time has come for the analysis of specific legislation. The rules assessed below relate, to some degree, to the right-duty to manage the continental shelf and are structured in line with the three dimensions of environmental conservation referred to in previous chapters: (i) conservation of living resources; (ii) prevention, reduction and control of marine pollution; and (iii) the conduction of marine scientific research. Such a step should provide a detailed picture of the domestic legal framework determining the Brazilian environmental jurisdiction on the continental shelf, both within and beyond 200 nm, so as to permit the assessment on whether there is margin for the country's domestic legislation to (i) enter in greater consistency with UNCLOS; (ii) to legally adapt to the "new" reality of the country having to manage an extended continental shelf; and (iii) display increased coherence/cohesion while regulating the multiple uses of the continental shelf.

[81]*Id.* section 38.

[82]*Id.* sections 115 to 124.

[83]*Id.* section 134, on offences in relation to discharge of harmful substances.

10.2.2 Managing and Conserving Brazilian Living Resources

The occurrence of living organisms on the Brazilian continental shelf is confirmed by scientific charts depicting the marine biological composition of that zone.[84] In fact, the economic potential and relevance of sedentary species for the country was at the core of the so-called "Lobster War" against France in 1963, due to French vessels capturing lobsters and other crustaceans of the Brazilian continental shelf.[85] In addition to traditional sedentary fisheries, one ought also to bear in mind the still unknown potential of the genetic resources of some of the species inhabiting the depths of the Brazilian continental margin. Surveys indicate an important presence of sponges in certain areas of the outer limits of our continental shelf, whose chemical and pharmacological properties are not yet well known.[86]

The status of deep-sea fisheries in Brazilian waters was worrisome in 2006, when fishing for shrimps was denounced as threatening deep marine ecosystems and corals. Researchers of the Center for Marine Biology, University of São Paulo, have found that "deep-sea trawling off the Brazilian coast – more than 200 meters deep – has been growing since late 1990s".[87] The destruction of corals and other deep-sea organisms by heavy gear nets has been verified by researchers in loco. Unfortunately, no new data or statistics could be found online in order to support this research, although the problem seems to persist, as the online profile of *Oceana Brasil*, on Facebook, denounced the continuity of such predatory practices as late as 2016.[88]

In 2009, the National Fisheries Act, no. 11.959/09, was enacted to tackle unsustainable fishing off the Brazilian coast. In fact, national regulation of those living organisms inhabiting the continental shelf was left to that Act, which is supplemented by a group of policies and plans of action. The Fisheries Act delineates the National Policy for the Sustainable Development of Aquaculture and Fisheries, thus regulating fishing activities in areas within Brazilian jurisdiction. Here, "fisheries" are considered aquatic animals and plants which can be researched or exploited on an amateur, scientific or commercial basis, a definition which encompasses the sedentary species defined in Art. 77 (4) UNCLOS. Regarding the *ratione loci* application of the National Fisheries Act, Art. 2 (X) includes the continental shelf in the list of "fishing activity areas", in line with international commitments assumed by Brazil. When defining the continental shelf, the Act

[84] *See* IBGE, Atlas Mar, *Atlas of the Marine Life*.

[85] *See* generally Azzam (1964).

[86] As of 2006, a total of 37 species of sponges had been identified on the Brazilian Northern Cone, off the Amazon River Basin, five of which were considered endemic at the time. For more, *see* Mothes et al. (2006), p. 675.

[87] Geraque (2006) online.

[88] Oceana Brasil, *Porque a Pesca de Arrasto do Camarão é um Grande Problema?* Facebook Page, available online at: https://www.facebook.com/oceanabrasil/photos/porque-a-pesca-de-arrasto/944183009023364/.

copies Art. 76 (1) UNCLOS, without mentioning the outer shelf nor the possibility of extended jurisdiction beyond 200 nm from the baselines.

Overall, the Fisheries Act envisages ample legislative and enforcement jurisdiction to Brazilian authorities with respect to fisheries in areas within national jurisdiction. For instance, Art. 5 (I) of the Act stipulates that the exercise of fishing activities shall only be carried out after the issuing of a *permission* by the competent authority, so as to ensure "the protection of ecosystems and the maintenance of ecological balance, observing the principles of preservation of biodiversity and the sustainable use of natural resources".[89] The Statute's wording clearly indicates Brazilian legislative and enforcement rights over fishing activities taking place on the continental shelf—an enforcement which aims at protecting ecosystems and preserving biodiversity. It is, in other words, a practical implementation of the right-duty to manage marine resources of the continental shelf, claimed elsewhere in this work.

In addition to that, and reinforcing the broad scope of coastal states' sovereign rights over fisheries within national jurisdiction, the Act determines that fishing activities may be *prohibited*, periodically or permanently, for the protection of (i) threatened species, areas or ecosystems; or (ii) for the reproductive process of species and other processes vital to the maintenance and recovery of fish stocks, among other purposes.[90] Finally, all fishing activities which employ prohibited or predatory equipment, techniques and methods are automatically prohibited, a rule that suggests legal ground for the domestic prohibition of bottom-trawling in the Brazilian Blue Amazon.[91]

Monitoring and control of fishing activities, i.e. enforcement measures, are considered important instruments for the sustainable management of Brazilian marine living resources, pursuant to Art. 7 (IX) of the National Fisheries Act, another demonstration of Brazilian jurisdictional assertion over all kinds of fishing activities within national jurisdiction. In general terms, environmental enforcement jurisdiction is a common competence in Brazil, i.e. shared between the federative entities—Union, States and Municipalities—given the significance of environmental goods.[92] At the federal level, enforcement powers are shared by the Navy, IBAMA and ICMBio, in federal marine protected areas, to monitor and enforce the Act in Brazilian maritime spaces.

Monitoring of fishing activities encompasses the different stages of fishing, cultivating, landing, conserving, transporting, processing, storing and commercializing the catches, as well as the *environmental monitoring of marine ecosystems*.[93]

[89]Brazilian National Fisheries Act, Art. 5 (I), on the exercise of fishing activities.

[90]Fisheries Act, Article 6 (I) and (II).

[91]*Id.* Article 6 (VI) (d).

[92]Art. 23 (III) (IV) (VI) (VII) (IX) and (XI), Brazilian Federal Constitution, on the common competence of the Union, States, Federal District and Municipalities to, among others, protect the environment, control pollution, and preserve the national fauna and flora.

[93]Fisheries Act, Art. 31.

In order to enhance the Fisheries Act's effectivity, enforcement jurisdiction is to be exercised in combination with the Environmental Crimes Act—9.605/98,[94] so as to have practices and activities damaging to fisheries and the marine environment punished pursuant to the Environmental Crimes Act and its regulatory decrees.[95]

The federal enforcing agency has been, since 1989, IBAMA—institute responsible for regulating and enforcing the conservation of marine biodiversity both on land, in internal waters, and marine areas. Prior to IBAMA, the Department for the Development of Fisheries was responsible for managing fisheries, but the organ lacked an environmental perspective. Upon the creation of IBAMA, social and economic perspectives were combined to a previously weak environmental *rationale*. Great institutional change took place in 2009, upon the creation of the Ministry of Fisheries and Aquaculture (MPA) and the passing of the National Policy for the Sustainable Development of Aquaculture and Fisheries (PNDSAP). At that moment, fisheries management was given new objectives and the entire division of domestic competences was revised, the main change being the creation of a *joint management* scheme, in which the MPA and the Ministry of the Environment began to conjointly draft and publish norms on fisheries.

In 2011, adoption of Complementary Law no. 140/11, on the administrative competences to manage the environment, brought about more changes—this time regarding competences' arrangement between the Union, States and Municipalities. With respect to fisheries management, member-states are chiefly responsible for controlling fisheries within the limits of their jurisdictions, even though federal and municipal bodies may be cumulatively called into action. Finally, in December 2015, the MPA was extinguished and all of its competences were fully transferred to the Department of Fisheries and Aquaculture in the Ministry of Agriculture, Livestock and Supply, as an attempt to reconcile environmental conservation and production needs, which nonetheless maintained the *joint management arrangement* with the MMA—having IBAMA and ICMBio as its enforcement organs.

Regrettably, the analysis of IBAMA's statistics on enforcement operations was extremely difficult, due to the Institute's outdated and incomplete website. The section on biodiversity, for instance, had just one single active link on fisheries,[96] while the last report with statistical data concerning fisheries available at the website dates from 2007. Such a lack of transparency hardens the work of monitoring NGOs and other civil society initiatives, thus contributing to the overall low implementation rate of domestic legislation on fisheries' conservation. And that is one of the easiest challenges ahead of Brazil, as the next items will show.

---

[94]Fisheries Act, Art. 33.

[95]Apart from those Acts, it should be reminded that regulations on this regard are supported by the *REVIMAR Plan*, mentioned previously, and its objectives to evaluate, monitor and promote the conservation of marine biodiversity with an ecosystem approach, aiming at establishing scientific bases and integrated actions capable of subsidizing conservation policies and actions and shared management strategies for the sustainable use of living resources.

[96]See IBAMA's website: http://ibama.gov.br/biodiversidade-aquatica/gestao-pesqueira/estatistica-pesqueira. Accessed 12 April 2020.

10.2.3 Marine Spatial Planning of the Brazilian Blue Amazon

In Brazil, the conservation of living marine organisms via MPAs is regulated by the Conservation Units Act, no. 9.985/00, and implemented under the National Plan for Protected Areas (PNAP).[97] On the one hand, the Conservation Units Act organizes protected areas in two main axes: of integral protection—the so-called "no-touch" areas, and units of sustainable use, in which exploitation is allowed as long as it respects ecological processes and maintains biodiversity levels. On the other hand, the National Plan emphasizes the objective to "assess the representativeness of existing conservation units between continental and marine biomes", pursuant to Art. 3 (1) (II).[98] In line with the Plan, public policies should aim at ensuring the maintenance of marine ecosystems' connectedness via designating networks of coastal and marine protected areas. For that to occur, a mandatory step is to define the scale and conceptual treatment of the "separation" between coastal and marine environments, in order to optimize the creation and effectiveness of maritime conservation units.

To that end, diverse initiatives for the constitution of "mosaics" of coastal and marine conservation units have been carried, with the federal government acting to support and articulate the execution of activities related to these initiatives, so as to spread the perception of conservation units as an instrument of fisheries management. The first coastal and marine mosaic was formally recognized by MMA Ordinance no. 150/2006, which included 33 conservation units of Atlantic forest and coastal and marine zones to the South of São Paulo. Iconic conservation units in the south of Bahia and Rio de Janeiro, such as *Abrolhos*, have also been designated since then.

Currently, there are approximately 338 coastal and marine protected areas covering approximately 25% of the Brazilian Blue Amazon. Those impressive numbers mean that the country has achieved the goal set forth at the end of the 10th Conference of the Parties to the CBD: the Aichi Targets.[99] A few reasons have influenced the designation of that many MPAs within the Brazilian Blue Amazon. Firstly, there was a favorable domestic political scenario for the creation of protected

---

[97]The National Plan for Protected Areas was enacted domestically following the 7th Conference of the Parties to the CBD, in 2004, Malaysia.

[98]According to the 2006 Conservation Units Plan, protected areas are "natural and semi-natural areas defined geographically, regulated, and managed with objectives of conservation and sustainable use of biodiversity", while ecosystems consist of a "dynamic complex of plant, animal and microorganism communities and their inorganic environment that interact as a functional unit".

[99]The initial Aichi Target 11 for marine biodiversity was to have 10% of national maritime spaces formally protected by some sort of area-based tool by 2020, thus having marine resources "conserved through effectively and equitably managed, ecologically representative and well-connected systems of protected areas and other effective area-based conservation measures, and integrated into the wider landscapes and seascapes". *See* 10th Conference of the Parties, CBD, Decision X/2, 18 to 29 October 2010, in Nagoya, Aichi Prefecture, Japan.

areas for sustainable use during the Lula and Rousseff presidential terms—2003 to 2016. Secondly, consideration by policy-makers of two large marine ecosystems (LME) off the Brazilian coast, the East and South areas, where similar strategies to manage natural resources were drafted. That occurred even though the largest part of Brazilian oil reserves is located off the South coast, which suggests that oil and gas activities were not a factor considered by Brazilian marine policy-makers when defining marine conservation strategies.

Yet, the greatest motive for Brazil's reaching the Aichi Target was the designation of two giant MPAs within the EEZ of the Brazilian Atlantic Archipelago of São Pedro e São Paulo, as well as the Vitória and Trindade Islands.[100] Within the MPAs, which are mostly of "sustainable use", there are areas of a "natural monument", which are no-touch zones for commercial activities. The MPAs combined add approx. 900,000 km^2 of open seas to Brazilian protected areas, a decision supported by environmentalists and backed the Ministries of Defense and the Navy. This author has co-published a peer-reviewed paper on the Brazilian jurisdictional assertions over the Archipelago, claiming that the declaration of the MPAs around the islands crowns the uncontested Brazilian jurisdiction over the islands' EEZ.[101]

Surrounding the Vitória-Trindade submarine chain, a submarine mount previously unknown to the Brazilian population,[102] its corals have been described as "a tropical forest at the bottom of the sea".[103] Altogether, there were 30 submarine mounts, between 30 and 150-meters deep. The list of living organisms inhabiting the mounts reaches 270 species of reef fish—24 of them threatened by extinction, one of the highest rates of diversity among all the islands of the Atlantic. All those ecological riches have been threatened by fishing and mining.[104] Following public consultations, the Federal Government declared an MPA in the region, of about 450,000 km^2, approximately the area of Sweden. Both MPAs will be co-managed by the Ministries of Environment and Defense, which is considered as an innovative approach for protected areas.

Implementation issues still persist, though. Designating such massive MPAs does not mean that immediate environmental, species and habitat conservation has been

---

[100]Decree no. 9.312 creates the MPA of the Trindade and Martim Vaz Archipelago and the Trinity and Martim Vaz Islands Natural Monument and Mount Columbia; while Decree no. 9.313/08 creates the MPA of the São Pedro and São Paulo Archipelago and the Natural Monument of the São Pedro and São Paulo Archipelago.

[101]*See* generally Ventura and Mello Filho (2020) Forthcoming.

[102]The submarine chain gained visibility in 2017 when a study on the submarine mounts made it to the cover of Science Magazine. A comprehensive MSR project started in February 2018 with the purpose to map out the biodiversity inhabiting such mounts and exploring its economic potential and relevance to ocean services—uniting researchers from Espírito Santo, Pará and Paraíba. *See* Pinheiro et al. (2015) online.

[103]Fellet (2018) online.

[104]The Brazilian National Department of Mineral Production (DNPM) has already granted two licenses for the exploitation of rhodolite banks (limestone kelp and other organisms) and coral reefs in the Vitória-Trindade chain.

achieved. Resort to marine spatial planning and the designation of area-based tools for the protection of the marine environment must come hand-in-hand with the ample and collaborative participation of all interested stakeholders. If not so, resistance to the MPAs and disrespect of protective measures are to be expected by the industry and individuals. In fact, due to lack of information, creating MPAs may be often seen as an obstacle to fishing and, therefore, to the national socioeconomic development. What opposers usually ignore is the key role of marine protected areas and their importance for fish reproduction, including the replenishment of stocks of the most consumed species. The phenomenon is a sort of "overflow", in which fish stocks located in protected areas grow and migrate to adjacent areas where fishermen can catch them freely. Thus, fishermen are soon to benefit from the establishment of MPAs.

Moreover, the creation of marine protected areas, if not followed by rigorous management plans, are doomed to fail on their main goal, environmental conservation. Yet, the marketing effect triggered by them is considerable and explains why the Brazilian government has opted to design such massive MPAs far from Brazil's mainland. Moreover, considerable problems concerning the management of such areas emerge: it is not enough to just declare them on paper, one must enforce legislation in the protected areas—a problem known to virtually every country in the world. In fact, before the designation of the two massive MPAs mentioned supra, whose efficacy is quite questionable, there was little attention within the Brazilian MPAs "mosaic" to large marine ecosystems.[105]

Overall, implementation of the Brazilian national plans—established in the PSRMs—has been deficient. The evaluation of the sustainable potential of living resources, as intended by the REVIMAR Action, foresaw the execution of twelve Marine Management Units. Due to budgetary difficulties and vessels shortage, only two were implemented: the sardine and lobster management unit; and the tunas one. Other aspects that seem to hinder implementation are the different views and perceptions of the ministries' representatives interested in this action, in particular the MMA, through IBAMA and ICMBio, and the Ministry for Fisheries and Aquaculture.[106] After all, the reconciliation between conservation and production is not as easy as one would have thought. The shared competences on fisheries management between the two ministries seems to have hampered general coordination and implementation of plans, thus causing immobilism and the discontinuity of living resources' monitoring.

Problems with implementation are shared by other coastal countries as well. Take, for instance, Portugal, where studies have shown that a boom of deep-seas MPAs did not lead to more effective protection, either due to the insufficient nature

[105]In fact, the Brazilian coastal environment is far more protected than the marine environment, at least concerning the amount of declared MPAs. *See* Santos and Schiavetti (2014), p. 454.

[106]The state administrative structure in Brazil (in particular the number of ministries and thematic combinations) historically varies with the Presidency, depending on the political agenda of the representative. Hence, certain tensions and challenges mentioned herein may reduce depending on the administrative structure currently in place.

of management measures, or the lack of rigor of the arrangements. Amongst the flaws are the lack of "management plans", as well as the concrete monitoring and enforcement of protective measures. For some OSPAR MPAs situated beyond 200 nm, there is still no management plan in place, as in the case of the *Josephine* submarine mount.[107]

Finally, reference should be made to Decree no. 4.810/2003, which regulates the operation of fishing vessels in Brazilian fishing areas and the high seas, referring a few times to fishing on the continental shelf. That diploma launches the general objective to sustainably exploit fishing resources with Brazilian and international waters—Art. 4 (VII), and declares the intention to deepen knowledge of living resources on the continental shelf as a goal of the National Policy for Developing Oceanic Fishing.[108] Yet, the Decree cannot be considered an environmental norm, but rather an administrative act dedicated to regulating the operation of national and foreign fishing fleets in areas under Brazilian jurisdiction, so as to reach the rational exploitation of fish stocks and species. In so doing, the Brazilian norm mirrors provisions of UNCLOS and UNFSA, thus reverence for the international legislation on the issue of living resources of the EEZ and the continental shelf.

In light of the implementation difficulties raised above, it would be advisable for the Brazilian authorities to engage in a few strategic steps. Firstly, to detect further priority continental shelf areas that deserve some sort of conservation, apart from enforcing management measures in the recently designated marine areas of São Pedro and São Paulo and Vitória and Martim Vaz. Secondly, the country ought to strengthen the National Coastal Management Program (GERCO). Concerning coastal ecosystems, it is the case not to develop newer policies, a step which would only add confusion to the current "spaghetti-bowl" of Brazilian marine environmental legislation, but to implement existing norms and materialize existing plans.[109] Thirdly, Brazilian authorities should specify strategies for the protection of marine systems and expand the protected areas of all large marine ecosystems, thus executing the Marine Protected Areas Project (also known as *GEF Mar*), approved in 2014 and financed by World Bank.[110] Finally, the country ought to approve and engage in very possible efforts to implement a National Policy for the Marine Biome (PNCMar), particularly its Title IV on the specially protected marine areas.[111]

[107]Ribeiro (2015), p. 62.

[108]Art. 4 (VI), Decree no. 4.810/2003.

[109]Such a view is also shared by Milton Asmus, President of the Forum "Conselho do Mar". *See* MMA (2018), p. 70.

[110]Detailed information on the *GEF Mar* project is available at: http://documents.worldbank.org/curated/en/608051468215124739/Brazil-BR-Marine-Protected-Areas-Project-P128968-Implementation-Status-Results-Report-Sequence-03. Accessed 12 April 2020.

[111]Art. 17, single paragraph, PNCMar: "Brazil shall stimulate and support international actions, programs and agencies aimed at defining specially protected areas beyond national jurisdictions, especially those potentially located in the South Atlantic Ocean basin".

10.2.4 Preventing, Reducing and Controlling Pollution from Activities on the Brazilian Continental Shelf

In Brazil, the Federal Constitution (Art. 225, analyzed supra) and ordinary legislation regulate the offshore oil and gas sector. For instance, the 1981 National Environmental Policy brought about important rules on environmental responsibility and liability.[112] In line with Art. 4, the Environmental Policy aims at imposing on polluters the obligation to recover and compensate damages caused, and imposing on users the obligation to pay contribution for the utilization of environmental resources with economic purposes. The hydrocarbons' industry fits like a glove into this provision, which does nothing more than domestically ratify the polluter-pays principle.[113]

10.2.4.1 Offshore Oil and Gas Drilling

Domestically, the Brazilian Oil Act, no. 9.966/2000 affirms Brazil's functional jurisdiction to manage and conserve the marine environment under national jurisdiction—both with respect to prescriptive and enforcement jurisdiction. That diploma is organized in titles that govern pollution prevention, control and response systems, as well as the discharge of oil and other dangerous substances offshore. To each of the malpractices, the Oil Act anticipates sanctions on three different dimensions: civil, administrative and criminal.[114]

With respect to the prevention of offshore oil pollution, Art. 28 of the Brazilian Oil Act enables the federal environmental agency, IBAMA, to define the location and limits of *ecologically sensitive areas*, upon previous consultation with Brazilian maritime authorities, a provision which is consistent with international regulations on the matter, such as the Particularly Sensitive Sea Areas, as instituted by the IMO. Additionally, when it comes to pollution *reduction* and *control*, the Brazilian oil pollution preparedness and response framework, which is composed of National Contingency Plans, determines that national plans be prepared through the consolidation of local and regional contingency plans.

Furthermore, the domestic Act which introduced the National Energy Policy decreed that oil, natural gas and other fluid hydrocarbons existing within the national territory—including mainland, territorial sea, continental shelf and the exclusive

---

[112]The Policy was enacted by Act no. 6.938/1981, as discussed in the previous chapter.

[113]The Polluter-Pays Principle was first formulated in 1972 by the Council of the Organization for Economic Co-operation and Development (OECD). Since then, the principle has made it to several international environmental agreements, in particular the Agenda 21, the 1992 Rio Declaration on Environment and Development, the 1990 International Convention on Oil Pollution Preparedness, Response and Co-operation (OPRC), as well as the 2015 Paris Agreement and others.

[114]Art. 25, Brazilian Act no. 9.966/2000.

economic zone—belong to the Union.[115] Offshore oil and gas activities, such as exploration, exploitation and maritime transportation, are to be legally executed on a monopolist manner by the Union, which can further delegate the activities to private parties, pursuant to Art. 17 of the Federal Constitution. In fact, those activities are to be regulated and audited by the Union, but may be exercised by companies incorporated under Brazilian law, with headquarters and administration in the country.[116]

That very same Act created the *Brazilian National Petroleum Agency* (ANP). It is important to notice, though, that ANP consists of a regulatory agency which aims primarily at regulating, contracting and inspecting the economic activities that are part of the oil, natural gas and biofuels industry. On a secondary basis, the Agency also has the mandate to enforce best practices for the conservation and rational use of oil, natural gas, their by-products and biofuels, as well as for the preservation of the environment.[117] Such a mandate is compatible with the international obligations set out in Arts. 145 and 146 UNCLOS, to which Brazil is bound.

The Agency attempts at reconciling safety and security standards with environmental conservation measures, so as to prevent the loss of lives and marine fauna and flora due to oil spills and other sorts of incidents. In fulfilling that mission, the Oil Agency counts on the work of national and regional environmental councils. At the national level, the National Council for the Environment (CONAMA) assumes the most relevant role of establishing general standards and principles, while state-level environmental agencies issue specific licenses and exercise environmental control and inspection.[118] By fostering such am complementary interaction between the ANP and environmental agencies, the Brazilian legal framework signals how relevant it is for environmental conservation norms to permeate all economic sectors. One of the results of such interaction is the requirement for oil companies to obtain environmental licenses in connection with authorizations and concessions issued by the Agency. Finally, the Agency defines responsibilities and operational clauses in case of offshore oil spills.

In case prevention of oil pollution does not work and an incident occurs, the Brazilian legislator has taken steps towards incorporating internationally negotiated standards into the Brazilian marine environmental framework. In so doing, Brazil has adopted a rigorous system of liability. Pursuant to Art. 37 (6) of the Federal Constitution, the public administration—be it federal, state, or municipal—has strict liability whenever offshore oil pollution incidents take place. In Brazil, such a strict

[115]Art. 3, Act no. 9.478/1997. This work has previously shown the degree to which Brazilian scholars and legislators wrongly consider the continental shelf and the EEZ to be part of the Brazilian territory. That understanding is not in accordance with UNCLOS, nor international law.

[116]Art. 5, idem.

[117]Art. 8 (IX), idem, on the mandate of the National Petroleum Agency.

[118]That division of labor is regulated by the previously mentioned Constitutional Complementary Act no. 140/2011, which specified the prescriptive and enforcement competences of federal, state-level, and local environmental agencies.

liability flows from the "integral risk theory".[119] Yet, the government is also to be held liable when it acts with fault, i.e. by omitting itself to undertake action to prevent environmental damage, in situations in which the omissive conduct can be proved.

Hence, in the case of an oilfield accident, the Federal Government must respond if it has omitted to supervise the operations of a specific oil company. Such a provision in line with the Art. 44 of the National Energy Policy, according to which the contract conceding exploratory rights to private companies shall stipulate that the concessionaire is responsible and liable for the acts of its representatives, and is to compensate any damage arising from both exploration and exploitation. The interested oil company and its partners must, thus, plan how to dispose waste material from the exploitation site; to assist the injured; to prevent oil from reaching the coast; to stop the leak; to capture oil which has already leaked, among other measures.

Finally, Brazilian norms on environmental liability impose the duty to repair damages to the environment on the polluter. Those who degrade the natural environment may be held liable for doing so. Liability of the polluter is also to be found in the Brazilian Civil Code, according to which "the person who, by an unlawful act, causes harm to another, is obliged to repair the damage".[120] Within Brazilian jurisdiction, environmental liability is essentially *strict*, as clarified by Art. 14 (1), Act no. 6.938/1981:

> Without prejudice to the application of the penalties provided for in this article, the polluter is obliged, regardless of the existence of fault, to indemnify or repair the damages caused to the environment and to third parties affected by their activity. The Public Prosecutor's Office of the Union and States shall have the right to file civil and criminal liability charges for damages inflicted onto the environment.[121]

Not only the concessionaire company, but also the natural persons responsible for the operation and related companies may respond administratively, as stated in Art. 25 (1) of the Brazilian Oil Act. Moreover, environmental liability is the focus of domestic Act no. 9.605/1998, on crimes against the environment, whose Art. 2 confirms that individuals and private companies may be held liable for environmental crimes.[122] In fact, companies may also be held criminally liable under Art. 3 of that same diploma. In case of offshore oil discharges, thus, in addition to

[119]Legal support to the strict liability regime is to be found in the Brazilian Constitution, Art. 225 (3), as well as in Act. No. 6.938/1981, Art. 14 (1). Internally, Brazilian courts have thoroughly embraced the "integral risk theory", so as to recognize the objective liability of public and private entities involved in environmental degradation incidents. For more on that theory, *see* Rodrigues (2016), p. 381.

[120]Art. 927, Act no. 10.406/2002, Civil Code.

[121]Art. 14 (1), Act no. 6.938/198. Free translation.

[122]Art. 2, Act no. 9.605/1998: "Who, in any way, contributes to the practice of the crimes listed in this Act, is subject to the penalties to which they are committed, to the extent of their culpability, as well as the director, the administrator, the member of the council and of the technical organ, the manager, the agent or agent of a legal person, who, knowing of the criminal conduct of another, ceases to impede the malpractice, when he/she could have acted to prevent it". Free translation.

managers, employees who are absent, companies can be charged with crimes defined both within Act no. 9.605/1998 and the Brazilian Criminal Code.

Hence, the three-fold constitutionally mandated environmental liability system encompasses the activities of oil extraction in the high seas, aiming to minimize and indemnify society for the damages caused by oil spills. Brazilian legislation in this regard is in consonance with UNCLOS, namely Art. 235, which calls upon states to ensure compliance with their international obligations relating to the protection and preservation of the marine environment. In addition to that, states are required to ensure through their domestic law the means of redress for obtaining prompt and adequate compensation damage caused by pollution to the marine environment by natural or legal persons under their jurisdiction.[123]

In order to exemplify such framework, it is indispensable to bring some of the most iconic case law within Brazilian courts and tribunals to the fore of this discussion. For instance, in 2007, the Brazilian Superior Court of Justice found that the Brazilian state's liability in case of *omission* is subjective (non-strict), even in cases of damage to the environment, since the illegality in omissive behavior is assessed from the perspective that the state should have acted as prescribed by law. The Court also decided that the Union has the duty to supervise activities related to mineral extraction, so that these activities abide by environmental conservation norms.[124]

With respect to the coastal state's powers over continental shelf activities, a major incident in Brazil has rendered a pertinent legal discussion for the purposes of this work. In 2011, an oil leak off the coast of Rio de Janeiro caused by Chevron[125] denoted the need for reforms in the Brazilian legal framework on marine pollution.[126] The incident happened in the context of expansion of the Brazilian oil and gas industry, upon the then still recent discovery of deep-sea oil fields. Such expansion, as the oil leak showed, met no equivalent enhancement of environmental standards for offshore oil and gas exploration in the country.

The Federal Public Prosecutor's Office filed two lawsuits against Chevron and the two companies responsible for the rig's operation and contingency plan: Transocean and Halliburton. The first suit was for civil damages, while the second one sought criminal sanction, claiming US$10 billion in damages and the arrest of the seventeen Chevron employees responsible for the faults that lead to disaster. Initially, the case was filed before the Federal Court in Rio, but the court declined jurisdiction on the case, as the exploitation site laid beyond the Brazilian territorial sea. According to the federal justices, Brazil would have no enforcement jurisdiction

[123] Art. 235, paragraph 2 UNCLOS.

[124] Superior Court of Justice, Special Appeal no. 647493, Justice João Otávio De Noronha, decision from 22 May 2007, judgment's entry.

[125] In November 2011, an offshore oil well operated by Chevron leaked approx. 3700 barrels of oil into the sea.

[126] Marcelo Varella identified the need to redesign the current oil and gas framework in Brazil, so as to increase possibilities of prevention and damage compensation. *See* Varella (2015), p. 242.

to pursue criminal charges for offenses taking place in the EEZ—even if the offenses are related to the sovereign rights to explore and exploit natural resources in the region. The case was sent to the Rio state court, which rejected the criminal action in 2013, deciding that the incident had occurred outside Brazilian criminal jurisdiction.[127] The case was returned to the federal justice and the imbroglio was finally settled, with Chevron being cleared by the 2nd Regional Federal Court. Despite pungent evidence, the Judges found that not one fish died due to the leak and acquitted the company and the persons involved in it.

The challenge for the Brazilian authorities remains, which is to lawfully assert criminal and civil jurisdiction over activities taking place on the continental shelf past 12 nm. National scholars have called for reforms of the regulatory system,[128] claiming that "sooner or later, the National Congress will have to create – or adapt – the regulatory framework for the exploration and production of oil in the extended continental shelf, whose regulation should be later structured by the ANP".[129] Comparatively, for instance,

> Australia may only exercise jurisdiction over its exclusive economic zone and continental shelf for purposes relating to economic exploitation and environmental protection. *This does not extend to criminal matters*. [. . .] Should Australia wish to exercise jurisdiction over an alleged crime occurring within its contiguous zone, exclusive economic zone, continental shelf or on the high seas, it can only do so under certain circumstances. Such an exercise of jurisdiction is called extra-territorial jurisdiction. Extra-territorial jurisdiction is provided in general international law and is *beyond the scope of UNCLOS* (emphasis added).[130]

Regarding prevention, reduction and control of marine pollution from oil and gas activities, one should also mention the Brazilian Policy for the Conservation of the Marine Biome (PNCMar), which embraces marine spatial planning as its main instrument both on the national and regional levels. According to the proposed Policy, marine planning shall contain measures to monitor, evaluate and control the environmental quality of marine ecosystems and resources, in light of the risk inherent to some activities and their potential negative impacts, such as oil spills.[131]

It is noteworthy, thus, that the Brazilian national legal system, in compliance with the demands of the international communities and the environmental law treaties, was equipped with a series of environmental liability measures for the direct and indirect polluter of biota. This book scrutinizes just a few of the several domestic statutes and provisions regarding the prevention, reduction and control of pollution from oil and gas activities on the continental shelf. Those norms included the Federal Constitution, the Civil Code, the National Environmental Policy, the National

---

[127] *Id.* 247.

[128] *Id.* 248.

[129] Silva (2015), p. 243.

[130] Jurisdiction at sea: international law and domestic law. *Inquiry into the arrangements surrounding crimes committed at sea*. Australian Parliament, Report of the Standing Committee on Social Policy and Legal Affairs, 24 June 2013, chapter 3, 27.

[131] Art. 7 (2) IV, PNCMar Bill.

Energy Policy—Act no. 9.478/97, the Environmental Crimes Act, and the Oil Act are instruments designed to control the environment and to supervise people in their activities to prevent, mitigate, recover and compensate damages to the marine environment.

As one can attest from the above, Brazil made use of its prescriptive jurisdiction for managing the country's continental shelf, without distinctions between inner or outer shelf. Domestic legislation on the conduct of offshore oil and gas activities essentially respect UNCLOS and other international legal obligations assumed by the Brazilian state, with but a few exceptions. The most inconvenient one, as assessed by this work, is Art. 3 (2) (c) of Decree no. 4.136/2002, which erroneously declare that Brazilian jurisdictional waters include those of the water column above the extended continental shelf.[132] It is doubtful, however, whether any legal operator in Brazil would implement such a provision and consider the country's jurisdiction to actually encompass the superjacent waters of the continental shelf beyond 200 nm. In fact, there are no traces of any such application of that provision in the Brazilian jurisprudence researched. It would be just the case to pass an amendment to the Decree in point, so as to fully adjust it to Art. 77 UNCLOS.

That very same Decree consolidated Brazilian enforcement jurisdiction over activities on or in connection with the continental shelf, namely regarding hydrocarbons exploitation. In order to prevent, reduce and control marine pollution from oil discharges, Brazilian norms imposes strict, solidary civil liability as a consequence of integral risk theory. In addition, the country also levies criminal liability on individuals, legal entities and company representatives, to the extent of their culpability. Yet to have domestic rules allowing for enforcement is not the same as actually enforcing, and challenges regarding the effective implementation of the Brazilian marine environmental framework for oil and gas activities remain.

10.2.4.2 Mining the Brazilian Continental Shelf

The Brazilian continental shelf has a considerable mining potential with regard to siliciclastic granules, carbonate granules, placers—diamond, gold, ilmenite, zircon, monazite and rutile, potassium, sulfur and phosphorite salts. Estimates also show polymetallic nodules on the outer continental shelf off the coast of Rio Grande do Sul, according to the georeferenced database "Geology of the Brazilian Legal Continental Shelf and Adjacent Ocean Areas", launched by the Brazilian Geological Service in 2008.[133] Widely used as fertilizer and source of phosphorus for the

---

[132] Art. 3 (2) (c), Decree no. 4.136/2002, which provides for the sanctions applicable to violations of national rules on the prevention, control and monitoring of pollution caused by the discharge of oil and other harmful or dangerous substances in waters under national jurisdiction.

[133] The Database presents a Geographic Information System containing all available information about the Brazilian legal continental shelf. It also contains a map of the Mineral Potential of the PCJB in the scale 1: 2,500,000. The initiative stems from joint efforts of the Brazilian Geological Service and the Brazilian Navy, within the scope of the REMPLAC Program, previously analyzed

chemical industry, phosphorite has been found on the outer continental shelf, as well as on the upper slope.[134] Besides, phosphorite deposits have also been found in areas of coastal resurgence, where the deeper waters rich in nutrients emerge towards the surface.[135]

Deep-sea mineral deposits of the Brazilian outer continental shelf and the Area are considered future alternatives for the international market of mineral commodities, especially metals that abound in polymetallic nodules at water depths of 500–2500 m, and polymetallic sulfides, at depths ranging from 2000 to 4000 m. Despite current researches and exploratory missions, the extraction technology for nodules, as well as for crusts, hydrates and sulfides, is still at an embryonic level in Brazil.[136] In other words, the deep-sea nodules and crusts are within reach, but have not yet been made viable on an industrial scale. In fact, marine mining usually takes place on the seabed within 75 km from the baselines, and the most sought resources comprise potassium salts[137] and limestone in a total to 1248 requests for offshore mining.[138] Apart from those, phosphate nodules have been confirmed on the continental shelf of Rio Grande do Sul,[139] while potassium and magnesium salts were tracked off the coasts of Sergipe and Alagoas at approximately 3000 m deep.[140]

In recent years, following the IX Sectorial Plan for Marine Resources, there has been an increase in applications for research on the Brazilian inner continental shelf, with more than 1.200 exploration licenses granted by the *National Mining Agency*

---

in this work. That the collection, analysis and publishing of geological data in a multi-institutional concerted effort was possible is praiseworthy and demonstrates a certain level of institutional maturity. Online, users can access two interactive maps depicting the mineral potential of the Brazilian continental shelf, within and beyond 200 nm. See: http://mapoteca.cprm.gov.br/programas/template.php.

[134]The "upper slope" is the region toward the deeper areas of the ocean, along the Brazilian continental margin.

[135]Souza (2010), p. 24.

[136]In 2010, there are a few offshore mining research projects under way. Among research projects developed in partnership between the Brazilian Geological Survey (CPRM), the Directorate of Hydrography and Navigation, of the Brazilian Navy, and Brazilian universities are the hydrothermal deposits, rich in zinc, copper, gold and silver, located on the Brazilian continental shelf and cobalt crusts from the international areas adjacent to the Brazilian continental shelf. These areas of research include the study of the geological conditions of the areas where these mineral sources exist. *See* Cavalcanti (2011), p. 75.

[137]The Brazilian Mining Agency recorded 815 requests for exploration and exploitation of potassium salts on the continental shelf, as of 2010.

[138]There were 270 requests for exploration and exploitation of offshore limestone. See ANM, Dez. 2010.

[139]Souza (2010), p. 25.

[140]In addition to mining in areas within national jurisdiction, Brazil is also currently engaged in the mineral exploration of the Area. On the Rio Grande Rise, in the South Atlantic Ocean, polymetallic nodules occur in the form of porous concretions of various sizes and shapes found in thin and discontinuous surface layers of the ocean floor, at an average depth of 5000 m. Seeking such resources, as well as an increased geopolitical presence in the South Atlantic Ocean, Brazil was the first country in the Southern Hemisphere to sign an Exploration Contract with the ISA. *Id.* 26.

(ANM). Nevertheless, the IX Sectorial Plan was crystal clear when it asserted that, despite the accumulated knowledge, there is a need for new geological geophysical geotechnical researches on a more detailed scale to evaluate the mineral potential of the continental shelf.[141] Transformation of marine minerals into products with high added value is a priority in Brazil, as it is expected to stimulate socioeconomic development.

A mining company which pioneered in exploring the Brazilian Blue Amazon is *TWB Mineração*, and the company's history offers pertinent lessons for the sustainable management of the Blue Amazon. After exploring the Brazilian continental shelf for almost two decades, the company has been prospecting for limestone algae in the region of Archipelago of Trindade and Martim Vaz. According to the company's executive manager, Luiz Eduardo Anchieta da Silva, the company seeks a another lithotamniun variation which is lighter and rich than similar species found near the coast.[142] Despite the promising result, the TWB got a setback. The company had its licenses canceled by the National Mining Agency, because the government considered that the activity was being conducted in international areas. This situation simply endorses the need for further detailed investigation on the Brazilian actual submarine frontiers, so that investments can be made without legal uncertainty.

However, despite its potentially positive socioeconomic impacts, mining is known to have a negative ecological footprint and to harm the marine environment. According to a 2011 Report on the mineral potential of the Brazilian continental shelf, the impact of deep-sea dredging operations depends on the nature of the physical impacts and the characteristics of the benthic communities at stake. Hence, lobster, herring, crabs and others species that move and feed on the seafloor may be endangered by offshore mineral dredging. Deep-water ecosystems may also suffer from the mining of polymetallic nodules, given that these operations remove along the fauna and epifauna which colonize the nodules' sites. The mining of hydrothermal sulfides (vents) is also likely to affect a biota of odd and little-known characteristics, as deep ocean ecosystems are the ones with the greatest biodiversity on the planet.[143]

In light of such ecological impacts, it is worrisome that current Brazilian legislation governing mineral exploration and exploitation makes no distinction between underwater and terrestrial areas. The Mining Code regulates the access to mineral resources, their research and exploitation regimes, as well as other aspects of the

[141] CIRM, IX Sectorial Plan for Marine Resources, 2016–2019, 10.

[142] Mr Anchieta da Silva has declared that "our research points to excellent product results in fruit growing, soybeans and especially sugarcane." See Brasil reivindica extensão maior da Amazônia Azul, *26 September 2011, Carlos Vasconcellos. Valor Econômico. Available online.*

[143] See Cavalcanti. at 87–92. Unfortunately, that was the newest report this study could find with public access online. In fact, the REMPLAC section of the CIRM website (https://www.marinha.mil.br/secirm/remplac) is outdated and lacks reports on the activities and measures carried out in the scope of the Program. Apart from that one, a Report on non-living resources of the Brazilian shelf was ordered by the Brazilian Ministry for Mines and Energy in 2009. For more, see Martins (2009).

mineral industry.[144] Thus, mining on the territorial sea, continental shelf and exclusive economic zone depends on a research permit from the National Mining Agency and a concession by the Minister for Mines and Energy, following the same procedure applicable to land permissions.[145]

Apart from the Mining Code, domestic environmental legislation regarding mining activities on the continental shelf include the National Environmental Policy, which conditions on- and offshore mining to three control instruments of potential risks of damages to the environment: the environmental impact assessment (EIA); the environmental licensing procedures; and the Recovery Plan for Degraded Areas.

The EIA, which precedes the environmental licensing of any mining activity, has its definition, norms, basic criteria and implementation guidelines established by the National Council for the Environment Resolution no. 001/1986, supplemented by Resolutions n° 009/1990 and n° 010/1990. Pursuant to those norms, detailed impact assessments are required to mining undertakings of every single mineral, except those for immediate use in civil construction enterprises.[146] The Assessment must be submitted to the competent environmental agency for analysis and approval, and then be made public. Approval of an EIA is a requisite for environmental licensing, which is required to locate, install or expand any mining activity.

Environmental licensing, on its turn, is regulated by CONAMA Resolution no. 237/1997, which assigns the federal environmental Institute IBAMA the duty to license ventures and activities in the territorial sea, continental shelf and exclusive economic zone.[147] Finally, with respect to the third pollution control instrument, mining companies are required to submit *Recovery Plans for Degraded Areas* upon submission of the EIA to the competent environmental agency.[148] Such plans disclose the technical solution chosen and considered appropriate by the licensed miner for the rehabilitation of the degraded area for future use past the mineral activity. Given mining's high risk of environmental damage, sch activities are also regulated by the Environmental Crimes Act, which specified the conditions under which environmental damage will be treated as a crime, with penalties ranging from fines and compensation to imprisonment. All that in line with international norms and regulations, especially UNCLOS, regarding the coastal state's powers over continental shelf activities.

Measures to prevent, reduce and control pollution from mining activities on the continental shelf also include area-based tools, particularly the designation of marine protected areas.[149] In this regard, several MPAs have been established alongside the

[144]The Mining Code was enacted by Decree-Law no. 227/1967, as amended by Act no. 9.314/1996.

[145]Art. 2, Brazilian Mining Code.

[146]Art. 1, Act no. 6.567/1978, amended by Act no. 8.982/1995.

[147]The federal environmental Institute, IBAMA, may delegate to state-level agencies the licensing of activities with a significant environmental impact at a regional level, standardizing, whenever possible, the requirements, pursuant to Art. 4 (2), CONAMA Resolution no. 237/1997.

[148]Art. 225 (2), Federal Constitution, as well as the entirety of Federal Decree no. 97.632/1989.

[149]Act no. 9.985/2000, or Conservation Units' Act.

Brazilian immense shore as a response to demands from environmental pressure groups. Yet, such domestic attempts at regulating marine mining activities via designation of MPAs may have, according to industry representatives, an undesirable side. The creation of marine protected areas without the confirmation of the environmental relevance of those areas and the abundance of mineral and energy resources with viable exploration, has blocked the consolidation of the marine mineral sector in Brazil, thus scaring investors off.[150]

The cause for such a backlash is that knowledge of the Brazilian continental shelf, even in shallow waters, is still embryonic, except for a few isolated areas. Only a thorough morpho-sedimentary survey of the seabed in detailed scale could generate basic knowledge that would enable the demarcation of the areas of relevant environmental interest, without over-dimensioning concrete problems. Such knowledge could also prevent the designation of MPAs with areas much larger than the actual needs to protect a given marine resources or ecosystem, often making it unfeasible to access marine natural resources at all. In this sense, Brazil ought to invest more in marine scientific research, so as to map out the environmental particularities and needs of its seafloor and deep-sea ecosystems, and perhaps render the environmental licensing procedure before domestic environmental agencies less problematic. Marine scientific research is precisely the focus of the next item.

10.2.5 Researching on the Brazilian Continental Shelf

Not long ago, Brazil signaled that it would commit itself to enhancing marine research and knowledge of the country's maritime spaces. It was so in 2015, upon the purchase of the state-of-the-art oceanographic R/V *Vital de Oliveira*.[151] Another illustration was the accomplishment in 2009 of the First Brazilian Trans-Atlantic Oceanographic Commission by the R/V *Cruzeiro do Sul*. Back at the day, Brazil advocated increased horizontal cooperation in the South Atlantic Ocean through workshops, which outlined bilateral action plans and joint research projects.

---

[150]Cavalcanti (2011), p. 63.

[151]With 78 m of length, accommodation for 140 people, including up to 50 researchers, technicians and students, and autonomy of 60 days at sea, the vessel is one of the largest scientific research vessels in the history of Brazil. It results from a public-private partnership between the Brazilian Ministry for Science, Technology and Industry (MCTI), the Navy, as well as the corporations Vale S.A and Petrobras, and was built in China for R$ 162 million (approximately US$ 41 million, as of August 2018). Apart from the R/V *Vital de Oliveira*, Brazil has other oceanographic R/Vs, such as the *Alpha Crucis*, *Alpha Delphini*, and *Wladimir Bernard*, operated by the Oceanographic Institute of the University of São Paulo; the R/V *Atlántico Sul*, operated by the Federal University of Rio Grande do Sul; and the R/V *Ary Rongel*, R/V *Cruzeiro do Sul*, and the Polar Vessel *Malmirante Maximiliano*, what suggests a certain attention to the issue of conducting MSR and perfecting knowledge about the Brazilian maritime space. Of those, the R/V Alpha Delphini is destined to mapping out the continental shelf off the São Paulo coast, where the sedimentary basins lodging the pre-salt oil reserves are. See CEMBRA Newsletter, 2015, Ano 1, n. 2, at 3. Available online.

Likewise, under the structure of the Community of Lusophone Countries (CPLP), Brazil pushed for ocean cooperation during the VI Conference of Heads of State and Government of the CPLP.[152] Besides, the Marine Biotechnology Action Plan (BIOMAR) endeavored to "promote and encourage the *study* and sustainable exploitation of the biotechnological potential of marine biodiversity in Brazilian jurisdictional waters and in other areas of national interest".[153]

Domestically, the *lex specialis* disciplining marine scientific research is Federal Decree no. 96.000/1988—also known as "Marine Scientific Research Act"—which provides for marine scientific research and investigation on the continental shelf and in waters under Brazilian jurisdiction. Of all the Brazilian marine environmental legislation scrutinized for this work, the Marine Scientific Research Act is certainly the most controversial one with respect to consistency with international law, in general, and UNCLOS in particular.

Upfront, the Decree considers as "scientific research" solely the set of works executed for purely scientific, non-commercial purposes. It then imposes considerable restrictions on researching the continental shelf, due to the economic and political sensitivity of that space. In line with Art. 2, all marine scientific research on the continental shelf shall only be carried out with *prior, express consent* from the Brazilian government. Furthermore, Art. 5 of the Decree restricts requests for marine research by *foreign entities*, conditioning it to several requirements, such as the previous signature of contracts or agreements with Brazilian institutions, or the submission of preliminary reports to the Navy prior to any international publication.[154] Formal applications for consent for marine research must be lodged before the Brazilian Navy 120 days before the desired kickstart of investigations. Moreover, Brazilian authorities avail themselves the right to *authorize* prospection and exploration of minerals and living resources only if the interested parties comply with the domestic legislation on such activities and other requirements by the Navy regarding national security and safety considerations.[155]

The domestic legal framework remains controversial with respect to the treatment given to the right to construct and authorize the construction and operation of artificial islands, installations, and fixed structures. Pursuant to Art. 14 (c) of the Decree, Brazil has the exclusive right to adopt regulations on the above-mentioned installations—regardless of whether on the continental shelf within or beyond 200 nm—and avails itself the right to deny consent to research projects which demand the construction and operation of any such structures.

Prima facie, one can spot a few incompatibilities between the Brazilian MSR Decree and core UNCLOS provisions on marine research. Art. 246 of the Convention, for instance, when dealing with research in the exclusive economic zone and on

[152]The CPLP Conference was held in Lisbon, in July 2008. At the end of the Conference, the CPLP Oceans Policy was adopted.

[153]Rede de Conservação da Biodiversidade Marinha (2017).

[154]Art. 5, single paragraph, and Art. 6 (I) to (VIII), Marine Scientific Research Act.

[155]Art. 18, idem.

the continental shelf, confirms that coastal states have the right to regulate, authorize and conduct marine research on their continental shelves, thus conditioning any research on that area to coastal state consent.[156] However, the Convention limits coastal states' right to withhold consent, under normal circumstances, in situations in which the research is for purely scientific purposes.[157] Clearly, not only Decree no. 96.000/1988 makes no reference to such situations, but domestic provisions have also codified additional requirements for the conduct of marine research by foreign entities. In fact, Art. 14, single paragraph, of the Brazilian Act stipulates that:

> No prospection or scientific research shall be authorized when it: a) causes losses to the commercial exploitation of natural resources, whether living or non-living; b) involves drilling on the continental shelf, using explosives or introducing substances harmful to the environment; c) demands the construction and operation of artificial islands or fixed installations and structures; d) the information provided is considered inaccurate or insufficient; and e) the State or international organization wishing to conduct the scientific investigation has obligations pending with Brazil, arising from previous expeditions.

Another controversial topic concerns the absence in the Brazilian legislation of any reference to a dual treatment between research on the inner and outer continental shelf. Such a dual system is present at Art. 246 (6) UNCLOS, regarding research projects on the continental shelf beyond 200 nm, which severely limits sovereign discretion to withhold consent—as opposed to Art. 246 (4). An exception to the obligation of coastal states to grant consent comes to play if the coastal state has ongoing exploratory or exploitation activities in the area, or expects to engages in such activities within a reasonable period of time, within the limits of good faith in international law. *Ipsis litteris*, UNCLOS Art. 246 (6) determines that

> coastal States may not exercise their discretion to withhold consent [. . .] in respect of marine scientific research projects to be undertaken in accordance with the provisions of this Part on the continental shelf, beyond 200 nautical miles from the baselines.

Note that the rule applicable to the outer continental shelf is drastically different than the one applicable to the inner shelf. States, therefore, ought to take those considerations into account when drafting national legislation. That does not seem, however, to have been the case of Brazil, as the country does not distinguish between consent on the continental shelf within or beyond 200 nm. Hence, in exercising its prescriptive jurisdiction on the continental shelf, Brazil has neglected relevant UNCLOS provisions, perhaps due to the lack of urgency concerning the regulation of the outer continental shelf at the time when the MSRA was enacted—1988, or given the stark sovereigntist approach adopted by Brazilian authorities towards the continental shelf and its riches.

Brazil's interpretation of the coastal state's jurisdiction regarding MSR opposes directly the understanding of Germany, according to whom

[156]Art. 246 (1) and (2), UNCLOS.

[157]Art. 246 (5), UNCLOS.

> although the traditional freedom of research suffered a considerable erosion by the Convention, this freedom will remain in force for States, international organizations and private entities in some maritime areas, e.g., the seabed beyond the continental shelf and the high seas. However, the exclusive economic zone and the continental shelf, which are of particular interest to marine scientific research, will be subject to a consent regime, a basic element of which is the obligation of the coastal State under article 246, paragraph 3, to grant its consent in normal circumstances. In this regard, promotion and creation of favorable conditions for scientific research, as postulated in the Convention, are general principles governing the application and interpretation of all relevant provisions of the Convention.[158]

Domestic enforcement powers, as prescribed in Art. 21 of the Brazilian MSR Decree, are owed to the Brazilian Navy and include the right to *inspect* activities on the continental shelf and in waters under Brazilian jurisdiction. Additionally, the Decree stipulates the mandatory presence onboard national and foreign R/Vs of Brazilian military and scientific personnel. Art. 22 (2) is crystal clear when it dictates that

> Brazilian representatives appointed as inspectors have the authority to halt, in waters under Brazilian jurisdiction, the collection of data, information or samples outside the period established in the ordinance that authorized the prospection or scientific research (free translation).

Domestic sanctions for those in breach of the rules stipulated in the MSR Decree include: (i) immediate suspension of any prospection or scientific research in progress, for a certain period; (ii) cancellation of the authorization granted for the research or scientific investigation in question; (iii) fine of 50–1000 times the highest reference value in force at the time of finding the breach; (iv) bar—for a certain period or permanently—of the research vessel from carrying out such activities in waters under Brazilian jurisdiction; (v) bar—for a certain period or permanently—of the responsible entities and sponsors from undertaking or sponsoring such activities in waters under Brazilian jurisdiction; and (vi) arrest of the research vessel and seizure of its scientific equipment, respecting the immunities recognized by international acts to which Brazil is bound, in the case of foreigners and international organizations.[159] Finally, Brazil demands those in breach of the rules to compensate the Brazilian state for damages eventually caused to the marine environment—as a result of prospecting, researching, exploring, mining, or exploiting the continental shelf and waters under Brazilian jurisdiction.[160]

Another key instrument regarding the conduct of marine scientific research is Resolution 003/2010, of the Interministerial Commission on Marine Resources (CIRM), regarding the Brazilian assertion of the right to regulate scientific research over the claimed outer continental shelf limits. Currently, Brazil acknowledges that the outer limits of its continental shelf have not been "definitively established", insofar as it awaits final and binding recommendations by the CLCS. Meanwhile, the country wishes to prevent undue exploration of non-living riches of the claimed

[158] *See* Germany, Declaration upon Accession to UNCLOS, 1994, available online.

[159] Art. 23, Brazilian MSR Decree.

[160] Art. 25, *id.*

outer limits, and rightfully so. In this context, CIRM Resolution no. 003/2010 requires research activities on the Brazilian postulated outer shelf to be conducted solely upon previous authorization of the Brazilian state, under no particular penalty, but the rebuttal of the unauthorized research activities and the eventual worsening of diplomatic relations between Brazil and foreign researching states.[161]

The action sparked controversy in the international community, which prompts this work to analyze the controversial issues. Firstly, coastal states' right to regulate exploration activities on the continental shelf stems both from the *ab initio and ipso facto* doctrine and the unilaterality of the delineation act. *Ab initio* means that the continental shelf rights do not depend on occupation or any express proclamation—UNCLOS Art. 77 (3), while *ipso facto* indicates that the act of delineating the outer limits is unilaterally exercisable by coastal states—UNCLOS Art. 76 (7). It is the international validity and recognition of such outer limits that depends on the CLCS recommendations. Correctly so, Alexandre da Silva held that the Brazilian decision is not contrary to international law, as the country is solely safeguarding its interests, just the way the United States did on past occasions, with the Truman Proclamations.[162]

A similar view is held by Rodrigo More, to whom there is no illegality in the Brazilian unilateral declaration contained in CIRM Resolution no. 003/2010, but on different grounds—grounds which are not entirely shared in this work.[163] To defend the legality of the cited Resolution, Rodrigo More summons an unusual distinction between the concepts of "right to explore"—supposedly related to prospection activities—and "right to conduct marine scientific research". For the scholar, exploration and marine scientific research are distinct legal concepts for the same activity, differing by destination: the right to explore derives from jurisdiction over the continental shelf—Art. 77 UNCLOS—and as such is due only to the coastal state. Marine scientific research, on the other hand, is permitted in the Area and lies beyond national continental shelves, thus falling under the regime of freedoms of the high seas.[164] Such ambiguity in both phrases (exploration and research), added to the merely declaratory nature of the CIRM Resolution, i.e. non-executive, would render the document consistent with UNCLOS, so the Brazilian scholar.[165]

Although More's conclusion is hereby endorsed, the author's distinction between exploration and scientific research does not seem to be based on the best interpretation of UNCLOS. Nowhere does the Convention raise a divide between "exploration" and "scientific research". *Ratione materiae*, both activities may be of an

[161]CIRM Resolution 003/2010, section A.

[162]Silva (2012), p. 308.

[163]More (2012), p. 66.

[164]More (2012), p. 66.

[165]In addition to that, there is no reason to believe that irreparable damage to the rights of researching states would arise, as in practical terms, eventual MSR that may be denied by Brazil can be later on conducted under the regime of the high seas or the Area, in case the Brazilian submissions are denied by the CLCS.

applied or pure nature, i.e. may serve commercial ends or the pure expansion of scientific knowledge on the functioning of marine systems. *Ratione loci*, both activities may occur on zones within or beyond national jurisdiction. More's view derives, perhaps, from a literal reading of the Convention. Given that Art. 77 UNCLOS grants coastal states' the sovereign right to *explore* and exploit their continental shelves, without mentioning "scientific research", and given that states expressly enjoy freedom of *scientific* research in the high seas—Art. 87 (f) UNCLOS), the Brazilian scholar may have established a strict link between exploration and areas under national jurisdiction, and scientific research in areas beyond. Even if that should have been the case, Art. 87 (f) UNCLOS subjects the exercise of the right to research in the high seas to Parts VI and XIII, thus suggesting a clear connection between exploration and research on the continental shelf. Finally, Art. 246 UNCLOS also distinguishes at no point between "exploration" and "scientific research".

Regardless of the controversy, CIRM Resolution no. 003/2010 has simultaneously demonstrated Brazil's respect for Art. 76 UNCLOS and the Convention's formal procedure to delineate outer continental shelf limits, while securing national control over activities happening on or in connection with the claimed portions of the seafloor beyond 200 nm. It is no evidence of blind nationalism, but a possible and legal interpretation of the rights codified in Part VI UNCLOS, an interpretation which does not unjustifiably or irreparably damages the rights and freedoms of other states over the outer limits.

For the Brazilian public authorities, the relevance of delineating the outer limits of the continental shelf lies, among others, on the fact that it will "extend" the areas under national jurisdiction, thus delimiting new "boundary lines" between Brazil and the international community. Such jurisdictional dilation impacts on four main dimensions: sovereign/defense, economic, scientific, and environmental,[166] which correspond to interests that have informed the Brazilian *modus operandi* in the law of the sea for decades. More recently, the need to raise awareness amid the national population as to the role of oceans in fulfilling those state interests has prompted the Brazilian Navy to coin the catch phrase which stands at the core of this research: The Blue Amazon. The delineation of the outer limits of the continental shelf consolidates that grandiose Brazilian Blue Amazon.

From the discussed above, Brazil does not seem to hamper unjustifiably marine scientific research, as such a practice is key to enhancing the world's scientific understanding of the oceans, a paramount pillar to better protecting the marine environment.[167] However, it is never enough to emphasize the need to adequate domestic legislation to UNCLOS Art. 246 (6), regarding the granting of consent for pure research projects on the outer continental shelf. Besides, it is also the case to reinforce how much the tide has changed regarding Brazilian ocean policies. The difficulties encountered in meeting the proposed goals are related to the scarcity of

[166]Mattos (1996), p. 65.

[167]*See* Brazilian Statement, DOALOS, Oceans and the Law of the Sea, 2015.

budgetary resources, the low availability of floating means for the shipment of researchers for the collection and sorting of scientific samples, the lack of qualified professionals for the processing and analysis of the material, the "apparent" lack of harmony between the various normative acts related to Biotechnology, biodiversity, genetic resources and biological materials.[168] This and other challenges are briefly mentioned in the conclusions below, without any intention to exhaust the problems lying ahead of the Brazilian "oceanic state", and without meaning to offer solution to all those marine environmental challenges.

References

Azzam I (1964) The dispute between France and Brazil over lobster fishing in the Atlantic. Int Comp Law Q 13(4):1453–1459

Brady H (2017) First photos of new amazon coral reef system released. National Geographic, January 30

Brown ED (1973) Maritime zones: a survey of claims. In: New Directions in the law of the sea. The Eastern Press, London

Cavalcanti VMM (2011) Plataforma continental: a última fronteira da mineração brasileira. Departamento Nacional de Produção Mineral, Brasília

Chircop A (2004) Operationalizing article 82 of the United Nations Convention on the law of the sea: a new role for the international seabed authority? Ocean Yearb 18:398–412

Churchill R, Lowe V (1999) The law of the sea. Manchester University Press, Manchester

ECORYS (2014) Study to investigate the state of knowledge of deep-sea mining, Final Report, SC E1/2013/04

Farranha AC (2014) Minutiae of the GERN Workshop. University of Brasília, Brasília

Fellet J (2018) A desconhecida cordilheira no litoral brasileiro que pode virar a maior reserva marinha do atlântico, BBC News <https://noticias.uol.com.br/meio-ambiente/ultimas-noticias/bbc/2018/01/26/a-desconhecida-cordilheira-no-litoral-brasileiro-que-pode-virar-a-maior-reserva-marinha-do-atlantico.htm>. Accessed 12 April 2020

Gavouneli M (2014) State jurisdiction in relation to the protection and preservation of the marine environment. In: The IMLI manual on international maritime law. Oxford University Press, Oxford, Chapter 1

Geraque E (2006) Pesca de arrasto ameaça corais no Brasil, Jornal Folha de São Paulo, 23 October, Available at https://www1.folha.uol.com.br/fsp/ciencia/fe2310200601.htm. Accessed 12 Apr 2020

Gianni M (2004) High seas bottom trawl fisheries and their impacts on the biodiversity of vulnerable deep-sea ecosystems: options for international action. IUCN, Gland

Goodwin EJ (2011) International Environmental Law and the conservation of coral reefs. Routledge Research in International Environmental Law, UK

Hart P (2010) Montara oil spill: a failure of sensible oilfield practice. The Oil Drum, 8 December

Huh N (2017) Article 246. In: Proelss A (ed) UNCLOS: a commentary. C.H. Beck, Nomos Verlag, Baden-Baden

Jayakumar S (2013) The continental shelf regime under UNCLOS In: The regulation of continental shelf development: rethinking international standards. Nijhoff, Leiden, pp 1–12

Kelsen H (2017) Reine Rechtslehre. Mit Einem Anhang: Das Problem Der Gerechtigkeit, 2nd ed, Hrsg. von Matthias Jestaedt, Mohr-Siebeck, Tübingen

[168]Rippel (2014), p. 45.

Lagoni R (2003) Marine protected areas in the exclusive economic zone. In: International marine environmental law: institutions, implementation and innovations. Kluwer Law, Leiden

Long R (2014) Principles and normative trends in EU ocean governance. In: The limits of maritime jurisdiction. Nijhoff, Leiden, pp 699–728

Maggio AR (2017) Article 77. In: Proelss A (ed) UNCLOS: a commentary. C. H. Beck, Hart, Nomos, Baden-Baden

Martins AJM (2009) Informação Sobre Recursos Marinhos Não Vivos. Ministério de Minas e Energia, Brasília

Mattos AM (1996) O novo direito do mar. Renovar, Rio de Janeiro

MMA (2018) O processo brasileiro de construção da estratégia e plano de ação nacionais para a biodiversidade (EPANB), Brasília

Molenaar EJ (2007) Current legal and institutional issues relating to the conservation and management of high seas deep-sea fisheries. FAO Fisheries Report, Rome, pp 113–139

More RF (2012) Quando cangurus voarem: a declaração unilateral brasileira sobre direito de pesquisa além dos limites da plataforma continental. Revista de Direito Internacional, Brasília 9(1):61–68

Mossop J (2015) Reconciling activities on the extended continental shelf with protection of the marine environment. In: Research handbook on international marine environmental law. Edward Elgar, London, pp 170–189

Mossop J (2016) The continental shelf beyond 200 nautical miles: rights and responsibilities. Oxford University Press, Oxford

Mothes B et al (2006) Esponjas (*Porifera, Demospongiae*) da plataforma continental ao largo do Estado do Amapá, Brasil. Revista Brasileira de Zoologia 23(3):667–677

Nelson D (2010) Maritime jurisdiction. In Max Planck Encyclopedia of Public International Law. Oxford University Press, Oxford

Nordquist MH, Grandy NR, Nandan SN, Rosenne S (eds) (2002) United Nations Convention on the law of the sea 1982: a commentary. Nijhoff, The Hague

Owen D, Chambers F (2006) The powers of the OSPAR Commission and coastal state parties to the OSPAR Convention to manage marine protected areas on the seabed beyond 200 nm from the baseline. WWF Germany, Frankfurt am Main

Pendleton GD (2005) State responsibility and the high seas marine environment: a legal theory for the protection of seamounts in the global commons. Pac Rim Law Policy J 14(2):486–514

Pinheiro H et al (2015) Fish biodiversity of the Vitória-Trindade Seamount Chain, Southwestern Atlantic: an updated database. Public Library of Science PLOS One

Plesmann W, Röben V (1991) Marine scientific research: state practice versus law of the sea. In: Law of the sea at the crossroads: the continuing search for a universally accepted regime. Duncker & Humblot, Berlin

Rede de Conservação da Biodiversidade Marinha (2017) Relatório de Atividades Do Planejamento Estratégico Integrado de Biodiversidade Marinha 2007–2016. Rede BIOMAR, São Paulo

Ribeiro MC (2015) Entre o apelo dos recursos minerais e a protecção dos ecossistemas vulneráveis do mar profundo em Portugal: enquadramento legal, sistema de competências e ordenamento. In: 20 anos da Convenção das Nações Unidas sobre o Direito do Mar. CIIMAR FDUP, Porto

Rippel MP (2014) A política nacional para o os recursos do mar: instrumento para conhecer e explorar a Amazônia azul. Escola de Guerra Naval, Rio de Janeiro

Rochette J et al (2014) Seeing beyond the horizon for deepwater oil and gas: strengthening the international regulation of offshore exploration and exploitation. Institut du développement durable et des relations internationales, Paris, p 38

Rodrigues MA (2016) Direito ambiental esquematizado. Saraiva, São Paulo

Santos C, Schiavetti A (2014) Spatial analysis of protected areas of the coastal/marine environment of Brazil. J Nat Conserv 22:453–461

Sharpless A (2016) New Movie "Deepwater Horizon" highlights threat of offshore oil drilling. The Huffington Post, 30 June. Available at: http://www.huffingtonpost.com/andrew-sharpless/new-movie-deepwater-horiz_b_12271918.html. Accessed 12 April 2020

Silva AP d (2012) Brasil e Canadá na Convenção das Nações Unidas sobre o Direito do Mar: Os esforços brasileiros e canadenses para aumentarem suas plataformas continentais. Política Hoje 21(1):291–325
Silva AP d (2015) O Brasil e o Direito Internacional do Mar Contemporâneo. Almedina, Coimbra
Souza KG (2010) O Futuro da exploração mineral em águas brasileiras e internacionais. Ciência e Cultura 62(3):23–25
Souza KLCM (2015) Critérios para cobrança da contribuição internacional pela utilização da plataforma continental estendida: panorama geral e impactos financeiros de sua aplicação quanto à exploração de petróleo na camada pré-sal no Brasil. Cadernos do Programa de Pós-Graduação em Direito da UFRGS 10(1):236–264
Stiles ML et al (2010) Impacts of bottom trawling on fisheries, tourism and the marine environment: a report to Oceana, available online at www.oceana.org. Accessed 13 Apr 2020
Tanaka Y (2015) Principles of international marine environmental law. In: Research handbook on international marine environmental law. Edward Elgar, Cheltenham, pp 31–56
Türk H (2012) The waning freedom of the seas: reflections on the contemporary law of the sea. Nijhoff, Leiden
Van Dover C (2012) Designating networks of chemosynthetic ecosystem reserves in the deep-sea. Mar Policy 36
Varella MD (2015) A necessidade de repensar os mecanismos de responsabilidade ambiental em caso de riscos de vazamento de petróleo na zona econômica exclusiva do Brasil. Revista de Direito Internacional 12(1):240–249
Ventura AMF (2018) Revisiting the critique against territorialism in the Law of the Sea: Brazilian state practice in light of the concepts of creeping jurisdiction and spoliative jurisdiction. Braz J Int Law 15(1):161–179
Ventura VAMF, Mello Filho EC (2020) The legal status of the São Pedro and São Paulo Archipelago in light of article 121 UNCLOS and the South China Sea Arbitral Award: uncontested right to EEZ and continental shelf or Brazilian 'creeping jurisdiction'. In: Global challenges and the law of the sea. Springer, Berlin
Wallerstein I (1974) The modern world system: capitalist agriculture and the origins of the European world economy in the sixteenth century. Academic Press, New York
Warner R (2008) Protecting the diversity of the depths: environmental regulation of bioprospecting and marine scientific research beyond national jurisdiction. Ocean Yearb 22:411–443
Wolfrum R (2000) Preservation of the marine environment. Kluwer Law, Leiden

Jurisprudence

PCA (2007) Arbitration regarding the delimitation of the maritime boundary between Guyana and Suriname, PCA Records, Award of 17 September 2007
ICJ (1976) Aegean Continental Shelf case, Greece v. Turkey, request for provisional measures, ICJ Reports

Chapter 11
Conclusions

Researches on the international law of the sea undertake a variety of problems and legal issues of relevance to academics, practitioners, activists and governmental authorities alike. Current hot topics include controversies on the negotiation of a legally binding instrument on the protection of biodiversity beyond areas of national jurisdiction; the reshaping of port state jurisdiction to tackle illegal, unreported and unregulated fishing; the development of multilateral and national strategies for an effective implementation of marine spatial planning; the drafting of an environmental management of the Area and deep-sea mining; the assessment of climate change effects in the functioning of ocean services; the study of ocean acidification and its consequences for populations of the globe from a legal perspective and the role of law in tackling that phenomenon, among others. A common place in those questions is the concern with the overall health of the marine environment and its resources.

Such a concern is at the very core of this book, the idea being to combine a research on marine environmental law and the performance of a particular state in that regard, Brazil. Hence, following the above-mentioned concern, this work has grappled with two main questions that navigate at the intersection between the law of the sea and international environmental law. Firstly, what is the material extent of coastal states' environmental jurisdiction—to legislate and to enforce—on the continental shelf within and beyond 200 nm? Secondly, are the Brazilian marine environmental policies and legislation for the Blue Amazon consistent with general international law and the law of the sea? A few key-words stand out from those two questions, namely "coastal states", "environmental jurisdiction", "continental shelf", and "Brazil". Such emphasis reflects an attempt to delineate the object under scrutiny and streamline both the researching and writing, without drifting away from original concerns.

Chapters 2 to 8 entertained the first research question, in a journey marked by the logical progression between the above-mentioned key-words: from the international regime applicable to the continental shelf, passing by the study of sovereignty and jurisdiction in the law of the sea with respect to the continental shelf, then the

V. Alencar Mayer Feitosa Ventura, *Environmental Jurisdiction in the Law of the Sea*,
https://doi.org/10.1007/978-3-030-50543-1_11

jurisdictional intersections between different maritime zones, to finally reach the environmental jurisdiction of coastal states on the continental shelf, its material extent and scope. The remaining Chaps. 9 and 10, dealt with the second research question, departing from a descriptive, panoramic view of the Brazilian ocean governance edifice—its policies and agents—towards the qualitative analysis Brazil's marine environmental legal framework consistency with the law of the sea.

Throughout the monography, a few core theses emerged alongside several incidental propositions which, if not entirely original, might contribute to the study of the continental shelf regime. These conclusions are grouped in thematic blocks of chapters, respecting the key-words referred to supra.

Chapters 2 and 3 placed the foundations of the work and dissected the general legal regime of the continental shelf within and beyond 200 nm. At the outset, it was noted that the UN Convention on the Law of the Sea consists of an international legally binding instrument which results from political tensions that marked international relations and the oceans between the end of World War II and the late 1970s. Such tensions were potentialized by historic events, such as the decolonization wave, calls for a just international order, and the realization of the oceans' multiple dimensions—surface, depth, subsoil and airspace. The Convention marked a shift from a dual-division of the oceans towards a multi-division, having codified regimes of rights and duties applicable to each of those maritime spaces.

A vital regime to this investigation was the continental shelf one or, in other words, "the international law of the continental shelf", which has existed for approximately 70 years—dating back to 1958, when the international community negotiated the first Convention on the Continental Shelf. Prior to that, there was mostly unilateral practice, each coastal state adopting different views on the definition, scope and width of the continental shelf. The CSC was then succeeded by UNCLOS, which embodied substantial upgrades concerning the ocean seabed.

The main pillars of the "new" continental shelf regime were the *natural prolongation* (Art. 76 (1) UNCLOS), the principle of *inherent entitlement* of the coastal state to the continental shelf (Art. 77 (3) UNCLOS), and the *sovereign and exclusive rights* of the coastal state over the continental shelf for the purpose of its exploration and exploitation of its resources (Art. 77 (1) and (2) UNCLOS). According to those principles, coastal states exercise sovereign rights *ab initio* over the natural resources of the submarine areas that extend beyond their territorial seas. Such rights do not depend on any express proclamation, nor occupation of those submarine areas.

An important part of the new continental shelf regime is dedicated to the possibility of coastal states delineating the outer limits of their continental shelves beyond the default 200 nm. Here, the book provided an in-depth view not only of the delineation procedure that precedes the international validation of outer continental shelf claims, but also the challenges faced by the international organizations charged with conducting and overseeing such procedure. The relevance of doing so lied on the need to understand the main nuances of the continental shelf regime, in particular the possibility of having different rules apply to the continental shelf within and beyond 200 nm.

The delineation procedure set out in Art. 76 UNCLOS has been widely respected by the international community. It is, therefore, consentaneous to the international law of the sea to claim that the delineation procedure *latu sensu* has acquired a customary nature, which ought to be respected including by non-parties to the Convention. There can occur, however, divergences as to the interpretation of technical terms employed at the Convention, such as "foot of the continental slope", which do not jeopardize the obligation to have outer continental shelf limits expressly recommended by the Commission on the Limits of the Continental Shelf (CLCS).

Upon the analysis of the tasks, overall performance and challenges lying ahead of the two UNCLOS-based institutions that are mandated to aid and monitor the delineation and delimitation of outer continental shelf limits, this work concluded that both the CLCS and the International Tribunal for the Law of the Sea (ITLOS) have performed satisfactorily thus far. Each body has a clear and precise role in upholding the coherent system legal regime applicable to the continental shelf. Yet, their mission is far from over, and the road ahead seems a rather bumpy one.

On the Commission's side, the key challenge concerns the massive workload in sight, with optimistic estimates shooting at another 40 years until the last outer continental shelf delineation. Reasons for that are the gigantesque amount of data scrutinized in every submission, added to the limited number of members of the Commission and their far-from-optimal working conditions. Furthermore, complexities of a technical nature and steep costs of gathering high-quality seafloor data are factors that may postpone not only the *issuing* of recommendations, but also the *adoption* of those recommendations by coastal states.

On the ITLOS' side, the Tribunal has faced questions regarding its jurisdiction to delimit and delineate outer continental shelves, apart from speculations as to the relation between the Tribunal and the CLCS. In its jurisprudence, the Tribunal has asserted jurisdiction to delimit the continental shelf in its entirety, within and beyond 200 nm, particularly due to the concept of a "single continental shelf". The Tribunal has also carved a distinction between the *delimitation* of opposing continental shelves beyond 200 nm and the *delineation* of outer limits. Finally, the judges have crafted the notion of a "grey area", in which one state exercises sovereign rights over the seabed, whereas another state, over the superjacent EEZ.

Furthermore, the Tribunal has not yet dealt with issues regarding the marine environmental protection of continental shelf ecosystems and habitats, neither to the environmental jurisdiction of coastal states on the continental shelf. Possible reasons for that are the still ongoing scrutiny of outer limits' claims by the CLCS; the insecurity faced by coastal states as to whether their claims will be upheld by the Commission; the lack of urgency in implementing outer continental shelf provisions—such as Art. 82 or Art. 246 (6) UNCLOS, in light of the currently inexistent exploitation of natural resources of the outer continental shelf, which has not prompted disputed relating to the environmental management of continental shelves, nor to eventual jurisdictional conflicts concerning the shelf beyond 200 nm.

That said, the legal regime of the continental shelf has still not been entirely understood, in particular the environmental jurisdiction of coastal states in the portion of the seabed beyond 200 nm. The entire Part VI UNCLOS makes no reference to the marine environment, neither to coastal states environmental rights and duties on the continental shelf. As such, it identified the need to clarify the *regulatory maneuver room* left to coastal states when governing their continental shelves, especially the portion beyond 200 nm. To assess that, this study delved into the issues of sovereignty and jurisdiction in the law of the sea.

Chapter 4 demonstrated that sovereignty and jurisdiction are interrelated concepts, both having shaped the law of the sea for a long time. Understood as a constitutive element of statehood, *sovereignty* conveys the meaning of a collection of rights, competences, and powers applicable within a certain territory. Its corollary, *jurisdiction*, is an instrumental concept which stems from sovereignty and consists of the competence to determine the administrative domain over which a legal authority extends. This book joined efforts with modern theories on jurisdiction, according to which the concept comprises not only rights, but also duties. In this sense, to say that a coastal state has jurisdiction implies that it is bound by specific obligations. The very concept of "sovereign rights" embodied this nuanced approach to sovereignty and jurisdiction in the law of the sea.

The chapter then emphasized that the emergence of new maritime zones prompted the shift from the black-and-white opposition between sovereignty and non-sovereignty (marginal sea vs. high seas), characteristic of the pre-UNCLOS era, into a polychrome, trichotomic scheme of sovereignty, functional jurisdiction, and non-sovereignty. The continental shelf lies precisely in the added category of functional jurisdiction, subject neither to the full powers of coastal states, nor the freedoms of the high seas as prescribed at UNCLOS Art. 87.

The functioning of the multizonal regime designed within UNCLOS is made possible by the principles of *legality* and *regression*, according to which jurisdiction shall not be presumed, and shall diminish the farther away from mainland one is. Those principle have not been enough to prevent conflicts arising from *concurrent or conflicting jurisdictions* between maritime zones, in particular the continental shelf, EEZ, high seas and the Area. Thus, issues such as the extent of coastal states rights over the EEZ, the respect for freedoms of the high seas; the interactions between coastal states' authority over the continental shelf and the legal regime applicable to the Area have made it to the spotlight. Such jurisdictional conflicts assume greater proportion when the subject matter in dispute is the protection of the marine environment.

Chapter 5 dealt with the jurisdictional intersections between the continental shelf and other maritime spaces, namely EEZ, high seas and the Area. Regarding the first one, it was said that, despite the merging of provisions for both zones in the Convention, as in the case of Art. 60 and 80, on artificial islands, installations and structures, the relationship between continental shelf and EEZ rules is marked by *autonomy* and *parallelism*. Both zones have upheld slightly differing rules, which run, however, in parallel to each other. They are zones in which coastal states exercise differing competences in differing degrees, as is the case of jurisdiction to manage and conserve natural resources, a power explicitly acknowledged to them over the EEZ, but not over the continental shelf.

The intersection between continental shelf and high seas rules is a rather complex and delicate one—which required an entire item of this work. Here, it was shown that the powers exercisable by the coastal state over the outer continental shelf relate *exclusively* to the seafloor, as UNCLOS preserved the legal status of the superjacent waters beyond the 200 nm as high seas.

Regarding the legal intersection between outer continental shelf rules and the regime of the Area, this book identified a problematic perception among international lawyers, that coastal states' aggressiveness in asserting jurisdiction over the outer continental shelf—via constant attempts to place as much ocean floor under national jurisdiction as possible—amounts to the decline of the common heritage principle. As abominable as national excessive claims may be, there seems to be an exaggerated emphasis on the imminence of conflictive scenarios between coastal states and the international community in the process of outer continental shelf delineation. On the issue of an alleged *a priori* "encroachment" of continental shelves over the Area, there is no such intrusion, for two reasons. Firstly, both regimes were born at the same time, upon the signature of UNCLOS. Secondly, the geological continental margin has always been there. What coastal states claim is merely jurisdiction over a submarine portion of their land territory.

Even if allegedly well-intentioned, alarmism against coastal states' jurisdictional expansion, depicted as one of the greatest threats to the common heritage principle, is prejudicial to an accurate analysis of the interactions between the legal regimes of Area and the continental shelf. Hyperbolic criticisms may pose risks to the consolidation of the continental shelf regime, in particular the portion extending beyond 200 nm, and obfuscate the fact that the road for encroaching on the Area can be made a lot more difficult than some of those criticisms may suggest. Overall, the efforts to create an international regime for the submerged spaces beyond national jurisdiction have been, to a large extent, successful.

From such intersections, this work identified a transparent confrontation between calls for a "renewed ethos" for the *mare liberum* doctrine—in which environmental rights are better placed in relation to traditional freedoms of the seas—and calls for a detachment from a "territorial mentality" that allegedly purports more losses than gains to a holistic environmental governance of the oceans. The chief question remains how to balance coastal states' jurisdiction with the freedoms of the high seas and the obligation of due regard for the rights of other states. For that, Chap. 6 analyzed coastal states' jurisdictional expansion in the second half of the last century, followed by a critique on the specialized literature that overemphasizes the aspect of illegality and abusiveness of coastal states' jurisdictional claims seawards.

Most doctrinal studies, when analyzing the legality of coastal states' jurisdictional claims seawards, prioritize the principle of freedom of navigation to the detriment of socioeconomic development and, more recently, marine environmental health. The practice of advancing jurisdictional assertions seaward is often depicted as excessive and undesirable in practically every scenario and, therefore, damaging to the maintenance of peace and order in the world oceans. Early unilateral claims prior to 1982 were considered to have violated customary law, while newer claims are said to infringe UNCLOS provisions. Following that rationale, the declaration of a 200 nm economic zone made by several Latin American States during the 1970s was considered contrary to customary law prior to 1982. Nowadays, the unnegotiated adoption of stricter environmental rules for vessels navigating the EEZ—as was the case of Portugal, Spain and France, following the 2003 *Prestige* incident—was also dismissed as an excessive measure.

Those claims amounted, so the traditional doctrine of the law of the sea, to a practice labeled as "creeping jurisdiction", which needs no introduction. This work offered a counterargument to the widespread and wholesale use of that phrase, employed to depict every unilateral measure considered excessive by naval powers, regardless of the context in which the measure is enforced. To do so, it divided two "epochs" in the law of the sea: the pre-UNCLOS era, and the times which followed the adoption of the Convention.

Concerning the pre-UNCLOS era, the widespread phrase "creeping jurisdiction" does not accurately depict the expansionist claims staged by coastal states. The concept is value-laden and describes an inherently wicked practice, which may not be the case with the systematic opposition to the *ordre publique* of the oceans before 1982. Hence, this work advanced the thesis according to which territorialist positions prior to UNCLOS were crucial, as they defied the model of colonial spoliation which inspired the law of the sea until that time. The opposite of the so-called "creeping jurisdiction" would, thus, be the continuation of a *spoliative jurisdiction*, one that connotes the colonialist origins of the law of the sea as a legal system that favored technologically advanced coastal states through overwhelming prestige to freedom of the seas. Such prestige was the direct result of the primary role played by maritime states in shaping the public order of the oceans over the course of history.

In that context, Brazil, the "leader of territorialists", assumed a leading role in seeking the expansion of coastal state powers farther away offshore. The country played an important part in catalyzing change, partially due to its gigantic area, economic status, and political clout. By affirming sovereignty over the 200-nm zone, in 1970, Brazil and other developing countries obtained decisive bargaining power for the international negotiations that took place during the Third Conference. Ultimately, Brazilian practice prior to the adoption of UNCLOS was instrumental to the emergence of the "new" law of the sea, one sensitive to social, economic and human needs.

Following those considerations, this book diagnosed the need for a Southern narrative of the law of the sea, one that objects traditional privileges and hegemony held by maritime and naval powers; a narrative that perceives the law of the sea as a compound of *juridico-political* constructs which stem from political struggles. It was so with the disputes for a territorial sea of twelve nautical miles, for a 200-nm EEZ, for an outer continental shelf, for an internationalized deep seabed subject to the common heritage principle, and, nowadays, for enhanced marine environmental protection.

Regarding coastal states' marine environmental jurisdiction, in particular, this work sided with the calls for a renewed ethos of the *mare liberum* doctrine, one that updates freedoms of the seas to the current historical moment of the consolidation of an increased *conscience environmentale*. Maritime states with particular security interests are the most unenthusiastic about coastal states' exercise of environmental jurisdiction on the continental shelf within and beyond 200 nm. In this regard, such outdated opposition between maritime security and environmental concerns needs to be overcome and make way to the more encompassing concept of "environmental security jurisdiction", so that coastal states may adopt protective environmental measures which may partially restrict specific freedoms of the high seas, provided such measures are justifiable and scientifically based.

Vessel-source pollution in the EEZ and continental shelf, for instance, is a dimension in which coastal states have reasons to bargain for expanded environmental jurisdiction. Similarly, hydrocarbon pollution and oil slicks following hydrocarbons' exploitation on the outer shelf, or damages to the seabed following bottom fishing or mining the deep ocean floor are also dimensions in which coastal states may exercise marine environmental jurisdiction—in accordance not only to UNCLOS but also to other international law instruments. Despite fears by naval powers of coastal states camouflaging abusive enclosures of the oceans as environmental concerns, coastal states' measures which aim at increasing the environmental security and quality of the maritime zones under national jurisdiction are not to be *a priori* dismissed as abusive and contrary to UNCLOS. An analysis of the particular context, as well as the rules other than UNCLOS, such as the Convention on Biological Diversity, should follow suit.

For the rest, i.e. the other environment-grounded measures which openly disguise trade or geopolitical interests—such as in the case of the Japanese scientific whaling program or the Chinese jurisdictional aspirations in the South China Sea, it should be noted that every push towards a jurisdiction expansion seaward triggers an equally powerful reaction from the international community. In this sense, it is risky and costly for coastal states to unilaterally advance abusive self-interests disguised as the protection of global commons, particularly so in the current moment, when the international community accepts that universal problems require negotiated solutions.

Having dismissed *a priori* criticisms to the exercise of marine environmental jurisdiction by coastal states, Chap. 7 set out to assess the nature and material extent of such environmental jurisdiction on the continental shelf—and there only. One of the most important findings of this work was that, due to a long-established narrative in the law of the sea contrary to coastal states' jurisdictional expansion seawards, coastal states' environmental jurisdiction on the continental shelf has been said to be significantly more limited than it actually is.

In the "battle of *ethoses*" for the interpretation of UNCLOS, this work sided with the call which insists not only on an environment-oriented interpretation of UNCLOS provisions, but also on the combined application of the Convention and CBD in areas within national jurisdiction. To this task, the theory of UNCLOS as a "living treaty" has greatly inspired the points argued in this work. Taken as a living instrument, UNCLOS is capable of changing and accommodating new challenges to the world oceans. It is undeniable that the international law of the sea, as any branch of law, undergoes permanent evolution and progressive development that is linked to states' practice and institutional and academic interpretation of UNCLOS provisions. Such an evolution through interpretation may offer maneuver room for legal operators to tackle the most pressing challenges to the Convention, without needing to hope for improbable implementing agreements or unlikely formal amendments.

Hence, Chap. 6 has shown that the "environmental UNCLOS" represented a giant leap towards the regulation of the marine environment, albeit in a fragmented and incomplete way. The Convention was drafted at a time of profound *prise de conscience environmentale*, in which the value of environmental conservation gains the hearts and minds of populations across the globe, having codified two dimensions of environmental concerns in a pioneer fashion: the conservation of living resources, as well as the prevention, reduction and control of marine pollution. Hence, the way in which the Convention codified the obligation to preserve and protect the marine environment—by coupling it with the sovereign rights to conserve and manage living resources—allows for the drawing of a general, overriding *right-duty to manage the marine environment within national jurisdiction*.

International law in general and the law of the sea in particular have played a significant role in reaffirming mechanisms to protect nature, by turning the terrestrial and marine environment into legal goods worthy of safeguarding. Nonetheless, even though UNCLOS joined such ecological efforts and accommodated an entire Part on the protection and preservation of the marine environment, the Convention did not specify the environmental jurisdiction that coastal state have over its extended continental shelf. In addition to that, Part XII contains mostly obligations which fall upon states to protect the marine environment against pollution. Thus, it remains unclear what the environmental *rights* of broad-margin states are, i.e. the limits of national regulatory powers on environmental matters concerning the extended shelf.

For the purposes of this work, coastal states' environmental jurisdiction over continental shelf activities was extracted from different sources: international customary law; the joint reading of UNCLOS' relevant provisions and the MEAs which eventually apply to the marine realm, such as the CBD and CITES. In fact, assessing such a jurisdiction is a job that demands a holistic reading of UNCLOS, its implementing agreements and its preparatory works, but not only that. Marine environmental matters extrapolate UNCLOS and peer into the domain of other subsystems of public international law. Such diagonal regime interaction is in line with a unifying approach to international law, one that prioritizes a coherent application of the discipline, instead of focusing on fragmentated parts and the tensions permeating inter-regime relations.

Starting with UNCLOS, the rights and duties contained in Art. 77 are not restricted to adopting laws, but extend to enforcing measures—not only with regard to the exploration of the continental shelf and the exploitation of its resources, but to the management of those resources, which also comprises conservation and protection schemes. The general environmental provision *par excellence* within UNCLOS is the dual-edged *right-duty to manage the marine environment under national jurisdiction*. Such a view, however, is not backed by a literal reading of the Convention, according to which coastal states have, on the one hand, sovereign rights to explore and exploit, and, on the other, a general obligation to protect and preserve the marine environment. Nothing more than that.

The concept of a "right-duty" is widely employed in Brazilian legal doctrine, namely in constitutional studies, to refer to a category of rights, in a sense of formulation containing a subjective *Anspruch* to a particular good, which is simultaneously an obligation to act or behave on a particular way. The right-duty suggested here does not apply exclusively to natural resources, for it is not identical to the sovereign rights prescribed in Art. 77 (1) UNCLOS. It also governs activities which do not directly interfere with natural resources, but which may pose harm to the marine environment at large. In other words, the right-duty to manage goes a step further than sovereign rights in providing international legal contours for coastal states' domestic environmental powers.

Having that in mind, the specific environmental duties which comprise the right-duty to manage the continental shelf are: *duty not to cause damage by pollution to the environment of other states*, Art. 194 (2) UNCLOS; *duty not to transfer damage or hazards* from one area to another or to transform one type of pollution into another, so Art. 195 UNCLOS; *duty to monitor risks and effects* of all sources of pollution to the marine environment, as well as the *duty to assess the potential effects of activities* which may cause substantial pollution of or significant and harmful changes to the marine environment, pursuant to Arts. 204 and 206 UNCLOS; obligation to *regulate, enforce and monitor measures towards the preservation of marine biodiversity*, pursuant to Arts. 5 to 8 CBD. Finally, states are compelled by the *duty to promote the sustainable development of marine natural resources*, an obligation which may be extracted not only from certain UNCLOS provisions, but also from key environmental treaties.

The relevance of emphasizing the existence of such a right-duty to manage within the UNCLOS' edifice lies on the fact that a literary reading of Art. 77 (1) of the Convention could eventually lead to the understanding that coastal states exercise sovereign rights over continental shelf resources for the exclusive purpose of *exploring* and *exploiting* those resources, nothing else. The deliberate absence of expressions such as "management" or "protect and preserve", or "marine environment" in Part VI of the Convention could, thus, guide to strict interpretations on the extent of coastal states' powers over that specific space. Such a literal interpretation would not survive a thorough legal analysis, based, among others, on the evolutive and purpose-oriented hermeneutics suggested at the Art. 31 (1) of the Vienna Convention on the Law of Treaties.[1]

The idea of a right-duty to manage the continental shelf is not to say that this work believes so blindly on the capacity of individual nation-states to solve trans-individual issues; that it neglects contemporary calls for collective action and for enhanced cooperation to tackle the deterioration of the world's oceans. Quite the

[1]Art. 31 (1), VCLT: A treaty shall be interpreted in good faith in accordance with the ordinary meaning to be given to the terms of the treaty in their context and in the light of its object and purpose.

contrary, the purpose is to offer collective action and cooperation a powerful complement, that of coastal states' domestic action, given those states' immediate susceptibility to marine environmental harms and, thus, their direct interest in the overall quality of the seas washing their shores. After all, coastal states have been attributed by UNCLOS the role of "keepers" of common, diffuse and collective concerns, particularly the protection and preservation of the marine environment. They are, in the eyes of the Convention, part of the solution and not just part of the problem.

Building on that idea, Chap. 8 assessed coastal states' material jurisdiction to prescribe and enforce rules on marine environmental matters. The premise underlying this chapter was that UNCLOS, as a product of its epoch, has limitations and only vaguely contains provision on the prescriptive and enforcement powers of coastal states on the continental shelf, both within and beyond 200 nm.

On the prescriptive environmental jurisdiction to conserve marine living resources, this work noted that the concept of "living organisms" is expressly limited to the sedentary species of Art. 77 (4) UNCLOS, thus not including general benthic fauna such as fishes that just eventually touch the seafloor. Besides, coastal states are attributed solely sovereign rights for the purposes of exploring the continental shelf and exploiting its resources. A literal interpretation of the Convention in this regard could prompt to the conclusion that the *management* and *conservation* of sedentary species of the outer continental shelf are left outside coastal states' sovereign rights, an interpretation that would not make justice to coastal states' environmental powers and obligations. In fact, it is illogical that provisions applicable to sedentary species within the 200-nm zone are not be valid for the continental shelf beyond 200 nm.

Coastal states have the obligation to protect the biodiversity of the continental shelf, both within and beyond 200 nm. Regarding fisheries' regulation, for instance, whenever living resources exist under the jurisdiction of the coastal state, there is municipal jurisdiction to protect, preserve and stimulate the sustainable and rational use of those resources. That is essentially an environmental power which flows from a holistic interpretation of UNCLOS Part XII and provisions of the CBD, such as Art. 4 (a), which can be read in such way as to impose conservation obligations vis-à-vis sedentary species.

A thorny question standing at the spotlight since the adoption of UNCLOS relates to the regime applicable to genetic resources. Here, this book favored the view which does not rule out the application of the CBD to the management and conservation of marine living resources within national jurisdiction, including genetic resources. In fact, the CBD concepts of "ecosystem" and "functional unit" are of particular relevance when determining the living resources of the outer continental shelf over which coastal states may exercise environmental jurisdiction. That is particularly relevant, for instance, for the fragile and pristine ecosystems of hydrothermal vents.

On the prescriptive environmental jurisdiction regarding the prevention, reduction and control of marine pollution, it was shown that UNCLOS outlines coastal states' general obligation to protect and preserve the marine environment and defines the obligation to take all measures consistent with the Convention that are necessary to prevent, reduce and control pollution of the marine environment—Arts. 192 and

194. Then, as a second step, Art. 208 establishes states' jurisdiction to *prescribe* laws and regulations for combatting marine pollution from all sources, thereby elaborating on the general obligations laid down previously.

The second half of Chap. 8 appraised coastal states' enforcement jurisdiction over the continental shelf. It found that those states have the right to take enforcement measures aimed at implementing national laws against activities which may harm living resources of their continental shelves—especially within, but also beyond 200 nm, pursuant to UNCLOS Arts. 73 and 77. Before reaching such conclusion, this work analyzed arguments pro and against coastal states' enforcement jurisdiction on the continental shelf, especially beyond 200 nm.

Those who are against enforcement rights on the extended shelf support their views on the fact that UNCLOS does not expressly provide for such jurisdiction. Those defending the legality of coastal states enforcing their rights on the outer shelf invoke the commentaries to the 1958 CSC, which saw implicit control powers to prevent violations of their rights—control meaning preventive and punishment powers. Such an interpretation prioritizes the effective achievement of coastal states' sovereign rights and functional jurisdiction over the continental shelf, without extending such rights *ratione loci* to the superjacent waters.

The exercise of such rights, however, is subject to the *obligation of due regard* when taking measures, as the Convention expressly prohibits "unjustifiable interferences" to the rights and freedoms of other states. Due to their conflictive potential, enforcement questions made it to international jurisprudence in several occasions—yet, always with regard to the EEZ, never the continental shelf beyond 200 nm. It is the case of ITLOS' *Virginia G* case and coastal states' right to "take the necessary enforcement measures" for the implementation of national legislation; or the *Arctic Sunrise* Arbitration and coastal states' right to enforce domestic laws relating to non-living resources in the EEZ on a *reasonable, necessary and proportionate* manner.

Coastal states must exercise environmental powers within the material limits of Art. 78 UNCLOS—must not infringe or result in any unjustifiable interference with navigation and other rights of other states. Yet, "unjustifiable" is a term passive of different interpretations, especially as time passes and new values inspire the international community. When France, Spain and Portugal decided to unilaterally ban the access of single-hull tankers from their EEZ, such a measure was considered by many as "unjustifiable" at the time, but certainly is not so nowadays. Thus, borderline cases in which coastal states cap rights and freedoms of high seas of other states, while exercising environmental jurisdiction above the outer continental shelf should be analyzed on a case-by-case basis.

As discussed in Chaps. 7 and 8, coastal states' environmental jurisdiction on the outer continental shelf is not a matter of black and white, but of different shades of grey. This work concluded that the coastal states' sovereign rights and jurisdiction over the continental shelf are far from absolute, but so are the traditional freedoms of the seas enshrined in Art. 87 UNCLOS. That is the so-called "mutual due regard", which falls upon coastal and other states alike. In current days, the balance between rights and obligations of coastal states and other states over the continental shelf necessarily involves taking environmental considerations seriously. As long as the protection of the environment is regarded as the Trojan horse of coastal states for advancing national jurisdiction seawards, the health of the world's oceans can be expected to decrease.

Building on the theoretical framework discussed up to this point, Chap. 9 mapped the seascape of marine environmental policies and laws in Brazil which apply to the management of the "Brazilian Blue Amazon". While a book is certainly not suited for exhausting such a seascape, should this work have triggered greater awareness as to the regulation and conservation of the Brazilian seafloor, it will have achieved its goal. Brazil relies on a complex web of policies, plans, and concrete actions that level the ground for the environmental governance of Brazilian waters and maritime spaces. Despite such a complexity, the individual elements of such a network can be said to complement themselves and to cover, in a fairly decent manner, the most relevant aspects of marine environmental governance. The macro-policies for the marine environmental governance of Brazilian seas are: the 1994 National Maritime Policy, the 1981 National Environmental Policy, and the 1980 National Policy for Marine Resources.

For the purposes of ocean governance, the 1980 National Policy for Marine Resources (PNRM) was key to this study. It governs the development of maritime activities focused on the use, exploration and exploitation of living, mineral and energy resources of the Brazilian maritime spaces, in a *rational and sustainable* way, in accordance with national interests and facing the country's socioeconomic development. The PNRM relies on the principles of precaution in the exploitation of marine resources; protection and conservation of biodiversity and genetic heritage in marine areas under national jurisdiction; and respect for the internationally accepted commitments by the Brazilian state.

Within the umbrella provided by the PNRM, several quinquennial plans thrive, each containing actions and measures aimed at a specific axis of ocean governance, such as conservation of biodiversity, monitoring of maritime activity, assessment of a given area's marine resource potential, etc. Currently, Brazil runs the IX Sectorial Plan for Marine Resources (PSRM), which is mostly grounded on concerns with "marine sustainability". Of the several *actions* outlined in previous PSRM's, those concerning the marine environment of the continental shelf are of particular interest to this study. The bulk of those policies, plans and actions amount to what could be termed a "Brazilian ocean strategy"—which has informed municipal ocean legislation since the 1970s.

Under the quinquennial Sectorial Plans for Marine Resources, specific actions have been designed and implemented, such as the REVIZEE or the LEPLAC—the former mapped out the living resources of the Brazilian EEZ and published extensive reports with the resulting conclusions, and the latter enabled the collection of massive amounts of data on the Brazilian seabed morphology which grounded the country's submissions for an outer continental shelf before the CLCS. Yet, not-so-successful actions also exist, and that is the particular case of REMPLAC. It was designed to evaluate the mineral potential of the Brazilian continental shelf, while simultaneously (i) depicting the physical environment of that continental shelf;

(ii) identifying and detailing areas of relevant mineral potential; (iii) collecting basic geological information for the management and integrated management of the shelf and the adjacent coastal zone. Nonetheless, the Action progresses on a rather slow rhythm, what suggests a lack of priority from national stakeholders to surveying the mineral potential of the Brazilian shelf. Thus, it is unlikely that mineral exploitation of deep-sea areas under national jurisdiction will start anytime soon—even though that may not be the case of the exploitation of offshore hydrocarbons, a superior Brazilian interest.

Every policy must count on domestic institutional actors in their implementation cycle. The first and crucial governmental body tasked with the coordination of the Actions referred to supra is the Interministerial Commission for Marine Resources (CIRM). From what this investigation could assess, CIRM presents a truly impressive service sheet throughout its almost 40 years of existence. It seeks to fill—and achieves, to a large extent—the institutional vacuum in the Brazilian marine space. Another chief actor in designing and upholding the Brazilian ocean governance scheme is the Brazilian Navy. Despite the Navy's awareness of its broader institutional role of not only protecting Brazilian waters and mainland, but also caring for the conservation of the marine environment, the latter is not the Navy's primary concern. Enforcement of marine environment-related regulations falls under the responsibilities of the Brazilian Institute for Renewable Resources and the Environment (IBAMA), a situation which could potentially trigger institutional conflicts between the Navy and IBAMA, due to the overlap of tasks, and makes one wonder whether a shared protagonism between these two institutions exists.

In addition to junctural uncertainties regarding the place of environmental public policies in the new government, Brazil struggles with more structural issues, namely the quests for coherence and effectiveness in complementing and enforcing the complex web of domestic marine environmental policies. This book faced two different views on that quest. For a parcel of the specialized literature, striving for coherence means reducing fragmentation in policy-making, understood here as the tendency of having different sectors and stakeholders overlap in domestic ocean decision-making spheres. Yet, one should also recognize the complexity inherent to the governance of the oceans. A quick glimpse at the policies, programs, actions and institutions participating in the Brazilian ocean governance reveals the complexity of such a process in the historic era that scientists have agreed to refer to as the "Anthropocene". Yet, Brazil is not alone in dealing with a "horrendogram" of domestic policies, rules, programs and agencies that interact on marine environmental issues.

This book considered both arguments compatible with each other. To acknowledge the intrinsic complexity of regulating the management of the marine environment is equivalent by no means to defending unnecessarily labyrinthine domestic rules and policies. Indeed, a too intricate ocean governance system is likely to lead to internal conflicts of formal competence, as well as to material contradiction, consequences which are to be avoided by policy- and law-makers. It is also far from implying that public authorities should refrain from harmonizing policies and plans for the marine environment. Quite the contrary, to expect a handful of documents to regulate all uses of the oceans is not consonant with reality. Admitting the inherent complicatedness of the process, due to the multiplicity of opposing interests at stake and the great variety of stakeholders, is a first step towards drawing effective strategies for the oceans.

In order to make that point, this work considered the Portuguese National Ocean Strategy and its vibrant objective to turn the Portuguese seas into a national project, i.e. to implement action plans capable of mobilizing stakeholders around crucial questions pertaining to the management of Portuguese maritime spaces. Such a clear objective is not easily extractable from the Brazilian ocean governance edifice—and this shows how a decentralized web of policies, plans and actions may blur essential goals. Brazil could certainly benefit from such a symbolism of raising the Brazilian seas to the status of a "national project", instead of a destiny, some sort of fate and predestination.

Noteworthy is also that the Portuguese strategy is not centered on the aspect of national sovereignty, defense and security, thus embracing "refreshed" objectives, such as innovation, technology, *stimuli* to the blue economy and marine environmental conservation. Brazil, on the other side, has been criticized by the literature for designing its national ocean policy from a stark military perspective—with some truth to it.

Regarding the effectiveness of the integrated ocean management in Brazil, the comprehensive package of laws and policies formally integrating all levels of government—municipal, state and federal—has been met with incipient implementation. The more incisive laws in relation to ocean and coastal management have the form of resolutions and not decrees or acts, thus hinting at the presumption of a weak system by those required to abide by the resolutions and recommendations. Besides, the policies are excessively concentrated in the Executive branch of government, which does not facilitate the effective regulation of marine issues at the national level. Furthermore, insufficient dialogue at the national level usually jeopardizes the selection of national interests which will make it to oceans policies—not interests picked in hermitically isolated offices in the Brazilian capital. Finally, the deficient flow of financial resources to ground-force agencies is also a reason for low implementation rates.

This work went on to scrutinize the *extended* Blue Amazon and the current status of the Brazilian submissions for outer continental shelf limits in the South Atlantic Ocean. For that purpose, Chap. 9 relied on concepts of a legal and international relations' nature. Following the implementation of the Continental Shelf Survey Plan (LEPLAC), Brazil forwarded *three submissions* for outer continental shelf limits to the CLCS. The first submission dated 2004 and claimed sovereign rights over approximately 911,000 km^2 of extended continental shelf. The CLCS agreed with approximately 79% of the claimed limits, what prompted Brazil to forward revised partial submissions in 2015, 2017 and 2018. Thus far, only the executive summaries of the Brazilian submissions have been made public, as part of the strategy chosen by the Brazilian delegation, pursuant to Rules 48 and 49 of the CLCS, in order to safeguard sensitive information on the Brazilian submarine areas from the eyes of third states.

The extended continental shelf will conform the final layout of the Brazilian maritime jurisdiction, thus giving shape to the what the Brazilian Navy has called the "Blue Amazon". By creating and spreading the idea of a Blue Amazon, with its slightly poetic touch, the Brazilian Navy placed itself as an important actor in the domestic political debate, thus proposing policies and highlighting the need for a well-equipped naval force to safeguard not only the country's interests in the adjacent waters but also the "ocean destiny" neglected by Brazil for decades, according to doctrines nurtured in the Navy.

This book dissected the concept of the "Blue Amazon" in its multifaceted-nature. The frenzy with the new concept steered a plethora of domestic publications on the Blue Amazon, its definition, objectives and practical implications for the Brazilian authorities. Somewhat regrettably, Brazilian scholars have misleadingly referred to the Blue Amazon as the "Brazilian maritime territory" or the "Brazilian jurisdictional waters", references which were dismissed, on legal grounds, throughout Chap. 9. Moreover, this work examined each of the Blue Amazon's pillars: (i) assurance of sovereignty national defense, via exercising politico-strategical influence in the South Atlantic Ocean; (ii) economic prosperity; (iii) scientific and technological innovation; and (iv) environmental conservation.

In defense terms, the Blue Amazon consists of the "vital area" of the so-called "Brazilian strategic contour", which also includes the South Atlantic Ocean, the West African coast and Antarctica. In economic terms, the Blue Amazon is widely perceived as a motor of economic development through technological advancements and innovation. Brazilian maritime zones are believed to form a "Brazilian oceanic complex" which, if managed well, should benefit national aquaculture and fisheries; recreational and leisure activities; renewable energies and offshore exploration; maritime transport; and marine sciences.

On the environmental side, some conceptual problems emerged. The environmental conservation dimension of the Blue Amazon is not left aside in theorization efforts embraced by Brazilian political strategists, though it is also not given much of a relevance either. Until now, most of the programs and plans for the integrated management of coastal and marine environments have been directed mainly to the prevention of degradation of strictly coastal environments.

Besides, another issue identified in this research refers to the link forced by the Brazilian Navy between safety of navigation and environmental conservation, a *rationale* according to which measures taken for increasing navigational safety in the Blue Amazon directly contribute to the environmental conservation of the area. For instance, the Brazilian Navy's website which is dedicated to the environmental dimension of the Blue Amazon clearly emphasizes safety of navigation over any other criterion for the principled environmental management of the Blue Amazon—a somewhat misleading approach. No matter how relevant navigational safety measures may be for the peaceful use and management of the marine spaces under national jurisdiction, that element certainly does not exhaust environmental concerns over marine ecosystems.

In the assessment of the extended Blue Amazon carried out in this work, benefits and risks of an extended Blue Amazon arose. On the side of benefits, tangible economic gains stand out, given the (not yet fully known) exploitation potential of living and non-living resources of the outer continental shelf, namely deep seabed minerals, hydrocarbons, and sedentary species. Another advantage relates to foreign policy achievements, viz. the strengthening of cooperation links with neighboring countries of the South Atlantic Ocean, given the Brazilian ability and willingness to provide technical assistance and consultancy to states currently preparing submissions for the delineation of outer continental shelf limits.

On the side of the risks, the most notable one, according to this work, is having the country ill-suited to manage the extended Blue Amazon both in legal and institutional terms. For instance, the situation of Brazilian official agencies engaged in marine conservation efforts did not look promising in the last years, as highlighted in Chap. 9. To make it worse, since 2014 a domestic political crisis has added to the unfavorable international context, thus shaking Brazilian economics and politics and throwing the country into a calamity that is referred to by scholars as the "international rollback" of Brazil.

Overall, there are praises and criticisms to be made to the "Brazilian ocean strategy". Predominantly, the national policies—in particular the PNRM—have been serving the interests of the Brazilian society. They are responsible for initiating an ongoing process which has lasted for almost 40 years, expected to continue for many years more. Much has been achieved, but there is still much work to be done.

It is necessary to improve *coordination* within such a complex web of plans and programs, which is expected to become difficult by the day, thus adding more pressure to the work of the CIRM. Another obstacle to effective policies is posed by recent budgetary cuts to environmental agencies, including those tasked with monitoring the oceans. Despite the afore-mentioned marine riches under Brazilian jurisdiction, it is hardly disputable that insufficient funds to marine scientific research will hamper increased knowledge of the shelf and harden the drafting of environmentally sound exploration, exploitation, and conservation strategies.

In addition to that, one should warn against the lack of or insufficient follow-up reports on the actions and objectives set out by each Action of the different PSRMs, as REMPLAC or REVIMAR. The CIRM's website is not updated, as of December 2018, and several actions have reports which date from years ago. The same situation was identified at the IBAMA website with respect to statistics on fisheries off Brazilian waters, the latest having been reported in 2007. Such carelessness is worrisome, what brings to surface yet another challenge to Brazilian marine environmental governance efforts: communication and dialogue. Public authorities ought to reach out for the interested public and better inform stakeholders about the objectives, actions and the consequences of all marine policies. That is a major challenge, as the specialty and technicality of public discussions may drive out crucial stakeholders and the population at large, a consequence that would irreparably crack the objective of developing a "maritime mentality" in Brazil.

The final chapter of this work dwelled on the question whether the Brazilian marine environmental legal framework, with particular regard to the continental shelf, is consistent with international law and UNCLOS. Following a field research in the Brazilian federal capital, Brasília, and 4 years of intensive examination of

Brazilian marine environmental rules, this chapter consisted of the *konzentrat* of the entire research. The thesis' main argument, with respect to the empirical investigation centered on Brazil, was that the country could perform better to increase (i) overall domestic legislative coherence on marine environmental matters, and (ii) the consistency of domestic rules with international ocean and environmental law.

Such questions matter, for, despite the troubled domestic political context, Brazil has started to exploit its offshore deep-sea hydrocarbon reserves to meet domestic market demands. This is a strategical sector in the country's reindustrialization agenda. However, enlargement of Brazil's jurisdiction seaward requires the carrying out of research capable of properly managing the exploration and commercialization of these marine resources, relevant both from an economic and ecological angle.

Hence, Chap. 10 set out with the major goal of answering to two core questions. Firstly, whether the Brazilian legal marine environmental framework is in accordance with general international law and the law of the sea, namely UNCLOS. To answer this question, it embraced the categorization between: conserving living resources; preventing, reducing and controlling pollution caused by the exploitation of non-living resources; and researching on the continental shelf. The answer to that first question was that yes, most of the Brazilian legislation examined in this work is consistent with UNCLOS, with but a few exceptions.

In short, Brazil has actively exercised its right-duty to manage the marine environment under national jurisdiction. Domestic norms concerning the environment in general, and the *marine* environment in particular, permeate both the 1988 Federal Constitution (Arts. 24, 31, 225, and others) and infraconstitutional legislation, such as Acts, Federal Decrees, and Resolutions. The Brazilian Ocean Act recognizes the Brazilian exclusive regulatory right concerning the uses and *conservation* of the continental shelf, especially the regulation of marine scientific research, *protection and preservation of the marine environment*, and the construction, operation and use of all types of artificial islands, facilities and structures. That is in fact, both a right and duty, as Brazilian authorities are bound to satisfy the requirement of regulating the conservation of the continental shelf and the protection of its environment. In other words, the country may not purport to enjoy solely the right to do so, without being obliged to it.

However, this work identified a few exceptions to the rule, cases in which Brazilian legislation deviates from UNCLOS. The most critical provisions relate to the coastal state's rights on marine scientific research, and erroneous clauses which consider "jurisdictional waters" the superjacent water column above the outer continental shelf. Regarding the former, Art. 5 of the Brazilian Marine Scientific Research Act requires the express consent of Brazilian prior to any marine scientific investigation on the continental shelf, without distinguishing between areas within and beyond national jurisdiction. This provision collides with UNCLOS Art. 246 (6), which severely limits coastal states' discretion to withhold consent for scientific research beyond 200 nm—implying that this area would be slightly more subject to freedom of scientific research in the high seas than to the continental shelf regime.

Secondly, Art. 3 of Decree no. 4.136/02, which disciplines domestic sanctions for oil pollution in "waters under national jurisdiction", considers that even the water column above the extended continental shelf falls under jurisdiction national. Such a provision is inconsistent with UNCLOS insofar as the Convention specifies that the waters above the outer continental shelf are not subject to national jurisdiction but to the regime of freedoms of the high seas. In both cases, legal amendments correctly implementing UNCLOS' terms might be needed.

Onto the second question, on whether there are any legal-environmental implications arising from the process of delineating outer continental shelf limits for the Brazilian state, the book showed that UNCLOS contains no express obligation to adapt national legislation to that "new" reality. Yet, there are legal-environmental implications for the domestic legal order of a coastal state endowed with an extended continental shelf. For one, coastal states are required both to implement Art. 82 UNCLOS and to adapt domestic legislation to the peculiarities of the legal regime of the outer continental shelf, namely with respect to marine scientific research and the employment of area-based tools for managing and conserving the region—such as the designation of deep-sea marine protected areas on the outer shelf. As attested by this work, Brazil has not carried out such modifications up to now. For the protection and security of the Blue Amazon, Brazil did not adopt new legislation, nor amend previous ones as of 2019.

This work further concluded that there is margin for the country's domestic legislation to (i) enter in greater consistency with UNCLOS; (ii) to legally adapt to the "new" reality of the country having to manage an extended continental shelf; and (iii) display increased coherence/cohesion while regulating the multiple uses of the continental shelf.

Brazil has an overall policy and regulatory situation that enables jurisdiction for the persecution of environmental goals within the Brazilian Blue Amazon. Having the appropriate policy and legal framework, however, is but the first step in the implementation process of successful marine environmental measures. Substantial outcomes in terms of increased sustainability or marine environmental conservation (or prevention of degradation) shall only be made possible by domestic political will and adequate funding schemes. Concrete challenges ahead for the Brazilian (oceanic) state include: tackling a fragmented ocean strategy; implementing more institutional coordination; opening more communication channels between government and affected stakeholders; devising and drafting a new administrative law of the sea, one which distinguishes between rules for the mainland and the sea; fostering increased political will for ocean management projects in a country with a diminished "maritime mentality"; ensuring more funding for ocean conservation projects in a scenario of financial scarcity and a "short blanket".

As of early 2020, political turmoil in Brazil gives little reason for hope of an enhanced and more coherent approach to ocean governance. The platform of the presidential candidates in the 2018 elections were disappointing, as all candidates ignored the seas, either not mentioning it or doing so *en passant*. It was the case of President Jair Bolsonaro and his 81-pages long electoral program, which made no reference to seas nor oceans. Worryingly, the President has emphatically shown on occasion some irritation with the so-called "Shiitism" of the previous staff that served the Ministry for the Environment.[2]

Yet, this cannot turn into an immobilizing argument to avoid facing domestic legal and institutional inconsistencies. Having the national legislative framework designed with as little conflict and overlaps as possible, and having the institutional agencies aware of clear mandates, objectives and coordination commitments with similar agencies, is a reasonable first step in long-term path towards a sustainable use of the Brazilian maritime spaces. With regard to the continental shelf, such a foundational work would signal to the international community that Brazil is not just seeking expanded jurisdiction seawards but embracing its duties and responsibilities by internally adopting coherent policies and regulations and reasonably exercising its enforcement powers.

If Brazil is to live up to twenty-first century challenges and reach the much-desired sustainable management of the Brazilian Blue Amazon, the perspective shift from "entitlement to" to "responsibility for" the oceans ought to be intensified. That can be reached, among other means, through progressive, purpose-oriented and ecological interpretations of both international law instruments, added to the effective enforcement of domestic marine environmental legislation consistent with UNCLOS the Convention. Hopefully, this work will have represented a small contribution to that end.

[2]AFP, *Planos de Bolsonaro para Amazônia preocupam defensores do meio ambiente*, 22 October 2018. Available at: https://exame.abril.com.br/mundo/planos-de-bolsonaro-para-amazonia-preocupam-defensores-do-meio-ambiente/. Accessed 12 April 2020.

The manufacturer's authorised representative in the EU is Springer Nature Customer Service Centre GmbH, Europaplatz 3, 69115 Heidelberg, Germany. If you have any concerns regarding our products, please contact ProductSafety@springernature.com

Printed and bound by CPI Group (UK) Ltd, Croydon, CR0 4YY

23/09/2026

02221535-0006